The
London Book of
ENGLISH
VERSE

The
London Book of
ENGLISH
VERSE

Selected by
HERBERT READ AND
BONAMY DOBRÉE

LONDON
Eyre & Spottiswoode
22 HENRIETTA STREET WC2

First published 1949
Second, revised, crown 8vo edition 1952
Reprinted 1956
Reprinted 1960
Reprinted 1963
Reprinted 1965
India paper edition 1953

3.4
Catalogue No. 6/2171/19
Printed in Great Britain
for Eyre & Spottiswoode (Publishers) Ltd.,
by Richard Clay (The Chaucer Press), Ltd.,
Bungay, Suffolk

GENERAL CONTENTS

INTRODUCTION

THE aim we have set ourselves in this anthology is to make a representative selection of English poetry, with historical limits which begin with Chaucer and end with our contemporary T. S. Eliot. This, admittedly, has been done before, and two anthologies in particular have for long enjoyed a popularity which must be challenged with good reasons, lest this fresh attempt seem an impertinence. There is, indeed, one reason sufficient in itself—the passage of time, with its attendant shift of sensibility. Sir Francis Palgrave's *Golden Treasury* was published in 1861. The first, or at any rate the earliest, editions of that volume remain the best: they have the integrity of the tempered taste of a man of his period. Editions which followed that careful sifting, however much they have brought that anthology 'up to date', represent so many dilutions of the original essence. The process of dilution has not yet been applied to *The Oxford Book of English Verse*, except at the hand of the compiler himself, who first issued his selection in 1900. We are now a little farther away from Sir Arthur Quiller-Couch's anthology than he was from Sir Francis Palgrave's; and most readers will agree that forty-eight years is long enough for a shift in sensibility to have taken place, and for a revision of values to be attempted. We have come, speaking in these terms, to what we may call a new literary generation, and our values cannot be the same. We live in a different world; we have had different experiences; the philosophic climate of opinion has altered.

We all have in our minds something that we loosely call essential poetry, what for convenience we may call absolute poetry; but the absolute, in poetry perhaps even more than in metaphysics, is something each man has to seize according to his limited capacities. Those capacities are, if not 'determined', at least coloured and swayed by the imponderable factors which we call 'the spirit of the age'. We glimpse the absolute through a veil of mundane pre-occupations, and as those preoccupations

vii

change, our values change, too. That is at once the justification for attempting this task anew and for not pretending to finality. We are not sincere if we pretend to reduce an affair of the sensibility, formed by whatever experiences may have befallen us, to the measured rectitude of a science; for science cares nothing for those values with which poetry is supremely concerned. Poetry cannot be selected by rules, by intellectual instruments of any kind: we have an immediate intuition of its essential quality, and it is according to this that our choice must fall.

But though the critic, in Montaigne's phrase, must be an *être ondoyant et divers*, our values are not so vague as to be beyond definition. Positively it may be difficult to say why one poem is included rather than another when we cannot deny poetic quality to either: we must confess to personal idiosyncrasies, counter-checked in this anthology because it is a work of collaboration. We had at least to justify our idiosyncrasies to one another, if not to the world at large; and if we have on occasion yielded to each other's pleadings for inclusion, or arguments for rejection, readers of this volume will possibly be the gainers. When it comes to negative values–to qualities which we have held should exclude certain poems, popular though they may have been, and even once our own favourites–there we can be more specific. If in the application of our standard we have rejected more than half the material offered by Palgrave and Quiller-Couch, there must be some definable barrier, some gauge of appreciation, which has sifted out what in 1860 or 1900 seemed perfect ore. We can mention two.

The first is a certain type of romanticism which we believe to be false, at any rate to be inferior. As an example we would suggest the difference there is between the romanticism of *Christabel* and that of *Kubla Khan*. The former springs from a conscious attempt to find symbols for emotions and intuitions for which none can be found in contemporary life, a deliberate search to express oneself by trying to assume the modes of feeling of another age; it does not achieve a more distinct reality, but rather, glozes over intuitional and emotional imprecisions in the poet. We meet the same sort of thing in *The Cottar's Saturday Night*, where Burns was trying to adapt the social consciousness of eighteenth century England to his own Scottish intuitions. In *Kubla Khan* we feel the instantaneous fusion of intuition, image, and word, which in one form or another we get in all good poetry, as we do in *The Holy Fair*.

The second barrier, more indicative of the shift in sensibility to which we have referred than anything else we can point to, is what we are almost compelled to describe as the pathological condition of sentimentality which set in about 1810 (Moore, Mrs. Hemans), and lasts until 1914 (Dowson, Flecker and the 'Georgians' generally). Sentimentality we would define as feeling more emotion about a thing or situation than the thing or situation warrants; or, alternatively, an imprecise emotion playing with words in the hope of attaining clarity. This sentimentality, which betrays itself not only in subject-matter, in rhythms, and in the choice of words, as well as in unnecessary verbiage, is not merely a question of the literary convention of a time. There was a literary convention towards the end of the sixteenth century; but though charged with sentiment of a distinctive kind, it is not sentimental. The convention is appropriate to the mood or emotion, and for this reason can bear a good deal of repetition without causing boredom or embarrassment.

A further reason why this collection inevitably differs from the two we have mentioned is that both Palgrave and Quiller-Couch chose poems 'chiefly lyrical'. Difficult as it is to define the lyric, it is clear what Palgrave was using as a basis, and it was much the basis used by Quiller-Couch. We give many more examples of the contemplative and epistolary, feeling that there is as great poetic integrity in Ben Jonson's poem inviting a friend to supper as in "See the chariot at hand here of love", or in Tennyson's lines to FitzGerald as in *In Memoriam*. Cotton's stanzas ("the rough magnanimity of the old English vein") we feel to be as good as Herrick's songs, though in a different way. Moreover we have tried to include long enough extracts from long poems to give a sense, though only an imperfect one, of the whole poem; we have not aimed at extracting 'anthology pieces', since the long poem has a contour, a rise and fall of rhythmical intensity, which is not felt in the detached purple patch. To isolate such patches is to give the false impression that all good poetry is necessarily lyrical. It is one of the characteristic achievements of English verse that it has demonstrated the poetic value of the conversational rhythm and tone.

We have tried, within our historical limits, to include every English poet of importance, and to represent every type of verse which is genuinely poetic, except for the dramatic, which needs its reference and its setting, and would have enlarged our scope too much. Once we had made our choice, we had to decide on what arrangement we should adopt. There are two easy and obvious methods: the chronological order of the poet's birth or death, which is the principle followed by most anthologists; or the alphabetical order of the poets' names, which produces an arbitrary result, but nevertheless has the merit of sometimes showing interesting comparisons in treatment, and, occasionally, amusing contrasts. But it seemed to us that such arrangements serve little purpose except for ease of reference (which can be supplied by indexes) and lead to no illumination. Two principles remained, one of which we adopted in the *London Book of English Prose*–namely, an order determined by the writers' motives. This principle, which we think to be of great use in considering prose, since it is normally written with a more definable aim than poetry, did not, when attempted, prove profitable when applied to the subtler approach, the more intuitive handling of words and ideas which characterise poetry. All poetry has a single inclusive aim: to move us, to pluck some chord, even to touch some single note, in the sensitive organism of our being. There are many chords waiting to be plucked, with soft or vigorous strokes, and in any one poem a poet may rove over their compass to produce pure melody or metrical counterpoint. The final result is an æsthetic unity which cannot be classified according to a simple intention.

We were left with the principle which we have adopted– arrangement in an order which we would venture to call 'organic'. However it began, however it may have developed, poetry can be arranged according to its emotional complexity and the depth of its reference, reflected in its formal structure, its interplay of stress and meaning, its music and its allusiveness; in short, according to its emotional pressure and its artifice in creation. Without attempting to carry out a systematic analysis, we have tried to indicate by our divisions the contrasts which clearly exist between poetic forms which are effortless and simple, and those which are sophisticated and complex, between the direct and allusive styles, between effects of unity and multiplicity, clarity and obscurity, between poems of action and poems of meditation, between objective description and subjective impressions. We have presented these divisions in an order which, while not smoothing out stimulating contrasts, yet allows the reader to proceed from what is easy in technique and sentiment to what is comparatively difficult. The steps at the end of any of these slopes may seem a little steeper than those which immediately follow at the beginning of the next, but nevertheless the result, we hope, is a *gradus ad Parnassum* in the true sense of that phrase–an order which will imperceptibly guide the reader from the relatively simple and accessible forms of the art to those major and infinitely more complicated forms which offer the enjoyment of illimitable vistas over the range and heights of mind and imagination, and which yet do not exclude those minor moods of irony, humour or satire in which the poet reflects on human errors, vanities and limitations.

The sections which then emerged might be briefly characterised as follows:

Book I

Narrative poetry, the most primitive form of verse, its form and origin determined by the desire to record and repeat a story of action in easily memorised words, but developing into something far from primitive. For recitation rather than song.

Book II

Songs and incantations which are essentially singable, or depend for their appeal on an inherent syllabic musical quality.

Book III

Lyrical verse the main effect of which is to convey a mood or emotion, without complications of reflection or intellect. The poetry of sentiment.

Book IV

Lyrical verse the main effect of which is to convey a notion or a conceit. The poetry of fancy and of curious meditation.

Book V

Descriptive verse of an objective type, relying on the exact observation of natural phenomena; enumerative, precise.

Book VI

Descriptive verse of an impressionistic type, which, though still relying on outward observation, is more concerned than that in the previous section to record the emotions which result from such observation, and to associate with the object the poet's memories and sentiments.

Book VII

Moralistic verse. The poet passes from memories and sentiments aroused by the object to generalisations and judgments.

Book VIII

Metaphysical verse. This section includes most of the religious verse to be found in our anthology. The poet is now primarily concerned to express an idea, or system of ideas, while still retaining the sensuous appeal of his medium.

Book IX

The symphonic poem. Here the emphasis has shifted to form rather than content, but it is the complexity of the emotions or ideas to be expressed, and the imperative need of comprehending a diversity of emotional responses within a single artistic form, which gives to this highest type of poetry its compelling distinction.

Book X

Satirical verse. This section has not the same unity or formal coherence as the rest, but it seemed desirable to separate a state of the poetic spirit in which poetic forms are used to express sentiments distinct from though often merging into those normally expected in poetry and usually mocking its traditional seriousness. We have included in this section some lighter occasional verses which verge on the satirical.

It will be seen that this arrangement is neither logical, psychological, nor, when it comes to matters of form, architectonic. Nor do we suggest that the arrangement is final, since poetry, no more than human life, can be fitted into pigeon-holes: many poems might well find a place in one, or even two, other sections. We offer the arrangement merely as agreeable means of ordering a body of material of infinite complexity: but having erected our structure, we venture to think that it displays not only Convenience and Beauty–to use the phrase of Sir John Vanbrugh, poet no less than architect–but also the quality he called State.

There were, of course, the minor details to consider, such as the spelling. To retain the old has certain advantages; it adds a flavour, induces an atmosphere: but spelling conventions have nothing to do with poetry. Moreover the old forms demand a reader happily at home with them, and for most, either they will be an obstacle, or they will produce an irrelevant spicing of 'quaintness'. We have therefore modernised freely, here or there retaining old forms, where to have abandoned them would have been to lose some subtlety of stress or meaning, or to destroy a rhyme. A few authors we have left untouched, such as Chaucer and Milton: Chaucer, because it is impossible to modernise him satisfactorily; Milton because many of his spellings are clearly deliberate, and it would be rash to attempt to distinguish between these and such as were mere accidents of printers' practice or the fashion of the time. A few poems of other authors we have also left untouched. We have freely used our discretion in the matter of capitals and italics, but have been very cautious in tampering with the punctuation.

As regards texts, we have in the main used the most recent ones, holding with Lord Chesterfield that the latest text is always the best, unless the editor is a fool; but we have frequently had recourse, or made reference to other texts or original editions. From the nineteenth century we have generally speaking made use of 'standard' editions. In the notes, kept as brief as possible, we usually indicate where the poem first appeared, and anything about it which seems of special interest.

We would like to thank those friends and colleagues who have given us the benefit of their special knowledge or infected us with their special enthusiasms. We are particularly indebted to Mr. Kenneth Muir for several suggestions, and for supplying us with a reliable text from the MSS. of Sir Thomas Wyatt's poems. Mr. Grigson first drew our attention to the forgotten work of William Diaper.

B. D.
H. R.

ACKNOWLEDGMENTS

OUR thanks are due to the authors, or their representatives, and the publishers concerned, for permission to include poems from the following sources:

Robert Bridges.	*Poetical Works.*	The Clarendon Press, Oxford.
Walter de la Mare.	*Collected Poems.*	Sir Walter de la Mare, Faber & Faber, Ltd., and Henry Holt & Co., Inc. (U.S.A.).
R. W. Dixon.	*Selected Poems.*	Oxford University Press.
Austin Dobson.	*Collected Poems.*	A. T. A. Dobson, Esq., and Oxford University Press.
H. D. (Hilda Doolittle).	*Collected Poems.*	Liveright Publishing Corporation (U.S.A.)
Ernest Dowson.	*Poetical Works.*	John Lane, The Bodley Head, Ltd., and Dodd, Mead & Co. (U.S.A.).
T. S. Eliot.	*Collected Poems 1909–1935.*	T. S. Eliot, Esq., Faber & Faber, Ltd., and Harcourt Brace & Co., Inc. (U.S.A.).
John Gray.	*The Long Road.*	Basil Blackwell & Mott, Ltd.
Julian Grenfell.		Lord Desborough.
Thomas Hardy.	*Collected Poems* and *The Dynasts.*	The Trustees of the Hardy Estate, and Macmillan & Co., Ltd.
W. E. Henley.	*Poems.*	The author's representative, Macmillan & Co., Ltd., and Charles Scribner's Sons (U.S.A.).
G. M. Hopkins.	*Poems.*	Oxford University Press.

xvi Acknowledgments

A. E. Housman.	*Collected Poems.*	The Trustees of the Estate, the Society of Authors, Jonathan Cape, Ltd., and Henry Holt & Co., Inc. (U.S.A.).
Robinson Jeffers.	*Cawdon.*	The Hogarth Press, Ltd.
Rudyard Kipling.	*A Diversity of Creatures.* *Many Inventions.* *Plain Tales from the Hills.*	Mrs. George Bambridge, Macmillan & Co., Ltd., and Doubleday, Doran Co. (Inc.), U.S.A.
	The Five Nations.	Mrs. George Bambridge, Methuen & Co., Ltd., and Doubleday, Doran Co. (Inc.), U.S.A.
Andrew Lang	*Poetical Works.*	Representatives of the late Andrew Lang, and Longmans, Green & Co., Ltd.
D. H. Lawrence.	*Collected Poems.*	Mrs. Frieda Lawrence, William Heinemann, Ltd., and Viking Press, Inc. (U.S.A.).
Vachel Lindsay.	*Collected Poems.*	Macmillan & Co., Ltd.
Marianne Moore.	*Selected Poems.*	Faber & Faber, Ltd.
Wilfred Owen.	*Poems.*	Chatto & Windus, Ltd.
Ezra Pound.	*Selected Poems* and *Draft of Thirty Cantos.*	Faber & Faber, Ltd., and New Directions (U.S.A.).
John Crowe Ransom.	*Selected Poems.*	Eyre & Spottiswoode, Ltd., and Alfred Knopf Inc. (U.S.A.)
Algernon Swinburne.	*Collected Poetical Works.*	William Heinemann, Ltd.
J. M. Synge.	*Poems and Translations.*	Allen & Unwin, Ltd.
Edward Thomas.	*Collected Poems* in the Faber Library Edition.	Mrs. Helen Thomas and Faber & Faber, Ltd.
Francis Thompson	*Poems.*	Burns Oates & Washbourne, Ltd.
Arthur Waley.	*170 Chinese Poems.*	Constable & Company, Ltd.
W. B. Yeats.	*Collected Poems* and *Last Poems and Plays.*	Mrs. W. B. Yeats and Macmillan & Co., Ltd.
Andrew Young.	*Collected Poems.*	Jonathan Cape, Ltd.

TABLE OF CONTENTS

Book I: NARRATIVE POETRY

xvii

Table of Contents

Book II: SONGS AND INCANTATIONS

Table of Contents

Table of Contents   xxiii

Table of Contents

Table of Contents　　　xxix

Book VII: GENERALIZATIONS AND JUDGEMENTS

Table of Contents   xxxi

Table of Contents

BOOK IX: THE SYMPHONIC POEM

B

Book X: SATIRICAL VERSE

Table of Contents

Book I

NARRATIVE POETRY

1 *The Cherry-tree Carol*

Joseph was an old man,
 and an old man was he,
When he wedded Mary,
 in the land of Galilee.

Joseph and Mary walked
 through an orchard good,
Where was cherries and berries,
 so red as any blood.

Joseph and Mary walked
 through an orchard green,
Where was berries and cherries
 as thick as might be seen.

O then bespoke Mary,
 so meek and so mild:
Pluck me one cherry, Joseph,
 for I am with child.

O then bespoke Joseph,
 with words most unkind:
'Let him pluck thee a cherry
 that brought thee with child.'

O then bespoke the babe,
 within his mother's womb:
'Bow down then the tallest tree,
 for my mother to have some.'

Then bowed down the highest tree
 unto his mother's hand;
Then she cried, 'See, Joseph,
 I have cherries at command.'

O then bespake Joseph:
  'I have done Mary wrong:
But cheer up, my dearest,
  and be not cast down.'

Then Mary plucked a cherry,
  as red as the blood,
Then Mary went home
  With her heavy load.

Then Mary took her babe,
  and sat him on her knee,
Saying, 'My dear son, tell me
  what this world will be.'

'O I shall be as dead, mother,
  as the stones in the wall;
O the stones in the streets, mother,
  shall mourn for me all.

'Upon Easter-day, mother,
  my uprising shall be;
O the sun and the moon, mother,
  shall both rise with me.'

ANON

2 *Lully, lulley*

Lully, lulley, lully, lulley,
The faucon hath borne my make away.

He bare him up, he bare him down,
He bare him into an orchard brown.

In that orchard there was an hall,
That was hanged with purple and pall.

And in that hall there was a bed,
It was hanged with gold so red.

And in that bed there lieth a knight,
His woundes bleeding day and night.

By that bedside kneeleth a may,
But she weepeth both night and day.

And by that bedside there standeth a stone,
Corpus Christi written thereon.

ANON

3 *The Laily* [1] *Worm and the Machrel of The Sea*

'I was but seven year auld
   When my mither she did dee,
My father married the ae warst woman
   The warld did ever see.

'For she has made me the laily worm
   That lies at the foot of the tree,
An' o' my sister Maisry
   The machrel of the sea.

'An' every Saturday at noon
   The machrel comes to me,
An' she takes my laily head,
   An' lays it on her knee,
An' kames it wi' a siller kame,
   An' washes it in the sea.

'Seven knights hae I slain
   Sin I lay at the foot of the tree;
An' ye war nae my ain father,
   The eighth ane ye should be.'

'Sing on your song, ye laily worm,
   That ye sung to me.'
'I never sung that song
   But what I would sing to ye.

'I was but seven year auld
   When my mither she did dee,
My father married the ae warst woman
   The warld did ever see.

[1] loathly

'She changed me to the laily worm
    That lies at the foot of the tree,
An my sister Maisry
    To the machrel of the sea.

'And every Saturday at noon
    The machrel comes to me,
An' she takes my laily head,
    An' lays it on her knee,
An' kames it with a siller kame,
    An' washes it in the sea.

'Seven knights hae I slain
    Sin I lay at the foot of the tree;
An' ye war nae my ain father,
    The eighth ane ye should be.'

He sent for his lady
    As fast as send could he:
'Whar is my son,
    That ye sent frae me,
And my daughter,
    Lady Maisry?'

'Your son is at our king's court,
    Serving for meat an' fee,
And your daughter is at our queen's court,
    A mary [1] sweet an' free.'

'Ye lee, ye ill woman,
    Sae loud as I hear ye lee,
For my son is the laily worm
    That lays at the foot of the tree,
And my daughter Maisry
    The machrel of the sea.'

She has ta'en a silver wan'
    An' gi'en him strokes three,
And he started up the bravest knight
    Your eyes did ever see.

[1] maid of honour

She has ta'en a small horn
    An' loud an' shrill blew she;
An' a' the fish came her 'till
    But the machrel of the sea:
'Ye shaped me ance an unseemly shape,
    An' ye'll never mare shape me.'

He has sent to the wood
    For hathorn an' whin,
An' he has ta'en that gay lady,
    An' there he did her burn.

                       ANON

4 *The Wife of Usher's Well*

There lived a wife at Usher's Well,
    And a wealthy wife was she;
She had three stout and stalwart sons,
    And sent them o'er the sea.

They hadna been a week from her,
    A week but barely one,
When word came to the carline wife [1]
    That her three sons were gone.

They hadna been a week from her,
    A week but barely three,
When came word to the carline wife
    That her sons she'd never see.

'I wish the wind may never cease,
    Nor fashes [2] in the flood,
Till my three sons come hame to me,
    In earthly flesh and blood.'

It fell about the Martinmass,
    When nights are lang and mirk,
The carline wife's three sons came hame,
    And their hats were o' the birk. [3]

[1] old woman   [2] troubles   [3] birch

It neither grew in syke [1] nor ditch,
    Nor yet in any sheugh [2];
But at the gates o' Paradise,
    That birk grew fair enough.

'Blow up the fire, my maidens,
    Bring water from the well;
For a' my house shall feast this night,
    Since my three sons are well.'

And she has made to them a bed,
    She's made it large and wide,
And she's ta'en her mantle her about,
    Sat down at the bed-side.

Up then crew the red, red cock,
    And up and crew the gray;
The eldest to the youngest said,
    ' 'Tis time we were away.'

The cock he hadna craw'd but once,
    And clapp'd his wings at a',
When the youngest to the eldest said,
    'Brother, we must awa'.'

'The cock doth craw, the day doth daw:
    The channerin' [3] worm doth chide;
Gin we be miss'd out o' our place,
    A sair pain we maun bide.

'Fare ye well, my mother dear!
    Farewell to barn and byre!
And fare ye well, the bonny lass
    That kindles my mother's fire!'

ANON

---

[1] march   [2] trench   [3] fretting

5 *Sir Patrick Spens*

The king sits in Dunfermline town
    Drinking the blood-red wine:
'O whar will I get guid sailor,
    To sail this ship of mine?'

Up and spake an eldern knight,
    Sat at the king's right knee;
'Sir Patrick Spens is the best sailor
    That sails upon the sea.'

The King has written a braid letter,
    And sign'd it wi' his hand,
And sent it to Sir Patrick Spens,
    Was walking on the sand.

The first line that Sir Patrick read,
    A loud laugh laughed he;
The next line that Sir Patrick read,
    The tear blinded his e'e.

'O wha is this has done this deed,
    This ill deed done to me,
To send me out this time o' the year,
    To sail upon the sea!

'Make haste, make haste, my merry men all,
    Our guid ship sails the morn':
'O say na sae, my master dear,
    For I fear a deadly storm.

'Late late yestre'en I saw the new moon,
    Wi' the auld moon in her arm,
And I fear, I fear, my dear master,
    That we will come to harm.'

O our Scots nobles were right loath
    To wet their cork-heel'd schoon;
But lang ere a' the play were play'd,
    Their hats they swam aboon.

O lang, lang may their ladies sit,
   Wi' their fans into their hand,
Or e'er they see Sir Patrick Spens
   Come sailing to the land.

O lang, lang may the ladies stand,
   Wi' their golden kames in their hair,
Waiting for their ain dear lords
   For they'll see them na mair.

Ha'f o'er, ha'f o'er to Aberdour,
   It's fifty fathom deep,
And their lies guid Sir Patrick Spens,
   Wi' the Scots lords at his feet.

ANON

6 *Lord Randal*

'O where hae you been, Lord Randal, my son?
And where hae you been, my handsome young man?'
'I hae been at the greenwood; mother, make my bed soon,
For I'm wearied wi' hunting, and fain would lie down.'

'An wha met ye there, Lord Randal, my son?
'And wha met ye there, my handsome young man?'
'O I met wi' my true-love; mother, make my bed soon,
For I'm wearied wi' hunting, and fain would lie down.'

'And what did she give you, Lord Randal, my son?
And what did she give you, my handsome young man?'
'Eels fried in a pan; mother, make my bed soon,
For I'm wearied wi' hunting, and fain would lie down.'

'And wha gat your leavings, Lord Randal, my son?
And wha gat your leavings, my handsome young man?'
'My hawks and my hounds; mother, make my bed soon,
For I'm wearied wi' hunting, and fain would lie down.'

'And what became of them, Lord Randal, my son?
And what became of them, my handsome young man?'
'They stretched their legs out and died; mother, make my bed
   soon,
For I'm wearied wi' hunting, and fain would lie down.'

'O I fear you are poisoned, Lord Randal, my son!
I fear you are poisoned, my handsome young man!'
'O yes, I am poisoned; mother, make my bed soon,
For I'm sick at the heart, and I fain would lie down.'

'What d'ye leave to your mother, Lord Randal, my son?
What d'ye leave to your mother, my handsome young man?'
'Four and twenty milk kye; mother, make my bed soon,
For I'm sick at the heart, and I fain would lie down.'

'What d'ye leave to your sister, Lord Randal, my son?
What d'ye leave to your sister, my handsome young man?'
'My gold and my silver; mother, make my bed soon,
For I'm sick at the heart, and I fain would lie down.'

'What d'ye leave to your brother, Lord Randal, my son?
What d'ye leave to your brother, my handsome young man?'
'My houses and my lands; mother, make my bed soon,
For I'm sick at the heart, and I fain would lie down.'

'What d'ye leave to your true-love, Lord Randal, my son?
What d'ye leave to your true-love, my handsome young man?'
'I leave her hell and fire; mother, make my bed soon,
For I'm sick at the heart, and I fain would lie down.'

ANON

7 *Helen of Kirconnell*

I wish I were where Helen lies,
Night and day on me she cries;
O that I were where Helen lies
    On fair Kirconnell lea!

Curst be the heart that thought the thought,
And curst the hand that fired the shot,
When in my arms burd Helen dropt,
    And died to succour me!

O think na ye my heart was sair,
When my Love dropt down and spake nae mair!
I laid her down wi' meikle care
    On fair Kirconnell lea.

As I went down the water-side,
None but my foe to be my guide,
None but my foe to be my guide
   On fair Kirconnell lea;

I lighted down my sword to draw,
I hacked him in pieces sma',
I hacked him in pieces sma',
   For her sake that died for me.

O Helen fair, beyond compare!
I'll make a garland o' thy hair
Shall bind my heart for evermair
   Until the day I dee!

O that I were where Helen lies!
Night and day on me she cries;
Out of my bed she bids me rise,
   Says, 'Haste, and come to me!'

O Helen fair! O Helen chaste!
If I were with thee, I were blest,
Where thou lies low and takes thy rest,
   On fair Kirconnell lea.

I wish my grave were growing green,
A winding-sheet drawn ower my een,
And I in Helen's arms lying,
   On fair Kirconnell lea.

I wish I were where Helen lies!
Night and day on me she cries;
And I am weary of the skies,
   Since my Love died for me.

ANON

8 *The Little Cart*

The little cart jolting and banging through the yellow haze of
   dusk;
The man pushing behind, the woman pulling in front.

They have left the city and do not know where to go.
'Green, green, those elm-tree leaves: *they* will cure my
hunger,
If only we could find some quiet place and sup on them together.'

The wind has flattened the yellow mother-wort:
Above it in the distance they see the walls of a house.
'*There* surely must be people living who'll give you something
to eat.'
They tap at the door, but no one comes: they look in, but the
kitchen is empty.
They stand hesitating in the lonely road and their tears fall like
rain.

ARTHUR WALEY: from the Chinese

9 *Ulysses hears the Prophecies of Tiresias*

'Arriv'd now at our ship, we launch'd, and set
Our mast up, put forth sail, and in did get
Our late-got cattle. Up our sails, we went,
My wayward fellows mourning now th' event.
A good companion yet, a foreright wind,
Circe (the excellent utt'rer of her mind)
Supplied our murmuring consorts with, that was
Both speed and guide to our adventurous pass.
All day our sails stood to the winds, and made
Our voyage prosp'rous. Sun then set, and shade
All ways obscuring, on the bounds we fell
Of deep Oceanus, where people dwell
Whom a perpetual cloud obscures outright,
To whom the cheerful sun lends never light,
Nor when he mounts the star-sustaining heaven,
Nor when he stoops earth, and sets up the even,
But night holds fix'd wings, feather'd all with banes,
Above those most unblest Cimmerians.
Here drew we up our ship, our sheep withdrew,
And walk'd the shore till we attain'd the view,
Of that sad region Circe had foreshadow'd;
And then the sacred off'rings to be vow'd
Eurylochus and Persimedes bore.
When I my sword drew, and earth's womb did gore

Till I a pit digg'd of a cubit round,
Which with the liquid sacrifice we crown'd,
First honey mix'd with wine, then sweet wine neat,
Then water pour'd in, last the flour of wheat.
Much I importun'd then the weak-neck'd dead,
And vow'd, when I the barren soil should tread
Of cliffy Ithaca, amidst my hall
To kill a heifer, my clear best of all,
And give in off'ring, on a pile compos'd
Of all the choice goods my whole house enclos'd.
And to Tiresias himself, alone,
A sheep coal-black, and the selectest one
Of all my flocks. When to the Pow'rs beneath,
The sacred nation that survive with death,
My pray'rs and vows had done devotions fit,
I took the off'rings, and upon the pit
Bereft their lives. Out gush'd the sable blood,
And round about me fled out of the flood
The souls of the deceas'd. There cluster'd then
Youths, and their wives, much-suff'ring aged men,
Soft tender virgins that but new came there
By timeless death, and green their sorrows were.
There men-at-arms, with armours all embrew'd,
Wounded with lances, and with faulchions hew'd,
In numbers, up and down the ditch, did stalk,
And threw unmeasur'd cries about their walk,
So horrid that a bloodless fear surpris'd
My daunted spirits. Straight then I advis'd
My friends to flay the slaughter'd sacrifice,
Put them in fire, and to the Deities,
Stern Pluto and Persephone, apply
Exciteful pray'rs. Then drew I from my thigh
My well-edg'd sword, stept in, and firmly stood
Betwixt the prease of shadows and the blood,
And would not suffer any one to dip
Within our off'ring his unsolid lip,
Before Tiresias that did all controul.
The first that press'd in was Elpenor's soul,
His body in the broad-way'd earth as yet
Unmourn'd, unburied by us, since we swet

With other urgent labours. Yet his smart
I wept to see, and rued it from my heart,
Enquiring how he could before me be
That came by ship? He, mourning, answer'd me:
"In Circe's house, the spite some spirit did bear,
And the unspeakable good liquor there,
Hath been my bane; for, being to descend
A ladder much in height, I did not tend
My way well down, but forwards made a proof
To tread the rounds, and from the very roof
Fell on my neck, and brake it; and this made
My soul thus visit this infernal shade.
And here, by them that next thyself are dear,
Thy wife, and father, that a little one
Gave food to thee, and by thy only son
At home behind thee left, Telemachus,
Do not depart by stealth, and leave me thus,
Unmourn'd, unburied, lest neglected I
Bring on thyself th' incensed Deity.
I know that, sail'd from hence, thy ship must touch
On th' isle Æaea; where vouchsafe thus much,
Good king, that, landed, thou wilt instantly
Bestow on me thy royal memory
To this grace, that my body, arms and all,
May rest consumed in fiery funeral;
And on the foamy shore a sepulchre
Erect to me, that after-times may hear
Of one so hapless. Let me these implore
And fix upon my sepulchre the oar
With which alive I shook the aged seas,
And had of friends the dear societies."
        I told the wretched soul I would fulfill
And execute to th' utmost point his will;
And, all the time we sadly talk'd, I still
My sword above the blood held when aside
The idol of my friend still amplified
His plaint, as up and down the shades he err'd.
Then my deceasèd mother's soul appear'd,
Fair daughter of Autolycus the great,
Grave Anticlea, whom, when forth I set

For sacred Ilion, I had left alive.
Her sight much mov'd me, and to tears did drive
My note of her decease; and yet not she
(Though in my ruth she held the high'st degree)
Would I admit to touch the sacred blood,
Till from Tiresias I had understood
What Circe told me. At the length did land
Theban Tiresias' soul, and in his hand
Sustain'd a golden sepulchre, knew me well,
And said: "O man unhappy, why to hell
Admitt'st thou dark arrival, and the light
The sun gives leav'st, to have the horrid sight
Of this black region, and the shadows here?
Now sheathe thy sharp sword, and the pit forbear,
That I the blood may taste, and then relate
The truth of those acts that affect thy fate."
        I sheath'd my sword, and left the pit, till he,
The black blood tasting, thus instructed me:
"Renown'd Ulysses! All unask'd I know
That all the cause of thy arrival now
Is to enquire thy wish'd retreat for home;
Which hardly God will let thee overcome,
Since Neptune still will his opposure try,
With all his laid-up anger, for the eye
His lov'd son lost to thee. And yet through all
Thy suff'ring course (which must be capital)
If both thine own affections, and thy friends,
Thou wilt contain, when thy access ascends
The three-fork'd island, having 'scap'd the seas,
Where ye shall find fed on the flow'ry leas
Fat flocks, and oxen, which the Sun doth own,
To whom are all things as well heard as shown,
And never dare one head of those to slay,
But hold unharmful on your wishèd way,
Though through enough affliction, yet secure
Your Fates shall land ye; but presage says sure,
If once ye spoil them, spoil to all thy friends,
Spoil to thy fleet, and if the justice ends
Short of thyself, it shall be long before,
And that length forc'd out with inflictions store,

When, losing all thy fellows, in a sail
Of foreign built (when most thy Fates prevail
In thy deliv'rance) thus th' event shall sort:
Thou shalt find shipwrack raging in thy port,
Proud men thy goods consuming, and thy wife
Urging with gifts, give charge upon thy life.
But all these wrongs revenge shall end to thee,
And force, or cunning, set with slaughter free
The house of all thy spoilers. Yet again
Thou shalt a voyage make, and come to men
That know no sea, nor ships, nor oars that are
Wings to a ship, nor mix with any fare
Salt's savoury vapour. Where thou first shalt land,
This clear-giv'n sign shall let thee understand,
That there those men remain: Assume ashore
Up to thy royal shoulder a ship oar,
With which, when thou shalt meet one on the way
That will in county admiration say
What dost thou with that wan [1] upon thy neck?
There fix that wan thy oar, and that shore deck
With sacred rites to Neptune; slaughter there
A ram, a bull, and (who for strength doth bear
The name of husband to a herd) a boar.
And, coming home, upon thy natural shore,
Give pious hecatombs to all the Gods,
Degrees observ'd. And then the periods
Of all thy labours in the peace shall end
Of easy death; which shall the less extend
His passion to thee, that thy foe, the Sea,
Shall not enforce it, but Death's victory
Shall chance in only-earnest-pray-vow'd age,
Obtain'd at home, quite emptied of his rage,
Thy subjects round about thee, rich and blest.
And here hath Truth summ'd up thy vital rest." '

GEORGE CHAPMAN: from the Greek of Homer

[1] winnowing fan

10 *Vision of Sorrow*

But how can I describe the doleful sight,
That in the shield so livelike fair did shine?
Sith in this world, I think was never wight
Could have set forth the half, not half so fine:
I can no more but tell how there is seen
Fair *Ilium* fall in burning red gledes down,
And from the soil great *Troy*, *Neptunus'* town.

Herefrom when scarce I could mine eyes withdraw,
That fill'd with tears as doth the springing well,
We passed on so far forth till we saw
Rude *Acheron*, a loathsome lake to tell,
That boils and bubs up swelth [1] as black as hell;
Where grisly *Charon*, at their fixed tide,
Still ferries ghosts unto the farther side.

The aged god no sooner Sorrow spied,
But hasting straight unto the bank apace,
With hollow call unto the rout he cried,
To swerve apart, and give the goddess place:
Straight it was done, when to the shore we pace,
Where, hand in hand as we then linked fast,
Within the boat we are together plac'd.

And forth we launch full fraughted to the brink,
When with the unwonted weight, the rusty keel
Began to crack as if the same should sink:
We hoise up mast and sail, that in a while
We fetch'd the shore, where scarcely we had while
For to arrive, but that we heard anon
A three sound bark confounded all in one.

We had not long forth pass'd, but that we saw
Black *Cerberus*, the hideous hound of hell,
With bristles rear'd, and with a three mouth'd jaw
Foredinning the ayer with his horrible yell,
Out of the deep dark cave where he did dwell:
The goddess straight he knew, and by and by,
He peas'd [2] and couch'd, while that we passed by.

---

[1] foul water   [2] became still

Thence come we to the horrour and the hell
The large great kingdoms, and the dreadful reign
Of *Pluto* in his throne where he did dwell,
The wide waste places, and the hugy plain,
The wailings, shrieks, and sundry sorts of pain,
The sighs, the sobs, the deep and deadly groan;
Earth, air, and all, resounding plaint and moan.

Here pul'd the babes, and here the maids unwed
With folded hands their sorry chance bewail'd,
Here wept the guiltless slain, and lovers dead,
That slew themselves when nothing else avail'd;
A thousand sorts of sorrows here that wail'd
With sighs, and tears, sobs, shrieks, and all yfere
That (oh alas) it was a hell to hear.

We stay'd us straight, and with a rueful fear,
Beheld this heavy sight; while from mine eyes
The vapour'd tears downstilled here and there,
And *Sorrow* eke in far more woeful wise,
Took on with plaint, up heaving to the skies
Her wretched hands, that with her cry the rout
'Gan all in heaps to swarm us round about.

Lo here, quoth Sorrow, Princes of renown,
That whilom sat on top of Fortune's wheel,
Now laid full low, like wretches whirled down,
Ev'n with one frown, that stay'd but with a smile:
And now behold the thing that thou erewhile,
Saw only in thought, and, what thou now shalt hear,
Recount the same to Kesar, King, and Peer.

THOMAS SACKVILLE

11   *The Despair of Troilus*

Departed out of parlement echone,
This Troilus, withouten wordes mo,
Unto his chambre spedde hym faste allone,
But if it were a man of his or two,
The which he bad out faste for to go,
Bycause he wolde slepen, as he seyde,
And hastily upon his bed hym leyde.

And as in wynter leves ben biraft,
Ech after other, til the tree be bare,
So that ther nys but bark and braunche ilaft,
Lith Troilus, byraft of ech welfare,
Ibounden in the blake bark of care,
Disposed wood [1] out of his wit to breyde,
So sore hym sat the chaungynge of Criseyde.

He rist hym up, and every dore he shette
And wyndow ek, and tho this sorwful man
Upon his beddes syde adown hym sette,
Ful lik a ded ymage, pale and wan;
And in his brest the heped wo bygan
Out breste, and he to werken in this wise
In his woodnesse, as I shal yow devyse.

Right as the wylde bole [2] bygynneth sprynge,
Now her, now ther, idarted to the herte,
And of his deth roreth in compleynynge,
Right so gan he aboute the chaumbre sterte,
Smytyng his brest ay with his fistes smerte;
His hed to the wal, his body to the grounde
Ful ofte he swapte, hymselven to confounde.

His eyen two, for piete of herte,
Out stremeden as swifte welles tweye;
The heighe sobbes of his sorwes smerte
His speche hym refte, unnethes myghte he seye,
'O deth, allas! why nyltow so me deye?
Acorsed be that day which that Nature
Shop [3] me to ben a layves creature!'

But after, when the furie and al the rage
Which that his herte twiste and faste threste,
By lengthe of tyme somwhat gan aswage
Upon his bed he leyde hym down to reste
But tho bygonne his teeris more out breste,
That wonder is the body may suffise
To half this wo, which that I yow devyse.

[1] madly   [2] bull   [3] created

Than seyde he thus, 'Fortune, allas the while
What have I don? What have I the agylt?
How myghtestow for rowthe me bygile?
Is ther no grace, and shal I thus be spilt? [1]
Shal thus Creiseyde awey, for that thow wilt?
Allas! how maistow in thyn herte fynde
To ben to me thus cruwel and unkynde?

'Have I the nought honoured al my lyve,
As thow wel woost, above the goddes alle?
Whi wiltow me fro joie thus deprive?
O Troilus, what may men now the calle
But wrecche of wrecches, out of honour falle
Into miserie, in which I wol bewaille
Criseyde, allas! till that the breth me faille?

'Allas, Fortune! if that my lif in joie
Displesed hadde unto thi foule envye,
Why ne haddestow my fader, kyng of Troye,
Byraft the lif, or don my bretheren dye,
Or slayn myself, that thus compleyne and crye,
I, combre-world, that may of nothyng serve,
But evere dye and nevere fulli sterve?

'If that Criseyde allone were me laft,
Nought roughte I whider thow woldest me steere;
And hire, allas! than hastow me biraft.
But everemore, lo, this is thi manere,
Te reve a wight that most is to hym deere,
To preve in that thi gerful [2] violence.
Thus am I lost, ther helpeth no diffence.

'O verrey lord, O Love! O god, allas!
That knowest best myn herte and al my thought,
What shal my sorwful lif don in this cas,
If I forgo that I so deere have bought?
Syn ye Criseyde and me han fully brought
Into youre grace, and bothe oure hertes seled,
How may ye suffre, allas! it be repeled?

     [1] killed   [2] changeable

'What shal I don? I shal, while I may dure
On lyve in torment and in cruwel peyne,
This infortune or this disaventure,
Allone as I was born, iwys, compleyne;
Ne nevere wol I seen it shyne or reyne,
But ende I wol, as Edippe, in derknesse
My sorwful lif, and dyen in distresse.

'O wery goost, that errest to and fro,
Why nyltow fleen out of the wofulleste
Body that evere myghte on grounde go?
O soule, lurkynge in this wo, unneste,
Fle forth out of myn herte, and lat it breste,
And folowe alwey Criseyde, thi lady dere.
Thi righte place is now no lenger here.

'O woful eyen two, syn youre disport
Was al to sen Criseydes eyen brighte,
What shal ye don but, for my discomfort,
Stonden for naught, and wepen out youre sighte,
Syn she is queynt,[1] that wont was yow to lighte?
In vayn fro this forth have ich eyen tweye
Ifourmed, syn youre vertu is aweye.

'O my Criseyde, O lady sovereigne
Of thilke woful soule that thus crieth,
Who shal now yeven comfort to my peyne?
Allas! no wight; but whan myn herte dieth,
My spirit, which that so unto yow hieth,
Receyve in gree, for that shal ay yow serve;
Forthi no fors is, though the body sterve.

'O ye loveris, that heigh upon the whiel
Ben set of Fortune, in good aventure,
God leve that ye fynde ay love of stiel[2],
And longe mote youre lif in joie endure!
But when ye comen by my sepulture,
Remembreth that youre felawe resteth there;
For I loved ek, though ich unworthi were.

---

[1] quenched   [2] true as steel

'O oold, unholsom, and myslyved man,
Calkas I mene, allas! what eileth the,
To ben a Grek, syn thow are born Troian?
O Calkas, which that wolt my bane be,
In corsed tyme was thow born for me!
As wolde blisful Jove, for his joie,
That I the hadde, wher I wolde, in Troie!'

A thousand sikes, hotter than the gleede [1],
Out of his brest ech after other wente,
Medled with pleyntes new, his wo to feede,
For which his woful teris nevere stente;
And shortly, so his peynes hym torente,
And wex so mat [2], that joie nor penaunce
He feleth non, but lith forth in a traunce.

GEOFFREY CHAUCER

12 *The Prioress's Tale*

Ther was in Asye, in a greet citee,
Amonges Cristene folk, a Jewerye,
Sustened by a lord of that contree
For foule usure and lucre of vileynye,
Hateful to Crist and to his compaignye;
And thurgh the strete men myghte ride or wende,
For it was free and open at eyther ende.

A litel scole of Cristen folk ther stood
Doun at the ferther ende, in which ther were
Children an heep, ycomen of Cristen blood,
That lerned in that scole yeer by yere
Swich manere doctrine as men used there,
This is to seyn, to syngen and to rede,
As smale children doon in hire childhede.

Among thise children was a wydwes sone,
A litel clergeon, seven yeer of age,
That day by day to scole was his wone,
An eek also, where as he saugh th' ymage
Of Cristes mooder, hadde he in usage,

---

[1] live coal   [2] dead

As hym was taught, to knele adoun and seye
His Ave Marie, as he goth by the weye.

Thus hath this wydwe hir litel sone ytaught
Oure blisful Lady, Cristes mooder deere,
To worshipe ay, and he forgat it naught,
For seely [1] child wol alday soone leere.
But ay, whan I remembre on this mateere,
Seint Nicholas stant evere in my presence,
For he so yong to Crist dide reverence.

This litel child, his litel book lernynge,
As he sat in the scole at his prymer,
He *Alma redemptoris* herde synge,
As children lerned hire antiphoner;
And as he dorste, he drough hym ner and ner,
And herkned ay the wordes and the noote,
Til he the firste vers koude al by rote.

Noght wiste he what this Latyn was to seye,
For he so yong and tendre was of age.
But on a day his felawe gan he preye
T'expounden hym this song in his langage,
Or telle hym why this song was in usage;
This preyde he hym to construe and declare
Ful often tyme upon his knowes bare.

His felawe, which that elder was than he,
Answerde hym thus: 'This song, I have herd seye,
Was maked of our blisful Lady free,
Hire to salue, and eek hire for to preye
To been oure help and socour whan we deye.
I kan namoore expounde in this mateere;
I lerne song, I kan but smal grammeere.'

'And is this song maked in reverence
Of Cristes mooder?' seyde this innocent.
'Now, certes, I wol do my diligence
To konne it al er Cristemasse be went.
Though that I for my prymer shal be shent,

---

[1] blessed

And shal be beten thries in an houre,
I wol it konne Oure Lady for to honoure!'

His felawe taughte hym homward prively,
Fro day to day, til he koude it by rote,
And thanne he song it wel and boldely,
Fro word to word, acordynge with the note.
Twies a day it passed thurgh his throte,
To scoleward and homward whan he wente:
On Cristes mooder set was his entente.

As I have seyd, thurghout the Juerie,
This litel child, as he cam to and fro,
Ful murily than wolde he synge and crie
O Alma redemptoris everemo.
The swetnesse hath his herte perced so
Of Cristes mooder that, to hire to preye,
He kan nat stynte of syngyng by the weye.

Oure firste foo, the serpent Sathanas,
That hath in Jues herte his waspes nest,
Up swal [1], and seide, 'O Hebrayk peple, allas!
If this to yow a thyng that is honest,
That swich a boy shal walken as hym lest
In youre despit, and synge of swich sentence
Which is agayn youre lawes reverence?'

Fro thennes forth the Jues han conspired
This innocent out of this world to chace.
An homycide therto han they hyred,
That in an aleye hadde a privee place;
And as the child gan forby for to pace,
This cursed Jew hym hente, and heeld hym faste,
And kitte his throte, and in a pit hym caste.

I seye that in a wardrobe they hym threwe
Where as thise Jewes purgen hire entraille.
O cursed folk of Herodes al newe,
What may youre yvel entente yow availle?
Mordre wol out, certeyn, it wol nat faille,

---

[1] uprose

And namely ther th'onour of God shal sprede;
The blood out crieth on youre cursed dede.

O martir, souded to [1] virginitee,
Now maystow syngen, folwynge evere in oon
The white Lamb celestial–quod she–
Of which the grete evaungelist Seint John,
In Pathmos wroot, which seith that they that goon
Biforn this Lamb, and synge a song al newe,
That nevere, flesshly, wommen they ne knewe.

This poure wydwe awaiteth al that nyght
After hir litel child, but he cam noght;
For which, as soone as it was dayes lyght,
With face pale of drede and bisy thoght,
She hath at scole and elleswhere hym soght,
Til finally she gan so fer espie
That he last seyn was in the Juerie.

With moodres pitee in hir brest enclosed,
She gooth, as she were half out of hir mynde,
To every place where she hath supposed
By liklihede hir litel child to fynde;
And evere on Cristes mooder meeke and kynde
She cride, and atte laste thus she wroghte,
Among the cursed Jues she hym soghte.

She frayneth [2] and she preyeth pitously
To every Jew that dwelte in thilke place,
To telle hire if hir child wente oght forby.
They seyde 'nay'; but Jhesu, of his grace,
Yaf in hir thoght, inwith a litel space,
That in that place after hir sone she cryde,
Where he was casten in a pit bisyde.

O grete God, that parfournest [3] thy laude
By mouth of innocentz, lo, heere thy myght!
This gemme of chastite, this emeraude,
And eek of martirdom the ruby bright,
Ther he with throte ykorven lay upright,

---

[1] confirmed in   [2] enquires   [3] fulfillest

He *Alma redemptoris* gan to synge
So loude that al the place gan to rynge.

The Cristene folk that thurgh the strete wente
In coomen for to wondre upon this thyng,
And hastily they for the provost sente;
He cam anon withouten tariyng,
And herieth [1] Crist that is of hevene kyng,
And eek his mooder, honour of mankynde,
And after that the Jewes leet he bynde.

This child with pitous lamentacioun
Up taken was, syngynge his song alway,
And with honour of greet processioun
They carien hym unto the nexte abbay.
His mooder swownynge by the beere lay;
Unnethe [2] myghte the peple that was theere
This newe Rachel brynge fro his beere.

With torment and with shameful deeth echon
This provost dooth thise Jewes for to sterve
That of this mordre wiste, and that anon.
He nolde no swich cursednesse observe.
'Yvele shal have that yvele wol deserve';
Therfore with wilde hors he dide hem drawe,
And after that he heng hem by the lawe.

Upon this beere ay lith this innocent
Biforn the chief auter, whil masse laste;
And after that, the abbot with his covent
Han sped hem for to burien hym ful faste;
And whan they hooly water on hym caste,
Yet spak this child, whan spreynd was hooly water,
And song *O Alma redemptoris mater!*

This abbot, which that was an hooly man,
As monkes been, or elles oghte be,
This yonge child to conjure he bigan,
And seyde, 'O deere child, I halse [3] thee,
In vertu of the hooly Trinitee,

---

[1] praises   [2] with difficulty   [3] conjure

Tel me what is thy cause for to synge,
Sith that thy throte is kut to my semynge?'

'My throte is kut unto my nekke boon,'
Seyd this child, "and, as by wey of kynde,
I sholde have dyed, ye, longe tyme agon.
But Jesu Crist, as ye in bookes fynde,
Wil that his glorie laste and be in mynde,
And for the worship of his Mooder deere
Yet may I synge *O Alma* loude and cleere.

'This welle of mercy, Cristes mooder sweete,
I loved alwey, as after my konnynge;
And whan that I my lyf sholde forlete [1],
To me she cam, and bad me for to synge
This anthem verraily in my deyynge,
As ye han herd, and whan that I hadde songe,
Me thoughte she leyde a greyn [2] upon my tonge.

'Wherefore I synge, and synge I moot certeyn,
In honour of that blisful Mayden free,
Til fro my tonge of taken is the greyn;
And after that thus seyde she to me:
"My litel child, now wol I fecche thee,
Whan that the greyn if fro thy tonge ytake.
Be nat agast, I wol thee nat forsake." '

This hooly monk, this abbot, hym meene I,
His tonge out caughte, and took awey the greyn,
And he yaf up the goost ful softely.
And whan this abbot hadde this wonder seyn,
His salte teeries trikled doun as reyn,
And gruf [3] he fil al plat upon the grounde,
And stille he lay as he had ben ybounde.

The covent eek lay on the pavement
Wepynge, and heryen Cristes mooder deere,
And after that they ryse, and forth been went,
And tooken awey this martir from his beere:
And in a tombe of marbul stones cleere

---

[1] lose   [2] pearl (?)   [3] face downward

Enclosen they his litel body sweete.
Ther he is now, God leve us for to meete!

O yonge Hugh of Lyncoln, slayn also
With cursed Jewes, as it is notable,
For it is but a litel while ago,
Preye eek for us, we synful folk unstable,
That, of his mercy, God so merciable
On us his grete mercy multiplie,
For reverence of his mooder Marie.
    Amen.

GEOFFREY CHAUCER

13 *Hero and Leander*

On Hellespont, guilty of true love's blood,
In view and opposite two cities stood,
Sea borderers, disjoin'd by Neptune's might;
The one Abydos, the other Sestos hight.
At Sestos Hero dwelt; Hero the fair,
Whom young Apollo courted for her hair,
And offer'd as a dower his burning throne,
Where she should sit for men to gaze upon.
The outside of her garments were of lawn,
The lining purple silk, with gilt stars drawn;
Her wide sleeves green, and bordered with a grove,
Where Venus in her naked glory strove
To please the careless and disdainful eyes
Of proud Adonis that before her lies.
Her kirtle blue, whereon was many a stain,
Made with the blood of wretched lovers slain.
Upon her head she ware a myrtle wreath,
From whence her veil reach'd to the ground beneath.
Her veil was artificial flowers and leaves,
Whose workmanship both man and beast deceives.
Many would praise the sweet smell as she passed,
When 'twas the odour which her breath forth cast;
And there for honey, bees have sought in vain,
And, beat from thence, have lighted there again.
About her neck hung chains of pebble-stone,
Which, lighten'd by her neck, like diamonds shone.

She ware no gloves, for neither sun nor wind
Would burn or parch her hands, but to her mind
Or warm or cool them, for they took delight
To play upon those hands, they were so white.
Buskins of shells all silvered used she,
And branch'd with blushing coral to the knee,
Where sparrows perch'd, of hollow pearl and gold,
Such as the world would wonder to behold:
Those with sweet water oft her handmaid fills,
Which, as she went, would chirrup through the bills.
Some say, for her the fairest Cupid pin'd,
And, looking in her face, was strooken blind.
But this is true, so like was one the other,
As he imagin'd Hero was his mother;
And oftentimes into her bosom flew,
About her naked neck his bare arms threw,
And laid his childish head upon her breast,
And with still panting rock'd, there took his rest.
So lovely fair was Hero, Venus' nun,
As Nature wept, thinking she was undone,
Because she took more from her than she left,
And of such wondrous beauty her bereft;
Therefore, in sign her treasure suffer'd wrack,
Since Hero's time hath half the world been black.
Amorous Leander, beautiful and young,
(Whose tragedy divine Musaeus sung)
Dwelt at Abydos; since him dwelt there none
For whom succeeding times make greater moan.
His dangling tresses that were never shorn,
Had they been cut and unto Colchos borne,
Would have allur'd the vent'rous youth of Greece
To hazard more than for the Golden Fleece.
Fair Cynthia wish'd his arms might be her sphere;
Grief makes her pale, because she moves not there.
His body was as straight as Circe's wand;
Jove might have sipt out nectar from his hand.
Even as delicious meat is to the taste,
So was his neck in touching, and surpast
The white of Pelops' shoulder. I could tell ye
How smooth his breast was, and how white his belly,

And whose immortal fingers did imprint
That heavenly path, with many a curious dint,
That runs along his back; but my rude pen
Can hardly blazon forth the loves of men,
Much less of powerful gods; let it suffice
That my slack muse sings of Leander's eyes,
Those orient cheeks and lips, exceeding his
That leapt into the water for a kiss
Of his own shadow, and despising many,
Died ere he could enjoy the love of any.
Had wild Hippolytus Leander seen,
Enamoured of his beauty had he been;
His presence made the rudest peasant melt,
That in the vast uplandish country dwelt;
The barbarous Thracian soldier, mov'd with naught,
Was mov'd with him, and for his favour sought.
Some swore he was a maid in man's attire,
For in his looks were all that men desire,
A pleasant smiling cheek, a speaking eye,
A brow for love to banquet royally;
And such as knew he was a man would say,
'Leander, thou art made for amorous play;
Why art thou not in love, and lov'd of all?
Though thou be fair, yet be not thine own thrall.'
        The men of wealthy Sestos, every year,
For his sake whom their goddess held so dear,
Rose-cheek'd Adonis, kept a solemn feast.
Thither resorted many a wand'ring guest
To meet their loves; such as had none at all,
Came lovers home, from this great festival;
For every street like to a firmament,
Glistered with breathing stars, who where they went,
Frighted the melancholy earth, which deem'd
Eternal heaven to burn, for so it seem'd
As if another Phaëton had got
The guidance of the sun's rich chariot.
But, far above the loveliest, Hero shin'd,
And stole away th' enchanted gazer's mind;
For like sea-nymphs' inveigling harmony,
So was her beauty to the standers by;

c

Nor that night-wandering pale and watery star
(When yawning dragons draw her thirling [1] car
From Latmus' mount up to the gloomy sky,
Where, crown'd with blazing light and majesty,
She proudly sits) more over-rules the flood
Than she the hearts of those that near her stood.
Even as, when gaudy nymphs pursue the chase,
Wretched Ixion's shaggy-footed race,
Incens'd with savage heat, gallop amain
From steep pine-bearing mountains to the plain;
So ran the people forth to gaze upon her,
And all that view'd her were enamour'd on her . . .

CHRISTOPHER MARLOWE

14 *The Courser and the Jennet*

But, lo! from forth a copse that neighbours by,
A breeding jennet, lusty, young, and proud,
Adonis' trampling courser doth espy,
And forth she rushes, snorts and neighs aloud:
    The strong-necked steed, being tied unto a tree,
    Breaketh his rein, and to her straight goes he.

Imperiously he leaps, he neighs, he bounds,
And now his woven girths he breaks asunder;
The bearing earth with his hard hoof he wounds,
Whose hollow womb resounds like heaven's thunder;
    The iron bit he crushes 'tween his teeth,
    Controlling what he was controlled with.

His ears up-prick'd; his braided hanging mane
Upon his compass'd crest now stand on end;
His nostrils drink the air, and forth again,
As from a furnace, vapours doth he send:
    His eye, which scornfully glisters like fire,
    Shows his hot courage and his high desire.

Sometime he trots, as if he told the steps,
With gentle majesty and modest pride;
Anon he rears upright, curvets and leaps,
As who should say, 'Lo! thus my strength is tried;

[1] flying like a missile

And this I do to captivate the eye
Of the fair breeder that is standing by.'

What recketh he his rider's angry stir,
His flattering 'Holla,' or his 'Stand, I say?'
What cares he now for curb or pricking spur?
For rich caparisons or trapping gay?
   He sees his love, and nothing else he sees,
   For nothing else with his proud sight agrees.

Look, when a painter would surpass the life,
In limning out a well-proportion'd steed,
His art with nature's workmanship at strife,
As if the dead the living should exceed;
   So did this horse excel a common one,
   In shape, in courage, colour, pace and bone.

Round-hoof'd, short-jointed, fetlocks shag and long,
Broad breast, full eye, small head, and nostril wide,
High crest, short ears, straight legs and passing strong,
Thin mane, thick tail, broad buttock, tender hide:
   Look, what a horse should have he did not lack,
   Save a proud rider on so proud a back.

Sometimes he scuds far off, and there he stares;
Anon he starts at stirring of a feather;
To bid the wind a base he now prepares,
And whe'r he run or fly they know not whether;
   For through his mane and tail the high wind sings,
   Fanning the hairs, who wave like feather'd wings.

He looks upon his love, and neighs unto her;
She answers him as if she knew his mind;
Being proud, as females are, to see him woo her,
She puts on outward strangeness, seems unkind,
   Spurns at his love and scorns the heat he feels,
   Beating his kind embracements with her heels.

Then, like a melancholy malcontent,
He vails his tail that, like a falling plume
Cool shadow to his melting buttock lent:
He stamps, and bites the poor flies in his fume.

His love, perceiving how he is enrag'd,
Grew kinder, and his fury was assuag'd.

His testy master goeth about to take him;
When lo! the unback'd breeder, full of fear,
Jealous of catching, swiftly doth forsake him,
With her the horse, and left Adonis there.
    As they were mad, unto the wood they hie them
    Out-stripping crows that strive to over-fly them.

All swoln with chafing, down Adonis sits,
Banning his boisterous and unruly beast:
And now the happy season once more fits,
That love-sick Love by pleading may be blest;
    For lovers say, the heart hath treble wrong
    When it is barr'd the aidance of the tongue.

An oven that is stopp'd, or river stay'd,
Burneth more hotly, swelleth with more rage:
So of concealed sorrow may be said;
Free vent of words love's fire doth assuage;
    But when the heart's attorney once is mute,
    The client breaks, as desperate in his suit.
WILLIAM SHAKESPEARE

15 *Sonnet or Dittie*

Mars in a fury gainst love's brightest Queen
  Put on his helm and took him to his lance:
On Erecynus' mount was Mavors seen,
  And there his ensigns did the god advance.
    And by heaven's greatest gates he stoutly swore,
    Venus should die for she had wrong'd him sore.

Cupid heard this and he began to cry,
  And wisht his mother's absence for a while:
Peace, fool, quoth Venus, is it I must die?
  Must it be Mars? with that she coin'd a smile:
    She trimm'd her tresses and did curl her hair,
    And made her face with beauty passing fair.

A fan of silver feathers in her hand,
   And in a coach of ebony she went:
She past the place where furious Mars did stand,
   And out her looks a lovely smile she sent,
     Then from her brows leapt out so sharp a frown,
     That Mars for fear threw all his armour down.

He vow'd repentance for his rash misdeed,
   Blaming his choler that had caus'd his woe:
Venus grew gracious, and with him agreed,
   But charg'd him not to threaten beauty so,
     For women's looks are such inchanting charms,
     As can subdue the greatest god in arms.

ROBERT GREENE

16 *The Ballad of Dowsabell*

Far in the country of *Arden*
There wond a knight hight *Cassemen*,
   as bold as Isenbras:
Fell was he and eager bent,
In battle and in tournament,
   as was the good sir *Topas*.
He had, as antique stories tell,
A daughter cleaped *Dowsabell*,
   a maiden fair and free:
And for she was her father's heir,
Full well she was ycond the leyre[1],
   of mickle curtesy.
The silk well could she twist and twine,
And make the fine Marchpine [2],
   and with the needle work,
And she could help the priest to say
His Mattins on a holyday,
   and sing a Psalme in Kirk.
She wore a frock of frolick green,
Might well beseem a maiden Queen,
   which seemly was to see.
A hood to that so neat and fine,
In colour like the colombine,
   ywrought full featously.

[1] knew the learning   [2] marzipan

Her feature all as fresh above,
As is the grass that grows by Dove,
   as lithe as lass of Kent:
Her skin as soft as Lemster wool,
As white as snow on peakish hull,
   or Swan that swims in Trent.
This maiden in a morn betime,
Went forth when May was in her prime,
   to get sweet Cetywall [1],
The honey-suckle, the Harlock,
The Lilly and the Lady-smock,
   to deck her summer hall.
Thus as she wandred here and there,
Ypicking of the bloomed Breere,
   she chanced to espie
A shepherd sitting on a bank,
Like *Chantecleer* he crowed crank [2],
   and pip'd with merry glee:
He leard his sheep as he him list,
When he would whistle in his fist,
   To feed about him round:
Whilst he full many a carol sung,
Until the fields and meadows rung,
   and that the woods did sound:
In favour this same shepherd's swain,
Was like the bedlam *Tamburlain*,
   which held proud Kings in awe:
But meek he was as Lamb might be,
Ylike that gentle Abel he,
   whom his lewd brother slew.
This shepherd wore a sheep gray cloak,
Which was of the finest loke [3],
   that could be cut with shear,
His mittens were of Bauzens [4] skin,
His cockers [5] were of Cordiwin
   his hood of Meniveere [6].
His aule and lingell in a thong,
His tar-box on a broad belt hung,
   his breech of Coyntrie [7] blew:
Full crisp and curled were his locks,

[1] garden valerian   [2] lustily   [3] lock   [4] badger's
[5] rustic high-shoes   [6] a kind of fur   [7] Coventry

His brow as white as *Albion* rocks,
  so like a lover true.
And piping still he spent the day,
So merry as the Popingay:
  which liked Dowsabell,
That would she ought or would she nought,
This lad would never from her thought:
  she in love-longing fell,
At length she tucked up her frock,
White as the Lily was her smock,
  she drew the shepherd nigh,
But then the shepherd pip'd a good,
That all his sheep forsook their food,
  to hear his melody.
Thy sheep, quoth she, cannot be lean,
That have a jolly shepherd's swain,
  the which can pipe so well.
Yea but (sayth he) their shepherd may,
If piping thus he pine away,
  In love of Dowsabell.
Of love fond boy take thou no keep,
Quoth she, look well unto thy sheep,
  lest they should hap to stray.
Quoth he, so had I done full well,
Had I not seen fair Dowsabell,
  come forth to gather May.
With that she gan to veil her head,
Her cheeks were like the Roses red,
  but not a word she said.
With that the shepherd 'gan to frown,
He threw his pretty pipes adown,
  and on the ground him laid.
Sayth she, I may not stay till night,
And leave my summer hall undight,
  and all for long of thee.
My coat saith he, nor yet my fold,
Shall neither sheep nor shepherd hold,
  except thou favour me.
Saith she, Yet lever I were dead,
Then I should lose my maidenhead,
  and all for love of men:

Saith he, Yet are you too unkind,
If in your heart you cannot find,
   to love us now and then:
And I to thee will be as kind,
As *Colin* was to *Rosalind*,
   of curtesy the flower;
Then I will be as true, quoth she,
As ever maiden yet might be,
   unto her Paramour:
With that she bent her snow-white knee,
Down by the shepherd kneeled she,
   and him she sweetely kist.
With that the shepherd whoop'd for joy,
Quoth he, there's never shepherd's boy,
   that ever was so blist.

MICHAEL DRAYTON

17 *La Belle Dame Sans Merci*

A BALLAD

O what can ail thee, knight-at-arms,
   Alone and palely loitering?
The sedge has wither'd from the lake,
   And no birds sing.

O what can ail thee, knight-at-arms!
   So haggard and so woe-begone?
The squirrel's granary is full,
   And the harvest's done.

I see a lilly on thy brow
   With anguish moist and fever dew,
And on thy cheek a fading rose
   Fast withereth too.

I met a lady in the meads,
   Full beautiful—a faery's child,
Her hair was long, her foot was light,
   And her eyes were wild.

I made a garland for her head,
 And bracelets too, and fragrant zone;
She look'd at me as she did love,
 And made sweet moan.

I set her on my pacing steed,
 And nothing else saw all day long,
For sidelong would she bend, and sing
 A faery's song.

She found me roots of relish sweet,
 And honey wild, and manna dew,
And sure in language strange she said–
 'I love thee true.'

She took me to her elfin grot,
 And there she wept, and sigh'd full sore.
And there I shut her wild wild eyes
 With kisses four.

And there she lulled me asleep,
 And there I dream'd–Ah! woe betide!
The latest dream I ever dream'd
 On the cold hill side.

I saw pale kings and princes too,
 Pale warriors, death-pale were they all;
They cried—'La Belle Dame sans Merci
 Hath thee in thrall!'

I saw their starved lips in the gloam,
 With horrid warning gaped wide,
And I awoke and found me here,
 On the cold hill side.

And this is why I sojourn here,
 Alone and palely loitering,
Though the sedge has wither'd from the lake,
 And no birds sing.

JOHN KEATS

18 *Proud Maisie*

Proud Maisie is in the wood,
    Walking so early;
Sweet Robin sits on the bush,
    Singing so rarely.

'Tell me, thou bonny bird,
When shall I marry me?'
'When six braw gentlemen
Kirkward shall carry ye.'

'Who makes the bridal bed,
Birdie, say truly?'
'The grey-headed sexton
That delves the grave duly.'

'The glowworm o'er grave and stone
Shall light thee steady;
The owl from the steeple sing
"Welcome, proud lady."'

SIR WALTER SCOTT

19 *Both Less and More*

I rode my horse to the hostel gate,
    And the landlord fed it with corn and hay:
His eyes were blear, he limped in his gait,
    His lip hung down, his hair was grey.

I entered in the wayside inn;
    And the landlady met me without a smile;
Her dreary dress was old and thin,
    Her face was full of piteous guile.

There they had been for threescore years:
    There was none to tell them they were great:
Not one to tell of our hopes and fears;
    And not far off was the churchyard gate.

RICHARD WATSON DIXON

20 *Eight O'Clock*

He stood, and heard the steeple
  Sprinkle the quarters on the morning town.
One, two, three, four, to market-place and people
  It tossed them down.

Strapped, noosed, nighing his hour,
  He stood and counted them and cursed his luck;
And then the clock collected in the tower
  Its strength, and struck.

A. E. HOUSMAN

21 *Amantium Irae*

In going to my naked bed, as one that would have slept,
I heard a wife sing to her child, that long before had wept;
She sighed sore, and sang full sweet to bring the babe to rest,
That would not rest but cried still, in sucking at her breast.
She was full weary of her watch, and grieved with her child,
She rocked it and rated it, until on her it smiled.
Then did she say, 'Now have I found this proverb true to
    prove,
The falling out of faithful friends, renewing is of love.'

Then took I paper, pen, and ink, this proverb for to write,
In register for to remain of such a worthy wight.
As she proceeded thus in song unto her little brat
Much matter uttered she of weight, in place whereas she sat:
And proved plain there was no beast, nor creature bearing
    life
Could well be known to live in love, without discord and strife.
Then kissed she her little babe, and sware, by God above,
The falling out of faithful friends, renewing is of love.

She said that neither king, ne prince, ne lord could live
    aright,
Until their puissance they did prove, their manhood, and their
    might:

When manhood shall be matched so, that fear can take no
    place,
Then weary works make warriors each other to embrace,
And leave their force that failed them, which did consume the
    rout
That might by force with love have lived the term of nature
    out.
Then did she sing, as one that thought no man could her
    reprove,
The falling out of faithful friends, renewing is of love.

She said she saw no fish, ne fowl, nor beast within her haunt.
That met a stranger in their kind, but could give it a taunt.
Since flesh might not endure, but rest must wrath succeed,
And force the fight to fall to play in pasture where they
    feed,
So noble Nature can well end the work she hath begun,
And bridle well that will not cease her tragedy in some.
Thus in her song she oft rehearsed, as did her well behove,
The falling out of faithful friends, renewing is of love.

'I marvel much, pardy,' quoth she, 'for to behold the rout,
To see man, woman, boy, and beast, to toss the world about;
Some kneel, some crouch, some beck, some check, and some
    can smoothly smile,
And some embrace others in arms, and there think many a
    wile;
Some stand aloof at cap and knee, some humble, and some
    stout,
Yet are they never friends in deed until they once fall out!'
Thus ended she her song, and said, before she did remove,
The falling out of faithful friends, renewing is of love.

RICHARD EDWARDS

22 *My Sister's Sleep*

She fell asleep on Christmas Eve:
    At length the long-ungranted shade
    Of weary eyelids overweigh'd
The pain nought else might yet relieve.

Our mother, who had leaned all day
   Over the bed from chime to chime,
   Then raised herself for the first time,
And as she sat her down, did pray.

Her little work-table was spread
   With work to finish. For the glare
   Made by her candle, she had care
To work some distance from the bed.

Without, there was a cold moon up,
   Of winter radiance sheer and thin;
   The hollow halo it was in
Was like an icy crystal cup.

Through the small room, with subtle sound
   Of flame, by vents the fireshine drove
   And reddened. In its dim alcove
The mirror shed a clearness round.

I had been sitting up some nights,
   And my tired mind felt weak and blank;
   Like a sharp strengthening wine it drank
The stillness and the broken lights.

Twelve struck. That sound, by dwindling years
   Heard in each hour, crept off; and then
   The ruffled silence spread again,
Like water that a pebble stirs.

Our mother rose from where she sat:
   Her needles, as she laid them down,
   Met lightly, and her silken gown
Settled: no other noise than that.

'Glory unto the Newly Born!'
   So, as said angels, she did say;
   Because we were in Christmas Day,
Though it would still be long till morn.

Just then in the room over us
  There was a pushing back of chairs,
  As some who had sat unawares
So late, now heard the hour, and rose.

With anxious softly-stepping haste
  Our mother went where Margaret lay,
  Fearing the sounds o'erhead—should they
Have broken her long watched-for rest!

She stopped an instant, calm, and turned;
  But suddenly turned back again;
  And all her features seemed in pain
With woe, and her eyes gazed and yearned.

For my part, I but hid my face,
  And held my breath, and spoke no word:
  There was none spoken; but I heard
The silence for a little space.

Our mother bowed herself and wept:
  And both my arms fell, and I said,
  'God knows I knew that she was dead.'
And there, all white, my sister slept.

Then kneeling, upon Christmas morn
  A little after twelve o'clock,
  We said, ere the first quarter struck,
'Christ's blessing on the newly born!'
                    DANTE GABRIEL ROSSETTI

23 *Patch-Shaneen*

Shaneen and Maurya Prendergast
  Lived west in Carnareagh,
  And they'd a cur-dog, cabbage plot,
  A goat, and cock of hay.

He was five foot one or two,
  Herself was four foot ten,
  And he went travelling asking meal
  Above through Caragh Glen.

She'd pick her bag of carrageen
Or perries through the surf,
Or loan as ass of Foxy Jim
To fetch her creel of turf.

Till on one windy Samhain night,
When there's stir among the dead,
He found her perished, stiff and stark,
Beside him in the bed.

And now when Shaneen travels far
From Droum to Ballyhyre
The women lay him sacks of straw,
Beside the seed of fire.

And when the grey cocks crow and flap
And winds are in the sky,
'Oh, Maurya, Maurya, are you dead?'
You'll hear Patch-Shaneen cry.

JOHN MILLINGTON SYNGE

24 *Billy in the Darbies*

Good of the Chaplain to enter Lone Bay
And down on his marrow-bones here and pray
For the likes just o' me, Billy Budd.–But look:
Through the port comes the moon-shine astray!
It tips the guard's cutlass and silvers this nook;
But 'twill die in the dawning of Billy's last day.
A jewel-block they'll make of me to-morrow,
Pendant pearl from the yard-arm-end
Like the ear-drop I gave to Bristol Molly–
Oh, 'tis me, not the sentence, they'll suspend.
Ay, Ay, all is up; and I must up too
Early in the morning, aloft from alow.
On an empty stomach, now, never it would do.
They'll give me a nibble–bit o' biscuit ere I go.
Sure, a messmate will reach me the last parting cup;
But turning heads away from the hoist and the belay,
Heaven knows who will have the running of me up!

No pipe to those halyards–But aren't it all a sham?
A blur's in my eyes; it is dreaming that I am.
A hatchet to my panzer? All adrift to go?
The drum roll to grog, and Billy never know?
But Donald he has promised to stand by the plank;
So I'll shake a friendly hand ere I sink.
But–no! It is dead then I'll be, come to think.
I remember Taff the Welshman when he sank.
And his cheek it was like the budding pink.
But me, they'll lash me in hammock, drop me deep
Fathoms down, fathoms down, how I'll dream fast asleep.
I feel it stealing now. Sentry, are you there?
Just ease these darbies at the wrist,
And roll me over fair.
I am sleepy, and the oozy weeds about me twist.

HERMAN MELVILLE

25 *The Ghosts*

Never stoops the soaring vulture
On his quarry in the desert,
On the sick or wounded bison,
But another vulture, watching
From his high aerial look-out,
Sees the downward plunge, and follows;
And a third pursues the second,
Coming from the invisible ether,
First a speck, and then a vulture,
Till the air is dark with pinions.

So disasters come not singly;
But as if they watched and waited,
Scanning one another's motions,
When the first descends, the others
Follow, follow, gathering flock-wise
Round their victim, sick and wounded,
First a shadow, then a sorrow,
Till the air is dark with anguish.

Now, o'er all the dreary Northland,
Mighty Peboan, the Winter,
Breathing on the lakes and rivers,
Into stone had changed their waters,

From his hair he shook the snow-flakes,
Till the plains were strewed with whiteness,
One uninterrupted level,
As if, stooping, the Creator
With his hand had smoothed them over.

Through the forest, wide and wailing,
Roamed the hunter on his snow-shoes;
In the village worked the women,
Pounded maize, or dressed the deerskin;
And the young men played together
On the ice the noisy ball-play,
On the plain the dance of snow-shoes.

One dark evening, after sundown,
In her wigwam Laughing Water
Sat with old Nokomis, waiting
For the steps of Hiawatha
Homeward from the hunt returning.

On their faces gleamed the fire-light,
Painting them with streaks of crimson,
In the eyes of old Nokomis
Glimmered like the watery moonlight,
In the eyes of Laughing Water
Glistened like the sun in water;
And behind them crouched their shadows
In the corners of the wigwam,
And the smoke in wreaths above them
Climbed and crowded through the smoke-flue.

Then the curtain of the doorway
From without was slowly lifted;
Brighter glowed the fire a moment,
And a moment swerved the smoke-wreath,
As two women entered softly,
Passed the doorway uninvited,
Without word of salutation,
Without sign of recognition,
Sat down in the farthest corner,
Crouching low among the shadows.

From their aspect and their garments,
Strangers seemed they in the village;
Very pale and haggard were they,
As they sat there sad and silent,

Trembling, cowering with the shadows.
    Was it the wind above the smoke-flue,
Muttering down into the wigwam?
Was it the owl, the Koko-koho,
Hooting from the dismal forest?
Sure a voice said in the silence:
'These are corpses clad in garments,
These are ghosts that come to haunt you,
From the kingdom of Ponemah,
From the land of the Hereafter!'
    Homeward now came Hiawatha
From his hunting in the forest,
With the snow upon his tresses,
And the red deer on his shoulders.
At the feet of Laughing Water
Down he threw his lifeless burden;
Nobler, handsomer she thought him,
Than when first he came to woo her;
First threw down the deer before her,
As a token of his wishes,
As a promise of the future.
    Then he turned and saw the strangers,
Cowering, crouching with the shadows;
Said within himself, 'Who are they?
What strange guests has Minnehaha?'
But he questioned not the strangers,
Only spake to bid them welcome
To his lodge, his food, his fireside.
    When the evening meal was ready,
And the deer had been divided,
Both the pallid guests, the strangers,
Springing from among the shadows,
Seized upon the choicest portions,
Seized the white fat of the roebuck,
Set apart for Laughing Water,
For the wife of Hiawatha;
Without asking, without thanking,
Eagerly devoured the morsels,
Flitted back among the shadows
In the corner of the wigwam.
    Not a word spake Hiawatha,

Not a motion made Nokomis,
Not a gesture Laughing Water;
Not a change came o'er their features:
Only Minnehaha softly
Whispered, saying, 'They are famished;
Let them do what best delights them;
Let them eat, for they are famished.'
Many a daylight dawned and darkened,
Many a night shook off the daylight
As the pine shakes off the snow-flakes
From the midnight of its branches;
Day by day the guests unmoving
Sat there silent in the wigwam;
But by night, in storm or starlight,
Forth they went into the forest,
Bringing fire-wood to the wigwam,
Bringing pine-cones for the burning,
Always sad and always silent.
And whenever Hiawatha
Came from fishing or from hunting,
When the evening meal was ready,
And the food had been divided,
Gliding from their darksome corner,
Came the pallid guests, the strangers,
Seized upon the choicest portions
Set aside for Laughing Water,
And without rebuke or question
Flitted back among the shadows.
Never once had Hiawatha
By a word or look reproved them;
Never once had old Nokomis
Made a gesture of impatience;
Never once had Laughing Water
Shown resentment at the outrage.
All had they endured in silence,
That the rights of guest and stranger,
That the virtue of free-giving,
By a look might not be lessened,
By a word might not be broken.
Once at midnight Hiawatha,
Ever wakeful, ever watchful,

In the wigwam, dimly lighted
By the brands that still were burning,
By the glimmering, flickering fire-light,
Heard a sighing, oft repeated,
Heard a sobbing, as of sorrow.

From his couch rose Hiawatha,
From his shaggy hides of bison,
Pushed aside the deer-skin curtain,
Saw the pallid guests, the shadows,
Sitting upright on their couches,
Weeping in the silent midnight.

And he said: 'O guests! why is it
That your hearts are so afflicted,
That you sob so in the midnight?
Has perchance the old Nokomis,
Has my wife, my Minnehaha,
Wronged or grieved you by unkindness,
Failed in hospitable duties?'

Then the shadows ceased from weeping,
Ceased from sobbing and lamenting,
And they said, with gentle voices:
'We are ghosts of the departed,
Souls of those who once were with you.
From the realms of Chibiabos
Hither have we come to try you,
Hither have we come to warn you.

'Cries of grief and lamentation
Reach us in the Blessed Islands;
Cries of anguish from the living,
Calling back their friends departed,
Sadden us with useless sorrow.
Therefore have we come to try you;
No one knows us, no one heeds us.
We are but a burden to you,
And we see that the departed
Have no place among the living.

'Think of this, O Hiawatha!
Speak of it to all the people,
That henceforward and for ever
They no more with lamentations
Sadden the souls of the departed

In the Islands of the Blessed.

'Do not lay such heavy burdens
In the graves of those you bury,
Not such weight of furs and wampum,
Not such weight of pots and kettles,
For the spirits faint beneath them.
Only give them food to carry,
Only give them fire to light them.

'Four days is the spirit's journey
To the land of ghosts and shadows,
Four its lonely night encampments;
Four times must their fires be lighted.
Therefore, when the dead are buried,
Let a fire, as night approaches,
Four times on the grave be kindled,
That the soul upon its journey
May not lack the cheerful fire-light,
May not grope about in darkness.

'Farewell, noble Hiawatha!
We have put you to the trial,
To the proof have put your patience,
By the insult of our presence,
By the outrage of our actions.
We have found you great and noble.
Fail not in the greater trial,
Faint not in the harder struggle.'

When they ceased, a sudden darkness
Fell and filled the silent wigwam.
Hiawatha heard a rustle
As of garments trailing by him,
Heard the curtain of the doorway
Lifted by a hand he saw not,
Felt the cold breath of the night air,
For a moment saw the starlight;
But he saw the ghosts no longer,
Saw no more the wandering spirits
From the kingdom of Ponemah,
From the land of the Hereafter.

HENRY WADSWORTH LONGFELLOW

26 *The Haystack in the Floods*

Had she come all the way for this,
To part at last without a kiss?
Yea, had she borne the dirt and rain
That her own eyes might see him slain
Beside the haystack in the floods?

Along the dripping leafless woods,
The stirrup touching either shoe,
She rode astride as troopers do;
With kirtle kilted to her knee,
To which the mud splash'd wretchedly;
And the wet dripp'd from every tree
Upon her head and heavy hair,
And on her eyelids broad and fair;
The tears and rain ran down her face.
By fits and starts they rode apace,
And very often was his place
Far off from her; he had to ride
Ahead, to see what might betide
When the roads cross'd; and sometimes, when
There rose a murmuring from his men,
Had to turn back with promises;
Ah me! she had but little ease;
And often for pure doubt and dread
She sobb'd, made giddy in the head
By the swift riding; while, for cold,
Her slender fingers scarce could hold
The wet reins; yea, and scarcely, too,
She felt the foot within her shoe,
Against the stirrup: all for this,
To part at last without a kiss
Beside the haystack in the floods.

For when they near'd that old soak'd hay,
They saw across the only way
That Judas, Godmar, and the three
Red running lions dismally

Grinn'd from his pennon, under which,
In one straight line along the ditch,
They counted thirty heads.
                   So then,
While Robert turn'd round to his men,
She saw at once the wretched end,
And, stooping down, tried hard to rend
Her coif the wrong way from her head,
And hid her eyes; while Robert said:
'Nay, love, 'tis scarcely two to one,
At Poictiers where we made them run
So fast—why, sweet my love, good cheer.
The Gascon frontier is so near,
Nought after this.'
                But, 'O,' she said,
'My God! my God! I have to tread
The long way back without you; then
The court at Paris; those six men;
The gratings of the Chatelet;
The swift Seine on some rainy day
Like this, and people standing by,
And laughing, while my weak hands try
To recollect how strong men swim,
All this, or else a life with him,
For which I should be damned at last,
Would God that this next hour were past!'

He answer'd not, but cried his cry,
'St. George for Marny!' cheerily;
And laid his hand upon her rein.
Alas! no man of all his train
Gave back that cheery cry again;
And, while for rage his thumb beat fast
Upon his sword-hilts, some one cast
About his neck a kerchief long,
And bound him.
             Then they went along
To Godmar; who said: 'Now Jehane,
Your lover's life is on the wane
So fast, that, if this very hour
You yield not as my paramour,

He will not see the rain leave off–
Nay, keep your tongue from gibe and scoff,
Sir Robert, or I slay you now.'

She laid her hand upon her brow,
Then gazed upon the palm, as though
She thought her forehead bled, and–'No,'
She said, and turn'd her head away,
As there were nothing else to say,
And everything were settled: red
Grew Godmar's face from chin to head:
'Jehane, on yonder hill there stands
My castle, guarding well my lands:
What hinders me from taking you,
And doing that I list to do
To your fair wilful body, while
Your knight lies dead?'
           A wicked smile
Wrinkled her face, her lips grew thin,
A long way out she thrust her chin:
'You know that I should strangle you
While you were sleeping; or bite through
Your throat, by God's help–ah!' she said,
'Lord Jesus, pity your poor maid!
For in such wise they hem me in,
I cannot choose but sin and sin,
Whatever happens: yet I think
They could not make me eat or drink,
And so should I just reach my rest.'
'Nay, if you do not my behest,
O Jehane! though I love you well,'
Said Godmar, 'would I fail to tell
All that I know.' 'Foul lies,' she said.
'Eh? lies my Jehane? by God's head,
At Paris folks would deem them true!
Do you know, Jehane, they cry for you,
"Jehane the brown! Jehane the brown!
Give us Jehane to burn or drown!"–
Eh–gag me Robert!–sweet my friend,
This were indeed a piteous end

For those long fingers, and long feet,
And long neck, and smooth shoulders sweet;
An end that few men would forget
That saw it–So, an hour yet:
Consider, Jehane, which to take
Of life or death!'
                              So scarce awake,
Dismounting, did she leave that place,
And totter some yards: with her face
Turn'd upward to the sky she lay,
Her head on a wet heap of hay,
And fell asleep: and while she slept,
And did not dream, the minutes crept
Round to the twelve again; but she,
Being waked at last, sigh'd quietly,
And strangely childlike came, and said:
'I will not.' Straightway Godmar's head,
As though it hung on strong wires, turn'd
Most sharply round, and his face burn'd.

For Robert–both his eyes were dry,
He could not weep, but gloomily
He seem'd to watch the rain; yea, too,
His lips were firm; he tried once more
To touch her lips; she reach'd out, sore
And vain desire so tortured them,
The poor grey lips, and now the hem
Of his sleeve brush'd them.
                              With a start
Up Godmar rose, thrust them apart;
From Robert's throat he loosed the bands
Of silk and mail; with empty hands
Held out, she stood and gazed, and saw,
The long bright blade without a flaw
Glide out from Godmar's sheath, his hand
In Robert's hair; she saw him bend
Back Robert's head; she saw him send
The thin steel down; the blow told well,
Right backward the knight Robert fell,
And moan'd as dogs do, being half dead,

Unwitting, as I deem: so then
Godmar turn'd grinning to his men,
Who ran, some five or six, and beat
His head to pieces at their feet

Then Godmar turn'd again, and said:
'So, Jehane, the first fitte is read!
Take note, my lady, that your way
Lies backward to the Chatelet!'
She shook her head and gazed awhile
At her cold hands with a rueful smile,
As though this thing had made her mad.

This was the parting that they had
Beside the haystack in the floods.

WILLIAM MORRIS

27 *Near Lanivet*, 1872

There was a stunted handpost just on the crest,
   Only a few feet high:
She was tired, and we stopped in the twilight-time for her
   rest,
   At the crossways close thereby.

She leant back, being so weary, against its stem,
   And laid her arms on its own,
Each open palm stretched out to each end of them,
   Her sad face sideways thrown.

Her white-clothed form at this dim-lit cease of day
   Made her look as one crucified
In my gaze at her from the midst of the dusty way,
   And hurriedly 'Don't,' I cried.

I do not think she heard. Loosing thence she said,
   As she stepped forth ready to go,
'I am rested now.–Something strange came into my head;
   I wish I had not leant so!'

And wordless we moved onward down from the hill
   In the west cloud's murked obscure,
And looking back we could see the handpost still
   In the solitude of the moor.

'It struck her too,' I thought, for as if afraid
  She heavily breathed as we trailed;
Till she said, 'I did not think how 'twould look in the
  shade,
  When I leant there like one nailed.'

I, lightly: 'There's nothing in it. For *you*, anyhow!'
  –'O I know there is not,' said she . . .
'Yet I wonder . . . If no one is bodily crucified now,
  In spirit one may be!'

And we dragged on and on, while we seemed to see
  In the running of Time's far glass
Her crucified, as she had wondered if she might be
  Some day.–Alas, alas!

THOMAS HARDY

28 *Helen and Corythos*

   Her failing spirits with derisive glee
And fondness he refresht: her anxious thoughts
Followed, and upon Corythos they dwelt.
Often he met her eyes, nor shun'd they his,
For, royal as she was and born of Zeus,
She was compassionate, and bow'd her head
To share her smiles and griefs with those below.
All in her sight were level, for she stood
High above all within the seagirt world.
At last she questioned Corythos what brought
His early footsteps thro such dangerous ways,
And from abode so peaceable and safe.
At once he told her why he came: she held
Her hand to Corythos: he stood ashamed
Not to have hated her: he lookt, he sigh'd,
He hung upon her words . . . what gentle words!
How chaste her countenance.
                 'What open brows
The brave and beauteous ever have!' thought she,
'But even the hardiest, when above their heads
Death is impending, shudder at the sight
Of barrows on the sands and bones exposed

And whitening in the wind, and cypresses
From Ida waiting for dissever'd friends."

WALTER SAVAGE LANDOR

29 *Gabriel meets Satan*

Which of those rebell Spirits adjudg'd to Hell
Com'st thou, escap'd thy prison, and transform'd,
Why satst thou like an enemie in waite
Here watching at the head of these that sleep?
　Know ye not then said *Satan*, fill'd with scorn,
Know ye not me? ye knew me once no mate
For you, there sitting where ye durst not soare;
Not to know mee argues your selves unknown,
The lowest of your throng; or if ye know,
Why ask ye, and superfluous begin
Your message, like to end as much in vain?
To whom thus *Zephon*, answering scorn with scorn.
Think not, revolted Spirit, thy shape the same,
Or undiminisht brightness, to be known
As when thou stoodst in Heav'n upright and pure;
That Glorie then, when thou no more wast good,
Departed from thee, and thou resembl'st now
Thy sin and place of doom obscure and foule.
But come, for thou, besure, shalt give account
To him who sent us, whose charge is to keep
This place inviolable, and these from harm.
　So spake the Cherube, and his grave rebuke
Severe in youthful beautie, added grace
Invincible: abasht the Devil stood,
And felt how awful goodness is, and saw
Vertue in her shape how lovly, saw, and pin'd
His loss; but chiefly to find here observ'd
His lustre visibly impar'd; yet seemd
Undaunted. If I must contend, said he,
Best with the best, the Sender not the sent,
Or all at once; more glorie will be wonn,
Or less be lost. Thy fear, said *Zephon* bold,
Will save us trial what the least can doe
Single against thee wicked and thence weak.

The Fiend repli'd not, overcome with rage;
But like a proud Steed reind, went hautie on,
Chaumping his iron curb: to strive or flie
He held it vain; awe from above had quelld
His heart, not else dismai'd. Now drew they nigh
The western point, where those half-rounding guards
Just met, & closing stood in squadron joind
Awaiting next command. To whom their Chief
Gabriel from the front thus called aloud.
    O friends, I hear the tread of nimble feet
Hasting this way, and now by glimps discerne
Ithuriel and *Zephon* through the shade,
And with them comes a third of Regal port,
But faded splendour wan; who by his gate
And fierce demeanour seems the Prince of Hell,
Not likely to part hence without contest;
Stand firm, for in his look defiance lours.
    He scarce had ended, when those two approach'd
And brief related whom they brought, wher found,
How busied, in what form and posture coucht.
    To whom with stern regard thus *Gabriel* spake.
Why hast thou, *Satan*, broke the bounds prescrib'd
To thy transgressions, and disturbd the charge
Of others, who approve not to transgress
By thy example, but have power and right
To question thy bold entrance on this place;
Imploi'd it seems to violate sleep, and those
Whose dwelling God hath planted here in bliss?
    To whom thus *Satan* with contemptuous brow.
Gabriel, thou hadst in Heav'n th' esteem of wise,
And such I held thee; but this question askt
Puts me in doubt. Lives ther who loves his pain?
Who would not, finding way, break loose from Hell,
Though thither doomd? Thou wouldst thy self, no doubt,
And boldly venture to whatever place
Farthest from pain, where thou mightst hope to change
Torment with ease, & soonest recompence
Dole with delight, which in this place I sought;
To thee no reason; who knowst only good,
But evil hast not tri'd: and wilt object
His will who bound us? let him surer barr

His Iron Gates, if he intends our stay
In that dark durance: thus much what was askt.
The rest is true, they found me where they say;
But that implies not violence or harme.

   Thus hee in scorn. The warlike Angel mov'd,
Disdainfully half smiling thus repli'd.
O loss of one in Heav'n to judge of wise,
Since *Satan* fell, whom follie overthrew,
And now returns him from his prison scap't,
Gravely in doubt whether to hold them wise
Or not, who ask what boldness brought him hither
Unlicenc't from his bounds in Hell prescrib'd;
So wise he judges it to fly from pain
However, and to scape his punishment.
So judge thou still, presumptuous, till the wrauth,
Which thou incurr'st by flying, meet thy flight
Seavenfold, and scourge that wisdom back to Hell,
Which taught thee yet no better, that no pain
Can equal anger infinite provok't.
But wherefore thou alone? wherefore with thee
Came not all Hell broke loose? is pain to them
Less pain, less to be fled, or thou then they
Les hardie to endure? courageous Chief,
The first in flight from pain, had'st thou alleg'd
To thy deserted host this cause of flight,
Thou surely hadst not come sole fugitive.

   To which the Fiend thus answerd frowning stern.
Not that I less endure, or shrink from pain,
Insulting Angel; well thou knowst I stood
Thy fiercest, when in Battel to thy side
The blasting volied Thunder made all speed
And seconded thy else not dreaded Spear.
But still thy words at random, as before,
Argue thy inexperience what behooves
From hard assaies and ill successes past
A faithful Leader, not to hazard all
Through wayes of danger by himself untri'd.
I therefore, I alone first undertook
To wing the desolate Abyss, and spie
This new created World, whereof in Hell
Fame is not silent, here in hope to find

Better abode, and my afflicted Powers
To settle here on Earth, or in mid Aire;
Though for possession put to try once more
What thou and thy gay Legions dare against;
Whose easier business were to serve thir Lord
High up in Heav'n, with songs to hymne his Throne,
And practis'd distances to cringe, not fight.

    To whom the warriour Angel soon repli'd.
To say and strait unsay, pretending first
Wise to flie again, professing next the Spie,
Argues no Leader, but a lyar trac't,
Satan, and couldst thou faithful add? O name,
O sacred name of faithfulness profan'd!
Faithful to whom? to thy rebellious crew?
Armie of Fiends, fit body to fit head;
Was this your discipline and faith ingag'd,
Your military obedience, to dissolve
Allegeance to th' acknowledg'd Power supream?
And thou sly hypocrite, who now wouldst seem
Patron of liberty, who more then thou
Once fawn'd, and cring'd and servilly ador'd
Heavn's awful Monarch? wherefore but in hope
To dispossess him, and thy self to reigne?
But mark what I arreede thee now, avant;
Flie thither whence thou fledst: if from this houre
Within these hallowd limits thou appeer,
Back to th' infernal pit I drag thee chaind,
And Seale thee so, as henceforth not to scorne
The facil gates of hell too slightly barrd.

    So threatn'd hee, but *Satan* to no threats
Gave heed, but waxing more in rage repli'd.

    Then when I am thy captive talk of chaines,
Proud limitarie Cherube, but ere then
Farr heavier load thy self expect to feel
From my prevailing arme, though Heavens King
Ride on thy wings, and thou with thy Compeers,
Us'd to the yoak, draw'st his triumphant wheels
In progress through the rode of Heav'n Star-pav'd.

    While thus he spake, th' Angelic Squadron bright
Turnd fierie red, sharpning in mooned hornes
Thir Phalanx, and began to hemm him round

With ported Spears, as thick as when a field
Of *Ceres* ripe for harvest waving bends
Her bearded Grove of ears, which way the wind
Swayes them; the careful Plowman doubting stands
Least on the threshing floore his hopeful sheaves
Prove chaff. On th' other side *Satan* allarm'd
Collecting all his might dilated stood,
Like *Teneriff* or *Atlas* unremov'd:
His stature reacht the Skie, and on his Crest
Sat horror Plum'd; nor wanted in his graspe
What seemd both Spear and Shield: now dreadful deeds
Might have ensu'd, nor onely Paradise
In this commotion, but the Starrie Cope
Of Heav'n perhaps, or all the Elements
At least had gon to rack, disturbd and torne
With violence of this conflict, had not soon
Th' Eternal to prevent such horrid fray
Hung forth in Heav'n his golden Scales, yet seen
Betwixt *Astrea* and the *Scorpion* signe,
Wherein all things created first he weighd,
The pendulous round Earth with ballanc't Aire
In counterpoise, now ponders all events,
Battels and Realms: in these he put two weights
The sequel each of parting and of fight;
The latter quick up flew, and kickt the beam;
Which *Gabriel* spying, thus bespake the Fiend.
   Satan, I know thy strength, and thou knowest mine,
Neither our own but giv'n; what follie then
To boast what Arms can doe, since thine no more
Then Heav'n permits, nor mine, though doubld now
To trample thee as mire: for proof look up,
And read thy Lot in yon celestial Sign
Where thou art weigh'd, & shown how light, how weak,
If thou resist. The Fiend lookt up and knew
His mounted scale aloft: nor more; but fled
Murmuring, and with him fled the shades of night.

JOHN MILTON

30 *The Archangel*

But bringing up the rear of this bright host
  A Spirit of a different aspect waved
His wings, like thunder-clouds above some coast
  Whose barren beach with frequent wrecks is paved;
His brow was like the deep when tempest-toss'd;
  Fierce and unfathomable thoughts engraved
Eternal wrath on his immortal face,
And *where* he gazed a gloom pervaded space.

As he drew near, he gazed upon the gate
  Ne'er to be enter'd more by him or sin,
With such a glance of supernatural hate,
  As made Saint Peter wish himself within;
He patter'd with his keys at a great rate,
  And sweated through his apostolic skin:
Of course his perspiration was but ichor,
Or some such other spiritual liquor.

The very cherubs huddled all together,
  Like birds when soars the falcon; and they felt
A tingling to the tip of every feather,
  And form'd a circle like Orion's belt
Around their poor old charge; who scarce knew whither
  His guards had led him, though they gently dealt
With royal manes (for by many stories,
And true, we learn the angels all are Tories).

As things were in this posture, the gate flew
  Asunder, and the flashing of its hinges
Flung over space an universal hue
  Of many-colour'd flame, until its tinges
Reach'd even our speck of earth, and made a new
  Aurora borealis spread its fringes
O'er the North Pole; the same seen, when ice-bound,
By Captain Parry's crew, in 'Melville Sound.'

And from the gate thrown open issued beaming
  A beautiful and mighty Thing of Light,
Radiant with glory, like a banner streaming
  Victorious from some world-o'erthrowing fight:
D

My poor comparisons must needs be teeming
　　With earthly likenesses, for here the night
Of clay obscures our best conceptions, saving
Johanna Southcote, or Bob Southey raving.

'Twas the archangel Michael: all men know
　　The make of angels and archangels, since
There's scarce a scribbler has not one to show,
　　From the fiends' leader to the angels' prince.
There also are some altar-pieces, though
　　I really can't say that they much evince
One's inner notions of immortal spirits;
But let the connoisseurs explain *their* merits.

Michael flew forth in glory and in good;
　　A goodly work of him from whom all glory
And good arise; the portal passed–he stood;
　　Before him the young cherubs and saints hoary–
(I say *young*, begging to be understood
　　By looks, not years; and should be very sorry
To state, they were not older than St. Peter,
But merely that they seem'd a little sweeter).

The cherubs and the saints bow'd down before
　　That arch-angelic hierarch, the first
Of essences angelical, who wore
　　The aspect of a god; but this ne'er nursed
Pride in his heavenly bosom, in whose core
　　No thought, save for his Maker's service, durst
Intrude, however glorified and high;
He knew him but the viceroy of the sky.

He and the sombre silent Spirit met–
　　They knew each other both for good and ill;
Such was their power, that neither could forget
　　His former friend and future foe; but still
There was a high, immortal, proud regret
　　In either's eye, and if 'twere less their will
Than destiny to make the eternal years
Their date of war, and their 'champ clos,' the spheres.

　　　　　　　　　　　GEORGE GORDON, LORD BYRON

31 *Saul : The Conclusion*

I know not too well how I found my way home in the night.
There were witnesses, cohorts about me, to left and to right,
Angels, powers, the unuttered, unseen, the alone, the aware:
I repressed, I got through them as hardly, as strugglingly there,
As a runner beset by the populace famished for news—
Life or death. The whole earth was awakened, hell loosed with
 her crews;
And the stars of night beat with emotion, and tingled and shot
Out in fire the strong pain of pent knowledge: but I fainted not,
For the Hand still impelled me at once and supported, sup-
 pressed
All the tumult, and quenched it with quiet, and holy behest,
Till the rapture was shut in itself, and the earth sank to rest.
Anon at the dawn, all that trouble had withered from earth—
Not so much, but I saw it die out in the day's tender birth;
In the gathered intensity brought to the grey of the hills;
In the shuddering forests' held breath; in the sudden wind-
 thrills;
In the startled wild beasts that bore off, each with eye sidling
 still
Though averted with wonder and dread; in the birds stiff and
 chill
That rose heavily, as I approached them, made stupid with
 awe:
E'en the serpent that slid away silent,—he felt the new law.
The same stared in the white humid faces upturned by the
 flowers;
The same worked in the heart of the cedar and moved the vine-
 bowers;
And the little brooks witnessing murmured, persistent and
 low,
With their obstinate, all but hushed voices—'E'en so, it is so!'
ROBERT BROWNING

Book II

SONGS AND INCANTATIONS

32 *A Maiden in the Moor*

Maiden in the mor lay,
  In the mor lay,
Sevenyst [1] fulle, sevenist fulle,
Maiden in the mor lay,
  In the mor lay,
Sevenistes fulle ant a day.

Welle was hire mete;
  Wat was hire mete?
  The primerole [2] ant the,–
  The primerole ant the,–
Welle was hire mete;
What was hire mete;–
  The primerole ant the violet.

Welle (was hire dryng [3]);
  Wat was hire dryng?
The chelde water of (the) welle-spring.

Welle was hire bour;
  Wat was hire bour?
The rede rose an te lilie flour.

ANON. 14TH CENTURY

33 *Hark, hark! the lark*

Hark! hark! the lark at heaven's gate sings,
  And Phoebus 'gins arise,
His steeds to water at those springs
  On chalic'd flowers that lies ;
And winking Mary-buds begin
  To ope their golden eyes:
With every thing that pretty is,
  My lady sweet, arise:
    Arise, arise;

WILLIAM SHAKESPEARE

[1] seven nights   [2] primrose   [3] drink

64

34 *Ariel's Song*

Come unto these yellow sands,
   And then take hands:
Curtsied when you have, and kiss'd,
   The wild waves whist,–
Foot it featly here and there;
And, sweet sprites, the burden bear.
     Hark, hark!
     The watch-dogs bark:
     Hark, hark! I hear
The strain of strutting Chanticleer.
              WILLIAM SHAKESPEARE

35 *A Birthday*

My heart is like a singing bird
   Whose nest is in a watered shoot;
My heart is like an apple-tree
   Whose boughs are bent with thickset fruit;
My heart is like a rainbow shell
   That paddles in a halcyon sea;
My heart is gladder than all these
   Because my love is come to me.

Raise me a dais of silk and down;
   Hang it with vair and purple dyes;
Carve it in doves and pomegranates,
   And peacocks with a hundred eyes;
Work it in gold and silver grapes,
   In leaves and silver fleurs-de-lys;
Because the birthday of my life
   Is come, my love is come to me.
              CHRISTINA ROSSETTI

36 *Song*

The feathers of the willow
Are half of them grown yellow
   Above the swelling stream;
And ragged are the bushes,
And rusty now the rushes,
   And wild the clouded gleam.

The thistle now is older,
His stalk begins to moulder,
　　His head is white as snow;
The branches all are barer,
The linnet's song is rarer,
　　The robin pipeth now.

RICHARD WATSON DIXON

37 *The Shepherd*

How sweet is the Shepherd's sweet lot;
From the morn to the evening he strays;
He shall follow his sheep all the day,
And his tongue shall be filled with praise.

For he hears the lamb's innocent call,
And he hears the ewe's tender reply;
He is watchful while they are in peace,
For they know when their Shepherd is nigh.

WILLIAM BLAKE

38 *Song*

Gold wings across the sea!
Grey light from tree to tree,
Gold hair beside my knee,
I pray thee come to me,
Gold wings!

　　The water slips,
The red-bill'd moorhen dips.
Sweet kisses on red lips;
Alas; the red rust grips,
And the blood-red dagger rips,
Yet, O knight, come to me!

Are not my blue eyes sweet?
The west wind from wheat
Blows cold across my feet;
Is it not time to meet
Gold wings across the sea?

White swans on the green moat,
Small feathers left afloat
By the blue-painted boat;
Swift running of the stoat;
Sweet gurgling note by note
Of sweet music.

       O gold wings,
Listen how gold hair sings,
And the Ladies' Castle rings
Gold wings across the sea.

I sit on a purple bed,
Outside the wall is red,
Thereby the apple hangs,
And the love-crazed knight

Kisses the long wet grass:
The weary days pass,—
Gold wings across the sea!

Gold wings across the sea!
Moonlight from tree to tree,
Sweet hair laid on my knee,
O, sweet knight, come to me.

Gold wings, the short night slips,
The white swan's long neck drips,
I pray thee, kiss my lips,
Gold wings across the sea.

             WILLIAM MORRIS

39 *Spring Quiet*

Gone were but the Winter,
  Come were but the Spring
I would go to a covert
  Where the birds sing.

Where in the whitethorn
  Singeth a thrush,
And a robin sings
  In the holly-bush.

Full of fresh scents
　　Are the budding boughs
Arching high over
　　A cool green house:

Full of sweet scents,
　　And whispering air
Which sayeth softly:
　　'We spread no snare;

'Here dwell in safety,
　　Here dwell alone,
With a clear stream
　　And a mossy stone.

'Here the sun shineth
　　Most shadily;
Here is heard an echo
　　Of the far sea,
Though far off it be.'

CHRISTINA ROSSETTI

40 *The Unquiet Grave*

'The wind doth blow to-day, my love,
　　And a few small drops of rain;
I never had but one true-love,
　　In cold grave she was lain.

'I'll do as much for my true-love
　　As any young man may;
I'll sit and mourn all at her grave
　　For a twelvemonth and a day.'

The twelvemonth and a day being up,
　　The dead began to speak:
'Oh who sits weeping on my grave,
　　And will not let me sleep?'

''Tis I, my love, sits on your grave,
　　And will not let you sleep;
For I crave one kiss of your clay-cold lips,
　　That is all I seek.'

'You crave one kiss of my clay-cold lips;
  But my breath smells earthy strong;
If you have one kiss of my clay-cold lips,
  Your time will not be long.

'Tis down in yonder garden green,
  Love, where we used to walk,
The finest flower that ere was seen
  Is withered to a stalk.

'The stalk is withered dry, my love,
  So will our hearts decay;
So make yourself content, my love,
  Till God calls you away.'

ANON

41 *Balade*

Hyd, Absolon, thy gilte tresses clere;
Ester, ley thou thy meknesse al adown;
Hyd, Jonathas, al thy frendly manere;
Penalopee and Marcia Catoun,
Make of youre wifhod no comparysoun;
Hyde ye youre beautes, Ysoude and Eleyne:
My lady cometh, that al this may disteyne [1].

Thy faire body, lat yt nat appere,
Lavyne; and thou, Lucresse of Rome toun,
And Polixene, that boghten love so dere,
And Cleopatre, with al thy passyoun,
Hyde ye your trouthe of love and your renoun;
And thou, Tisbe, that hast for love swich peyne:
My lady cometh, that al this may disteyne.

Herro, Dido, Laudomia, alle yfere [2],
And Phillis, hangyng for thy Demonphoun,
And Canace, espied by thy chere,
Ysiphile, betrayed with Jasoun,
Maketh of your trouthe neythir boost ne soun;
Nor Ypermystre or Adriane, ye tweyne:
My lady cometh, that al this may disteyne.

GEOFFREY CHAUCER

[1] bedim   [2] together

42 *Song* : *Spring and Winter*

When daisies pied and violets blue
  And lady-smocks all silver-white
And cuckoo-buds of yellow hue
  Do paint the meadows with delight,
The cuckoo then, on every tree,
Mocks married men; for thus sings he,
                    Cuckoo;
Cuckoo, cuckoo: O, word of fear,
Unpleasing to a married ear!

When shepherds pipe on oaten straws,
  And merry larks are ploughmen's clocks,
When turtles tread, and rooks, and daws,
  And maidens bleach their summer smocks,
The cuckoo then, on every tree,
Mocks married men; for thus sings he,
                    Cuckoo;
Cuckoo, cuckoo: O, word of fear,
Unpleasing to a married ear!

When icicles hang by the wall,
  And Dick the shepherd blows his nail,
And Tom bears logs into the hall,
  And milk comes frozen home in pail,
When blood is nipp'd, and ways be foul,
Then nightly sings the staring owl,
                    Tu-who;
Tu-whit, tu-who–a merry note,
While greasy Joan doth keel the pot.

When all aloud the wind doth blow,
  And coughing drowns the parson's saw,
And birds sit brooding in the snow,
  And Marian's nose looks red and raw,
When roasted crabs hiss in the bowl,
Then nightly sings the staring owl,
                    Tu-who;
Tu-whit, tu-who–a merry note,
While greasy Joan doth keel the pot.
                    WILLIAM SHAKESPEARE

43 *Song*

Whenas the rye reach to the chin,
And chopcherry, chopcherry ripe within,
Strawberries swimming in the cream,
And schoolboys playing in the stream;
Then oh, then oh, then oh, my true Love said,
Till that time come again
She could not live a maid.

GEORGE PEELE

44 *Hey nonny no!*

Hey nonny no!
Men are fools that wish to die!
Is 't not fine to dance and sing
When the bells of death do ring?
Is 't not fine to swim in wine,
And turn upon the toe
And sing hey nonny no,
When the winds do blow,
And the seas do flow?
Hey nonny no!

ANON

45 *Fara diddle dyno*

Ha ha! ha ha! This world doth pass
    Most merrily I'll be sworn,
For many an honest Indian ass
    Goes for a unicorn.
            Fara diddle dyno,
            This is idle fyno.

Tie hie! tie hie! O sweet delight!
    He tickles this age that can
Call Tullia's ape a marmasyte
    And Leda's goose a swan.
            Fara diddle dyno,
            This is idle fyno.

So so! so so! Fine English days!
   For false play is no reproach,
For he that doth the coachman praise
   May safely use the coach.
      Fara diddle dyno,
      This is idle fyno.

ANON

46 *Song*

And can the physician make sick men well?
And can the magician a fortune divine?
Without lily, germander, and sops-in-wine,
     With sweet-briar
     And bon-fire
     And strawberry wire
     And columbine.

Within and out, in and out, round as a ball,
With hither and thither, as straight as a line,
With lily, germander, and sops-in-wine,
     With sweet-briar
     And bon-fire
     And strawberry wire
     And columbine.

When Saturn did live, there lived no poor,
The king and the beggar with roots did dine,
With lily, germander, and sops-in-wine,
     With sweet-briar
     And bon-fire
     And strawberry wire
     And columbine.

ANON

47 *Apollo's Song*

Apollo :

   Which way, and whence the lightning flew,
   Or how it burned, bright, and blue,
   Design, and figure by your lights :
   Then forth, and show the several flights
   Your birds have made, or what the wing,
   Or voice in Augury doth bring.

Which hand the Crow cried on, how high
The Vulture, or the Erne did fly;
What wing the Swan made, and the Dove,
The Stork, and which did get above:
Show all the birds of food or prey,
But pass by the unlucky Jay,
The Night-Crow, Swallow, or the Kite,
Let those have neither right,
                              Nor part

Chorus :

In this night's art.

BEN JONSON

48 *Karolin's Song*

Though I am young, and cannot tell,
    Either what Death, or Love is well,
Yet I have heard, they both bear darts,
    And both do aim at human hearts:
And then again, I have been told
    Love wounds with heat, as Death with cold;
So that I fear, they do but bring
    Extremes to touch, and mean one thing.

As in a ruin, we it call
    One thing to be blown up, or fall;
Or to our end, like way may have,
    By a flash of lightning, or a wave:
So Love's inflamed shaft, or brand,
    May kill, as soon as Death's cold hand;
Except Love's fires the virtue have
    To fright the frost out of the grave.

BEN JONSON

49 *The Song in Making of the Arrows*

My shag-hair Cyclops, come, let's ply
Our Lemnian hammers lustily;
        By my wife's sparrows,
        I swear these arrows
        Shall singing fly
    Through many a wanton's eye.

These headed are with golden blisses,
These silver ones feathered with kisses,
    But this of lead
    Strikes a clown dead,
    When in a dance
    He falls in a trance,
To see his black-brow lass not buss him,
And then whines out for death t'untruss him.
So, so, our work being done let's play,
Holiday (boys), cry Holiday!

                    JOHN LILY

50 *Patrico's Song*

The faery beam upon you,
The stars to glister on you;
    A Moon of light,
    In the Noon of night,
Till the firedrake hath o'er-gone you.
The wheel of fortune guide you,
The Boy with the bow beside you,
    Run aye in the way,
    Till the bird of day,
And the luckier lot betide you.

To the old, long life and treasure;
To the young, all health and pleasure;
    To the fair, their face
    With eternal grace;
And the soul to be lov'd at leisure.
To the witty, all clear mirrors,
To the foolish their dark errors;
    To the loving sprite,
    A secure delight :
To the jealous his own false terrors.

                    BEN JONSON

51 *New Hampshire*

Children's voices in the orchard
Between the blossom- and the fruit-time :
Golden head, crimson head,
Between the green tip and the root.

Black wing, brown wing, hover over
Twenty years and the spring is over;
To-day grieves, to-morrow grieves,
Cover me over, light-in-leaves;
Golden head, black wing,
Cling, swing,
Spring, sing,
Swing up into the apple-tree.

THOMAS STEARNS ELIOT

52 *To Mistress Margaret Hussy*

Merry Margaret,
As midsummer flower,
Gentle as falcon
Or hawk of the tower:
With solace and gladness,
Much mirth and no madness,
All good and no badness;
So joyously,
So maidenly,
So womanly
Her demeaning
In every thing,
Far, far passing
Than I can indite,
Or suffice to write
Of Merry Margaret
As midsummer flower,
Gentle as falcon
Or hawk of the tower.
As patient and still
And as full of good will
As fair Isaphill [1],
Coliander,
Sweet pomander,
Good cassander,
Steadfast of thought,
Well made, well wrought,
Far may be sought

[1] Hypsipyle

Ere that ye can find
So courteous, so kind
As Merry Margaret,
This midsummer flower,
Gentle as falcon
Or hawk of the tower.

JOHN SKELTON

53 *When that I was and a little Tiny Boy*

When that I was and a little tiny boy,
  With hey, ho, the wind and the rain;
A foolish thing was but a toy,
  For the rain it raineth every day.

But when I came to man's estate,
  With hey, ho, the wind and the rain;
'Gainst knaves and thieves men shut their gates,
  For the rain it raineth every day.

But when I came, alas! to wive,
  With hey, ho, the wind and the rain;
By swaggering could I never thrive,
  For the rain it raineth every day.

But when I came unto my beds,
  With hey, ho, the wind and the rain;
With toss-pots still had drunken heads,
  For the rain it raineth every day.

A great while ago the world begun,
  With hey, ho, the wind and the rain;
But that's all one, our play is done,
  And we'll strive to please you every day.

WILLIAM SHAKESPEARE

54 *When daffodils begin to peer*

When daffodils begin to peer,
  With heigh! the doxy, over the dale,
Why, then comes in the sweet of the year;
  For the red blood reigns in the winter's pale.

The white sheet bleaching on the hedge,
  With heigh! the sweet birds, O, how they sing!
Doth set my pugging tooth on edge ;
  For a quart of ale is a dish for a king.

The lark, that tirra-lirra chants,
  With heigh! with heigh! the thrush and the jay,
Are summer songs for me and my aunts,
  While we lie tumbling in the hay.

WILLIAM SHAKESPEARE

55 *Epilogue*

Puck :

Now the hungry lion roars,
  And the wolf behowls the moon;
Whilst the heavy ploughman snores,
  All with weary task fordone,
Now the wasted brands do glow,
  Whilst the screech-owl, screeching loud,
Puts the wretch that lies in woe
  In remembrance of a shroud.
Now it is the time of night
  That the graves all gaping wide,
Every one lets forth his sprite,
  In the churchway-paths to glide :
And we fairies, that do run
  By the triple Hecate's team,
From the presence of the sun,
  Following darkness like a dream,
Now are we frolic. Not a mouse
Shall disturb this hallow'd house :
I am sent with broom before,
To sweep the dust behind the door.

Oberon :

Through the house give glimmering light
  By the dead and drowsy fire;
Every elf and fairy sprite
  Hop as light as bird from brier;
And this ditty after me
Sing and dance it trippingly.

Titania :

> First, rehearse your song by rote,
> To each word a warbling note :
> Hand in hand, with fairy grace,
> Will we sing, and bless this place.

Oberon :

> Now, until the break of day,
> Through this house each fairy stray.
> To the best bride-bed will we,
> Which by us shall blessed be;
> And the issue there create
> Ever shall be fortunate.
> So shall all the couples three
> Ever true in loving be;
> And the blots of Nature's hand
> Shall not in their issue stand :
> Never mole, hare-lip, nor scar,
> Nor mark prodigious, such as are
> Despised in nativity,
> Shall upon their children be.
> With this field-dew consecrate,
> Every fairy take his gait,
> And each several chamber bless,
>   Through this palace, with sweet peace;
> Ever shall in safety rest,
> And the owner of it blest.
>   Trip away;
>   Make no stay;
> Meet me all by break of day.

Puck :

> If we shadows have offended,
> Think but this, and all is mended,
> That you have but slumber'd here
> While these visions did appear.
> And this weak and idle theme,
> No more yielding but a dream,
> Gentles, do not reprehend :
> If you pardon, we will mend.
> And, as I'm an honest Puck,
> If we have unearned luck

Now to 'scape the serpent's tongue,
We will make amends ere long;
Else the Puck a liar call :
So, good night unto you all.
Give me your hands, if we be friends,
And Robin shall restore amends.

WILLIAM SHAKESPEARE

56 *Sweet Content*

Art thou poor, yet hast thou golden slumbers?
    O sweet content!
Art thou rich, yet is thy mind perplexed?
    O punishment!
Dost thou laugh to see how fools are vexed
To add to golden numbers, golden numbers?
O sweet content! O sweet, O sweet content!
  Work apace, apace, apace, apace;
  Honest labour bears a lovely face;
Then hey nonny nonny, hey nonny nonny!

Canst drink the waters of the crisped spring?
    O sweet content!
Swimm'st thou in wealth, yet sink'st in thine own tears?
    O punishment!
Then he that patiently want's burden bears
No burden bears, but is a king, a king!
O sweet content! O sweet, O sweet content!
  Work apace, apace, apace, apace;
  Honest labour bears a lovely face;
Then hey nonny nonny, hey nonny nonny!

THOMAS DEKKER

57 *Syrinx*

Pan's Syrinx was a girl indeed,
Though now she's turned into a reed;
From that dear reed Pan's pipe does come,
A pipe that strikes Apollo dumb;
Nor flute, nor lute, nor gittern can
So chant it as the pipe of Pan :

Cross-gartered swains and dairy girls,
With faces smug and round as pearls,
When Pan's shrill pipe begins to play,
With dancing wear out night and day:
The bagpipe's drone his hum lays by
When Pan sounds up his minstrelsy;
His minstrelsy! oh, base! this quill—
Which at my mouth with wind I fill—
Puts me in mind, though her I miss,
That still my Syrinx' lips I kiss.

JOHN LILY

58 *The Dance*

Robin is a lovely lad,
No lass a smoother ever had.
Tommy hath a look as bright
As is the rosy morning light.
Tib is dark and brown of hue,
But like her colour firm and true.
Jinny hath a lip to kiss
Wherein a spring of nectar is.
Simkin well his mirth can place
And words to win a woman's grace.
Sib is all in all to me,
There is no queen of love but she.
Let us in a lover's round
Circle all this happy ground.
Softly, softly trip and go,
The light foot fairies jet it so.
Forward then and back again,
Here and there and everywhere,
Winding to and winding fro,
Skipping high and louting low.
And like lovers hand in hand
March around and make a stand.

GEORGE MASON AND JOHN EARSDEN

59 *Gorbo and Batte*

Gorbo, as thou cam'st this way
By yonder little hill,
Or as thou through the fields didst stray
Saw'st thou my Daffadill?

She's in a frock of Lincoln green
The colour maids delight,
And never hath her beauty seen
But through a vale of white.

Than Roses richer to behold
That trim up lovers' bowers,
The Pansy and the Marigold
The Phoebus Paramours.

Gorbo :

Thou well describ'st the Daffadill,
It is not full an hour
Since by the spring near yonder hill
I saw that lovely flower.

Batte :

Yet my fair flower thou didst not meet,
Nor news of her didst bring,
And yet my Daffadill more sweet,
Than that by yonder spring.

Gorbo :

I saw a shepherd that doth keep
In yonder field of Lillies,
Was making (as he fed his sheep)
A wreath of Daffadillies.

Batte :

Yet Gorbo thou delud'st me still
My flower thou didst not see,
For know my pretty Daffadill
Is worn of none but me.

To shew itself but near her seat,
No Lilly is so bold,
Except to shade her from the heat,
Or keep her from the cold :

Gorbo :

Through yonder vale as I did pass,
Descending from the hill,
I met a smirking bonny lass,
They call her Daffadill :

Whose presence as along she went,
The pretty flowers did greet,
As though their heads they downward bent,
With homage to her feet.

And all the shepherds that were nigh,
From top of every hill,
Unto the valleys loud did cry,
There goes sweet Daffadill.

Batte :

I gentle shepherd, now with joy
Thou all my flocks dost fill,
That's she alone kind shepherd's boy,
Let us to Daffadill.

MICHAEL DRAYTON

60 *Bethsabe Bathing*

Hot sun, cool fire, temper'd with sweet air,
Black shade, fair nurse, shadow my white hair:
Shine, sun; burn, fire; breathe, air, and ease me;
Black shade, fair nurse, shroud me and please me:
Shadow, my sweet nurse, keep me from burning,
Make not my glad cause cause of mourning.
Let not my beauty's fire
Inflame unstaid desire,
Nor pierce any bright eye
That wand'reth lightly.

GEORGE PEELE

61 *Rosalind's Madrigal*

Love in my bosom like a bee
Doth suck his sweet;
Now with his wings he plays with me,
Now with his feet.

Within mine eyes he makes his nest,
His bed amidst my tender breast;
My kisses are his daily feast,
And yet he robs me of my rest.
    Ah, wanton, will ye?

And if I sleep, then percheth he
    With pretty flight,
And makes his pillow of my knee
    The livelong night.
Strike I my lute, he tunes the string;
He music plays if so I sing;
He lends me every lovely thing;
Yet cruel he my heart doth sting.
    Whist, wanton, still ye!

Else I with roses every day
    Will whip you hence,
And bind you, when you long to play,
    For your offence.
I'll shut mine eyes to keep you in,
I'll make you fast it for your sin,
I'll count your power not worth a pin.
Alas! what hereby shall I win
    If he gainsay me?

What if I beat the wanton boy
    With many a rod?
He will repay me with annoy,
    Because a god.
Then sit thou safely on my knee,
And let thy bower my bosom be;
Lurk in mine eyes, I like of thee.
O Cupid, so thou pity me,
    Spare not, but play thee!

THOMAS LODGE

62 *Fine Knacks for Ladies*

Fine knacks for ladies, cheap, choice, brave and new!
  Good pennyworths! but money cannot move.
I keep a fair but for the fair to view;
  A beggar may be liberal of love.
Though all my wares be trash, the heart is true.

Great gifts are guiles and look for gifts again;
  My trifles come as treasures from my mind.
It is a precious jewel to be plain;
  Sometimes in shell the Orient's pearls we find.
Of others take a sheaf, of me a grain.

Within this pack pins, points, laces, and gloves,
  And divers toys fitting a country fair.
But in my heart, where duty serves and loves,
  Turtles and twins, court's brood, a heavenly pair.
Happy the heart that thinks of no removes!

JOHN DOWLAND

63 *Come away, sweet love*

Come away, come, sweet love! The golden morning breaks;
All the earth, all the air of love and pleasure speaks.
        Teach thine arms then to embrace,
            And sweet
            Rosy
          Lips to kiss,
        And mix our souls in mutual bliss;
        Eyes were made for beauty's grace,
            Viewing,
            Rueing
          Love-long pain
        Procured by beauty's rude disdain.

Come away, come, sweet love! The golden morning wastes,
While the sun from his sphere his fiery arrows casts
        Making all the shadows fly,
            Playing,
            Staying
          In the grove
        To entertain the stealth of love

Thither, sweet love, let us hie,
    Flying,
    Dying
  In desire
Winged with sweet hopes and heavenly fire.

Come away, come, sweet love! Do not in vain adorn
Beauty's grace, that should rise like to the naked morn.
    Lilies on the riverside
      And fair
      Cyprian
    Flowers new-blown
Desire no beauties but their own,
Ornament is nurse of pride;
    Pleasure
    Measure
Love's delight.
Haste then, sweet love, our wished flight!

JOHN DOWLAND

64 *Perigot and Willye*

Perigot.	It fell upon a holly eve,
Willye.	hey ho hollidaye,
Per.	When holly fathers wont to shrieve:
Wil.	now gynneth this roundelay.
Per.	Sitting upon a hill so hye
Wil.	hey ho the high hill,
Per.	The while my flocke did feede thereby,
Wil.	the while the shepheard selfe did spill:
Per.	I saw the bouncing Bellibone,
Wil.	hey ho Bonibell,
Per.	Tripping over the dale alone,
Wil.	She can trippe it very well:
Per.	Well decked in a frocke of gray,
Wil.	hey ho gray is greete [1],
Per.	And in a Kirtle of greene saye [2],
Wil.	the greene is for maydens meete:
Per.	A chapelet on her head she wore,
Wil.	hey ho chapelet,

[1] weeping   [2] a serge-like cloth

Per.	Of sweete Violets therein was store,
Wil.	she sweeter than the Violet.
Per.	My sheepe did leave theyr wonted foode,
Wil.	hey ho seely sheepe,
Per.	And gazed on her, as they were wood,
Wil.	woode as he, that did them keepe.
Per.	As the bonilasse passed bye,
Wil.	hey ho bonilasse,
Per.	She roude [1] at me with glauncing eye,
Wil.	as cleare as the christall glasse:
Per.	All as the Sunnye beame so bright,
Wil.	hey ho the Sunne beame,
Per.	Glaunceth from *Phoebus* face forthright,
Wil.	so love into thy hart did streame:
Per.	Or as the thunder cleaves the cloudes,
Wil.	hey ho the Thonder,
Per.	Wherein the lightsome levin shroudes,
Wil.	so cleaves thy soule a sonder:
Per.	Or as Dame *Cynthias* silver raye
Wil.	hey ho the Moonelight,
Per.	Upon the glyttering wave doth playe:
Wil.	such play is a pitteous plight.
Per.	The glaunce into my heart did glide,
Wil.	hey ho the glyder,
Per.	Therewith my soule was sharply gryde [2],
Wil.	such woundes soone wexen wider.
Per.	Hasting to rauch the arrow out,
Wil.	hey ho Perigot.
Per.	I left the head in my hart roote:
Wil.	it was a desperate shot.
Per.	There itranckleth ay more and more,
Wil.	hey ho the arrowe,
Per.	Ne can I find salve for my sore:
Wil.	love is a curelesse sorrowe.
Per.	And though my bale with death I bought,
Wil.	hey ho heavie cheere,
Per.	Yet should thilk lasse not from my thought:
Wil.	so you may buye gold to deare.
Per.	But whether in paynefull love I pyne,
Wil.	hey ho pinching payne,

[1] roue : to shoot with arrows   [2] pierced

Per.	Or thrive in welth, she shalbe mine.
Wil.	but if thou can her obteine.
Per.	And if for gracelesse greefe I dye,
Wil.	hey ho gracelesse griefe,
Per.	Witnesse, shee slewe with me with her eye:
Wil.	let thy follye be the priefe.
Per.	And you, that sawe it, simple shepe,
Wil.	hey ho the fayre flocke,
Per.	For priefe, thereof, my deathe shall weepe,
Wil.	and mone with many a mocke.
Per.	So learnd I love on a hollye eve,
Wil.	hey ho holidaye,
Per.	That ever since my hart did greve.
Wil.	now endeth our roundelay.

EDMUND SPENSER

65 *An Ode*

As it fell upon a day
In the merry month of May,
Sitting in a pleasant shade
Which a grove of myrtles made,
Beasts did leap and birds did sing,
Trees did grow and plants did spring;
Every thing did banish moan
Save the nightingale alone.
She, poor bird, as all forlorn,
Lean'd her breast against a thorn,
And there sung the dolefull'st ditty
That to hear it was great pity.
Fie, fie, fie, now would she cry:
Teru, teru, by and by:
That to hear her so complain
Scarce I could from tears refrain;
For her griefs so lively shown
Made me think upon mine own.
Ah, thought I, thou mourn'st in vain,
None takes pity on thy pain:
Senseless trees, they cannot hear thee,
Ruthless beasts, they will not cheer thee;
King Pandion he is dead,
All thy friends are lapped in lead:

All thy fellow birds do sing
Careless of thy sorrowing:
Even so, poor bird, like thee
None alive will pity me.

RICHARD BARNFIELD

66 *Batte's Song*

What is Love but the desire
Of the thing that fancy pleaseth?
A holy and resistless fire,
Weak and strong alike that ceaseth,
Which not heaven hath power to let,
Nor wise nature cannot smother,
Whereby *Phoebus* doth beget
On the universal mother.
That the everlasting Chain,
Which together all things tied,
And unmoved them retain
And by which they shall abide:
That consent we clearly find;
All things doth together draw,
And so strong in every kind,
Subjects them to nature's law.
Whose high virtue number teaches
In which everything doth move,
From the lowest depth that reaches
To the height of heaven above:
Harmony that wisely found,
When the cunning hand doth strike
Whereas every amorous sound,
Sweetly marries with his like.
The tender cattle scarcely take
From their damm's the fields to prove,
But each seeketh out a mate,
Nothing lives that doth not love:
Not so much as but the plant
As nature everything doth pair,
By it if the male it want
Doth dislike and will not bear:

Nothing then is like to love
In the which all creatures be.
From it ne'er let me remove
Nor let it remove from me.

MICHAEL DRAYTON

67 *The Satyr's Leave-Taking*

Thou divinest, fairest, brightest,
Thou most powerful maid, and whitest,
Thou most vertuous and most blessed,
Eyes of stars, and golden tressed
Like *Apollo*, tell me sweetest
What new service now is meetest
For the *Satyr*? shall I stray
In the middle air and stay
The sailing Rack, or nimbly take
Hold by the Moon, and gently make
Suit to the pale Queen of night
For a beam to give thee light?
Shall I dive into the Sea,
And bring thee Coral, making way
Through the rising waves that fall
In snowy fleeces; dearest, shall
I catch the wanton Fawns, or Flies,
Whose woven wings the Summer dyes
Of many colours? get thee fruit?
Or steal from Heaven old *Orpheus'* Lute?
All these I'll venture for, and more,
To do her service all these woods adore.
Holy Virgin, I will dance
Round about these woods as quick
As the breaking light, and prick
Down the lawns, and down the vails
Faster than the Wind-mill sails
So I take my leave, and pray
All the comforts of the day,
Such as *Phoebus* heat doth send
On the earth, may still befriend
Thee, and this arbour.

JOHN FLETCHER

68 *Song*

Phoebus, arise,
And paint the sable skies
With azure, white, and red;
Rouse Memnon's mother from her Tithon's bed,
That she thy carrier may with roses spread;
The nightingales thy coming each where sing;
Make an eternal spring,
Give life to this dark world which lieth dead;
Spread forth thy golden hair
In larger locks than thou was wont before,
And, emperor-like, decore
With diadem of pearl thy temples fair:
Chase hence the ugly night,
Which serves but to make dear thy glorious light.
This is that happy morn,
That day, long-wished day,
Of all my life so dark
(If cruel stars have not my ruin sworn,
And fates not hope betray),
Which, only white, deserves
A diamond for ever should it mark:
This is the morn should bring unto this grove
My love, to hear and recompense my love.
Fair king, who all preserves,
But show thy blushing beams,
And thou two sweeter eyes
Shalt see, than those which by Peneus' streams
Did once thy heart surprise;
Nay, suns, which shine as clear
As thou when two thou did to Rome appear.
Now, Flora, deck thyself in fairest guise;
If that ye, winds, would hear
A voice surpassing far Amphion's lyre,
Your stormy chiding stay;
Let Zephyr only breathe,
And with her tresses play,
Kissing sometimes those purple ports of death.
The winds all silent are,
And Phoebus in his chair,

Ensaffroning sea and air,
Makes vanish every star:
Night like a drunkard reels
Beyond the hills to shun his flaming wheels;
The fields with flow'rs are deck'd in every hue,
The clouds bespangle with bright gold their blue:
Here is the pleasant place,
And ev'rything, save her, who all should grace.
                               WILLIAM DRUMMOND

69 *Song*

Sabrina fair,
      Listen where thou art sitting
Under the glassie, cool, translucent wave,
      In twisted braids of Lillies knitting
The loose train of thy amber-dropping hair,
      Listen for dear honours sake,
      Goddess of the silver lake,
            Listen and save!

Listen, and appear to us,
In name of great Oceanus,
By the earth-shaking Neptune's mace,
And Tethys' grave majestick pace;
By hoary Nereus' wrincled look,
And the Carpathian wisard's hook;
By scaly Triton's winding shell,
And old soothsaying Glaucus' spell;
By Leucothea's lovely hands,
And her son that rules the strands;
By Thetis' tinsel-slipper'd feet,
And the songs of Sirens sweet;
By dead Parthenope's dear tomb,
And fair Ligea's golden comb,
Wherewith she sits on diamond rocks
Sleeking her soft alluring locks;
By all the Nymphs that nightly dance
Upon thy streams with wily glance;
Rise, rise, and heave thy rosie head
From thy coral-pav'n bed

And bridle in thy headlong wave,
Till thou our summons answered have.

Sabrina, *rises, attended by Water-Nymphs, and sings.*

Listen and save.

By the rushy-fringed bank,
Where grows the Willow and the Osier dank,
    My sliding Chariot stayes,
Thickset with Agate, and the azurn sheen
Of Turkis blew, and Emrauld green
    That in the channel strayes;
Whilst from off the waters fleet
Thus I set my printless feet
O're the Cowslip's Velvet head,
    That bends not as I tread.
Gentle swain at thy request
    I am here.

JOHN MILTON

70 *On his Mistress, the Queen of Bohemia*

You meaner beauties of the night,
    That poorly satisfy our eyes
More by your number than your light,
    You common people of the skies;
    What are you when the moon shall rise?

You curious chanters of the wood,
    That warble forth Dame Nature's lays,
Thinking your passions understood
    By your weak accents; what's your praise,
    When Philomel her voice shall raise?

You violets that first appear,
    By your pure purple mantles known
Like the proud virgins of the year,
    As if the spring were all your own;
    What are you when the rose is blown?

So, when my mistress shall be seen
    In form and beauty of her mind,
By virtue first, then choice, a Queen,
    Tell me if she were not designed
    Th' eclipse and glory of her kind?

SIR HENRY WOTTON

71 *Laura Sleeping*

Winds whisper gently whilst she sleeps,
   And fan her with your cooling wings;
Whilst she her drops of beauty weeps,
   From pure, and yet unrivall'd springs.

Glide over beauty's field her face,
   To kiss her lip, and cheek be bold,
But with a calm, and stealing pace;
   Neither too rude; nor yet too cold.

Play in her beams, and crisp her hair,
   With such a gale, as wings soft Love,
And with so sweet, so rich an air,
   As breathes from the Arabian grove.

A breath as hushed as lover's sigh;
   Or that unfolds the morning door:
Sweet, as the winds, that gently fly,
   To sweep the Spring's enamell'd floor.

Murmur soft music to her dreams,
   That pure, and unpolluted run,
Like to the new-born crystal streams,
   Under the bright enamour'd sun.

But when she waking shall display
   Her light, retire within your bar,
Her breath is life, her eyes are day,
   And all mankind her creatures are.

                 CHARLES COTTON

72 *Piping Peace*

You virgins that did late despair
   To keep your wealth from cruel men,
Tie up in silk your careless hair:
   Soft peace is come again.

Now lovers' eyes may gently shoot
   A flame that will not kill;
The drum was angry, but the lute
   Shall whisper what you will.

E

Sing Io, Io; for his sake
  That hath restored your drooping heads;
With choice of sweetest flowers make
  A garden where he treads;

Whilst we whole groves of laurel bring,
  A petty triumph for his brow,
Who is the Master of our spring
  And all the bloom we owe.

JAMES SHIRLEY

73 *Songs at Amala's Wedding*

By female voices

We have bathed, where none have seen us,
  In the lake and in the fountain,
    Underneath the charmed statue
Of the timid, bending Venus,
  When the water-nymphs were counting
In the waves the stars of night,
    And those maidens started at you,
Your limbs shone through so soft and bright.
  But no secrets dare we tell,
    For thy slaves unlace thee,
    And he, who shall embrace thee,
  Waits to try thy beauty's spell.

By male voices

We have crowned thee queen of women,
  Since love's love, the rose, hath kept her
    Court within thy lips and blushes,
And thine eye, in beauty swimming,
  Kissing, we rendered up the sceptre,
At whose touch the startled soul
    Like an ocean bounds and gushes,
And spirits bend at thy control.
  But no secrets dare we tell,
    For thy slaves unlace thee,
    And he, who shall embrace thee,
  Is at hand, and so farewell.

THOMAS LOVELL BEDDOES

74 *Fear no more the heat o' the sun*

Fear no more the heat o' the sun,
  Nor the furious winter's rages;
Thou thy worldly task hast done,
  Home art gone, and ta'en thy wages;
Golden lads and girls all must,
As chimney-sweepers, come to dust.

Fear no more the frown o' the great,
  Thou art past the tyrant's stroke:
Care no more to clothe and eat;
  To thee the reed is as the oak:
The sceptre, learning, physic, must
All follow this, and come to dust.

Fear no more the lightning-flash,
  Nor the all-dread thunder-stone;
Fear not slander, censure rash;
  Thou hast finished joy and moan;
All lovers young, all lovers must
Consign to thee, and come to dust.

No exorciser harm thee!
  Nor no witchcraft charm thee!
Ghost unlaid forbear thee!
  Nothing ill come near thee!
Quiet consummation have;
And renowned be thy grave!
                    WILLIAM SHAKESPEARE

75 *Autolycus' Song*

Lawn as white as driven snow;
Cyprus black as e'er was crow;
Gloves as sweet as damask roses;
Masks for faces and for noses;
Bugle-bracelet, necklace-amber,
Perfume for a lady's chamber;
Golden quoifs and stomachers,
For my lads to give their dears;

Pins and poking-sticks of steel;
What maids lack from head to heel:
Come buy of me, come; come buy, come buy;
Buy, lads, or else your lasses cry;
Come buy.

WILLIAM SHAKESPEARE

76 *There came a wind like a bugle*

There came a wind like a bugle;
It quivered through the grass,
And a green chill upon the heat
So ominous did pass
We barred the windows and the doors
As from an emerald ghost;
The doom's electric moccasin
That very instant passed.
On a strange mob of panting trees,
And fences fled away,

And rivers where the houses ran
The living looked that day.
The bell within the steeple wild
The flying tidings whirled.
How much can come
And much can go,
And yet abide the world!

EMILY DICKINSON

77 *Song*

The splendour falls on castle walls
    And snowy summits old in story:
The long light shakes across the lakes,
    And the wild cataract leaps in glory.
Blow, bugle, blow, set the wild echoes flying,
Blow, bugle; answer, echoes, dying, dying, dying.

O hark, O hear! how thin and clear,
    And thinner, clearer, farther going!
O sweet and far from cliff and scar
    The horns of Elfland faintly blowing!

Blow, let us hear the purple glens replying:
Blow, bugle; answer, echoes, dying, dying, dying.

O love, they die in yon rich sky,
    They faint on hill or field or river:
Our echoes roll from soul to soul,
    And grow for ever and for ever.
Blow, bugle, blow, set the wild echoes flying,
And answer, echoes, answer, dying, dying, dying.

ALFRED, LORD TENNYSON

78 *The Flower-fed Buffaloes*

The flower-fed buffaloes of the spring
In the days of long ago,
Ranged where the locomotives sing
And the prairie flowers lie low:—
The tossing, blooming, perfumed grass
Is swept away by the wheat,
Wheels and wheels and wheels spin by
In the spring that still is sweet.
But the flower-fed buffaloes of the spring
Left us, long ago.
They gore no more, they bellow no more,
They trundle around the hills no more:—
With the Blackfeet, lying low,
With the Pawnees, lying low,
Lying low.

VACHEL LINDSAY

79 *To* ——

Music, when soft voices die,
Vibrates in the memory—
Odours, when sweet violets sicken,
Live within the sense they quicken.

Rose leaves, when the rose is dead,
Are heaped for the beloved's bed;
And so thy thoughts, when thou art gone,
Love itself shall slumber on.

PERCY BYSSHE SHELLEY

80 *The Sick Rose*

O Rose, thou art sick!
The invisible worm
That flies in the night,
In the howling storm,

Has found out thy bed
Of crimson joy,
And his dark secret love
Does thy life destroy.

WILLIAM BLAKE

81 *Serenade*

Stars of the summer night!
    Far in yon azure deeps,
Hide, hide your golden light!
    She sleeps!
My lady sleeps!
    Sleeps!

Moon of the summer night!
    Far down yon western steeps,
Sink, sink in silver light!
    She sleeps!
My lady sleeps!
    Sleeps!

Wind of the summer night!
    Where yonder woodbine creeps,
Fold, fold thy pinions light!
    She sleeps!
My lady sleeps!
    Sleeps!

Dreams of the summer night!
    Tell her, her lover keeps
Watch! while in slumbers light
    She sleeps!
My lady sleeps!
    Sleeps!

HENRY WADSWORTH LONGFELLOW

82 *To Celia*

Come my Celia, let us prove,
While we may, the sports of love;
Time will not be ours, for ever:
He, at length, our good will sever.
Spend not then his gifts in vaine.
Suns, that set, may rise again:
But if once we lose this light,
'Tis, with us, perpetual night.
Why should we defer our joys?
Fame, and rumour are but toys.
Cannot we delude the eyes
Of a few poor household spies?
Or his easier ears beguile,
So removed by our wile?
'Tis no sin, love's fruit to steal,
But the sweet theft to reveal:
To be taken, to be seen,
These have crimes accounted been.

*

Kiss me, sweet: The wary lover
Can your favours keep, and cover,
When the common courting jay
All your bounties will betray.
Kiss again: no creature comes.
Kiss, and score up wealthy sums
On my lips, thus hardly sund'red,
While you breathe. First give a hundred,
Then a thousand, then another
Hundred, then unto the tother
Add a thousand, and so more:
Till you equal with the store,
All the grass that *Romney* yields,
Or the sands in *Chelsea* fields,
Or the drops in silver *Thames*,
Or the stars, that gild his streams,
In the silent summer-nights,
When youths ply their stol'n delights.
That the curious may not know
How to tell 'em, as they flow,

And the envious, when they find
What their number is, be pin'd.

BEN JONSON

83 *Song*

Now I see thy looks were feigned
Quickly lost and quickly gained.
Soft thy skin like wool of wethers,
Heart unconstant, light as feathers;
Tongue untrusty, subtle sighted;
Wanton will with change delighted.
    Siren pleasant, foe to reason,
      Cupid plague thee for thy treason!

Of thine eye I made my mirror,
From thy beauty came my error;
All thy words I counted witty,
All thy sighs I deemed pity;
Thy false tears that me aggrieved
First of all my trust deceived.
    Siren pleasant, foe to reason,
      Cupid plague thee for thy treason!

Feign'd acceptance when I asked,
Lovely words with cunning masked,
Holy vows but heart unholy.
Wretched man! my trust was folly.
Lily-white and pretty winking,
Solemn vows but sorry thinking.
    Siren pleasant, foe to reason,
      Cupid plague thee for thy treason!

Now I see, O seemly cruel,
Others warm them at my fuel.
Wit shall guide me in this durance
Since in love is no assurance.
Change thy pasture, take thy pleasure,
Beauty is a fading treasure.
    Siren pleasant, foe to reason,
      Cupid plague thee for thy treason!

Prime youth lasts not, age will follow
And make white those tresses yellow;
Wrinkled face for looks delightful
Shall acquaint the dame despiteful;
And when time shall date thy glory
Then too late thou wilt be sorry.
    Siren pleasant, foe to reason,
    Cupid plague thee for thy treason!
                                    THOMAS LODGE

84 *To Mistress Margery Wentworth*

With margerain gentle,
    The flower of goodlihead,
Enbroider'd the mantle
    Is of your maidenhead.
Plainly I cannot glose;
    Ye be, as I devine,
The pretty primrose,
    The goodly columbine.
With margerain gentle,
    The flower of goodlihead,
Enbroider'd the mantle
    Is of your maidenhead.
Benign, courteous, and meek,
    With wordes well devised;
In you, who list to seek,
    Be virtues well comprised.
With margerain gentle,
    The flower of goodlihead,
Enbroider'd the mantle
    Is of your maidenhead.
                                    JOHN SKELTON

85 *Song*

Sweet Echo, sweetest Nymph, that liv'st unseen
        Within thy airy shell
    By slow Meander's margent green,
And in the violet-imbroider'd vale
        Where the love-lorn Nightingale
Nightly to thee her sad Song mourneth well:

Canst thou not tell me of a gentle Pair
That likest thy Narcissus are?
O if thou have
Hid them in some flow'ry cave,
Tell me but where,
Sweet Queen of Parly, Daughter of the Sphear,
So may'st thou be translated to the skies,
And give resounding grace to all Heav'ns Harmonies!

JOHN MILTON

86 *Song*

O're the smooth enamel'd green
Where no print of step hath been,
Follow me as I sing
And touch the warbled string.
Under the shady roof
Of branching Elm-Star-proof
Follow me.
I will bring you where she sits,
Clad in splendor as befits
Her deity.
Such a rural Queen
All Arcadia hath not seen.

JOHN MILTON

87 *Shepherd's Song*

'Come down, O maid, from yonder mountain height:
What pleasure lives in height (the shepherd sang)
In height and cold, the splendour of the hills?
But cease to move so near the Heavens, and cease
To glide a sunbeam by the blasted Pine,
To sit a star upon the sparkling spire;
And come, for Love is of the valley, come,
For Love is of the valley, come thou down
And find him; by the happy threshold, he,
Or hand in hand with Plenty in the maize,
Or red with spirted purple of the vats,
Or foxlike in the vine; nor cares to walk
With Death and Morning on the silver horns,
Nor wilt thou snare him in the white ravine,

Nor find him dropt upon the firths of ice,
That huddling slant in furrow-cloven falls
To roll the torrent out of dusky doors:
But follow; let the torrent dance thee down
To find him in the valley; let the wild
Lean-headed Eagles yelp alone, and leave
The monstrous ledges there to slope, and spill
Their thousand wreaths of dangling water-smoke,
That like a broken purpose waste in air:
So waste not thou; but come; for all the vales
Await thee; azure pillars of the hearth
Arise to thee; the children call, and I
Thy shepherd pipe, and sweet is every sound,
Sweeter thy voice, but every sound is sweet;
Myriads of rivulets hurrying thro' the lawn,
The moan of doves in immemorial elms,
And murmuring of innumerable bees.'

ALFRED, LORD TENNYSON

88 *It was a lover and his lass*

It was a lover and his lass,
    With a hey, and a ho, and a hey nonino,
That o'er the green corn-field did pass,
    In the spring time, the only pretty ring time,
When birds do sing, hey ding a ding, ding;
Sweet lovers love the spring.

Between the acres of the rye,
    With a hey, and a ho, and a hey nonino,
These pretty country folks would lie,
    In the spring time, the only pretty ring time,
When birds do sing, hey ding a ding, ding;
Sweet lovers love the spring.

This carol they began that hour,
    With a hey, and a ho, and a hey nonino,
How that life was but a flower
    In the spring time, the only pretty ring time,
When birds do sing, hey ding a ding, ding;
Sweet lovers love the spring.

And therefore take the present time,
  With a hey, and a ho, and a hey nonino;
For love is crowned with the prime
  In the spring time, the only pretty ring time,
When birds do sing, hey ding a ding, ding;
Sweet lovers love the spring.

WILLIAM SHAKESPEARE

89 *Montrose To his Mistress*

My dear and only love, I pray
  This noble world of thee,
Be govern'd by no other sway
  But purest monarchy.
For if confusion have a part,
  Which virtuous souls abhorr,
And hold a synod in thy heart,
  I'll never love thee more.

Like Alexander I will reign,
  And I will reign alone,
My thoughts shall evermore disdain
  A rival on my throne.
He either fears his fate too much,
  Or his deserts are small,
That puts it not unto the touch,
  To win or lose it all.

But I must rule, and govern still,
  And always give the law,
And have each subject at my will,
  And all to stand in awe.
But 'gainst my battery if I find
  Thou shun'st the prize so sore,
As that thou set'st me up a blind,
  I'll never love thee more.

Or in the empire of thy heart,
  Where I should solely be,
Another do pretend a part,
  And dares to vie with me,

Or if committees thou erect,
   And goes on such a score,
I'll sing and laugh at thy neglect,
   And never love thee more.

But if thou wilt be constant then,
   And faithful of thy word,
I'll make thee glorious by my pen,
   And famous by my sword.
I'll serve thee in such noble ways
   Was never heard before:
I'll crown and deck thee all with bays,
   And love thee evermore.

JAMES GRAHAM,
MARQUIS OF MONTROSE

90 *To Helen*

Helen, thy beauty is to me
   Like those Nicean barks of yore,
That gently, o'er a perfumed sea,
   The weary, wayworn wanderer bore
   To his own native shore.

On desperate seas long wont to roam,
   Thy hyacinth hair, thy classic face,
Thy Naiad airs have brought me home
   To the glory that was Greece
   And the grandeur that was Rome.

Lo! in yon brilliant window-niche
   How statue-like I see thee stand,
The agate lamp within thy hand!
   Ah, Psyche, from the regions which
   Are Holy Land!

EDGAR ALLAN POE

91 *Callicles' Song*

Through the black, rushing smoke-bursts,
Thick breaks the red flame;
All Etna heaves fiercely
Her forest-clothed frame.

Not here, O Apollo!
Are haunts meet for thee.
But, where Helicon breaks down
In cliff to the sea,

Where the moon-silver'd inlets
Send far their light voice
Up the still vale of Thisbe,
O speed, and rejoice!

On the sward at the cliff-top
Lie strewn the white flocks,
On the cliff-side the pigeons
Roost deep in the rocks.

In the moonlight the shepherds,
Soft lull'd by the rills,
Lie wrapt in their blankets
Asleep on the hills.

–What forms are these coming
So white through the gloom?
What garments out-glistening
The gold-flower'd broom?

What sweet-breathing presence
Out-perfumes the thyme?
What voices enrapture
The night's balmy prime?–

'Tis Apollo comes leading
His choir, the Nine.
–The leader is fairest,
But all are divine.

They are lost in the hollows!
They stream up again!
What seeks on this mountain
The glorified train?–

They bathe on this mountain,
In the spring by their road;
Then on to Olympus,
Their endless abode.

–Whose praise do they mention?
Of what is it told?–
What will be for ever;
What was from of old.

First hymn they the Father
Of all things; and then,
The rest of immortals,
The action of men.

The day in his hotness,
The strife with the palm;
The night in her silence,
The stars in their calm.

MATTHEW ARNOLD

92 *Ilion, Ilion*

Ilion, Ilion, dreamy Ilion, pillared Ilion, holy Ilion,
City of Ilion when wilt thou be melody born?
Blue Scamander, yellowing Simois from the heart of piny Ida
Everwhirling from the molten snows upon the mountainthrone,
Roll Scamander, ripple Simois, ever onward to a melody
Manycircled, overflowing thoro' and thoro' the flowery level
of unbuilt Ilion,
City of Ilion, pillared Ilion, shadowy Ilion, holy Ilion,
  To a music merrily flowing, merrily echoing
  When wilt thou be melody born?

Manygated, heavywalléd, manytowered city of Ilion,
From the silver, lilyflowering meadowlevel
  When wilt thou be melody born?
Ripple onward, echoing Simois,
Ripple ever with a melancholy moaning,
  In the rushes to the dark blue brimméd Ocean, yellowing
Simois,
To a music from the golden twanging harpwire heavily drawn.
  Manygated, heavywalléd, manytowered city of Ilion,
  To a music sadly flowing, slowly falling,
  When wilt thou be melody born?

ALFRED, LORD TENNYSON

93 *A Fancy*

First shall the heavens want starry light,
 The seas be robbed of their waves;
The day want sun, and sun want bright,
  The night want shade, the dead men graves;
   The April flowers and leaf and tree,
   Before I false my faith to thee.

First shall the tops of highest hills
 By humble plains be overpried;
And poets scorn the Muses' quills,
  And fish forsake the water-glide,
   And Iris lose her coloured weed,
   Before I fail thee at thy need.

First direful hate shall turn to peace,
 And love relent in deep disdain;
And death his fatal stroke shall cease,
  And envy pity every pain,
   And pleasure mourn, and sorrow smile
   Before I talk of any guile.

First time shall stay his stayless race,
 And winter bless his brows with corn,
And snow bemoisten July's face,
  And winter spring, and summer mourn,
   Before my pen by help of fame
   Cease to recite thy sacred name.

        THOMAS LODGE

94 *Ah Fading Joy*

Ah fading joy, how quickly art thou past!
 Yet we thy ruin haste:
As if the Cares of Human Life were few,
 We seek out new,
And follow Fate that does too fast pursue.

See how on ev'ry Bough the Birds express
 In their sweet notes their happiness.
 They all enjoy and nothing spare;
But on their Mother Nature lay their care:

Why then should Man, the Lord of all below,
  Such troubles choose to know,
As none of all his Subjects undergo?

Hark, hark, the Waters fall, fall, fall
  And with a Murmuring sound
  Dash, dash, upon the ground,
    To gentle slumbers call.

JOHN DRYDEN

95 *She Walks in Beauty*

She walks in beauty, like the night
  Of cloudless climes and starry skies;
And all that's best of dark and bright
  Meet in her aspect and her eyes:
Thus mellow'd to that tender light
  Which heaven to gaudy day denies.

One shade the more, one ray the less,
  Had half impair'd the nameless grace
Which waves in every raven tress,
  Or softly lightens o'er her face;
Where thoughts serenely sweet express
  How pure, how dear their dwelling-place.

And on that cheek, and o'er that brow,
  So soft, so calm, yet eloquent,
The smiles that win, the tints that glow,
  But tell of days in goodness spent,
A mind at peace with all below,
  A heart whose love is innocent!

GEORGE GORDON, LORD BYRON

96 *To Anthea, Who may Command Him Anything*

Bid me to live, and I will live
  Thy Protestant to be!
Or bid me love, and I will give
  A loving heart to thee.

A heart as soft, a heart as kind,
　　A heart as sound and free
As in the whole world thou canst find,
　　That heart I'll give to thee.

Bid that heart stay, and it will stay
　　To honour thy decree:
Or bid it languish quite away,
　　And't shall do so for thee.

Bid me to weep, and I will weep
　　While I have eyes to see:
And, having none, yet I will keep
　　A heart to weep for thee.

Bid me despair, and I'll despair,
　　Under the Cypress tree:
Or bid me die, and I will dare
　　E'en Death, to die for thee.

Thou art my life, my love, my heart,
　　The very eyes of me:
And hast command of every part
　　To live and die for thee.

ROBERT HERRICK

97 *Song*

Sweet Cupid, ripen her desire,
　　Thy joyful harvest may begin;
If age approach a little nigher,
　　'Twill be too late to get it in.

Cold winter storms lay standing corn,
　　Which once too ripe will never rise,
And lovers wish themselves unborn
　　When all their joys lie in their eyes.

Then, sweet, let us embrace and kiss.
　　Shall beauty shale upon the ground?
If age bereave us of this bliss,
　　Then will no more such sport be found.

WILLIAM CORKINE

98 *Rose-cheek'd Laura*

Rose-cheekt *Laura*, come
Sing thou smoothly with thy beauty's
Silent music, either other
    Sweetly gracing.

Lovely forms do flow
From concent divinely framed;
Heav'n is music, and thy beauty's
    Birth is heavenly.

These dull notes we sing
Discords need for helps to grace them;
Only beauty purely loving
    Knows no discord,

But still moves delight,
Like clear springs renew'd by flowing,
Ever perfect, ever in them-
    selves eternal.

                THOMAS CAMPION

99 *To my lady Mirriel Howard*

My little lady I may not leave behind,
  But do her service needës now I must;
Benign, courteous, of gentle heart and mind,
  Whom Fortune and Fate plainly have dicust [1]
Long to enjoy pleasure, delight, and lust:
The embudded blossoms of roses red of hue,
With lilies white your beauty doth renew.

Compare you I may to Cydippe, the maid,
  That of Acontius, when she found the bill [2]
In her bosom, lord, how she was afraid!
The ruddy shame-facedness in her visage fill,
  Which manner of abashment became her not ill!
Right so, madam, the roses red of hue
With lilies white your beauty doth renew.

                JOHN SKELTON

[1] determined
[2] love-verses which Acontius had written on the apple

100 *Love still has something of the Sea*

Love still has something of the sea
    From whence his mother rose;
No time his slaves from doubt can free,
    Nor give their thoughts repose:

They are becalm'd in clearest days,
    And in rough weather tost;
They wither under cold delays,
    Or are in tempests lost.

One while they seem to touch the port,
    Then straight into the main
Some angry wind in cruel sport
    The vessel drives again.

At first disdain and pride they fear,
    Which if they chance to 'scape,
Rivals and falsehood soon appear
    In a more dreadful shape.

By such degrees to joy they come,
    And are so long withstood,
So slowly they receive the sum,
    It hardly does them good.

'Tis cruel to prolong a pain;
    And to defer a joy,
Believe me, gentle Celemene,
    Offends the winged boy.

An hundred thousand oaths your fears
    Perhaps would not remove;
And if I gaz'd a thousand years
    I could no deeper love.

SIR CHARLES SEDLEY

101 *To a Lady, asking him how long he would
love her*

> It is not, Celia, in our power
>   To say how long our love will last;
> It may be we within this hour
>   May lose those joys we now do taste:
> The blessed, that immortal be,
> From change in love are only free.
>
> Then, since we mortal lovers are,
>   Ask not how long our love will last;
> But, while it does, let us take care
>   Each minute be with pleasure passed.
> Were it not madness to deny
> To live, because we're sure to die?
>
> SIR GEORGE ETHEREGE

102 *Menaphon's Song*

> Some say Love
> Foolish Love
>   Doth rule and govern all the Gods,
> I say Love,
> Inconstant Love
>   Sets mens senses far at odds.
> Some swear Love
> Smooth'd face Love
>   Is sweetest sweet that men can have:
> I say Love,
> Sour Love
>   Makes virtue yield as beauty's slave.
> A bitter sweet, a folly worst of all
> That forceth wisdom to be folly's thrall
> Love is sweet,
> Wherein sweet?
>   In fading pleasures that do pain.
> Beauty sweet.
> Is that sweet
>   That yieldeth sorrow for a gain?

If Love's sweet,
Herein sweet,
  That minute's joys are monthly woes.
Tis not sweet,
That is sweet
  Nowhere, but where repentance grows.
Then love who list if beauty be so sour:
Labour for me, Love rest in Princes' bower.

ROBERT GREENE

103 *Ode of Anacreon*

The women tell me every day
That all my bloom has past away.
'Behold,' the pretty wantons cry,
'Behold this mirror with a sigh;
The locks upon thy brow are few,
And, like the rest, they're withering too!'
Whether decline has thinn'd my hair,
I'm sure I neither know nor care;
But this I know, and this I feel,
As onward to the tomb I steal,
That still as death approaches nearer,
The joys of life are sweeter, dearer;
And had I but an hour to live,
That little hour to bliss I'd give.

THOMAS MOORE

104 *How happy the Lover*

How happy the lover,
  How easy his chain,
How pleasing his pain!
How sweet to discover
  He sighs not in vain.
For love ev'ry creature
Is form'd by his nature;
No joys are above
The pleasures of love.

In vain are our graces,
    In vain are your eyes,
    If love you despise;
When age furrows faces,
    'Tis time to be wise.
Then use the short blessing,
That flies in possessing:
No joys are above
The pleasures of love.

JOHN DRYDEN

105 *Pack, Clouds, Away*

Pack, clouds, away, and welcome day,
    With night we banish sorrow;
Sweet air blow soft, mount larks aloft
    To give my love good-morrow!
Wings from the wind to please her mind,
    Notes from the lark I'll borrow;
Bird prune thy wing, nightingale sing,
    To give my love good-morrow;
        To give my love good-morrow
        Notes from them both I'll borrow.

Wake from thy nest, Robin red-breast,
    Sing, birds, in every furrow;
And from each hill, let music shrill
    Give my fair love good-morrow!
Blackbird and thrush in every bush,
    Stare, linnet and cock-sparrow!
You pretty elves, amongst yourselves
    Sing my fair Love good-morrow;
        To give my love good-morrow
        Sing, birds, in every furrow.

THOMAS HEYWOOD

106 *To the Virgins to make much of Time*

Gather ye rosebuds while ye may,
    Old Time is still a-flying:
And this same flower that smiles to-day
    To-morrow will be dying.

The glorious lamp of heaven, the Sun,
　　The higher he's a-getting,
The sooner will his race be run,
　　And nearer he's to setting.

That age is best which is the first,
　　When Youth and Blood are warmer;
But being spent, the worse, and worst
　　Times still succeed the former.

Then be not coy, but use your time,
　　And while ye may, go marry:
For having lost but once your prime
　　You may for ever tarry.

ROBERT HERRICK

107 *To Electra*

I dare not ask a kiss;
　　I dare not beg a smile;
Lest having that, or this,
　　I might grow proud the while.

No, no, the utmost share
　　Of my desire, shall be
Only to kiss that air,
　　That lately kissed thee.

ROBERT HERRICK

108 *To Daffodils*

Fair daffodils, we weep to see
　　You haste away so soon;
As yet the early-rising Sun
　　Has not attain'd his noon.
　　　　Stay, stay,
　　Until the hasting day
　　　　Has run
　　But to the evensong;
And, having pray'd together, we
　　Will go with you along.

We have short time to stay, as you,
　　We have as short a Spring;
As quick a growth to meet decay,
　　As you, or anything.
　　　　We die,
　　As hours do, and dry
　　　　Away,
　　Like to the Summer's rain;
Or as the pearls of Morning's dew,
　　Ne'er to be found again.
ROBERT HERRICK

109 *To Blossoms*

Fair pledges of a fruitful tree,
　　Why do ye fall so fast?
　　Your date is not so past;
But you may stay yet here a while,
　　To blush and gently smile;
　　　　And go at last.

What! were ye born to be
　　An hour or half's delight;
　　And so to bid good-night?
'Twas pity Nature brought ye forth
　　Merely to show your worth,
　　　　And lose you quite.

But you are lovely leaves, where we
　　May read how soon things have
　　Their end, though ne'er so brave:
And after they have shown their pride,
　　Like you a while: they glide
　　　　Into the grave.
ROBERT HERRICK

110 *Delight in Disorder*

A sweet disorder in the dress
Kindles in clothes a wantonness:
A lawn about the shoulders thrown
Into a fine distraction:

An erring lace, which here and there
Enthralls the crimson stomacher:
A cuff neglectful, and thereby
Ribbons to flow confusedly:
A winning wave, deserving note,
In the tempestuous petticoat:
A careless shoe-string, in whose tie
I see a wild civility:
Do more bewitch me than when art
Is too precise in every part.

ROBERT HERRICK

111 *Clerimont's Song*

Still to be neat, still to be drest,
As you were going to a feast;
Still to be powd'red, still perfum'd:
Lady, it is to be presum'd,
Though art's hid causes are not found,
All is not sweet, all is not sound.

Give me a look, give me a face,
That makes simplicity a grace;
Robes loosely flowing, hair as free:
Such sweet neglect more taketh me,
Than all th'adulteries of art.
They strike mine eyes, but not my heart.

BEN JONSON

112 *Upon Julia's Clothes*

Whenas in silks my Julia goes,
Then, then, methinks, how sweetly flows
The liquefaction of her clothes.

Next, when I cast mine eyes and see
That brave vibration each way free;
O how that glittering taketh me!

ROBERT HERRICK

113 *The Night-Piece, to Julia*

Her eyes the glow-worm lend thee,
The shooting stars attend thee
    And the elves also,
    Whose little eyes glow
Like the sparks of fire, befriend thee.

No Will-o'-th'-Wisp mislight thee,
Nor snake, or slow-worm bite thee;
    But on, on thy way
    Not making a stay,
Since ghost there's none to affright thee.

Let not the dark thee cumber:
What though the moon does slumber?
    The stars of the night
    Will lend thee their light
Like tapers clear without number.

Then Julia let me woo thee,
Thus, thus to come unto me;
    And when I shall meet
    Thy silv'ry feet
My soul I'll pour into thee.

ROBERT HERRICK

114 *To Dianeme*

Sweet, be not proud of those two eyes
Which starlike sparkle in their skies;
Nor be you proud, that you can see
All hearts your captives; yours yet free:
Be you not proud of that rich hair
Which wantons with the love-sick air;
Whenas that ruby, which you wear,
Sunk from the tip of your soft ear,
Will last to be a precious stone
When all your world of beauty's gone.

ROBERT HERRICK

115 *Her Rambling*

My mistress when she goes
To pull the pink and rose
Along the river bounds,
And trippeth on the grounds,
And runs from rocks to rocks
With lovely scattered locks,
Whilst amorous wind doth play
With hairs so golden gay,
The water waxeth clear,
The fishes draw her near,
The sirens sing her praise,
Sweet flowers perfume her ways,
And Neptune, glad and fain,
Yields up to her his reign.

THOMAS LODGE

116 *O Mistress Mine, where are you Roaming?*

O mistress mine! where are you roaming?
O! stay and hear; your true love's coming.
    That can sing both high and low.
Trip no further, pretty sweeting;
Journeys end in lovers meeting,
    Every wise man's son doth know.

What is love? 'tis not hereafter;
Present mirth hath present laughter;
    What's to come is still unsure:
In delay there lies no plenty;
Then come kiss me, sweet-and-twenty,
    Youth's a stuff will not endure.

WILLIAM SHAKESPEARE

117 *Ruth*

She stood breast high amid the corn,
Clasp'd by the golden light of morn,
Like the sweetheart of the sun,
Who many a glowing kiss had won.

On her cheek an autumn flush,
Deeply ripened;–such a blush
In the midst of brown was born,
Like red poppies grown with corn.

Round her eyes her tresses fell,
Which were blackest none could tell,
But long lashes veil'd a light,
That had else been all too bright.

And her hat, with shady brim,
Made her tressy forehead dim;–
Thus she stood amid the stooks,
Praising God with sweetest looks:–

Sure, I said, heav'n did not mean,
Where I reap thou shouldst but glean,
Lay thy sheaf adown and come,
Share my harvest and my home.

THOMAS HOOD

118 *The Solitary Reaper*

Behold her, single in the field,
Yon solitary Highland Lass!
Reaping and singing by herself;
Stop here, or gently pass!
Alone she cuts and binds the grain,
And sings a melancholy strain;
O listen! for the Vale profound
Is overflowing with the sound.

No Nightingale did ever chaunt
More welcome notes to weary bands
Of travellers in some shady haunt,
Among Arabian sands:
A voice so thrilling ne'er was heard
In spring-time from the Cuckoo-bird,
Breaking the silence of the seas
Among the farthest Hebrides.

Will no one tell me what she sings?–
Perhaps the plaintive numbers flow
For old, unhappy, far-off things,
And battles long ago:
Or is it some more humble lay,
Familiar matter of to-day?
Some natural sorrow, loss, or pain,
That has been, and may be again?

Whate'er the theme, the Maiden sang
As if her song could have no ending;
I saw her singing at her work,
And o'er the sickle bending;–
I listened, motionless and still;
And, as I mounted up the hill,
The music in my heart I bore,
Long after it was heard no more.

WILLIAM WORDSWORTH

119 *For Anne Gregory*

'Never shall a young man,
Thrown into despair
By those great honey-coloured
Ramparts at your ear,
Love you for yourself alone
And not your yellow hair.'

'But I can get a hair-dye
And set such colour there,
Brown, or black, or carrot,
That young men in despair
May love me for myself alone
And not my yellow hair.'

'I heard an old religious man
But yesternight declare
That he had found a text to prove
That only God, my dear,
Could love you for yourself alone
And not your yellow hair.'

WILLIAM BUTLER YEATS

120 *Lines : When the Lamp is Shattered*

When the lamp is shattered
The light in the dust lies dead—
　When the cloud is scattered
The rainbow's glory is shed.
　When the lute is broken,
Sweet tones are remembered not;
　When the lips have spoken,
Loved accents are soon forgot.

　As music and splendour
Survive not the lamp and the lute,
　The heart's echoes render
No song when the spirit is mute:—
　No song but sad dirges,
Like the wind through a ruined cell,
　Or the mournful surges
That ring the dead seaman's knell.

　When hearts have once mingled
Love first leaves the well-built nest;
　The weak one is singled
To endure what it once possessed.
　O Love! who bewailest
The frailty of all things here,
　Why choose you the frailest
For your cradle, your home, and your bier?

　Its passions will rock thee
As the storms rock the ravens on high;
　Bright reason will mock thee,
Like the sun from a wintry sky.
　From thy nest every rafter
Will rot, and thine eagle home
　Leave thee naked to laughter,
When leaves fall and cold winds come.

PERCY BYSSHE SHELLEY

121 *Oh! snatch'd away in Beauty's Bloom*

Oh! snatch'd away in beauty's bloom,
On thee shall press no ponderous tomb;
   But on thy turf shall roses rear
   Their leaves, the earliest of the year;
   And the wild cypress wave in tender gloom:

And oft by yon blue gushing stream
   Shall Sorrow lean her drooping head,
And feed deep thought with many a dream,
   And lingering pause and lightly tread;
   Fond wretch! as if her step disturb'd the dead!

Away! we know that tears are vain,
   That death nor heeds nor hears distress:
Will this unteach us to complain?
   Or make one mourner weep the less?
And thou—who tell'st me to forget,
Thy looks are wan, thine eyes are wet.

GEORGE GORDON, LORD BYRON

122 *Song*

My Luve is like a red, red rose,
   That's newly sprung in June:
My Luve is like the melodie,
   That's sweetly play'd in tune.

As fair art thou, my bonie lass,
   So deep in luve am I;
And I will luve thee still, my Dear,
   Till a' the seas gang dry.

Till a' the seas gang dry, my Dear,
   And the rocks melt wi' the sun;
And I will luve thee still, my Dear,
   While the sands o' life shall run.

And fare-thee-well, my only Luve!
   And fare-thee-well, a while!
And I will come again, my Luve,
   Tho' 'twere ten thousand mile!

ROBERT BURNS

123 *When we two parted*

When we two parted
  In silence and tears,
Half broken-hearted
  To sever for years,
Pale grew thy cheek and cold,
  Colder thy kiss;
Truly that hour foretold
  Sorrow to this.

The dew of the morning
  Sunk chill on my brow—
It felt like the warning
  Of what I feel now.
Thy vows are all broken,
  And light is thy fame;
I hear thy name spoken,
  And share in its shame.

They name thee before me,
  A knell to mine ear;
A shudder comes o'er me—
  Why wert thou so dear?
They know not I knew thee,
  Who knew thee too well:—
Long, long shall I rue thee,
  Too deeply to tell.

In secret we met—
  In silence I grieve,
That thy heart could forget,
  Thy spirit deceive.
If I should meet thee
  After long years,
How should I greet thee?—
  With silence and tears.

                    GEORGE GORDON, LORD BYRON

F

124 *Of a' the airts the wind can blaw*

Of a' the airts the wind can blaw,
   I dearly like the west,
For there the bonie lassie lives,
   The lassie I lo'e best:
There's wild-woods grow, and rivers row,
   And mony a hill between:
But day and night my fancy's flight
   Is ever wi' my Jean.

I see her in the dewy flowers,
   I see her sweet and fair:
I hear her in the tunefu' birds,
   I hear her charm the air:
There's not a bonie flower that springs,
   By fountain, shaw, or green;
There's not a bonie bird that sings,
   But minds me o' my Jean.

ROBERT BURNS

125 *The Banks o' Doon*

Ye flowery banks o' bonie Doon,
   How can ye blume sae fair?
How can ye chant, ye little birds,
   And I sae fu' o care!
Thou'll break my heart, thou bonie bird,
   That sings upon the bough;
Thou minds me o' the happy days
   When my fause Luve was true.
Thou'll break my heart, thou bonie bird,
   That sings beside thy mate;
For sae I sat, and sae I sang,
   And wist na o' my fate.

Aft hae I rov'd by bonie Doon,
   To see the woodbine twine;
And ilka bird sang o' its Luve,
   And sae did I o' mine.

Wi' lightsome heart I pu'd a rose,
  Upon a morn in June;
How like that rose my blooming morn,
  Sae darkly set ere noon!
Wi' lightsome heart I pu'd a rose,
  Upon its thorny tree;
But my fause Luver staw my rose,
  And left the thorn wi' me.

ROBERT BURNS

126 *There be None of Beauty's Daughters*

There be none of Beauty's daughters
  With a magic like thee;
And like music on the waters
  Is thy sweet voice to me:
When, as if its sound were causing
The charmed ocean's pausing,
The waves lie still and gleaming,
And the lull'd winds seem dreaming.

And the midnight moon is weaving
  Her bright chain o'er the deep;
Whose breast is gently heaving,
  As an infant's asleep:
So the spirit bows before thee,
To listen and adore thee;
With a full but soft emotion,
Like the swell of Summer's ocean.

GEORGE GORDON, LORD BYRON

127 *Oft, in the Stilly Night*

Oft, in the stilly night,
  Ere Slumber's chain has bound me,
Fond Memory brings the light
  Of other days around me;
    The smiles, the tears,
    Of boyhood's years,

The words of love then spoken;
    The eyes that shone,
    Now dimm'd and gone,
  The cheerful hearts now broken!
Thus, in the stilly night,
  Ere Slumber's chain hath bound me,
Sad Memory brings the light
  Of other days around me.

When I remember all
  The friends, so link'd together,
I've seen around me fall,
  Like leaves in wintry weather;
    I feel like one,
    Who treads alone
  Some banquet-hall deserted,
    Whose lights are fled,
    Whose garlands dead,
  And all but he departed!
Thus, in the stilly night,
  Ere Slumber's chain has bound me,
Sad Memory brings the light
  Of other days around me.

                    THOMAS MOORE

128 *So, we'll go no more a roving*

So, we'll go no more a roving
  So late into the night,
Though the heart be still as loving,
  And the moon be still as bright.

For the sword outwears its sheath,
  And the soul wears out the breast,
And the heart must pause to breathe,
  And love itself have rest.

Though the night was made for loving,
  And the day returns too soon,
Yet we'll go no more a roving
  By the light of the moon.

        GEORGE GORDON, LORD BYRON

129 *Sang*

My Peggy is a young thing,
   Just enter'd in her teens,
Fair as the day, and sweet as May,
Fair as the day, and always gay.
   My Peggy is a young thing,
     And I'm not very auld,
   Yet well I like to meet her at
     The wawking [1] of the fauld.

My Peggy speaks sae sweetly,
   Whene'er we meet alane,
I wish nae mair to lay my care
I wish nae mair of a' that's rare.
   My Peggy speaks sae sweetly,
     To a' the lave [2] I'm cauld ;
But she gars a' my spirits glow
     At wawking of the fauld.

My Peggy smiles sae kindly,
   Whene'er I whisper love,
That I look down on a' the town,
That I look down upon a crown.
   My Peggy smiles sae kindly,
     It makes me blythe and bauld,
And naething gi'es me sic delight,
     As wawking of the fauld.

My Peggy sings sae saftly,
   When on my pipe I play ;
By a' the rest it is confest,
By a' the rest that she sings best.
   My Peggy sings sae saftly,
     And in her sangs are tald,
With innocence, the wale [3] of sense,
     At wawking of the fauld.
                   ALLAN RAMSAY

[1] keeping watch on   [2] the rest   [3] choice

130 *The Rigs o' Barley*

It was upon a Lammas night,
    When corn rigs are bonie,
Beneath the moon's unclouded light,
    I held awa to Annie;
The time flew by, wi' tentless heed;
    Till, 'tween the late and early,
Wi' sma' persuasion she agreed
    To see me thro' the barley.
        Corn rigs, an' barley rigs,
            An' corn rigs are bonie:
            I'll ne'er forget that happy night,
            Amang the rigs wi' Annie.

The sky was blue, the wind was still,
    The moon was shining clearly;
I set her down, wi' right good will,
    Amang the rigs o' barley:
I ken't her heart was a' my ain;
    I lov'd her most sincerely;
I kiss'd her owre and owre again,
    Amang the rigs o' barley.
        Corn rigs, an' barley rigs, &c.

I lock'd her in my fond embrace;
    Her heart was beating rarely:
My blessings on that happy place,
    Amang the rigs o' barley!
But by the moon and stars so bright,
    That shone that hour so clearly!
She ay shall bless that happy night
    Amang the rigs o' barley.
        Corn rigs, an' barley rigs, &c.

I hae been blythe wi' comrades dear;
    I hae been merry drinking;
I hae been joyfu' gath'rin gear;
    I hae been happy thinking:

But a' the pleasures e'er I saw,
    Tho' three times doubl'd fairly–
That happy night was worth them a',
    Amang the rigs o' barley.
        Corn rigs, an' barley rigs, &c.
                                    ROBERT BURNS

131 *The War-Song of Dinas Vawr*

The mountain sheep are sweeter,
But the valley sheep are fatter;
We therefore deemed it meeter
To carry off the latter.
We made an expedition;
We met a host, and quelled it;
We forced a strong position,
And killed the men who held it.

On Dyfed's richest valley,
Where herds of kine were brousing,
We made a mighty sally,
To furnish our carousing.
Fierce warriors rushed to meet us;
We met them, and o'erthrew them:
They struggled hard to beat us;
But we conquered them, and slew them.

As we drove our prize at leisure,
The king marched forth to catch us:
His rage surpassed all measure,
But his people could not match us.
He fled to his hall-pillars;
And, ere our force we led off,
Some sacked his house and cellars,
While others cut his head off.

We there, in strife bewild'ring,
Spilt blood enough to swim in:
We orphaned many children,
And widowed many women.

The eagles and the ravens
We glutted with our foemen;
The heroes and the cravens,
The spearmen and the bowmen.

We brought away from battle,
And much their land bemoaned them,
Two thousand head of cattle,
And the head of him who owned them:
Ednyfed, king of Dyfed,
His head was borne before us;
His wine and beasts supplied our feasts,
And his overthrow, our chorus.

THOMAS LOVE PEACOCK

132 *Seamen Three*

Seamen three! What men be ye?
Gotham's three wise men we be.
Whither in your bowl so free?
To rake the moon from out the sea.
The bowl goes trim. The moon doth shine.
And our ballast is old wine;
And your ballast is old wine.

Who art thou, so fast adrift?
I am he they call Old Care.
Here on board we will thee lift.
No: I may not enter there.
Wherefore so? 'Tis Jove's decree,
In a bowl Care may not be;
In a bowl Care may not be.

Fear ye not the waves that roll?
No: in charmed bowl we swim.
What the charm that floats the bowl?
Water may not pass the brim.
The bowl goes trim. The moon doth shine.
And our ballast is old wine;
And your ballast is old wine.

THOMAS LOVE PEACOCK

133 *To Signora Cuzzoni*

May 25, 1724

Little *Siren* of the stage,
Charmer of an idle age,
Empty warbler, breathing lyre,
Wanton gale of fond desire,
Bane of every manly art,
Sweet enfeebler of the heart,
O, too pleasing in thy strain,
Hence, to southern climes again;
Tuneful mischief, vocal spell,
To this island bid farewell;
Leave us as we ought to be,
Leave the *Britons* rough and free.

AMBROSE PHILIPS

Book III

THE POETRY OF SENTIMENT

134 *As You came from the Holy Land*

As you came from the holy land
   of Walsinghame
Met you not with my true love
   by the way as you came?

How shall I know your true love
   That have met many one
As I went to the holy land
   That have come that have gone?

She is neither white nor brown
   But as the heavens fair;
There is none hath a form so divine
   In the earth or the air.

Such an one did I meet good Sir,
   Such an Angelic face,
Who like a queen like a nymph did appear,
   by her gait by her grace:

She hath left me here all alone,
   All alone as unknown;
Who sometimes did me lead with her self,
   And me lov'd as her own:

What's the cause that she leaves you alone
   And a new way doth take:
Who loved you once as her own
   And her joy did you make?

I have lov'd her all my youth,
   but now old as you see,
Love likes not the falling fruit
   From the withered tree:

Know that love is a careless child
   And forgets promise past:
He is blind he is deaf when he list
   And in faith never fast:

His desire is a dureless content
   And a trustless joy;
He is won with a world of despair
   And is lost with a toy:

Of women kind such indeed is the love
   Or the word Love abus'd
Under which many childish desires
   And conceits are excus'd:

But Love is a durable fire
   In the mind ever burning:
never sick never old never dead
   from itself never turning.

                   SIR WALTER RALEIGH

135 *A Cradle Hymn*

Hush! my dear, lie still and slumber,
Holy angels guard thy bed!
Heav'nly blessings without number
Gently falling on thy head.

Sleep my babe; thy food and raiment,
House and home, thy friends provide
All without thy care or payment,
All thy wants are well supply'd.

How much better thou'rt attended
Than the Son of God could be,
When from heav'n he descended
And became a child like thee?

Soft and easy is thy cradle;
Coarse and hard thy Saviour lay;
When his birthplace was a stable,
And his softest bed was hay.

Blessed Babe! what glorious features,
Spotless fair, divinely bright!
Must he dwell with brutal creatures?
How could angels bear the sight?

Was there nothing but a manger
Cursed sinners could afford,
To receive the heav'nly stranger?
Did they thus affront their Lord?

Soft, my child; I did not chide thee,
Tho' my song might sound too hard;
'Tis thy nurse [1] that sits beside thee,
And her arm shall be thy guard.

Yet to read the shameful story
How the Jews abus'd their King,
How they serv'd the Lord of glory,
Makes me angry while I sing.

See the kinder shepherds round him
Telling wonders from the sky;
There they sought him, there they found him,
With his virgin Mother by.

See the lovely Babe a-dressing,
Lovely Infant how he smil'd!
When he wept, the Mother's blessing
Sooth'd and hush'd the holy Child.

Lo! he slumbers in his manger
Where the horned oxen feed;
Peace, my Darling, here's no danger,
Here's no ox anear thy bed.

'Twas to save thee, child, from dying,
Save my dear from burning flame,
Bitter groans, and endless crying,
That thy blest Redeemer came.

[1] Here you may use the words mother, sister, neighbour, friend, etc.

May'st thou live to know and fear him,
Trust and love him all thy days!
Then go dwell for ever near him,
See his face, and sing his praise!

I could give thee thousand kisses,
Hoping what I most desire;
Not a mother's fondest wishes
Can to greater joys aspire.

ISAAC WATTS

136 *Balulalow*

O my deir hert, young Jesus sweit,
Prepare thy creddil in my spreit,
And I sall rock thee in my hert
And never mair from thee depart.

But I shall praise thee evermoir
With sangis sweit unto thy gloir;
The knees of my hert sall I bow,
And sing that richt *Balulalow!*

JAMES, JOHN, AND ROBERT WEDDERBURN

137 *Though Regions-far Divided*

Though regions-far divided
    And tedious tracts of time,
By my misfortune guided
    Make absence thought a crime;
Though we were set asunder
    As far as East from West,
Love still should work this wonder,
    Thou should'st be in my breast.

How slow alas are paces
    Compared to thoughts that fly
In moment back to places,
    Whole ages scarce descry.
The body must have pauses;
    The mind requires no rest;
Love needs no second causes
    To guide thee to my breast.

Accept in that poor dwelling,
 But welcome, nothing great,
With pride no turrets swelling
 But lowly as the seat;
Where, though not much delighted,
 In peace thou mayst be blest,
Unfeasted yet unfrighted,
 By rivals, in my breast.

But this is not the diet
 That doth for glory strive;
Poor beauties seek in quiet
 To keep one heart alive.
The price of his ambition,
 That looks for such a guest
Is hopeless of fruition
 To beat an empty breast.

See then my last lamenting.
 Upon a cliff I'll sit,
Rock Constancy presenting,
 Till I grow part of it;
My tears a quicksand feeding
 Whereon no foot can rest,
My sighs a tempest breeding
 About my stony breast.

Those arms wherin wide open
 Love's fleet was wont to put,
Shall laid across betoken
 That haven's mouth is shut.
Mine eyes no light shall cherish
 For ships at sea distrest,
But darkling let them perish
 Or split against my breast.

Yet if I can discover
 When thine before it rides,
To show I was thy lover
 I'll smooth my rugged sides.

And so much better measure
  Afford thee than the rest,
Thou shalt have no displeasure
  By knocking at my breast.
                            AURELIAN TOWNSHEND

138 *How should I be so pleasant?*

How should I
Be so pleasant,
In my semblant,
As my fellows be?
  Not long ago
It chanced so
As I did walk alone,
I heard a man
That now and than
Himself did thus bemoan:
  'Alas,' he said,
'I am betray'd
And utterly undone,
Whom I did trust
And think so just
Another man hath won.
  'My service due
And heart so true
On her I did bestow,
I never meant
For to repent
In wealth nor yet in woe.
  'Love did assign
Her to be mine
And not to love none new;
But who can bind
The fickle kind
That never will be true?
  'Each western wind
Hath turn'd her mind
And blown it clean away,

Thereby my wealth
My mirth and health
Are driven to great decay.
  'Fortune did smile
A right short while
And never said me nay,
With pleasant plays
And joyful days
My time to pass away.
  'Alas, ah las!
The time so was
So never shall it be,
Since she is gone
And I alone
Am left as ye may see.
  'Where is the oath
Where is the troth
That she to me did give?
Such feigned words
With silly bourds [1]
Let no wise man believe.
  'For even as I
Thus woefully
Unto myself complain,
If ye then trust
Needs learn ye must
To sing my song in vain.'
  How should I
Be so pleasant,
In my semblant,
As my fellows be?

SIR THOMAS WYATT

139 *Farewell, unkist*

What should I say,
  Since faith is dead,
And truth away
  From you is fled?
  Should I be led

---

[1] jests

With doubleness?
Nay, nay, Mistress!

I promised you,
   And you promised me,
To be as true,
   As I would be.
   But since I see
Your double heart,
Farewell my part!

Though for to take,
   It is not my mind
But to forsake
   [I am not blind] [1]
   And as I find
So will I trust,
Farewell, unjust!

Can ye say nay?
   But you said
That I alway
   Should be obey'd,
   And thus betray'd
Ere that I wist.
Farewell, unkist!

                              SIR THOMAS WYATT

140 *With Serving Still*

With serving still
   This have I won,
For my goodwill
   To be undone.

And for redress
   Of all my pain,
Disdainfulness
   I have again.

   [1] line missing in text.

And for reward
  Of all my smart,
Lo, thus unheard
  I must depart!

Wherefore all ye
  That after shall
By fortune be
  As I am, thrall,

Example take
  What I have won;
Thus for her sake
  To be undone!

SIR THOMAS WYATT

141 *Say Nay*

And wilt thou leave me thus?
Say nay, say nay, for shame
To save thee from the blame
Of all my grief and grame.
And wilt thou leave me thus?
  Say nay, say nay!

And wilt thou leave me thus
That hath lov'd thee so long,
In wealth and woe among?
And is thy heart so strong
As for to leave me thus?
  Say nay, say nay!

And wilt thou leave me thus
That hath given thee my heart,
Never for to depart,
Neither for pain nor smart:
And wilt thou leave me thus?
  Say nay, say nay!

And wilt thou leave me thus,
And have no more pity,
Of him that loveth thee?
Helas! thy cruelty!
And wilt thou leave me thus!
   Say nay, say nay!

   Sir Thomas Wyatt

142 *Rondeau*

What no, perdie! ye may be sure!
Think not to make me to your lure,
With words and cheer so contrarying,
Sweet and sour counter-weighing,
Too much it were still to endure.
Truth is tried, where craft is in ure,
But though ye have had my heartës cure,
Trow ye! I dote without ending?
   What no, perdie!

Though that with pain I do procure
For to forget that once was pure;
Within my heart shall still that thing
Unstable, unsure, and wavering,
Be in my mind without recure?
   What no, perdie!

   Sir Thomas Wyatt

143 *Shall I come, sweet Love, to thee?*

Shall I come, sweet Love, to thee,
   When the ev'ning beams are set?
Shall I not excluded be?
   Will you find no feigned let?
Let me not, for pity, more,
Tell the long hours at your door.

Who can tell what thief or foe,
   In the covert of the night,
For his prey will work my woe,
   Or through wicked foul despite:

So may I die unredrest,
Ere my long love be possest.

But to let such dangers pass,
Which a lover's thoughts disdain,
'Tis enough in such a place
    To attend love's joys in vain.
Do not mock me in thy bed,
While these cold nights freeze me dead.

THOMAS CAMPION

144 *My Sweetest Lesbia*

My sweetest Lesbia let us live and love,
And though the sager sort our deeds reprove,
Let us not weigh them: heav'n's great lamps do dive
Into their west, and straight again revive,
But soon as once set is our little light,
Then must we sleep one ever-during night.

If all would live their lives in love like me,
Then bloody swords and armour should not be,
No drum nor trumpet peaceful sleeps should move,
Unless alarm came from the camp of love:
But fools do live, and waste their little light,
And seek with pain their ever-during night.

When timely death my life and fortune ends,
Let not my hearse be vext with mourning friends,
But let all lovers rich in triumph come,
And with sweet pastimes grace my happy tomb;
And Lesbia close up thou my little light,
And crown with love my ever-during night.

THOMAS CAMPION

145 *Where She her Sacred Bower Adorns*

Where she her sacred bower adorns
    The rivers clearly flow;
The groves and meadows swell with flowers,
    The winds all gently blow.

Her sun-like beauty shines so fair,
    Her Spring can never fade:
Who then can blame the life that strives
    To harbour in her shade?

Her grace I sought, her love I wooed;
    Her love though I obtain,
No time, no toil, no vow, no faith,
    Her wished grace can gain.
Yet truth can tell my heart is hers,
    And her I will adore;
And from that love when I depart,
    Let heav'n view me no more.

Her roses with my prayers shall spring;
    And when her trees I praise,
Their boughs shall blossom, mellow fruit
    Shall straw her pleasant ways.
The words of hearty zeal have power
    High wonders to effect;
O why should then her princely ear
    My words, or zeal neglect?

If she my faith misdeems, or worth,
    Woe-worth my hapless fate:
For though time can my truth reveal,
    That time will come too late.
And who can glory in the worth,
    That cannot yield him grace?
Content in ev'rything is not,
    Nor joy in ev'ry place.

But from her bower of joy since I
    Must now excluded be,
And she will not relieve my cares,
    Which none can help but she;
My comfort in her love shall dwell,
    Her love lodge in my breast,
And though not in her bower, yet I
    Shall in her temple rest.

                              THOMAS CAMPION

146 *Madrigal: Love Vagabonding*

Sweet nymphs, if, as ye stray,
Ye find the froth-born goddess of the sea,
All blubber'd, pale, undone,
Who seeks her giddy son,
That little god of love,
Whose golden shafts your chastest bosoms prove,
Who, leaving all the heavens, hath run away;
If aught to him that finds him she'll impart,
Tell her he nightly lodgeth in my heart.

WILLIAM DRUMMOND

147 *The Dream of the Romaunt of the Rose*

Within my twenty yer of age,
Whan that Love taketh his cariage
Of yonge folk, I wente soone
To bedde, as I was wont to done,
And faste I slepte; and in slepyng
Me mette such a swevenyng [1]
That lyked me wonders wel.
But in that sweven is never a del [2]
That it nys afterward befalle,
Ryght as this drem wol tel us alle.

Now this drem wol I ryme aright
To make your hertes gaye and lyght,
For Love it prayeth, and also
Commaundeth me that it be so.
And if there any aske me,
Whether that it be he or she,
How this book, [the] which is here
Shal hatte,[3] that I rede you here;
It is the Romance of the Rose,
In which al the art of love I close.

The mater fayre is of to make;
God graunt me in gree [4] that she it take
For whom that it begonnen is!
And that is she that hath, ywis,

---

[1] dreaming   [2] part, whit   [3] be called   [4] favour

So mochel pris; and therto she
So worthy is biloved to be,
That she wel ought, of pris and ryght,
Be cleped Rose of every wight.
    That it was May me thoughte tho–
It is fyve yer or more ago–
That it was May, thus dremed me,
In tyme of love and jolite,
That al thing gynneth waxen gay,
For ther is neither busk nor hay
In May, that it nyl shrouded ben,
And it with newe leves wren.[1]
These wodes eek recoveren grene,
That drie in wynter ben to sene:
And the erthe wexith proud withalle,
For swote dewes that on it falle,
And the pore estat forget
In which that wynter had it set.
And than bycometh the ground so proud
That it wole have a newe shroud,
And makith so queynt his robe and faire
That it have hewes an hundred payre
Of gras and flouris, ynde [2] and pers,[3]
And many hewes ful dyvers.
That is the robe I mene, iwis,
Through which the ground to preisen is.
    The byrdes that han left her song,
While thei suffride cold so strong,
In wedres gryl and derk to sighte,
Ben in May, for the sonne brighte,
So glade that they shewe in syngyng
That in her hertis is sich lykyng
That they mote syngen and be light.
Than doth the nyghtyngale hir myght
To make noyse and syngen blythe.
Than is blisful many sithe [4]
The chelaundre [5] and papyngay.[6]
Than yonge folk entenden ay

[1] covered   [2] indigo   [3] blue-gray
[4] many a time   [5] lark   [6] woodpecker

Forto ben gay and amorous,
The tyme is than so saverous.
Hard is the hert that loveth nought
In May, whan al this mirth is wrought,
Whan he may on these braunches here
The smale briddes syngen clere
Her blisful swete song pitous.
And in this sesoun delytous,
Whan love affraieth alle thing,
Me thought a-nyght, in my sleping,
Right in my bed, ful redily,
That it was by the morowe erly,
And up I roos, and gan me clothe.
Anoon I wissh myn hondis bothe;
A sylvre nedle forth y drough
Out of an aguler ¹ queynt ynough,
And gan this nedle threde anon;
For out of toun me list to gon
The song of briddes forto here,
That in thise buskes syngen clere.
And in the swete seson that leef is,
With a thred bastyng my slevis,
Alone I wente in my plaiyng,
The smale foules song harknyng,
That peyned hem, ful many peyre,
To synge on bowes blosmed feyre.
Jolif and gay, ful of gladnesse,
Toward a ryver gan I me dresse,
That I herd renne faste by;
For fairer plaiyng non saugh I
Than playen me by that ryver.
For from an hill that stood ther ner,
Cam doun the strem ful stif and bold,
Cleer was the water, and as cold
As any welle is, soth to seyne;
And somdel lasse it was than Seyne,
But it was strayghter wel away.
And never saugh I, er that day,
The watir that so wel lyked me;
And wondir glad was I to se

¹ needle-case

That lusty place and that ryver.
And with that watir, that ran so cler,
My face I wyssh.   Tho saugh I well
The botme paved everydell
With gravel, ful of stones shene.
The medewe softe, swote and grene,
Beet right on the watir syde.
Ful cler was than the morowtyde,
And ful attempre, out of drede.

GEOFFREY CHAUCER

148 *The Rose-Bud*

To the Lady Jane Wharton

Queen of Fragrance, lovely Rose,
The Beauties of thy Leaves disclose!
The Winter's past, the Tempests fly,
Soft Gales breathe gently thro' the Sky;
The Lark sweet warbling on the Wing
Salutes the gay Return of Spring:
The silver Dews, the vernal Show'rs,
Call forth a bloomy Waste of Flow'rs;
The joyous Fields, the shady Woods,
Are cloth'd with Green, or swell with Buds;
Then haste thy Beauties to disclose,
Queen of Fragrance, lovely Rose!

Thou, beauteous Flow'r, a welcome Guest,
Shalt flourish on the Fair-one's Breast,
Shalt grace her Hand, or deck her Hair,
The Flow'r most sweet, the Nymph most fair;
Breathe soft, ye Winds! be calm, ye Skies!
Arise ye flow'ry Race, arise!
And haste thy Beauties to disclose,
Queen of Fragrance, lovely Rose!

But thou, fair Nymph, thy self survey
In this sweet Offspring of a Day;
That Miracle of Face must fail,
Thy Charms are sweet, but Charms are frail:
Swift as the short-liv'd Flow'r they fly,
At Morn they bloom, at Evening die:

Tho' Sickness yet a while forbears,
Yet Time destroys, what Sickness spares;
Now *Helen* lives alone in Fame,
And *Cleopatra*'s but a Name;
Time must indent that heav'nly Brow,
And thou must be, what they are now.
    This Moral to the Fair disclose,
Queen of Fragrance, lovely Rose.

WILLIAM BROOME

149 *Ye know my heart . . .*

Ye know my heart, my Lady dear,
    That since the time I was your thrall
I have been yours both whole and clear,
    Though my reward hath been but small:
So am I yet and more than all.
    And ye know well how I have serv'd,
As if ye prove it shall appear,
        How well, how long,
        How faithfully:
        And suffered wrong
        How patiently!
Then since that I have never swerv'd,
Let not my pains be undeserv'd.

Ye know also though ye say nay
    That you alone are my desire;
And you alone it is that may
    Assuage my fervent flaming fire.
Succour me then I you require.
    Ye know it were a just request
Since ye do cause my heat, I say
        If that I burn
        That ye will warm,
        And not to turn
        All to my harm,
Sending such flame from frozen breast
Against all right for my unrest.

And I know well how frowardly
  Ye have mistaken my true intent,
And hitherto how wrongfully
  I have found cause for to repent.
But death shall rid me readily
  If your [hard] heart doth not relent,
And I know well all this ye know,
    That I and mine,
    And all I have,
    Ye may assign,
    To spill or save.
Why are ye then so cruel foe
Unto your own that loveth you so?

SIR THOMAS WYATT

150 *The Passionate Shepherd to His Love*

Come live with me, and be my love,
And we will all the pleasures prove
That hills and valleys, dales and fields,
And all the craggy mountains yields.

There we will sit upon the rocks,
Seeing the shepherds feed their flocks
By shallow rivers, to whose falls
Melodious birds sing madrigals.

And I will make thee beds of roses
With a thousand fragrant posies,
A cap of flowers and a kirtle
Embroider'd all with leaves of myrtle.

A gown made of the finest wool
Which from our pretty lambs we pull,
Fair lined slippers for the cold,
With buckles of the purest gold;

A belt of straw and ivy buds,
With coral clasps and amber studs,
And if these pleasures may thee move,
Come live with me, and be my love.

The shepherd swains shall dance and sing
For thy delight each May-morning:
If these delights thy mind may move,
Then live with me, and be my love.

CHRISTOPHER MARLOWE

151 *The Nymph's Reply to the Shepherd*

If all the world and love were young,
And truth in every Shepherd's tongue,
These pretty pleasures might me move,
To live with thee, and be thy love.

Time drives the flocks from field to fold,
When Rivers rage, and Rocks grow cold,
And Philomel becometh dumb,
The rest complains of cares to come.

The flowers do fade, and wanton fields,
To wayward winter reckoning yields,
A honey tongue, a heart of gall,
Is fancy's spring, but sorrow's fall.

Thy gowns, thy shoes, thy beds of Roses,
Thy cap, thy kirtle, and thy posies,
Soon break, soon wither, soon forgotten:
In folly ripe, in reason rotten.

Thy belt of straw and Ivy buds,
Thy Coral clasps and Amber studs,
All these in me no means can move,
To come to thee, and be thy love.

But could youth last, and love still breed,
Had joys no date, nor age no need,
Then these delights my mind might move,
To live with thee, and be thy love.

SIR WALTER RALEIGH

152 *The Shepherd's Wife's Song*

Ah what is love? It is a pretty thing,
As sweet unto a shepherd as a king,
    And sweeter too:
For kings have cares that wait upon a Crown,
And cares can make the sweetest love to frown:
    Ah then, ah then,
If country loves such sweet desires do gain,
What Lady would not love a Shepherd Swain?

His flocks are folded, he comes home at night,
As merry as a king in his delight,
    And merrier too:
For kings bethink them what the state require,
Where Shepherds careless carol by the fire.
    Ah then, ah then,
If country loves such sweet desires gain,
What Lady would not love a Shepherd Swain?

He kisseth first, then sits as blithe to eat
His cream and curds, as doth the king his meat;
    And blither too:
For kings have often fears when they do sup,
Where Shepherds dread no poison in their cup.
    Ah then, ah then,
If country loves such sweet desires gain,
What Lady would not love a Shepherd Swain?

To bed he goes, as wanton then I ween,
As is a king in dalliance with a Queen;
    More wanton too:
For kings have many griefs affects to move,
Where Shepherds have no greater grief than love:
    Ah then, ah then,
If country loves such sweet desires gain,
What Lady would not love a Shepherd Swain?

Upon his couch of straw he sleeps as sound,
As doth the king upon his bed of down,
    More sounder too:

For cares cause kings full oft their sleep to spill,
Where weary Shepherds lie and snort their fill:
    Ah then, ah then,
If country loves such sweet desires gain,
What Lady would not love a Shepherd Swain?

Thus with his wife he spends the year as blithe,
As doth the king at every tide or sithe,[1]
    And blither too:
For kings have wars and broils to take in hand,
Where Shepherds laugh, and love upon the land.
    Ah then, ah then,
If country loves such sweet desires gain,
What Lady would not love a Shepherd Swain?

ROBERT GREENE

153 *Chromis*

Thelgon. Chromis

Thel.   *Chromis* my joy, why drop thy rainy eyes?
    And sullen clouds hang on thy heavy brow?
    Seems that thy net is rent, and idle lies;
    Thy merry pipe hangs broken on a bough:
      But late thy time in hundred joys thou spent'st;
      Now time spends thee, while thou in vain lament'st.

Chrom. *Thelgon*, my pipe is whole, and nets are new:
    But nets and pipe contemn'd, and idle lie:
    My little reed, that late so merry blew,
    Tunes sad notes to his master's misery:
      Time is my foe, and hates my rugged rimes:
      And I as much hate both that hate, and times.

Thel.   What is it then that causeth thy unrest?
    Or wicked charms? or love's new-kindled fire?
    Ah! much I fear love eats thy tender breast;
    Too well I know his never quenched ire,
      Since I *Amyntas* lov'd, who me disdains,
      And loves in me nought but my grief and pains.

[1] time

Chrom.   No lack of love did ever breed my smart:
      I only learn'd to pity others' pain,
      And ward my breast from his deceiving art:
      But one I love, and he loves me again;
        In love this only is my greatest sore,
        He loves so much, and I can love no more.

      But when the fishers' trade, once highly priz'd,
      And justly honour'd in those better times,
      By every lozel-groom I see despis'd;
      No marvel if I hate my jocund rimes,
        And hang my pipe upon a willow bough:
        Might I grieve ever, if I grieve not now.

Thel.   Ah foolish boy! why should'st thou so lament
      To be like him, whom thou dost like so well?
      The Prince of fishers thousand tortures rent.
      To heav'n, lad, thou art bound: the way by hell.
        Would'st thou ador'd, and great and merry be,
        When he was mockt, debas'd, and dead for thee?

      Men's scorns should rather joy, than sorrow move;
      For then thou highest art, when thou art down.
      Their storms of hate should more blow up my love;
      Their laughters my applause, their mocks my crown.
        Sorrow for him, and shame let me betide,
        Who for me wretch in shame and sorrow died.

Chrom.   Thelgon, 'tis not my self for whom I plain,
      My private loss full easy could I bear,
      If private loss might help the public gain:
      But who can blame my grief, or chide my fear,
        Since now the fisher's trade, and honour'd name
        Is made the common badge of scorn and shame?

      Little know they the fisher's toilsome pain,
      Whose labour with his age, still growing, spends not:
      His care and watchings (oft misspent in vain)
      The early morn begins, dark evening ends not.
        Too foolish men, that think all labour stands
        In travel of the feet, and tired hands!

Ah wretched fishers! born to hate and strife;
To others good, but to your rape and spoil.
This is the briefest sum of fisher's life,
To sweat, to freeze, to watch, to fast, to toil,
   Hated to love, to live despis'd, forlorn,
   A sorrow to himself, all others scorn.

Thel. Too well I know the fisher's thankless pain,
Yet bear it cheerfully, nor dare repine.
To grudge at loss is fond, (too fond and vain)
When highest causes justly it assign.
   Who bites the stone, and yet the dog condemns,
   Much worse is than the beast he so contemns.

Chromis, how many fishers dost thou know,
That rule their boats, and use their nets aright?
That neither wind, nor time, nor tide foreslow?
Such some have been; but (ah!) by tempests' spite
   Their boats are lost; while we may sit and moan,
   That few were such, and now those few are none.

Chrom. Ah cruel spite, and spiteful cruelty,
That thus hath robb'd our joy, and desert shore!
No more our seas shall hear your melody;
Your songs and shrilling pipes shall sound no more:
   Silent our shores, our seas are vacant quite.
   Ah spiteful cruelty, and cruel spite!

Thel. In stead of these a crew of idle grooms,
Idle, and bold, that never saw the seas,
Fearless succeed, and fill their empty rooms:
Some lazy live, bathing in wealth and ease:
   Their floating boats with waves have leave to play,
   Their rusty hooks all year keep holy-day.

Here stray their skiffs, themselves are never here,
Ne'er saw their boats: ill mought they fishers be:
Mean time some wanton boy the boat doth steer,
(Poor boat the while!) that cares as much as he:
   Who in a brook a whirry cannot row,
   Now backs the seas, before the seas he know.

Chrom. Ah foolish lads, that think with waves to play,
And rule rough seas, which never knew command!
First in some river thy new skill assay,
Till time and practice teach thy weakly hand:
    A thin, thin plank keeps in thy vital breath:
    Death ready waits. Fond boys, to play with death!

Thel. Some stretching in their boats supinely sleep,
Seasons in vain recall'd, and winds neglecting:
Other their hooks and baits in poison steep,
Neptune himself with deathful drugs infecting:
    The fish their life and death together drink,
    And dead pollute the seas with venom'd stink.

Some teach to work, but have no hands to row:
Some will be eyes, but have no light to see:
Some will be guides, but have no feet to go:
Some deaf, yet ears; some dumb, yet tongues will be:
    Dumb, deaf, lame, blind, and maim'd; yet fishers all:
    Fit for no use, but store an hospital.

Some greater, scorning now their narrow boat,
In mighty hulks and ships (like courts) do dwell;
Slaving the skiffs that in their seas do float;
Their silken sails with winds do proudly swell;
    Their narrow bottoms stretch they large and wide,
    And make full room for luxury and pride.

Self did I see a swain not long ago,
Whose lordly ship kept all the rest in awe:
About him thousand boats do waiting row;
His frowns are death, his word is firmest law;
    While all the fisher-boys their bonnets vail,
    And far adore their lord with strucken sail.

His ear is shut to simple fisher-swain.
For *Gemma's* self (a sea-nymph great and high)
Upon his boat attended long in vain:
What hope, poor fisher-boy may come him nigh?
    His speech to her, and presence he denied.
    Had *Neptune* come, *Neptune* he had defied.

G

Where Tiber's swelling waves his banks o'erflow,
There princely fishers dwell in courtly halls:
The trade they scorn, their hands forget to row;
Their trade, to plot their rising, others falls;
    Into their seas to draw the lesser brooks,
    And fish for steeples high with golden hooks.

Chrom. *Thelgon*, how canst thou well that fisher blame,
Who in his art so highly doth excel,
That with himself can raise the fishers' name?
Well may he thrive, that spends his art so well.
    Ah, little needs their honour to depress:
    Little it is; yet most would have it less.

Thel. Alas poor boy! thy shallow-swimming sight
Can never dive into their deepest art;
Those silken shews so dim thy dazzl'd sight.
Could'st thou unmask their pomp, unbreast their heart,
    How would'st thou laugh at this rich beggarie!
    And learn to hate such happy miserie!

Panting ambition spurs their tired breast:
Hope chain'd to doubt, fear linkt to pride and threat,
(Too ill yok't pairs) give them no time to rest;
Tyrants to lesser boats, slaves to the great.
    That man I rather pity, than adore,
    Who fear'd by others much, fears others more.

Most cursed town, where but one tyrant reigns:
(Though less his single rage on many spent)
But much more misery that soul remains,
When many tyrants in one heart are pent:
    When thus thou serv'st, the comfort thou canst have
    From greatness is, thou art a greater slave.

Chrom. Ah wretched swains, that live in fishers' trade;
With inward griefs, and outward wants distressed;
While every day doth more your sorrow lade;
By others scorn'd, and by your selves oppressed!
    The great the greater serve, the lesser these:
    And all their art is how to rise and please.

Algon. Those fisher-swains, from whom our trade doth flow,
That by the King of seas their skill were taught;
As they their boats on Jordan wave did row,
And catching fish, were by a Fisher caught;
    (Ah blessed chance! much better was the trade,
    That being fishers, thus were fishes made).

Those happy swains, in outward shew unblest,
Were scourg'd, were scorn'd, yet was this loss their
      gain:
By land, by sea, in life, in death, distrest;
But now with King of seas securely reign:
    For that short woe in this base earthly dwelling,
    Enjoying joy all excellence excelling.

Then do not thou, my boy, cast down thy mind,
But seek to please with all thy busy care
The King of seas; so shalt thou surely find
Rest, quiet, joy, in all this troublous fare.
    Let not thy net, thy hook, thy singing cease:
    And pray these tempests may be turn'd to peace.

Of Prince of waters, Sovereign of seas,
Whom storms and calms, whom winds and waves obey;
If ever that great Fisher did thee please,
Chide thou the winds, and furious waves allay:
    So on thy shore the fisher-boys shall sing
    Sweet songs of peace to our sweet peace's King.
                    PHINEAS FLETCHER

154 *Myra*

I, with whose colours Myra dressed her head,
  I, that ware posies of her own hand-making,
I, that mine own name in the chimneys read
  By Myra finely wrought ere I was waking;
    Must I look on, in hope time coming may
    With change bring back my turn again to play?

I, that on Sunday at the church-stile found
  A garland sweet, with true-love knots in flowers,
Which I to wear about mine arm was bound,
    That each of us might know that all was ours;
      Must I now lead an idle life in wishes,
      And follow Cupid for his loaves and fishes?

I, that did wear the ring her mother left,
  I, for whose love she gloried to be blamed,
I, with whose eyes her eyes committed theft,
    I, who did make her blush when I was named;
      Must I lose ring, flowers, blush, theft, and go naked,
      Watching with sighs, till dead love be awakened?

I, that, when drowsy Argus fell asleep,
  Like jealousy o'erwatched with desire,
Was ever warned modesty to keep,
    While her breath, speaking, kindled Nature's fire;
      Must I look on a-cold, while others warm them?
      Do Vulcan's brothers in such fine nets arm them?

Was it for this that I might Myra see
  Washing the water, with her beauties, white?
Yet would she never write her love to me.
    Thinks wit of change, while thoughts are in delight?
      Mad girls must safely love, as they may leave;
      No man can print a kiss; lines may deceive.
                    FULKE GREVILLE, LORD BROOKE

155 *Cloris and Mertilla*

Chaste Cloris doth disclose the shames
Of the Felician frantic Dames,
Mertilla strives t'appease her woe,
To golden wishes then they go.

Mer. Why how now *Cloris*, what, thy head
        Bound with forsaken Willow?
      Is the cold ground become thy bed?
        The grass become thy pillow?

O let not those life-lightning eyes
In this sad veil be shrouded,
Which into mourning puts the Skies,
To see them over-clouded.

Clor. O my *Mertilla* do not praise
These Lamps so dimly burning,
Such sad and sullen lights as these
Were only made for mourning:
Their objects are the barren Rocks
With aged Moss o'er shaded;
Now whilst the Spring lays forth her Locks
With blossoms bravely braided.

Mer. O *Cloris*, can there be a Spring,
O my dear Nymph, there may not,
Wanting thine eyes it forth to bring,
Without which Nature cannot:
Say what it is that troubleth thee
Encreast by thy concealing,
Speak; sorrows many times we see
Are lesned by revealing.

Clor. Being of late too vainly bent
And but at too much leisure;
Not with our Groves and Downs content,
But surfeiting in pleasure;
Felicia's Fields I would go see,
Where fame to me reported,
The choice Nymphs of the world to be
From meaner beauties sorted;
Hoping that I from them might draw
Some graces to delight me,
But there such monstrous shapes I saw,
That to this hour affright me.
Through the thick hair, that thatch'd their Brows,
Their eyes upon me stared,
Like to those raging frantique Froes [1]
For *Bacchus* Feasts prepared:
Their Bodies, although straight by kind,
Yet they so monstrous make them,

[1] frows: ungainly women?

That for huge Bags blown up with wind,
You very well may take them.
Their Bowels in their Elbows are,
Whereon depend their Paunches,
And their deformed Arms by far
Made larger than their Haunches:
For their behaviour and their grace,
Which likewise should have priz'd them,
Their manners were as beastly base
As th'rags that so disguis'd them;
All Anticks, all so impudent,
So fashion'd out of fashion,
As black *Cocytus* up had sent
Her Fry into this nation,
Whose monstrousness doth so perplex
Of Reason and deprives me,
That for their sakes I loath my sex,
Which to this sadness drives me.

Mer. O my dear *Cloris* be not sad,
Nor with these Furies daunted,
But let these female fools be mad,
With hellish pride inchanted;
Let not thy noble thoughts descend
So low as their affections;
Whom neither counsel can amend,
Nor yet the Gods' corrections:
Such mad folks ne'r let us bemoan,
But rather scorn their folly,
And since we two are here alone,
To banish melancholy,
Leave we this lowly creeping vane
Not worthy admiration,
And in a brave and lofty strain,
Let's exercise our passion,
With wishes of each other's good,
From our abundant treasures,
And in this jocond sprightly mood:
Thus alter we our measures.

Mer. O I could wish this place were strew'd with Roses,
And that this Bank were thickly thrumm'd with Grass

As soft as Sleave, or Sarcenet ever was,
Whereon my *Cloris* her sweet self reposes.

Clor. O that these Dews Rosewater were for thee,
These Mists Perfumes that hang upon these thicks,
And that the Winds were all Aromatics,
Which, if my wish could make them, they should be.

Mer. O that my Bottle one whole Diamond were,
So fill'd with Nectar that a Fly might sup,
And at one draught that thou mightst drink it up,
Yet a Carouse not good enough I fear.

Clor. That all the Pearl, the Seas, or Indias have
Were well dissolv'd and thereof made a Lake,
Thou therein bathing, and I by to take
Pleasure to see thee clearer than the Wave.

Mer. O that the Horns of all the Herds we see,
Were of fine gold, or else that every horn
Were like to that one of the Unicorn,
And of all these, not one but were thy Fee.

Clor. O that their Hooves were Ivory, or some thing,
Than the pur'st Ivory far more Christalline,
Fill'd with the food wherewith the Gods do dine,
To keep thy Youth in a continual Spring.

Mer. O that the sweets of all the Flowers that grow,
The labouring air would gather into one,
In Gardens, Fields, nor Meadows leaving none,
And all their Sweetness upon thee would throw.

Clor. Nay that those sweet harmonious strains we hear,
Amongst the lively Birds' melodious Lays,
As they recording sit upon the Sprays,
Were hovering still for Music at thine ear.

Mer. O that thy name were carv'd on every Tree,
That as these plants still great, and greater grow,
Thy name dear Nymph might be enlarged so,
That every Grove and Coppice might speak thee.

Clor. Nay, would thy name upon their Rinds were set,
And by the Nymphs so oft and loudly spoken,
As that the Echoes to that language broken
Thy happy name might hourly counterfet.

Mer. O let the Spring still put stern winter by,
And in rich Damask let her revel still,
As it should do if I might have my will,
And thou mightst still walk on her Tapestry;
And thus since Fate no longer time allows
Under this broad and shady Sycamore,
Where now we sit, as we have oft before;
Those yet unborn shall offer up their Vows.

MICHAEL DRAYTON

156 *The Sun Rising*

Busy old fool, unruly Sun,
Why dost thou thus,
Through windows, and through curtains, call on us?
Must to thy motions lovers' seasons run?
Saucy pedantic wretch, go chide
Late school-boys and sour prentices,
Go tell court-huntsmen, that the king will ride,
Call country ants to harvest offices;
Love, all alike, no season knows, nor clime,
Nor hours, days, months, which are the rags of time.

Thy beams, so reverend, and strong
Why shouldst thou think?
I could eclipse and cloud them with a wink,
But that I would not lose her sight so long:
If her eyes have not blinded thine,
Look, and to-morrow late, tell me,
Whether both th'Indias of spice and mine
Be where thou left'st them, or lie here with me.
Ask for those kings whom thou saw'st yesterday,
And thou shalt hear, 'All here in one bed lay.'

She's all states, and all princes, I,
Nothing else is.
Princes do but play us; compar'd to this,
All honour's mimic; all wealth alchemy.
Thou, Sun, art half as happy, as we,
In that the world's contracted thus;
Thine age asks ease, and since thy duties be
To warm the world, that's done in warming us.

Shine here to us, and thou art everywhere;
This bed thy centre is, these walls, thy sphere.

JOHN DONNE

157 *Description of Spring*

The soote [1] season, that bud and bloom forth brings,
With green hath clad the hill, and eke the vale.
The nightingale with feathers new she sings;
The turtle to her make [2] hath told her tale.
Summer is come, for every spray now springs,
The hart hath hung his old head on the pale;
The buck in brake his winter coat he flings;
The fishes flete [3] with new repaired scale;
The adder all her slough away she slings;
The swift swallow pursueth the flies smale;
The busy bee her honey now she mings;[4]
Winter is worn that was the flowers' bale.
　　And thus I see among these pleasant things
　　Each care decays, and yet my sorrow springs!

HENRY HOWARD, EARL OF SURREY

158 *Sonnet*

Happy ye leaves when as those lilly hands,
　　which hold my life in their dead doing might,
　　shall handle you and hold in loves soft bands,
　　lyke captives trembling at the victors sight.
And happy lines, on which with starry light,
　　those lamping eyes will deigne sometimes to look
　　and reade the sorrowes of my dying spright,
　　written with teares in harts close bleeding book.
And happy rymes bath'd in the sacred brooke,
　　of *Helicon* whence she derived is,
　　when ye behold that Angels blessed looke
　　my soule's long lacked foode, my heaven's blis.
Leaves, lines, and rymes, seeke her to please alone,
　　whom if ye please, I care for other none.

EDMUND SPENSER

---

[1] sweet　　　[2] mate　　　[3] float　　　[4] bethinks herself of

159 *Sonnet*

Being my selfe captyved here in care,
    my hart, whom none with servile bands can tye,
    but the fayre tresses of your golden hayre,
    breaking his prison forth to you doth fly.
Lyke as a byrd that in one's hand doth spy
    desired food, to it doth make his flight:
    even so my hart, that wont on your fayre eye
    to feed his fill, flyes backe unto your sight.
Doe you him take, and in your bosome bright,
    gently encage, that he may be your thrall:
    perhaps he there may learne with rare delight,
    to sing your name and prayses over all.
That it hereafter may you not repent,
    him lodging in your bosome to have lent.
EDMUND SPENSER

160 *Sonnet*

Since there's no help, come, let us kiss and part,
Nay, I have done, you get no more of me,
And I am glad, yea, glad with all my heart,
That thus so cleanly I myself can free.
Shake hands for ever, cancel all our vows,
And when we meet at any time again,
Be it not seen in either of our brows
That we one jot of former love retain.
Now at the last gasp of Love's latest breath,
When his pulse failing, Passion speechless lies,
When Faith is kneeling by his bed of death,
And Innocence is closing up his eyes,
    Now, if thou wouldst, when all have given him over,
    From death to life thou might'st him yet recover.
MICHAEL DRAYTON

161 *They flee from me*

They flee from me, that sometime did me seek
With naked foot, stalking in my chamber:
I have seen them gentle, tame, and meek,
That now are wild, and do not remember

That sometime they put themselves in danger
To take bread at my hand; and now they range
Busily seeking with a continual change.

Thanked be fortune it hath been otherwise
Twenty times better; but once, in special,
In thin array, after a pleasant guise,
When her loose gown from her shoulders did fall,
And she me caught in her armes long and small,
Therewithal sweetly did me kiss,
And softly said, 'Dear heart, how like you this?'

It was no dream; I lay broade waking:
But all is turned, thorough my gentleness,
Into a strange fashion of forsaking;
And I have leave to go of her goodness:
And she also to use new-fangledness.
But since that I so kindely am served,
I would fain know what she hath deserved.

SIR THOMAS WYATT

162 *Past ruin'd Ilion*

Past ruin'd Ilion Helen lives,
   Alcestis rises from the shades;
Verse calls them forth; 'tis verse that gives
   Immortal youth to mortal maids.

Soon shall Oblivion's deepening veil
   Hide all the peopled hills you see,
The gay, the proud, while lovers hail
   In distant ages you and me.

The tear for fading beauty check,
   For passing glory cease to sigh;
One form shall rise above the wreck,
   One name, Ianthe, shall not die.

WALTER SAVAGE LANDOR

163 *Sonnet*

Shall I compare thee to a summer's day?
Thou art more lovely and more temperate:
Rough winds do shake the darling buds of May,
And summer's lease hath all too short a date:
Sometime too hot the eye of heaven shines,
And often is his gold complexion dimm'd,
And every fair from fair sometime declines,
By chance, or nature's changing course, untrimm'd;
But thy eternal summer shall not fade,
Nor lose possession of that fair thou ow'st;
Nor shall Death brag thou wander'st in his shade,
When in eternal lines to time thou grow'st:
  So long as men can breathe, or eyes can see,
  So long lives this, and this gives life to thee.
WILLIAM SHAKESPEARE

164 *Sonnet*

When in disgrace with fortune and men's eyes,
I all alone beweep my outcast state,
And trouble deaf heaven with my bootless cries,
And look upon myself and curse my fate,
Wishing me like to one more rich in hope,
Featur'd like him, like him with friends possest,
Desiring this man's art, and that man's scope,
With what I most enjoy contented least;
Yet in these thoughts myself almost despising,
Haply I think on thee, and then my state,
(Like to the lark at break of day arising)
From sullen earth sings hymns at heaven's gate;
  For thy sweet love remember'd such wealth brings
  That then I scorn to change my state with kings.
WILLIAM SHAKESPEARE

165 *Sonnet*

When to the sessions of sweet silent thought
I summon up remembrance of things past,
I sigh the lack of many a thing I sought,
And with old woes new wail my dear time's waste:

Then can I drown an eye, unus'd to flow,
For precious friends hid in death's dateless night,
And weep afresh love's long since cancell'd woe,
And moan the expense of many a vanish'd sight:
Then can I grieve at grievances foregone,
And heavily from woe to woe tell o'er
The sad account of fore-bemoaned moan,
Which I new pay, as if not paid before.
   But if the while I think on thee, dear friend,
   All losses are restor'd, and sorrows end.
WILLIAM SHAKESPEARE

166 *Sonnet*

Full many a glorious morning have I seen
Flatter the mountain-tops with sovereign eye,
Kissing with golden face the meadows green,
Gilding pale streams with heavenly alchymy;
Anon permit the basest clouds to ride
With ugly rack on his celestial face,
And from the forlorn world his visage hide,
Stealing unseen to west with this disgrace:
Even so my sun one early morn did shine
With all-triumphant splendour on my brow;
But, out, alack! he was but one hour mine,
The region cloud hath mask'd him from me now.
   Yet him for this my love no whit disdaineth;
   Suns of the world may stain when heaven's sun staineth.
WILLIAM SHAKESPEARE

167 *Sonnet*

Not marble, nor the gilded monuments
Of princes, shall outlive this powerful rime,
But you shall shine more bright in these contents
Than unswept stone, besmear'd with sluttish time.
When wasteful war shall statues overturn,
And broils root out the work of masonry,
Nor Mars his sword, nor war's quick fire, shall burn
The living record of your memory.

'Gainst death, and all-oblivious enmity,
Shall you pace forth, your praise shall still find room,
Even in the eyes of all posterity
That wear this world out to the ending doom.
  So, till the judgement that yourself arise,
  You live in this, and dwell in lovers' eyes.
WILLIAM SHAKESPEARE

168 *Sonnet*

Like as the waves make towards the pebbled shore,
So do our minutes hasten to their end,
Each changing place with that which goes before,
In sequent toil all forwards do contend.
Nativity, once in the main of light,
Crawls to maturity, wherewith being crown'd,
Crooked eclipses 'gainst his glory fight,
And Time that gave doth now his gift confound.
Time doth transfix the flourish set on youth,
And delves the parallels in beauty's brow,
Feeds on the rarities of nature's truth,
And nothing stands but for his scythe to mow.
  And yet to times in hope my verse shall stand,
  Praising thy worth, despite his cruel hand.
WILLIAM SHAKESPEARE

169 *Sonnet*

That time of year thou mayst in me behold
When yellow leaves, or none, or few, do hang
Upon those boughs which shake against the cold,
Bare ruin'd choirs, where late the sweet birds sang.
In me thou see'st the twilight of such day
As after sunset fadeth in the west,
Which by and by black night doth take away,
Death's second self that seals up all in rest.
In me thou see'st the glowing of such fire,
That on the ashes of his youth doth lie,
As the death-bed, whereon it must expire
Consum'd with that which it was nourish'd by.

This thou perceiv'st, which makes thy love more strong
To love that well, which thou must leave ere long.
WILLIAM SHAKESPEARE

170 *Sonnet*

Let me not to the marriage of true minds
Admit impediments; love is not love
Which alters when it alteration finds,
Or bends with the remover to remove:
O, no! it is an ever-fixèd mark,
That looks on tempests and is never shaken;
It is the star to every wandering bark,
Whose worth's unknown, although his height be taken.
Love's not Time's fool, though rosy lips and cheeks
Within his bending sickle's compass come;
Love alters not with his brief hours and weeks,
But bears it out even to the edge of doom.
    If this be error and upon me prov'd,
    I never writ, nor no man ever lov'd.
WILLIAM SHAKESPEARE

171 *Sonnet*

When in the chronicle of wasted time
I see descriptions of the fairest wights,
And beauty making beautiful old rime,
In praise of ladies dead, and lovely knights,
Then in the blazon of sweet beauty's best,
Of hand, of foot, of lip, of eye, of brow,
I see their antique pen would have express'd
Even such a beauty as you master now.
So all their praises are but prophecies
Of this our time, all you prefiguring,
And, for they look'd but with divining eyes,
They had not skill enough your worth to sing:
    For we, which now behold these present days,
    Have eyes to wonder, but lack tongues to praise.
WILLIAM SHAKESPEARE

172 *Sonnet*

Not mine own fears, nor the prophetic soul
Of the wide world, dreaming on things to come,
Can yet the lease of my true love control,
Suppos'd as forfeit to a confin'd doom.
The mortal moon hath her eclipse endur'd,
And the sad augurs mock their own presage;
Incertainties now crown themselves assur'd,
And peace proclaims olives of endless age.
Now with the drops of this most balmy time
My love looks fresh, and Death to me subscribes,
Since, spite of him, I'll live in this poor rime,
While he insults o'er dull and speechless tribes:
   And thou in this shalt find thy monument,
    When tyrants' crests and tombs of brass are spent.
WILLIAM SHAKESPEARE

173 *When thou must home*

When thou must home to shades of under ground
And there arriv'd, a new admired guest,
The beauteous spirits do ingirt thee round,
White Iope, blithe Helen, and the rest,
To hear the stories of thy finisht love
From that smooth tongue whose music hell can move;

Then wilt thou speak of banqueting delights,
Of masks and revels which sweet youth did make,
Of Tourneys and great challenges of knights,
And all these triumphs for thy beauty's sake:
When thou hast told these honours done to thee,
Then tell, O tell, how thou didst murder me.
THOMAS CAMPION

174 *Sonnet*

How many paltry, foolish, painted things,
That now in coaches trouble every street,
Shall be forgotten, whom no Poet sings,
Ere they be well wrapt in their winding-sheet!

Where I to thee eternity shall give,
When nothing else remaineth of these days,
And Queens hereafter shall be glad to live
Upon the alms of thy superfluous praise.
Virgins and matrons, reading these my rimes,
Shall be so much delighted with thy story
That they shall grieve they lived not in these times,
To have seen thee, their sex's only glory.
  So shalt thou fly above the vulgar throng,
  Still to survive in my immortal song.

MICHAEL DRAYTON

175 *Sonnet*

An evil spirit, your beauty haunts me still,
Wherewith, alas, I have been long possest,
Which ceaseth not to tempt me to each ill,
Nor gives me once but one poor minute's rest;
In me it speaks, whether I sleep or wake,
And when by means to drive it out I try,
With greater torments then it me doth take,
And tortures me in most extremity;
Before my face it lays down my despairs,
And hastes me on unto a sudden death,
Now tempting me to drown myself in tears,
And then in sighing to give up my breath.
  Thus am I still provoked to every evil
  By this good wicked spirit, sweet angel-devil.

MICHAEL DRAYTON

176 *Sonnet*

The expense of spirit in a waste of shame
Is lust in action, and till action, lust
Is perjur'd, murderous, bloody, full of blame,
Savage, extreme, rude, cruel, not to trust;
Enjoy'd no sooner but despised straight,
Past reason hunted, and no sooner had,
Past reason hated, as a swallow'd bait,
On purpose laid to make the taker mad:

Mad in pursuit, and in possession so,
Had, having, and in quest to have extreme,
A bliss in proof, and prov'd, a very woe,
Before, a joy propos'd; behind, a dream;
 All this the world well knows, yet none knows well
 To shun the heaven that leads men to this hell.

WILLIAM SHAKESPEARE

177 *Sonnet*

Two loves I have of comfort and despair,
Which like two spirits do suggest me still:
The better angel is a man right fair,
The worser spirit a woman colour'd ill.
To win me soon to hell, my female evil
Tempteth my better angel from my side,
And would corrupt my saint to be a devil,
Wooing his purity with her foul pride.
And whether that my angel be turn'd fiend
Suspect I may, yet not directly tell;
But being both from me, both to each friend,
I guess one angel in another's hell:
 Yet this shall I ne'er know, but live in doubt,
 Till my bad angel fire my good one out.

WILLIAM SHAKESPEARE

178 *To Lucasta, Going beyond the Seas*

If to be absent were to be
  Away from thee;
  Or that when I am gone,
  You or I were alone;
Then my *Lucasta* might I crave
Pity from blust'ring wind, or swallowing wave.

But I'll not sigh one blast or gale
  To swell my sail,
  Or pay a tear to 'suage
  The foaming blue-Gods rage;
For whether he will let me pass
Or no, I'm still as happy as I was.

Though Seas and Land betwixt us both,
    Our Faith and Troth,
      Like separated souls,
      All time and space controls:
Above the highest sphere we meet
Unseen, unknown, and greet as Angels greet.

So then we do anticipate
    Our after-fate,
      And are alive i' th' skies,
      If thus our lips and eyes
Can speak like spirits unconfin'd
In Heav'n, their earthy bodies left behind.
                    RICHARD LOVELACE

179 *To Lucasta, going to the Wars*

Tell me not (Sweet) I am unkind,
    That from the Nunnery
Of thy chaste breast, and quiet mind,
    To War and Arms I fly.

True; a new Mistress now I chase,
    The first Foe in the Field;
And with a stronger Faith imbrace
    A Sword, a Horse, a Shield.

Yet this Inconstancy is such,
    As you too shall adore;
I could not love thee (Dear) so much,
    Lov'd I not Honour more.
                    RICHARD LOVELACE

180 *Gratiana dancing and singing*

See! with what constant Motion
Even, and glorious, as the Sun,
  Gratiana steers that Noble Frame,
Soft as her breast, sweet as her voice
That gave each winding Law and poise,
  And swifter then the wings of Fame.

She beat the happy Pavement
By such a Star made Firmament,
   Which now no more the Roof envies;
But swells up high with *Atlas* ev'n,
Bearing the brighter, nobler Heav'n,
   And in her, all the Deities.

Each step trod out a Lover's thought
And the Ambitious hopes he brought,
   Chain'd to her brave feet with such arts,
Such sweet command, and gentle awe,
As when she ceas'd, we sighing saw
   The floor lay pav'd with broken hearts.

So did she move; so did she sing
Like the Harmonious spheres that bring
   Unto their Rounds their music's aid;
Which she performed such a way,
As all th' inamoured world will say
   The *Graces* danced, and *Apollo* play'd.

Richard Lovelace

181 *To Althea, from Prison*

When Love with unconfined wings
   Hovers within my Gates;
And my divine *Althea* brings
   To whisper at the Grates:
When I lie tangled in her hair,
   And fetter'd to her eye;
The *Gods* that wanton in the Air,
   Know no such Liberty.

When flowing Cups run swiftly round
   With no allaying *Thames*,
Our careless heads with Roses bound,
   Our hearts with Loyal Flames;
When thirsty grief in Wine we steep,
   When Healths and draughts go free,
Fishes that tipple in the Deep,
   Know no such Liberty.

When (like committed Linnets) I
　With shriller throat shall sing
The sweetness, Mercy, Majesty,
　And glories of my KING;
When I shall voice aloud, how Good
　He is, how Great should be;
　　Inlarged Winds that curl the Flood,
　　Know no such Liberty.

Stone Walls do not a Prison make,
　Nor Iron bars a Cage;
Minds innocent and quiet take
　That for an Hermitage;
If I have freedom in my Love,
　And in my soul am free;
Angels alone that soar above,
　Enjoy such liberty.
　　　　　　　　　RICHARD LOVELACE

182 *On a Girdle*

That which her slender waist confin'd,
Shall now my joyful temples bind;
No Monarch but would give his Crown,
His Arms might do what this has done.

It is my Heaven's extremest Sphere,
The pale which held the lovely Dear,
My joy, my grief, my hope, my Love,
Do all within this Circle move.

A narrow compass, and yet there
Dwells all that's good, and all that's fair:
Give me but what this Ribbon tied,
Take all the sun goes round beside.
　　　　　　　　　EDMUND WALLER

183 *Song*

　　Go, lovely rose!
Tell her that wastes her time, and me,
　　That now she knows,
　When I resemble her to thee,
How sweet, and fair, she seems to be.

Tell her that's young,
And shuns to have her graces spied,
That hadst thou sprung
In deserts, where no men abide,
Thou must have uncommended died.

Small is the worth
Of beauty from the light retir'd:
Bid her come forth,
Suffer her self to be desir'd
And not blush so to be admir'd.

Then die! that she
The common fate of all things rare
May read in thee:
How small a part of time they share,
That are so wondrous sweet, and fair!

EDMUND WALLER

184 *Epithalamion Teratos*

Come, come dear Night, Love's mart of kisses,
    Sweet close of his ambitious line,
The fruitful summer of his blisses,
    Love's glory doth in darkness shine.
O come soft rest of cares, come Night,
    Come naked Virtue's only tire,
The reaped harvest of the light,
    Bound up in sheaves of sacred fire.
        Love calls to war,
            Sighs his alarms,
        Lips his swords are,
            The field his arms.

Come, Night, and lay thy velvet hand
    On glorious Day's outfacing face;
And all thy crowned flames command,
    For torches to our nuptial grace.
        Love calls to war,
            Sighs his alarms,
        Lips his swords are,
            The field his arms.

No need have we of factious Day,
    To cast, in envy of thy peace,
Her balls of discord in thy way:
    Here Beauty's day doth never cease,
Day is abstracted here,
And varied in a triple sphere,
Hero, Alcmane, Mya, so outshine thee,
Ere thou come here, let Thetis thrice refine thee.
            Love calls to war,
                Sighs his alarms,
            Lips his swords are,
                The field his arms.

            The evening star I see:
                Rise youths, the evening star
                Helps Love to summon war;
                Both now embracing be.
Rise, youths, Love's rite claims more than banquets, rise:
Now the bright marigolds, that deck the skies,
Phoebus' celestial flowers, that, contrary
To his flowers here, ope when he shuts his eye,
And shut when he doth open, crown your sports:
Now Love in Night, and Night in Love exhorts
Courtship and dances: all your parts employ,
And suit Night's rich expansure with your joy.
Love paints his longings in sweet virgin eyes:
Rise, youths, Love's rite claims more than banquets; rise.

    Rise, virgins, let fair nuptial loves enfold
Your fruitless breasts: the maidenheads ye hold
Are not your own alone, but parted are;
Part in disposing them your parents share,
And that a third part is; so must ye save
Your loves a third, and you your thirds must have.
Love paints his longings in sweet virgins' eyes:
Rise, youths, Love's rite claims more than banquets; rise.

    Herewith the amorous spirit, that was so kind
To Teras' hair, and comb'd it down with wind.
Still as it comet-like brake from her brain,
Would needs have Teras gone, and did refrain
To blow it down; which staring up, dismay'd
The timorous feast; and she no longer stay'd;

But, bowing to the bridegroom and the bride,
Did, like a shooting exhalation, glide
Out of their sights: the turning of her back
Made them all shriek, it look'd so ghastly black.
O hapless Hero! that most hapless cloud
Thy soon-succeeding tragedy foreshow'd.
Thus all the nuptial crew to joys depart,
But much-wrong'd Hero stood Hell's blackest dart:
Whose wound because I grieve so to display,
I use digressions thus t'increase the day.

GEORGE CHAPMAN

185 *His Golden Locks Time hath to Silver Turned*

His golden locks time hath to silver turn'd;
    O time too swift, O swiftness never ceasing!
His youth 'gainst time and age hath ever spurn'd,
    But spurn'd in vain; youth waneth by increasing:
Beauty, strength, youth, are flowers but fading seen;
Duty, faith, love, are roots, and ever green.

His helmet now shall make a hive for bees;
    And lovers' sonnets turned to holy psalms,
A man-at-arms must now serve on his knees,
    And feed on prayers, which are age's alms:
But though from court to cottage he depart,
His saint is sure of his unspotted heart.

And when he saddest sits in homely cell,
    He'll teach his swains this carol for a song,—
'Blest be the hearts that wish my sovereign well,
    Curst be the souls that think her any wrong.'
Goddess, allow this aged man his right,
To be your beadsman now that was your knight.

GEORGE PEELE

186 *Song*

Ah stay! ah turn! ah whither would you fly
    Too charming, too relentless Maid?
I follow not to Conquer but to Die,
    You of the fearful are afraid.

In vain I call; for she like fleeting Air,
 When prest by some tempestuous Wind,
Flies swifter from the Voice of my Despair,
 Nor casts one pitying Look behind.

WILLIAM CONGREVE

187 *Hesperus's Hymn to Cynthia*

Queen, and *Huntress*, chaste, and fair,
Now the *Sun* is laid to sleep,
Seated, in thy silver chair,
State in wonted manner keep:
 Hesperus intreats thy light,
 Goddess, excellently bright.

Earth, let not thy envious shade
Dare it's self to interpose;
Cynthia's shining orb was made
Heaven to clear, when day did close:
 Bless us then with wished sight,
 Goddess, excellently bright.

Lay thy bow of pearl apart,
And thy crystal-shining quiver;
Give unto the flying hart
Space to breathe, how short soever:
 Thou that mak'st a day of night,
 Goddess, excellently bright.

BEN JONSON

188 *The Triumph of Charis*

See the Chariot at hand here of Love
 Wherein my Lady rideth!
Each that draws, is a Swan, or a Dove,
 And well the Car Love guideth;
As she goes, all hearts do duty
  Unto her beauty;
And enamour'd, do wish, so they might
  But enjoy such a sight,
That they still were, to run by her side,
Through Swords, through Seas, whither she would ride.

Do but look on her eyes, they do light
   All that Love's world compriseth!
Do but look on her Hair, it is bright
   As Love's star when it riseth!
Do but mark her forehead's smoother
      Than words that soothe her!
And from her arched brows, such a grace
      Sheds it's self through the face,
As alone there triumphs to the life
All the Gain, all the Good, of the Elements' strife.

Have you seen but a bright Lily grow,
   Before rude hands have touch'd it?
Ha' you mark'd but the fall o' the Snow
   Before the soil hath smutch'd it?
Ha' you felt the wool of Beaver?
      Or Swan's Down ever?
Or have smelt o' the bud o' the Briar?
      Or the Nard in the fire?
Or have tasted the bag of the Bee?
O so white! O so soft! O so sweet is she!

BEN JONSON

189 *To Castara*

We saw and woo'd each others eyes,
My soul contracted then with thine,
And both burnt in one sacrifice
By which our Marriage grew divine.

Let wilder youth, whose soul is sense,
Prophane the Temple of delight;
And purchase endless penitence,
With the stol'n pleasure of one night.

Time's ever ours, while we despise
The sensual idol of our clay;
For though the Sun do set and rise,
We joy one everlasting day,

Whose light no jealous clouds obscure
While each to us shine innocent;
The troubled stream is still impure,
With virtue flies away content.

And though opinion often err,
We'll court the modest smile of fame;
For sin's black danger circles her,
Who hath infection in her name.

Thus when to one dark silent room,
Death shall our loving coffins thrust,
Fame will build columns on our tomb,
And add a perfume to our dust.

WILLIAM HABINGTON

190 *An Anniversary*

The day is curl'd about agen
To view the splendor she was in;
When first with hallow'd hands
The holy man knit the mysterious bands;
When you two your contracted Souls did move,
Like *Cherubims* above,
And did make Love;
As your un-understanding issue now
In a glad sigh, a smile, a tear, a Vow.

Tell me, O self-reviving Sun,
In thy Perigrination,
Hast thou beheld a pair
Twist their soft beams like these in their chaste air;
As from bright numberless imbracing rays
Are sprung th'industrious days;
So when they gaze,
And change their fertile Eyes with the new morn,
A beauteous Offspring is shot forth, not born.

Be witness then, all-seeing Sun,
Old Spy, thou that thy race hast run,
In full five thousand Rings;
To thee were ever purer Offerings
Sent on the Wings of Faiths? and thou, oh Night!
Curtain of their delight,
By these made bright,
Have you not marked their Cœlestial play,
And no more peek'd the gaieties of the day?

Come then pale Virgins, Roses strow,
   Mingled with *Io*'s as you go;
     The snowy Ox is kill'd,
The Fane with pros'lyte Lads and Lasses fill'd,
You too may hope the same *seraphic* joy,
    Old time cannot destroy,
     Nor fulness cloy,
When like these, you shall stamp by Sympathies,
Thousands of new-born-loves with your chaste eyes.

RICHARD LOVELACE

191 *Song*

Go, and catch a falling star,
   Get with child a mandrake root,
Tell me where all past years are,
   Or who cleft the Devil's foot,
Teach me to hear mermaids singing,
Or to keep off envy's stinging,
    And find
    What wind
Serves to advance an honest mind.

If thou beest born to strange sights,
   Things invisible to see,
Ride ten thousand days and nights,
   Till age snow white hairs on thee,
Thou, when thou return'st, wilt tell me,
All strange wonders that befell thee,
    And swear,
    No where
Lives a woman true, and fair.

If thou find'st one, let me know,
   Such a pilgrimage were sweet;
Yet do not, I would not go,
   Though at next door we might meet,
Though she were true, when you met her,
And last, till you write your letter,
    Yet she
    Will be
False, ere I come, to two or three.

JOHN DONNE

192 *The Relic*

When my grave is broke up again
Some second guest to entertain,
(For graves have learn'd that woman-head,
To be to more than one a bed)
    And he that digs it, spies
A bracelet of bright hair about the bone,
    Will not he let'us alone,
And think that there a loving couple lies,
Who thought that this device might be some way
To make their souls, at the last busy day,
Meet at this grave, and make a little stay?

If this fall in a time, or land,
Where mis-devotion doth command,
Then, he that digs us up, will bring
Us to the bishop, and the king,
    To make us relics; then
Thou shalt be a Mary Magdalen, and I
    A something else thereby;
All women shall adore us, and some men;
And since at such time, miracles are sought,
I would have that age by this paper taught
What miracles we harmless lovers wrought.

First we loved well and faithfully,
Yet knew not what we loved, nor why,
Difference of sex no more we knew,
Than our guardian angels do;
    Coming and going, we
Perchance might kiss, but not between those meals;
    Our hands ne'er touch'd the seals,
Which nature, injured by late law, sets free.
These miracles we did; but now alas,
All measure, and all language, I should pass,
Should I tell what a miracle she was.

JOHN DONNE

193 *The Dream*

Dear love, for nothing less than thee
Would I have broke this happy dream;
  It was a theme
For reason, much too strong for fantasy.
Therefore thou waked'st me wisely; yet
My dream thou brok'st not, but continued'st it.
Thou art so true that thoughts of thee suffice
To make dreams truths; and fables histories;
Enter these arms, for since thou thought'st it best,
Not to dream all my dream, let's act the rest.

As lightning, or a taper's light,
Thine eyes, and not thy noise wak'd me;
  Yet I thought thee
(For thou lovest truth) an angel, at first sight;
But when I saw thou sawest my heart,
And knew'st my thoughts, beyond an angel's art,
When thou knew'st what I dreamt, when thou knew'st when
Excess of joy would wake me, and cam'st then,
I must confess, it could not choose but be
Profane, to think thee any thing but thee.

Coming and staying show'd thee, thee,
But rising makes me doubt, that now
  Thou art not thou.
That love is weak where fear's as strong as he;
'Tis not all spirit, pure, and brave,
If mixture it of fear, shame, honour have;
Perchance as torches which must ready be,
Men light and put out, so thou deal'st with me;
Thou cam'st to kindle, go'st to come; then I
Will dream that hope again, but else would die.

JOHN DONNE

194 *Twickenham Garden*

Blasted with sighs, and surrounded with tears,
 Hither I come to seek the spring,
And at mine eyes, and at mine ears,
 Receive such balms, as else cure every thing.
 But O! self-traitor, I do bring

The spider Love, which transubstantiates all,
And can convert manna to gall;
And that this place may thoroughly be thought
True Paradise, I have the serpent brought.

'Twere wholesomer for me, that winter did
    Benight the glory of this place,
And that a grave frost did forbid
    These trees to laugh and mock me to my face;
    But that I may not this disgrace
Indure, nor yet leave loving, Love let me
Some senseless piece of this place be;
Make me a mandrake, so I may grow here,
Or a stone fountain weeping out my year.

Hither with crystal phials, lovers come,
    And take my tears, which are love's wine,
And try your mistress' tears at home,
    For all are false, that taste not just like mine.
    Alas! hearts do not in eyes shine,
Nor can you more judge women's thoughts by tears,
Than by her shadow, what she wears.
O perverse sex, where none is true but she,
Who's therefore true, because her truth kills me.
                                        JOHN DONNE

195 *Actuality*

O for some honest lover's ghost,
        Some kind unbodied post
        Sent from the shades below!
        I strangely long to know,
Whether the nobler chaplets wear,
Those that their mistress' scorn did bear,
        Or those that were used kindly.

For whatsoe'er they tell us here
        To make those sufferings dear,
        'Twill there I fear be found,
        That to the being crown'd
T' have loved alone will not suffice,
Unless we also have been wise,
        And have our loves enjoy'd.

What posture can we think him in,
    That here unlov'd again
    Departs, and's thither gone,
    Where each sits by his own?
Or how can that elysium be,
Where I my mistress still must see
    Circled in others' arms?

For there the judges all are just,
    And Sophonisba must
    Be his whom she held dear,
    Not his who loved her here.
The sweet Philoclea, since she died,
Lies by her Pirocles his side,
    Not by Amphialus.

Some bays, perchance, or myrtle bough,
    For difference crowns the brow
    Of those kind souls that were
    The noble martyrs here;
And if that be the only odds,
(As who can tell?) ye kinder gods,
    Give me the woman here.

JOHN SUCKLING

196 *Constancy*

Out upon it, I have loved
    Three whole days together;
And am like to love three more,
    If it prove fair weather.

Time shall moult away his wings,
    Ere he shall discover
In the whole wide world again
    Such a constant lover.

But the spite on 't is, no praise
    Is due at all to me:
Love with me had made no stays,
    Had it any been but she.

Had it any been but she,
    And that very face,
There had been at least ere this
    A dozen dozen in her place.

JOHN SUCKLING

197 *Song*

Why so pale and wan, fond lover?
    Prithee, why so pale?
Will, when looking well can't move her,
    Looking ill prevail?
    Prithee, why so pale?

Why so dull and mute, young sinner?
    Prithee, why so mute?
Will, when speaking well can't win her,
    Saying nothing do 't?
    Prithee, why so mute?

Quit, quit, for shame, this will not move:
    This cannot take her.
If of herself she will not love,
    Nothing can make her:
    The devil take her!

JOHN SUCKLING

198 *Song*

No, no, fair heretic, it needs must be
    But an ill love in me,
    And worse for thee.

For were it in my power,
To love thee now this hour
    More than I did the last:

T'would then so fall,
    I might not love at all.
Love that can flow, and can admit increase,
Admits as well an ebb, and may grow less.

True love is still the same; the torrid zones,
    And those more frigid ones,
    It must now know.

H

For love, grown cold or hot,
　　Is lust or friendship, not
　　　The thing we have.

For that's a flame would die,
　Held down or up too high:

　　Then think I love more than I can express,
　　And would love more, could I but love thee less.
　　　　　　　　　　　　　　　　JOHN SUCKLING

199   *A Song*

Absent from thee I languish still;
　Then ask me not, When I return?
The straying Fool 'twill plainly kill,
　To wish all day, all night to mourn.

Dear, from thine arms then let me fly,
　That my fantastic mind may prove,
The Torments it deserves to try,
　That tears my fixt heart from my love.

When wearied with a world of woe,
　To thy safe bosom I retire,
Where love and peace and truth does flow,
　May I contented there expire.

Lest once more wand'ring from that Heav'n,
　I fall on some base heart unblest;
Faithless to thee, false, unforgiven,
　And lose my everlasting rest.
　　　　　　　　　　JOHN WILMOT, EARL OF ROCHESTER

200   *Love and Life. A Song*

All my past life is mine no more,
　The flying hours are gone:
Like transitory dreams giv'n o'er,
Whose images are kept in store,
　By memory alone.

The time that is to come is not;
　How can it then be mine?
The present moment's all my lot;
And that, as fast as it is got,
　Phillis, is only thine.

Then talk not of inconstancy,
　　False hearts, and broken vows;
If I, by miracle, can be
This live-long minute true to thee,
　　'Tis all that Heav'n allows.
JOHN WILMOT, EARL OF ROCHESTER

201   *A Song*

My dear Mistress has a heart
　　Soft as those kind looks she gave me;
When with love's resistless art,
　　And her eyes, she did enslave me.
But her constancy's so weak,
　　She's so wild, and apt to wander;
That my jealous heart would break,
　　Should we live one day asunder.

Melting joys about her move,
　　Killing pleasures, wounding blisses;
She can dress her eyes in love,
　　And her lips can arm with kisses.
Angels listen when she speaks,
　　She's my delight, all mankind's wonder:
But my jealous heart would break,
　　Should we live one day asunder.
JOHN WILMOT, EARL OF ROCHESTER

202   *Song*

O, no more, no more, too late
　　Sighs are spent; the burning tapers
Of a life as chaste as fate,
　　Pure as are unwritten papers,
Are burnt out: no heat, no light
Now remains; 'tis ever night.

Love is dead; let lovers' eyes,
　　Locked in endless dreams,
　　　Th' extremes of all extremes,

Ope no more, for now Love dies,
　　Now Love dies,–implying
　　Love's martyrs must be ever ever dying.

JOHN FORD

203 *Song*

Of thee, kind boy, I ask no red and white,
　　To make up my delight:
　　No odd becoming graces,
Black eyes, or little know-not-whats in faces;
Make me but mad enough, give me good store
Of love for her I court:
　　I ask no more,
'Tis love in love that makes the sport.

There's no such thing as that we beauty call,
　　It is mere cosenage all;
　　For though some long ago
Like t' certain colours mingled so and so,
That doth not tie me now from choosing new.
If I a fancy take
　　To black and blue,
That fancy doth it beauty make.

'Tis not the meat, but 'tis the appetite
　　Makes eating a delight,
　　And if I like one dish
More than another, that a pheasant is;
What in our watches, that in us is found;
So to the height and nick
　　We up be wound,
No matter by what hand or trick.

JOHN SUCKLING

204 *The Mower's Song*

My mind was once the true survey
Of all these meadows fresh and gay;
And in the greenness of the grass
Did see its hopes as in a glass;
When *Juliana* came, and she
What I do to the grass, does to my thoughts and me.

But these, while I with sorrow pine,
Grew more luxuriant still and fine;
That not one blade of grass you spied,
But had a flower on either side;
When *Juliana* came, and she
What I do to the grass, does to my thoughts and me.

Unthankful meadows, could you so
A fellowship so true forego,
And in your gaudy May-games meet,
While I lay trodden under feet?
When *Juliana* came, and she
What I do to the grass, does to my thoughts and me.

But what you in compassion ought,
Shall now by my revenge be wrought:
And flowr's, and grass, and I and all,
Will in one common ruin fall.
For *Juliana* comes, and she
What I do to the grass, does to my thoughts and me.

And thus, ye meadows, which have been
Companions of my thoughts more green,
Shall now the heraldry become
With which I shall adorn my tomb;
For *Juliana* comes, and she
What I do to the grass, does to my thoughts and me.

ANDREW MARVELL

205 *To Delia*

Unto the boundless Ocean of thy beauty,
    Runs this poor River, charg'd with streams of zeal:
    Returning thee the tribute of my duty,
    Which here my love, my youth, my plaints reveal.
Here I unclasp the Book of my charg'd soul,
    Where I have cast th'accounts of all my care:
    Here have I summ'd my sighs, here I inrol
    How they were spent for thee; look what they are:
Look on the dear expenses of my youth,
    And see how just I reckon with thine eyes:
    Examine well thy beauty with my truth,
    And cross my cares ere greater sums arise.

Read it (sweet maid) though it be done but slightly;
Who can shew all his love, doth love but lightly.

SAMUEL DANIEL

206 *No, no, poor suff'ring Heart*

No, no, poor suff'ring Heart, no Change endeavour,
Choose to sustain the smart, rather than leave her;
My ravish'd Eyes behold such Charms about her,
I can die with her, but not live without her.
One tender Sigh of hers to see me languish,
Will more than pay the Price of my past Anguish:
Beware, O cruel Fair, how you smile on me,
'Twas a kind Look of yours that has undone me.

Love has in store for me one happy Minute,
And She will end my pain who did begin it;
Then no day void of Bliss, or Pleasure leaving,
Ages shall die away without perceiving:
Cupid shall guard the Door the more to please us,
And keep out Time and Death, when they would seize us:
Time and Death shall depart, and say in flying,
Love has found out a way to Live by Dying.

JOHN DRYDEN

207 *Macheath and Polly*

Mac. Were I laid on Greenland's coast,
          And in my arms embrac'd my lass,
       Warm amidst eternal frost,
          Too soon the half-year's night would pass.

Polly Were I sold on Indian soil,
           Soon as the burning day was closed,
        I could mock the sultry toil,
           When on my charmer's breast reposed.

Mac. And I would love you all the day,
Polly Every night would kiss and play;
Mac. If with me you'd fondly stray
Polly Over the hills and far away.

JOHN GAY

208 *Song*

Can love be controll'd by advice?
  Will Cupid our mothers obey?
Though my heart was as frozen as ice,
  At his flame 'twould have melted away.

When he kiss'd me, so closely he press'd,
  'Twas so sweet, that I must have complied,
So I thought it both safest and best
  To marry, for fear you should chide.

JOHN GAY

209 *The Nightingale*

The nightingale, as soon as April bringeth
  Unto her rested sense a perfect waking,
While late bare earth, proud of new clothing, springeth,
  Sings out her woes, a thorn her song-book making,
  And mournfully bewailing,
Her throat in tunes expresseth
What grief her breast oppresseth
  For Tereus' force on her chaste will prevailing.
O Philomela fair, O take some gladness,
That here is juster cause of plaintful sadness:
Thine earth now springs, mine fadeth;
Thy thorn without, my thorn my heart invadeth.

Alas, she hath no other cause of anguish
  But Tereus' love, on her by strong hand wroken,[1]
  Wherein she suff'ring, all her spirits languish,
Full womanlike complains her will was broken.
  But I, who, daily craving,
Cannot have to content me,
Have more cause to lament me,
  Since wanting is more woe then too much having.
O Philomela fair, O take some gladness,
That here is juster cause of plaintful sadness:
Thine earth now springs, mine fadeth;
Thy thorn without, my thorn my heart invadeth.

SIR PHILIP SIDNEY

[1] wreaked

210 *Heart Exchange*

My true love hath my heart, and I have his,
By just exchange one for the other given:
I hold his dear, and mine he cannot miss;
There never was a bargain better driven.
His heart in me keeps me and him in one;
My heart in him his thoughts and senses guides:
He loves my heart, for once it was his own;
I cherish his, because in me it bides.
His heart his wound received from my sight;
My heart was wounded with his wounded heart;
For, as from me on him his hurt did light,
So still me-thought in me his hurt did smart:
Both equal hurt in this change sought our bliss:
My true love hath my heart and I have his.

SIR PHILIP SIDNEY

211 *To my Inconstant Mistress*

When thou, poor Excommunicate
    From all the joys of love, shalt see
The full reward and glorious fate
    Which my strong faith shall purchase me,
    Then curse thine own inconstancy.

A fairer hand than thine shall cure
    That heart, which thy false oaths did wound;
And to my soul, a soul more pure
    Than thine, shall by Love's hand be bound,
    And both with equal glory crown'd.

Then shalt thou weep, entreat, complain
    To love, as I did once to thee;
When all thy tears shall be as vain
    As mine were then: for thou shalt be
    Damn'd for thy false Apostacy.

THOMAS CAREW

212 *To Roses in the Bosom of Castara*

Yee blushing virgins happy are
In the chaste nunn'ry of her breasts,
For he'd prophane so chaste a fair,
Who e'er should call them *Cupid*'s nests.

Transplanted thus how bright ye grow,
How rich a perfume do ye yield?
In some close garden, cowslips so
Are sweeter than ith' open field.

In those white cloisters live secure
From the rude blasts of wanton breath,
Each hour more innocent and pure,
Till you shall wither into death.

Then that which living gave you room,
Your glorious sepulchre shall be.
There wants no marble for a tomb,
Whose breast hath marble been to me.
                                        WILLIAM HABINGTON

213 *To* ——

One word is too often profaned
    For me to profane it,
One feeling too falsely disdained
    For thee to disdain it;
One hope is too like despair
    For prudence to smother,
And pity from thee more dear
    Than that from another.

I can give not what men call love,
    But wilt thou accept not
The worship the heart lifts above
    And the Heavens reject not,—
The desire of the moth for the star,
    Of the night for the morrow,
The devotion to something afar
    From the sphere of our sorrow?
                                        PERCY BYSSHE SHELLEY

214 *Song*

My silks and fine array,
　My smiles and languish'd air,
By love are driv'n away;
　And mournful lean Despair
Brings me yew to deck my grave:
　Such end true lovers have.

His face is fair as heav'n,
　When springing buds unfold;
O why to him was't giv'n,
　Whose heart is wintry cold?
His breast is love's all worship'd tomb,
　Where all love's pilgrims come.

Bring me an axe and spade,
　Bring me a winding sheet;
When I my grave have made,
　Let winds and tempests beat:
Then down I'll lie, as cold as clay.
　True love doth pass away!

WILLIAM BLAKE

215 *Song*

Never seek to tell thy love
Love that never told can be;
For the gentle wind does move
Silently, invisibly.

I told my love, I told my love,
I told her all my heart,
Trembling, cold, in ghastly fears–
Ah, she doth depart.

Soon as she was gone from me
A traveller came by
Silently, invisibly–
O, was no deny.

WILLIAM BLAKE

216 *Love*

All thoughts, all passions, all delights,
Whatever stirs this mortal frame,
All are but ministers of Love,
   And feed his sacred flame.

Oft in my waking dreams do I
Live o'er again that happy hour,
When midway on the mount I lay,
   Beside the ruined tower.

The moonshine, stealing o'er the scene
Had blended with the lights of eve;
And she was there, my hope, my joy,
   My own dear Genevieve!

She leant against the armed man,
The statue of the armed knight;
She stood and listened to my lay,
   Amid the lingering light.

Few sorrows hath she of her own.
My hope! my joy! my Genevieve!
She loves me best, whene'er I sing
   The songs that make her grieve.

I played a soft and doleful air,
I sang an old and moving story–
An old rude song, that suited well
   That ruin wild and hoary.

She listened with a flitting blush,
With downcast eyes and modest grace;
For well she knew, I could not choose
   But gaze upon her face.

I told her of the knight that wore
Upon his shield a burning brand;
And that for ten long years he wooed
   The Lady of the Land.

I told her how he pined: and ah!
The deep, the low, the pleading tone
With which I sang another's love,
    Interpreted my own.

She listened with a flitting blush,
With downcast eyes, and modest grace
And she forgave me, that I gazed
    Too fondly on her face!

But when I told the cruel scorn
That crazed that bold and lovely Knight,
And that he crossed the mountain-woods,
    Nor rested day nor night;

That sometimes from the savage den,
And sometimes from the darksome shade
And sometimes starting up at once
    In green and sunny glade,—

There came and looked him in the face
An angel beautiful and bright;
And that he knew it was a Fiend,
    This miserable Knight!

And that, unknowing what he did,
He leaped amid a murderous band,
And saved from outrage worse than death
    The Lady of the Land!

And how she wept, and clasped his knees;
And how she tended him in vain—
And ever strove to expiate
    The scorn that crazed his brain;—

And that she nursed him in a cave;
And how his madness went away,
When on the yellow forest-leaves
    A dying man he lay;—

His dying words—but when I reached
That tenderest strain of all the ditty,
My faltering voice and pausing harp
    Disturbed her soul with pity!

All impulses of soul and sense
Had thrilled my guileless Genevieve;
The music and the doleful tale,
   The rich and balmy eve;

And hopes, and fears that kindle hope,
An undistinguishable throng,
And gentle wishes long subdued,
   Subdued and cherished long!

She wept with pity and delight,
She blushed with love, and virgin shame;
And like the murmur of a dream,
   I heard her breathe my name.

Her bosom heaved–she stepped aside,
As conscious of my look she stepped–
Then suddenly, with timorous eye,
   She fled to me and wept.

She half enclosed me with her arms,
She pressed me with a meek embrace;
And bending back her head, looked up,
   And gazed upon my face.

'Twas partly love, and partly fear,
And partly 'twas a bashful art,
That I might rather feel, than see,
   The swelling of her heart.

I calmed her fears, and she was calm,
And told her love with virgin pride;
And so I won my Genevieve,
   My bright and beauteous Bride.
                  SAMUEL TAYLOR COLERIDGE

217 *The Hour of Death*

"Il est dans la Nature d'aimer à se livrer à l'idée même qu'on
redoute."—Corinne.

Leaves have their time to fall,
And flowers to wither at the north wind's breath,
   And stars to set–but all,
Thou hast *all* seasons for thine own, O Death!

Day is for mortal care,
Eve, for glad meetings round the joyous hearth,
　　Night, for the dreams of sleep, the voice of prayer—
But all for thee, thou mightiest of the earth.

　　The banquet hath its hour—
Its feverish hour, of mirth, and song, and wine;
　　There comes a day for grief's o'erwhelming power,
A time for softer tears—but all are thine.

　　Youth and the opening rose
May look like things too glorious for decay,
　　And smile at thee—but thou art not of those
That wait the ripen'd bloom to seize their prey.

　　Leaves have their time to fall,
And flowers to wither at the north wind's breath,
　　And stars to set—but all,
Thou hast *all* seasons for thine own, O Death!

　　We know when moons shall wane,
When summer birds from far shall cross the sea,
　　When autumn's hue shall tinge the golden grain—
But who shall teach us when to look for thee!

　　Is it when spring's first gale
Comes forth to whisper where the violets lie?
　　Is it when roses in our paths grow pale?—
They have *one* season—*all* are ours to die!

　　Thou art where billows foam,
Thou art where music melts upon the air;
　　Thou art around us in our peaceful home,
And the world calls us forth—and thou art there.

　　Thou art where friend meets friend,
Beneath the shadow of the elm to rest—
　　Thou art where foe meets foe, and trumpets rend
The skies, and swords beat down the princely crest.

　　Leaves have their time to fall,
And flowers to wither at the north wind's breath,
　　And stars to set—but all—
Thou hast *all* seasons for thine own, O Death!

FELICIA HEMANS

218 *Vitae summa brevis spem nos vetat incohare longam*

> They are not long, the weeping and the laughter,
>   Love and desire and hate:
> I think they have no portion in us after
>   We pass the gate.
>
> They are not long, the days of wine and roses:
>   Out of a misty dream
> Our path emerges for a while, then closes
>   Within a dream.
>
> ERNEST DOWSON

219 *Blows the wind to-day*

> Blows the wind to-day, and the sun and the rain are flying,
>   Blows the wind on the moors to-day and now,
> Where about the graves of the martyrs the whaups are crying,
>   My heart remembers how!
>
> Grey recumbent tombs of the dead in desert places,
>   Standing stones on the vacant wine-red moor,
> Hills of sheep, and the howes of the silent vanished races,
>   And winds, austere and pure:
>
> Be it granted me to behold you again in dying,
>   Hills of home! and to hear again the call;
> Hear about the graves of the martyrs the peewees crying,
>   And hear no more at all.
>
> ROBERT LOUIS STEVENSON

220 *Thus piteously Love closed*

> Thus piteously Love closed what he begat:
> The union of this ever-diverse pair!
> These two were rapid falcons in a snare,
> Condemned to do the flitting of the bat.

Lovers beneath the singing sky of May,
They wandered once; clear as the dew on flowers:
But they fed not on the advancing hours:
Their hearts held cravings for the buried day.
Then each applied to each that fatal knife,
Deep questioning, which probes to endless dole.
Ah, what a dusty answer gets the soul
When hot for certainties in this our life!–
In tragic hints here see what evermore,
Moves dark as yonder midnight ocean's force,
Thundering like ramping hosts of warrior horse,
To throw that faint thin line upon the shore!

GEORGE MEREDITH

221　*Those Various Scalpels*

those
various sounds consistently indistinct, like intermingled echoes
    struck from thin glasses successively at random–the
        inflection disguised : your hair, the tails of two
    fighting-cocks head to head in stone–like sculptured scimi-
        tars re-
        peating the curve of your ears in reverse order : your eyes,
        flowers of ice

and
snow sown by tearing winds on the cordage of disabled ships ;
    your raised hand,
    an ambiguous signature: your cheeks, those rosettes
        of blood on the stone floors of French châteaux, with
    regard to which the guides are so affirmative–those regrets
        of the retoucher on the contemporary stone : your other
        hand,

a
bundle of lances all alike, partly hid by emeralds from Persia
    and the fractional magnificence of Florentine
        goldwork–a collection of little objects–
    sapphires set with emeralds and pearls with a moonstone
        made fine
        with enamel in gray, yellow, and dragon-fly blue; a
        lemon, a

pear
and three bunches of grapes, tied with silver: your dress, a
    magnificent square
  cathedral tower of uniform
    and at the same time, diverse appearance–a
  species of vertical vineyard rustling in the storm
    of conventional opinion. Are they weapons or scalpels?
    Whetted

to
brilliance by the hard majesty of that sophistication which is
    superior to opportunity, these things are rich
  instruments with which to experiment; naturally. But
    why dissect destiny with instruments which
  are more highly specialised than the tissues of destiny
    itself?

MARIANNE MOORE

Book IV

THE POETRY OF FANCY

222 *Sudden Light*

I have been here before,
    But when or how I cannot tell:
I know the grass beyond the door,
    The sweet keen smell,
The sighing sound, the lights around the shore.

You have been mine before,—
    How long ago I may not know:
But just when at that swallow's soar
    Your neck turned so,
Some veil did fall,—I knew it all of yore.

Has this been thus before?
    And shall not thus time's eddying flight
Still with our lives our love restore
    In death's despite,
And day and night yield one delight once more?

                   DANTE GABRIEL ROSSETTI

223 *Summer Dawn*

Pray but one prayer for me 'twixt thy closed lips,
    Think but one thought of me up in the stars.
The summer night waneth, the morning light slips,
    Faint and grey 'twixt the leaves of the aspen, betwixt the
        cloud-bars
That are patiently waiting there for the dawn:
    Patient and colourless, though Heaven's gold
Waits to float through them along with the sun.
Far out in the meadows, above the young corn
    The heavy elms wait, and restless and cold
The uneasy wind rises; the roses are dun;

Through the long twilight they pray for the dawn,
Round the lone house in the midst of the corn.
  Speak but one word to me over the corn,
  Over the tender, bow'd locks of the corn.

WILLIAM MORRIS

224 *Sonnet*

To one who has been long in city pent,
  'Tis very sweet to look into the fair
  And open face of heaven,–to breathe a prayer
Full in the smile of the blue firmament.
Who is more happy, when, with heart's content
  Fatigued he sinks into some pleasant lair
  Of wavy grass, and reads a debonair
And gentle tale of love and languishment?
Returning home at evening, with an ear
  Catching the notes of Philomel,–an eye
Watching the sailing cloudlet's bright career,
  He mourns that day so soon has glided by:
E'en like the passage of an angel's tear
  That falls through the clear ether silently.

JOHN KEATS

225 *Virtue*

Sweet day, so cool, so calm, so bright,
The bridal of the earth and sky:
The dew shall weep thy fall to-night;
        For thou must die.

Sweet rose, whose hue angry and brave
Bids the rash gazer wipe his eye:
Thy root is ever in its grave,
        And thou must die.

Sweet spring, full of sweet days and roses,
A box where sweets compacted lie;
My musick shows ye have your closes,
        And all must die.

Only a sweet and virtuous soul,
Like season'd timber, never gives;
But though the whole world turn to coal,
    Then chiefly lives.

GEORGE HERBERT

226 *Song*

The world is young to-day:
    Forget the gods are old,
    Forget the years of gold
When all the months were May.

A little flower of Love
    Is ours, without a root,
    Without the end of fruit,
Yet–take the scent thereof.

There may be hope above,
    There may be rest beneath;
    We see them not, but Death
Is palpable–and Love.

DIGBY MACKWORTH DOLBEN

227 *The night is freezing fast*

The night is freezing fast,
    To-morrow comes December;
    And winterfalls of old
Are with me from the past;
    And chiefly I remember
    How Dick would hate the cold.

Fall, winter, fall; for he,
    Prompt hand and headpiece clever,
    Has woven a winter robe,
And made of earth and sea
    His overcoat for ever,
    And wears the turning globe.

A. E. HOUSMAN

228 *To Meadows*

Ye have been fresh and green,
    Ye have been fill'd with flowers:
And ye the walks have been
    Where maids have spent their hours.

You have beheld, how they
    With wicker arks did come
To kiss, and bear away
    The richer cowslips home.

Y'ave heard them sweetly sing,
    And seen them in a round;
Each virgin, like a spring.
    With honey-suckles crown'd.

But now we see none here
    Whose silv'ry feet did tread,
And with dishevell'd hair
    Adorn'd this smoother mead.

Like unthrifts, having spent
    Your stock and needy grown,
Y'are left here to lament
    Your poor estates, alone.

ROBERT HERRICK

229 *The Burial*

All the flowers of the spring
Meet to perfume our burying;
These have but their growing prime,
And man does flourish but his time.
Survey our progress from our birth—
We are set, we grow, we turn to earth,
Courts adieu, and all delights,
All bewitching appetites!
Sweetest breath and clearest eye,
Like perfumes go out and die;

And consequently this is done
As shadows wait upon the sun.
Vain the ambition of kings
Who seek by trophies and dead things
To leave a living name behind,
And weave but nets to catch the wind.

JOHN WEBSTER

230 *Sonnet*

It is a beauteous evening, calm and free,
The holy time is quiet as a Nun
Breathless with adoration; the broad sun
Is sinking down in its tranquillity;
The gentleness of heaven broods o'er the Sea:
Listen! the mighty Being is awake,
And doth with his eternal motion make
A sound like thunder–everlastingly.
Dear Child! dear Girl! that walkest with me here,
If thou appear untouched by solemn thought,
Thy nature is not therefore less divine:
Thou liest in Abraham's bosom all the year;
And worshipp'st at the Temple's inner shrine,
God being with thee when we know it not.

WILLIAM WORDSWORTH

231 *Dover Beach*

The sea is calm to-night.
The tide is full, the moon lies fair
Upon the straits;–on the French coast the light
Gleams and is gone; the cliffs of England stand,
Glimmering and vast, out in the tranquil bay.
Come to the window, sweet is the night-air!
Only, from the long line of spray
Where the sea meets the moon-blanch'd land,
Listen! you hear the grating roar
Of pebbles which the waves draw back, and fling,
At their return, up the high strand,
Begin, and cease, and then again begin,
With tremulous cadence slow, and bring
The eternal note of sadness in.

Sophocles long ago
Heard it on the Ægæan, and it brought
Into his mind the turbid ebb and flow
Of human misery: we
Find also in the sound a thought,
Hearing it by this distant northern sea.

The sea of faith
Was once, too, at the full, and round earth's shore
Lay like the folds of a bright girdle furl'd.
But now I only hear
Its melancholy, long, withdrawing roar,
Retreating to the breath
Of the night-wind down the vast edges drear
And naked shingles of the world.

Ah, love, let us be true
To one another! for the world, which seems
To lie before us like a land of dreams,
So various, so beautiful, so new,
Hath really neither joy, nor love, nor light,
Nor certitude, nor peace, nor help for pain:
And we are here as on a darkling plain
Swept with confused alarms of struggle and flight,
Where ignorant armies clash by night.

Matthew Arnold

232 *The Odyssey*

As one that for a weary space has lain
    Lull'd by the song of Circe and her wine
    In gardens near the pale of Proserpine,
Where that Æææan isle forgets the main,
And only the low lutes of love complain,
    And only shadows of wan lovers pine—
    As such an one were glad to know the brine
Salt on his lips, and the large air again—
So gladly from the songs of modern speech
    Men turn, and see the stars, and feel the free

Shrill wind beyond the close of heavy flowers,
And through the music of the languid hours
They hear like Ocean on a western beach
The surge and thunder of the Odyssey.

ANDREW LANG

233 *His Last Sonnet*

Bright star! would I were steadfast as thou art—
    Not in lone splendour hung aloft the night
And watching, with eternal lids apart,
    Like Nature's patient, sleepless Eremite,
The moving waters at their priestlike task
    Of pure ablution round earth's human shores,
Or gazing on the new soft fallen mask
    Of snow upon the mountains and the moors—
No—yet still steadfast, still unchangeable,
    Pillow'd upon my fair love's ripening breast,
To feel for ever its soft fall and swell,
    Awake for ever in a sweet unrest,
Still, still to hear her tender-taken breath,
And so live ever—or else swoon to death.

JOHN KEATS

234 *The Cypress curtain of the night*

The Cypress curtain of the night is spread,
And over all a silent dew is cast.
The weaker cares by sleep are conquered;
But I alone, with hideous grief, aghast,
In spite of Morpheus' charms, a watch do keep
Over mine eyes, to banish careless sleep.

Yet oft my trembling eyes through faintness close,
And then the Map of hell before me stands,
Which Ghosts do see, and I am one of those
Ordain'd to pine in sorrow's endless bands,
Since from my wretched soul all hopes are reft
And now no cause of life to me is left.

Grief, sieze my soul, for that will still endure,
When my craz'd body is consum'd and gone,
Bear it to thy black den, there keep it sure,
Where thou ten thousand souls dost tire upon.
But all do not afford such food to thee
As this poor one, the worser part of me.

THOMAS CAMPION

235 *Echo*

Come to me in the silence of night;
  Come in the speaking silence of a dream;
Come with soft rounded cheeks and eyes as bright
    As sunlight on a stream;
      Come back in tears,
O memory, hope, love of finished years.

O dream how sweet, too sweet, too bitter sweet,
  Whose wakening should have been in Paradise,
Where souls brimfull of love abide and meet;
    Where thirsting longing eyes
      Watch the slow door
That opening, letting in, lets out no more.

Yet come to me in dreams, that I may live
  My very life again though cold in death;
Come back to me in dreams, that I may give
    Pulse for pulse, breath for breath:
      Speak low, lean low,
As long ago, my love, how long ago.

CHRISTINA ROSSETTI

236 *A Complaint by Night*

Alas! so all things now do hold their peace !
Heaven and earth disturbed in no thing;
The beasts, the air, the birds their song do cease;
The nightes chare [1] the stars about doth bring.

---

[1] chariot

Calm is the sea; the waves work less and less:
So am not I, whom love, alas! doth wring,
Bringing before my face the great increase
Of my desires, whereat I weep and sing,
In joy and woe, as in a doubtful ease.
For my sweet thoughts sometime do pleasure bring;
But by and by, the cause of my disease
Gives me a pang, that inwardly doth sting,
   When that I think what grief it is again,
    To live and lack the thing should rid my pain.
Henry Howard, Earl of Surrey

237 *Sleep*

Come, Sleep! O Sleep, the certain knot of peace,
The baiting-place of wit, the balm of woe,
The poor man's wealth, the prisoner's release,
Th' indifferent judge between the high and low;
With shield of proof shield me from out the prease
Of those fierce darts Despair at me doth throw:
O make in me those civil wars to cease;
I will good tribute pay, if thou do so.
Take thou of me smooth pillows, sweetest bed,
A chamber deaf of noise and blind of light,
A rosy garland and a weary head:
And if these things, as being thine in right,
Move not thy heavy grace, thou shalt in me,
Livelier than elsewhere, Stella's image see.
Sir Philip Sidney

238 *Care-charmer Sleep*

Care-charmer Sleep, son of the sable night,
   Brother to death, in silent darkness born:
   Relieve my languish, and restore the light,
   With dark forgetting of my care return.
And let the day be time enough to mourn
   The shipwrack of my ill adventured youth:
   Let waking eyes suffice to wail their scorn,
   Without the torments of the night's untruth.

Cease dreams, th'Images of day desires,
  To model forth the passions of the morrow:
Never let rising Sun approve you liars,
  To add more grief to aggravate my sorrow.
Still let me sleep, imbracing clouds in vain,
And never wake to feel the day's disdain.

SAMUEL DANIEL

239 *To Sleep*

O soft embalmer of the still midnight!
  Shutting, with careful fingers and benign,
Our gloom-pleased eyes, embower'd from the light,
  Enshaded in forgetfulness divine;
O soothest Sleep! if so it please thee, close,
  In midst of this thine hymn, my willing eyes,
Or wait the amen, ere thy poppy throws
  Around my bed its lulling charities;
Then save me, or the passed day will shine
Upon my pillow, breeding many woes;
  Save me from curious conscience, that still hoards
Its strength for darkness, burrowing like a mole;
  Turn the key deftly in the oiled wards,
And seal the hushed casket of my soul.

JOHN KEATS

240 *Nuptial Sleep*

At length their long kiss severed, with sweet smart:
  And as the last slow sudden drops are shed
  From sparkling eaves where all the storm has fled,
So singly flagged the pulses of each heart.
Their bosoms sundered, with the opening start
  Of married flowers to either side outspread
  From the knit stem; yet still their mouths, burnt red,
Fawned on each other where they lay apart.

Sleep sank them lower than the tide of dreams,
  And their dreams watched them sink, and slid away.
Slowly their souls swam up again, through gleams
  Of watered light and dull drowned waifs of day;
Till from some wonder of new woods and streams
  He woke, and wondered more: for there she lay.

DANTE GABRIEL ROSSETTI

241　*The Visionary*

Silent is the house: all are laid asleep:
One alone looks out o'er the snow-wreaths deep,
Watching every cloud, dreading every breeze
That whirls the 'wildering drift, and bends the groaning trees.

Cheerful is the hearth, soft the matted floor;
Not one shivering gust creeps through pane or door;
The little lamp burns straight, its rays shoot strong and far:
I trim it well, to be the wanderer's guiding-star.

Frown, my haughty sire! chide, my angry dame!
Set your slaves to spy; threaten me with shame:
But neither sire nor dame, nor prying serf shall know
What angel nightly tracks that waste of frozen snow.

What I love shall come like visitant of air,
Safe in secret power from lurking human snare;
Who loves me, no word of mine shall e'er betray,
Though for faith unstained my life must forfeit pay.

Burn then, little lamp; glimmer straight and clear—
Hush! a rustling wing stirs, methinks, the air:
He for whom I wait thus ever comes to me;
Strange Power! I trust thy might; trust thou my constancy.

EMILY BRONTË

242　*In the Seven Woods*

I have heard the pigeons of the Seven Woods
Make their faint thunder, and the garden bees
Hum in the lime-tree flowers; and put away
The unavailing outcries and the old bitterness
That empty the heart. I have forgot awhile
Tara uprooted, and new commonness
Upon the throne and crying about the streets
And hanging its paper flowers from post to post,
Because it is alone of all things happy.
I am contented, for I know that Quiet
Wanders laughing and eating her wild heart

Among pigeons and bees, while that Great Archer,
Who but awaits His hour to shoot, still hangs
A cloudy quiver over Parc-na-lee.

WILLIAM BUTLER YEATS

243 *My heart leaps up*

My heart leaps up when I behold
  A rainbow in the sky;
So was it when my life began;
So is it now I am a man;
So be it when I shall grow old,
  Or let me die!
The Child is father of the Man
And I could wish my days to be
Bound each to each by natural piety.

WILLIAM WORDSWORTH

244 *A Garden Song*

(To W. E. H.)

Here, in this sequestered close,
Bloom the hyacinth and rose;
Here beside the modest stock
Flaunts the flaring hollyhock;
Here, without a pang, one sees
Ranks, conditions, and degrees.

All the seasons run their race
In this quiet resting place;
Peach, and apricot, and fig
Here will ripen, and grow big
Here is store and overplus,–
More had not Alcinous!

Here, in alleys cool and green,
Far ahead the thrush is seen;
Here along the southern wall
Keeps the bee his festival;
All is quiet else–afar
Sounds of toil and turmoil are.

Here be shadows large and long;
Here be spaces meet for song;
Grant, O garden-god, that I,
Now that mood and moment please,–
Find the fair Pierides!

HENRY AUSTIN DOBSON

245 *To the Cuckoo*

O blithe New-comer! I have heard,
I hear thee and rejoice.
O Cuckoo! shall I call thee Bird,
Or but a wandering Voice;

While I am lying on the grass
Thy twofold shout I hear;
From hill to hill it seems to pass
At once far off, and near.

Though babbling only to the Vale,
Of sunshine and of flowers,
Thou bringest unto me a tale
Of visionary hours.

Thrice welcome, darling of the Spring!
Even yet thou art to me
No bird, but an invisible thing,
A voice, a mystery;

The same whom in my schoolboy days
I listened to; that Cry
Which made me look a thousand ways
In bush, and tree, and sky.

To seek thee did I often rove
Through woods and on the green;
And thou wert still a hope, a love;
Still longed for, never seen.

And I can listen to thee yet;
Can lie upon the plain
And listen, till I do beget
That golden time again.

O blessèd Bird! the earth we pace
Again appears to be
An unsubstantial, faery place;
That is fit home for Thee!

WILLIAM WORDSWORTH

246 *The Lark Ascending*

He rises and begins to round,
He drops the silver chain of sound,
Of many links without a break,
In chirrup, whistle, slur and shake,
All intervolved and spreading wide,
Like water-dimples down a tide
Where ripple ripple overcurls
And eddy into eddy whirls;
A press of hurried notes that run
So fleet they scarce are more than one,
Yet changeingly the trills repeat
And linger ringing while they fleet,
Sweet to the quick o' the ear, and dear
To her beyond the handmaid ear,
Who sits beside our inner springs,
Too often dry for this he brings,
Which seems the very jet of earth
At sight of sun, her music's mirth,
As up he wings the spiral stair,
A song of light, and pierces air
With fountain ardour, fountain play,
To reach the shining tops of day,
And drink in everything discerned
An ecstasy to music turned
Impelled by what his happy bill
Disperses; drinking, showering still,
Unthinking save that he may give
His voice the outlet, there to live
Renewed in endless notes of glee,
So thirsty of his voice is he,
For all to hear and all to know
That he is joy, awake, aglow,

The tumult of the heart to hear
Through pureness filtered crystal-clear,
And know the pleasure sprinkled bright
By simple singing of delight,
Shrill, irreflective, unrestrained,
Rapt, ringing, on the jet sustained
Without a break, without a fall,
Sweet-silvery, sheer lyrical,
Perennial, quavering up the chord
Like myriad dews of sunny sward
That trembling into fulness shine,
And sparkle dropping argentine;
Such wooing as the ear receives
From zephyr caught in choric leaves
Of aspens when their chattering net
Is flushed to white with shivers wet;
And such the water-spirit's chime
On mountain heights in morning's prime,
Too freshly sweet to seem excess,
Too animate to need a stress;
But wider over many heads
The starry voice ascending spreads,
Awakening, as it waxes thin,
The best in us to him akin;
And every face to watch him raised
Puts on the light of children praised,
So rich our human pleasure ripes
When sweetness on sincereness pipes,
Though nought be promised from the seas,
But only a soft-ruffling breeze
Sweep glittering on a still content,
Serenity in ravishment.

For singing till his heaven fills,
'Tis love of earth that he instils,
And ever winging up and up,
Our valley is his golden cup,
And he the wine which overflows
To lift us with him as he goes:
The woods and brooks, the sheep and kine,
He is, the hills, the human line,

The meadows green, the fallows brown,
The dreams of labour in the town;
He sings the sap, the quickened veins;
The wedding song of sun and rains
He is, the dance of children, thanks
Of sowers, shout of primrose-banks,
And eye of violets while they breathe;
All these the circling song will wreathe,
And you shall hear the herb and tree,
The better heart of men shall see,
Shall feel celestially, as long
As you crave nothing save the song.

Was never voice of ours could say
Our inmost in the sweetest way,
Like yonder voice aloft, and link
All hearers in the song they drink.
Our wisdom speaks from failing blood,
Our passion is too full in flood,
We want the key of his wild note
Of truthful in a tuneful throat,
The song seraphically free
Of taint of personality,
So pure that it salutes the suns,
The voice of one for millions,
In whom the millions rejoice
For giving their one spirit voice.

Yet men have we, whom we revere,
Now names, and men still housing here,
Whose lives, by many a battle-dint
Defaced, and grinding wheels on flint,
Yield substance, though they sing not, sweet
For song our highest heaven to greet:
Whom heavenly singing gives us new,
Enspheres them brilliant in our blue,
From firmest base to farthest leap,
Because their love of Earth is deep,
And they are warriors in accord
With life to serve, and pass reward,
So touching purest and so heard
In the brain's reflex of yon bird:

I

Wherefore their soul in me, or mine,
Through self-forgetfulness divine,
In them, that song aloft maintains,
To fill the sky and thrill the plains
With showerings drawn from human stores,
As he to silence nearer soars,
Extends the world at wings and dome,
More spacious making more our home,
Till lost on his aërial rings
In light, and then the fancy sings.

GEORGE MEREDITH

247 *The Woodspurge*

The wind flapped loose, the wind was still,
Shaken out dead from tree and hill:
I had walked on at the wind's will,—
I sat now, for the wind was still.

Between my knees my forehead was,—
My lips, drawn in, said not Alas!
My hair was over in the grass,
My naked ears heard the day pass.

My eyes, wide open, had the run
Of some ten weeds to fix upon;
Among those few, out of the sun,
The woodspurge flowered, three cups in one.

From perfect grief there need not be
Wisdom or even memory:
One thing then learnt remains to me,—
The woodspurge has a cup of three.

DANTE GABRIEL ROSSETTI

248 *A Contemplation upon Flowers*

Brave flowers, that I could gallant it like you
And be as little vain;
You come abroad, and make a harmless show,
And to your beds of Earth again;

You are not proud, you know your birth
For your embroider'd garments are from Earth:

You do obey your months, and times, but I
Would have it ever spring,
My fate would know no winter, never die
Nor think of such a thing;
Oh that I could my bed of Earth but view
And smile, and look as cheerfully as you:

Oh teach me to see death, and not to fear
But rather to take truce;
How often have I seen you at a bier,
And there look fresh and spruce;
You fragrant flowers then teach me that my breath
Like yours may sweeten, and perfume my death.

HENRY KING

249 *To a Snowflake*

What heart could have thought you?–
Past our devisal
(O filigree petal!)
Fashioned so purely,
Fragilely, surely,
From what Paradisal
Imagineless metal,
Too costly for cost?
Who hammered you, wrought you,
From argentine vapour?–
'God was my shaper.
Passing surmisal,
He hammered, He wrought me,
From curled silver vapour,
To lust of His mind:–
Thou could'st not have thought me!
So purely, so palely,
Tinily, surely,
Mightily, frailly,
Insculped and embossed,
With His hammer of wind,
And His graver of frost.'

FRANCIS THOMPSON

250 *The Poetry of a Root Crop*

Underneath their eider-robe
Russet swede and golden globe,
Feathered carrot burrowing deep,
Steadfast wait in charmèd sleep;
Treasure-houses wherein lie,
Locked by angels' alchemy,
Milk and hair, and blood, and bone,
Children of the barren stone;
Children of the flaming Air,
With his blue eye keen and bare,
Spirit-peopled smiling down
On frozen field and toiling town—
Toiling town that will not heed
God His voice for rage and greed;
Frozen fields that surpliced lie,
Gazing patient at the sky;
Like some marble carven nun,
With folded hands when work is done,
Who mute upon her tomb doth pray,
Till the resurrection day.

CHARLES KINGSLEY

251 *Sonnet*

The world is too much with us; late and soon,
Getting and spending, we lay waste our powers:
Little we see in Nature that is ours;
We have given our hearts away, a sordid boon!
This Sea that bares her bosom to the moon;
The winds that will be howling at all hours,
And are up-gathered now like sleeping flowers;
For this, for everything, we are out of tune;
It moves us not.—Great God! I'd rather be
A Pagan suckled in a creed outworn;
So might I, standing on this pleasant lea,
Have glimpses that would make me less forlorn;
Have sight of Proteus rising from the sea;
Or hear old Triton blow his wreathèd horn.

WILLIAM WORDSWORTH

252 *Westminster Bridge*

Earth has not anything to show more fair:
Dull would he be of soul who could pass by
A sight so touching in its majesty:
This City now doth, like a garment, wear
The beauty of the morning; silent, bare,
Ships, towers, domes, theatres, and temples lie
Open unto the fields, and to the sky;
All bright and glittering in the smokeless air.
Never did sun more beautifully steep
In his first splendour, valley, rock, or hill;
Ne'er saw I, never felt, a calm so deep!
The river glideth at his own sweet will:
Dear God! the very houses seem asleep;
And all that mighty heart is lying still!

WILLIAM WORDSWORTH

253 *I wandered lonely as a cloud*

I wandered lonely as a cloud
That floats on high o'er vales and hills,
When all at once I saw a crowd,
A host, of golden daffodils;
Beside the lake, beneath the trees,
Fluttering and dancing in the breeze.

Continuous as the stars that shine
And twinkle on the milky way,
They stretched in never-ending line
Along the margin of a bay:
Ten thousand saw I at a glance,
Tossing their heads in sprightly dance.

The waves beside them danced; but they
Out-did the sparkling waves in glee:
A poet could not but be gay,
In such a jocund company:
I gazed—and gazed—but little thought
What wealth the show to me had brought:

For oft, when on my couch I lie
In vacant or in pensive mood,
They flash upon that inward eye
Which is the bliss of solitude;
And then my heart with pleasure fills
And dances with the daffodils.

WILLIAM WORDSWORTH

254 *The Moon*

With how sad steps, O Moon, thou climb'st the skies!
How silently, and with how wan a face!
What, may it be that even in heav'nly place
That busy archer his sharp arrows tries!
Sure, if that long-with-love-acquainted eyes
Can judge of love, thou feel'st a lover's case,
I read it in thy looks; thy languisht grace,
To me, that feel the like, thy state descries.
Then, ev'n of fellowship, O Moon, tell me,
Is constant love deem'd there but want of wit?
Are beauties there as proud as here they be?
Do they above love to be lov'd, and yet
Those lovers scorn whom that love doth possess?
Do they call virtue there ungratefulness?

SIR PHILIP SIDNEY

255 *To the Moon*

Art thou pale for weariness
Of climbing heaven and gazing on the earth,
    Wandering companionless
Among the stars that have a different birth,—
And ever changing, like a joyless eye
That finds no object worth its constancy?

    Thou chosen sister of the Spirit,
That gazes on thee till in thee it pities . . .

PERCY BYSSHE SHELLEY

256 *Stanzas*

Away! the moor is dark beneath the moon,
  Rapid clouds have drank the last pale beam of even:
Away! the gathering winds will call the darkness soon,
  And profoundest midnight shroud the serene lights of
    heaven.

Pause not! the time is past! Every voice cries, Away!
  Tempt not with one last tear thy friend's ungentle mood:
Thy lover's eye, so glazed and cold, dares not entreat thy stay:
  Duty and dereliction guide thee back to solitude.

Away, away! to thy sad and silent home;
  Pour bitter tears on its desolated hearth;
Watch the dim shades as like ghosts they go and come,
  And complicate strange webs of melancholy mirth.

The leaves of wasted autumn woods shall float around thine
    head;
  The blooms of dewy spring shall gleam beneath thy feet:
But thy soul or this world must fade in the frost that binds
    the dead,
  Ere midnight's frown and morning's smile, ere thou and
    peace may meet.

The cloud shadows of midnight possess their own repose,
  For the weary winds are silent, or the moon is in the deep:
Some respite to its turbulence unresting ocean knows;
  Whatever moves, or toils, or grieves, hath its appointed
    sleep.

Thou in the grave shalt rest—yet till the phantoms flee
  Which that house and heath and garden made dear to thee
    erewhile,
Thy remembrance, and repentance, and deep musings are not
    free
  From the music of two voices and the light of one sweet
    smile.

PERCY BYSSHE SHELLEY

257 *Sonnet*

Black pitchy night, companion of my woe,
The inn of care, the nurse of dreary sorrow,
Why lengthenest thou thy darkest hours so,
Still to prolong my long-time-looked-for morrow?
Thou sable shadow, image of despair,
Portrait of hell, the air's black mourning weed,
Recorder of revenge, remembrancer of care,
The shadow and the veil of every sinful deed;
Death like to thee, so live thou still in death,
The grave of joy, prison of day's delight;
Let heavens withdraw their sweet ambrosian breath,
Nor moon nor stars lend thee their shining light;
   For thou alone renew'st that old desire,
   Which still torments me in day's burning fire.

MICHAEL DRAYTON

258 *Hark! now everything is still*

Hark! now everything is still,
The screech-owl and the whistler shrill
Call upon our dame aloud,
And bid her quickly don her shroud.

Much you had of land and rent;
Your length in clay's now competent.
A long war disturb'd your mind;
Here your perfect peace is signed.
Of what is't fools make such vain keeping?—
Sin their conception, their birth weeping,
Their life a general mist of error,
Their death a hideous storm of terror.
Strew your hair with powders sweet,
Don clean linen, bathe your feet,
And (the foul fiend more to check)
A crucifix let bless your neck:
'Tis now full tide 'tween night and day;
End your groan, and come away.

JOHN WEBSTER

259 *The Wizard's Funeral*

For me, for me, two horses wait,
Two horses stand before my gate:
Their vast black plumes on high are cast,
Their black manes swing in the midnight blast,
Red sparkles from their eyes fly fast.
But can they drag the hearse behind,
Whose black plumes mystify the wind?
What a thing for this heap of bones and hair!
Despair, despair!
Yet think of half the world's winged shapes
Which have come to thee wondering:
At thee the terrible idiot gapes,
At thee the running devil japes,
And angels stoop to thee and sing
From the soft midnight that enwraps
Their limbs, so gently, sadly fair;–
Thou seest the stars shine through their hair.
The blast again, ho, ho, the blast!
I go to a mansion that shall outlast;
And the stoled priest who steps before
Shall turn and welcome me at the door.
                              RICHARD WATSON DIXON

260 *Death's Emissaries*

Victorious men of earth, no more
    Proclaim how wide your empires are;
Though you bind in every shore
    And your triumphs reach as far
        As night or day,
    Yet you, proud monarchs, must obey
And mingle with forgotten ashes, when
Death calls ye to the crowd of common men.

Devouring Famine, Plague, and War,
    Each able to undo mankind,
Death's servile emissaries are;
    Nor to these alone confined,
        He hath at will
    More quaint and subtle ways to kill.

A smile or kiss, as he will use the art,
Shall have the cunning skill to break a heart.

JAMES SHIRLEY

261 *Sonnet on his Deceased Wife*

Methought I saw my late espoused Saint
  Brought to me like ALCESTIS from the grave,
  Whom Jove's great Son to her glad Husband gave,
  Rescu'd from death by force though pale and faint.
Mine as whom washt from spot of child-bed taint,
  Purification in the old Law did save,
  And such, as yet once more I trust to have
  Full sight of her in Heaven without restraint,
Came vested all in white, pure as her mind:
  Her face was vail'd; yet to my fancied sight,
  Love, sweetness, goodness, in her person shin'd
So clear, as in no face with more delight.
  But O as to embrace me she enclin'd
  I wak'd, she fled, and day brought back my night.

JOHN MILTON

262 *The Apparition*

When by thy scorn, O murd'ress, I am dead,
And that thou think'st thee free
From all solicitation from me,
Then shall my ghost come to thy bed,
And thee, feign'd vestal, in worse arms shall see:
Then thy sick taper will begin to wink,
And he, whose thou art then, being tir'd before,
Will, if thou stir, or pinch to wake him, think
    Thou call'st for more,
And in false sleep, will from thee shrink:
And then, poor aspen wretch, neglected thou
Bath'd in a cold quicksilver sweat wilt lie
    A verier ghost than I.
What I will say, I will not tell thee now,
Lest that preserve thee; and since my love is spent,
I'd rather thou shouldst painfully repent,
Than by my threatenings rest still innocent.

JOHN DONNE

263 *Sonnet*

It is not death, that sometime in a sigh
This eloquent breath shall take its speechless flight;
That sometime these bright stars, that now reply
In sunlight to the sun, shall set in night;
That this warm conscious flesh shall perish quite,
And all life's ruddy springs forget to flow;
That thoughts shall cease, and the immortal spright
Be lapp'd in alien clay and laid below;
It is not death to know this,–but to know
That pious thoughts, which visit at new graves
In tender pilgrimage, will cease to go
So duly and so oft,–and when grass waves
Over the past-away, there may be then
No resurrection in the minds of men.

THOMAS HOOD

264 *Say not, the struggle nought availeth*

Say not, the struggle nought availeth,
    The labour and the wounds are vain,
The enemy faints not, nor faileth,
    And as things have been they remain.

If hopes were dupes, fears may be liars;
    It may be, in yon smoke concealed,
Your comrades chase e'en now the fliers,
    And, but for you, possess the field.

For while the tired waves, vainly breaking,
    Seem here no painful inch to gain,
Far back, through creeks and inlets making,
    Comes silent, flooding in, the main,

And not by eastern windows only,
    When daylight comes, comes in the light,
In front, the sun climbs slow, how slowly,
    But westward, look, the land is bright.

ARTHUR HUGH CLOUGH

265 *Ode*

How sleep the Brave, who sink to Rest,
By all their Country's Wishes blest!
When Spring, with dewy Fingers cold,
Returns to deck their hallow'd Mold,
She there shall dress a sweeter Sod,
Than Fancy's Feet have ever trod.

By Fairy Hands their Knell is rung,
By Forms unseen their Dirge is sung;
There Honour comes, a Pilgrim grey,
To bless the Turf that wraps their Clay,
And Freedom shall awhile repair,
To dwell a weeping Hermit there!

WILLIAM COLLINS

266 *The Virginian Voyage*

You brave Heroic minds,
Worthy your Country's Name;
That Honour still pursue,
Go, and subdue,
Whilst loit'ring Hinds
Lurk here at home, with shame.

Britons, you stay too long,
Quickly aboard bestow you,
And with a merry Gale
Swell your stretch'd Sail,
With Vows as strong,
As the Winds that blow you.

Your Course securely steer,
West and by South forth keep,
Rocks, Lee-shores, nor Shoals,
When EOLUS scowls,
You need not fear,
So absolute the Deep.

And cheerfully at Sea,
Success you still entice,
   To get the Pearl and Gold,
   And ours to hold,
VIRGINIA,
Earth's only Paradise.

Where Nature hath in store
Fowl, Venison, and Fish,
   And the fruitfull'st Soil,
   Without your Toil,
Three Harvests more,
All greater than your Wish.

And the ambitious Vine
Crowns with his purple Mass,
   The cedar reaching high
   To kiss the Sky
The Cypress, Pine
And useful Sassafras.

To whom, the golden Age
Still Nature's laws doth give,
   No other Cares that tend,
   But them to defend
From Winter's rage,
That long there doth not live.

When as the luscious smell
Of that delicious Land,
   Above the Seas that flows,
   The clear Wind throws,
Your Hearts to swell
Approaching the dear Strand.

In kenning of the Shore
(Thanks to God first given,)
   O you the happy'st men,
   Be frolic then,
Let Cannons roar,
Frighting the wide Heaven.

And in Regions far
Such Heroes bring ye forth,
   As those from whom We came,
   And plant Our name,
Under that Star
Not known unto our North.

And as there Plenty grows
Of Laurel everywhere,
   APOLLO's Sacred tree,
   You may it see,
A Poet's Brows
To crown, that may sing there.

Thy Voyages attend,
Industrious HACKLUIT,
   Whose Reading shall inflame
   Men to seek Fame,
And much to commend
To after-Times thy Wit.

MICHAEL DRAYTON

267 *Ulysses and the Siren*

Syren.   Come worthy Greek, Ulysses come
Possess these shores with me:
The winds and Seas are troublesome,
And here we may be free.
   Here may we sit, and view their toil
That travail on the deep,
And joy the day in mirth the while,
And spend the night in sleep.

Ulys.   Faire Nymph, if fame, or honour were
To be attain'd with ease,
Then would I come and rest me there,
And leave such toils as these.
   But here it dwells, and here must I
With danger seek it forth:
To spend the time luxuriously
Becomes not men of worth.

Syren. *Ulysses*, O be not deceiv'd
With that unreal name:
This honour is a thing conceiv'd,
And rests on others' fame.
　　Begotten only to molest
Our peace, and to beguile
(The best thing of our life) our rest,
And give us up to toil.

Ulys. Delicious Nymph, suppose there were
Nor honour, nor report,
Yet manliness would scorn to wear
The time in idle sport.
　　For toil doth give a better touch,
To make us feel our joy:
And ease finds tediousness as much
As labour yields annoy.

Syren. Then pleasure likewise seems the shore
Whereto tends all your toil,
Which you forgo to make it more,
And perish oft the while.
　　Who may disport them diversly,
Find never tedious day,
And ease may have variety,
As well as action may.

Ulys. But natures of the noblest frame,
These toils, and dangers please,
And they take comfort in the same,
As much as you in ease.
　　And with the thought of actions past
Are recreated still;
When pleasure leaves a touch at last,
To show that it was ill.

Syren. That doth opinion only cause,
That's out of custom bred,
Which makes us many other laws
Than ever Nature did.
　　No widows wail for our delights,
Our sports are without blood,
The world we see by warlike wights,
Receives more hurt then good.

Ulys.   But yet the state of things require
These motions of unrest,
And these great Spirits of high desire,
Seem born to turn them best.
  To purge the mischiefs that increase
And all good order mar:
For oft we see a wicked peace,
To be well chang'd for war.

Syren.   Well, well Ulysses then I see
I shall not have thee hear,
And therefore I will come to thee,
And take my fortunes there.
  I must be won that cannot win,
Yet lost were I not won:
For beauty hath created bin,
T'undo, or be undone.

SAMUEL DANIEL

268 *In Time of 'The Breaking of Nations'*

Only a man harrowing clods
  In a slow silent walk
With an old horse that stumbles and nods
  Half asleep as they stalk.

Only thin smoke without flame
  From the heaps of couch-grass;
Yet this will go onward the same
  Though Dynasties pass.

Yonder a maid and her wight
  Come whispering by:
War's annals will cloud into night
  Ere their story die.

THOMAS HARDY

269 *From Milton*

And did those feet in ancient time
Walk upon England's mountains green?
And was the holy Lamb of God
On England's pleasant pastures seen?

And did the Countenance Divine
Shine forth upon our clouded hills?
And was Jerusalem builded here
Among these dark Satanic Mills?

Bring me my Bow of burning gold:
Bring me my Arrows of desire:
Bring me my Spear: O clouds unfold!
Bring me my Chariot of fire.

I will not cease from Mental Fight,
Nor shall my Sword sleep in my hand
Till we have built Jerusalem
In England's green and pleasant Land.

WILLIAM BLAKE

270 *Chorus*

Life of Life! thy lips enkindle
  With their love the breath between them;
And thy smiles before they dwindle
  Make the cold air fire; then screen them
In those looks, where whoso gazes
Faints, entangled in their mazes.

Child of Light! thy limbs are burning
  Through the vest which seems to hide them;
As the radiant lines of morning
  Through the clouds ere they divide them;
And this atmosphere divinest
Shrouds thee wheresoe'er thou shinest.

Fair are others; none beholds thee,
  But thy voice sounds low and tender
Like the fairest, for it folds thee
  From the sight, that liquid splendour,
And all feel, yet see thee never,
As I feel now, lost for ever!

Lamp of Earth! where'er thou movest
  Its dim shapes are clad with brightness,
And the souls of whom thou lovest
  Walk upon the winds with lightness,
Till they fail, as I am failing,
Dizzy, lost, yet unbewailing!

PERCY BYSSHE SHELLEY

271   *Chorus*

Before the beginning of years
  There came to the making of man
Time, with a gift of tears;
  Grief, with a glass that ran;
Pleasure, with pain for leaven;
  Summer, with flowers that fell;
Remembrance fallen from heaven,
  And madness risen from hell;
Strength without hands to smite;
  Love that endures for a breath;
Night, the shadow of light,
  And life, the shadow of death.

And the high gods took in hand
  Fire, and the falling of tears,
And a measure of sliding sand
  From under the feet of the years,
And froth and drift of the sea;
  And dust of the labouring earth;
And bodies of things to be
  In the houses of death and of birth;
And wrought with weeping and laughter,
  And fashioned with loathing and love,
With life before and after
  And death beneath and above,
For a day and a night and a morrow,
  That his strength might endure for a span
With travail and heavy sorrow,
  The holy spirit of man.

From the winds of the north and the south
  They gathered as unto strife;
They breathed upon his mouth,
  They filled his body with life;
Eyesight and speech they wrought
  For the veils of the soul therein,
A time for labour and thought,
  A time to serve and to sin;
They gave him light in his ways,
  And love, and a space for delight,
And beauty and length of days,
  And night, and sleep in the night.
His speech is a burning fire;
  With his lips he travaileth;
In his heart is a blind desire,
  In his eyes foreknowledge of death;
He weaves, and is clothed with derision;
  Sows, and he shall not reap;
His life is a watch or a vision
  Between a sleep and a sleep.

ALGERNON CHARLES SWINBURNE

272 *Chorus*

The world's great age begins anew,
  The golden years return,
The earth doth like a snake renew
  Her winter weeds outworn:
Heaven smiles, and faiths and empires gleam,
Like wrecks of a dissolving dream.

A brighter Hellas rears its mountains
  From waves serener far;
A new Peneus rolls his fountains
  Against the morning star.
Where fairer Tempes bloom, there sleep
Young Cyclads on a sunnier deep.

A loftier Argo cleaves the main,
  Fraught with a later prize;
Another Orpheus sings again,
  And loves, and weeps, and dies.

A new Ulysses leaves once more
Calypso for his native shore.

Oh, write no more the tale of Troy,
    If earth Death's scroll must be!
Nor mix with Laian rage the joy
    Which dawns upon the free:
Although a subtler Sphinx renew
Riddles of death Thebes never knew

Another Athens shall arise,
    And to remoter time
Bequeath, like sunset to the skies,
    The splendour of its prime;
And leave, if nought so bright may live,
All earth can take or Heaven can give.

Saturn and Love their long repose
    Shall burst, more bright and good
Than all who fell, than One who rose,
    Than many unsubdued:
Not gold, not blood, their altar dowers,
But votive tears and symbol flowers.

Oh, cease! must hate and death return?
    Cease! must men kill and die?
Cease! drain not to its dregs the urn
    Of bitter prophecy.
The world is weary of the past,
Oh, might it die or rest at last!

                              PERCY BYSSIE SHELLEY

273 *Chorus*

Behold what furies still
Torment their tortur'd breast,
Who by their doing ill,
Have wrought the worlds unrest.
Which when being most distrest,
Yet more to vex their sprite,
The hideous face of sin
(In forms they most detest)

Stands ever in their sight.
Their conscience still within
Th'eternal 'larum is
That ever-barking dog that calls upon their miss.

No means at all to hide
Man from himself can find:
No way to start aside
Out from the hell of mind.
But in himself confin'd
He still see sin before;
And winged-footed pain,
That swiftly comes behind,
The which is ever-more
The sure and certain gain
Impiety doth get,
And wanton loose respect, that doth itself forget.

And *Cleopatra* now,
Well sees the dangerous way
She took, and car'd not how,
Which led her to decay.
And likewise makes us pay
For her disordered lust,
The int'rest of our blood:
Or live a servile prey,
Under a hand unjust,
As others shall think good.
This hath her riot won:
And thus she hath her state, herself and us undone.

Now every mouth can tell,
What close was muttered:
How that she did not well,
To take the course she did.
For now is nothing hid,
Of what fear did restrain;
No secret closely done,
But now is uttered.
The text is made most plain
The flatt'ry gloz'd upon,

The bed of sin reveal'd,
And all the luxury that shame would have conceal'd.

The scene is broken down
And all uncover'd lies,
The purple actors known
Scarce men, whom men despise.
The complots of the wise,
Prove imperfections smok'd:
And all what wonder gave
To pleasure-gazing eyes,
Lies scatt'red, dasht, all broke.
Thus much beguiled have
Poor unconsiderate wights,
These momentary pleasures, fugitive delights.

SAMUEL DANIEL

274 *Troynovant*

Troynovant is now no more a City:
    O great pity! is't not pity?
  And yet her towers on tiptoe stand,
  Like pageants built in fairy land,
      And her marble arms,
      Like to magic charms
  Bind thousands fast unto her,
That for her wealth and beauty daily woo her.
  Yet for all this, is't not pity?
Troynovant is now no more a City.

Troynovant is now a summer arbour,
    Or the nest wherein doth harbour
  The Eagle, of all birds that fly,
  The sovereign, for his piercing eye.
      If you wisely mark,
      Tis besides a park
  Where runs (being newly born)
With the fierce Lion, the fair Unicorn,
    Or else it is a wedding hall,
Where four great kingdoms hold a festival.

Troynovant is now a bridal chamber,
  Whose roof is gold, floor is of amber,
 By virtue of that holy light,
 That burns in *Hymen*'s hand, more bright,
   Than the silver moon,
   Or the torch at noon.
 Hark what the Echoes say!
Britain till now ne'er kept a holiday:
 For *Jove* dwells here: And 'tis no pity,
 If *Troynovant* be now no more a City.
                              THOMAS DEKKER

275 *Now winter nights enlarge*

  Now winter nights enlarge
  The number of their hours;
And clouds their storms discharge
  Upon the airy towers.
Let now the chimneys blaze
  And cups o'erflow with wine,
Let well-tun'd words amaze
  With harmony divine.
Now yellow waxen lights
  Shall wait on honey Love
While youthful revels, masks, and courtly sights,
  Sleep's leaden spells remove.

  This time doth well dispense
  With lovers' long discourse;
Much speech hath some defence,
  Though beauty no remorse.
All do not all things well;
  Some measures comely tread;
Some knotted riddles tell;
  Some poems smoothly read.
The Summer hath his joys,
  And Winter his delights;
Though Love and all his pleasures are but toys,
  They shorten tedious nights.
                              THOMAS CAMPION

276 *Will you come?*

Will you come?
Will you come
Will you ride
So late
At my side?
O, will you come?

Will you come?
Will you come
If the night
Has a moon,
Full and bright?
O, will you come?

Would you come?
Would you come
If the noon
Gave light,
Not the moon?
Beautiful, would you come?

Would you have come?
Would you have come
Without scorning,
Had it been
Still morning?
Beloved, would you have come?

If you come
Haste and come.
Owls have cried;
It grows dark
To ride.
Beloved, beautiful, come.

EDWARD THOMAS

277 *The Mermaiden's Vesper Hymn*

Troop home to silent grots and caves!
  Troop home! and mimic as you go
The mournful winding of the waves
  Which to their dark abysses flow.

At this sweet hour, all things beside
  In amorous pairs to covert creep;
The swans that brush the evening tide
  Homeward in snowy couples keep.

In his green den the murmuring seal
  Close by his sleek companion lies;
While singly we to bedward steal,
  And close in fruitless sleep our eyes.

In bowers of love men take their rest,
  In loveless bowers we sigh alone,
With bosom-friends are others blest,–
  But we have none! but we have none!
                                    GEORGE DARLEY

278 *The Phoenix*

O blest unfabled Incense Tree,
That burns in glorious Araby,
With red scent chalicing the air,
Till earth-life grow Elysian there!

Half buried to her flaming breast
In this bright tree, she makes her nest,
Hundred-sunned Phoenix! when she must
Crumble at length to hoary dust!

Her gorgeous death-bed! her rich pyre
Burnt up with aromatic fire!
Her urn, sight high from spoiler men!
Her birthplace when self-born again!

The mountainless green wilds among,
Here ends she her unechoing song!
With amber tears and odorous sighs
Mourned by the desert where she dies!
                                    GEORGE DARLEY

279 *Song*

Now sleeps the crimson petal, now the white;
Nor waves the cypress in the palace walk;
Nor winks the gold fin in the porphyry font:
The fire-fly wakens: waken thou with me.

Now droops the milk white peacock like a ghost,
And like a ghost she glimmers on to me.

Now lies the Earth all Danae to the stars,
And all thy heart lies open unto me.

Now slides the silent meteor on, and leaves
A shining furrow, as thy thoughts in me.

Now folds the lily all her sweetness up,
And slips into the bosom of the lake:
So fold thyself, my dearest, thou, and slip
Into my bosom and be lost in me.

ALFRED, LORD TENNYSON

280 *An African Song*

Haste, ye purple gleams of light,
　　Haste and gild the spacious skies;
Haste, ye eagles, take your flight,
　　Haste and bid the morning rise.

Now the eastern curtain draws;
　　Now the red'ning splendor gleams,
Now the purple plum'd maccaws
　　Skim along the silver streams.

Now the fragrant-scented thorn,
　　Trembles with the gummy dew;
Now the pleasures of the morn,
　　Swell upon the eager view.

Whither does my archer stay?
　　Whither is my Narva fled?
What can keep his soul away,
　　From the transports of Mored?

THOMAS CHATTERTON

281 *To the Evening Star*

Thou fair-hair'd angel of the evening,
Now, whilst the sun rests on the mountains, light
Thy bright torch of love; thy radiant crown
Put on, and smile upon our evening bed!
Smile on our loves, and, while thou drawest the
Blue curtains of the sky, scatter thy silver dew
On every flower that shuts its sweet eyes
In timely sleep. Let thy west wind sleep on
The lake; speak silence with thy glimmering eyes,
And wash the dusk with silver. Soon, full soon,
Dost thou withdraw; then the wolf rages wide,
And the lion glares thro' the dun forest:
The fleeces of our flocks are cover'd with
Thy sacred dew: protect them with thine influence.

WILLIAM BLAKE

282 *To the Muses*

Whether on Ida's shady brow,
   Or in the chambers of the East,
The chambers of the sun, that now
   From antient melody have ceas'd;

Whether in Heav'n ye wander fair,
   Or the green corners of the earth,
Or the blue regions of the air,
   Where the melodious winds have birth;

Whether on chrystal rocks ye rove,
   Beneath the bosom of the sea
Wand'ring in many a coral grove,
   Fair Nine, forsaking Poetry!

How have you left the antient love
   That bards of old enjoy'd in you!
The languid strings do scarcely move!
   The sound is forc'd, the notes are few.

WILLIAM BLAKE

283 *To Night*

Swiftly walk o'er the western wave,
        Spirit of Night!
Out of the misty eastern cave,
Where, all the long and lone daylight,
Thou wovest dreams of joy and fear,
Which make thee terrible and dear,—
        Swift be thy flight!

Wrap thy form in a mantle gray,
        Star-inwrought!
Blind with thine hair the eyes of Day;
Kiss her until she be wearied out,
Then wander o'er city, and sea, and land,
Touching all with thine opiate wand—
        Come, long-sought!

When I arose and saw the dawn,
        I sighed for thee;
When light rode high, and the dew was gone,
And noon lay heavy on flower and tree,
And the weary Day turned to his rest,
Lingering like an unloved guest,
        I sighed for thee.

Thy brother Death came, and cried,
        Wouldst thou me?
Thy sweet child Sleep, the filmy-eyed,
Murmured like a noontide bee,
Shall I nestle near thy side?
Wouldst thou me?—And I replied,
        No, not thee!

Death will come when thou art dead,
        Soon, too soon—
Sleep will come when thou art fled;
Of neither would I ask the boon
I ask of thee, beloved Night—
Swift be thine approaching flight,
        Come soon, soon!

                                PERCY BYSSHE SHELLEY

284 *Fragment*

I walk'd along a stream for pureness rare,
  Brighter than sunshine, for it did acquaint
    The dullest sight with all the glorious prey,
    That in the pebble-paved channel lay.

No molten crystal, but a richer mine,
  Even Nature's rarest alchemy ran there,
Diamonds resolv'd, and substance more divine,
  Through whose bright gliding current might appear
A thousand naked nymphs, whose ivory shine,
  Enamelling the banks, made them more dear
    Then ever was that glorious palace gate,
    Where the day-shining sun in triumph sate.

Upon this brim the eglantine and rose,
  The tamarisk, olive, and th' almond tree
As kind companions in one union grows,
  Folding their twining arms, as oft we see
Turtle-taught lovers either other close,
  Lending to dullness feeling sympathy.
    And as a costly valance o'er a bed,
    So did their garland-tops the brook o'erspread.

Their leaves that differed both in shape and show,
  (Though all were green yet difference such in green)
Like to the checkered bent of Iris' bow,
  Prided the running main as it had been—
                GERVASE MARKHAM

285 *The Peaceful Western Wind*

The peaceful western wind
The winter storms hath tam'd,
And nature in each kind
The kind heat hath inflam'd:
The forward buds so sweetly breathe
  Out of their earthy bowers,
That heav'n which views their pomp beneath
  Would fain be deckt with flowers.

See how the morning smiles
On her bright eastern hill,
And with soft steps beguiles
Them that lie slumbring still.
The music-loving birds are come
From cliffs and rocks unknown
To see the trees and briars bloom
That late were overflown.

What Saturn did destroy,
Love's Queen revives again;
And now her naked boy
Doth in the fields remain,
Where he such pleasing change doth view
In ev'ry living thing,
As if the world were born anew
To gratify the Spring.

If all things life present,
Why die my comforts then?
Why suffers my content?
Am I the worst of men?
O, beauty, be not thou accus'd
Too justly in this case:
Unkindly if true love be us'd,
'Twill yield thee little grace.

THOMAS CAMPION

286 *Dorus's Song*

O sweet woods, the delight of solitariness!
O how much I do like your solitariness!
Where man's mind hath a freed consideration,
Of goodness, to receive lovely direction;
Where senses do behold th' order of heav'nly host,
And wise thoughts do behold what the Creator is:
Contemplation here holdeth his only seat,
Bounded with no limits, born with a wing of hope,
Climbs even unto the stars, Nature is under it;
Nought disturbs thy quiet, all to thy service yields;
Each sight draws on a thought,—thought, mother of science;

Sweet birds kindly do grant harmony unto thee;
Fair trees' shade is enough fortification,
Nor danger to thy self, if be not in thy self.

O sweet woods, the delight of solitariness!
O how much I do like your solitariness!
Here no treason is hid, veiled in innocence,
Nor Envy's snaky eye, finds any harbour here,
Nor flatterers' venomous insinuations,
Nor cunning humorists' puddled opinions,
Nor courteous ruining of proffered usury,
Nor time prattled away, cradle of ignorance,
Nor causeless duty, nor comber of arrogance,
Nor trifling title of vanity dazzleth us,
Nor golden manacles stand for a paradise;
Here Wrong's name is unheard, Slander a monster is;
Keep thy sprite from abuse, here no abuse doth haunt:
What man grafts in a tree, dissimulation?

O sweet woods, the delight of solitariness!
O how well I do like your solitariness!
Yet, dear soul, if a soul clos'd in a mansion
As sweet as violets, fair as a lily is,
Straight as a cedar, a voice stains the canary-bird's,
Whose shade Safety doth hold, Danger avoideth her:
Such wisdom, that in her lives Speculation:
Such goodness, that in her Simplicity triumphs;
Where Envy's snaky eye winketh or else dieth,
Slander wants a pretext, Flattery gone beyond:
Oh, if such a one have bent to a lonely life
Her steps, glad we receive, glad we receive her eyes:
And think not she doth hurt our solitariness,
For such company decks such solitariness.
                                        SIR PHILIP SIDNEY

287 *Doralicia's Song*

In time we see that silver drops
    The craggy stones make soft:
The slowest snail in time, we see,
    Doth creep and climb aloft.

With feeble puffs the tallest pine
    In tract of time doth fall:
The hardest heart in time doth yield
    To Venus' luring call.

Where chilling frost a-late did nip,
    There flasheth now a fire:
Where deep disdain bred noisome hate,
    There kindleth now desire.

Time causeth hope to have his hap,
    What care in time not eas'd?
In time I loath'd that now I love,
    In both content and pleas'd.

ROBERT GREENE

288 *A Copy of Verses sent by Cleone to Aspasia*

Perilla! to thy fates resign'd,
    Think not what years are gone,
While Atalanta lookt behind
    The golden fruit roll'd on.

Albeit another may have lost
    The plaything at her breast,
Albeit the one she cherisht most,
    It but endears the rest.

Youth, my Perilla, clings on Hope,
    And looks into the skies
For brighter day; she fears to cope
    With grief, she shrinks at sighs.

Why should the memory of the past
    Make you and me complain?
Come, as we could not hold it fast
    We'll play it o'er again.

WALTER SAVAGE LANDOR

289 *Song: to the Masquers representing Stars*

Advance your Choral motions now,
    You music-loving lights:
This night concludes the nuptial vow,
    Make this the best of nights:
So bravely crown it with your beams
    That it may live in fame
As long as *Rhenus* or the *Thames*
    Are known by either name.

Once move again, yet nearer move
    Your forms at willing view;
Such fair effects of joy and love
    None can express but you.
Then revel midst your airy Bowers
    Till all the clouds do sweat,
That pleasure may be pour'd in showers
    On this triumphant Seat.

Long since hath lovely *Flora* thrown
    Her Flowers and Garlands here;
Rich *Ceres* all her wealth hath shown,
    Proud of her dainty cheer.
Chang'd then to human shape, descend,
    Clad in familiar weed,
That every eye may here commend
    The kind delights you breed.

THOMAS CAMPION

290 *Well I remember*

Well I remember how you smiled
    To see me write your name upon
The soft sea-sand . . . "*O! what a child!
    You think you're writing upon stone!*"
I have since written what no tide
    Shall ever wash away, what men
Unborn shall read o'er ocean wide
    And find Ianthe's name agen.

WALTER SAVAGE LANDOR

291 *Dream-Pedlary*

If there were dreams to sell,
  What would you buy?
Some cost a passing bell;
  Some a light sigh,
That shakes from Life's fresh crown
Only a roseleaf down.
If there were dreams to sell,
  Merry and sad to tell,
    And the crier rung the bell,
      What would you buy?

A cottage lone and still,
  With bowers nigh,
Shadowy, my woes to still,
  Until I die.
Such pearl from Life's fresh crown
Fain would I shake me down.
  Were dreams to have at will,
  This would best heal my ill,
    This would I buy.

But there were dreams to sell,
  Ill didst thou buy;
Life is a dream, they tell,
  Waking, to die.
Dreaming a dream to prize,
In wishing ghosts to rise;
  And, if I had the spell
  To call the buried, well,
    Which one would I?

If there are ghosts to raise,
  What shall I call,
Out of hell's murky haze,
  Heaven's blue pall?
Raise my loved long-lost boy
To lead me to his joy,—
  There are no ghosts to raise;
  Out of death lead no ways;
    Vain is the call.

Know'st thou not ghosts to sue?
    No love thou hast.
Else lie, as I will do,
    And breathe thy last.
So out of Life's fresh crown
Fall like a rose-leaf down.
    Thus are the ghosts to woo;
    Thus are all dreams made true,
        Ever to last!

THOMAS LOVELL BEDDOES

292 *Love is a sickness*

Love is a sickness full of woes,
    All remedies refusing:
A plant that with most cutting grows,
    Most barren with best using.
                Why so?
More we enjoy it, more it dies,
If not enjoy'd, it sighing cries,
                Hey ho.

Love is a torment of the mind,
    A tempest everlasting;
And Jove hath made it of a kind,
    Not well, nor full nor fasting.
                Why so?
More we enjoy it, more it dies
If not enjoy'd, it sighing cries,
                Hey ho.

SAMUEL DANIEL

293 *Ode*

Now each creature joys the other,
    passing happy days and hours;
One Bird reports unto another,
    in the fall of silver showers;
Whilst the earth (our common mother)
    hath her bosom deckt with flowers.

Whilst the greatest Torch of heaven
   with bright rays warms FLORA's lap,
Making nights and days both even,
   cheering plants with fresher sap:
My field of flowers quite bereaven,
   wants refresh of better hap.

ECHO, daughter of the Air,
   (babbling guest of Rocks and hills,)
Knows the name of my fierce Fair,
   and sounds the accents of my ills.
Each thing pities my despair,
   whilst that she her Lover kills.

Whilst that she (O cruel Maid)
   doth me and my true love despise;
My life's flourish is decayed,
   that depended on her eyes:
But her will must be obeyed,
   and well he ends for love who dies.

SAMUEL DANIEL

294 *Are they shadows?*

Are they shadows that we see?
And can shadows pleasure give?
Pleasures only shadows be
Cast by bodies we conceive,
And are made the things we deem,
In those figures which they seem.
But these pleasures vanish fast,
Which by shadows are exprest:
   Pleasures are not, if they last,
   In their passing, is their best.
   Glory is most bright and gay
   In a flash, and so away.
Feed apace then greedy eyes
On the wonder you behold.
   Take it sudden as it flies
   Though you take it not to hold:

When your eyes have done their part,
Thought must length it in the heart.

SAMUEL DANIEL

295 *Melancholy*

Were but that sigh a penitential breath
That thou art mine: It would blow with it death,
T' inclose me in my marble: Where I'ld be
Slave to the tyrant worms, to set thee free.
What should we envy? Though with larger sail
Some dance upon the Ocean: yet more frail
And faithless is that wave, than where we glide,
Blest in the safety of a private tide.
We still have land in ken. And 'cause our boat
Dares not affront the weather, we'll ne'er float
Far from the shore. To daring them each cloud
Is big with thunder, every wind speaks loud.
    And though wild rocks about the shore appear
    Yet virtue will find room to anchor there.

WILLIAM HABINGTON

296 *Love's Nightingale*

Though now 'tis neither May nor June,
And nightingales are out of tune,
Yet in these leaves, fair One, there lies
(Sworn servant to your sweetest eyes)
A nightingale, who may she spread
In your white bosom her chaste bed,
Spite of all the maiden snow
Those pure untrodden paths can show,
You straight shall see her wake and rise
Taking fresh life from your fair eyes.
And with claspt wings proclaim a spring,
Where Love and she shall sit and sing.
For lodg'd so near your sweetest throat
What nightingale can lose her note?
Nor let her kindred birds complain
Because she breaks the year's old reign;
For let them know she's none of those
Hedge-quiristers whose music owes

Only such strains as serve to keep
Sad shades, and sing dull night asleep.
No, she's a priestess of that grove,
The holy chapel of chaste Love,
Your virgin bosom. Then what e'er
Poor laws divide the public year,
Whose revolutions wait upon
The wild turns of the wanton sun,
Be you the Lady of Love's year:
Where your eyes shine his suns appear:
There all the year is Love's long spring.
  There all the year
Love's nightingales shall sit and sing.

RICHARD CRASHAW

297 *Destiny*

Chide, chide no more away
The fleeting daughters of the day,
Nor with impatient thoughts out-run
  The lazy Sun,
Or think the hours do move too slow;
  Delay is kind,
And we too soon shall find
That which we seek, yet fear to know.

The mystic dark decrees
Unfold not of the Destinies,
Nor boldly seek to antedate
  The laws of Fate,
Thy anxious search awhile forbear,
  Suppress thy haste,
And know that Time at last
Will crown thy hope, or fix thy fear.

THOMAS STANLEY

298 *To Leuconöe*

Seek not, for thou shalt not find it, what my end, what thine
  shall be;
Ask not of Chaldaea's science what God wills, Leuconöe:
Better far, what comes, to bear it. Haply many a wintry blast
Waits thee still: and this, it may be, Jove ordains to be thy last

Which flings now the flagging sea-wave on the obstinate sand-
  stone reef.
Be thou wise: fill up the wine-cup; shortening, since the time is
  brief,
Hopes that reach into the future. While I speak, hath stol'n
  away
Jealous Time. Mistrust To-morrow, catch the blossom of
  To-day.

CHARLES STUART CALVERLEY

299 Song

Fly hence, shadows, that do keep
Watchful sorrows charm'd in sleep!
Though the eyes be overtaken,
Yet the heart doth ever waken
Thoughts, chain'd up in busy snares
Of continual woes and cares:
Love and griefs are so exprest
As they rather sigh than rest.
Fly hence, shadows, that do keep
Watchful sorrows charm'd in sleep!

JOHN FORD

300 To his Coy Mistress

Had we but World enough, and time,
This coyness Lady were no crime.
We would sit down, and think which way
To walk, and pass our long Love's Day.
Thou by the *Indian Ganges* side
Should'st Rubies find: I by the Tide
Of *Humber* would complain. I would
Love you ten years before the Flood:
And you should if you please refuse
Till the Conversion of the *Jews*.
My vegetable Love should grow
Vaster than Empires, and more slow.
An hundred years should go to praise
Thine Eyes, and on thy Forehead Gaze.
Two hundred to adore each Breast:
But thirty thousand to the rest.

An Age at least to every part,
And the last Age should show your Heart.
For Lady you deserve this State;
Nor would I love at lower rate.
  But at my back I always hear
Time's winged Chariot hurrying near:
And yonder all before us lie
Desarts of vast Eternity.
Thy Beauty shall no more be found,
Nor, in thy marble Vault, shall sound
My echoing Song: then Worms shall try
That long preserv'd Virginity:
And your quaint Honour turn to dust;
And into ashes all my Lust.
The Grave's a fine and private place,
But none I think do there embrace.
  Now therefore, while the youthful hew
Sits on thy skin like morning dew,
And while thy willing Soul transpires
At every pore with instant Fires,
Now let us sport us while we may;
And now, like am'rous birds of prey,
Rather at once our Time devour,
Than languish in his slow-chapt pow'r.
Let us roll all our Strength, and all
Our sweetness, up into one Ball:
And tear our Pleasures with rough strife,
Thorough the Iron gates of Life.
Thus, though we cannot make our Sun
Stand still, yet we will make him run.

ANDREW MARVELL

301 *To a Lady, that Desired I would Love Her*

Now you have freely given me leave to love,
        What will you do?
Shall I your mirth, or passion move
        When I begin to woo?
Will you torment, or scorn, or love me too?

Each petty Beauty can disdain, and I,
      'Spite of your hate,
Without your leave can see, and die.
      Dispense a nobler fate!
'Tis easy to destroy: you may create.

Then give me leave to love, and love me too:
      Now with design
To raise, as Love's curst rebels do,
      When puling poets whine,
Fame to their Beauty, from their blubber'd eyne.

Grief is a puddle, and reflects not clear
      Your Beauty's rays;
Joys are pure streams: your eyes appear
      Sullen in sadder lays:
In cheerful numbers they shine bright with praise,

Which shall not mention, to express you fair,
      Wounds, flames, and darts,
Storms in your brow, nets in your hair,–
      Suborning all your parts,
Or to betray, or torture captive hearts.

I'll make your eyes like morning suns appear,
      As mild, and fair;
Your brow as crystal smooth, and clear;
      And your dishevell'd hair
Shall flow like a calm region of the air.

Rich Nature's store (which is the Poet's treasure)
      I'll spend to dress
Your beauties, if your mine of pleasure
      In equal thankfulness
You but unlock, so we each other bless.

THOMAS CAREW

302 *Whiteness, or Chastity*

Tell me, where doth *Whiteness* grow,
Not on beds of Scythian snow;
Nor on alabaster hills;
Nor in Canaan's milky rills;

Nor the dainty living land
Of a young Queen's breast or hand;
Nor on cygnet's lovely necks;
Nor in lap of virgin wax;
Nor upon the soft and sleek
Pillows of the lilies' cheek;
Nor the precious smiling heirs
Of the morning's pearly tears;
Nor the silver-shaming grace
Of the moon's unclouded face:
No; All these candors
Are but the handsome slanders
Cast on the name of genuine WHITENESS, which
Doth Thee alone, fair CHASTITY, inrich.

JOSEPH BEAUMONT

303 *Song from Endymion*

'O Sorrow,
Why dost borrow
The natural hue of health, from vermeil lips?–
To give maiden blushes
To the white rose bushes?
Or is it thy dewy hand the daisy tips?

'O Sorrow,
Why dost borrow
The lustrous passion from a falcon-eye?–
To give a glow-worm light?
Or, on a moonless night,
To tinge, on syren shores, the salt sea-spray?

'O Sorrow,
Why dost borrow
The mellow ditties from a mourning tongue?–
To give at evening pale
Unto the nightingale,
That thou mayst listen the cold dews among?

'O Sorrow,
Why dost borrow
Heart's lightness from the merriment of May?—
A lover would not tread
A cowslip on the head,
Though he should dance from eve till peep of day—
Nor any drooping flower
Held sacred for thy bower,
Wherever he may sport himself and play.

'To Sorrow,
I bade good-morrow,
And thought to leave her far away behind;
But cheerly, cheerly,
She loves me dearly;
She is so constant to me, and so kind:
I would deceive her,
And so leave her,
But ah! she is so constant and so kind.'

JOHN KEATS

304 *Epitaph on the Countess Dowager of Pembroke*

Underneath this sable hearse
Lies the subject of all verse:
Sidney's sister, Pembroke's mother:
Death, ere thou hast slain another,
Fair, and learn'd, and good as she,
Time shall throw a dart at thee.

WILLIAM BROWNE

305 *Epitaph on Sir Philip Sidney*

Silence augmenteth grief, writing increaseth rage,
Stal'd are my thoughts, which lov'd and lost the wonder of our
    age:
Yet quicken'd now with fire, though dead with frost ere now,
Enrag'd I write I know not what; dead, quick, I know not how.

Hard-hearted minds relent, and rigour's tears abound,
And envy strangely rues his end, in whom no fault she found.
Knowledge her light hath lost; valour hath slain her knight.
Sidney is dead; dead is my friend; dead is the world's delight.

Place pensive wails his fall whose presence was her pride,
Time crieth out, 'My ebb is come; his life was my spring tide.'
Fame mourns in that she lost the ground of her reports;
Each living wight laments his lack, and all in sundry sorts.

He was (woe worth that word!) to each well-thinking mind
A spotless friend, a matchless man, whose virtue ever shin'd,
Declaring in his thoughts, his life, and that he writ,
Highest conceits, longest foresights, and deepest works of wit.

He, only like himself, was second unto none,
Whose death (though life) we rue, and wrong, and all in vain
    do moan.
Their loss, not him, wail they, that fill the world with cries,
Death slew not him, but he made death his ladder to the skies.

Now sink of sorrow I, who live, the more the wrong,
Who wishing death, whom death denies, whose thread is all
    too long;
Who tied to wretched life, who looks for no relief,
Must spend my ever dying days, in never ending grief.

Heart's ease and only I, like parallels run on,
Whose equal length keep equal breadth, and never meet in
    one;
Yet for not wronging him, my thoughts, my sorrow's cell,
Shall not run out, though leak they will, for liking him so well.

Farewell to you my hopes, my wonted waking dreams,
Farewell sometimes enjoyed joy; eclipsed are thy beams.
Farewell self-pleasing thoughts, which quietness brings forth;
And farewell friendship's sacred league, uniting minds of
    worth.

And farewell merry heart, the gift of guiltless minds,
And all sports which, for life's restore, variety assigns;
Let all that sweet is void; in me no mirth may dwell.
Philip, the cause of all this woe, my life's content farewell!

Now rhyme, the son of rage, which art no kin to skill,
And endless grief, which deads my life, yet knows not how to
  kill,
Go, seek that hapless tomb, which if ye hap to find,
Salute the stones, that keep the limbs, that held so good a
  mind.

FULKE GREVILLE, LORD BROOKE

306 *On my First Daughter*

Here lies to each her parent's ruth,
Mary, the daughter of their youth:
Yet, all heaven's gifts, being heaven's due,
It makes the father, less, to rue.
At six months' end, she parted hence
With safety of her innocence;
Whose soul heaven's Queen (whose name she bears),
In comfort of her mother's tears,
Hath plac'd amongst her virgin-train:
Where, while that sever'd doth remain,
This grave partakes the fleshly birth.
Which cover lightly, gentle earth.

BEN JONSON

307 *On my First Son*

Farewell, thou child of my right hand, and joy,
  My sin was too much hope of thee, lov'd boy,
Seven years th' wert lent to me, and I thee pay,
  Exacted by thy fate, on the just day.
O I could lose all father now. For why
  Will man lament the state he should envy?
To have so soon scap'd world's and flesh's rage,
  And, if no other misery, yet age?
Rest in soft peace, and ask'd, say here doth lie
  BEN: JONSON his best piece of *poetry*.

For whose sake, hence-forth, all his vows be such
As what he loves may never like too much.

BEN JONSON

308 *Epitaph on S.P. a Child of Q. El. Chapel*

Weep with me all you that read
This little story:
And know, for whom a tear you shed,
Death's self is sorry.
'Twas a child, that so did thrive
In grace, and feature,
As Heaven and Nature seem'd to strive
Which own'd the creature.
Years he numb'red scarce thirteen
When Fates turn'd cruel,
Yet three fill'd Zodiacs had he been
The stage's jewel;
And did act (what now we moan)
Old men so duly,
As, sooth, the Parcæ thought him one,
He play'd so truly.
So, by error, to his fate
They all consented;
But viewing him since (alas, too late)
They have repented
And have sought (to give new birth)
In baths to steep him;
But, being so much too good for earth,
Heaven vows to keep him.

BEN JONSON

309 *An Epitaph upon* —

Enough: and leave the rest to Fame.
'Tis to commend her but to name.
Courtship, which living she declin'd,
When dead to offer were unkind.
Where never any could speak ill,
Who would officious praises spill?

Nor can the truest wit or friend,
Without detracting, her commend.
To say she liv'd a virgin chaste,
In this age loose and all unlac't;
Nor was, when vice is so allow'd,
Of virtue or asham'd, or proud;
That her soul was on Heaven so bent
No minute but it came and went;
That ready her last debt to pay
She summ'd her life up ev'ry day;
Modest as morn; as mid-day bright;
Gentle as ev'ning; cool as night;
'Tis true: but all so weakly said;
'Twere more significant, *She's Dead.*

ANDREW MARVELL

310 *Upon a Child*

Here a pretty baby lies
Sung asleep with lullabies;
Pray be silent, and not stir
Th' easy earth that covers her.

ROBERT HERRICK

311 *An Epitaph*

Here lies a most beautiful lady,
Light of step and heart was she;
I think she was the most beautiful lady
That ever was in the West Country.

But beauty vanishes: beauty passes;
However rare — rare it be;
And when I crumble, who will remember
This lady of the West Country?

WALTER DE LA MARE

312 *Ariel's Song*

Full fathom five thy father lies;
  Of his bones are coral made:
Those are pearls that were his eyes:
  Nothing of him that doth fade,
But doth suffer a sea-change
  Into something rich and strange.
Sea-nymphs hourly ring his knell:
Hark! now I hear them,–ding-dong, bell.

WILLIAM SHAKESPEARE

313 *A Land Dirge*

Call for the robin-redbreast and the wren,
Since o'er shady groves they hover,
And with leaves and flowers do cover
The friendless bodies of unburied men.
Call unto his funeral dole
The ant, the field-mouse, and the mole,
To rear him hillocks that shall keep him warm,
And (when gay tombs are robb'd) sustain no harm;
But keep the wolf far thence, that's foe to men,
For with his nails he'll dig them up again.

JOHN WEBSTER

314 *Dirge in the Woods*

A wind sways the pines,
    And below
Not a breath of wild air;
Still as the mosses that glow
On the flooring and over the lines
Of the roots here and there.
The pine-tree drops its dead;
They are quiet, as under the sea.
Overhead, overhead

Rushes life in a race,
As the clouds the clouds chase;
  And we go,
And we drop like the fruits of the tree,
   Even we,
   Even so.

GEORGE MEREDITH

315 *Witches' Charm*

The owl is abroad, the bat, and the toad,
 And so is the cat-a-mountain,
The ant, and the mole sit both in a hole,
 And frog peeps out o' the fountain;
The dogs, they do bay, and the timbrels play,
 The spindle is now a-turning;
The moon it is red, and the stars are fled,
 But all the sky is a burning:
The ditch is made, and our nails the spade,
With pictures full, of wax, and of wool;
Their livers I stick, with needles quick;
There lacks but the blood, to make up the flood.
 Quickly DAME, then, bring your part in,
 Spur, spur, upon little MARTIN,
 Merrily, merrily, make him sail,
 A worm in his mouth, and a thorn in's tail,
 Fire above, and fire below,
 With a whip i' your hand, to make him go.

   O, now she's come!
   Let all be dumb.

BEN JONSON

316 *The Curse of Kehama*

  I charm thy life
 From the weapons of strife,
 From stone and from wood,
 From fire and from flood,
 From the serpent's tooth,
 And the beasts of blood:
 From Sickness I charm thee,

And Time shall not harm thee;
　But Earth which is mine,
　Its fruits shall deny thee;
　And Water shall hear me,
　And know thee and fly thee;
And the Winds shall not touch thee
　When they pass by thee,
And the Dews shall not wet thee,
　When they fall nigh thee:
　And thou shalt seek Death
　To release thee, in vain;
　Thou shalt live in thy pain
　While Kehama shall reign,
　With a fire in thy heart,
　And a fire in thy brain;
　And Sleep shall obey me,
　　And visit thee never,
And the Curse shall be on thee
　For ever and ever.

ROBERT SOUTHEY

317 *The Minstrel's Song*

Oh! sing unto my roundelay;
　Oh! drop the briny tear with me;
Dance no more at holiday;
　Like a running river be.
　　My love is dead,
　　Gone to his death-bed,
　　All under the willow-tree.

Black his crine as the winter night,
　White his rode [1] as the summer snow,
Red his face as the morning light;
　Cold he lies in the grave below.
　　My love is dead,
　　Gone to his death-bed,
　　All under the willow-tree.

Sweet his tongue as the throstle's note,
　Quick in dance as thought can be,

[1] complexion

Deft his tabour, cudgel stout;
  Oh! he lies by the willow-tree.
    My love is dead,
    Gone to his death-bed,
    All under the willow-tree.

Hark! the raven flaps his wing,
  In the briared dell below;
Hark! the death-owl loud doth sing
  To the night-mares, as they go.
    My love is dead,
    Gone to his death-bed,
    All under the willow-tree.

See! the white moon shines on high,
  Whiter is my true love's shroud,
Whiter than the morning sky,
  Whiter than the evening cloud.
    My love is dead,
    Gone to his death-bed,
    All under the willow-tree.

Here, upon my true love's grave,
  Shall the barren flowers be laid;
Not one holy saint to save
  All the celness [1] of a maid.
    My love is dead,
    Gone to his death-bed,
    All under the willow-tree.

With my hands I'll dente [2] the briars,
  Round his holy corse to gre [3],
Elfin fairy, light your fires,
  Here, my body still shall be.
    My love is dead,
    Gone to his death-bed,
    All under the willow-tree.

Come, with acorn-cup and thorn,
  Drain my hartys blood away;
Life and all its good I scorn,
  Dance by night, or feast by day.

[1] coldness   [2] fasten   [3] grow

My love is dead,
Gone to his death-bed,
All under the willow-tree.

Water-witches, crowned with reytes [1],
Bear me to your lethal tide.
I die; I come; my true love waits.
Thus the damsel spake and died.

THOMAS CHATTERTON

318 *Celanta at the Well of Life*

Gently dip, but not too deep,
For fear you make the golden beard to weep.
Fair maiden, white and red,
Comb me smooth, and stroke my head,
And thou shalt have some cockell-bread.
Gently dip, but not too deep,
For fear thou make the golden beard to weep.
Fair maid, white and red,
Comb me smooth, and stroke my head,
And every hair a sheaf shall be,
And every sheaf a golden tree.

GEORGE PEELE

319 *Thrice toss these Oaken ashes in the air*

Thrice toss these Oaken ashes in the air,
Thrice sit thou mute in this inchanted chair;
And thrice three times tie up this true loves knot,
And murmur soft, she will, or she will not.

Go burn these pois'nous weeds in yon blue fire,
These Screech-owls' feathers and this prickling briar;
This Cypress gathered at a dead man's grave;
That all thy fears and cares, an end may have.

Then come, you Fairies, dance with me a round;
Melt her hard heart with your melodious sound:
In vain are all the charms I can devise:
She hath an Art to break them with her eyes.

THOMAS CAMPION

[1] water-flags

320 *The Mad Maid's Song*

Good-morrow to the day so fair;
　　Good-morning Sir to you;
Good-morrow to mine own torn hair
　　Bedabbled with the dew.

Good-morning to this primrose too;
　　Good-morrow to each maid;
That will with flowers the tomb bestrew,
　　Wherein my love is laid.

Ah! Woe is me, woe, woe is me,
　　Alack and well-a-day!
For pity, Sir, find out that bee,
　　Which bore my love away.

I'll seek him in your bonnet brave;
　　I'll seek him in your eyes;
Nay, now I think th'ave made his grave
　　I'th'bed of strawberries.

I'll seek him there; I know, ere this,
　　The cold, cold earth doth shake him;
But I will go, or send a kiss
　　By you, Sir, to awake him.

Pray, hurt him not; though he be dead,
　　He knows well who do love him,
And who with green turfs rear his head,
　　And who do rudely move him.

He's soft and tender (pray take heed)
　　With bands of cowslips bind him;
And bring him home, but 'tis decreed
　　That I shall never find him.

ROBERT HERRICK

321 *Song*

Oh roses for the flush of youth,
　　And laurel for the perfect prime;
But pluck an ivy branch for me
　　Grown old before my time.

Oh violets for the grave of youth,
　　And bay for those dead in their prime;
Give me the withered leaves I chose
　　Before in the old time.

CHRISTINA ROSSETTI

322 *A Dirge*

Why were you born when the snow was falling?
You should have come to the cuckoo's calling,
Or when grapes are green in the cluster,
Or, at least, when lithe swallows muster
　　For their far off flying
　　From summer dying.

Why did you die when the lambs were cropping?
You should have died at the apples' dropping,
When the grasshopper comes to trouble,
And the wheat-fields are sodden stubble,
　　And all winds go sighing
　　For sweet things dying.

CHRISTINA ROSSETTI

323 *Up-hill*

Does the road wind up-hill all the way?
　　Yes, to the very end.
Will the day's journey take the whole long day?
　　From morn to night, my friend.

But is there for the night a resting-place?
　　A roof for when the slow dark hours begin.
May not the darkness hide it from my face?
　　You cannot miss that inn.

Shall I meet other wayfarers at night?
   Those who have gone before.
Then must I knock, or call when just in sight?
   They will not keep you standing at that door.

Shall I find comfort, travel-sore and weak?
   Of labour you shall find the sum.
Will there be beds for me and all who seek?
   Yea, beds for all who come.

CHRISTINA ROSSETTI

324 *Lucy*

She dwelt among the untrodden ways
   Beside the springs of Dove,
A maid whom there were none to praise
   And very few to love:

A violet by a mossy stone
   Half hidden from the eye!
–Fair as a star, when only one
   Is shining in the sky.

She lived unknown, and few could know
   When Lucy ceased to be;
But she is in her grave, and, oh,
   The difference to me!

WILLIAM WORDSWORTH

325 *Song*

   'A widow bird sate mourning
    Upon a wintry bough.'

Heigho! the lark and the owl!
   One flies the morning, and one lulls the night:–
Only the nightingale, poor fond soul,
   Sings like the fool through darkness and light.

'A widow bird sate mourning for her love
   Upon a wintry bough;
The frozen wind crept on above,
   The freezing stream below.

'There was no leaf upon the forest bare,
    No flower upon the ground,
And little motion in the air
    Except the mill-wheel's sound.'

PERCY BYSSHE SHELLEY

326 *Dirge*

A voice from the waters :

The swallow leaves her nest,
The soul my weary breast;
But therefore let the rain
    On my grave
Fall pure; for why complain
Since both will come again
    O'er the wave?
The wind dead leaves and snow
Doth hurry to and fro;
And, once, a day shall break
    O'er the wave,
When a storm of ghosts shall shake
The dead, until they wake
    In the grave.

THOMAS LOVELL BEDDOES

327 *Lines*

Shall earth no more inspire thee,
    Thou lonely dreamer, now?
Since passion may not fire thee,
    Shall nature cease to bow?

Thy mind is ever moving
    In regions dark to thee;
Recall its useless roving;
    Come back, and dwell with me.

I know my mountain-breezes
    Enchant and soothe thee still,
I know my sunshine pleases,
    Despite thy wayward will.

When day with evening blending,
   Sinks from the summer sky,
I've seen thy spirit bending
   In fond idolatry.

I've watched thee every hour;
   I know my mighty sway:
I know my magic power
   To drive thy griefs away.

Few hearts to mortals given,
   On earth so wildly pine;
Yet few would ask a heaven
   More like this earth than thine.

Then let my winds caress thee;
   Thy comrade let me be:
Since nought beside can bless thee,
   Return—and dwell with me.

EMILY BRONTË

328 *Chorus*

Yea, the coneys are scared by the thud of hoofs,
And their white scuts flash at their vanishing heels,
And swallows abandon the hamlet-roofs.

The mole's tunnelled chambers are crushed by wheels,
The lark's eggs scattered, their owners fled;
And the hedgehog's household the sapper unseals.[1]

The snail draws in at the terrible tread,
But in vain; he is crushed by the felloe-rim;
The worm asks what can be overhead,

And wriggles deep from a scene so grim,
And guesses him safe; for he does not know
What a foul red flood will be soaking him!

[1] Variation: 'And the hare's hid litter the sapper unseals.'

Beaten about by the heel and toe
Are butterflies, sick of the day's long rheum,
To die of a worse than the weather-foe.

Trodden and bruised to a miry tomb
Are ears that have greened but will never be gold,
And flowers in the bud that will never bloom.

THOMAS HARDY

329 *Lines*

The cold earth slept below,
    Above the cold sky shone;
And all around, with a chilling sound,
    From caves of ice and fields of snow,
    The breath of night like death did flow
        Beneath the sinking moon.

The wintry hedge was black,
    The green grass was not seen,
The birds did rest on the bare thorn's breast,
    Whose roots, beside the pathway track,
    Had bound their folds o'er many a crack
        Which the frost had made between.

Thine eyes glowed in the glare
    Of the moon's dying light;
As a fen-fire's beam on a sluggish stream
    Gleams dimly, so the moon shone there,
    And it yellowed the strings of thy raven hair,
        That shook in the wind of night.

The moon made thy lips pale, beloved–
    The wind made thy bosom chill–
The night did shed on thy dear head
    Its frozen dew, and thou didst lie
    Where the bitter breath of the naked sky
        Might visit thee at will.

PERCY BYSSHE SHELLEY

330 *Desdemona's Song*

The poor soul sat sighing by a sycamore tree,
    Sing all a green willow;
Her hand on her bosom, her head on her knee,
    Sing willow, willow, willow:
The fresh streams ran by her, and murmur'd her moans;
    Sing willow, willow, willow:
Her salt tears fell from her, and soften'd the stones;–
    Sing willow, willow, willow:
I call'd my love false love; but what said he then?
    Sing willow, willow, willow:
If I court moe women, you'll couch with moe men.

WILLIAM SHAKESPEARE

331 *Fall, leaves, fall*

Fall, leaves, fall; die, flowers, away;
Lengthen night, and shorten day!
Every leaf speaks bliss to me,
Fluttering from the autumn tree.

I shall smile when wreaths of snow
Blossom where the rose should grow;
I shall sing when night's decay
Ushers in a drearier day.

EMILY BRONTË

332 *Song*

Care charming sleep, thou easer of all woes,
Brother to death, sweetly thy self dispose
On this afflicted Prince, fall like a Cloud
In gentle show'rs, give nothing that is loud,
Or painful to his slumbers; easy, sweet,
And as a purling stream, thou son of night,
Pass by his troubled senses; sing his pain

Like hollow murmuring wind, or silver Rain,
Into this Prince gently, Oh gently slide,
And kiss him into slumbers like a Bride.

JOHN FLETCHER

333 *A little child, a limber elf*

A little child, a limber elf,
Singing, dancing to itself,
A fairy thing with red round cheeks,
That always finds, and never seeks,
Makes such a vision to the sight
As fills a father's eyes with light;
And pleasures flow in so thick and fast
Upon his heart, that he at last
Must needs express his love's excess
With words of unmeant bitterness.
Perhaps 'tis pretty to force together
Thoughts so all unlike each other;
To mutter and mock a broken charm,
To dally with wrong that does no harm.
Perhaps 'tis tender too and pretty
At each wild word to feel within
A sweet recoil of love and pity.
And what, if in a world of sin
(O sorrow and shame should this be true!)
Such giddiness of heart and brain
Comes seldom save from rage and pain,
So talks as it's most used to do.

SAMUEL TAYLOR COLERIDGE

334 *Sephestia's Song to her Child*

Weep not my wanton smile upon my knee:
When thou art old there's grief enough for thee.
      Mother's wag, pretty boy,
      Father's sorrow, father's joy.
      When thy father first did see
      Such a boy by him and me,

He was glad, I was woe,
Fortune changed made him so,
When he left his pretty boy,
Last his sorrow, first his joy.
Weep not my wanton smile upon my knee:
When thou art old there's grief enough for thee.
Streaming tears that never stint,
Like pearl drops from a flint
Fell by course from his eyes,
That one anothers' place supplies:
Thus he griev'd in every part,
Tears of blood fell from his heart,
When he left his pretty boy,
Father's sorrow, father's joy.
Weep not my wanton smile upon my knee:
When thou art old there's grief enough for thee.
The wanton smiled, father wept:
Mother cried, baby leapt:
More he crowed, more we cried;
Nature could not sorrow hide.
He must go, he must kiss
Child and mother, baby bliss:
For he left his pretty boy,
Father's sorrow, father's joy.
Weep not my wanton smile upon my knee:
When thou art old there's grief enough for thee.

ROBERT GREENE

335 *Lullaby*

Golden slumbers kiss your eyes,
Smiles awake you when you rise
Sleep, pretty wantons, do not cry,
And I will sing a lullaby;
Rock them, rock them, lullaby.

Care is heavy, therefore sleep you;
You are care, and care must keep you.
Sleep, pretty wantons, do not cry,
And I will sing a lullaby:
Rock them, rock them, lullaby.

THOMAS DEKKER

336 *The Fairies' Song*

You spotted snakes with double tongue,
    Thorny hedgehogs, be not seen;
Newts, and blind-worms, do no wrong;
    Come not near our Fairy Queen.

    Philomel, with melody,
    Sing in our sweet lullaby;
Lulla, lulla, lullaby;
        lulla, lulla, lullaby:
    Never harm,
    Nor spell, nor charm,
    Come our lovely lady nigh;
    So, good night, with lullaby.

Weaving spiders come not here;
    Hence, you long-legg'd spinners, hence!
Beetles black, approach not near;
    Worm nor snail, do no offence.

    Philomel, with melody,
    Sing in our sweet lullaby;
Lulla, lulla, lullaby;
        lulla, lulla, lullaby:
    Never harm,
    Nor spell, nor charm,
    Come our lovely lady nigh;
    So, good night, with lullaby.

                              WILLIAM SHAKESPEARE

337 *Echo's Song*

Slow, slow, fresh fount, keep time with my salt tears;
    Yet slower, yet, o faintly gentle springs:
List to the heavy part the music bears,
    Woe weeps out her division, when she sings.
        Droop herbs, and flowers;
        Fall grief in showers;
        Our beauties are not ours.

O, I could still
Like melting snow upon some craggy hill,
   Drop, drop, drop, drop,
Since nature's pride is now a wither'd daffodill.

BEN JONSON

338 *An Hymn*

Drop, drop, slow tears,
   and bathe those beauteous feet,
Which brought from heav'n
   the news and Prince of peace:
Cease not, wet eyes,
   his mercies to intreat;
To cry for vengeance
   sin doth never cease:
In your deep floods
   drown all my faults and fears;
Nor let his eye
   see sin, but through my tears.

PHINEAS FLETCHER

339 *Lament*

Chaste maids which haunt fair Aganippe's well,
And you in Tempe's sacred shade who dwell,
Let fall your harps, cease tunes of joy to sing,
Dishevelled make all Parnassus ring
With anthems sad; thy music, Phoebus, turn
In doleful plaints, whilst joy itself doth mourn:
Dead is thy darling who decor'd thy bays,
Who oft was wont to cherish thy sweet lays,
And to a trumpet raise thine amorous style,
That floating Delos envy might this isle.
You Acidalian archers break your bows,
Your brandons quench, with tears blot beauty's snows,
And bid your weeping mother yet again
A second Adon's death, nay Mars's plain.
His eyes once were your darts, nay, even his name,
Wherever heard, did every heart inflame:
Tagus did court his love with golden streams,
Rhine with his towns, fair Seine with all she claims.

But ah! poor lovers, death did them betray,
And, not suspected, made their hopes his prey.
Tagus bewails his loss with golden streams,
Rhine with his towns, fair Seine with all she claims.
Moeliades sweet courtly nymphs deplore,
From Thule to Hydaspes' pearly shore.
  Delicious meads, whose chequer'd plain forth brings
White, golden, azure flowers, which once were kings,
In mourning black their shining colours dye,
Bow down their heads, whilst sighing zephyrs fly.
Queen of the fields, whose blush makes blush the morn,
Sweet rose, a prince's death in purple mourn;
O hyacinths, for aye your AI keep still,
Nay, with more marks of woe your leaves now fill;
And you, O flower of Helen's tears first born,
Into those liquid pearls again you turn;
Your green locks, forests, cut; in weeping myrrhs,
The deadly cypress, and ink-dropping firs,
Your palms and myrtles change; from shadows dark,
Wing'd syrens, wail; and you, sad echoes, mark
The lamentable accents of their moan,
And plain that brave Moeliades is gone.
Stay, sky, thy turning course, and now become
A stately arch unto the earth, his tomb;
Over which aye the wat'ry Iris keep,
And sad Electra's sisters which still weep.
Moeliades sweet courtly nymphs deplore,
From Thule to Hydaspes' pearly shore.

WILLIAM DRUMMOND

340   *Weep you no more*

Weep you no more, sad fountains;
  What need you flow so fast?
Look how the snowy mountains
  Heaven's sun doth gently waste.
    But my sun's heavenly eyes
      View not your weeping,
      That now lies sleeping
    Softly, now softly lies
      Sleeping.

Sleep is a reconciling,
  A rest that peace begets.
Doth not the sun rise smiling
    When fair at ev'n he sets?
      Rest you then, rest, sad eyes,
        Melt not in weeping
        While she lies sleeping
      Softly, now softly lies
        Sleeping.

JOHN DOWLAND

341 *Lines*

A slumber did my spirit seal;
  I had no human fears:
She seemed a thing that could not feel
  The touch of earthly years.

No motion has she now, no force;
  She neither hears nor sees;
Rolled round in earth's diurnal course,
  With rocks, and stones, and trees.

WILLIAM WORDSWORTH

342 *A Lament*

O world! O life! O time!
On whose last steps I climb,
  Trembling at that where I had stood before;
When will return the glory of your prime?
    No more–Oh, never more!

Out of the day and night
A joy has taken flight;
  Fresh spring, and summer, and winter hoar,
Move my faint heart with grief, but with delight
    No more–Oh, never more!

PERCY BYSSHE SHELLEY

L

343 *The Indian Serenade*

I arise from dreams of thee
In the first sweet sleep of night,
When the winds are breathing low,
And the stars are shining bright:
I arise from dreams of thee,
And a spirit in my feet
Hath led me—who knows how?
To thy chamber window, Sweet!

The wandering airs they faint
On the dark, the silent stream—
The Champak odours fail
Like sweet thoughts in a dream;
The nightingale's complaint,
It dies upon her heart;
As I must on thine,
Oh, belovèd as thou art!

Oh lift me from the grass!
I die! I faint! I fail!
Let thy love in kisses rain
On my lips and eyelids pale.
My cheek is cold and white, alas!
My heart beats loud and fast;
Oh! press it to thine own again,
Where it will break at last.

PERCY BYSSHE SHELLEY

344 *Heaven-Haven*

A nun takes the veil

I have desired to go
  Where springs not fail,
To fields where flies no sharp and sided hail
  And a few lilies blow.

And I have asked to be
  Where no storms come,
Where the green swell is in the havens dumb,
  And out of the swing of the sea.
GERARD MANLEY HOPKINS

345 *Lullaby*

Upon my lap my sovereign sits
  And sucks upon my breast.
Meanwhile his love sustains my life,
  And gives my body rest.
    Sing lullaby, my little boy,
    Sing lullaby, my only joy.

When thou hast taken thy repast,
  Repose, my babe, on me;
So may thy mother and thy nurse
  Thy cradle also be.
    Sing lullaby, my little boy,
    Sing lullaby, my only joy.

I grieve that duty doth not work
  All what my wishing would,
Because I would not be to thee
  But in the best I should.
    Sing lullaby, my little boy,
    Sing lullaby, my only joy.

Yet as I am, and as I may,
  I must and will be thine,
Though all too little for thyself,
  Vouchsafing to be mine.
    Sing lullaby, my little boy,
    Sing lullaby, my only joy.
RICHARD VERSTEGAN

346 *Grace for a Child*

Here a little child I stand
Heaving up my either hand;

Cold as paddocks though they be,
Here I lift them up to Thee,
For a benison to fall
On our meat, and on us all. *Amen.*

ROBERT HERRICK

347 *Infant Joy*

'I have no name:
'I am but two days old.'
What shall I call thee?
'I happy am,
'Joy is my name.'
Sweet joy befall thee!

Pretty joy!
Sweet joy but two days old,
Sweet joy I call thee:
Thou dost smile,
I sing the while,
Sweet joy befall thee!

WILLIAM BLAKE

348 *Songs of Innocence: Introduction*

Piping down the valleys wild,
Piping songs of pleasant glee,
On a cloud I saw a child,
And he laughing said to me:

'Pipe a song about a Lamb !'
So I piped with merry chear.
'Piper, pipe that song again;'
So I piped: he wept to hear.

'Drop thy pipe, thy happy pipe;
'Sing thy songs of happy chear:'
So I sung the same again,
While he wept with joy to hear.

'Piper, sit thee down and write
'In a book, that all may read.'
So he vanish'd from my sight,
And I pluck'd a hollow reed,

And I made a rural pen,
And I stain'd the water clear,
And I wrote my happy songs
Every child may joy to hear.

WILLIAM BLAKE

349 *The Lamb*

Little Lamb, who made thee?
  Dost thou know who made thee?
Gave thee life, & bid thee feed
By the stream & o'er the mead;
Gave thee clothing of delight,
Softest clothing, woolly, bright;
Gave thee such a tender voice,
Making all the vales rejoice?
  Little Lamb, who made thee?
  Dost thou know who made thee?

Little Lamb, I'll tell thee,
  Little Lamb, I'll tell thee:
He is called by thy name,
For he calls himself a Lamb.
He is meek, & he is mild;
He became a little child.
I a child, & thou a lamb,
We are called by his name.
  Little Lamb, God bless thee!
  Little Lamb, God bless thee!

WILLIAM BLAKE

350 *The Tyger*

Tyger! Tyger! burning bright
In the forests of the night,
What immortal hand or eye
Could frame thy fearful symmetry?

In what distant deeps or skies
Burnt the fire of thine eyes?
On what wings dare he aspire?
What the hand dare seize the fire?

And what shoulder, & what art,
Could twist the sinews of thy heart?
And when thy heart began to beat,
What dread hand? & what dread feet?

What the hammer? what the chain?
In what furnace was thy brain?
What the anvil? what dread grasp
Dare its deadly terrors clasp?

When the stars threw down their spears,
And water'd heaven with their tears,
Did he smile his work to see?
Did he who made the Lamb make thee?

Tyger! Tyger! burning bright
In the forests of the night,
What immortal hand or eye,
Dare frame thy fearful symmetry?

WILLIAM BLAKE

351 *Songs of Experience: Introduction*

Hear the voice of the Bard!
Who Present, Past, & Future sees;
The Holy Word
Whose ears have heard
That walk'd among the ancient trees,

Calling the lapsed Soul,
And weeping in the evening dew;
That might controll
The starry pole,
And fallen, fallen light renew!

'O Earth, O Earth, return!
'Arise from out the dewy grass;
'Night is worn,
'And the morn
'Rises from the slumberous mass.

'Turn away no more;
'Why wilt thou turn away?
'The starry floor,
'The wat'ry shore,
'Is giv'n thee till the break of day.'

WILLIAM BLAKE

352 *Morning*

To find the Western path
Right thro' the Gates of Wrath
I urge my way;
Sweet Mercy leads me on:
With soft repentant moan
I see the break of day.

The war of swords & spears
Melted by dewy tears
Exhales on high;
The Sun is freed from fears
And with soft grateful tears
Ascends the sky.

WILLIAM BLAKE

353 *The Clod and the Pebble*

'Love seeketh not Itself to please,
'Nor for itself hath any care,
'But for another gives its ease,
'And builds a Heaven in Hell's despair.'

So sung a little Clod of Clay
Trodden with the cattle's feet,
But a Pebble of the brook
Warbled out these metres meet:

'Love seeketh only Self to please,
'To bind another to Its delight,
'Joys in another's loss of ease,
'And builds a Hell in Heaven's despite.'

WILLIAM BLAKE

354 *The Garden of Love*

I went to the Garden of Love,
And saw what I never had seen:
A Chapel was built in the midst,
Where I used to play on the green.

And the gates of this Chapel were shut,
And 'Thou shalt not' writ over the door;
So I turn'd to the Garden of Love
That so many sweet flowers bore;

And I saw it filled with graves,
And tomb-stones where flowers should be;
And Priests in black gowns were walking their rounds,
And binding with briars my joys & desires.

WILLIAM BLAKE

355 *Lines*

Clear had the day been from the dawn,
All chequer'd was the sky,
The clouds, like scarfs of cobweb lawn,
Veil'd heaven's most glorious eye.
The wind had no more strength than this,
—That leisurely it blew—
To make one leaf the next to kiss
That closely by it grew.
The rills, that on the pebbles play'd,
Might now be heard at will;
This world the only music made,
Else every thing was still.

The flowers, like brave embroider'd girls,
    Look'd as they most desired
To see whose head with orient pearls
    Most curiously was tyred.
And to itself the subtle air
    Such sovreignty assumes,
That it receiv'd too large a share
    From Nature's rich perfumes. . . .

MICHAEL DRAYTON

356 *Into Battle*

The naked earth is warm with Spring,
    And with green grass and bursting trees
Leans to the sun's gaze glorying,
    And quivers in the sunny breeze;

And life is Colour and Warmth and Light,
    And a striving evermore for these;
And he is dead who will not fight,
    And who dies fighting has increase.

The fighting man shall from the sun
    Take warmth, and life from the glowing earth;
Speed with the light-foot winds to run,
    And with the trees to newer birth;
And find, when fighting shall be done,
    Great rest, and fullness after dearth.

All the bright company of Heaven
    Hold him in their high comradeship,
The Dog-star, and the Sisters Seven,
    Orion's Belt and sworded hip.

The woodland trees that stand together,
    They stand to him each one a friend;
They gently speak in the windy weather;
    They guide to valley and ridge's end.

The kestrel hovering by day,
  And the little owls that call by night,
Bid him be swift and keen as they,
  As keen of ear, as swift of sight.

The blackbird sings to him, 'Brother, brother,
  If this be the last song you shall sing
Sing well, for you may not sing another;
  Brother, sing.'

In dreary doubtful waiting hours,
  Before the brazen frenzy starts,
The horses show him nobler powers;–
  O patient eyes, courageous hearts!

And when the burning moment breaks,
  And all things else are out of mind,
And only Joy of Battle takes
  Him by the throat and makes him blind,

Through joy and blindness he shall know,
  Not caring much to know, that still
Nor lead nor steel shall reach him, so
  That it be not the Destined Will.

The thundering line of battle stands,
  And in the air Death moans and sings;
But Day shall clasp him with strong hands,
  And Night shall fold him in soft wings.

JULIAN GRENFELL

357 *To the Rev. Mr. Newton*

An Invitation into the Country

The swallows in their torpid state
  Compose their useless wing,
And bees in hives as idly wait
  The call of early Spring.

The keenest frost that binds the stream,
    The wildest wind that blows,
Are neither felt nor fear'd by them,
    Secure of their repose.

But man, all feeling and awake,
    The gloomy scene surveys,
With present ills his heart must ache,
    And pant for brighter days.

Old Winter, halting o'er the mead,
    Bids me and Mary mourn;
But lovely Spring peeps o'er his head,
    And whispers your return.

Then April with her sister May
    Shall chase him from the bowers,
And weave fresh garlands every day,
    To crown the smiling hours.

And if a tear that speaks regret
    Of happier times appear,
A glimpse of joy that we have met
    Shall shine, and dry the tear.

WILLIAM COWPER

358 *A Song*

Ask me no more, where Jove bestows,
When June is past, the fading rose?
For in your Beauties orient deep
'These flowers, as in their causes, sleep.

Ask me no more, whither do stray
The golden atoms of the day?
For in pure love heaven did prepare
Those powders to inrich your hair.

Ask me no more, whither doth haste
The Nightingale, when May is past?
For in your sweet dividing throat
She winters, and keeps warm her note.

Ask me no more, where those stars light,
That downwards fall in dead of night?
For in your eyes they sit, and there
Fixed, become as in their sphere.

Ask me no more, if east or west
The Phœnix builds her spicy nest?
For unto you at last she flies,
And in your fragrant bosom dies.

THOMAS CAREW

359 *Rose Aylmer*

Ah what avails the sceptred race,
    Ah what the form divine!
What every virtue, every grace!
    Rose Aylmer, all were thine.
Rose Aylmer, whom these wakeful eyes
    May weep, but never see,
A night of memories and of sighs
    I consecrate to thee.

WALTER SAVAGE LANDOR

360 *Dirce*

Stand close around, ye Stygian set,
    With Dirce in one boat conveyed!
Or Charon, seeing, may forget
    That he is old and she a shade.

WALTER SAVAGE LANDOR

361 *An Ode for Ben Jonson*

Ah Ben!
    Say how, or when
    Shall we thy guests
Meet at those lyric feasts,
    Made at the Sun,
The Dog, the Triple Tun?

Where we such clusters had,
As made us nobly wild, not mad;
And yet each verse of thine
Out-did the meat, out-did the frolic wine.

My Ben!
Or come again:
Or send to us
Thy wit's great overplus;
But teach us yet
Wisely to husband it,
Lest we that talent spend:
And having once brought to an end
That precious stock; the store
Of such a wit the world should have no more.

ROBERT HERRICK

362 *Memorabilia*

Ah, did you once see Shelley plain,
And did he stop and speak to you
And did you speak to him again?
How strange it seems and new!

But you were living before that,
And also you are living after;
And the memory I started at—
My starting moves your laughter.

I crossed a moor, with a name of its own
And a certain use in the world no doubt,
Yet a hand's-breadth of it shines alone
'Mid the blank miles round about:

For there I picked up on the heather
And there I put inside my breast
A moulted feather, an eagle-feather!
Well, I forget the rest.

ROBERT BROWNING

363 *Lines on the Mermaid Tavern*

Souls of Poets dead and gone,
What Elysium have ye known,
Happy field or mossy cavern,
Choicer than the Mermaid Tavern?
Have ye tippled drink more fine
Than mine host's Canary wine?
Or are fruits of Paradise
Sweeter than those dainty pies
Of venison? O generous food!
Drest as though bold Robin Hood
Would, with his maid Marian,
Sup and bowse from horn and can.

I have heard that on a day
Mine host's sign-board flew away,
Nobody knew whither, till
An astrologer's old quill
To a sheepskin gave the story,
Said he saw you in your glory,
Underneath a new-old sign
Sipping beverage divine,
And pledging with contented smack
The Mermaid in the Zodiac.

Souls of Poets dead and gone,
What Elysium have ye known,
Happy field or mossy cavern,
Choicer than the Mermaid Tavern?

JOHN KEATS

364 *The Monk*

I saw a Monk of Charlemaine
Arise before my sight:
I talk'd with the Grey Monk as we stood
In beams of infernal light.

Gibbon arose with a lash of steel,
And Voltaire with a wracking wheel:
The Schools, in clouds of learning roll'd,
Arose with War in iron & gold.

'Thou lazy Monk,' they sound afar,
'In vain condemning glorious War;
    'And in your Cell you shall ever dwell:
'Rise, War, & bind him in his Cell!'

The blood red ran from the Grey Monk's side,
His hands & feet were wounded wide,
    His body bent, his arms & knees
Like to the roots of ancient trees.

When Satan first the black bow bent
And the Moral Law from the Gospel rent,
    He forg'd the Law into a Sword
And spill'd the blood of mercy's Lord.

Titus! Constantine! Charlemaine!
O Voltaire! Rousseau! Gibbon! Vain
    Your Grecian Mocks & Roman Sword
Against this image of his Lord!

For a Tear is an Intellectual thing,
And a Sigh is the Sword of an Angel King,
    And the bitter groan of a Martyr's woe
Is an Arrow from the Almightie's Bow.

WILLIAM BLAKE

365 *A Song*

If Wine and Musick have the Pow'r,
To ease the Sickness of the Soul;
Let Phoebus ev'ry String explore;
And Bacchus fill the sprightly Bowl.
Let Them their friendly Aid imploy,
To make my Cloe's Absence light;
And seek for Pleasure, to destroy
    The Sorrows of this live-long Night.

But She to Morrow will return:
Venus, be Thou to Morrow great;
Thy Myrtles strow, Thy Odours burn;
And meet Thy Fav'rite Nymph in State.

Kind Goddess, to no other Pow'rs
Let Us to Morrow's Blessings own:
Thy darling Loves shall guide the Hours;
And all the Day be Thine alone.

MATTHEW PRIOR

366 *Drinking*

The thirsty Earth soaks up the Rain,
And drinks, and gapes for Drink again.
The Plants suck in the Earth, and are
With constant Drinking fresh and fair.
The Sea it self, which one would think
Should have but little need of Drink,
Twice ten thousand Rivers up,
So fill'd that they o'er-flow the Cup.
The busy Sun (and one would guess
By 's drunken fiery Face no less)
Drinks up the Sea, and when he 'as done,
The Moon and Stars drink up the Sun.
They drink and dance by their own Light,
They drink and revel all the Night.
Nothing in Nature's sober found,
But an eternal Health goes round.
Fill up the Bowl then, fill it high,
Fill all the Glasses there, for why
Should ev'ry Creature Drink but I,
Why, Man of Morals, tell me why?

ABRAHAM COWLEY

367 *To Live Merrily and to Trust to Good Verses*

Now is the time for mirth,
  Nor cheek, or tongue be dumb;
For, with the flowery earth,
  The golden pomp is come.

The golden pomp is come;
  For now each tree does wear
(Made of her pap and gum)
  Rich beads of amber here.

Now reigns the rose, and now
　Th' Arabian dew besmears
My uncontrolled brow
　And my retorted hairs.

Homer, this health to thee,
　In sack of such a kind
That it would make thee see
　Though thou wert ne'er so blind.

Next, Virgil I'll call forth,
　To pledge this second health
In wine, whose each cup's worth
　An Indian commonwealth.

A goblet next I'll drink
　To Ovid and suppose,
Made he the pledge, he'd think
　The world had all one nose.

Then this immensive cup
　Of aromatic wine,
Catullus, I quaff up
　To that terse muse of thine.

Wild I am now with heat:
　O Bacchus, cool thy rays!
Or, frantic, I shall eat
　Thy thyrse, and bite the bays.

Round, round the roof does run;
　And being ravisht thus,
Come, I will drink a tun
　To my Propertius.

Now, to Tibullus, next,
　This flood I drink to thee:
But stay; I see a text,
　That this presents to me.

Behold, Tibullus lies
　Here burnt, whose small return
Of ashes, scarce suffice
　To fill a little urn.

Trust to good verses then;
   They only will aspire,
   When pyramids, as men,
     Are lost, i' th' funeral fire.

And when all bodies meet
   In Lethe to be drown'd;
Then only numbers sweet
   With endless life are crown'd.

ROBERT HERRICK

368 *His Poetry his Pillar*

Only a little more
   I have to write,
   Then I'll give o'er,
And bid the world good-night.

'Tis but a flying minute
   That I must stay,
   Or linger in it;
And then I must away.

O time that cut'st down all
   And scarce leav'st here
   Memorial
Of any men that were.

How many lie forgot
   In vaults beneath?
   And piecemeal rot
Without a fame in death?

Behold this living stone
   I rear for me,
   Ne'er to be thrown
Down, envious Time, by thee.

Pillars let some set up
   (If so they please)
   Here is my hope,
And my Pyramides.

ROBERT HERRICK

369 *The Lady's Song*

A quire of bright Beauties in Spring did appear,
To choose a *May*-lady to govern the Year;
All the Nymphs were in White, and the Shepherds in Green,
The Garland was giv'n, and *Phillis* was Queen;
But *Phillis* refus'd it, and sighing did say,
I'll not wear a Garland while *Pan* is away.

While *Pan* and fair *Syrinx*, are fled from our Shore,
The Graces are banish'd, and Love is no more:
The soft God of Pleasure that warm'd our Desires
Has broken his Bow, and extinguish'd his Fires,
And vows that himself, and his Mother, will mourn,
Till *Pan* and fair *Syrinx* in Triumph return.

Forbear your Addresses, and Court us no more,
For we will perform what the Deity swore:
But, if you dare think of deserving our Charms,
Away with your Sheephooks, and take to your Arms:
Then Laurels and Myrtles your Brows shall adorn,
When *Pan*, and his Son, and fair *Syrinx*, return.

JOHN DRYDEN

370 *Never love unless you can*

Never love unless you can
Bear with all the faults of man:
Men sometimes will jealous be,
Though but little cause they see;
   And hang the head, as discontent,
   And speak what straight they will repent.

Men that but one Saint adore,
Make a show of love to more:
Beauty must be scorn'd in none,
Though but truly serv'd in one:
   For what is courtship, but disguise?
   True hearts may have dissembling eyes.

Men when their affairs require,
Must a while themselves retire:
Sometimes hunt, and sometimes hawk,
And not ever sit and talk.
    If these, and such like you can bear,
    Then like, and love, and never fear.

THOMAS CAMPION

371 *Farewell, rewards and fairies*

*A Proper New Ballad, entitled The Fairies' Fare-
well or God-a-Mercy Will; to be sung or whistled to
the tune of the Madow Brow by the Learned; by the
Unlearned, to the tune of Fortune.*

Farewell, rewards and fairies,
    Good housewives now may say,
For now foul sluts in dairies
    Do fare as well as they;
And though they sweep their hearths no less
    Than maids were wont to do,
Yet who of late for cleanliness
    Finds sixpence in her shoe?

Lament, lament old abbeys,
    The fairies lost command,
They did but change priests' babies,
    But some have chang'd your land;
And all your children stol'n from thence
    Are now grown puritanes
Who live as changelings ever since
    For love of your domains.

At morning and at evening both,
    You merry were and glad;
So little care of sleep and sloth
    These pretty ladies had;
When Tom came home from labour,
    Or Ciss to milking rose,
Then merrily went their tabor,
    And nimbly went their toes.

Witness those rings and roundelays
   Of theirs which yet remain,
Were footed in Queen Mary's days
   On many a grassy plain.
But since of late Elizabeth
   And later James came in,
They never danc'd on any heath
   As when the time had been.

By which we note the fairies
   Were of the old profession,
Their songs were *Ave Maries*,
   Their dances were procession;
But now alas, they all are dead
   Or gone beyond the seas,
Or further from religion fled,
   Or else they take their ease.

A tell-tale in their company
   They never could endure,
And whoso kept not secretly
   Their mirth, was punished sure.
It was a just and Christian deed
   To pinch such black and blue;
Oh, how the commonwealth doth need
   Such justices as you!

Now they have left our quarters,
   A register they have,
Who can preserve their charters,
   A man both wise and grave.
A hundred of their merry pranks,
   By one that I could name
Are kept in store; con twenty thanks
   To William for the same.

To William Churne of Staffordshire
   Give laud and praises due;
Who every meal can mend your cheer
   With tales both old and true.

To William all give audience,
   And pray you for his noddle;
For all the fairies' evidence
   Were lost if it were addle.

RICHARD CORBET

372 *For my Own Monument*

As Doctors give physic by way of prevention,
   Matt alive and in health, of his tomb-stone took care,
For delays are unsafe, and his pious intention
   May haply be never fulfill'd by his Heir.

Then take Matt's word for it, the Sculptor is paid,
   That the Figure is fine, pray believe your own eye,
Yet credit but lightly what more may be said,
   For we flatter our selves, and teach marble to lie.

Yet counting as far as to fifty his years,
   His virtues and vices were as other men's are,
High hopes he conceiv'd, and he smother'd great fears,
   In a life party-colour'd, half pleasure, half care.

Nor to business a drudge, nor to faction a slave,
   He strove to make int'rest and freedom agree,
In public employments industrious and grave,
   And alone with his friends, Lord how merry was he.

Now in equipage stately, now humbly on foot,
   Both fortunes he tried, but to neither would trust,
And whirl'd in the round, as the wheel turn'd about,
   He found riches had wings, and knew man was but dust.

This verse little polish'd, tho' mighty sincere
   Sets neither his titles nor merit to view,
It says that his relics collected lie here,
   And no mortal yet knows too if this may be true.

Fierce robbers there are that infest the highway,
   So Matt may be kill'd, and his bones never found,
False witness at court, and fierce tempests at sea,
   So Matt may yet chance to be hang'd, or be drown'd.

If his bones lie in earth, roll in sea, fly in air,
  To Fate we must yield, and the thing is the same,
And if passing thou giv'st him a smile, or a tear,
  He cares not—yet prithee be kind to his Fame.

MATTHEW PRIOR

373 *The Earthly Paradise*

Of Heaven or Hell I have no power to sing,
I cannot ease the burden of your fears,
Or make quick-coming death a little thing,
Or bring again the pleasure of past years,
Nor for my words shall ye forget your tears,
Or hope again for aught that I can say,
The idle singer of an empty day.

But rather, when aweary of your mirth,
From full hearts still unsatisfied ye sigh,
And, feeling kindly unto all the earth,
Grudge every minute as it passes by,
Made the more mindful that the sweet days die—
Remember me a little then I pray,
The idle singer of an empty day.

The heavy trouble, the bewildering care
That weighs us down who live and earn our bread,
These idle verses have no power to bear;
So let me sing of names remembered,
Because they, living not, can ne'er be dead,
Or long time take their memory quite away
From us poor singers of an empty day.

Dreamer of dreams, born out of my due time,
Why should I strive to set the crooked straight?
Let it suffice me that my murmuring rhyme
Beats with light wing against the ivory gate,
Telling a tale not too importunate
To those who in the sleepy region stay,
Lulled by the singer of an empty day.

Folk say, a wizard to a northern king
At Christmas-tide such wondrous things did show,
That through one window men beheld the spring,
And through another saw the summer glow,
And through a third the fruited vines a-row,
While still, unheard, but in its wonted way,
Piped the drear wind of that December day.

So with this Earthly Paradise it is,
If ye will read aright, and pardon me,
Who strive to build a shadowy isle of bliss
Midmost the beating of the steely sea,
Where tossed about all hearts of men must be;
Whose ravening monsters mighty men shall slay,
Not the poor singer of an empty day.

WILLIAM MORRIS

Book V

DESCRIPTIONS AND OBSERVATIONS

374 *Evening*

The light passes
from ridge to ridge,
from flower to flower—
the hypaticas, wide-spread
under the light
grow faint—
the petals reach inward,
the blue tips bend
toward the bluer heart
and the flowers are lost.

The cornel-buds are still white,
but shadows dart
from the cornel-roots—
black creeps from root to root,
each leaf
cuts another leaf on the grass,
shadow seeks shadow,
then both leaf
and leaf-shadow are lost.

H. D.

375 *November*

The mellow year is hasting to its close;
The little birds have almost sung their last,
Their small notes twitter in the dreary blast—
That shrill-piped harbinger of early snows;
The patient beauty of the scentless rose,
Oft with the Morn's hoar crystal quaintly glass'd,
Hangs, a pale mourner for the summer past,
And makes a little summer where it grows:
In the chill sunbeam of the faint brief day
The dusky waters shudder as they shine,

The russet leaves obstruct the straggling way
Of cosy brooks, which no deep banks define,
And the gaunt woods, in ragged scant array,
Wrap their old limbs with sombre ivy twine.

HARTLEY COLERIDGE

376 *A Frosty Day*

Grass afield wears silver thatch;
  Palings all are edged with rime;
Frost-flowers pattern round the latch;
  Cloud nor breeze dissolve the clime:

When the waves are solid floor,
  And the clods are iron-bound,
And the boughs are crystall'd hoar,
  And the red leaf nailed aground.

When the fieldfare's flight is slow,
  And a rosy vapour rim,
Now the sun is small and low,
  Belts along the region dim.

When the ice-crack flies and flaws,
  Shore to shore, with thunder shock,
Deeper than the evening daws,
  Clearer than the village clock.

When the rusty blackbird strips,
  Bunch by bunch, the coral thorn;
And the pale day-crescent dips,
  New to heaven, a slender horn.

LORD DE TABLEY

377 *Mouse's Nest*

I found a ball of grass among the hay
And progged it as I passed and went away;
And when I looked I fancied something stirred,
And turned agen and hoped to catch the bird—
When out an old mouse bolted in the wheats
With all her young ones hanging at her teats;

She looked so odd and so grotesque to me,
I ran and wondered what the thing could be,
And pushed the knapweed bunches where I stood;
Then the mouse hurried from the craking brood.
The young ones squeaked, and as I went away
She found her nest again among the hay.
The water o'er the pebbles scarce could run
And broad old cesspools glittered in the sun.

JOHN CLARE

378 *Clock-a-Clay*

In the cowslip pips I lie,
Hidden from the buzzing fly,
While green grass beneath me lies,
Pearled with dew like fishes' eyes,
Here I lie, a clock-a-clay,
Waiting for the time of day.

While grassy forest quakes surprise,
And the wild wind sobs and sighs,
My gold home rocks as like to fall,
On its pillar green and tall;
When the pattering rain drives by
Clock-a-clay keeps warm and dry.

Day by day and night by night,
All the week I hide from sight;
In the cowslip pips I lie,
In rain and dew still warm and dry;
Day and night, and night and day,
Red, black-spotted clock-a-clay.

My home shakes in wind and showers,
Pale green pillar topped with flowers,
Bending at the wild wind's breath,
Till I touch the grass beneath;
Here I live, lone clock-a-clay,
Watching for the time of day.

JOHN CLARE

379 *The Dead Crab*

A rosy shield upon its back,
That not the hardest storm could crack,
From whose sharp edge projected out
Black pin-point eyes staring about;
Beneath, the well-knit cote-armure
That gave to its weak belly power;
The clustered legs with plated joints
That ended in stiletto points;
The claws like mouths it held outside:–
I cannot think this creature died
By storm or fish or sea-fowl harmed
Walking the sea so heavily armed;
Or does it make for death to be
Oneself a living armoury?

ANDREW YOUNG

380 *The Elm Beetle*

So long I sat and conned
That naked bole
With the strange hieroglyphics scored
That those small priests,
The beetle-grubs, had bored,
Telling of gods and kings and beasts
And the long journey of the soul
Through magic-opened gates
To where the throned Osiris waits,
That when at last I woke
I stepped from an Egyptian tomb
To see the wood's sun-spotted gloom,
And rising cottage smoke
That leaned upon the wind and broke,
Roller-striped fields, and smooth cow-shadowed pond.

ANDREW YOUNG

381 *The Maÿ Tree*

I've a-come by the Maÿ-tree all times o' the year,
  When leaves wer a-springèn,
  When vrost wer a-stingèn,
When cool-winded mornèn did show the hills clear,
When night were bedimmèn the vields vur an' near.

When, in zummer, his head wer as white as a sheet,
  Wi' white buds a-zwellèn,
  An' blossom, sweet smellèn,
While leaves wi' green leaves on his boughzides did meet,
A-sheädèn the dëaisies down under our veet.

When the zun, in the Fall, wer a-wanderèn wan,
  An' haws on his head
  Did sprinkle en red,
Or bright drops o' raïn wer a-hung loosely on
To the tips o' the sprigs when the scud wer a-gone.

An' when, in the winter, the zun did goo low,
  An' keen win' did huffle,[1]
  But never could ruffle
The hard vrozen feäce o' the water below,
His limbs wer a-fringed wi' the vrost or the snow.
WILLIAM BARNES

382 *Autumn*

A touch of cold in the Autumn night—
I walked abroad,
And saw the ruddy moon lean over a hedge
Like a red-faced farmer.
I did not stop to speak, but nodded,
And round about were the wistful stars
With white faces like town children.
THOMAS ERNEST HULME

[1] bluster

383 *Conversion*

Light-hearted I walked into the valley wood
In the time of hyacinths,
Till beauty like a scented cloth
Cast over, stifled me. I was bound
Motionless and faint of breath
By loveliness that is her own eunuch.

Now pass I to the final river
Ignominiously, in a sack, without sound,
As any peeping Turk to the Bosphorus.

THOMAS ERNEST HULME

384 *Inversnaid*

This darksome burn, horseback brown,
His rollrock highroad roaring down,
In coop and in comb the fleece of his foam
Flutes and low to the lake falls home.

A windpuff-bonnet of fáwn-fróth
Turns and twindles over the broth
Of a pool so pitchblack, féll-frowning,
It round and rounds Despair to drowning.

Degged with dew, dappled with dew
Are the groins of the braes that the brook treads through,
Wiry heathpacks, flitches of fern,
And the beadbonny ash that sits over the burn.

What would the world be, once bereft
Of wet and of wildness? Let them be left,
O let them be left, wildness and wet;
Long live the weeds and the wilderness yet.

GERARD MANLEY HOPKINS

385 *Nightingale and Flowers*

Thou hearest the Nightingale begin the Song of Spring.
The Lark sitting upon his earth bed, just as the morn
Appears, listens silent; then springing from the waving Corn-
field, loud
He leads the Choir of Day: trill, trill, trill, trill,
Mounting upon the wings of light into the Great Expanse,
Reechoing against the lovely blue & shining heavenly Shell,
His little throat labours with inspiration; every feather
On throat & breast & wings vibrates with the effluence
Divine.
All Nature listens silent to him, & the awful Sun
Stands still upon the Mountain looking on this little Bird
With eyes of soft humility & wonder, love & awe.
Then loud from their green covert all the Birds begin their
Songs:
The Thrush, the Linnet & the Goldfinch, Robin & the Wren
Awake the Sun from his sweet reverie upon the Mountain.
The Nightingale again assays his song, and thro' the day
And thro' the night warbles luxuriant, every Bird of Song
Attending his loud harmony with admiration & love.
This is a Vision of the Beulah over Ololon.

Thou perceivest the Flowers put forth their precious Odours,
And none can tell how from so small a center comes such
sweets,
Forgetting that within that Center Eternity expands
Its ever during doors that Og & Anak fiercely guard.
First, e'er the morning breaks, joy opens in the flowery
bosoms,
Joy even to tears, which the Sun rising dries; first the Wild
Thyme
And Meadow-sweet, downy & soft waving among the reeds,
Light springing on the air, lead the sweet Dance: they wake
The Honeysuckle sleeping on the Oak; the flaunting beauty
Revels along upon the wind; the White-thorn, lovely May,
Opens her many lovely eyes listening; the Rose still sleeps,
None dare to wake her; soon she bursts her crimson curtain'd
bed

And comes forth in the majesty of beauty; every Flower,
The Pink, the Jessamine, the Wall-flower, the Carnation,
The Jonquil, the mild Lily, opes her heavens; every Tree
And Flower & Herb soon fill the air with an innumerable
    Dance,
Yet all in order sweet & lovely. Men are sick with Love.
Such is a Vision of the lamentation of Beulah over Ololon.

WILLIAM BLAKE

386   *A Summer Day*

O perfect Light, which shaid [1] away
    The darkness from the light,
And set a ruler o'er the day,
    Another o'er the night—

Thy glory, when the day forth flies,
    More vively [2] doth appear
Than at mid day unto our eyes
    The shining sun is clear.

The shadow of the earth anon
    Removes and drawis by,
While in the East, when it is gone,
    Appears a clearer sky.

Which soon perceive the little larks,
    The lapwing and the snipe,
And tune their songs, like Nature's clerks,
    O'er meadow, muir, and stripe. [3]

Our hemisphere is polisht clean,
    And lighten'd more and more,
While everything is clearly seen
    Which seemit dim before:

Except the glistering astres [4] bright,
    Which all the night were clear,
Offuskit [5] with a greater light
    No longer do appear.

---

[1] parted   [2] vividly   [3] rill   [4] stars   [5] obscured

The golden globe incontinent
   Sets up his shining head,
And o'er the earth and firmament
   Displays his beams abroad.

For joy the birds with boulden [1] throats
   Against his visage sheen [2]
Take up their kindly musick notes
   In woods and gardens green.

The dew upon the tender crops.
   Like pearlis white and round,
Or like to melted silver drops,
   Refreshes all the ground.

The misty reek, the clouds of rain,
   From tops of mountains skails,[3]
Clear are the highest hills and plain,
   The vapours take the vales.

The ample heaven of fabrick sure
   In cleanness does surpass
The crystal and the silver pure,
   Or clearest polisht glass.

The time so tranquil is and still
   That nowhere shall ye find,
Save on a high and barren hill,
   An air of peeping wind.

All trees and simples, great and small,
   That balmy leaf do bear,
Than they were painted on a wall
   No more they move or stir.

Calm is the deep and purple sea,
   Yea, smoother than the sand;
The waves that weltering wont to be
   Are stable like the land.

---

[1] swollen   [2] bright   [3] clears

M

So silent is the cessile [1] air
  That every cry and call
The hills and dales and forest fair
  Again repeats them all.

The flourishes and fragrant flowers,
  Through Phoebus' fostering heat,
Refresht with dew and silver showers
  Cast up an odour sweet.

The cloggit [2] busy humming bees,
  That never think to drone,
On flowers and flourishes of trees
  Collect their liquor brown.

The Sun, most like a speedy post
  With ardent course ascends;
The beauty of the heavenly host
  Up to our zenith tends.

The burning beams down from his face
  So fervently can beat,
That man and beast now seek a place
  To save them from the heat.

The herds beneath some leafy tree
  Amidst the flowers they lie;
The stable ships upon the sea
  Tend up their sails to dry.

With gilded eyes and open wings
  The cock his courage shows;
With claps of joy his breast he dings, [3]
  And twenty times he crows.

The dove with whistling wings so blue
  The winds can fast collect;
Her purple pens turn many a hue
  Against the sun direct.

[1] yielding   [2] clogged   [3] beats

Now noon is went; gone is midday,
    The heat doth slake at last;
The sun descends down West away,
    For three of clock is past.

The rayons of the sun we see
    Diminish in their strength;
The shade of every tower and tree
    Extendit is in length.

Great is the calm, for everywhere
    The wind is setting down;
The reek throws right up in the air
    From every tower and town.

The gloming comes; the day is spent;
    The sun goes out of sight;
And painted is the occident
    With purple sanguine bright.

Our west horizon circular
    From time the sun be set
Is all with rubies, as it were,
    Or roses red o'erfret.

What pleasure were to walk and see,
    Endlong a river clear,
The perfect form of every tree
    Within the deep appear.

O then it were a seemly thing,
    While all is still and calm,
The praise of God to play and sing
    With cornet and with shalm!

All labourers draw home at even,
    And can to other say,
Thanks to the gracious God of heaven,
    Which sent this summer day.
                ALEXANDER HUME

387 *Patrolling Barnegat*

Wild, wild the storm, and the sea high running,
Steady the roar of the gale, with incessant undertone muttering,
Shouts of demoniac laughter fitfully piercing and pealing,
Waves, air, midnight, their savagest trinity lashing,
Out on the shadows there milk-white combs careering,
On beachy slush and sand spirts of snow fierce slanting,
Where through the murk the easterly death-wind breasting,
Through cutting swirl and spray watchful and firm advancing,
(That in the distance! is that a wreck? is the red signal flaring?)
Slush and sand of the beach tireless till daylight wending,
Steadily, slowly, through hoarse roar never remitting,
Along the midnight edge by those milk-white combs careering,
A group of dim, weird forms, struggling, the night confronting,
That savage trinity warily watching.

WALT WHITMAN

388 *Philoctetes*

Suppos'd to be written at Lemnos

On this lone Isle, whose rugged rocks affright
The cautious pilot, ten revolving years
Great Pæan's son, unwonted erst to tears,
Wept o'er his wound: alike each rolling light
Of heaven he watch'd, and blam'd its lingering flight.
By day the sea-mew screaming round his cave
Drove slumber from his eyes, the chiding wave,
And savage howlings chas'd his dreams by night.
Hope still was his: in each low breeze, that sigh'd
Thro' his rude grot, he heard a coming oar,
In each white cloud a coming sail he spied;
Nor seldom listen'd to the fancied roar
Of Oeta's torrents, or the hoarser tide
That parts fam'd Trachis from th'Euboic shore.

THOMAS RUSSELL

389 *The Flying Fish*

Of the birds that fly in the farthest sea
six are stranger than others be:
under its tumble, among the fish,
six are a marvel passing wish.

First is a hawk, exceeding great;
he dwelleth alone; he hath no mate;
his neck is wound with a yellow ring;
on his breast is the crest of a former king.

The second bird is exceeding pale,
from little head to scanty tail;
she is striped with black on either wing,
which is rose-lined, like a princely thing.

Though small the bulk of the brilliant third,
of all blue birds 'tis the bluest bird;
they fly in bands; and, seen by day,
by the side of them the sky is grey.

I mind the fifth, I forget the fourth,
unless that it comes from the east by north.
The fifth is an orange white-billed duck;
he diveth for fish, like the god of Luck;

he hath never a foot on which to stand;
for water yields and he loves not land.
This is the end of many words
save one, concerning marvellous birds.

The great-faced dolphin is first of fish;
he is devil-eyed and devilish;
of all the fishes is he most brave,
he walks the sea like an angry wave.

The second the fishes call their lord;
himself a bow, his face is a sword;
his sword is armed with a hundred teeth,
fifty above and fifty beneath.

The third hath a scarlet suit of mail;
the fourth is naught but a feeble tail;
the fifth is a whip with a hundred strands,
and every arm hath a hundred hands.

The last strange fish is the last strange bird;
Of him no sage hath ever heard;
he roams the sea in a gleaming horde
in fear of the dolphin and him of the sword.

He leaps from the sea with a silken swish;
he beats the air does the flying fish.
His eyes are round with excess of fright,
bright as the drops of his pinions' flight.

In sea and sky he hath no peace;
for the five strange fish are his enemies;
and the five strange fowls keep watch for him;
they know him well by his crystal gleam.

Oftwhiles, sir Sage, on my junk's white deck
have I seen this fish-bird come to wreck,
oftwhiles (fair deck) 'twixt bow and poop
have I seen this piteous sky-fish stoop.

Scaled bird, how his snout and gills dilate,
all quivering and roseate:
he pants in crystal and mother-of-pearl
while his body shrinks and his pinions furl.

His beauty passes like bubbles blown;
the white bright bird is a fish of stone;
the bird so fair, for its putrid sake,
is flung to the dogs in the junk's white wake.

JOHN GRAY

390 *Noon Quatrains*

The day grows hot, and darts his rays
From such a sure and killing place,
That this half world are fain to fly
The danger of his burning eye.

His early glories were benign,
Warm to be felt, bright to be seen,
And all was comfort, but who can
Endure him when Meridian?

Of him we as of Kings complain,
Who mildly do begin to reign,
But to the Zenith got of pow'r,
Those whom they should protect devour.

Has not another Phaethon
Mounted the chariot of the sun,
And, wanting art to guide his horse,
Is hurried from the sun's due course?

If this hold on, our fertile lands,
Will soon be turn'd to parched sands,
And not an onion that will grow
Without a Nile to overflow.

The grazing herds now droop and pant,
E'en without labour fit to faint,
And willingly forsook their meat,
To seek out cover from the heat.

The lagging ox is now unbound,
From larding the new turn'd up ground,
Whilst Hobbinal alike o'er-laid,
Takes his coarse dinner to the shade.

Cellars and grottos now are best
To eat and drink in, or to rest,
And not a soul above is found
Can find a refuge under ground.

When pagan tyranny grew hot,
Thus persecuted Christians got
Into the dark but friendly womb
Of unknown subterranean Rome.

And as that heat did cool at last,
So a few scorching hours o'er pass'd,
In a more mild and temp'rate ray
We may again enjoy the day.

CHARLES COTTON

391 *Evening Quatrains*

The day's grown old, the fainting sun
Has but a little way to run,
And yet his steeds, with all his skill,
Scarce lug the chariot down the hill.

With labour spent, and thirst opprest,
Whilst they strain hard to gain the West,
From fetlocks hot drops melted light,
Which turn to meteors in the night.

The shadows now so long do grow,
That brambles like tall cedars show,
Mole-hills seem mountains, and the ant
Appears a monstrous elephant.

A very little, little flock
Shades thrice the ground that it would stock;
Whilst the small stripling following them,
Appears a mighty Polypheme.

These being brought into the fold,
And by the thrifty master told,
He thinks his wages are well paid,
Since none are either lost or stray'd.

Now lowing herds are each-where heard,
Chains rattle in the villain's yard,
The cart's on tail set down to rest,
Bearing on high the Cuckold's crest.

The hedge is stripped, the clothes brought in,
Nought's left without should be within,
The bees are hiv'd, and hum their charm,
Whilst every house does seem a swarm.

The cock now to the roost is prest;
For he must call up all the rest;
The sow's fast pegg'd within the sty,
To still her squeaking progeny.

Each one has had his supping mess,
The cheese is put into the press,
The pans and bowls clean scalded all,
Rear'd up against the milk-house wall.

And now on benches all are sat
In the cool air to sit and chat,
Till Phœbus, dipping in the West,
Shall lead the world the way to rest.

CHARLES COTTON

392 *Description of a City Shower*

Careful Observers may foretell the Hour
(By sure Prognosticks) when to dread a Show'r:
While Rain depends, the pensive Cat gives o'er
Her Frolicks, and pursues her Tail no more.
Returning Home at Night, you'll find the Sink
Strike your offended Sense with double Stink.
If you be wise, then go not far to Dine,
You'll spend in Coach-hire more than save in Wine.
A coming Show'r your shooting Corns presage,
Old Aches throb, your hollow Tooth will rage.
Saunt'ring in Coffee-house is *Dulman* seen;
He damns the Climate, and complains of Spleen.

Mean while the South rising with dabbled Wings,
A Sable Cloud a-thwart the Welkin flings,
That swill'd more Liquor than it could contain,
And like a Drunkard gives it up again.
Brisk *Susan* whips her Linen from the Rope,
While the first drizzling Show'r is born aslope,
Such is that Sprinkling which some careless Quean
Flirts on you from her Mop, but not so clean.
You fly, invoke the Gods; then turning, stop
To rail; she singing, still whirls on her Mop.
Not yet, the Dust had shunn'd th'unequal Strife,
But aided by the Wind, fought still for Life;
And wafted with its Foe by violent Gust,
'Twas doubtful which was Rain, and which was Dust.

Ah! where must needy Poet seek for Aid,
When Dust and Rain at once his Coat invade;
His only Coat, where Dust confus'd with Rain,
Roughen the Nap, and leave a mingled Stain.

Now in contiguous Drops the Flood comes down,
Threat'ning with Deluge this *Devoted* Town.
To Shops in Crowds the daggled Females fly,
Pretend to cheapen Goods, but nothing buy.
The Templer spruce, while ev'ry Spout's a-broach,
Stays till 'tis fair, yet seems to call a Coach.
The tuck'd-up Sempstress walks with hasty Strides,
While Streams run down her oil'd Umbrella's Sides.
Here various Kinds by various Fortunes led,
Commence Acquaintance underneath a Shed.
Triumphant Tories, and desponding Whigs,
Forget their Feuds, and join to save their Wigs.

Box'd in a Chair the Beau impatient sits,
While Spouts run clatt'ring o'er the Roof by Fits;
And ever and anon with frightful Din
The Leather sounds, he trembles from within.
So when *Troy* Chair-men bore the Wooden Steed,
Pregnant with *Greeks*, impatient to be freed,
(Those Bully *Greeks*, who, as the Moderns do,
Instead of paying Chair-men, run them thro'.)
Laoco'n struck the Outside with his Spear,
And each imprison'd Hero quak'd for Fear.

Now from all Parts the swelling Kennels flow,
And bear their Trophies with them as they go:
Filth of all Hues and Odours seem to tell
What Street they sail'd from, by their Sight and Smell.
They, as each Torrent drives, with rapid Force
From *Smithfield*, or St. *Pulchre*'s shape their Course,
And in huge Confluent join at *Snow-Hill* Ridge,
Fall from the *Conduit* prone to *Holborn-Bridge*.
Sweepings from Butchers' Stalls, Dung, Guts, and Blood,
Drown'd Puppies, stinking Sprats, all drench'd in Mud,
Dead Cats and Turnip-Tops come tumbling down the Flood.

JONATHAN SWIFT

393 *Vigil*

Lived on one's back,
In the long hours of repose
Life is a practical nightmare–
Hideous asleep or awake.

Shoulders and loins
Ache – – –!
Ache, and the mattress,
Run into boulders and hummocks,
Glows like a kiln, while the bedclothes–
Tumbling, importunate, daft–
Ramble and roll, and the gas,
Screwed to its lowermost,
An inevitable atom of light,
Haunts, and a stertorous sleeper
Snores me to hate and despair.

All the old time
Surges malignant before me;
Old voices, old kisses, old songs
Blossom derisive about me;
While the new days
Pass me in endless procession:
A pageant of shadows
Silently, leeringly wending
On . . . and still on . . . still on!

Far in the stillness a cat
Languishes loudly. A cinder
Falls, and the shadows
Lurch to the leap of the flame.   The next man to me
Turns with a moan; and the snorer,
The drug like a rope at his throat,
Gasps, gurgles, snorts himself free, as the night-nurse,
Noiseless and strange,
Her bull's eye half-lanterned in apron,
(Whispering me, 'Are ye no sleepin' yet?')
Passes, list-slippered and peering,
Round . . . and is gone.

Sleep comes at last–
Sleep full of dreams and misgivings–
Broken with brutal and sordid
Voices and sounds that impose on me,
Ere I can wake to it,
The unnatural, intolerable day.

WILLIAM ERNEST HENLEY

394 *The Night Nurse goes her Round*

Droop under doves' wings silent, breathing shapes
white coverlids dissimulate; in hope
of opiate aid to round the ledge where gapes
the sootblack gulf in which obtuse minds grope

for very nothing, vast and undefined,
in starless depths no astrolabe can probe.
The moving form, as doomed to pass and wind,
unwind and pass anew, in sleep-dyed robe

of firmamental silence more than hue,
watches the doorway of the tired's escape
only. Fatigue gone on; I left behind

with moths' feet, wordless whispering; or find
reality, white coiffe and scarlet cape;
and dreams are what a dream should be, or true.

JOHN GRAY

395 *The Letter*

Preface:–After I parted with Yüan Chên, I suddenly dreamt
one night that I saw him. When I awoke, I found that a letter
from him had just arrived and, enclosed in it, a poem on the
paulovnia flower.

We talked together in the Yung-shou Temple;
We parted to the north of the Hsin-ch'ang ward.
Going home–I shed a few tears,
Grieving about things,–not sorry for you.
Long, long the Lan-t'ien road;
You said yourself you would not be able to write.
Reckoning up your halts for eating and sleeping–
By this time you've crossed the Shang mountains.

Last night the clouds scattered away;
A thousand leagues, the same moonlight scene.
When dawn came, I dreamt I saw your face;
It must have been that you were thinking of me.
In my dream, I thought I held your hand
And asked you to tell me what your thoughts were.
And *you* said: 'I miss you bitterly,
But there's no one here to send to you with a letter.'
When I awoke, before I had time to speak,
A knocking on the door sounded 'Doong, doong!'
They came and told me a messenger from Shang-chou
Had brought a letter,–a single scroll from you!
Up from my pillow I suddenly sprang out of bed,
And threw you my clothes, all topsy-turvy.
I undid the knot and saw the letter within;
A single sheet with thirteen lines of writing.
At the top it told the sorrows of an exile's heart;
At the bottom it described the pains of separation.
The sorrows and pains took up so much space
There was no room left to talk about the weather!
　　　　But you said that when you wrote
You were staying for the night to the east of Shang-chou;
Sitting alone, lighted by a solitary candle
Lodging in the mountain hostel of Yang-Ch'êng.
　　　　Night was late when you finished writing,
The mountain moon was slanting towards the west.
What is it lies aslant across the moon?
A single tree of purple *paulovnia* flowers–
Paulovnia flowers just on the point of falling
Are a symbol to express 'thinking of an absent friend.'
Lovingly–you wrote on the back side,
To send in the letter, your 'Poem of the Paulovnia Flower.'
The Poem of the Paulovnia Flower has eight rhymes;
Yet these eight couplets have cast a spell on my heart.
They have taken hold of this morning's thoughts
And carried them to yours, the night you wrote your letter.
The whole poem I read three times;
Each verse ten times I recite.
So precious to me are the fourscore words,
That each letter changes into a bar of gold.

　　　　　　　　　　　　ARTHUR WALEY
　　　　　　　　　　　　(from the Chinese)

396 *Currente calamo*

Quick, painter, quick, the moment seize
Amid the snowy Pyrenees;
More evanescent than the snow,
The pictures come, are seen, and go:
Quick, quick, *currente calamo*.
  I do not ask the tints that fill
The gate of day 'twixt hill and hill;
I ask not for the hues that fleet
Above the distant peaks; my feet
Are on a poplar-bordered road,
Where with a saddle and a load
A donkey, old and ashen-grey,
Reluctant works his dusty way.
Before him, still with might and main
Pulling his rope, the rustic rein,
A girl: before both him and me,
Frequent she turns and lets me see,
Unconscious, lets me scan and trace
The sunny darkness of her face
And outlines full of southern grace.
  Following I notice, yet and yet,
Her olive skin, dark eyes deep set,
And black, and blacker e'en than jet,
The escaping hair that scantly showed,
Since o'er it in the country mode,
For winter warmth and summer shade,
The lap of scarlet cloth is laid.
And then, back-falling from the head,
A crimson kerchief overspread
Her jacket blue; thence passing down,
A skirt of darkest yellow-brown,
Coarse stuff, allowing to the view
The smooth limb to the woollen shoe.
  But who—here's some one following too,—
A priest, and reading at his book!
Read on, O priest, and do not look;
Consider,—she is but a child,—
Yet might your fancy be beguiled.

Read on, O priest, and pass and go!
But see, succeeding in a row,
Two, three, and four, a motley train,
Musicians wandering back to Spain;
With fiddle and with tambourine,
A man with women following seen.
What dresses, ribbon-ends, and flowers!
And,–sight to wonder at for hours,–
The man,–to Phillip has he sat?–
With butterfly-like velvet hat;
One dame his big bassoon conveys,
On one his gentle arm he lays;
They stop, and look, and something say,
And to 'España' ask the way.
    But while I speak, and point them on;
Alas! my dearer friends are gone,
The dark-eyed maiden and the ass
Have had the time the bridge to pass.
Vainly, beyond it far descried,
Adieu, and peace with you abide,
Grey donkey, and your beauteous guide.
The pictures come, the pictures go,
Quick, quick, *currente calamo.*

ARTHUR HUGH CLOUGH

397 *The Storm*

Behold, slow-settling o'er the lurid grove,
Unusual darkness broods, and growing gains
The full possession of the sky, surcharg'd
With wrathful vapour, from the secret beds
Where sleep the mineral generations drawn.
Thence nitre, sulphur, and the fiery spume
Of fat bitumen, steaming on the day,
With various-tinctur'd trains of latent flame,
Pollute the sky, and in yon baleful cloud
A red'ning gloom, a magazine of fate,
Ferment; till, by the touch ethereal rous'd,
The dash of clouds, or irritating war
Of fighting winds while all is calm below,

They furious spring. A boding silence reigns
Dread through the dun expanse, save the dull sound
That from the mountain, previous to the storm,
Rolls o'er the mutt'ring earth, disturbs the flood,
And stirs the forest-leaf without a breath.
Prone to the lowest vale the aerial tribes
Descend; the tempest-loving raven scarce
Dares wing the dubious dusk. In rueful gaze
The cattle stand, and on the scowling heavens
Cast a deploring eye, by man forsook–
Who to the crowded cottage hies him fast,
Or seeks the shelter of the downward cave.
    'Tis listening fear and dumb amazement all,
When to the startl'd eye the sudden glance
Appears far south eruptive through the cloud,
And following slower in explosion vast
The thunder raises his tremendous voice.
At first, heard solemn o'er the verge of heaven,
The tempest growls; but, as it nearer comes
And rolls its awful burden on the wind,
The lightnings flash a larger curve, and more
The noise astounds, till over head a sheet
Of livid flame discloses wide, then shuts
And opens wider, shuts and opens still
Expansive, wrapping ether in a blaze.
Follows the loosen'd aggravated roar,
Enlarging, deep'ning, mingling, peal on peal
Crushed horrible, convulsing heaven and earth.
    Down comes a deluge of sonorous hail,
Or prone-descending rain. Wide-rent, the clouds
Pour a whole flood; and yet, its flame unquench'd,
The inconquerable lightning struggles through,
Ragged and fierce or in red whirling balls,
And fires the mountains with redoubl'd rage.
Black from the stroke, above, the smould'ring pine
Stands a sad shatter'd trunk; and, stretch'd below,
A lifeless group the blasted cattle lie,
Here the soft flocks, with that same harmless look
They wore alive, and ruminating still
In fancy's eye, and there the frowning bull,
And ox half-rais'd. Struck on the castl'd cliff,

The venerable tower and spiry fane
Resign their aged pride. The gloomy woods
Start at the flash, and from their deep recess,
Wide-flaming out, their trembling inmates shake.
Amid Carnarvon's mountains rages loud
The repercussive roar; with mighty crush,
Into the flashing deep, from the rude rocks
Of Penmanmaur heap'd hideous to the sky,
Tumble the smitten cliffs; and Snowdon's peak,
Dissolving, instant yields his wintry load.
Far seen the heights of heathy Cheviot blaze,
And Thule bellows through her utmost isles.

JAMES THOMSON

398 *Autumn*

But see, the fading many-coloured woods,
Shade deep'ning over shade, the country round
Imbrown,–a crowded umbrage, dusk, and dun,
Of every hue from wan declining green
To sooty dark. These now the lonesome muse,
Low-whispering, lead into their leaf-strown walks;
And give the season in its latest view.

Meantime, light-shadowing all, a sober calm
Fleeces unbounded ether, whose least wave
Stands tremulous, uncertain where to turn
The gentle current: while, illumin'd wide,
The dewy-skirted clouds imbibe the sun,
And through their lucid veil his soften'd force
Shed o'er the peaceful world. Then is the time
For those whom wisdom and whom nature charm
To steal themselves from the degenerate crowd,
And soar above this little scene of things;
To tread low-thoughted vice beneath their feet,
To soothe the throbbing passions into peace,
And woo lone quiet in her silent walks.

Thus solitary and in pensive guise
Oft let me wander o'er the russet mead
And through the sadden'd grove, where scarce is heard
One dying strain to cheer the woodman's toil.

Haply some widow'd songster pours his plaint
Far in faint warblings through the tawny copse;
While congregated thrushes, linnets, larks,
And each wild throat whose artless strains so late
Swell'd all the music of the swarming shades,
Robb'd of their tuneful souls, now shivering sit
On the dead tree, a dull despondent flock,
With not a brightness waving o'er their plumes,
And nought save chattering discord in their note.
Oh! let not, aim'd from some inhuman eye,
The gun the music of the coming year
Destroy, and harmless, unsuspecting harm,
Lay the weak tribes, a miserable prey,
In mingled murder fluttering on the ground.

JAMES THOMSON

399   *To Penshurst*

Thou art not, PENSHURST, built to envious show,
   Of touch, or marble; nor canst boast a row
Of polish'd pillars, or a roof of gold:
   Thou hast no lanthorn, whereof tales are told;
Or stair, or courts; but stand'st an ancient pile,
   And these grudg'd at, art reverenc'd the while.
Thou joy'st in better marks, of soil, of air,
   Of wood, of water: therein thou art fair.
Thou hast thy walks for health, as well as sport:
   Thy *Mount*, to which the *Dryads* do resort,
Where PAN, & BACCHUS their high feasts have made,
   Beneath the broad beech, and the chest-nut shade;
That taller tree, which of a nut was set,
   At his great birth, where all the *Muses* met.
There, in the writhed bark, are cut the names
   Of many a SYLVANE, taken with his flames.
And thence, the ruddy *Satyrs* oft provoke,
   The lighter *Fauns*, to reach thy *Ladies'* oak.
Thy copse too, nam'd of GAMAGE, thou hast there,
   That never fails to serve thee season'd deer,
When thou would'st feast, or exercise thy friends.
   The lower land, that to the river bends,

Thy sheep, thy bullocks, kine, and calves do feed:
  The middle grounds thy mares, and horses breed.
Each bank doth yield thee coneys; and the tops
  Fertile of wood, ASHORE, and SYDNEY's copse,
To crown thy open table, doth provide
  The purpled pheasant, with the speckled side:
The painted patriarch lies in every field,
  And for thy mess, is willing to be kill'd.
And if the high swol'n *Medway* fail thy dish,
  Thou hast thy ponds, that pay thee tribute fish,
Fat, aged carps, that run into thy net.
  And pikes, now weary their own kind to eat,
As loth, the second draught, or cast to stay,
  Officiously, at first, themselves betray.
Bright eels, that emulate them, and leap on land,
  Before the fisher, or into his hand.
Then hath thy orchard fruit, thy garden flowers,
  Fresh as the air, and new as are the hours.
The early cherry, with the later plum,
  Fig, grape, and quince, each in his time doth come:
The blushing apricot, and woolly peach
  Hang on thy walls, that every child may reach.
And though thy walls be of the country stone,
  They're rear'd with no man's ruin, no man's groan,
There's none, that dwell about them, wish them down;
  But all come in, the farmer, and the clown:
And no one empty-handed, to salute
  Thy lord, and lady, though they have no suit.
Some bring a capon, some a rural cake,
  Some nuts, some apples; some that think they make
The better cheeses, bring 'em; or else send
  By their ripe daughters, whom they would commend
This way to husbands; and whose baskets bear
  An emblem of themselves, in plum, or pear.
But what can this (more than express their love)
  Add to thy free provisions, far above
The need of such? whose liberal board doth flow,
  With all that hospitality doth know!
Where comes no guest, but is allow'd to eat,
  Without his fear, and of thy lord's own meat:

Where this same beer, and bread, and self-same wine,
  That is his Lordship's, shall be also mine.
And I not fain to sit (as some, this day,
  At great men's tables) and yet dine away.
Here no man tells my cups; nor, standing by,
  A waiter, doth my gluttony envy:
But gives me what I call, and lets me eat,
  He knows, below, he shall find plenty of meat,
Thy tables hoard not up for the next day,
  Nor, when I take my lodging, need I pray
For fire, or lights, or livery: all is there;
  As if thou, then, wert mine, or I reign'd here:
There's nothing I can wish, for which I stay.
  That found king JAMES, when hunting late, this way,
With his brave son, the Prince, they saw thy fires
  Shine bright on every hearth as the desires
Of thy *Penates* had been set on flame,
  To entertain them; or the country came,
With all their zeal, to warm their welcome here.
  What (great, I will not say, but) sudden cheer
Did'st thou, then, make 'em! and what praise was heap'd
  On thy good lady, then! who, therein, reap'd
The just reward of her high huswifery;
  To have her linen, plate, and all things nigh,
When she was far: and not a room, but drest,
  As if it had expected such a guest!
These, PENSHURST, are thy praise, and yet not all.
  Thy lady's noble, fruitful, chaste withal.
His children, thy great lord may call his own:
  A fortune, in this age, but rarely known.
They are, and have been taught religion: Thence
  Their gentler spirits have suck'd innocence.
Each morn, and even, they are taught to pray,
  With the whole household, and may, every day,
Read, in their virtuous parents' noble parts,
  The mysteries of manners, arms, and arts.
Now, PENSHURST, they that will proportion thee
  With other edifices, when they see
Those proud, ambitious heaps, and nothing else,
  May say, their lords have built, but thy lord dwells.

                                        BEN JONSON

400 *The Calm*

Our storm is past, and that storm's tyrannous rage
A stupid calm, but nothing it, doth 'suage.
The fable is inverted, and far more
A block afflicts, now, than a stork before.
Storms chafe, and soon wear out themselves, or us;
In calms, Heaven laughs to see us languish thus.
As steady as I could wish my thoughts were,
Smooth as thy mistress' glass, or what shines there,
The sea is now. And, as these isles which we
Seek, when we can move, our ships rooted be.
As water did in storms, now pitch runs out;
As lead, when a fir'd church becomes one spout.
And all our beauty, and our trim, decays,
Like courts removing, or like ended plays.
The fighting-place now seamen's rags supply;
And all the tackling is a frippery.
No use of lanthorns; and in one place lay
Feathers and dust, to-day and yesterday.
Earth's hollownesses, which the world's lungs are,
Have no more wind than the upper vault of air.
We can nor lost friends nor sought foes recover,
But meteor-like, save that we move not, hover.
Only the calenture together draws
Dear friends, which meet dead in great fishes' jaws;
And on the hatches as on altars lies
Each one, his own priest and own sacrifice.
Who live, that miracle do multiply,
Where walkers in hot ovens do not die.
If in despite of these, we swim, that hath
No more refreshing than a brimstone bath;
But from the sea into the ship we turn,
Like parboil'd wretches, on the coals to burn.
Like Bajazet encag'd, the shepherds' scoff,
Or like slack-sinewed Sampson, his hair off,
Languish our ships. Now as a myriad
Of ants durst th'emperor's loved snake invade,
The crawling gallies, sea-gulls, finny chips,
Might brave our pinnaces, now bed-rid ships,

Whether a rotten state, and hope of gain,
Or to disuse me from the queasy pain
Of being belov'd, and loving, or the thirst
Of honour, or fair death, out-push'd me first,
I lose my end; for here, as well as I,
A desperate may live, and coward die.
Stag, dog, and all which from, or towards flies,
Is paid with life, or pray, or doing dies.
Fate grudges us all, and doth subtly lay
A scourge, 'gainst which we all forget to pray.
He that at sea prays for more wind, as well
Under the poles may beg cold, heat in hell.
What are we then? How little more, alas,
Is man now, than, before he was? he was
Nothing; for us, we are for nothing fit;
Chance, or ourselves, still disproportion it.
We have no power, no will, no sense; I lie,
I should not then thus feel this misery.

JOHN DONNE

401   *The Garden*

How vainly men themselves amaze
To win the Palm, the Oak, or Bays;
And their uncessant Labours see
Crown'd from some single Herb or Tree,
Whose short and narrow-verged Shade
Does prudently their Toils upbraid;
While all Flow'rs and all Trees do close
To weave the Garlands of repose.

Fair quiet, have I found thee here,
And Innocence thy Sister dear!
Mistaken long; I sought you then
In busy Companies of Men.
Your sacred Plants, if here below,
Only among the Plants will grow.
Society is all but rude,
To this delicious Solitude.

No white nor red was ever seen
So am'rous as this lovely green.
Fond Lovers, cruel as their Flame,
Cut in these Trees their Mistress' name.
Little, Alas, they know, or heed,
How far these Beauties Hers exceed!
Fair Trees! where s'e'er your barks I wound,
No Name shall but your own be found.

When we have run our Passion's heat,
Love hither makes his best retreat.
The *Gods*, that mortal Beauty chase,
Still in a Tree did end their race.
Apollo hunted *Daphne* so,
Only that She might Laurel grow.
And *Pan* did after *Syrinx* speed,
Not as a nymph, but for a Reed.

What wond'rous Life in this I lead!
Ripe Apples drop about my head;
The Luscious Clusters of the Vine
Upon my Mouth do crush their Wine;
The Nectaren, and curious Peach,
Into my hands themselves do reach;
Stumbling on Melons, as I pass,
Insnar'd with Flow'rs, I fall on Grass.

Mean while the Mind, from pleasure less,
Withdraws into its happiness:
The Mind, that Ocean where each kind
Does straight its own resemblance find;
Yet it creates, transcending these,
Far other Worlds, and other Seas;
Annihilating all that's made
To a green Thought in a green Shade.

Here at the Fountain's sliding foot,
Or at some Fruit-tree's mossy root,
Casting the Body's Vest aside,
My Soul into the boughs does glide:

There like a Bird it sits, and sings,
Then whets, and combs its silver Wings;
And, till prepar'd for longer flight,
Waves in its Plumes the various Light.

Such was that happy Garden-state,
While Man there walk'd without a Mate:
After a Place so pure, and sweet,
What other Help could yet be meet!
But 'twas beyond a Mortal's share
To wander solitary there:
Two Paradises 'twere in one
To live in Paradise alone.

How well the skilful Gard'ner drew
Of flow'rs and herbs this Dial new;
Where from above the milder Sun
Does through a fragrant Zodiack run;
And, as it works, th'industrious Bee
Computes its time as well as we.
How could such sweet and wholesome Hours
Be reckon'd but with herbs and flow'rs!

ANDREW MARVELL

402　*Song of Venus*

Fairest Isle, all Isles Excelling,
　　Seat of Pleasures, and of Loves;
Venus here will choose her Dwelling,
　　And forsake her *Cyprian* Groves.

Cupid, from his Fav'rite Nation,
　　Care and Envy will Remove;
Jealousy that poisons Passion,
　　And Despair that dies for Love.

Gentle Murmurs, sweet Complaining,
　　Sighs that blow the Fire of Love;
Soft Repulses, kind Disdaining,
　　Shall be all the Pains you prove.

> Ev'ry Swain shall pay his Duty,
>   Grateful ev'ry Nymph shall prove;
> And as these Excel in Beauty,
>   Those shall be Renown'd for Love.

JOHN DRYDEN

403 *Bermudas*

Where the remote *Bermudas* ride
In th' Ocean's bosom unespy'd,
From a small Boat, that row'd along,
The list'ning Winds receiv'd this Song.
  What should we do but sing his Praise
That led us through the wat'ry Maze,
Unto an Isle so long unknown,
And yet far kinder than our own?
Where he the huge Sea-Monsters wracks,
That lift the Deep upon their Backs.
He lands us on a grassy Stage;
Safe from the Storms, and Prelate's rage.
He gave us this eternal Spring,
Which here enamels everything;
And sends the Fowls to us in care,
On daily Visits through the Air.
He hangs in shades the Orange bright,
Like golden Lamps in a green Night.
And does in the Pomgranates close
Jewels more rich than *Ormus* shows.
He makes the Figs our mouths to meet;
And throws the Melons at our feet.
But Apples plants of such a price,
No Tree could ever bear them twice.
With Cedars, chosen by his hand,
From *Lebanon*, he stores the Land.
And makes the hollow Seas, that roar,
Proclaim the Ambergris on shore,
He cast (of which we rather boast)
The Gospel's Pearl upon our Coast.
And in these Rocks for us did frame
A Temple, where to sound his Name.
Oh let our Voice his Praise exalt,
Till it arrive at Heaven's Vault:

Which thence (perhaps) rebounding, may
Echo beyond the *Mexique Bay*.
Thus sung they, in the *English* boat,
An holy and a cheerful Note,
And all the way, to guide their Chime,
With Falling Oars they kept the time.

ANDREW MARVELL

404 *The Nymph Complaining for the Death of her Faun*

The wanton Troopers riding by
Have shot my Faun and it will die.
Ungentle men! They cannot thrive
To kill thee.　Thou ne'er didst alive
Them any harm: alas nor could
Thy death yet do them any good.
I'm sure I never wisht them ill;
Nor do I for all this; nor will:
But, if my simple Pray'rs may yet
Prevail with Heaven to forget
Thy murder, I will join my Tears
Rather then fail.　But, O my fears!
It cannot die so. Heaven's King
Keeps register of every thing:
And nothing may we use in vain.
Ev'n beasts must be with justice slain;
Else Men are made their *Deodands*.[1]
Though they should wash their guilty hands
In this warm life blood, which doth part
From thine, and wound me to the Heart,
Yet could they not be clean: their Stain
Is dy'd in such a Purple Grain.
There is not such another in
The World, to offer for their Sin.

　　Unconstant *Sylvio*, when yet
I had not found him counterfeit,
One morning (I remember well)
Ty'd in this silver Chain and Bell,

---

[1] forfeits to God

Gave it to me: nay and I know
What he said then; I'm sure I do.
Said He, look how your Huntsman here
Hath taught a Faun to hunt his *Dear*
But *Sylvio* soon had me beguil'd.
This waxed tame, while he grew wild,
And quite regardless of my Smart,
Left me his Faun, but took his Heart.

Thenceforth I set my self to play
My solitary time away,
With this: and very well content,
Could so mine idle Life have spent.
For it was full of sport; and light
Of foot, and heart; and did invite,
Me to its game: it seem'd to bless
Its self in me. How could I less
Than love it? O I cannot be
Unkind, t'a Beast that loveth me.

Had it liv'd long, I do not know
Whether it too might have done so
As *Sylvio* did: his Gifts might be
Perhaps as false or more than he.
But I am sure, for aught that I
Could in so short a time espy,
Thy love was far more better then [1]
The love of false and cruel men.

With sweetest milk, and sugar, first
I it at mine own fingers nurst.
And as it grew, so every day
It wax'd more white and sweet than they.
It had so sweet a Breath! And oft
I blusht to see its foot more soft,
And white, (shall I say than my hand?)
NAY any Lady's of the Land.

It is a wond'rous thing, how fleet
'Twas on those little silver feet.
With what a pretty skipping grace,
It oft would challenge me the Race:
And when't had left me far away,
'Twould stay, and run again, and stay.

[1] than

For it was nimbler much than Hinds;
And trod, as on the four Winds.
    I have a garden of my own,
But so with Roses over grown,
And Lilies, that you would it guess
To be a little Wilderness.
And all the Spring time of the year
It only loved to be there.
Among the beds of Lilies, I
Have sought it oft, where it should lie;
Yet could not, till it self would rise,
Find it, although before mine Eyes.
For, in the flaxen Lilies' shade,
It like a bank of Lilies laid.
Upon the Roses it would feed,
Until its Lips ev'n seem'd to bleed:
And then to me 'twould boldly trip,
And print those Roses on my Lip.
But all its chief delight was still
On Roses thus its self to fill:
And its pure virgin Limbs to fold
In whitest sheets of Lilies cold.
Had it liv'd long, it would have been
Lilies without, Roses within.
    O help! O help! I see it faint:
And die as calmly as a Saint.
See how it weeps. The Tears do come
Sad, slowly dropping like a Gum.
So weeps the wounded Balsam: so
The holy Frankincense doth flow.
The brotherless *Heliades*
Melt in such Amber Tears as these.
    I in a golden Vial will
Keep these two crystal Tears; and fill
It till it do o'erflow with mine;
Then place it in *Diana*'s Shrine.
    Now my sweet Faun is vanish'd to
Whither the Swans and Turtles go:
In fair *Elizium* to endure,
With milk-white Lambs, and Ermines pure.
O do not run too fast: for I

Will but bespeak thy Grave, and die.
  First my unhappy Statue shall
Be cut in Marble; and withal,
Let it be weeping too: but there
Th' Engraver sure his Art may spare;
For I so truly thee bemoan,
That I shall weep though I be Stone:
Until my Tears, still dropping, wear
My breast, themselves engraving there.
There at my feet shalt thou be laid,
Of purest Alabaster made:
For I would have thine Image be
White as I can, though not as Thee.

ANDREW MARVELL

405 *The Ditty*

Young Colin Clout, a lad of peerless meed,
Full well could dance, and deftly tune the reed;
In ev'ry wood his carols sweet were known,
At ev'ry wake his nimble feats were shown.
When in the ring the rustic routs he threw,
The damsels' pleasures with his conquests grew;
Or when aslant the cudgel threats his head,
His danger smites the breast of ev'ry maid,
But chief of Marian. Marian loved the swain,
The parson's maid, and neatest of the plain.
Marian, that soft could stroke the udder'd cow,
Or lessen with her sieve the barley mow;
Marbled with sage the hard'ning cheese she press'd,
And yellow butter Marian's skill confess'd;
But Marian, now devoid of country cares,
Nor yellow butter nor sage cheese prepares.
For yearning love the witless maid employs,
And love, say swains, all busy heed destroys.
Colin makes mock at all her piteous smart,
A lass that Cic'ly hight, had won his heart,
Cic'ly the western lass that tends the kee,[1]
The rival of the Parson's maid was she.

---

[1] kine

In dreary shade now Marian lies along,
And mixt with sighs thus wails in plaining song:

Ah! woful day! ah, woful noon and morn!
When first by thee my younglings white were shorn,
Then first, I ween, I cast a lover's eye,
My sheep were silly, but more silly I.
Beneath the shears they felt no lasting smart,
They lost but fleeces, while I lost a heart.

Ah, Colin! canst thou leave thy sweetheart true!
What I have done for thee will Cic'ly do?
Will she thy linen wash or hosen darn,
And knit thee gloves made of her own-spun yarn?
Will she with huswife's hand provide thy meat,
And ev'ry Sunday morn thy neckcloth plait?
Which o'er thy kersey doublet spreading wide,
In service-time drew Cic'ly's eyes aside.

Where-e'er I gad I cannot hide my care,
My new disasters in my look appear.
White as the curd my ruddy cheek is grown,
So thin my features that I'm hardly known:
Our neighbours tell me oft in joking talk
Of ashes, leather, oatmeal, bran, and chalk;
Unwittingly of Marian they divine,
And wist not that with thoughtful love I pine.
Yet Colin Clout, untoward shepherd swain,
Walks whistling blithe, while pitiful I plain.

Whilom with thee 'twas Marian's dear delight
To moil all day, and merry-make at night.
If in the soil you guide the crooked share,
Your early breakfast is my constant care.
And when with even hand you strow the grain,
I fright the thievish rooks from off the plain.
In misling days when I my thresher heard,
With nappy beer I to the barn repair'd;
Lost in the music of the whirling flail,
To gaze on thee I left the smoking pail;
In harvest when the sun was mounted high,
My leathern bottle did thy drought supply;

When-e'er you mow'd I follow'd with the rake,
And have full oft been sunburnt for thy sake;
When in the welkin gathering showers were seen,
I lagg'd the last with Colin on the green;
And when at eve returning with thy car,
Awaiting heard the jingling bells from far;
Straight on the fire the sooty pot I plac't,
To warm thy broth I burnt my hands for haste,
When hungry thou stood'st staring, like an oaf,
I slic'd the luncheon from the barley loaf,
With crumbled bread I thicken'd well thy mess.
Ah, love me more, or love thy pottage less!

    Last Friday's eve, when as the sun was set,
I, near yon stile, three sallow gypsies met.
Upon my hand they cast a poring look,
Bid me beware, and thrice their heads they shook;
They said that many crosses I must prove,
Some in my worldly gain, but most in love.
Next morn I miss'd three hens and our old cock,
And off the hedge two pinners and a smock.
I bore these losses with a Christian mind,
And no mishaps could feel, while thou wert kind.
But since, alas! I grew my Colin's scorn,
I've known no pleasure, night, or noon, or morn.
Help me, ye gypsies, bring him home again,
And to a constant lass give back her swain.

    Have I not sat with thee full many a night,
When dying embers were our only light,
When ev'ry creature did in slumbers lie,
Besides our cat, my Colin Clout, and I?
No troublous thoughts the cat or Colin move,
While I alone am kept awake by love.

    Remember, Colin, when at last year's wake,
I bought the costly present for thy sake,
Couldst thou spell o'er the posy on thy knife,
And with another change thy state of life?
If thou forget'st, I wot, I can repeat,
My memory can tell the verse so sweet.

As this is graved upon this knife of thine,
So is thy image on this heart of mine.
But woe is me! Such presents luckless prove,
For knives, they tell me, always sever love.

Thus Marian wail'd, her eyes with tears brimful,
When Goody Dobbins brought her cow to bull.
With apron blue to dry her tears she sought,
Then saw the cow well served, and took a groat.

JOHN GAY

406 *The Cave of Despair*

So as they traveild, lo they gan espy
    An armed knight towards them gallop fast,
    That seemed from some feared foe to fly,
    Or other griesly thing, that him agast.
    Still as he fled, his eye was backward cast,
    As if his feare still followed him behind;
    Als flew his steed, as he his bands had brast,
    And with his winged heeles did tread the wind,
As he had beene a fole of *Pegasus* his kind.

Nigh as he drew, they might perceive his head
    To be unarmd, and curld uncombed heares
    Upstaring stiffe, dismayd with uncouth dread;
    Nor drop of bloud in all his face appeares
    Nor life in limbe: and to increase his feares,
    In fowle reproch of knighthoods faire degree,
    About his neck an hempen rope he weares,
    That with his glistring armes does ill agree;
But he of rope or armes has now no memoree.

The *Redcrosse* knight toward him crossed fast,
    To weet, what mister wight was so dismayd:
    There him he finds all sencelesse and aghast,
    That of him selfe he seemd to be afrayd;
    Whom hardly he from flying forward stayd,
    Till he these wordes to him deliver might;
    Sir knight, aread who hath ye thus arayd,
    And eke from whom make ye this hasty flight:
For never knight I saw in such misseeming plight.

He answerd nought at all, but adding new
  Feare to his first amazment, staring wide
  With stony eyes, and hartlesse hollow hew,
  Astonisht stood, as one that had aspide
  Infernall furies, with their chaines untide.
  Him yet againe, and yet againe bespake
  The gentle knight; who nought to him replide,
  But trembling every joynt did inly quake,
And foltring tongue at last these words seemd forth to shake.

For Gods deare love, Sir knight, do me not stay;
  For loe he comes, he comes fast after mee.
  Eftlooking backe would faine have runne away;
  But he him forst to stay, and tellen free
  The secret cause of his perplexitie:
  Yet nathemore by his bold hartie speach,
  Could his bloud-frosen hart emboldned bee,
  But through his boldnesse rather feare did reach,
Yet forst, at last he made through silence suddein breach

And am I now in safetie sure (quoth he)
  From him, that would have forced me to dye?
  And is the point of death now turnd fro mee,
  That I may tell this haplesse history?
  Feare nought: (quoth he) no daunger now is nye.
  Then shall I you recount a ruefull cace,
  (Said he) the which with this unlucky eye
  I late beheld, and had not greater grace
Me reft from it, had bene partaker of the place.

I lately chaunst (Would I had never chaunst)
  With a faire knight to keepen companee,
  Sir *Terwin* hight, that well himselfe advaunst
  In all affaires, and was both bold and free,
  But not so happie as mote happie bee:
  He lov'd, as was his lot, a Ladie gent,
  That him againe lov'd in the least degree:
  For she was proud, and of too high intent,
And joyd to see her lover languish and lament.

From whom returning sad and comfortlesse,
  As on the way together we did fare,
  We met that villen (God from him me blesse)

N

That cursed wight, from whom I scapt why leare,
　　A man of hell, that cals himselfe *Despaire*:
　　Who first us greets, and after faire areedes
　　Of tydings strange, and of adventures rare:
　　So creeping close, as Snake in hidden weedes,
Inquireth of our states, and of our knightly deedes.

Which when he knew, and felt our feeble harts
　　Embost with bale, and bitter byting griefe,
　　Which love had launched with his deadly darts,
　　With wounding words and termes of foule repriefe
　　He pluckt from us all hope of due reliefe,
　　That earst us held in love of lingring life;
　　Then hopelesse hartlesse, gan the cunning thiefe
　　Persuade us die, to stint all further strife:
To me he lent this rope, to him a rustie knife.

With which sad instrument of hastie death,
　　That wofull lover, loathing lenger light,
　　A wide way made to let forth living breath.
　　But I more fearefull, or more luckie wight,
　　Dismayd with that deformed dismall sight,
　　Fled fast away, halfe dead with dying feare:
　　Ne yet assur'd of life by you, Sir knight,
　　Whose like infirmitie like chaunce may beare:
But God you never let his charmed speeches heare.

How may a man (said he) with idle speach
　　Be wonne, to spoyle the Castle of his health?
　　I wote (quoth he) whom triall late did teach,
　　That like would not for all this worldes wealth:
　　His subtill tongue, like dropping honny, mealt'th
　　Into the hart, and searcheth every vaine,
　　That ere one be aware, by secret stealth
　　His powre is reft, and weaknesse doth remaine.
O never Sir desire to try his guilefull traine.

Certes (said he) hence shall I never rest,
　　Till I that treachours art have heard and tride;
　　And you Sir knight, whose name mote I request,
　　Of grace do me unto his cabin guide.
　　I that hight *Trevisan* (quoth he) will ride

Against my liking backe, to doe you grace:
But nor for gold nor glee will I abide
By you, when ye arrive in that same place;
For lever had I die, then see his deadly face.

Ere long they come, where that same wicked wight
  His dwelling has, low in an hollow cave,
  Farre underneath a craggie clift ypight,
  Darke, dolefull, drearie, like a greedie grave,
  That still for carrion carcases doth crave:
  On top whereof aye dwelt the ghastly Owle,
  Shrieking his balefull note, which ever drave
  Farre from that haunt all other chearefull fowle;
And all about it wandring ghostes did waile and howle.

And all about old stockes and stubs of trees,
  Whereon nor fruit, nor leafe was ever seene,
  Did hang upon the ragged rocky knees;
  On which had many wretches hanged beene,
  Whose carcases were scattered on the greene,
  And throwne about the cliffs. Arrived there,
  That bare-head knight for dread and dolefull teene,[1]
  Would faine have fled, ne durst approchen neare,
But th' other forst him stay, and comforted in feare.

That darkesome cave they enter, where they find
  That cursed man, low sitting on the ground,
  Musing full sadly in his sullein mind;
  His griesie lockes, long growen, and unbound,
  Disordred hong about his shoulders round,
  And hid his face; through which his hollow eyne
  Lookt deadly dull, and stared as astound;
  His raw-bone cheekes through penurie and pine,
Were shronke into his jawes, as he did never dine.

His garment nought but many ragged clouts,
  With thornes together pind and patched was,
  The which his naked sides he wrapt abouts;
  And him beside there lay upon the gras
  A drearie corse, whose life away did pas,

---

[1] grief

All wallowd in his owne yet luke-warme blood,
That from his wound yet welled fresh alas;
In which a rustie knife fast fixed stood,
And made an open passage for the gushing flood.

EDMUND SPENSER

407 *The Bower of Bliss*

Eftsoones they heard a most melodious sound,
   Of all that mote delight a daintie eare,
   Such as attonce might not on living ground,
   Save in this Paradise, be heard elswhere:
   Right hard it was, for wight, which did it heare,
   To read, what manner musicke that mote bee:
   For all that pleasing is to living eare,
   Was there consorted in one harmonee,
Birdes, voices, instruments, windes, waters, all agree.

The joyous birdes shrouded in chearefull shade,
   Their notes unto the voice attempred sweet;
   Th' Angelicall soft trembling voices made
   To th' instruments divine respondence meet:
   The silver sounding instruments did meet
   With the base murmure of the waters fall:
   The waters fall with difference discreet,
   Now soft, now loud, unto the wind did call:
The gentle warbling wind low answered to all.

There, whence that Musick seemed heard to bee,
   Was the faire Witch her selfe now solacing,
   With a new lover, whom through sorceree
   And witchcraft, she from farre did thither bring:
   There she had him now laid a slombering,
   In secret shade, after long wanton joyes:
   Whilst round about them pleasauntly did sing
   Many faire Ladies, and lascivious boyes,
That ever mixt their song with light licentious toyes.

And all that while, right over him she hong,
   With her false eyes fast fixed in his sight,
   As seeking medicine, whence she was stong,
   Or greedily depasturing delight:
   And oft inclining downe with kisses light,

For feare of waking him, his lips bedewd,
And through his humid eyes did sucke his spright,
Quite molten into lust and pleasure lewd;
Wherewith she sighed soft, as if his case she rewd.

The whiles some one did chaunt this lovely lay;
Ah see, who so faire thing doest faine to see,
In springing flowre the image of thy day;
Ah see the Virgin Rose, how sweetly shee
Doth first peepe forth with bashfull modestee,
That fairer seemes, the lesse ye see her may;
Lo see soone after, how more bold and free
Her bared bosome she doth broad display;
Loe see soone after, how she fades, and falles away.

So passeth, in the passing of a day,
Of mortall life the leafe, the bud, the flowre,
Ne more doth flourish after first decay,
That earst was sought to decke both bed and bowre,
Of many a Ladie, and many a Paramowre:
Gather therefore the Rose, whilest yet is prime,
For soone comes age, that will her pride deflowre:
Gather the Rose of love, whilest yet is time,
Whilest loving thou mayst loved be with equall crime.

He ceast, and then gan all the quire of birdes
Their diverse notes t' attune unto his lay,
As in approvance of his pleasing words.
The constant paire heard all, that he did say,
Yet swarved not, but kept their forward way,
Through many covert groves, and thickets close,
In which they creeping did at last display
That wanton Ladie, with her lover lose,
Whose sleepie head she in her lap did soft dispose.

Upon a bed of Roses she was laid,
As faint through heat, or dight to pleasant sin,
And was arayd, or rather disarayd,
All in a vele of silke and silver thin,
That hid no whit her alablaster skin,

But rather shewd more white, if more might bee:
More subtile web *Arachne* cannot spin,
Nor the fine nets, which oft we woven see
Of scorched deaw, do not in th' aire more lightly flee.

Her snowy brest was bare to readie spoile
Of hungry eies, which n'ote therewith be fild,
And yet through languour of her late sweet toile,
Few drops, more cleare then Nectar, forth distild,
That like pure Orient perles adowne it trild,
And her faire eyes sweet smyling in delight,
Moistened their fierie beames, with which she thrild
Fraile harts, yet quenched not; like starry light
Which sparckling on the silent waves, does seeme more bright.

The young man sleeping by her, seemd to bee
Some goodly swayne of honorable place,
That certes it great pittie was to see
Him his nobilitie so foule deface;
A sweet regard, and amiable grace,
Mixed with manly sternnesse did appeare
Yet sleeping, in his well proportioned face,
And on his tender lips the downy heare
Did now but freshly spring, and silken blossomes beare.

His warlike armes, the idle instruments
Of sleeping praise, were hong upon a tree,
And his brave shield, full of old moniments,
Was fowly ra'st, that none the signes might see;
Ne for them, ne for honour cared hee,
Ne ought, that did to his advauncement tend,
But in lewd loves, and wastfull luxuree,
His dayes, his goods, his bodie he did spend:
O horrible enchantment, that him so did blend.

EDMUND SPENSER

408 *Sonnet*

Comming to kisse her lyps, (such grace I found)
Me seemd I smelt a gardin of sweet flowres:
that dainty odours from them threw around
for damzels fit to decke their lovers bowres.

Her lips did smell lyke unto Gillyflowers,
  her ruddy cheekes lyke unto Roses red:
  her snowy browes lyke budded Bellamoures,
  her lovely eyes lyke Pincks but newly spred.
Her goodly bosome lyke a Strawberry bed,
  her neck lyke to a bounch of Cullambynes:
  her brest lyke lillyes, ere theyr leaves be shed,
  her nipples lyke yong blossomd Iessemynes.
Such fragrant flowres doe give most odorous smell,
  but her sweet odour did them all excell.

                                    EDMUND SPENSER

409 *Ozymandias*

I met a traveller from an antique land
Who said: Two vast and trunkless legs of stone
Stand in the desert . . . Near them, on the sand,
Half sunk, a shattered visage lies, whose frown,
And wrinkled lip, and sneer of cold command,
Tell that its sculptor well those passions read
Which yet survive, stamped on these lifeless things,
The hand that mocked them, and the heart that fed:
And on the pedestal these words appear:
'My name is Ozymandias, king of kings:
Look on my works, ye Mighty, and despair!'
Nothing beside remains. Round the decay
Of that colossal wreck, boundless and bare
The lone and level sands stretch far away.

                              PERCY BYSSHE SHELLEY

410 *To the Earl of Dorset*

Copenhagen, March 9, 1709

From frozen climes, and endless tracts of snow,
From streams which northern winds forbid to flow,
What present shall the muse to *Dorset* bring,
Or how, so near the pole, attempt to sing?
The hoary winter here conceals from sight
All pleasing objects that to verse invite.

The hills and dales, and the delightful woods,
The flow'ry plains, and silver-streaming floods,
By snow disguis'd, in bright confusion lie,
And with one dazzling waste fatigue the eye.

No gentle breathing breeze prepares the spring,
No birds within the desert region sing.
The ships, unmov'd, the boist'rous winds defy,
While rattling chariots o'er the ocean fly.
The vast *Leviathan* wants room to play,
And spout his waters in the face of day.
The starving wolves along the main sea prowl,
And to the moon in icy valleys howl.
For many a shining league the level main
Here spreads itself into a glassy plain:
There solid billows of enormous size,
Alps of green ice, in wild disorder rise.

And yet but lately have I seen, ev'n here,
The winter in a lovely dress appear.
E're yet the clouds let fall the treasur'd snow,
Or winds begun thro' hazy skies to blow,
At ev'ning a keen eastern breeze arose,
And the descending rain unsully'd froze.
Soon as the silent shades of night withdrew,
The ruddy morn disclos'd at once to view
The face of nature in a rich disguise,
And brighten'd ev'ry object to my eyes:
For ev'ry shrub, and ev'ry blade of grass,
And ev'ry pointed thorn, seem'd wrought in glass;
In pearls and rubies rich the hawthorns show,
While through the ice the crimson berries glow.
The thick-sprung reeds the wat'ry marshes yield,
Seem'd polish'd lances in a hostile field.
The stag in limpid currents, with surprise,
Sees crystal branches on his forehead rise:
The spreading oak, the beech, and tow'ring pine,
Glaz'd over, in the freezing aether shine.
The frighted birds the rattling branches shun,
That wave and glitter in the distant sun.

When if a sudden gust of wind arise,
The brittle forest into atoms flies,
The crackling wood beneath the tempest bends,
And in a spangled show'r the prospect ends:
Or, if a southern gale the region warm,
And by degrees unbind the wintry charm,
The traveller a miry country sees,
And journeys sad beneath the dropping trees:
Like some deluded peasant, *Merlin* leads
Thro' fragrant bow'rs, and thro' delicious meads,
While here inchanted gardens to him rise,
And airy fabricks there attract his eyes,
His wand'ring feet the magick paths pursue;
And while he thinks the fair illusion true,
The trackless scenes disperse in fluid air,
And woods and wilds and thorny ways appear;
A tedious road the weary wretch returns,
And, as he goes, the transient vision mourns.

AMBROSE PHILIPS

411 *Masar*

Once a fair city, courted then by kings,
Mistress of nations, throng'd by palaces,
Raising her head o'er destiny, her face
Glowing with pleasure, and with palms refreshed,
Now, pointed at by Wisdom or by Wealth,
Bereft of beauty, bare of ornaments,
Stood, in the wilderness of woe, Masar.
Ere far advancing, all appear'd a plain.
Treacherous and fearful mountains, far advanced.
Her glory so gone down, at human step
The fierce hyæna, frighted from the walls,
Bristled his rising back, his teeth unsheathed,
Drew the long growl and with slow foot retired.
Still were remaining some of ancient race,
And ancient arts were now their sole delight.
With Time's first sickle they had marked the hour
When at their incantation would the Moon
Start back, and shuddering shed blue blasted light.
The rifted rays they gather'd, and immersed

In potent portion of that wondrous wave
Which, hearing rescued Israel, stood erect,
And led her armies through his crystal gates.
　　Hither—none shared her way, her counsel none—
Hied the Masarian Dalica: 'twas night,
And the still breeze fell languid on the waste.
She, tired with journey long, and ardent thoughts,
Stopt; and before the city she descried
A female form emerge above the sands:
Intent she fix'd her eyes, and on herself
Relying, with fresh vigor bent her way;
Nor disappear'd the woman, but exclaim'd—
One hand retaining tight her folded vest—
'Stranger! who loathest life, there lies Masar.
Begone, nor tarry longer, or, ere morn,
The cormorant, in his solitary haunt
Of insulated rock or sounding cove,
Stands on thy bleached bones, and screams for prey.
My lips can scatter them a hundred leagues,
So shrivell'd in one breath, as all the sands
We tread on, could not in as many years.
Wretched who die nor raise their sepulchre!
Therefor begone.'
　　　　　　　But, Dalica, unaw'd,—
Tho, in her wither'd but still firm right-hand
Held up with imprecations, hoarse and deep,
Glimmer'd her brazen sickle, and inclosed
Within its figur'd curve the fading moon—
Spake thus aloud. 'By yon bright orb of Heaven,
In that most sacred moment when her beam
Guided first thither by the forked shaft,
Strikes thro' the crevice of Arishtah's tower—'
'Sayst thou?' astonished cried the sorceress,
'Woman of outer darkness, fiend of death,
From what inhuman cave, what dire abyss,
Hast thou invisible that spell o'erheard?
What potent hand hath touched thy quicken'd corse,
What song dissolved thy cearments; who unclosed
Those faded eyes, and fill'd them from the stars?
But if with inextinguished light of life
Thou breathest, soul and body unamerst,

Then, whence that invocation; who hath dared
Those hallow'd words, divulging, to profane?'
Then Dalica–
     'To heaven, not earth, addrest,
Prayers for protection cannot be profane.'
 Here the pale sorceress turn'd her face aside,
Wildly, and mutter'd to herself, amazed,
'I dread her who, alone, at such an hour,
Can speak so strangely; who can thus combine
The words of reason with our gifted rites;
Yet will I speak once more–If thou hast seen
The city of Charoba, hast thou marked
The steps of Dalica?'
     'What then?'
          'The tongue
Of Dalica has then our rites divulged.'
'Whose rites?'
    'Her sister's, mother's, and her own.'
'Never.'
   'How sayst thou never? one would think,
Presumptuous, thou wert, Dalica.'
       'I am,
Woman, and who art thou?' with close embrace,
Clung the Masarian round her neck, and cried
'Art thou, then, not my sister? ah, I fear
The golden lamps and jewels of a court
Deprive thine eyes of strength and purity:
O Dalica, mine watch the waning moon,
For ever patient in our mother's art,
And rest on Heaven suspended, where the founts
Of Wisdom rise, where sound the wings of Power:
Studies intense of strong and stern delight!
And thou too, Dalica, so many years
Wean'd from the bosom of thy native land,
Returnest back, and seekest true repose.
O what more pleasant than the short-breath'd sigh,
When laying down your burden at the gate,
And dizzy with long wandering, you embrace
The cool and quiet of a homespun bed.'
 'Alas,' said Dalica, 'tho' all commend
This choice, and many meet with no controul,

Yet, none pursue it! Age, by Care opprest,
Feels for the couch, and drops into the grave.
The tranquil scene lies further still from Youth.
Phrenzied Ambition and desponding Love
Consume Youth's fairest flow'rs; compar'd with Youth
Age has a something something like repose.
Myrthyr, I seek not here a boundary
Like the horizon, which, as you advance,
Keeping its form and color, still recedes:
But mind my errand, and my suit perform.
    Twelve years ago Charoba first could speak.
If her indulgent father asked her name,
She would indulge him too, and would reply
"*What? why, Charoba*"—rais'd with sweet surprize,
And proud to shine a teacher in her turn.
Shew her the graven sceptre; what its use?–
'Twas to beat dogs with, and to gather flies.
She thought the crown a plaything to amuse
Herself, and not the people, for she thought
Who mimick infant words might infant toys:
But while she watched grave elders look with awe
On such a bauble, she withheld her breath;
She was afraid her parents should suspect
They had caught childhood from her in a kiss;
She blushed for shame, and fear'd–for she believ'd,
Yet was not courage wanting in the child. . . .'

                              WALTER SAVAGE LANDOR

412 *Sea Eclogue*

Meroe. Otys, begin—
Since he is gone, I'll fetch him to my Arms
By sacred Spells, and Force of Magic Charms.
Search in the Slime, you'll find the Cramp-fish there,
That, chilling stops whatever swims too near:
You'll find the Fish, that stays the labouring Ship,
Tho' ruffling Winds drive o'er the noisy Deep:
So *Phorbas*, while from me he perjur'd flies,
Is struck benumb'd, and fix'd with strange Surprize.
    Look down auspicious Moon; too well you know
    What Love will force, and potent Charms can do.

Take here, and drain the Sepia's inky Juice,
Sprinkle the Sea, and say, I thus infuse
Sad gloomy Thoughts into the perjur'd Swain,
'Till he relenting sigh, and turn to love again.
  Look down auspicious Moon; too well you know
What Love will force, and potent Charms can do.
  Wreath three times thrice three Reeds, and sev'n times round
The Chaplets wave (strange Virtues have been found.
In Numbers hid; and Energy divine,
In figur'd Spells, and the mysterious Trine.)
  Look down auspicious Moon; too well you know
What Love will force, and potent Charms can do.
  Take here the rav'nous Dog, and wound him thro'.
Then cry aloud, *Phorbas*, I strike for you;
So may his Soul be pierc'd with fretting Pain,
'Till he relenting sigh, and turn to love again.
  Look down auspicious Moon; too well you know
What Love will force, and potent Charms can do.
  Go fetch dry Weeds; They lie on yonder Isle;
Then raise in corner'd Squares the artful Pile,
And force the kindled Heap with flaming Oil:
So may his tortur'd Soul in Anguish mourn,
And as the Pile, so may the Triton burn.
  Look down auspicious Moon; too well you know
What Love will force, and potent Charms can do.
  I hear the holloaing Elves, and Midnight Shriek
Of wand'ring Ghosts, who now unbodied seek
Their lost Abodes, and restless ever roam;
Affright, ye Elves, and bring my *Phorbas* home.
  Look down auspicious Moon; too well you know
What Love will force, and potent Charms can do.
  While now the Flames consume the sacred Heap,
Sing, *Otys*; Try to lull my Soul asleep;
Delightful Sounds, when form'd by studious Art
Will kind Relief a while, and slumb'ring Ease impart;
They quell sad Thoughts, and raise from black Despair
The troubled Mind, and still the Voice of Care.
  Otys. Love once assay'd to swim; in wanton Play
He labouring strove to cut the liquid way:
He prest the Waters with extended Arms,
And as he mov'd, display'd a thousand Charms.

When tir'd with Sport, he would at length have flown,
His Wings were clog'd with Wet, and useless grown,
Flutt'ring he strove, but Moisture prest him down.
The God of Love is now to Seas confin'd,
No Triton must be proud, or Nymph unkind.
   Mer. Cease, *Otys*; see, the Flame already dies,
Choak'd with dark smoky Fumes, that circling rise,
Moisture imbib'd preserves the reeking Heap:
Sad sign!—
Nor will he burn, nor shall I cease to weep.
In vain we strive: No artful Spell can move,
No Charm will force unwilling Souls to love.

WILLIAM DIAPER

413 *Doron's Description of Samela*

Like to Diana in her Summer weed
Girt with a crimson robe of brightest die,
     goes fair Samela.
Whiter than be the flocks that straggling feed,
When washt by Arethusa's Fount they lie:
     is fair Samela.
As fair Aurora in her morning gray
Deckt with the ruddy glister of her love,
     is fair Samela.
Like lovely Thetis on a calmed day,
When as her brightness Neptune's fancy move,
     shines fair Samela.
Her tresses gold, her eyes like glassy streams,
Her teeth are pearl, the breasts are ivory,
     of fair Samela.
Her cheeks like rose and lily yield forth gleams,
Her brows bright arches fram'd of ebony;
     Thus fair Samela.
Passeth fair Venus in her bravest hew,
And Juno in the shew of majesty,
     for she's Samela.
Pallas in wit, all three if you well view,
For beauty, wit, and matchless dignity
     yield to Samela.

ROBERT GREENE

414 *A Prayer for my Daughter*

Once more the storm is howling, and half hid
Under this cradle-hood and coverlid
My child sleeps on. There is no obstacle
But Gregory's wood and one bare hill
Whereby the haystack- and roof-levelling wind,
Bred on the Atlantic, can be stayed;
And for an hour I have walked and prayed
Because of the great gloom that is in my mind.

I have walked and prayed for this young child an hour
And heard the sea-wind scream upon the tower,
And under the arches of the bridge, and scream
In the elms above the flooded stream;
Imagining in excited reverie
That the future years had come,
Dancing to a frenzied drum,
Out of the murderous innocence of the sea.

May she be granted beauty and yet not
Beauty to make a stranger's eye distraught,
Or hers before a looking-glass, for such,
Being made beautiful overmuch,
Consider beauty a sufficient end,
Lose natural kindness and maybe
The heart-revealing intimacy
That chooses right, and never find a friend.

Helen being chosen found life flat and dull
And later had much trouble from a fool,
While that great Queen, that rose out of the spray,
Being fatherless could have her way
Yet chose a bandy-leggèd smith for man.
It's certain that fine women eat
A crazy salad with their meat
Whereby the Horn of Plenty is undone.

In courtesy I'd have her chiefly learned;
Hearts are not had as a gift but hearts are earned
By those that are not entirely beautiful;
Yet many, that have played the fool

For beauty's very self, has charm made wise,
And many a poor man that has roved,
Loved and thought himself beloved,
From a glad kindness cannot take his eyes.

May she become a flourishing hidden tree
That all her thoughts may like the linnet be,
And have no business but dispensing round
Their magnanimities of sound,
Nor but in merriment begin a chase,
Nor but in merriment a quarrel.
O may she live like some green laurel
Rooted in one dear perpetual place.

My mind, because the minds that I have loved,
The sort of beauty that I have approved,
Prosper but little, has dried up of late,
Yet knows that to be choked with hate
May well be of all evil chances chief.
If there's no hatred in a mind
Assault and battery of the wind
Can never tear the linnet from the leaf.

An intellectual hatred is the worst,
So let her think opinions are accursed.
Have I not seen the loveliest woman born
Out of the mouth of Plenty's horn,
Because of her opinionated mind
Barter that horn and every good
By quiet natures understood
For an old bellows full of angry wind?

Considering that, all hatred driven hence,
The soul recovers radical innocence
And learns at last that it is self-delighting,
Self-appeasing, self-affrighting,
And that its own sweet will is Heaven's will;
She can, though every face should scowl
And every windy quarter howl
Or every bellows burst, be happy still.

And may her bridegroom bring her to a house
Where all's accustomed, ceremonious;
For arrogance and hatred are the wares
Peddled in the thoroughfares.
How but in custom and in ceremony
Are innocence and beauty born?
Ceremony's a name for the rich horn,
And custom for the spreading laurel tree.

WILLIAM BUTLER YEATS

415 *Elegy on his Mistress*

By our first strange and fatal interview,
By all desires which thereof did ensue,
By our long starving hopes, by that remorse
Which my words' masculine persuasive force
Begot in thee, and by the memory
Of hurts, which spies and rivals threaten'd me,
I calmly beg. But by thy father's wrath,
By all pains, which want and divorcement hath,
I conjure thee, and all the oaths which I
And thou have sworn to seal joint constancy,
Here I unswear, and overswear them thus:
Thou shalt not love by ways so dangerous.
Temper, O fair love, love's impetuous rage;
Be my true mistress still, not my feign'd page.
I'll go, and, by thy kind leave, leave behind
Thee, only worthy to nurse in my mind,
Thirst to come back; O! if thou die before,
My soul from other lands to thee shall soar.
Thy (else almighty) beauty cannot move
Rage from the seas, nor thy love teach them love,
Nor tame wild Boreas' harshness; thou hast read
How roughly he in pieces shivered
Fair Orithea, whom he swore he lov'd.
Fall ill or good, 'tis madness to have prov'd
Dangers unurg'd; feed on this flattery,
That absent lovers one in th'other be.
Dissemble nothing, not a boy, nor change
Thy body's habit, nor mind; be not strange

To thyself only. All will spy in thy face
A blushing womanly discovering grace;
Richly cloth'd apes, are call'd apes, and as soon
Eclips'd as bright, we call the moon the moon.
Men of France, changeable cameleons,
Spitals of diseases, shops of fashions,
Love's fuellers, and the rightest company
Of players, which upon the world's stage be,
Will quickly know thee, and no less, alas!
Th'indifferent Italian, as we pass
His warm land, well content to think thee page,
Will hunt thee with such lust, and hideous rage,
As Lot's fair guests were vex'd. But none of these,
Nor spongy hydroptic Dutch shall thee displease,
If thou stay here. O stay here, for, for thee
England is only a worthy gallery,
To walk in expectation, till from thence
Our greatest king call thee to his presence.
When I am gone, dream me some happiness;
Nor let thy looks our long-hid love confess;
Nor praise, nor dispraise me, nor bless nor curse
Openly love's force, nor in bed fright thy nurse
With midnight's startings, crying out, O! O!
Nurse, O! my love is slain; I saw him go
O'er the white Alps alone; I saw him, I,
Assail'd, fight, taken, stabb'd, bleed, fall, and die.
Augur me better chance, except dread Jove
Think it enough for me to'have had thy love.

JOHN DONNE

416 *The Fear of Death*

The *Sisiphus* is he, whom noise and strife
Seduce from all the soft retreats of life,
To vex the government, disturb the laws:
Drunk with the fumes of popular applause,
He courts the giddy crowd to make him great,
And sweats and toils in vain, to mount the sovereign seat.
For still to aim at pow'r and still to fail,
Ever to strive, and never to prevail,

What is it, but, in reason's true account
To heave the stone against the rising mount?
Which urg'd, and labour'd, and forc'd up with pain,
Recoils, and rolls impetuous down, and smokes along the
    plain.
Then still to treat thy ever-craving mind
With ev'ry blessing, and of ev'ry kind,
Yet never fill thy rav'ning appetite;
Though years and seasons vary thy delight,
Yet nothing to be seen of all the store,
But still the wolf within thee barks for more;
This is the fable's Moral, which they tell
Of fifty foolish virgins damn'd in hell
To leaky vessels, which the liquor spill;
To vessels of their sex, which none could ever fill.
As for the dog, the furies, and their snakes,
The gloomy caverns, and the burning lakes,
And all the vain infernal trumpery,
They neither are, nor were, nor e'er can be.
But here on earth, the guilty have in view
The mighty pains to mighty mischiefs due;
Racks, prisons, poisons, the *Tarpeian* Rock,
Stripes, hangmen, pitch, and suffocating smoke;
And last, and most, if these were cast behind,
Th' avenging horror of a conscious mind,
Whose deadly fear anticipates the blow,
And sees no end of punishment and woe;
But looks for more, at the last gasp of breath:
This makes an Hell on Earth, and life a death.
Mean time when thoughts of death disturb thy head;
Consider, *Ancus* great and good is dead;
Ancus thy better far, was born to die;
And thou, dost thou bewail mortality?
So many monarchs with their mighty state,
Who rul'd the world, were over-rul'd by fate.
That haughty king, who lorded o'er the main,
And whose stupendous bridge did the wild waves restrain,
(In vain they foam'd, in vain they threat'ned wreck,
While his proud legions march'd upon their back:)
Him death, a greater monarch, overcame;
Nor spar'd his guards the more, for their immortal name.

The *Roman* chief, the *Carthaginian* dread,
Scipio, the thunder bolt of war, is dead,
And like a common slave, by fate in triumph led.
The founders of invented arts are lost;
And wits who made eternity their boast.
Where now is *Homer*, who possesst the throne?
Th' immortal work remains, the mortal author's gone.
Democritus, perceiving age invade,
His body weak'n'd and his mind decay'd,
Obey'd the summons with a cheerful face;
Made haste to welcome death, and met him half the race.
That stroke ev'n *Epicurus* could not bar,
Though he in wit surpass'd mankind, as far
As does the midday sun the midnight star.
And thou, dost thou disdain to yield thy breath,
Whose very life is little more than death?
More than one half by lazy sleep possest;
And when awake, thy soul but nods at best,
Day-dreams and sickly thoughts revolving in thy breast.
Eternal troubles haunt thy anxious mind,
Whose cause and cure thou never hop'st to find;
But still uncertain, with thyself at strife,
Thou wander'st in the labyrinth of life.
O! if the foolish race of man, who find
A weight of cares still pressing on their mind,
Could find as well the cause of this unrest,
And all this burden lodg'd within the breast;
Sure they would change their course, nor live as now,
Uncertain what to wish or what to vow.
Uneasy both in country and in town,
They search a place to lay their burden down.
One, restless in his palace, walks abroad,
And vainly thinks to leave behind the load:
But straight returns; for he's as restless there:
And finds there's no relief in open air.
Another to his villa would retire,
And spurs as hard as if it were on fire
No sooner enter'd at his country door,
But he begins to stretch, and yawn, and snore;
Or seeks the city which he left before.
Thus every man o'er works his weary will,

To shun himself, and to shake off his ill:
The shaking fit returns, and hangs upon him still.
No prospect of repose, nor hope of ease;
The wretch is ignorant of his disease;
Which known would all his fruitless trouble spare;
For he would know the world not worth his care;
Then would he search more deeply for the cause;
And study nature well, and nature's laws:
For in this moment lies not the debate,
But on our future, fix'd, eternal state;
That never changing state, which all must keep,
Whom death has doom'd to everlasting sleep.
Why are we then so fond of mortal life,
Beset with dangers, and maintain'd with strife?
A life, which all our care can never save;
One fate attends us; and one common grave.
Besides, we tread but a perpetual round;
We ne'er strike out, but beat the former ground,
And the same mawkish joys in the same track are found.
For still we think an absent blessing best,
Which cloys, and is no blessing when possest;
A new arising wish expels it from the breast.
The feav'rish thirst of life increases still;
We call for more and more, and never have our fill;
Yet know not what to-morrow we shall try,
What dregs of life in the last draught may lie:
Nor, by the longest life we can attain,
One moment from the length of death we gain;
For all behind belongs to his eternal reign.
When once the Fates have cut the mortal thread,
The man as much to all intents is dead,
Who dies to-day, and will as long be so,
As he who died a thousand years ago.

JOHN DRYDEN

417 *On Zacheus*

Me thinks, I see, with what a busy haste,
Zacheus climb'd the Tree: But O, how fast,
How full of speed, canst thou imagine (when
Our Saviour call'd) he powder'd down agen!

He ne'er made trial, if the boughs were sound,
Or rotten; nor how far 'twas to the ground:
There was no danger fear'd; at such a call,
He'll venture nothing, that dare fear a fall;
Needs must he down, by such a *Spirit* driven,
Nor could he fall unless he fell to *Heaven*.
Down came *Zacheus*, ravisht from the tree;
Bird that was shot ne'er dropt so quick as he.

FRANCIS QUARLES

418 *Low Barometer*

The south-wind strengthens to a gale,
Across the moon the clouds fly fast,
The house is smitten as with a flail,
The chimney shudders to the blast.

On such a night, when Air has loosed
Its guardian grasp on blood and brain,
Old terrors then of god or ghost
Creep from their caves to life again;

And Reason kens he herits in
A haunted house.   Tenants unknown
Assert their squalid lease of sin
With earlier title than his own.

Unbodied presences, the pack'd
Pollution and remorse of Time,
Slipp'd from oblivion reënact
The horrors of unhouseld crime.

Some men would quell the thing with prayer
Whose sightless footsteps pad the floor,
Whose fearful trespass mounts the stair
Or bursts the lock'd forbidden door.

Some have seen corpses long interr'd
Escape from hallowing control,
Pale charnel forms–nay ev'n have heard
The shrilling of a troubled soul,

That wanders till the dawn hath cross'd
The dolorous dark, or Earth hath wound
Closer her storm-spredd cloke, and thrust
The baleful phantoms underground.

ROBERT BRIDGES

419 *Lucifer in Starlight*

On a starred night Prince Lucifer uprose.
Tired of his dark dominion swung the fiend
Above the rolling ball in cloud part screened,
Where sinners hugged their spectre of repose.
Poor prey to his hot fit of pride were those.
And now upon his western wing he leaned,
Now his huge bulk o'er Afric's sands careened,
Now the black planet shadowed Arctic snows.
Soaring through wider zones that pricked his scars
With memory of the old revolt from Awe,
He reached a middle height, and at the stars,
Which are the brain of heaven, he looked, and sank.
Around the ancient track marched, rank on rank,
The army of unalterable law.

GEORGE MEREDITH

Book VI

IMPRESSIONS AND MEMORIES

420 *The Linnet*

Upon this leafy bush
   With thorns and roses in it,
Flutters a thing of light,
   A twittering linnet,
And all the throbbing world
   Of dew and sun and air
By this small parcel of life
   Is made more fair:
As if each bramble spray
   And mounded gold-wreathed furze,
Harebell and little thyme,
   Were only hers;
As if this beauty and grace
   Did to one bird belong,
And, at a flutter of wing,
   Might vanish in song.

WALTER DE LA MARE

421 *Snake*

A snake came to my water-trough
On a hot, hot day, and I in pyjamas for the heat,
To drink there.

In the deep, strange-scented shade of the great dark carob-tree
I came down the steps with my pitcher
And must wait, must stand and wait, for there he was at the
   trough before me.

He reached down from a fissure in the earth-wall in the gloom
And trailed his yellow-brown slackness soft-bellied down, over
   the edge of the stone trough
And rested his throat upon the stone bottom,

372

And where the water had dripped from the tap, in a small
 clearness,
He sipped with his straight mouth,
Softly drank through his straight gums, into his slack long
 body,
Silently.

Someone was before me at my water-trough,
And I, like a second comer, waiting.

He lifted his head from his drinking, as cattle do,
And looked at me vaguely, as drinking cattle do,
And flickered his two-forked tongue from his lips, and mused
 a moment,
And stooped and drank a little more,
Being earth-brown, earth-golden from the burning bowels of
 the earth,
On the day of Sicilian July, with Etna smoking.

The voice of my education said to me
He must be killed,
For in Sicily the black, black snakes are innocent, the gold are
 venomous.

And voices in me said, If you were a man
You would take a stick and break him now, and finish
 him off.

But I must confess how I liked him,
How glad I was he had come like a guest in quiet, to drink at
 my water-trough
And depart peaceful, pacified, and thankless,
Into the burning bowels of this earth!

Was it cowardice, that I dared not kill him?
Was it perversity, that I longed to talk to him?
Was it humility, to feel so honoured?
I felt so honoured.

And yet those voices:
If you were not afraid, you would kill him!

And truly I was afraid, I was most afraid,
But even so, honoured still more
That he should seek my hospitality
From out the dark door of the secret earth.

He drank enough
And lifted his head, dreamily, as one who has drunken,
And flickered his tongue like a forked night on the air, so black,
Seeming to lick his lips,
And looked around like a god, unseeing, into the air,
And slowly turned his head,
And slowly, very slowly, as if thrice adream,
Proceeded to draw his slow length curving round
And climb again the broken bank of my wall-face.

And as he put his head into that dreadful hole,
And as he slowly drew up, snake-easing his shoulders, and
entered farther,
A sort of horror, a sort of protest against his withdrawing into
that horrid black hole,
Deliberately going into the blackness, and slowly drawing
himself after,
Overcame me now his back was turned.

I looked round, I put down my pitcher,
I picked up a clumsy log
And threw it at the water-trough with a clatter.

I think it did not hit him,
But suddenly that part of him that was left behind convulsed
in undignified haste,
Writhed like lightning, and was gone
Into the black hole, the earth-lipped fissure in the wall-front,
At which, in the intense still noon, I stared with fascination.

And immediately I regretted it.
I thought how paltry, how vulgar, what a mean act!
I despised myself and the voices of my accursed human
education.
And I thought of the albatross,
And I wished he would come back, my snake.

For he seemed to me again like a king,
Like a king in exile, uncrowned in the underworld,
Now due to be crowned again.

And so, I missed my chance with one of the lords
Of life.
And I have something to expiate;
A pettiness.

D. H. Lawrence

422 *Under the Woods*

When these old woods were young
The thrushes' ancestors
As sweetly sung
In the old years.

There was no garden here,
Apples nor mistletoe;
No children dear
Ran to and fro.

New then was this thatched cot,
But the keeper was old,
And he had not
Much lead or gold.

Most silent beech and yew:
As he went round about
The woods to view
Seldom he shot.

But now that he is gone
Out of most memories;
Still lingers on,
A stoat of his,

But one, shrivelled and green,
And with no scent at all,
And barely seen
On this shed wall.

Edward Thomas

423 *Tor House*

If you should look for this place after a handful of lifetimes:
Perhaps of my planted forest a few
May stand yet, dark-leaved Australians or the coast cypress, haggard
With storm-drift; but fire and axe are devils.
Look for foundations of sea-worn granite, my fingers had the art
To make stone love stone, you will find some remnant.
But if you should look in your idleness after ten thousand years:
It is the granite knoll on the granite
And lava tongue in the midst of the bay, by the mouth of the Carmel
River-valley, these four will remain
In the change of names. You will know it by the wild sea-fragrance of wind
Though the ocean may have climbed or retired a little;
You will know it by the valley inland that our sun and our moon were born from
Before the poles changed; and Orion in December
Evenings was strung in the throat of the valley like a lamp-lighted bridge.
Come in the morning you will see white gulls
Weaving a dance over blue water, the wane of the moon
Their dance-companion, a ghost walking
By daylight, but wider and whiter than any bird in the world.
My ghost you needn't look for; it is probably
Here, but a dark one, deep in the granite, not dancing on wind
With the made wings and the day moon.

ROBINSON JEFFERS

424 *The Churchyard on the Sands*

My love lies in the gates of foam,
  The last dear wreck of shore:
The naked sea-marsh binds her home,
  The sand her chamber door.

The grey gull flaps the written stones,
  The ox-birds chase the tide;
And near the narrow field of bones
  Great ships at anchor ride.

Black piers with crust of dripping green,
  One foreland, like a hand,
O'er intervals of grass between
  Dim lonely dunes of sand.

A church of silent weathered looks,
  A breezy reddish tower,
A yard whose mounded resting-nooks
  Are tinged with sorrel flower.

In peace the swallow's eggs are laid
  Along the belfry walls;
The tempest does not reach her shade,
  The rain her silent halls.

But sails are sweet in summer sky,
  The lark throws down a lay;
The long salt levels steam and dry,
  The cloud-heart melts away.

But patches of the sea-pink shine,
  The pied crows poise and come;
The mallow hangs, the bindweeds twine,
  Where her sweet lips are dumb.

The passion of the wave is mute;
  Nor sound or ocean shock;
No music save the rilling flute
  That marks the curlew flock.

But yonder when the wind is keen,
  And rainy air is clear,
The merchant city's spires are seen,
  The toil of men grows near.

Along the coast-way grind the wheels
  Of endless carts of coal;
And on the sides of giant keels
  The shipyard hammers roll.

The world creeps here upon the shout,
  And stirs my heart in pain;
The mist descends and blots it out,
  And I am strong again.

Strong and alone, my dove, with thee;
 And, tho' mine eyes be wet,
There's nothing in the world to me
 So dear as my regret.

I would not change my sorrow, sweet,
 For others' nuptial hours;
I love the daisies at thy feet
 More than their orange flowers.

My hand alone shall tend thy tomb
 From leaf-bud to leaf-fall,
And wreathe around each season's bloom
 Till autumn ruins all.

Let snowdrops, early in the year,
 Droop o'er her silent breast;
And bid the later cowslip rear
 The amber of its crest.

Come hither, linnets tufted-red,
 Drift by, O wailing tern;
Set pure vale lilies at her head,
 At her feet lady-fern.

Grow, samphire, at the tidal brink,
 Wave, pansies of the shore,
To whisper how alone I think
 Of her for evermore.

Bring blue sea-hollies thorny, keen,
 Long lavender in flower;
Grey wormwood like a hoary queen,
 Stanch mullein like a tower.

O sea-wall mounded long and low
 Let iron bounds be thine;
Nor let the salt wave overflow
 That breast I held divine.

Nor float its sea-weed to her hair,
 Nor dim her eyes with sands:
No fluted cockle burrow where
 Sleep folds her patient hands.

Tho' thy crest feel the wild sea's breath,
　Tho' tide-weight tear thy root,
Oh, guard the treasure house, where Death
　Has bound my darling mute.

Tho' cold her pale lips to reward
　With Love's own mysteries,
Ah, rob no daisy from her sward,
　Rough gale of eastern seas!

Ah, render sere no silent bent,
　That by her head-stone waves;
Let noon and golden summer blent
　Pervade these ocean graves.

And, ah, dear heart, in thy still nest,
　Resign this earth of woes,
Forget the ardours of the west,
　Neglect the morning glows.

Sleep, and forget all things but one,
　Heard in each wave of sea,–
How lonely all the years will run
　Until I rest by thee.

LORD DE TABLEY

425 *London Snow*

When men were all asleep the snow came flying,
In large white flakes falling on the city brown,
Stealthily and perpetually settling and loosely lying,
　Hushing the latest traffic of the drowsy town;
Deadening, muffling, stifling its murmurs failing;
Lazily and incessantly floating down and down:
　Silently sifting and veiling road, roof and railing;
Hiding difference, making unevenness even,
Into angles and crevices softly drifting and sailing.
　All night it fell, and when full inches seven
It lay in the depth of its uncompacted lightness,
The clouds blew off from a high and frosty heaven;
　And all woke earlier for the unaccustomed brightness
Of the winter dawning, the strange unheavenly glare:
The eye marvelled–marvelled at the dazzling whiteness;

The ear hearkened to the stillness of the solemn air;
No sound of wheel rumbling nor of foot falling,
And the busy morning cries came thin and spare.
　　Then boys I heard, as they went to school, calling,
They gathered up the crystal manna to freeze
Their tongues with tasting, their hands with snowballing;
　　Or rioted in a drift, plunging up to the knees;
Or peering up from under the white-mossed wonder,
'O look at the trees!' they cried, 'O look at the trees!'
　　With lessened load a few carts creak and blunder,
Following along the white deserted way,
A country company long dispersed asunder:
　　When now already the sun, in pale display
Standing by Paul's high dome, spread forth below
His sparkling beams, and awoke the stir of the day.
　　For now doors open, and war is waged with the snow;
And trains of sombre men, past tale of number,
Tread long brown paths, as toward their toil they go:
　　But even for them awhile no cares encumber
Their minds diverted; the daily word is unspoken,
The daily thoughts of labour and sorrow slumber
At the sight of the beauty that greets them, for the charm they
　　have broken.

ROBERT BRIDGES

426 *After the Gale*

Who has not walked upon the shore,
And who does not the morning know,
The day the angry gale is o'er,
The hour the wind has ceased to blow?

The horses of the strong south-west
Are pastured round his tropic tent,
Careless how long the ocean's breast
Sob on and sigh for passion spent.

The frightened birds, that fled inland
To house in rock and tower and tree,
Are gathering on the peaceful strand,
To tempt again the sunny sea;

Whereon the timid ships steal out
And laugh to find their foe asleep,
That lately scattered them about,
And drave them to the fold like sheep.

The snow-white clouds he northward chased
Break into phalanx, line, and band:
All one way to the south they haste,
The south, their pleasant fatherland.

From distant hills their shadows creep,
Arrive in turn and mount the lea,
And flit across the downs, and leap
Sheer off the cliff upon the sea;

And sail and sail far out of sight.
But still I watch their fleecy trains,
That piling all the south with light,
Dapple in France the fertile plains.

ROBERT BRIDGES

427 *On a Bank as I sat a-Fishing*

A Description of The Spring

And now all nature seem'd in love;
The lusty sap began to move;
New juice did stir th' embracing vines,
And birds had drawn their valentines;
The jealous trout, that, low did lie,
Rose at a well-dissembl'd fly:
There stood my friend, with patient skill,
Attending of his trembling quill.
Already were the eaves possess'd
With the swift pilgrim's daubed nest:
The groves already did rejoice
In Philomel's triumphing voice.
    The show'rs were short, the weather mild,
The morning fresh, the evening smil'd.
    Joan takes her neat-rubb'd pail, and now
She trips to milk the sand-red cow;

Where, for some sturdy football swain,
Joan strokes a syllabub or twain.
    The fields and gardens were beset
With tulip, crocus, violet;
And now, though late, the modest rose
Did more than half a blush disclose.
Thus all look'd gay, all full of cheer,
To welcome the new liveried year.

                              SIR HENRY WOTTON

428 *Grongar Hill*

Silent Nymph, with curious eye!
Who, the purple ev'ning, lie
On the mountain's lonely van,
Beyond the noise of busy man,
Painting fair the form of things,
While the yellow linnet sings;
Or the tuneful nightingale
Charms the forest with her tale;
Come with all thy various hues,
Come, and aid the sister Muse;
Now while Phoebus riding high
Gives lustre to the land and sky!
Grongar Hill invites my song,
Draw the landskip bright and strong;
Grongar, in whose mossy cells
Sweetly-musing Quiet dwells;
Grongar, in whose silent shade,
For the modest Muses made,
So oft I have, the evening still,
At the fountain of a rill,
Sate upon a flow'ry bed,
With my hand beneath my head;
While stray'd my eyes o'er Towy's flood,
Over mead, and over wood,
From house to house, from hill to hill,
'Till Contemplation had her fill.
    About his chequer'd sides I wind,
And leave his brooks and meads behind,

And groves, and grottoes where I lay,
And vistoes shooting beams of day:
Wide and wider spreads the vale;
As circles on a smooth canal:
The mountains round, unhappy fate!
Sooner or later, of all height!
Withdraw their summits from the skies,
And lessen as the others rise:
Still the prospect wider spreads,
Adds a thousand woods and meads,
Still it widens, widens still,
And sinks the newly-risen hill.

Now, I gain the mountain's brow,
What a landskip lies below!
No clouds, no vapours intervene,
But the gay, the open scene
Does the face of nature show,
In all the hues of heaven's bow!
And, swelling to embrace the light,
Spreads around beneath the sight.

Old castles on the cliffs arise,
Proudly tow'ring in the skies!
Rushing from the woods, the spires
Seem from hence ascending fires!
Half his beams Apollo sheds
On the yellow mountain-heads!
Gilds the fleeces of the flocks:
And glitters on the broken rocks!

Below me trees unnumber'd rise,
Beautiful in various dyes:
The gloomy pine, the poplar blue,
The yellow beech, the sable yew,
The slender fir, that taper grows,
The sturdy oak with broad-spread boughs.
And beyond the purple grove,
Haunt of Phillis, queen of love!
Gaudy as the op'ning dawn,
Lies a long and level lawn
On which a dark hill, steep and high,
Holds and charms the wand'ring eye!
Deep are his feet in Towy's flood,

His sides are cloath'd with waving wood,
And ancient towers crown his brow,
That cast an awful look below;
Whose ragged walls the ivy creeps,
And with her arms from falling keeps;
So both a safety from the wind
On mutual dependence find.
　　'Tis now the raven's bleak abode;
'Tis now th'appartment of the toad;
And there the fox securely feeds;
And there the pois'nous adder breeds
Concealed in ruins, moss and weeds;
While, ever and anon, there falls
Huge heaps of hoary moulder'd walls.
Yet time has seen, that lifts the low,
And level lays the lofty brow,
Has seen this broken pile compleat,
Big with the vanity of state;
But transient is the smile of Fate!
A little rule, a little sway,
A sun-beam in a winter's day,
Is all the proud and mighty have
Between the cradle and the grave.
　　And see the rivers how they run,
Thro' woods and meads, in shade and sun,
Sometimes swift, and sometimes slow,
Wave succeeding wave they go
A various journey to the deep,
Like human life to endless sleep!
Thus is nature's vesture wrought,
To instruct our wand'ring thought;
Thus she dresses green and gay,
To disperse our cares away.
　　Ever charming, ever new,
When will the landskip tire the view!
The fountain's fall, the river's flow,
The woody vallies, warm and low;
The windy summit, wild and high,
Roughly rushing on the sky!
The pleasant seat, the ruin'd tow'r,
The naked rock, the shady bow'r;

The town and village, dome and farm,
Each give each a double charm,
As pearls upon an Æthiop's arm.
  See on the mountain's southern side,
Where the prospect opens wide,
Where the evening gilds the tide;
How close and small the hedges lie!
What streaks of meadows cross the eye!
A step methinks may pass the stream,
So little distant dangers seem;
So we mistake the future's face,
Ey'd thro' Hope's deluding glass;
As yon summits soft and fair
Clad in colours of the air,
Which, to those who journey near,
Barren, and brown, and rough appear;
Still we tread tir'd the same coarse way,
The present's still a cloudy day.
  O may I with myself agree,
And never covet what I see:
Content me with an humble shade,
My passions tam'd, my wishes laid;
For while our wishes wildly roll,
We banish quiet from the soul:
'Tis thus the busy beat the air;
And misers gather wealth and care.
  Now, ev'n now, my joys run high,
As on the mountain-turf I lie;
While the wanton Zephyr sings,
And in the vale perfumes his wings;
While the waters murmur deep;
While the shepherd charms his sheep;
While the birds unbounded fly,
And with musick fill the sky,
Now, ev'n now, my joys run high.
  Be full, ye courts, be great who will;
Search for Peace with all your skill:
Open wide the lofty door,
Seek her on the marble floor,
In vain ye search, she is not there;
In vain ye search the domes of care!

Grass and flowers Quiet treads,
On the meads, and mountain-heads,
Along with Pleasure, close ally'd,
Ever by each other's side:
And often, by the murm'ring rill,
Hears the thrush, while all is still,
Within the groves of Grongar Hill.

JOHN DYER

429 *Ode to Evening*

If ought of Oaten Stop, or Pastoral Song,
May hope, chaste Eve, to soothe thy modest Ear,
　　Like thy own solemn Springs,
　　Thy Springs, and dying Gales,
O Nymph reserv'd, while now the bright-hair'd Sun
Sits in yon western Tent, whose cloudy Skirts,
　　With Brede ethereal wove,
　　O'erhang his wavy Bed:
Now Air is hush'd, save where the weak-ey'd Bat,
With short shrill Shriek flits by on leathern Wing,
　　Or where the Beetle winds
　　His small but sullen Horn,
As oft he rises 'midst the twilight Path,
Against the Pilgrim born in heedless Hum:
　　Now teach me, Maid compos'd,
　　To breathe some soften'd Strain,
Whose Numbers stealing thro' thy dark'ning Vale,
May not unseemly with its Stillness suit,
　　As musing slow, I hail
　　Thy genial lov'd Return!

For when thy folding Star arising shews
His paly Circlet, at his warning Lamp
　　The fragrant Hours, and Elves
　　Who slept in Flow'rs the Day,
And many a Nymph who wreaths her Brows with Sedge,
And sheds the fresh'ning Dew, and lovelier still,
　　The Pensive Pleasures sweet
　　Prepare thy shadowy Car.

Then lead, calm Vot'ress, where some sheety Lake,
Cheers the lone Heath, or some time-hallow'd Pile,
   Or up-land Fallows grey
   Reflect its last cool Gleam.
But when chill blust'ring Winds, or driving Rain,
Forbid my willing Feet, be mine the Hut,
   That from the Mountain's Side,
   Views Wilds, and swelling Floods,
And Hamlets brown, and dim-discover'd Spires,
And hears their simple Bell, and marks o'er all
   Thy Dewy Fingers draw
   The gradual dusky Veil.

While Spring shall pour his Show'rs, as oft he wont,
And bathe thy breathing Tresses, meekest Eve!
   While Summer loves to sport,
   Beneath thy ling'ring Light;
While sallow Autumn fills thy Lap with Leaves,
Or Winter yelling thro' the troublous Air,
   Affrights thy shrinking Train,
   And rudely rends thy Robes,
So long sure-found beneath thy sylvan Shed,
Shall Fancy, Friendship, Science, rose-lip'd Health,
   Thy gentlest Influence own,
   And hymn thy fav'rite Name!

WILLIAM COLLINS

430 *Ode to Autumn*

Season of mists and mellow fruitfulness,
   Close bosom-friend of the maturing sun;
Conspiring with him how to load and bless
   With fruit the vines that round the thatch-eaves run;
To bend with apples the moss'd cottage-trees,
   And fill all fruit with ripeness to the core;
     To swell the gourd, and plump the hazel shells
With a sweet kernel; to set budding more,
   And still more, later flowers for the bees,
   Until they think warm days will never cease,
     For Summer has o'er brimm'd their clammy cells.

Who hath not seen thee oft amid thy store?
  Sometimes whoever seeks abroad may find
Thee sitting careless on a granary floor,
  Thy hair soft-lifted by the winnowing wind;
Or on a half-reap'd furrow sound asleep,
  Drows'd with the fume of poppies, while thy hook
    Spares the next swath and all its twined flowers:
And sometimes like a gleaner thou dost keep
  Steady thy laden head across a brook;
  Or by a cider-press, with patient look,
    Thou watchest the last oozings hours by hours.

Where are the songs of Spring? Ay, where are they?
  Think not of them, thou hast thy music too,—
While barred clouds bloom the soft-dying day,
  And touch the stubble-plains with rosy hue;
Then in a wailful choir the small gnats mourn
  Among the river sallows, borne aloft
    Or sinking as the light wind lives or dies;
And full-grown lambs loud bleat from hilly bourn;
  Hedge-crickets sing; and now with treble soft
  The red-breast whistles from a garden-croft;
    And gathering swallows twitter in the skies.

                                         JOHN KEATS

431 *A Beautiful Night*

How lovely is the heaven of this night,
How deadly still its earth! The forest brute
Has crept into his cave, and laid himself
Where sleep has made him harmless like the lamb;
The horrid snake, his venom now forgot,
Is still and innocent as the honied flower
Under his head: and man, in whom are met
Leopard and snake,—and all the gentleness
And beauty of the young lamb and the bud,
Has let his ghost out, put his thoughts aside
And lent his senses unto death himself;
Whereby the King and beggar all lie down
On straw or purple-tissue, are but bones

And air, and blood, equal to one another
And to the unborn and buried: so we go
Placing ourselves among the unconceived
And the old ghosts, wantonly, smilingly,
For sleep is fair and warm–

THOMAS LOVELL BEDDOES

432 *To Night*

So thou art come again, old black-winged Night,
  Like an huge bird, between us and the sun,
Hiding, with out-stretched form, the genial light;
  And still, beneath thine icy bosom's dun
And cloudy plumage, hatching fog-breathed blight,
  And embryo storms, and crabbed frosts, that shun
Day's warm caress. The owls from ivied loop
  Are shrieking homage, as thou cowerest high,
Like sable crow pausing in eager stoop
  On the dim world thou gluttest thy clouded eye,
Silently waiting latest time's fell whoop
  When thou shalt quit thine eyrie in the sky,
    To pounce upon the world with eager claw,
    And tomb time, death, and substance in thy maw.

THOMAS LOVELL BEDDOES

433 *Contemplation*

This morning saw I, fled the shower,
The earth reclining in a lull of power:
The heavens, pursuing not their path,
Lay stretched out naked after bath,
Or so it seemed; field, water, tree, were still,
Nor was there any purpose on the calm-browed hill.

The hill, which sometimes visibly is
Wrought with unresting energies,
Looked idly; from the musing wood,
And every rock, a life renewed
Exhaled like an unconscious thought
When poets, dreaming unperplexed,
Dream that they dream of nought.

Nature one hour appears a thing unsexed,
Or to such serene balance brought
That her twin natures cease their sweet alarms,
And sleep in one another's arms.
The sun with resting pulses seems to brood,
And slacken its command upon my unurged blood.

The river has not any care
Its passionless water to the sea to bear;
The leaves have brown content;
The wall to me has freshness like a scent,
And takes half animate the air,
Making one life with its green moss and stain;
And life with all things seems too perfect blent
For anything of life to be aware.
The very shades on hill, and tree, and plain,
Where they have fallen doze, and where they doze remain.
No hill can idler be than I;
No stone its inter-particled vibration
Investeth with a stiller lie;
No heaven with a more urgent rest betrays
The eyes that on it gaze.
We are too near akin that thou shouldst cheat
Me, Nature, with thy fair deceit.
In poets floating like a water-flower
Upon the bosom of the glassy hour,
In skies that no man sees to move,
Lurk untumultuous vortices of power,
For joy too native, and for agitation
Too instant, too entire for sense thereof,
Motion like gnats when autumn suns are low,—
Perpetual as the prisoned feet of love
On the heart's floors with painèd pace that go.
From stones and poets you may know,
Nothing so active is, as that which least seems so.

For he, that conduit running wine of song,
Then to himself does most belong,
When he his mortal house unbars
To the importunate and thronging feet
That round our corporal walls unheeded beat;

Till, all containing, he exalt
His stature to the stars, or stars
Narrow their heaven to his fleshly vault:
When, like a city under ocean,
To human things he grows a desolation,
And is made a habitation
For the fluctuous universe
To lave with unimpeded motion.
He scarcely frets the atmosphere
With breathing, and his body shares
The immobility of rocks;
His heart's a drop-well of tranquillity;
His mind more still is than the limbs of fear,
And yet its unperturbed velocity
The spirit of the simoon mocks.
He round the solemn centre of his soul
Wheels like a dervish, while his being is
Streamed with the set of the world's harmonies,
In the long draft of whatsoever sphere
He lists the sweet and clear
Clangour of his high orbit on to roll,
So gracious is his heavenly grace;
And the bold stars does hear,
Every one in his airy soar,
For evermore
Shout to each other from the peaks of space,
As thwart ravines of azure shouts the mountaineer.

FRANCIS THOMPSON

434 *A Nocturnal Reverie*

In such a night, when every louder wind
Is to its distant cavern safe confin'd;
And only gentle Zephyr fans his wings,
And lonely Philomel, still waking, sings;
Or from some tree, fam'd for the owl's delight,
She, hollowing clear, directs the wand'rer right:
In such a night, when passing clouds give place,
Or thinly vail the heav'ns mysterious face;
When in some river, overhung with green,
The waving moon and trembling leaves are seen;

When freshen'd grass now bears it self upright,
And makes cool banks to pleasing rest invite,
Whence springs the woodbind, and the bramble-rose,
And where the sleepy cowslip shelter'd grows;
Whilst now a paler hue the foxglove takes,
Yet checquers still with red the dusky brakes:
When scatter'd glow-worms, but in twilight fine,
Shew trivial beauties, watch their hour to shine;
Whilst Salisb'ry stands the test of every light,
In perfect charms, and perfect virtue bright:
When odours, which declin'd repelling day,
Thro' temp'rate air uninterrupted stray;
When darken'd groves their softest shadows wear,
And falling waters we distinctly hear;
When thro' the gloom more venerable shows
Some ancient fabrick, awful in repose,
While sunburnt hills their swarthy looks conceal,
And swelling haycocks thicken up the vale:
When the loos'd horse now, as his pasture leads,
Comes slowly grazing thro' th' adjoining meads,
Whose stealing pace, and lengthen'd shade we fear,
Till torn up forage in his teeth we hear:
When nibbling sheep at large pursue their food,
And unmolested kine rechew the cud;
When curlews cry beneath the village-walls,
And to her straggling brood the partridge calls;
Their shortliv'd jubilee the creatures keep,
Which but endures, whilst tyrant-man does sleep;
When a sedate content the spirit feels,
And no fierce light disturbs, whilst it reveals;
But silent musings urge the mind to seek
Something, too high for syllables to speak;
Till the free soul to a compos'dness charm'd,
Finding the elements of rage disarm'd,
O'er all below a solemn quiet grown,
Joys in th' inferiour world, and thinks it like her own:
In such a night let me abroad remain,
Till morning breaks, and all's confus'd again;
Our cares, our toils, our clamours are renew'd,
Or pleasures, seldom reach'd, again pursu'd.

ANNE, COUNTESS OF WINCHILSEA

435 *Night*

It is the hush of night, and all between
Thy margin and the mountains, dusk, yet clear,
Mellow'd and mingling, yet distinctly seen,
Save darken'd Jura, whose capt heights appear
Precipitously steep; and drawing near,
There breathes a living fragrance from the shore,
Of flowers yet fresh with childhood; on the ear
Drops the light drip of the suspended oar,
Or chirps the grasshopper one good-night carol more;

He is an evening reveller, who makes
His life an infancy, and sings his fill;
At intervals, some bird from out the brakes
Starts into voice a moment, then is still.
There seems a floating whisper on the hill,
But that is fancy, for the starlight dews
All silently their tears of love instil,
Weeping themselves away, till they infuse
Deep into Nature's breast the spirit of her hues.

Ye stars! which are the poetry of heaven
If in your bright leaves we would read the fate
Of men and empires,—'tis to be forgiven,
That in our aspirations to be great,
Our destinies o'erleap their mortal state,
And claim a kindred with you; for ye are
A beauty and a mystery, and create
In us such love and reverence from afar,
That fortune, fame, power, life, have named themselves a star.

All heaven and earth are still—though not in sleep,
But breathless, as we grow when feeling most;
And silent, as we stand in thoughts too deep:—
All heaven and earth are still: From the high host
Of stars, to the lull'd lake and mountain-coast,
All is concenter'd in a life intense,
Where not a beam, nor air, nor leaf is lost,
But hath a part of being, and a sense
Of that which is of all Creator and defence.

Then stirs the feeling infinite, so felt
In solitude, where we are *least* alone;
A truth, which through our being then doth melt
And purifies from self: it is a tone,
The soul and source of music, which makes known
Eternal harmony, and sheds a charm,
Like to the fabled Cytherea's zone,
Binding all things with beauty;–'twould disarm
The spectre Death, had he substantial power to harm.

Not vainly did the early Persian make
His altar the high places and the peak
Of earth-o'ergazing mountains, and thus take
A fit and unwall'd temple, there to seek
The Spirit in whose honour shrines are weak,
Uprear'd of human hands. Come, and compare
Columns and idol-dwellings, Goth or Greek,
With Nature's realms of worship, earth and air,
Nor fix on fond abodes to circumscribe thy pray'r!

Thy sky is changed!–and such a change! Oh night,
And storm, and darkness, ye are wondrous strong,
Yet lovely in your strength, as is the light
Of a dark eye in woman! Far along,
From peak to peak, the rattling crags among
Leaps the live thunder! Not from one lone cloud,
But every mountain now hath found a tongue,
And Jura answers, through her misty shroud,
Back to the joyous Alps, who call to her aloud!

And this is in the night:–Most glorious night!
Thou wert not sent for slumber! Let me be
A sharer in thy fierce and far delight,–
A portion of the tempest and of thee!
How the lit lake shines, a phosphoric sea,
And the big rain comes dancing to the earth!
And now again 'tis black;–and now, the glee
Of the loud hills shakes with its mountain-mirth,
As if they did rejoice o'er a young earthquake's birth.

GEORGE GORDON, LORD BYRON

436 *She was a Phantom of delight*

She was a Phantom of delight
When first she gleamed upon my sight;
A lovely Apparition sent
To be a moment's ornament;
Her eyes as stars of Twilight fair;
Like Twilight's, too, her dusky hair;
But all things else about her drawn
From May-time and the cheerful Dawn;
A dancing Shape, an Image gay,
To haunt, to startle, and way-lay.

I saw her upon nearer view,
A Spirit, yet a Woman too!
Her household motions light and free,
And steps of virgin-liberty;
A countenance in which did meet
Sweet records, promises as sweet;
A Creature not too bright or good
For human nature's daily food;
For transient sorrows, simple wiles,
Praise, blame, love, kisses, tears, and smiles.

And now I see with eye serene
The very pulse of the machine;
A Being breathing thoughtful breath,
A Traveller between life and death;
The reason firm, the temperate will,
Endurance, foresight, strength, and skill;
A perfect Woman, nobly planned,
To warn, to comfort, and command;
And yet a Spirit still, and bright
With something of angelic light.

WILLIAM WORDSWORTH

437 *Three years she grew in sun and shower*

Three years she grew in sun and shower,
Then Nature said, 'A lovelier flower
On earth was never sown;

This Child I to myself will take;
She shall be mine, and I will make
A Lady of my own.

'Myself will to my darling be
Both law and impulse: and with me
The Girl, in rock and plain,
In earth and heaven, in glade and bower,
Shall feel an overseeing power
To kindle or restrain.

'She shall be sportive as the fawn
That wild with glee across the lawn
Or up the mountain springs;
And hers shall be the breathing balm,
And hers the silence and the calm
Of mute insensate things.

'The floating clouds their state shall lend
To her; for her the willow bend;
Nor shall she fail to see
Even in the motions of the Storm
Grace that shall mould the Maiden's form
By silent sympathy.

'The stars of midnight shall be dear
To her; and she shall lean her ear
In many a secret place
Where rivulets dance their wayward round,
And beauty born of murmuring sound
Shall pass into her face.

'And vital feelings of delight
Shall rear her form to stately height,
Her virgin bosom swell;
Such thoughts to Lucy I will give
While she and I together live
Here in this happy dell.'

Thus Nature spake—The work was done—
How soon my Lucy's race was run!
She died, and left to me

> This heath, this calm, and quiet scene;
> The memory of what has been,
> And never more will be.
> WILLIAM WORDSWORTH

438 *Frost at Midnight*

The Frost performs its secret ministry,
Unhelped by any wind. The owlet's cry
Came loud–and hark, again! loud as before.
The inmates of my cottage all at rest,
Have left me to that solitude, which suits
Abstruser musings: save that at my side
My cradled infant slumbers peacefully.
'Tis calm indeed! so calm, that it disturbs
And vexes meditation with its strange
And extreme silentness. Sea, hill, and wood,
This populous village! Sea, and hill, and wood,
With all the numberless goings-on of life,
Inaudible as dreams! the thin blue flame
Lies on my low-burnt fire, and quivers not;
Only that film, which fluttered, on the grate
Still flutters there, the sole unquiet thing.
Methinks, its motion in this hush of nature
Gives it dim sympathies with me who live
Making it a companionable form,
Whose puny flaps and freaks the idling Spirit
By its own moods interprets, every where
Echo or mirror seeking of itself,
And makes a toy of Thought.
But O! how oft,
How oft, at school with most believing mind,
Presageful, have I gazed upon the bars,
To watch that fluttering *stranger*! and as oft
With unclosed lids, already had I dreamt
Of my sweet birth-place, and the old church-tower,
Whose bells, the poor man's only music, rang
From morn to evening, all the hot Fair-day,
So sweetly, that they stirred and haunted me
With a wild pleasure, falling on mine ear
Most like articulate sounds of things to come!
So gazed I, till the soothing things I dreamt

Lulled me to sleep, and sleep prolonged my dreams!
And so I brooded all the following morn,
Awed by the stern preceptor's face, mine eye
Fixed with mock study on my swimming book:
Save if the door half opened, and I snatched
A hasty glance, and still my heart leaped up,
For still I hoped to see the *stranger*'s face.
Townsman, or aunt, or sister more beloved,
My play-mate when we both were clothed alike!

Dear Babe, that sleepest cradled by my side,
Whose gentle breathings, heard in this deep calm,
Fill up the interspersed vacancies
And momentary pauses of the thought!
My babe so beautiful! it thrills my heart
With tender gladness, thus to look at thee,
And think that thou shalt learn far other lore,
And in far other scenes! For I was reared
In the great city, pent 'mid cloisters dim,
And saw nought lovely but the sky and stars.
But *thou*, my babe! shalt wander like a breeze
By lakes and sandy shores, beneath the crags
Of ancient mountain, and beneath the clouds,
Which image in their bulk both lakes and shores
And mountain crags: so shalt thou see and hear
The lovely shapes and sounds intelligible
Of that eternal language, which thy God
Utters, who from eternity doth teach
Himself in all, and all things in himself.
Great universal Teacher! he shall mould
Thy spirit, and by giving make it ask.

Therefore all seasons shall be sweet to thee,
Whether the summer clothe the general earth
With greenness, or the redbreast sit and sing
Betwixt the tufts of snow on the bare branch
Of mossy apple-tree, while the nigh thatch
Smokes in the sun-thaw; whether the eave-drops fall
Heard only in the trances of the blast,
Or if the secret ministry of frost
Shall hang them up in silent icicles,
Quietly shining to the quiet Moon.

SAMUEL TAYLOR COLERIDGE

439 *The Deserted Village*

Sweet Auburn! loveliest village of the plain,
Where health and plenty cheer'd the labouring swain,
Where smiling spring its earliest visit paid,
And parting summer's lingering blooms delay'd.
Dear lovely bowers of innocence and ease,
Seats of my youth, when every sport could please,
How often have I loiter'd o'er thy green,
Where humble happiness endear'd each scene!
How often have I paus'd on every charm,
The shelter'd cot, the cultivated farm,
The never failing brook, the busy mill,
The decent church that topt the neighbouring hill,
The hawthorn bush, with seats beneath the shade,
For talking age and whispering lovers made!
How often have I blest the coming day,
When toil remitting lent its turn to play,
And all the village train, from labour free,
Led up their sports beneath the spreading tree,
While many a pastime circled in the shade,
The young contending as the old survey'd;
And many a gambol frolick'd o'er the ground,
And sleights of art and feats of strength went round.
And still as each repeated pleasure tir'd,
Succeeding sports the mirthful band inspir'd;
The dancing pair that simply sought renown,
By holding out, to tire each other down;
The swain mistrustless of his smutted face,
While secret laughter titter'd round the place;
The bashful virgin's sidelong looks of love,
The matron's glance that would those looks reprove,
These were thy charms, sweet village! sports like these,
With sweet succession, taught e'en toil to please;
These round thy bowers their cheerful influence shed,
These were thy charms–but all these charms are fled.

Sweet smiling village, loveliest of the lawn,
Thy sports are fled, and all thy charms withdrawn;
Amidst thy bowers the tyrant's hand is seen,
And desolation saddens all thy green:

One only master grasps the whole domain,
And half a tillage stints thy smiling plain;
No more thy glassy brook reflects the day,
But, chok'd with sedges, works its weedy way;
Along thy glades, a solitary guest,
The hollow sounding bittern guards its nest;
Amidst thy desert walks the lapwing flies,
And tires their echoes with unvaried cries.
Sunk are thy bowers in shapeless ruin all,
And the long grass o'ertops the mouldering wall,
And, trembling, shrinking from the spoiler's hand,
Far, far away thy children leave the land.

Ill fares the land, to hastening ills a prey,
Where wealth accumulates, and men decay:
Princes and lords may flourish, or may fade;
A breath can make them, as a breath has made:
But a bold peasantry, their country's pride,
When once destroy'd, can never be supplied.

A time there was, ere England's griefs began,
When every rood of ground maintain'd its man;
For him light labour spread her wholesome store,
Just gave what life requir'd, but gave no more:
His best companions, innocence and health;
And his best riches, ignorance of wealth.

But times are alter'd; trade's unfeeling train
Usurp the land and dispossess the swain;
Along the lawn, where scatter'd hamlets rose,
Unwieldy wealth and cumbrous pomp repose;
And every want to luxury allied,
And every pang that folly pays to pride.
Those gentle hours that plenty bade to bloom,
Those calm desires that ask'd but little room,
Those healthful sports that grac'd the peaceful scene,
Liv'd in each look, and brighten'd all the green;
These, far departing, seek a kinder shore,
And rural mirth and manners are no more.

Sweet Auburn! parent of the blissful hour,
Thy glades forlorn confess the tyrant's power.

Here, as I take my solitary rounds,
Amidst thy tangling walks, and ruin'd grounds,
And, many a year elaps'd, return to view
Where once the cottage stood, the hawthorn grew,
Remembrance wakes with all her busy train,
Swells at my breast, and turns the past to pain.

In all my wanderings round this world of care,
In all my griefs—and God has given my share—
I still had hopes my latest hours to crown,
Amidst these humble bowers to lay me down;
To husband out life's taper at the close,
And keep the flame from wasting by repose:
I still had hopes, for pride attends us still,
Amidst the swains to show my book-learn'd skill,
Around my fire an evening group to draw,
And tell of all I felt, and all I saw;
And as a hare, whom hounds and horns pursue,
Pants to the place from whence at first he flew,
I still had hopes, my long vexations past,
Here to return—and die at home at last . . .

Sweet was the sound, when oft at evening's close
Up yonder hill the village murmur rose;
There, as I passed with careless steps and slow,
The mingling notes came soften'd from below;
The swain responsive as the milkmaid sung,
The sober herd that low'd to meet their young;
The noisy geese that gabbled o'er the pool,
The playful children just let loose from school;
The watchdog's voice that bay'd the whispering wind,
And the loud laugh that spoke the vacant mind;
These all in sweet confusion sought the shade,
And fill'd each pause the nightingale had made.
But now the sounds of population fail,
No cheerful murmurs fluctuate in the gale,
No busy steps the grass-grown footway tread,
But all the bloomy flush of life is fled.
All but yon widow'd, solitary thing,
That feebly bends beside the plashy spring;

She, wretched matron, forc'd, in age, for bread,
To strip the brook with mantling cresses spread,
To pick her wintry faggot from the thorn,
To seek her nightly shed, and weep till morn;
She only left of all the harmless train,
The sad historian of the pensive plain . . .

    Beside yon straggling fence that skirts the way,
With blossom'd furze unprofitably gay,
There, in his noisy mansion, skill'd to rule,
The village master taught his little school;
A man severe he was, and stern to view,
I knew him well, and every truant knew;
Well had the boding tremblers learn'd to trace
The day's disasters in his morning face;
Full well they laugh'd with counterfeited glee
At all his jokes, for many a joke had he;
Full well the busy whisper, circling round,
Convey'd the dismal tidings when he frown'd;
Yet he was kind, or, if severe in aught,
The love he bore to learning was in fault;
The village all declar'd how much he knew;
'Twas certain he could write and cipher too;
Lands he could measure, terms and tides presage,
And e'en the story ran that he could gauge;
In arguing too the parson own'd his skill,
For e'en though vanquish'd, he could argue still;
While words of learned length and thundering sound
Amaz'd the gazing rustics rang'd around,
And still they gaz'd, and still the wonder grew,
That one small head could carry all he knew.

    But past is all his fame. The very spot
Where many a time he triumph'd is forgot.
Near yonder thorn, that lifts its head on high,
Where once the signpost caught the passing eye,
Low lies that house where nut-brown draughts inspir'd,
Where grey-beard mirth, and smiling toil retir'd,
Where village statesmen talk'd with looks profound,
And news much older than their ale went round.

Imagination fondly stoops to trace
The parlour splendours of that festive place;
The whitewash'd wall, the nicely sanded floor,
The varnish'd clock that click'd behind the door;
The chest contriv'd a double debt to pay,
A bed by night, a chest of drawers by day;
The pictures plac'd for ornament and use,
The twelve good rules, the royal game of goose;
The hearth, except when winter chill'd the day,
With aspen boughs, and flowers and fennel gay;
While broken teacups, wisely kept for show,
Rang'd o'er the chimney, glisten'd in a row.

Vain transitory splendour! could not all
Reprieve the tottering mansion from its fall!
Obscure it sinks, nor shall it more impart
An hour's importance to the poor man's heart;
Thither no more the peasant shall repair
To sweet oblivion of his daily care;
No more the farmer's news, the barber's tale,
No more the woodman's ballad shall prevail;
No more the smith his dusky brow shall clear,
Relax his ponderous strength, and lean to hear;
The host himself no longer shall be found
Careful to see the mantling bliss go round;
Nor the coy maid, half willing to be prest,
Shall kiss the cup to pass it to the rest.

Yes! let the rich deride, the proud disdain,
These simple blessings of the lowly train,
To me more dear, congenial to my heart,
One native charm, than all the gloss of art;
Spontaneous joys, where nature has its play,
The soul adopts, and owns their firstborn sway:
Lightly they frolic o'er the vacant mind,
Unenvied, unmolested, unconfin'd.
But the long pomp, the midnight masquerade,
With all the freaks of wanton wealth array'd,
In these, ere triflers half their wish obtain,
The toiling pleasure sickens into pain;
And, e'en while fashion's brightest arts decoy,
The heart distrusting asks, if this be joy?

OLIVER GOLDSMITH

440 *Prologue to 'The Good-Natur'd Man'*

Prest by the load of life, the weary mind
Surveys the general toil of human kind;
With cool submission joins the labouring train,
And social sorrow loses half its pain:
Our anxious Bard, without complaint, may share
This bustling season's epidemic care;
Like Cæsar's pilot, dignified by fate,
Tost in one common storm with all the great;
Distrest alike, the statesman and the wit,
When one a borough courts, and one the pit.
The busy candidates for power and fame,
Have hopes, and fears, and wishes, just the same;
Disabled both to combat, or to fly,
Must hear all taunts, and hear without reply.
Uncheck'd on both, loud rabbles vent their rage,
As mongrels bay the lion in a cage.
Th'offended burgess hoards his angry tale,
For that blest year when all that vote may rail;
Their schemes of spite the poet's foes dismiss,
Till that glad night when all that hate may hiss.
This day the powder'd curls and golden coat,
Says swelling Crispin, begg'd a cobbler's vote.
This night our wit, the pert apprentice cries,
Lies at my feet, I hiss him, and he dies.
The great, 'tis true, can charm th' electing tribe;
The bard may supplicate, but cannot bribe.
Yet judg'd by those, whose voices ne'er were sold,
He feels no want of ill-persuading gold;
But confident of praise, if praise be due,
Trusts without fear, to merit, and to you.

SAMUEL JOHNSON

441 *Love of England*

England, with all thy faults, I love thee still,
My country! and while yet a nook is left
Where English minds and manners may be found,
Shall be constrain'd to love thee. Though thy clime
Be fickle, and thy year, most part deform'd

With dripping rains, or wither'd by a frost,
I would not yet exchange thy sullen skies
And fields without a flower, for warmer France
With all her vines; nor for Ausonia's groves
Of golden fruitage and her myrtle bowers.
To shake thy senate, and from heights sublime
Of patriot eloquence to flash down fire
Upon thy foes, was never meant my task;
But I can feel thy fortunes, and partake
Thy joys and sorrows with as true a heart
As any thunderer there. And I can feel
Thy follies too, and with a just disdain
Frown at effeminates, whose very looks
Reflect dishonour on the land I love.
How, in the name of soldiership and sense,
Should England prosper, when such things, as smooth
And tender as a girl, all-essenced o'er
With odours, and as profligate as sweet,
Who sell their laurel for a myrtle wreath,
And love when they should fight; when such as these
Presume to lay their hand upon the ark
Of her magnificent and awful cause?
Time was when it was praise and boast enough
In every clime, and travel where we might,
That we were born her children; praise enough
To fill the ambition of a private man,
That Chatham's language was his mother-tongue,
And Wolfe's great name compatriot with his own.
Farewell those honours, and farewell with them
The hope of such hereafter. They have fallen
Each in his field of glory: one in arms,
And one in council–Wolfe upon the lap
Of smiling Victory that moment won,
And Chatham, heart-sick of his country's shame!
They made us many soldiers. Chatham still
Consulting England's happiness at home,
Secured it by an unforgiving frown
If any wrong'd her. Wolfe, where'er he fought,
Put so much of his heart into his act,
That his example had a magnet's force,
And all were swift to follow whom all loved.

Those suns are set. Oh, rise some other such!
Or all that we have left, is empty talk
Of old achievements, and despair of new.

WILLIAM COWPER

442 *The Stricken Deer*

I was a stricken deer that left the herd
Long since; with many an arrow deep infix'd
My panting side was charg'd, when I withdrew
To seek a tranquil death in distant shades.
There was I found by One who had Himself
Been hurt by the archers. In His side He bore,
And in His hands and feet, the cruel scars.
With gentle force soliciting the darts,
He drew them forth, and heal'd and bade me live.
Since then, with few associates, in remote
And silent woods I wander, far from those
My former partners of the peopled scene;
With few associates, and not wishing more.
Here much I ruminate, as much I may,
With other views of men and manners now
Than once, and others of a life to come.
I see that all are wanderers, gone astray
Each in his own delusions; they are lost
In chace of fancied happiness, still woo'd
And never won. Dream after dream ensues,
And still they dream that they shall still succeed,
And still are disappointed. Rings the world
With the vain stir. I sum up half mankind,
And add two-thirds of the remaining half,
And find the total of their hopes and fears
Dreams, empty dreams. The million flit as gay
As if created only like the fly,
That spreads his motley wings in the eye of noon,
To sport their season, and be seen no more.
The rest are sober dreamers, grave and wise,
And pregnant with discoveries new and rare.
Some write a narrative of wars, and feats
Of heroes little known, and call the rant
A history: describe the man, of whom

His own coevals took but little note,
And paint his person, character, and views,
As they had known him from his mother's womb.
They disentangle from the puzzled skein
In which obscurity has wrapp'd them up,
The threads of politic and shrewd design
That ran through all his purposes, and charge
His mind with meanings that he never had,
Or having, kept conceal'd. Some drill and bore
The solid earth, and from the strata there
Extract a register, by which we learn
That He who made it, and reveal'd its date
To Moses, was mistaken in its age.
Some more acute, and more industrious still,
Contrive creation; travel nature up
To the sharp peak of her sublimest height,
And tells us whence the stars; why some are fix'd,
And planetary some; what gave them first
Rotation, from what fountain flow'd their light.
Great contest follows, and much learned dust
Involves the combatants, each claiming truth,
And truth disclaiming both: and thus they spend
The little wick of life's poor shallow lamp
In playing tricks with nature, giving laws
To distant worlds, and trifling in their own.
Is 't not a pity now, that tickling rheums
Should ever tease the lungs and blear the sight
Of oracles like these? Great pity too,
That having wielded the elements, and built
A thousand systems, each in his own way,
They should go out in fume and be forgot!
Ah! what is life thus spent? and what are they
But frantic who thus spend it? all for smoke,—
Eternity for bubbles proves at last
A senseless bargain. When I see such games
Play'd by the creatures of a Power who swears
That He will judge the earth, and call the fool
To a sharp reckoning that has lived in vain;
And when I weigh this seeming wisdom well,
And prove it in the infallible result
So hollow and so false,—I feel my heart

Dissolve in pity, and account the learn'd,
If this be learning, most of all deceived.
Great crimes alarm the conscience, but it sleeps
While thoughtful man is plausibly amused.
Defend me therefore, common sense, say I,
From reveries so airy, from the toil
Of dropping buckets into empty wells,
And growing old in drawing nothing up!
    'Twere well, says one sage erudite, profound,
Terribly arch'd and aquiline his nose,
And overbuilt with most impending brows—
'Twere well, could you permit the world to live
As the world pleases. What's the world to you?
Much. I was born of woman, and drew milk,
As sweet as charity, from human breasts.
I think, articulate, I laugh and weep,
And exercise all functions of a man.
How then should I and any man that lives
Be strangers to each other? Pierce my vein,
Take of the crimson stream meandering there,
And catechise it well. Apply your glass,
Search it, and prove now if it be not blood
Congenial with thine own: and if it be,
What edge of subtlety canst thou suppose
Keen enough, wise and skilful as thou art,
To cut the link of brotherhood, by which
One common Maker bound me to the kind?
True; I am no proficient, I confess,
In arts like yours. I cannot call the swift
And perilous lightnings from the angry clouds,
And bid them hide themselves in earth beneath;
I cannot analyse the air, nor catch
The parallax of yonder luminous point
That seems half quench'd in the immense abyss;
Such powers I boast not—neither can I rest
A silent witness of the headlong rage
Or heedless folly by which thousands die,
Bone of my bone, and kindred souls to mine.
    God never meant that man should scale the heavens
By strides of human wisdom. In His works,
Though wondrous, He commands us in His Word

To seek Him rather where His mercy shines.
The mind indeed, enlighten'd from above,
Views Him in all; ascribes to the grand cause
The grand effect; acknowledges with joy
His manner, and with rapture tastes His style.
But never yet did philosophic tube,
That brings the planets home into the eye
Of observation, and discovers, else
Not visible, His family of worlds,
Discover Him that rules them: such a veil
Hangs over mortal eyes, blind from the birth,
And dark in things divine. Full often too
Our wayward intellect, the more we learn
Of nature, overlooks her Author more;
From instrumental causes proud to draw
Conclusions retrograde, and mad mistake.
But if His Word once teach us, shoot a ray
Through all the heart's dark chambers, and reveal
Truths undiscern'd but by that holy light,
Then all is plain. Philosophy baptized
In the pure fountain of eternal love
Has eyes indeed; and viewing all she sees,
As meant to indicate a God to man,
Gives Him his praise, and forfeits not her own.
Learning has borne such fruit in other days
On all her branches: piety has found
Friends in the friends of science, and true prayer
Has flow'd from lips wet with Castalian dews.
Such was thy wisdom, Newton, childlike sage!
Sagacious reader of the works of God,
And in His Word sagacious. Such too thine,
Milton, whose genius had angelic wings,
And fed on manna. And such thine, in whom
Our British Themis gloried with just cause,
Immortal Hale! for deep discernment praised,
And sound integrity not more, than famed
For sanctity of manners undefiled.

WILLIAM COWPER

443 *The Created Universe*

Oh! bless'd of Heaven, whom not the languid songs
Of Luxury, the siren! not the bribes
Of sordid Wealth, nor all the gaudy spoils
Of pageant Honour, can seduce to leave
Those ever-blooming sweets, which from the store
Of Nature fair Imagination culls
To charm the enliven'd soul! What though not all
Of mortal offspring can attain the heights
Of envied life; though only few possess
Patrician treasures or imperial state;
Yet Nature's care, to all her children just,
With richer treasures and an ampler state,
Endows at large whatever happy man
Will deign to use them. His the city's pomp,
The rural honours his. Whate'er adorns
The princely dome, the column, and the arch,
The breathing marbles and the sculptured gold,
Beyond the proud possessor's narrow claim,
His tuneful breast enjoys. For him, the Spring
Distils her dews, and from the silken gem
Its lucid leaves unfolds; for him, the hand
Of Autumn tinges every fertile branch
With blooming gold and blushes like the morn.
Each passing Hour sheds tribute from her wings;
And still new beauties meet his lonely walk,
And loves unfelt attract him. Not a breeze
Flies o'er the meadow, not a cloud imbibes
The setting sun's effulgence, not a strain
From all the tenants of the warbling shade
Ascends, but whence his bosom can partake
Fresh pleasure, unreproved. Nor thence partakes
Fresh pleasure only; for the attentive mind,
By this harmonious action on her powers,
Becomes herself harmonious; wont so oft
In outward things to meditate the charm
Of sacred order, soon she seeks at home
To find a kindred order, to exert
Within herself this elegance of love
This fair-inspired delight; her temper'd powers

Refine at length, and every passion wears
A chaster, milder, more attractive mien.
But if to ampler prospects, if to gaze
On Nature's form, where, negligent of all
These lesser graces, she assumes the port
Of that Eternal Majesty that weigh'd
The world's foundations, if to these the mind
Exalts her daring eye, then mightier far
Will be the change, and nobler. Would the forms
Of servile custom cramp her generous powers?
Would sordid policies, the barbarous growth
Of ignorance and rapine, bow her down
To tame pursuits, to indolence and fear?
Lo! she appeals to Nature, to the winds
And rolling waves, the sun's unwearied course,
The elements and seasons; all declare
For what the Eternal Maker has ordain'd
The powers of man; we feel within ourselves
His energy divine; he tells the heart,
He meant, he made us to behold and love
What he beholds and loves, the general orb
Of life and being; to be great like him,
Beneficent and active. Thus the men
Whom Nature's works can charm, with God himself
Hold converse; grow familiar, day by day,
With his conceptions, act upon his plan;
And form to his, the relish of their souls.

MARK AKENSIDE

444 *Nature*

O ye dales
Of Tyne, and ye most ancient woodlands; where,
Oft as the giant flood obliquely strides,
And his banks open, and his lawns extend,
Stops short the pleased traveller to view
Presiding o'er the scene some rustic tower
Founded by Norman or by Saxon hands:
O ye Northumbrian shades, which overlook
The rocky pavement and the mossy falls
Of solitary Wensbeck's limpid stream;

How gladly I recall your well-known seats
Beloved of old, and that delightful time
When all alone, for many a summer's day,
I wander'd through your calm recesses, led
In silence by some powerful hand unseen.
    Nor will I e'er forget you; nor shall e'er
The graver tasks of manhood, or the advice
Of vulgar wisdom, move me to disclaim
Those studies which possess'd me in the dawn
Of life, and fix'd the colour of my mind
For every future year: whence even now
From sleep I rescue the clear hours of morn,
And, while the world around lies overwhelm'd
In idle darkness, am alive to thoughts
Of honourable fame, of truth divine
Or moral, and of minds to virtue won
By the sweet magic of harmonious verse.

Mark Akenside

445 *Influence of Natural Objects*

Wisdom and Spirit of the universe!
Thou Soul, that art the Eternity of thought!
And giv'st to forms and images a breath
And everlasting motion! not in vain,
By day or star-light, thus from my first dawn
Of childhood didst thou intertwine for me
The passions that build up our human soul;
Not with the mean and vulgar works of Man;
But with high objects, with enduring things,
With life and nature; purifying thus
The elements of feeling and of thought,
And sanctifying by such discipline
Both pain and fear,–until we recognise
A grandeur in the beatings of the heart.

    Nor was this fellowship vouchsafed to me
With stinted kindness. In November days,
When vapours rolling down the valleys made
A lonely scene more lonesome; among woods
At noon; and 'mid the calm of summer nights,

When, by the margin of the trembling lake,
Beneath the gloomy hills, homeward I went
In solitude, such intercourse was mine:
Mine was it in the fields both day and night,
And by the waters, all the summer long.
And in the frosty season, when the sun
Was set, and, visible for many a mile,
The cottage-windows through the twilight blazed,
I heeded not the summons: happy time
It was indeed for all of us; for me
It was a time of rapture! Clear and loud
The village-clock tolled six–I wheeled about,
Proud and exulting like an untired horse
That cares not for his home–All shod with steel
We hissed along the polished ice, in games
Confederate, imitative of the chase
And woodland pleasures,–the resounding horn,
The pack loud-chiming, and the hunted hare.
So through the darkness and the cold we flew,
And not a voice was idle: with the din
Smitten, the precipices rang aloud;
The leafless trees and every icy crag
Tinkled like iron; while far-distant hills
Into the tumult sent an alien sound
Of melancholy, not unnoticed, while the stars,
Eastward, were sparkling clear, and in the west
The orange sky of evening died away.

Not seldom from the uproar I retired
Into a silent bay, or sportively
Glanced sideway, leaving the tumultuous throng,
To cut across the reflex of a star;
Image, that, flying still before me, gleamed
Upon the glassy plain: and oftentimes,
When we had given our bodies to the wind,
And all the shadowy banks on either side
Came sweeping through the darkness, spinning still
The rapid line of motion, then at once
Have I, reclining back upon my heels,
Stopped short; yet still the solitary cliffs
Wheeled by me–even as if the earth had rolled

P

With visible motion her diurnal round!
Behind me did they stretch in solemn train,
Feebler and feebler, and I stood and watched
Till all was tranquil as a summer sea.

WILLIAM WORDSWORTH

446 *A Grammarian's Funeral*

Shortly after the Revival of Learning in Europe

Let us begin and carry up this corpse,
    Singing together.
Leave we the common crofts, the vulgar thorpes
    Each in its tether
Sleeping safe on the bosom of the plain,
    Cared-for till cock-crow:
Look out if yonder be not day again
    Rimming the rock-row!
That's the appropriate country; there, man's thought,
    Rarer, intenser,
Self-gathered for an outbreak, as it ought,
    Chafes in the censer.
Leave we the unlettered plain its herd and crop;
    Seek we sepulture
On a tall mountain, cited to the top,
    Crowded with culture!
All the peaks soar, but one the rest excels;
    Clouds overcome it;
No! yonder sparkle is the citadel's
    Circling its summit.
Thither our path lies; wind we up the heights:
    Wait ye the warning?
Our low life was the level's and the night's:
    He's for the morning.
Step to a tune, square chests, erect each head,
    'Ware the beholders!
This is our master, famous calm and dead,
    Borne on our shoulders.

Sleep, crop and herd! sleep, darkling thorpe and croft,
    Safe from the weather!
He, whom we convoy to his grave aloft,
    Singing together,

He was a man born with thy face and throat,
    Lyric Apollo!
Long he lived nameless: how should spring take note
    Winter would follow?
Till lo, the little touch, and youth was gone!
    Cramped and dimished,
Moaned he, 'New measures, other feet anon!
    'My dance is finished?'
No, that's the world's way: (keep the mountain-side,
    Make for the city!)
He knew the signal, and stepped on with pride
    Over men's pity;
Left play for work, and grappled with the world
    Bent on escaping:
'What's in the scroll,' quoth he, 'thou keepest furled?
    'Show me their shaping,
'Theirs who most studied man, the bard and sage,–
    'Give!'–So, he gowned him,
Straight got by heart that book to its last page:
    Learned, we found him.
Yea, but we found him bald too, eyes like lead,
    Accents uncertain:
'Time to taste life,' another would have said,
    'Up with the curtain!'
This man said rather, 'Actual life comes next?
    'Patience a moment!
'Grant I have mastered learning's crabbed text,
    'Still there's the comment.
'Let me know all! Prate not of most or least,
    'Painful or easy!
'Even to the crumbs I'd fain eat up the feast,
    'Ay, nor feel queasy.'
Oh, such a life as he resolved to live,
    When he had learned it,
When he had gathered all books had to give!
    Sooner, he spurned it.
Image the whole, then execute the parts–
    Fancy the fabric
Quiet, ere you build, ere steel strike fire from quartz,
    Ere mortar dab brick!

(Here's the town-gate reached: there's the market-place
    Gaping before us.)
Yea, this in him was the peculiar grace
    (Hearten our chorus!)
That before living he'd learn how to live–
    No end to learning:
Earn the means first–God surely will contrive
    Use for our earning.
Others mistrust and say, 'But time escapes:
    'Live now or never!'
He said, 'What's time? Leave Now for dogs and apes!
    'Man has Forever.'
Back to his book then: deeper drooped his head:
    Calculus racked him:
Leaden before, his eyes grew dross of lead:
    Tussis attacked him.
'Now, master, take a little rest!'–not he!
    (Caution redoubled,
Step two abreast, the way winds narrowly!)
    Not a whit troubled
Back to his studies, fresher than at first,
    Fierce as a dragon
He (soul-hydroptic with a sacred thirst)
    Sucked at the flagon.
Oh, if we draw a circle premature,
    Heedless of far gain,
Greedy for quick returns of profit, sure
    Bad is our bargain!
Was it not great? did not he throw on God,
    (He loves the burthen)–
God's task to make the heavenly period
    Perfect the earthen?
Did not he magnify the mind, show clear
    Just what it all meant?
He would not discount life, as fools do here,
    Paid by instalment.
He ventured neck or nothing–heaven's success
    Found, or earth's failure:
'Wilt thou trust death or not?' He answered 'Yes':
    'Hence with life's pale lure!'

That low man seeks a little thing to do,
    Sees it and does it:
This high man, with a great thing to pursue,
    Dies ere he knows it:
That low man goes on adding one to one,
    His hundred's soon hit:
This high man, aiming at a million,
    Misses an unit.
That, has the world here–should he need the next
    Let the world mind him!
This, throws himself on God, and unperplexed
    Seeking shall find him.
So, with the throttling hands of death at strife,
    Ground he at grammar;
Still, thro' the rattle, parts of speech were rife:
    While he could stammer
He settled *Hoti*'s business–let it be!–
    Properly based *Oun*–
Gave us the doctrine of the enclitic *De*,
    Dead from the waist down.
Well, here's the platform, here's the proper place:
    Hail to your purlieus,
All ye highfliers of the feathered race,
    Swallows and curlews!
Here's the top-peak; the multitude below
    Live, for they can, there:
This man decided not to Live but Know–
    Bury this man there?
Here–here's his place, where meteors shoot, clouds form,
    Lightnings are loosened,
Stars come and go! Let joy break with the storm,
    Peace let the dew send!
Lofty designs must close in like effects:
    Loftily lying,
Leave him–still loftier than the world suspects,
    Living and dying.
                        ROBERT BROWNING

447 *On the Late Massacre in Piedmont*

Avenge O Lord thy slaughter'd Saints, whose bones
    Lie scatter'd on the Alpine mountains cold;
      Ev'n them who kept thy truth so pure of old,
When all our fathers worship't Stocks and Stones,
Forget not: in thy book record their groanes
    Who were thy Sheep, and in their antient Fold
    Slayn by the bloody Piemontese that roll'd
Mother with Infant down the Rocks. Their moans
The Vales redoubl'd to the Hills, and they
    To Heav'n. Their martyr'd blood and ashes sow
    O'er all the Italian fields where still doth sway
The triple Tyrant: that from these may grow
    A hunder'd-fold, who having learnt thy way
    Early may fly the Babylonian woe.

JOHN MILTON

448 *The Day of Judgment*

An Ode, Attempted in English Sapphick

When the fierce North wind with his airy forces,
Rears up the *Baltic* to a foaming fury;
And the red lightning, with a storm, of hail, comes
    Rushing amain down;

How the poor sailors stand amaz'd, and tremble!–
While the hoarse thunder, like a Bloody Trumpet,
Roars a loud onset to the gaping waters,
    Quick to devour them:

Such shall the noise be, and the wild disorder,
(If things eternal may be like these Earthly)
Such the dire terror, when the Great Archangel
    Shakes the Creation,

Tears the strong pillars of the vault of Heav'n,
Breaks up old marble, the repose of princes;–
See–the graves open,–and the bones arising,
    Flames all around 'em!

Hark, the shrill outcries of the guilty wretches!
Lively bright horror, and amazing anguish
Stare thro' their eyelids, while the living worm lies
   Gnawing within them.

Thoughts, like old vultures, prey upon their heart-
 strings,
And the smart twinges, when the eye beholds the
Lofty Judge frowning, and a flood of vengeance
   Rolling afore Him.

Hopeless immortals! how they scream and shiver,
While devils push them to the pit wide-yawning
Hideous and gloomy to receive them headlong
   Down to the centre:

Stop here, my fancy: (all away ye horrid
Doleful ideas) come arise to Jesus;
How He sits Godlike! and the saints around Him
   Thron'd, yet adoring!

O may I sit there when He comes triumphant,
Dooming the nations! then ascend to glory,
While our Hosannas all along the passage,
   Shout the Redeemer.
       ISAAC WATTS

449 *The Immortal*

The Immortal stood frozen amidst
The vast rock of eternity times
And times, a night of vast durance,
Impatient, stifled, stiffen'd, hard'ned;

Till impatience no longer could bear
The hard bondage: rent, rent, the vast solid,
With a crash from immense to immense,

Cracked across into numberless fragments.
The Prophetic wrath, struggling for vent,
Hurls apart, stamping furious to dust
And crumbling with bursting sobs, heaves
The black marble on high into fragments.

Hurl'd apart on all sides as a falling
Rock, the innumerable fragments away
Fell asunder; & horrible vacuum
Beneath him, & on all sides round,

Falling, falling, Los fell & fell,
Sunk precipitant, heavy, down, down,
Times on times, night on night, day on day–
Truth has bounds, Error none–falling, falling,
Years on years, & ages on ages
Still he fell thro' the void, still a void
Found for falling, day & night without end;
For tho' day or night was not, their spaces
Were measur'd by his incessant whirls
In the horrid vacuity bottomless.

The Immortal revolving, indignant,
First in wrath threw his limbs like the babe
New born into our world: wrath subsided,
And contemplative thoughts first arose:
Then aloft his head rear'd in the Abyss
And his downward-borne fall chang'd oblique

Many ages of groans, till there grew
Branchy forms organising the Human
Into finite inflexible organs;

Till in process from falling he bore
Sidelong on the purple air, wafting
The weak breeze in efforts o'erwearied.

Incessant the falling Mind labour'd,
Organising itself, till the Vacuum
Became element, pliant to rise
Or to fall or to swim or to fly,
With ease searching the dire vacuity.

WILLIAM BLAKE

450   *The Sea of Death*

A Fragment

                    –Methought I saw
Life swiftly treading over endless space;
And, at her foot-print, but a bygone pace,

The ocean-past, which, with increasing wave,
Swallow'd her steps like a pursuing grave.
Sad were my thoughts that anchor'd silently
On the dead waters of that passionless sea,
Unstirr'd by any touch of living breath:
Silence hung over it, and drowsy Death,
Like a gorged sea-bird, slept with folded wings
On crowded carcasses–sad passive things
That wore the thin grey surface, like a veil
Over the calmness of their features pale.

And there were spring-faced cherubs that did sleep
Like water-lilies on that motionless deep,
How beautiful! with bright unruffled hair
On sleek unfretted brows, and eyes that were
Buried in marble tombs, a pale eclipse!
And smile-bedimpled cheeks, and pleasant lips,
Meekly apart, as if the soul intense
Spake out in dreams of its own innocence:
And so they lay in loveliness, and kept
The birth-night of their peace, that Life e'en wept
With very envy of their happy fronts;
For there were neighbour brows scarr'd by the brunts
Of strife and sorrowing–where Care had set
His crooked autograph, and marr'd the jet
Of glossy locks, with hollow eyes forlorn,
And lips that curl'd in bitterness and scorn–
Wretched,–as they had breathed of this world's pain,
And so bequeath'd it to the world again
Through the beholder's heart in heavy sighs.

So lay they garmented in torpid light,
Under the pall of a transparent night,
Like solemn apparitions lull'd sublime
To everlasting rest,–and with them Time
Slept, as he sleeps upon the silent face
Of a dark dial in a sunless place.

THOMAS HOOD

451 *The Blessed Damozel*

The blessed damozel leaned out
    From the gold bar of Heaven;
Her eyes were deeper than the depth
    Of waters stilled at even;
She had three lilies in her hand,
    And the stars in her hair were seven.

Her robe, ungirt from clasp to hem,
    No wrought flowers did adorn,
But a white rose of Mary's gift,
    For service meetly worn;
Her hair that lay along her back
    Was yellow like ripe corn.

Herseemed she scarce had been a day
    One of God's choristers;
The wonder was not yet quite gone
    From that still look of hers;
Albeit, to them she left, her day
    Had counted as ten years.

(To one, it is ten years of years.
    . . . Yet now, and in this place,
Surely she leaned o'er me—her hair
    Fell all about my face. . . .
Nothing: the autumn-fall of leaves.
    The whole year sets apace.)

It was the rampart of God's house
    That she was standing on;
By God built over the sheer depth
    The which is Space begun;
So high, that looking downward thence
    She scarce could see the sun.

It lies in Heaven, across the flood
    Of ether, as a bridge.
Beneath, the tides of day and night
    With flame and darkness ridge
The void, as low as where this earth
    Spins like a fretful midge.

Around her, lovers, newly met
  'Mid deathless love's acclaims,
Spoke evermore among themselves
  Their heart-remembered[1] names;
And the souls mounting up to God
  Went by her like thin flames.

And still she bowed herself and stooped
  Out of the circling charm;
Until her bosom must have made
  The bar she leaned on warm,
And the lilies lay as if asleep
  Along her bended arm.

From the fixed place of Heaven she saw
  Time like a pulse shake fierce
Through all the worlds. Her gaze still strove
  Within the gulf to pierce
Its path; and now she spoke as when
  The stars sang in their spheres.

The sun was gone now; the curled moon
  Was like a little feather
Fluttering far down the gulf; and now
  She spoke through the still weather.
Her voice was like the voice the stars
  Had when they sang together.

(Ah sweet! Even now, in that bird's song,
  Strove not her accents there,
Fain to be hearkened? When those bells
  Possessed the mid-day air,
Strove not her steps to reach my side
  Down all the echoing stair?)

'I wish that he were come to me,
  For he will come,' she said.
'Have I not prayed in Heaven?—on earth,
  Lord, Lord, has he not pray'd?
Are not two prayers a perfect strength?
  And shall I feel afraid?

[1] *variant :* virginal new

'When round his head the aereole clings,
    And he is clothed in white,
I'll take his hand and go with him
    To the deep wells of light;
As unto a stream we will step down,
    And bathe there in God's sight.

'We two will stand beside that shrine,
    Occult, withheld, untrod,
Whose lamps are stirred continually
    With prayer sent up to God;
And see our old prayers, granted, melt
    Each like a little cloud.

'We two will lie i' the shadow of
    That living mystic tree
Within whose secret growth the Dove
    Is sometimes felt to be,
While every leaf that His plumes touch
    Saith His Name audibly.

'And I myself will teach to him,
    I myself, lying so,
The songs I sing here; which his voice
    Shall pause in, hushed and slow,
And find some knowledge at each pause,
    Or some new thing to know.'

(Alas! We two, we two, thou say'st!
    Yea, one wast thou with me
That once of old. But shall God lift
    To endless unity
The soul whose likeness with thy soul
    Was but its love for thee?)

'We two,' she said, 'will seek the groves
    Where the lady Mary is,
With her five handmaidens, whose names
    Are five sweet symphonies,
Cecily, Gertrude, Magdalen,
    Margaret and Rosalys.

'Circlewise sit they, with bound locks
　　And foreheads garlanded;
Into the fine cloth white like flame
　　Weaving the golden thread,
To fashion the birth-robes for them
　　Who are just born, being dead.

'He shall fear, haply, and be dumb:
　　Then will I lay my cheek
To his, and tell about our love,
　　Not once abashed or weak:
And the dear Mother will approve
　　My pride, and let me speak.

'Herself shall bring us, hand in hand,
　　To him round whom all souls
Kneel, the clear-ranged unnumbered heads
　　Bowed with their aureoles:
And angels meeting us shall sing
　　To their citherns and citoles.

'There will I ask of Christ the Lord
　　Thus much for him and me:–
Only to live as once on earth
　　With Love,–only to be,
As then awhile, for ever now
　　Together, I and he.'

She gazed and listened and then said,
　　Less sad of speech than mild,–
'All this is when he comes.' She ceased.
　　The light thrilled towards her, fill'd
With angels in strong level flight.
　　Her eyes prayed, and she smil'd.

(I saw her smile.) But soon their path
　　Was vague in distant spheres:
And then she cast her arms along
　　The golden barriers,
And laid her face between her hands,
　　And wept. (I heard her tears.)

DANTE GABRIEL ROSSETTI

452 *Saturn*

Deep in the shady sadness of a vale
Far sunken from the healthy breath of morn,
Far from the fiery noon, and eve's one star,
Sat grey-hair'd Saturn, quiet as a stone,
Still as the silence round about his lair;
Forest on forest hung about his head
Like cloud on cloud. No stir of air was there,
Not so much life as on a summer's day
Robs not one light seed from the feather'd grass,
But where the dead leaf fell, there did it rest.
A stream went voiceless by, still deaden'd more
By reason of his fallen divinity
Spreading a shade: the Naiad 'mid her reeds
Press'd her cold finger closer to her lips.

Along the margin-sand large foot-marks went,
No further than to where his feet had stray'd,
And slept there since. Upon the sodden ground
His old right hand lay nerveless, listless, dead,
Unsceptred; and his realmless eyes were closed;
While his bow'd head seem'd list'ning to the Earth,
His ancient mother, for some comfort yet.

It seem'd no force could wake him from his place;
But there came one, who with a kindred hand
Touch'd his wide shoulders, after bending low
With reverence, though to one who knew it not.
She was a Goddess of the infant world;
By her in stature the tall Amazon
Had stood a pigmy's height: she would have ta'en
Achilles by the hair and bent his neck;
Or with a finger stay'd Ixion's wheel.
Her face was large as that of Memphian sphinx,
Pedestal'd haply in a palace court,
When sages look'd to Egypt for their lore.
But oh! how unlike marble was that face:
How beautiful, if sorrow had not made
Sorrow more beautiful than Beauty's self.
There was a listening fear in her regard,
As if calamity had but begun;

As if the vanward clouds of evil days
Had spent their malice, and the sullen rear
Was with its stored thunder labouring up.
One hand she press'd upon that aching spot
Where beats the human heart, as if just there,
Though an immortal, she felt cruel pain:
The other upon Saturn's bended neck
She laid, and to the level of his ear
Leaning with parted lips, some words she spake
In solemn tenour and deep organ tone:
Some mourning words, which in our feeble tongue
Would come in these like accents; O how frail
To that large utterance of the early Gods!
'Saturn, look up!–though wherefore poor old King?
I have no comfort for thee, no not one:
I cannot say, "O wherefore sleepest thou?"
For heaven is parted from thee, and the earth
Knows thee not, thus afflicted, for a God;
And ocean too, with all its solemn noise,
Has from thy sceptre pass'd; and all the air
Is emptied of thine hoary majesty.
Thy thunder, conscious of the new command,
Rumbles reluctant o'er our fallen house;
And thy sharp lightning in unpractised hands
Scorches and burns our once serene domain.
O aching time! O moments big as years!
All as ye pass swell out the monstrous truth,
And press it so upon our weary griefs
That unbelief has not a space to breathe.
Saturn, sleep on:–O thoughtless, why did I
Thus violate thy slumbrous solitude?
Why should I ope thy melancholy eyes?
Saturn, sleep on! while at thy feet I weep.'

JOHN KEATS

453 *A Forsaken Garden*

In a coign of the cliff between lowland and highland,
  At the sea-down's edge between windward and lee,
Walled round with rocks as an inland island,
  The ghost of a garden fronts the sea.

A girdle of brushwood and thorn encloses
    The steep square slope of the blossomless bed
Where the weeds that grew green from the graves of its roses
        Now lie dead.

The fields fall southward, abrupt and broken,
    To the low last edge of the long lone land.
If a step should sound or a word be spoken,
    Would a ghost not rise at the strange guest's hand?
So long have the grey bare walks lain guestless,
    Through branches and briars if a man make way,
He shall find no life but the sea-wind's, restless
        Night and day.

The dense hard passage is blind and stifled
    That crawls by a track none turn to climb
To the strait waste place that the years have rifled
    Of all but the thorns that are touched not of time.
The thorns he spares when the rose is taken;
    The rocks are left when he wastes the plain.
The wind that wanders, the weeds wind-shaken,
        These remain.

Not a flower to be pressed of the foot that falls not;
    As the heart of a dead man the seed-plots are dry;
From the thicket of thorns whence the nightingale calls not,
    Could she call, there were never a rose to reply.
Over the meadows that blossom and wither
    Rings but the note of a sea-bird's song;
Only the sun and the rain come hither
        All year long.

The sun burns sere and the rain dishevels
    One gaunt bleak blossom of scentless breath.
Only the wind here hovers and revels
    In a round where life seems barren as death.
Here there was laughing of old, there was weeping,
    Haply, of lovers none ever will know,
Whose eyes went seaward a hundred sleeping
        Years ago.

Heart handfast in heart as they stood, 'Look thither,'
  Did he whisper? 'look forth from the flowers to the sea;
For the foam-flowers endure when the rose-blossoms wither,
  And men that love lightly may die–but we?'
And the same wind sang and the same waves whitened,
  And or ever the garden's last petals were shed,
In the lips that had whispered, the eyes that had lightened,
    Love was dead.

Or they loved their life through, and then went whither?
  And were one to the end–but what end who knows?
Love deep as the sea as a rose must wither,
  As the rose-red seaweed that mocks the rose.
Shall the dead take thought for the dead to love them?
  What love was ever as deep as a grave?
They are loveless now as the grass above them
    Or the wave.

All are at one now, roses and lovers,
  Not known of the cliffs and the fields and the sea.
Not a breath of the time that has been hovers
  In the air now soft with a summer to be.
Not a breath shall there sweeten the seasons hereafter
  Of the flowers or the lovers that laugh now or weep,
When as they that are free now of weeping and laughter
    We shall sleep.

Here death may deal not again for ever;
  Here change may come not till all change end.
From the graves they have made they shall rise up never,
  Who have left nought living to ravage and rend.
Earth, stones, and thorns of the wild ground growing,
  While the sun and the rain live, these shall be;
Till a last wind's breath upon all these blowing
    Roll the sea.

Till the slow sea rise and the sheer cliff crumble,
  Till terrace and meadow the deep gulfs drink,
Till the strength of the waves of the high tides humble
  The fields that lessen, the rocks that shrink,

Here now in his triumph where all things falter,
　Stretched out on the spoils that his own hand spread,
As a god self-slain on his own strange altar,
　　　Death lies dead.

ALGERNON CHARLES SWINBURNE

454 *On First looking into Chapman's Homer*

　　Much have I travell'd in the realms of gold,
　　　　And many goodly states and kingdoms seen;
　　　　Round many western islands have I been
　　Which bards in fealty to Apollo hold.
　　Oft of one wide expanse had I been told
　　　　That deep-brow'd Homer ruled as his demesne;
　　　　Yet did I never breathe its pure serene
　　Till I heard Chapman speak out loud and bold:
　　Then felt I like some watcher of the skies
　　　　When a new planet swims into his ken;
　　Or like stout Cortez when with eagle eyes
　　　　He stared at the Pacific–and all his men
　　Look'd at each other with a wild surmise–
　　　　Silent, upon a peak in Darien.

JOHN KEATS

455 *From 'An Epistle'*

　　And may my humble dwelling stand
　　Upon some chosen spot of land;
　　A pond before full to the brim,
　　Where cows may cool, and geese may swim;
　　Behind a green, like velvet neat,
　　Soft to the eye, and to the feet,
　　Where od'rous plants in evening fair
　　Breathe all around ambrosial air,
　　From Eurus, foe to kitchen-ground,
　　Fenc'd by a slope with bushes crown'd,
　　Fit dwelling for the feather'd throng,
　　Who pay their quit-rents with a song;
　　With op'ning views of hills and dales,
　　Which sense and fancy too regales,

Where the half-cirque, which vision bounds,
Like amphitheatre surrounds;
And woods impervious to the breeze,
Thick phalanx of embodied trees,
From hills thro' plains in dusk array
Extended far repel the day.
Here stillness, height, and solemn shade
Invite, and contemplation aid:
Here nymphs from hollow oaks relate
The dark decrees and will of fate,
And dreams beneath the spreading beach
Inspire, and docile fancy teach;
While soft as breezy breath of wind,
Impulses rustle thro' the mind:
Here Dryads, scorning Phœbus ray,
While Pan melodious pipes away,
In measur'd motions frisk about,
'Till old Silenus puts them out:
There see the clover, pea, and bean,
Vie in variety of green;
Fresh pastures speckl'd o'er with sheep;
Brown fields their fallow sabbaths keep;
Plump Ceres golden tresses wear,
And poppy-topknots deck her hair;
And silver stream thro' meadows stray,
And Naiads on the margin play;
And lesser nymphs on side of hills
From play-thing urns pour down the rills.

Thus shelter'd free from care and strife,
May I enjoy a calm thro' life;
See faction, safe in low degree,
As men at land see storms at sea;
And laugh at miserable elves
Not kind, so much as to themselves,
Curst with such souls of base alloy,
As can possess, but not enjoy,
Debarr'd the pleasure to impart
By av'rice, sphincter of the heart,
Who wealth, hard earn'd by guilty cares,
Bequeath untouch'd to thankless heirs.

May I, with look ungloom'd by guile,
And wearing virtue's livery-smile;
Prone the distressed to relieve,
And little trespasses forgive;
With income not in fortune's pow'r,
And skill to make a busy hour;
With trips to town, life to amuse,
To purchase books, and hear the news,
To see old friends, brush off the clown,
And quicken taste at coming down;
Unhurt by sickness' blasting rage,
And slowly mellowing in age,
When fate extends its gath'ring gripe,
Fall off like fruit grown fully ripe,
Quit a worn being without pain,
Perhaps to blossom soon again . . .

   Thus, thus I steer my bark, and sail
On even keel with gentle gale.
At helm I make my reason sit,
My crew of passions all submit.
If dark and blust'ring prove some nights
Philosophy puts forth her lights;
Experience holds the cautious glass,
To shun the breakers, as I pass;
And frequent throws the wary lead,
To see what dangers may be hid.
And once in seven years I'm seen
At Bath, or Tunbridge to careen.
Tho' pleas'd to see the dolphins play,
I mind my compass and my way;
With store sufficient for relief
And wisely still prepar'd to reef;
Nor wanting the dispersive bowl
Of cloudy weather in the soul,
I make (may heaven propitious send
Such wind and weather to the end)
Neither becalm'd, nor over-blown,
Life's voyage to the world unknown.

MATTHEW GREEN

456 *This Lime-tree Bower my Prison*

Addressed to Charles Lamb, of the India House, London

Well, they are gone, and here must I remain,
This lime-tree bower my prison! I have lost
Beauties and feelings, such as would have been
Most sweet to my remembrance even when age
Had dimmed mine eyes to blindness! They, meanwhile,
Friends, whom I never more may meet again,
On springy heath, along the hill-top edge,
Wander in gladness, and wind down, perchance,
To that still roaring dell, of which I told;
The roaring dell, o'erwooded, narrow, deep,
And only speckled by the mid-day sun;
Where its slim trunk the ash from rock to rock
Flings arching like a bridge;–that branchless ash,
Unsunned and damp, whose few poor yellow leaves
Ne'er tremble in the gale, yet tremble still,
Fanned by the water-fall! and there my friends
Behold the dark green file of long lank weeds,
That all at once (a most fantastic sight!)
Still nod and drip beneath the dripping edge
Of the blue clay-stone.

                Now, my friends emerge
Beneath the wide wide Heaven–and view again
The many-steepled tract magnificent
Of hilly fields and meadows, and the sea,
With some fair bark, perhaps, whose sails light up
The slip of smooth clear blue betwixt two Isles
Of purple shadow! Yes! they wander on
In gladness all; but thou, methinks, most glad,
My gentle-hearted Charles! for thou hast pined
And hungered after Nature, many a year,
In the great City pent, winning thy way
With sad yet patient soul, through evil and pain
And strange calamity! Ah! slowly sink
Behind the western ridge, thou glorious Sun!
Shine in the slant beams of the sinking orb,

Ye purple heath-flowers! richlier burn, ye clouds!
Live in the yellow light, ye distant groves!
And kindle, thou blue Ocean! So my Friend
Struck with deep joy may stand, as I have stood,
Silent with swimming sense; yea, gazing round
On the wide landscape, gaze till all doth seem
Less gross than bodily; and of such hues
As veil the Almighty Spirit, when yet he makes
Spirits perceive his presence.

                                    A delight
Comes sudden on my heart, and I am glad
As I myself were there! Nor in this bower,
This little lime-tree bower, have I not marked
Much that has soothed me. Pale beneath the blaze
Hung the transparent foliage; and I watched
Some broad and sunny leaf, and loved to see
The shadow of the leaf and stem above,
Dappling its sunshine! And that walnut-tree
Was richly tinged, and a deep radiance lay
Full on the ancient ivy, which usurps
Those fronting elms, and now, with blackest mass,
Makes their dark branches gleam a lighter hue
Through the late twilight; and though now the bat
Wheels silent by, and not a swallow twitters,
Yet still the solitary humble-bee
Sings in the bean-flower! Henceforth I shall know
That Nature ne'er deserts the wise and pure;
No plot so narrow, be but Nature there,
No waste so vacant, but may well employ
Each faculty of sense, and keep the heart
Awake to Love and Beauty! and sometimes
'Tis well to be bereft of promised good,
That we may lift the soul, and contemplate
With lively joy the joys we cannot share.
My gentle-hearted Charles! when the last rook
Beat its straight path along the dusky air
Homewards, I blest it! deeming, its black wing
(Now a dim speck, now vanishing in light)
Had cross'd the mighty orb's dilated glory,
While thou stood'st gazing; or when all was still,

Flew creeking o'er thy head, and had a charm
For thee, my gentle-hearted Charles, to whom
No sound is dissonant which tells of life.

SAMUEL TAYLOR COLERIDGE

457 *Eloisa to Abelard*

In these deep solitudes and awful cells,
Where heav'nly-pensive contemplation dwells,
And ever-musing melancholy reigns;
What means this tumult in a vestal's veins?
Why rove my thoughts beyond this last retreat?
Why feels my heart its long-forgotten heat?
Yet, yet I love!–From Abelard it came,
And Eloisa yet must kiss the name.

Dear fatal name! rest ever unreveal'd,
Nor pass these lips in holy silence seal'd:
Hide it, my heart, within that close disguise,
Where, mix'd with God's, his lov'd Idea lies:
Oh write it not, my hand–the name appears
Already written–wash it out, my tears!
In vain lost Eloisa weeps and prays,
Her heart still dictates, and her hand obeys.

Relentless walls! whose darksome round contains
Repentant sighs, and voluntary pains:
Ye rugged rocks! which holy knees have worn;
Ye grots and caverns shagg'd with horrid thorn!
Shrines! where their vigils pale-ey'd virgins keep,
And pitying saints, whose statues learn to weep!
Though cold like you, unmov'd, and silent grown,
I have not yet forgot my self to stone.
All is not Heaven's while Abelard has part,
Still rebel nature holds out half my heart;
Nor pray'rs nor fasts its stubborn pulse restrain,
Nor tears, for ages taught to flow in vain.

Soon as thy letters trembling I unclose,
That well-known name awakens all my woes.
Oh name for ever sad! for ever dear!
Still breath'd in sighs, still usher'd with a tear.
I tremble too, where'er my own I find,
Some dire misfortune follows close behind.

Line after line my gushing eyes o'erflow,
Led through a sad variety of woe:
Now warm in love, now with'ring in thy bloom,
Lost in a convent's solitary gloom!
There stern religion quench'd th' unwilling flame,
There died the best of passions, love and fame.

   Yet write, oh write me all, that I may join
Griefs to thy griefs, and echo sighs to thine.
Nor foes nor fortune take this pow'r away;
And is my Abelard less kind than they?
Tears still are mine, and those I need not spare;
Love but demands what else were shed in prayer;
No happier task these faded eyes pursue;
To read and weep is all they now can do.

   Then share thy pain, allow that sad relief;
Ah, more than share it! give me all thy grief.
Heav'n first taught letters for some wretch's aid,
Some banish'd lover, or some captive maid;
They live, they speak, they breathe what love inspires,
Warm from the soul, and faithful to its fires;
The virgin's wish without her fears impart,
Excuse the blush, and pour out all the heart,
Speed the soft intercourse from soul to soul,
And waft a sigh from Indus to the Pole.

   Thou know'st how guiltless first I met thy flame,
When Love approach'd me under Friendship's name;
My fancy form'd thee of angelic kind,
Some emanation of th' all-beauteous Mind.
Those smiling eyes, attemp'ring ev'ry ray,
Shone sweetly lambent with celestial day;
Guiltless I gaz'd; heav'n listen'd while you sung;
And truths divine came mended from that tongue.
From lips like those what precept fail'd to move?
Too soon they taught me 'twas no sin to love.
Back thro' the paths of pleasing sense I ran,
Nor wish'd an angel whom I lov'd a man.
Dim and remote the joys of saints I see;
Nor envy them that heav'n I lose for thee.

   How oft, when press'd to marriage, have I said,
Curse on all laws but those which love has made!

Love, free as air, at sight of human ties,
Spreads his light wings, and in a moment flies.
Let wealth, let honour, wait the wedded dame,
August her deed, and sacred be her fame;
Before true passion all those views remove;
Fame, wealth, and honour! what are you to love?
The jealous god, when we profane his fires,
Those restless passions in revenge inspires;
And bids them make mistaken mortals groan,
Who seek in love for aught but love alone.
Should at my feet the world's great master fall,
Himself, his throne, his world, I'd scorn 'em all:
Not Cæsar's empress would I deign to prove;
No, make me mistress to the man I love;
If there be yet another name more free,
More fond than mistress, make me that to thee!
Oh happy state! when souls each other draw,
When love is liberty, and nature, law:
All then is full, possessing and possest,
No craving void left aching in the breast:
Ev'n thought meets thought, ere from the lips it part,
And each warm wish springs mutual from the heart.
This sure is bliss (if bliss on earth there be),
And once the lot of Abelard and me.

    Alas, how chang'd! what sudden horrors rise!
A naked lover bound and bleeding lies!
Where, where was Eloise? her voice, her hand,
Her poniard, had oppos'd the dire command.
Barbarian stay! that bloody stroke restrain;
The crime was common, common be the pain.
I can no more; by shame, by rage supprest,
Let tears, and burning blushes speak the rest.

    Canst thou forget that sad, that solemn day,
When victims at yon altar's foot we lay?
Canst thou forget what tears that moment fell,
When, warm in youth, I bade the world farewell?
As with cold lips I kiss'd the sacred veil,
The shrines all trembled, and the lamps grew pale:
Heav'n scarce believ'd the conquest it survey'd,
And saints with wonder heard the vows I made.

Yet then, to those dread altars as I drew,
Not on the Cross my eyes were fix'd, but you:
Not grace, or zeal, love only was my call,
And if I lose thy love, I lose my all.
Come! with thy looks, thy words, relieve my woe;
Those still at least are left thee to bestow.
Still on that breast enamour'd let me lie,
Still drink delicious poison from thy eye,
Pant on thy lip, and to thy heart be prest;
Give all thou canst—and let me dream the rest.
Ah no! instruct me other joys to prize,
With other beauties charm my partial eyes!
Full in my view set all the bright abode,
And make my soul quit Abelard for God.

Ah think at least thy flock deserves thy care,
Plants of thy hand, and children of thy pray'r.
From the false world in early youth they fled,
By thee to mountains, wilds, and deserts led.
You rais'd these hallow'd walls; the desert smil'd,
And Paradise was open'd in the wild.
No weeping orphan saw his father's stores
Our shrines irradiate, or emblaze the floors;
No silver saints, by dying misers giv'n,
Here brib'd the rage of ill-requited heav'n;
But such plain roofs as piety could raise,
And only vocal with the Maker's praise.
In these lone walls (their day's eternal bound),
These moss-grown domes with spiry turrets crown'd,
Where awful arches make a noon-day night;
And the dim windows shed a solemn light;
Thy eyes diffus'd a reconciling ray,
And gleams of glory brighten'd all the day.
But now no face divine contentment wears,
'Tis all blank sadness, or continual tears.
See how the force of others' pray'rs I try,
(O pious fraud of am'rous charity!)
But why should I on others' pray'rs depend?
Come thou, my father, brother, husband, friend!
Ah, let thy handmaid, sister, daughter, move,
And all those tender names in one, thy love!

The darksome pines, that o'er yon rocks reclin'd,
Wave high, and murmur to the hollow wind,
The wandering streams that shine between the hills,
The grots that echo to the tinkling rills,
The dying gales that pant upon the trees,
The lakes that quiver to the curling breeze;
No more these scenes my meditation aid,
Or lull to rest the visionary maid:
But o'er the twilight groves, and dusky caves,
Long-sounding aisles and intermingled graves,
Black Melancholy sits, and round her throws
A death-like silence, and a dread repose:
Her gloomy presence saddens all the scene,
Shades ev'ry flow'r, and darkens every green,
Deepens the murmur of the falling floods,
And breathes a browner horror on the woods,

   Yet here for ever, ever must I stay;
Sad proof how well a lover can obey!
Death, only death can break the lasting chain;
And here, ev'n then, shall my cold dust remain,
Here all its frailties, all its flames resign,
And wait till 'tis no sin to mix with thine.

   Ah wretch! believ'd the spouse of God in vain,
Confess'd within the slave of love and man.
Assist me, Heaven! but whence arose that pray'r?
Sprung it from piety, or from despair?
Ev'n here, where frozen chastity retires,
Love finds an altar for forbidden fires.
I ought to grieve, but cannot what I ought;
I mourn the lover, not lament the fault;
I view my crime, but kindle at the view,
Repent old pleasures, and solicit new;
Now turn'd to heaven, I weep my past offence,
Now think of thee, and curse my innocence.
Of all affliction taught a lover yet,
'Tis sure the hardest science to forget!
How shall I lose the sin, yet keep the sense,
And love th' offender, yet detest th' offence?
How the dear object from the crime remove,
Or how distinguish penitence from love?

Unequal task! a passion to resign,
For hearts so touch'd, so pierc'd, so lost as mine.
Ere such a soul regains its peaceful state,
How often must it love, how often hate!
How often hope, despair, resent, regret,
Conceal, disdain—do all things but forget!
But let Heav'n seize it, all at once 'tis fir'd;
Not touch'd, but rapt; not waken'd, but inspir'd!
Oh come! Oh teach me nature to subdue,
Renounce my love, my life, my self—and you.
Fill my fond heart with God alone, for he
Alone can rival, can succeed to thee.

How happy is the blameless Vestal's lot!
The world forgetting, by the world forgot:
Eternal sunshine of the spotless mind!
Each pray'r accepted, and each wish resign'd;
Labour and rest, that equal periods keep;
'Obedient slumbers that can wake and weep';
Desires compos'd, affections ever ev'n;
Tears that delight, and sighs that waft to Heav'n.
Grace shines around her with serenest beams,
And whisp'ring angels prompt her golden dreams.
For her th' unfading rose of Eden blooms,
And wings of seraphs shed divine perfumes;
For her the Spouse prepares the bridal ring;
For her white virgins hymeneals sing;
To sounds of heav'nly harps, she dies away,
And melts in visions of eternal day.

Far other dreams my erring soul employ,
Far other raptures, of unholy joy:
When at the close of each sad, sorrowing day,
Fancy restores what vengeance snatch'd away,
Then conscience sleeps, and leaving nature free,
All my loose soul unbounded springs to thee.
Oh curst, dear horrors of all-conscious night!
How glowing guilt exalts the keen delight!
Provoking demons all restraint remove,
And stir within me ev'ry source of love.
I hear thee, view thee, gaze o'er all thy charms,
And round thy phantom glue my clasping arms.

I wake–no more I hear, no more I view,
The phantom flies me, as unkind as you.
I call aloud; it hears not what I say;
I stretch my empty arms; it glides away:
To dream once more I close my willing eyes;
Ye soft illusions, dear deceits, arise!
Alas no more! methinks we wand'ring go
Through dreary wastes, and weep each other's woe,
Where round some mould'ring tow'r pale ivy creeps,
And low-brow'd rocks hang nodding o'er the deeps.
Sudden you mount! you beckon from the skies;
Clouds interpose, waves roar, and winds arise.
I shriek, start up, the same sad prospect find,
And wake to all the griefs I left behind.

For thee the fates, severely kind, ordain
A cool suspense from pleasure and from pain;
Thy life a long dead calm of fix'd repose;
No pulse that riots, and no blood that glows.
Still as the sea, ere winds were taught to blow,
Or moving spirit bade the waters flow;
Soft as the slumbers of a saint forgiv'n,
And mild as opening gleams of promis'd heav'n.

Come Abelard! for what hast thou to dread?
The torch of Venus burns not for the dead;
Nature stands check'd; Religion disapproves;
Ev'n thou art cold–yet Eloisa loves.
Ah hopeless, lasting flames! like those that burn
To light the dead, and warm th' unfruitful urn.

What scenes appear where'er I turn my view!
The dear ideas, where I fly, pursue,
Rise in the grove, before the altar rise,
Stain all my soul, and wanton in my eyes!
I waste the Matin lamp in sighs for thee,
Thy image steals between my God and me;
Thy voice I seem in ev'ry hymn to hear,
With ev'ry bead I drop too soft a tear.
When from the censer clouds of fragrance roll,
And swelling organs lift the rising soul,
One thought of thee puts all the pomp to flight,
Priests, tapers, temples, swim before my sight:

In seas of flame my plunging soul is drown'd,
While altars blaze, and angels tremble round.

While prostrate here in humble grief I lie,
Kind, virtuous drops just gath'ring in my eye,
While praying, trembling, in the dust I roll,
And dawning grace is op'ning on my soul:
Come, if thou dar'st, all charming as thou art!
Oppose thyself to heav'n; dispute my heart;
Come, with one glance of those deluding eyes
Blot out each bright idea of the skies;
Take back that grace, those sorrows and those tears,
Take back my fruitless penitence and pray'rs;
Snatch me, just mounting, from the blest abode,
Assist the fiends and tear me from my God!

No, fly me, fly me! far as pole from pole;
Rise Alps between us! and whole oceans roll!
Ah come not, write not, think not once of me,
Nor share one pang of all I felt for thee.
Thy oaths I quit, thy memory resign;
Forget, renounce me, hate whate'er was mine.
Fair eyes, and tempting looks (which yet I view!),
Long lov'd, ador'd ideas! all adieu!
Oh grace serene! oh virtue heavenly fair!
Divine oblivion of low-thoughted care!
Fresh blooming hope, gay daughter of the sky!
And faith, our early immortality!
Enter each mild, each amicable guest;
Receive, and wrap me in eternal rest!

See in her cell sad Eloisa spread,
Propt on some tomb, a neighbour of the dead.
In each low wind methinks a spirit calls,
And more than echoes talk along the walls.
Here, as I watch'd the dying lamps around,
From yonder shrine I heard a hollow sound.
Come, sister, come! (it said, or seem'd to say)
Thy place is here, sad sister, come away!
Once like thyself, I trembled, wept, and pray'd,
Love's victim then, tho' now a sainted maid:
But all is calm in this eternal sleep;
Here grief forgets to groan, and love to weep;

Ev'n superstition loses ev'ry fear:
For God, not man, absolves our frailties here.
  I come, I come! prepare your roseate bowers,
Celestial palms, and ever-blooming flow'rs.
Thither, where sinners may have rest, I go,
Where flames refin'd in breasts seraphic glow:
Thou, Abelard! the last sad office pay,
And smooth my passage to the realms of day:
See my lips tremble, and my eye-balls roll,
Suck my last breath, and catch my flying soul!
Ah no—in sacred vestments may'st thou stand,
The hallow'd taper trembling in thy hand,
Present the Cross before my lifted eye,
Teach me at once, and learn of me to die.
Ah then, thy once lov'd Eloisa see!
It will be then no crime to gaze on me.
See from my cheek the transient roses fly!
See the last sparkle languish in my eye!
Till ev'ry motion, pulse, and breath be o'er;
And ev'n my Abelard be lov'd no more.
O Death all-eloquent! you only prove
What dust we doat on, when 'tis man we love.
  Then too, when fate shall thy fair frame destroy
(That cause of all my guilt, and all my joy),
In trance ecstatic may thy pangs be drown'd,
Bright clouds descend, and angels watch thee round;
From opening skies may streaming glories shine,
And saints embrace thee with a love like mine.
  May one kind grave unite each hapless name,
And graft my love immortal on thy fame.
Then, ages hence, when all my woes are o'er,
When this rebellious heart shall beat no more;
If ever chance two wand'ring lovers brings,
To Paraclete's white walls, and silver springs,
O'er the pale marble shall they join their heads,
And drink the falling tears each other sheds;
Then sadly say, with mutual pity mov'd,
O may we never love as these have lov'd!
From the full choir, when loud hosannas rise,
And swell the pomp of dreadful sacrifice,

Amid that scene, if some relenting eye
Glance on the stone where our cold relics lie,
Devotion's self shall steal a thought from heav'n,
One human tear shall drop, and be forgiv'n.
And sure if fate some future bard shall join
In sad similitude of griefs to mine,
Condemn'd whole years in absence to deplore,
And image charms he must behold no more;
Such if there be, who loves so long, so well,
Let him our sad, our tender story tell;
The well-sung woes will soothe my pensive ghost;
He best can paint 'em who shall feel 'em most.

ALEXANDER POPE

458 *The Exequy*

To his matchlesse never to be forgotten friend

Accept thou Shrine of my dead Saint,
Instead of Dirges this complaint;
And for sweet flowers to crown thy hearse,
Receive a strew of weeping verse
From thy griev'd friend, whom thou might'st see
Quite melted into tears for thee.

Dear loss! since thy untimely fate
My task hath been to meditate
On thee, on thee: thou art the book,
The library whereon I look
Though almost blind. For thee (lov'd clay)
I languish out, not live the day,
Using no other exercise
But what I practise with mine eyes:
By which wet glasses I found out
How lazily time creeps about
To one that mourns: this, only this
My exercise and bus'ness is:
So I compute the weary hours
With sighs dissolved into showers.

Nor wonder if my time go thus
Backward and most preposterous;

Thou hast benighted me, thy set
This Eve of blackness did beget,
Who was't my day, (though overcast
Before thou had'st thy Noon-tide past)
And I remember must in tears,
Thou scarce had'st seen so many years
As Day tells hours. By thy clear Sun
My life and fortune first did run;
But thou wilt never more appear
Folded within my Hemisphere,
Since both thy light and motion
Like a fled Star is fall'n and gone,
And twixt me and my soul's dear wish
An earth now interposed is,
Which such a strange eclipse doth make
As ne'er was read in Almanake.

I could allow thee for a time
To darken me and my sad Clime,
Were it a month, a year, or ten,
I would thy exile live till then;
And all that space my mirth adjourn,
So thou wouldst promise to return;
And putting off thy ashy shroud
At length disperse this sorrow's cloud.

But woe is me! the longest date
Too narrow is to calculate
These empty hopes: never shall I
Be so much blest as to descry
A glimpse of thee, till that day come
Which shall the earth to cinders doom,
And a fierce fever must calcine
The body of this world like thine,
(My Little World!). That fit of fire
Once off, our bodies shall aspire
To our soul's bliss: then we shall rise,
And view our selves with clearer eyes
In that calm Region, where no night
Can hide us from each other's sight.

Q

Mean time, thou hast her, earth: much good
May my harm do thee. Since it stood
With Heaven's will I might not call
Her longer mine, I give thee all
My short-liv'd right and interest
In her, whom living I lov'd best:
With a most free and bounteous grief,
I give thee what I could not keep.
Be kind to her, and prithee look
Thou write into thy Dooms-day book
Each parcel of this Rarity
Which in thy Casket shrin'd doth lie:
See that thou make thy reck'ning straight,
And yield her back again by weight;
For thou must audit on thy trust
Each grain and atom of this dust,
As thou wilt answer *Him* that lent,
Not gave thee, my dear Monument.

So close the ground, and 'bout her shade
Black curtains draw, my *Bride* is laid.

Sleep on my *Love* in thy cold bed
Never to be disquieted!
My last good night! Thou wilt not wake
Till I thy fate shall overtake:
Till age, or grief, or sickness must
Marry my body to that dust
It so much loves; and fill the room
My heart keeps empty in thy Tomb.
Stay for me there; I will not fail
To meet thee in that hollow Vale.
And think not much of my delay;
I am already on the way,
And follow thee with all the speed
Desire can make, or sorrows breed.
Each minute is a short degree,
And ev'ry hour a step towards thee.
At night when I betake to rest,
Next morn I rise nearer my West
Of life, almost by eight hours' sail,
Then when sleep breath'd his drowsy gale.

Thus from the Sun my Bottom steers,
And my day's Compass downward bears:
Nor labour I to stem the tide
Through which to *Thee* I swiftly glide.

'Tis true, with shame and grief I yield,
Thou like the *Van* first took'st the field,
And gotten hast the victory
In thus adventuring to die
Before me, whose more years might crave
A just precedence in the grave.
But hark! My pulse like a soft Drum
Beats my approach, tells *Thee* I come;
And slow howere my marches be,
I shall at last sit down by *Thee*.

The thought of this bids me go on,
And wait my dissolution
With hope and comfort. *Dear* (forgive
The crime) I am content to live
Divided, with but half a heart,
Till we shall meet and never part.

HENRY KING

459 *An Elegy*

Since you must go, and I must bid farewell,
    Hear Mistress, your departing servant tell
What it is like: and do not think they can
    Be idle words, though of a parting Man;
It is as if a night should shade noon-day,
    Or that the Sun was here, but forc't away;
And we were left under that Hemisphere,
    Where we must feel it Dark for half a year.
What fate is this to change men's days and hours,
    To shift their seasons, and destroy their powers!
Alas I ha' lost my heat, my blood, my prime,
    Winter is come a Quarter e're his Time,
My health will leave me; and when you depart,
    How shall I do sweet Mistress for my heart?

You would restore it? No, that's worth a fear,
  As if it were not worthy to be there:
O, keep it still; for it had rather be
  Your sacrifice, than here remain with me.
And so I spare it: Come what can become
  Of me, I'll softly tread unto my Tomb;
Or like a Ghost walk silent amongst men,
  Till I may see both it and you agen.

BEN JONSON

460 *To Mr. H. Lawes on his Airs*

Harry whose tuneful and well measur'd Song
  First taught our English Musick how to span
  Words with just note and accent, not to scan
  With Midas Ears, committing short and long;
Thy worth and skill exempts thee from the throng,
  With praise enough for Envy to look wan;
  To after age thou shalt be writ the man
  That with smooth aire couldst humor best our tonge.
Thou honour'st Verse, and Verse must send her wing
  To honour thee, the Priest of Phœbus quire,
  That tun'st their happiest lines in Hymn, or Story.
Dante shall give Fame leave to set thee higher
  Than his Casella whom he woo'd to sing
  Met in the milder shades of Purgatory.

JOHN MILTON

461 *To the Memory of Mr. Oldham*

Farewell, too little and too lately known,
Whom I began to think and call my own;
For sure our souls were near alli'd, and thine
Cast in the same poetic mould with mine.
One common note on either lyre did strike,
And knaves and fools we both abhorr'd alike.
To the same goal did both our studies drive:
The last set out the soonest did arrive.
Thus Nisus fell upon the slippery place,
Whilst his young friend perform'd and won the race.

O early ripe! to thy abundant store
What could advancing Age have added more?
It might (what Nature never gives the young)
Have taught the numbers of thy native tongue.
But Satire needs not those, and wit will shine
Through the harsh cadence of a rugged line.
A noble error, and but seldom made,
When poets are by too much force betray'd.
Thy gen'rous fruits, though gather'd ere their prime,
Still shew'd a quickness; and maturing time
But mellows what we write to the dull sweets of rhyme.
Once more, hail, and farewell! farewell, thou young
But ah! too short, Marcellus of our tongue!
Thy brows with ivy and with laurels bound;
But fate and gloomy night encompass thee around.

JOHN DRYDEN

462 *On the Earl of Strafford's Trial and Death*

Great Strafford! worthy of that name, though all
Of thee could be forgotten, but thy fall,
Crusht by imaginary treason's weight,
Which too much merit did accumulate:
As chymists gold from brass by fire would draw,
Pretexts are into treason forg'd by law.
His wisdom such, at once it did appear
Three kingdoms wonder, and three kingdoms fear;
Whilst single he stood forth, and seem'd, although
Each had an army, as an equal foe.
Such was his force of eloquence, to make
The hearers more concern'd than he that spake;
Each seem'd to act that part he came to see,
And none was more a looker-on than he;
So did he move our passion, some were known
To wish, for the defence, the crime their own.
Now private pity strove with public hate,
Reason with rage, and eloquence with fate:
Now they could him, if he could them forgive;
He's not too guilty, but too wise to live;
Less seem those facts which Treason's nick-name bore,
Than such a fear'd ability for more.

They after death their fears of him express,
His innocence, and their own guilt confess.
Their legislative frenzy they repent;
Enacting it should make no precedent.
This fate he could have 'scap'd, but would not lose
Honour for life, but rather nobly chose
Death from their fears, than safety from his own,
That his last action all the rest might crown.

JOHN DENHAM

463 *Elegy written in a Country Churchyard*

The Curfew tolls the knell of parting day,
   The lowing herd wind slowly o'er the lea,
The plowman homeward plods his weary way,
   And leaves the world to darkness and to me.

Now fades the glimmering landscape on the sight,
   And all the air a solemn stillness holds,
Save where the beetle wheels his droning flight,
   And drowsy tinklings lull the distant folds:

Save that from yonder ivy-mantled tow'r
   The mopeing owl does to the moon complain
Of such as, wand'ring near her secret bow'r,
   Molest her ancient solitary reign.

Beneath those rugged elms, that yew-tree's shade,
   Where heaves the turf in many a mould'ring heap,
Each in his narrow cell for ever laid,
   The rude Forefathers of the hamlet sleep.

The breezy call of incense-breathing Morn,
   The swallow twitt'ring from the straw-built shed,
The cock's shrill clarion, or the echoing horn,
   No more shall rouse them from their lowly bed.

For them no more the blazing hearth shall burn,
   Or busy housewife ply her evening care:
No children run to lisp their sire's return,
   Or climb his knee the envied kiss to share.

Oft did the harvest to their sickle yield,
   Their furrow oft the stubborn glebe has broke:
How jocund did they drive their team afield!
   How bow'd the woods beneath their sturdy stroke!

Let not Ambition mock their useful toil,
   Their homely joys, and destiny obscure;
Nor Grandeur hear with a disdainful smile
   The short and simple annals of the poor.

The boast of heraldry, the pomp of pow'r,
   And all that beauty, all that wealth e'er gave,
Awaits alike th' inevitable hour.
   The paths of glory lead but to the grave.

Nor you, ye Proud, impute to These the fault,
   If Mem'ry o'er their Tomb no Trophies raise,
Where through the long-drawn aisle and fretted vault
   The pealing anthem swells the note of praise.

Can storied urn or animated bust
   Back to its mansion call the fleeting breath?
Can Honour's voice provoke the silent dust,
   Or Flatt'ry soothe the dull cold ear of death?

Perhaps in this neglected spot is laid
   Some heart once pregnant with celestial fire;
Hands, that the rod of empire might have sway'd,
   Or wak'd to extasy the living lyre.

But Knowledge to their eyes her ample page
   Rich with the spoils of time did ne'er unroll;
Chill Penury repress'd their noble rage,
   And froze the genial current of the soul.

Full many a gem of purest ray serene,
   The dark unfathom'd caves of ocean bear:
Full many a flower is born to blush unseen,
   And waste its sweetness on the desert air.

Some village-Hampden, that with dauntless breast
   The little Tyrant of his fields withstood,
Some mute inglorious Milton here may rest,
   Some Cromwell guiltless of his country's blood.

Th' applause of list'ning senates to command,
  The threats of pain and ruin to despise,
To scatter plenty o'er a smiling land,
  And read their hist'ry in a nation's eyes,

Their lot forbad: nor circumscrib'd alone
  Their growing virtues, but their crimes confin'd;
Forbad to wade through slaughter to a throne,
  And shut the gates of mercy on mankind,

The struggling pangs of conscious truth to hide,
  To quench the blushes of ingenuous shame,
Or heap the shrine of Luxury and Pride
  With incense kindled at the Muse's flame.

Far from the madding crowd's ignoble strife,
  Their sober wishes never learn'd to stray;
Along the cool sequester'd vale of life
  They kept the noiseless tenor of their way.

Yet ev'n these bones from insult to protect
  Some frail memorial still erected nigh,
With uncouth rhimes and shapeless sculpture deck'd,
  Implores the passing tribute of a sigh.

Their name, their years, spelt by th' unletter'd muse,
  The place of fame and elegy supply:
And many a holy text around she strews,
  That teach the rustic moralist to die.

For who to dumb Forgetfulness a prey,
  This pleasing anxious being e'er resign'd,
Left the warm precincts of the cheerful day,
  Nor cast one longing ling'ring look behind?

On some fond breast the parting soul relies,
  Some pious drops the closing eye requires;
E'en from the tomb the voice of Nature cries,
  E'en in our Ashes live their wonted Fires.

For thee, who mindful of th' unhonour'd Dead,
  Dost in these lines their artless tale relate;
If chance, by lonely contemplation led,
  Some kindred spirit shall inquire thy fate,–

Haply some hoary-headed Swain may say,
'Oft have we seen him at the peep of dawn
Brushing with hasty steps the dews away
    To meet the sun upon the upland lawn.

'There at the foot of yonder nodding beech,
    That wreathes its old fantastic roots so high,
His listless length at noontide would he stretch,
    And pore upon the brook that babbles by.

'Hard by yon wood, now smiling as in scorn,
    Mutt'ring his wayward fancies he would rove,
Now drooping, woeful-wan, like one forlorn,
    Or craz'd with care, or cross'd in hopeless love.

'One morn I miss'd him on the custom'd hill,
    Along the heath, and near his fav'rite tree;
Another came; nor yet beside the rill,
    Nor up the lawn, nor at the wood was he:

'The next, with dirges due in sad array
    Slow thro' the church-way path we saw him borne.–
Approach and read (for thou can'st read) the lay,
    Grav'd on the stone beneath yon aged thorn.'

The Epitaph

Here rests his head upon the lap of Earth
    A Youth, to Fortune and to Fame unknown.
Fair Science frown'd not on his humble birth,
    And Melancholy mark'd him for her own.

Large was his bounty, and his soul sincere,
    Heav'n did a recompense as largely send:
He gave to Mis'ry all he had, a tear,
    He gain'd from Heav'n ('twas all he wish'd) a friend.

No farther seek his merits to disclose,
    Or draw his frailties from their dread abode,
(There they alike in trembling hope repose,)
    The bosom of his Father and his God.

THOMAS GRAY

464 *Artemis Prologizes*

I am a goddess of the ambrosial courts,
And save by Here, Queen of Pride, surpassed
By none whose temples whiten this the world.
Through heaven I roll my lucid moon along;
I shed in hell o'er my pale people peace;
On earth I, caring for the creatures, guard
Each pregnant yellow wolf and fox-bitch sleek,
And every feathered mother's callow brood,
And all that love green haunts and loneliness.
Of men, the chaste adore me, hanging crowns
Of poppies red to blackness, bell and stem,
Upon my image at Athenai here;
And this dead Youth, Asclepios bends above,
Was dearest to me.   He, my buskined step
To follow through the wild-wood leafy ways,
And chase the panting stag, or swift with darts
Stop the swift ounce, or lay the leopard low,
Neglected homage to another god:
Whence Aphrodite, by no midnight smoke
Of tapers lulled, in jealousy despatched
A noisome lust that, as the gadbee stings,
Possessed his stepdame Phaidra for himself
The son of Theseus her great absent spouse.
Hippolutos exclaiming in his rage
Against the fury of the Queen, she judged
Life insupportable; and, pricked at heart
An Amazonian stranger's race should dare
To scorn her, perished by the murderous cord:
Yet, ere she perished, blasted in a scroll
The fame of him her swerving made not swerve.
And Theseus, read, returning, and believed,
And exiled, in the blindness of his wrath,
The man without a crime who, last as first,
Loyal divulged not to his sire the truth.
Now Theseus from Poseidon had obtained
That of his wishes should be granted three,
And one he imprecated straight—'Alive
'May ne'er Hippolutos reach other lands!'
Poseidon heard, ai ai!   And scarce the prince

Had stepped into the fixed boots of the car
That give the feet a stay against the strength
Of the Henetian horses, and around
His body flung the rein, and urged their speed
Along the rocks and shingles of the shore,
When from the gaping wave a monster flung
His obscene body in the coursers' path.
These, mad with terror, as the sea-bull sprawled
Wallowing about their feet, lost care of him
That reared them; and the master-chariot-pole
Snapping beneath their plunges like a reed,
Hippolutos, whose feet were trammelled fast,
Was yet dragged forward by the circling rein
Which either hand directed; nor they quenched
The frenzy of their flight before each trace,
Wheel-spoke and splinter of the woeful car,
Each boulder-stone, sharp stub and spiny shell,
Huge fish-bone wrecked and wreathed amid the sands
On that detested beach, was bright with blood
And morsels of his flesh: then fell the steeds
Head foremost, crashing in their mooned fronts,
Shivering with sweat, each white eye horror-fixed.
His people, who had witnessed all afar,
Bore back the ruins of Hippolutos.
But when his sire, too swoln with pride, rejoiced
(Indomitable as a man foredoomed)
That vast Poseidon had fulfilled his prayer,
I, in a flood of glory visible,
Stood o'er my dying votary and, deed
By deed, revealed, as all took place, the truth.
Then Theseus lay the woefullest of men,
And worthily; but ere the death-veils hid
His face, the murdered prince full pardon breathed
To his rash sire. Whereat Athenai wails.
    So I, who ne'er forsake my votaries,
Lest in the cross-way none the honey-cake
Should tender, nor pour out the dog's hot life;
Lest at my fane the priests disconsolate
Should dress my image with some faded poor
Few crowns, made favours of, nor dare object
Such slackness to my worshippers who turn

Elsewhere the trusting heart and loaded hand,
As they had climbed Olumpos to report
Of Artemis and nowhere found her throne–
I interposed: and, this eventful night,–
(While round the funeral pyre the populace
Stood with fierce light on their black robes which bound
Each sobbing head, while yet their hair they clipped
O'er the dead body of their withered prince,
And, in his palace, Theseus prostrated
On the cold hearth, his brow cold as the slab
'Twas bruised on, groaned away the heavy grief–
As the pyre fell, and down the cross logs crashed
Sending a crowd of sparkles through the night,
And the gay fire, elate with mastery,
Towered like a serpent o'er the clotted jars
Of wine, dissolving oils and frankincense,
And splendid gums like gold),–my potency
Conveyed the perished man to my retreat
In the thrice-venerable forest here.
And this white-bearded sage who squeezes now
The berried plant, is Phoibos' son of fame,
Asclepios, whom my radiant brother taught
The doctrine of each herb and flower and root,
To know their secret'st virtue and express
The saving soul of all: who so has soothed
With lavers the torn brow and murdered cheeks,
Composed the hair and brought its gloss again,
And called the red bloom to the pale skin back,
And laid the strips and jagged ends of flesh
Even once more, and slacked the sinew's knot
Of every tortured limb–that now he lies
As if mere sleep possessed him underneath
These interwoven oaks and pines. Oh cheer
Divine presenter of the healing rod,
Thy snake, with ardent throat and lulling eye,
Twines his lithe spires around! I say, much cheer!
Proceed thou with thy wisest pharmacies!
And ye, white crowd of woodland sister-nymphs,
Ply, as the sage directs, these buds and leaves
That strew the turf around the twain! While I
Await, in fitting silence, the event.

ROBERT BROWNING

465 *Stella's Birthday*

This day, whate'er the Fates decree,
Shall still be kept with joy by me:
This day then, let us not be told,
That you are sick, and I grown old,
Nor think on our approaching ills,
And talk of spectacles and pills;
To morrow will be time enough
To hear such mortifying stuff.
Yet, since from reason may be brought
A better and more pleasing thought,
Which can in spite of all decays,
Support a few remaining days:
From not the gravest of divines,
Accept for once some serious lines.

Although we now can form no more
Long schemes of life, as heretofore;
Yet you, while time is running fast,
Can look with joy on what is past.

Were future happiness and pain,
A mere contrivance of the brain,
As atheists argue, to entice,
And fit their proselytes for vice;
(The only comfort they propose,
To have companions in their woes.)
Grant this the case, yet sure 'tis hard,
That virtue, styl'd its own reward,
And by all sages understood
To be the chief of human good,
Should acting, die, nor leave behind
Some lasting pleasure in the mind,
Which by remembrance will assuage,
Grief, sickness, poverty, and age;
And strongly shoot a radiant dart,
To shine through life's declining part.

Say, Stella, feel you no content,
Reflecting on a life well spent?
Your skilful hand employ'd to save
Despairing wretches from the grave;

And then supporting with your store,
Those whom you dragg'd from death before:
(So Providence on mortals waits,
Preserving what it first creates)
Your gen'rous boldness to defend
An innocent and absent friend;
That courage which can make you just,
To merit humbled in the dust:
The detestation you express
For vice in all its glitt'ring dress:
That patience under tort'ring pain,
Where stubborn stoics would complain.

Must these like empty shadows pass,
Or forms reflected from a glass?
Or mere chimæra's in the mind,
That fly and leave no marks behind?
Does not the body thrive and grow
By food of twenty years ago?
And, had it not been still supplied,
It must a thousand times have died.
Then, who with reason can maintain,
That no effects of food remain?
And, is not virtue in mankind
The nutriment that feeds the mind?
Upheld by each good action past,
And still continued by the last:
Then, who with reason can pretend,
That all effects of virtue end?

Believe me, Stella, when you show
That true contempt for things below,
Nor prize your life for other ends
Than merely to oblige your friends;
Your former actions claim their part,
And join to fortify your heart.
For virtue in her daily race,
Like Janus, bears a double face;
Looks back with joy where she has gone,
And therefore goes with courage on.
She at your sickly couch will wait,
And guide you to a better state.

O then, whatever heav'n intends,
Take pity on your pitying friends;
Nor let your ills affect your mind,
To fancy they can be unkind.
Me, surely me, you ought to spare,
Who gladly would your suff'rings share;
Or give my scrap of life to you,
And think it far beneath your due;
You, to whose care so oft I owe,
That I'm alive to tell you so.

JONATHAN SWIFT

466 *Inviting a Friend to Supper*

To-night, grave sir, both my poor house, and I
   Do equally desire your company:
Not that we think us worthy such a guest,
   But that your worth will dignify our feast,
With those that come; whose grace may make that seem,
   Something, which, else, could hope for no esteem.
It is the fair acceptance, Sir, creates
   The entertainment perfect: not the cates.
Yet shall you have, to rectify your palate,
   An olive, capers, or some better sallade
Ush'ring the mutton; with a short-leg'd hen,
   If we can get her, full of eggs, and then,
Limons, and wine for sauce: to these, a coney
   Is not to be despaired of, for our money;
And, though fowl, now, be scarce, yet there are clerks,
   The sky not falling, think we may have larks.
I'll tell you of more, and lie, so you will come:
   Of partrich, pheasant, wood-cock, of which some
May yet be there; and godwit, if we can:
   Knat, rail, and ruffe too. How so'ere, my man
Shall read a piece of VIRGIL, TACITUS,
   LIVY, or of some better book to us,
Of which we'll speak our minds, amidst our meat;
   And I'll profess no verses to repeat:
To this, if aught appear, which I not know of,
   That will the pastry, not my paper, show of.

Digestive cheese, and fruit there sure will be;
    But that, which most doth take my *Muse*, and me,
Is a pure cup of rich *Canary*-wine,
    Which is the *Mermaid*'s, now, but shall be mine:
Of which had HORACE, or ANACREON tasted,
    Their lives, as do their lines, till now had lasted.
Tobacco, Nectar, or the *Thespian* spring,
    Are all but LUTHER's beer, to this I sing.
Of this we will sup free, but moderately,
    And we will have no *Pooly'*, or *Parrot* by;
Nor shall our cups make any guilty men:
    But, at our parting, we will be, as when
We innocently met. No simple word,
    That shall be utter'd at our mirthful board,
Shall make us sad next morning: or afright
    The liberty, that we'll enjoy to-night.

                                        BEN JONSON

467 *Going to Church*

                    I

I woke at three; for I was bid
    To breakfast with the Dean at nine,
And thence to Church. My curtain slid,
    I found the dawning Sunday fine;
And could not rest, so rose. The air
    Was dark and sharp; the roosted birds
Cheep'd, 'Here am I, Sweet; are you there?'
    On Avon's misty flats the herds
Expected, comfortless the day,
    Which slowly fired the clouds above;
The cock scream'd somewhere far away;
    In sleep the matrimonial dove
Was crooning; no wind waked the wood,
    Nor moved the midnight river-damps,
Nor thrill'd the poplar; quiet stood
    The chestnut with its thousand lamps;
The moon shone yet, but weak and drear,
    And seem'd to watch, with bated breath,
The landscape, all made sharp and clear
    By stillness, as a face by death.

2

My pray'rs for her being done, I took
  Occasion by the quiet hour
To find and know, by Rule and Book,
  The rights of love's beloved power.

3

Fronting the question without ruth,
  Nor ignorant that, evermore,
If men will stoop to kiss the Truth,
  She lifts them higher than before,
I, from above, such light required
  As now should once for all destroy
The folly which at times desired
  A sanction for so great a joy.

4

Thenceforth, and through that pray'r, I trod
  A path with no suspicions dim.
I loved her in the name of God,
  And for the ray she was of Him;
I ought to admire much more, not less;
  Her beauty was a godly grace;
The mystery of loveliness,
  Which made an altar of her face,
Was not of the flesh, though that was fair,
  But a most pure and living light
Without a name, by which the rare
  And virtuous spirit flamed to sight.
If oft, in love, effect lack'd cause
  And cause effect, 'twere vain to soar
Reasons to seek for that which was
  Reason itself, or something more.
My joy was no idolatry
  Upon the ends of the vile earth bent,
For when I loved her most then I
  Most yearn'd for more divine content.
That other doubt, which, like a ghost,
  In the brain's darkness haunted me,
Was thus resolved: Him loved I most,
  But her I loved most sensibly.

Lastly, my giddiest hope allow'd
　　No selfish thought, or earthly smirch;
And forth I went, in peace, and proud
　　To take my passion into Church;
Grateful and glad to think that all
　　Such doubts would seem entirely vain
To her whose nature's lighter fall
　　Made no divorce of heart from brain.

5

I found them, with exactest grace
　　And fresh as Spring, for Spring attired;
And by the radiance in her face
　　I saw she felt she was admired;
And through the common luck of love,
　　A moment's fortunate delay,
To fit the little lilac glove,
　　Gave me her arm; and I and they
(They true to this and every hour,
　　As if attended on by Time),
Enter'd the Church while yet the tower
　　Was noisy with the finish'd chime.

6

Her soft voice, singularly heard
　　Beside me, in her chant, withstood
The roar of voices, like a bird
　　Sole warbling in a windy wood;
And, when we knelt, she seem'd to be
　　An angel teaching me to pray;
And all through the high Liturgy
　　My spirit rejoiced without allay,
Being, for once, borne clearly above
　　All banks and bars of ignorance,
By this bright spring-tide of pure love
　　And floated in a free expanse,
Whence it could see from side to side,
　　The obscurity from every part,
Winnow'd away and purified
　　By the vibrations of my heart.

COVENTRY PATMORE

468 *Dispraise of a Courtly Life*

Walking in bright Phœbus' blaze,
Where with heat opprest I was,
I got to a shady wood,
Where green leaves did newly bud,
And of grass was plenty dwelling,
Deckt with pied flowers sweetly smelling.
In this wood a man I met,
On lamenting wholly set;
Ruing change of wonted state,
Whence he was transformed late;
Once to shepherds' God retaining,[1]
Now in servile Court remaining.
There he wand'ring, malcontent,
Up and down perplexed went,
Daring not to tell to me,
Spake unto a senseless tree,
One among the rest electing,
These same words, or this effecting:
'My old mates I grieve to see
Void of me in field to be,
Where we once our lovely sheep
Lovingly like friends did keep;
Oft each other's friendship proving,
Never striving but in loving.
But may love abiding be
In poor shepherd's base degree?
It belongs to such alone
To whom art of love is known:
Seely shepherds are not witting
What in art of love is fitting.
Nay, what need the art to those
To whom we our love disclose?
It is to be used then
When we do but flatter men:
Friendship true, in heart assured,
Is by Nature's gifts procured.

[1] being retainer to

Therefore shepherds, wanting skill,
Can love's duties best fulfil;
Since they know not how to feign,
Nor with love to cloak disdain,
Like the wiser sort, whose learning
Hides their inward will of harming.
Well was I, while under shade
Oaten reeds me music made;
Striving with my mates in song,
Mixing mirth our songs among:
Greater was the shepherd's treasure
Then this false, fine, courtly pleasure;
Where, how many creatures be,
So many puft in mind I see;
Like to Juno's birds of pride,
Scarce each other can abide:
Friends like to black swans appearing,
Sooner these than those in hearing.
Therefore, Pan, if thou mayst be
Made to listen unto me,
Grant, I say (if seely man
May make treaty to god Pan),
That I, without thy denying,
May be still to thee relying.
Only for my two loves' sake,
In whose love I pleasure take;
Only two do me delight
With their ever-pleasing sight;
Of all men to thee retaining,
Grant me with those two remaining.
So shall I to thee always
With my reed's sound mighty praise;
And first lamb that shall befal,
Yearly deck thine altar shall;
If it please thee be reflected,
And I from thee not rejected.'
So I left him in that place,
Taking pity on his case;
Learning this among the rest,
That the mean estate is best;

Better filled with contenting,
Void of wishing and repenting.
                    SIR PHILIP SIDNEY

469 *A Letter to Ben Jonson*

*Mr. Francis Beaumont's Letter to Ben Jonson, written before he
and Mr. Fletcher came to London, with two of the precedent
Comedies then not finisht, which deferrd their merry meetings
at the Mermaid.*

The Sun which doth the greatest comfort bring
To absent friends, because the self-same thing
They know they see however absent, is
Here our best Hay-maker (forgive me this,
It is our Country's style). In this warm shine,
I lie and dream of your full Mermaid wine.
Oh we have water mixt with Claret Lees,
Drink apt to bring in drier heresies
Than beer, good only for the Sonnet's strain,
With fustian metaphors to stuff the brain,
So mixt, that given to the thirstiest one,
'Twill not prove alms, unless he have the stone:
I think with one draught man's invention fades,
Two Cups had quite spoil'd *Homer's Iliads*;
'Tis Liquor that will find out *Sutcliff's* wit,
Lie where he will, and make him write worse yet;
Fill'd with such moisture in most grievous qualms,
Did *Robert Wisdome* write his singing Psalms;
And so must I do this, and yet I think
It is a potion sent us down to drink
By special Providence, keeps us from fights,
Makes us not laugh, when we make legs to Knights.
'Tis this that keeps our minds fit for our States,
A Medicine to obey our Magistrates:
For we do live more free than you, no hate,
No envy at one another's *happy* State
Moves us, we are all equal every whit:
Of Land that God gives men here is their wit,
If we consider fully: for our best
And gravest man will, with his main house jest,

Scarce please you; we want subtilty to do
The City tricks, lie, hate, and flatter too:
Here are none that can bear a painted show,
Strike when you winch, and then lament the blow:
Who like Mills set the right way for to grind,
Can make their gains alike with every wind:
Only some fellows with the subtil'st pate
Amongst us, may perchance equivocate
At selling of a Horse, and that's the most.
Methinks the little wit I had is lost
Since I saw you, for wit is like a rest
Held up at Tennis, which men do the best,
With the best gamesters: What things have we seen,
Done at the Mermaid! heard words that have been
So nimble, and so full of subtill flame,
As if that every one from whence they came,
Had meant to put his whole wit in a jest,
And had resolv'd to live a fool, the rest
Of his dull life; then when there hath been thrown
Wit able enough to justify the Town
For three days past, wit that might warrant be
For the whole City to talk foolishly
Till that were cancel'd, and when that was gone,
We left an air behind us, which alone,
Was able to make the two next companies
Right witty; though but downright fools, more wise.
When I remember this, and see that now
The Country gentlemen begin to allow
My wit for dry bobs, then I needs must cry,
I see my days of ballating grow nigh;
I can already riddle, and can sing
Catches, sell bargains, and I fear shall bring
My self to speak the hardest words I find,
Over as oft as any, with one wind,
That takes no medicines: But one thought of thee
Makes me remember all these things to be
The wit of our young men, fellows that show
No part of good, yet utter all they know:
Who like trees of the Guard, have growing souls.
Only strong destiny, which all controls,

I hope hath left a better fate in store,
For me thy friend, than to live ever poor,
Banisht unto this home; fate once again
Bring me to thee, who can'st make smooth and plain
The way of Knowledge for me, and then I,
Who have no good but in thy company,
Protest it will my greatest comfort be
To acknowledge all I have to flow from thee.
Ben, when these Scenes are perfect, we'll taste wine;
I'll drink thy Muse's health, thou shalt quaff mine.

FRANCIS BEAUMONT

470 *Letter to Viscount Cobham*

Sincerest Critic of my Prose, or Rhyme,
Tell how thy pleasing STOWE employs the Time,
Say, COBHAM, what amuses thy Retreat?
Or Stratagems of War, or Schemes of State?
Dost thou recal to Mind with Joy, or Grief,
Great MALBRO's Actions? That immortal Chief,
Whose slightest Trophy rais'd in each Campaign,
More than suffic'd to signalise a Reign?
Does thy remembrance rising warm thy Heart,
With Glory past, where Thou thy self hadst Part,
Or dost thou grieve indignant, now to see,
The fruitless End of all thy Victory?
To see th'Audacious Foe, so late subdu'd,
Dispute those Terms for which so long they su'd,
As if BRITANNIA now were sunk so low,
To beg that Peace she wonted to bestow.
Be far that Guilt! be never known that Shame!
That ENGLAND shou'd retract her rightful Claim,
Or ceasing to be dreaded and ador'd,
Stain with her Pen the Lustre of her Sword.
Or dost thou give the Winds afar to blow
Each vexing Thought, and heart-devouring Woe,
And fix thy Mind alone on rural Scenes,
To turn the level'd Lawns to liquid Plains,
To raise the creeping Rills from humble Beds,
And force the latent Springs to lift their Heads,

On wat'ry Columns, Capitals to rear,
That mix their flowing Curls with upper Air?
Or dost Thou, weary grown, these Works neglect,
No Temples, Statues, Obelisks erect,
But catch the morning Breeze from fragrant Meads,
Or shun the noontide Ray in wholesome Shades,
Or slowly walk along the mazy Wood,
To meditate on all that's wise and good?
For Nature bountiful in thee has join'd,
A Person pleasing with a worthy Mind,
Not given the Form alone, but Means, and Art,
To draw the Eye, or to allure the Heart.
Poor were the Praise in Fortune to excel,
Yet want the Way to use that Fortune well.
While thus adorn'd, while thus with Virtue crown'd,
At Home in Peace, Abroad in Arms renown'd,
Graceful in Form, and winning in Address
While well you think, what aptly you express,
With Health, with Honour, with a fair Estate,
A Table free, and eloquently neat,
What can be added more to mortal Bliss?
What can he want who stands possest of this?
What can the fondest wishing Mother more
Of Heaven attentive for her Son implore?
And yet a Happiness remains unknown,
Or to Philosophy reveal'd alone;
A Precept, which unpractis'd renders vain,
Thy flowing Hopes, and Pleasure turns to Pain.
Shou'd Hope, and Fear thy Heart alternate tear,
Or Love, or Hate, or Rage, or anxious Care,
Whatever Passions may thy Mind infest,
(Where is that Mind which Passions ne'er molest?)
Amidst the Pangs of such intestine Strife,
Still think the present Day, the last of Life;
Defer not till to Morrow to be wise,
To Morrow's Sun to thee may never rise.
Or should to Morrow chance to cheer thy Sight,
With her enliv'ning and unlookt-for Light,
How grateful will appear her dawning Rays!
As Favours unexpected doubly please.

Who thus can think and who such thoughts pursues,
Content may keep his Life, or calmly lose;
All Proofs of this Thou may'st thy self receive.
When Leisure from Affairs will give thee Leave,
Come, see thy Friend, retir'd without Regret,
Forgetting Care, or striving to forget;
In easy Contemplation soothing Time
With Morals much, and now and then with Rhyme,
Not so robust in Body, as in Mind,
And always undejected, tho' declin'd;
Not wondering at the World's new wicked Ways,
Compar'd with those of our Fore-fathers' Days,
For Virtue now is neither more or less,
And Vice is only varied in the Dress;
Believe it, Men have ever been the same,
And all the Golden Age, is but a Dream.

WILLIAM CONGREVE

471 *To Edward FitzGerald*

Old Fitz, who from your suburb grange,
    Where once I tarried for a while,
Glance at the wheeling Orb of change,
    And greet it with a kindly smile;
Whom yet I see as there you sit
    Beneath your sheltering garden-tree,
And while your doves about you flit,
    And plant on shoulder, hand and knee,
Or on your head their rosy feet,
    As if they knew your diet spares
Whatever moved in that full sheet
    Let down to Peter at his prayers;
Who live on milk and meal and grass;
    And once for ten long weeks I tried
Your table of Pythagoras,
    And seem'd at first 'a thing enskied'
(As Shakespeare has it) airy-light
    To float above the ways of men,
Then fell from that half-spiritual height
    Chill'd, till I tasted flesh again

One night when earth was winter-black,
    And all the heavens flash'd in frost;
And on me, half-asleep, came back
    That wholesome heat the blood had lost,
And set me climbing icy capes
    And glaciers, over which there roll'd
To meet me long-arm'd vines with grapes
    Of Eschol hugeness; for the cold
Without, and warmth within me, wrought
    To mould the dream; but none can say
That Lenten fare makes Lenten thought,
    Who reads your golden Eastern lay,
Than which I know no version done
    In English more divinely well;
A planet equal to the sun
    Which cast it, that large infidel
Your Omar; and your Omar drew
    Full-handed plaudits from our best
In modern letters, and from two,
    Old friends outvaluing all the rest,
Two voices heard on earth no more;
    But we old friends are still alive,
And I am nearing seventy-four,
    While you have touch'd at seventy-five,
And so I send a birthday line
    Of greeting; and my son, who dipt
In some forgotten book of mine
    With sallow scraps of manuscript,
And dating many a year ago,
    Has hit on this, which you will take
My Fitz, and welcome, as I know
    Less for its own than for the sake
Of one recalling gracious times,
    When, in our younger London days,
You found some merit in my rhymes,
    And I more pleasure in your praise.

ALFRED, LORD TENNYSON

Book VII
GENERALIZATIONS AND JUDGMENTS

472 *Eternity*

He who binds to himself a joy
Does the winged life destroy;
But he who kisses the joy as it flies
Lives in eternity's sun rise.

WILLIAM BLAKE

473 *Like as the Damask Rose*

Like as the Damask Rose you see,
Or like the Blossom on the Tree,
Or like the dainty Flower of May,
Or like the Morning to the Day,
Or like the Sun or like the Shade,
Or like the Gourd which Jonas had:

Even such is Man; whose thread is spun,
Drawn out, and cut, and so is done.
The Rose withers, the Blossom blasteth,
The Flower fades, the Morning hasteth,
The Sun sets, the Shadow flies,
The Gourd consumes, and Man he dies.

Like to the Grass that's newly sprung,
Or like the Tale that's new begun,
Or like the bird that's here today,
Or like the pearled Dew of May,
Or like an Hour, or like a Span,
Or like the singing of a Swan.

Even such is Man, who lives by breath;
Is here, now there, in life, in death.
The Grass withers, the Tale is ended,
The Bird is flown, the Dew's ascended.
The Hour is short, the Span not long,
The Swan's near death; Man's life is done.

471

Like to the Bubble in the Brook,
Or, in a Glass, much like a look,
Or like a Shuttle in Weaver's hand;
Or like the Writing on the Sand,
Or like a Thought, or like a Dream,
Or like the gliding of the Stream;

Even such is Man, who lives by breath;
Is here, now there, in life, and death,
The Bubble's cut, the Look's forgot,
The Shuttle's flung, the Writing's blot,
The Thought is past, the Dream is gone,
The Water glides; Man's life is done.

Like to an Arrow from the Bow,
Or like swift course of Wat'ry flow,
Or like the time 'twixt Flood and Ebb;
Or like the Spider's tender Webb,
Or like a Race, or like a Goal,
Or like the dealing of a Dole:

Even such is Man, whose brittle state
Is always subject unto Fate.
The Arrow's shot, the Flood soon spent,
The Time no Time, the Webb soon rent,
The Race soon run, the Goal soon won;
The Dole soon dealt; Man's life first done.

Like to the Lightning from the sky,
Or like a Post that quick doth die,
Or like a Quaver in short song,
Or like a Journey three days long,
Or like the Snow when Summer's come,
Or like the Pear, or like the Plum:

Even such is Man, who heaps up sorrow,
Lives but this day, and dies tomorrow.
The Lightning's past, the Post must go,
The Song is short, the Journey's so,
The Pear doth rot, the Plum doth fall,
The Snow dissolves, and so must all.

Like to the Seed put in Earth's Womb,
Or like dead Lazarus in his Tomb,
Or like Tabitha, being asleep,
Or Jonas like, within the Deep.
Or like the Night, or Stars by day,
Which seem to vanish clean away:

Even so this Death, Man's life bereaves,
But being dead, Man death deceives,
The Seed it springeth, Lazarus standeth,
Tabitha walks, and Jonas landeth.
The Night is past, the Stars remain:
So Man that dies, shall live again.

FRANCIS QUARLES (?)

474 *Fancy*

Ever let the Fancy roam,
Pleasure never is at home:
At a touch sweet Pleasure melteth,
Like to bubbles when rain pelteth;
Then let winged Fancy wander
Through the thought still spread beyond her:
Open wide the mind's cage-door,
She'll dart forth, and cloudward soar.
O sweet Fancy! let her loose;
Summer's joys are spoilt by use,
And the enjoying of the Spring
Fades as does its blossoming;
Autumn's red-lipp'd fruitage too,
Blushing through the mist and dew,
Cloys with tasting: What do then?
Sit thee by the ingle, when
The sear faggot blazes bright,
Spirit of a winter's night;
When the soundless earth is muffled,
And the caked snow is shuffled
From the ploughboy's heavy shoon;
When the Night doth meet the Noon
In a dark conspiracy
To banish Even from her sky.

Sit thee there, and send abroad
With a mind self-overaw'd,
Fancy, high-commission'd:–send her!
She has vassals to attend her:
She will bring, in spite of frost,
Beauties that the earth hath lost;
She will bring thee, all together,
All delights of summer weather;
All the buds and bells of May,
From dewy sward or thorny spray
All the heaped Autumn's wealth,
With a still-mysterious stealth:
She will mix these pleasures up
Like three fit wines in a cup,
And thou shalt quaff it:–thou shalt hear
Distant harvest-carols clear;
Rustle of the reaped corn;
Sweet birds antheming the morn:
And, in the same moment–hark!
'Tis the early April lark,
Or the rooks, with busy caw,
Foraging for sticks and straw.
Thou shalt, at one glance, behold
The daisy and the marigold;
White-plum'd lilies, and the first
Hedge-grown primrose that hath burst;
Shaded hyacinth, alway
Sapphire queen of the mid-May;
And every leaf, and every flower
Pearled with the self-same shower.
Thou shalt see the field-mouse peep
Meagre from its celled sleep;
And the snake all winter-thin
Cast on sunny bank its skin;
Freckled nest-eggs thou shalt see
Hatching in the hawthorn-tree,
When the hen-bird's wing doth rest
Quiet on her mossy nest;
Then the hurry and alarm
When the bee-hive casts its swarm;

Acorns ripe down-pattering,
While the autumn breezes sing.

Oh, sweet Fancy! let her loose;
Every thing is spoilt by use:
Where's the cheek that doth not fade,
Too much gaz'd at? Where's the maid
Whose lip mature is ever new?
Where's the eye, however blue,
Doth not weary? Where's the face
One would meet in every place?
Where's the voice, however soft,
One would hear so very oft?
At a touch sweet Pleasure melteth
Like to bubbles when rain pelteth.
Let, then, winged Fancy find
Thee a mistress to thy mind:
Dulcet-eyed as Ceres' daughter,
Ere the God of Torment taught her
How to frown and how to chide;
With a waist and with a side
White as Hebe's, when her zone
Slipt its golden clasp, and down
Fell her kirtle to her feet,
While she held the goblet sweet,
And Jove grew languid.–Break the mesh
Of the Fancy's silken leash;
Quickly break her prison-string
And such joys as these she'll bring.–
Let the winged Fancy roam,
Pleasure never is at home.

JOHN KEATS

475 *To a Highland Girl*
At Inversneyde, upon Loch Lomond

Sweet Highland Girl, a very shower
Of beauty is thy earthly dower!
Twice seven consenting years have shed
Their utmost beauty on thy head:

And these grey rocks; that household lawn;
Those trees, a veil just half withdrawn;
This fall of water that doth make
A murmur near the silent lake;
This little bay; a quiet road
That holds in shelter thy abode—
In truth together do ye seem
Like something fashioned in a dream;
Such Forms as from their covert peep
When earthly cares are laid asleep!
But, O fair Creature! in the light
Of common day, so heavenly bright,
I bless Thee, Vision as thou art,
I bless thee with a human heart;
God shield thee to thy latest years!
Thee, neither know I, nor thy peers;
And yet my eyes are filled with tears.

With earnest feeling I shall pray
For thee when I am far away:
For never saw I mien, or face,
In which more plainly I could trace
Benignity and home-bred sense
Ripening in perfect innocence.
Here scattered, like a random seed,
Remote from men, Thou dost not need
The embarrassed look of shy distress,
And maidenly shamefacedness:
Thou wear'st upon thy forehead clear
The freedom of a Mountaineer:
A face with gladness overspread!
Soft smiles, by human kindness bred!
And seemliness complete, that sways
Thy courtesies, about thee plays;
With no restraint, but such as springs
From quick and eager visitings
Of thoughts that lie beyond the reach
Of thy few words of English speech:
A bondage sweetly brooked, a strife
That gives thy gestures grace and life!

So have I, not unmoved in mind,
Seen birds of tempest-loving kind–
Thus beating up against the wind.

What hand but would a garland cull
For thee who art so beautiful?
O happy pleasure! here to dwell
Beside thee in some heathy dell;
Adopt your homely ways, and dress,
A Shepherd, thou a Shepherdess!
But I could frame a wish for thee
More like a grave reality:
Thou art to me but as a wave
Of the wild sea; and I would have
Some claim upon thee, if I could,
Though but of common neighbourhood.
What joy to hear thee, and to see!
Thy Elder Brother I would be,
Thy Father–anything to thee!

Now thanks to Heaven! that of its grace
Hath led me to this lonely place.
Joy have I had! and going hence
I bear away my recompense.
In spots like these it is we prize
Our Memory, feel that she hath eyes:
Then, why should I be loth to stir?
I feel this place was made for her;
To give new pleasure like the past,
Continued long as life shall last.
Nor am I loth, though pleased at heart,
Sweet Highland Girl! from thee to part;
For I, methinks, till I grow old,
As fair before me shall behold,
As I do now, the cabin small,
The lake, the bay, the waterfall;
And Thee, the Spirit of them all!

WILLIAM WORDSWORTH

R

476 *Hester*

When maidens such as Hester die,
Their place ye may not well supply,
Though ye among a thousand try,
    With vain endeavour.

A month or more hath she been dead,
Yet cannot I by force be led
To think upon the wormy bed,
    And her together.

A springy motion in her gait,
A rising step, did indicate
Of pride and joy no common rate,
    That flush'd her spirit.

I know not by what name beside
I shall it call:—if 'twas not pride,
It was a joy to that allied,
    She did inherit.

Her parents held the Quaker rule,
Which doth the human feeling cool,
But she was train'd in Nature's school,
    Nature had blest her.

A waking eye, a prying mind,
A heart that stirs, is hard to bind,
A hawk's keen sight ye cannot blind,
    Ye could not Hester.

My sprightly neighbour, gone before
To that unknown and silent shore,
Shall we not meet, as heretofore,
    Some summer morning,

When from thy cheerful eyes a ray
Hath struck a bliss upon the day,
A bliss that would not go away,
    A sweet fore-warning?

CHARLES LAMB

477 *To a Mouse*

On Turning Her up in Her Nest with the Plough,
November, 1785.

Wee, sleeket, cowrin, tim'rous beastie,
O, what a panic's in thy breastie!
Thou need na start awa sae hasty,
           Wi' bickerin brattle! [1]
I wad be laith to rin an' chase thee,
           Wi' murderin' pattle! [2]

I'm truly sorry man's dominion,
Has broken nature's social union,
An' justifies that ill opinion,
           Which makes thee startle
At me, thy poor, earth-born companion,
           An' fellow-mortal!

I doubt na, whyles, but thou may thieve;
What then? poor beastie, thou maun live!
A daimen icker in a thrave [3]
           'S a sma' request;
I'll get a blessin wi' the lave,
           An' never miss 't!

Thy wee bit housie, too, in ruin!
It's silly wa's the win's are strewin'
An' naething, now, to big a new ane,
           O' foggage green!
An' bleak December's winds ensuin,
           Baith snell [4] an' keen!

Thou saw the fields laid bare an' waste,
An' weary winter comin fast,
An' cozie here, beneath the blast,
           Thou thought to dwell–
Till crash! the cruel coulter past
           Out thro' thy cell.

That wee bit heap o' leaves an' stibble,
Has cost thee mony a weary nibble!

---

[1] speedy scamper   [2] stick to break clods
[3] an occasional ear in twenty-four sheaves   [4] biting

Now thou's turn'd out, for a' thy trouble,
　　But house or hald,[1]
To thole [2] the winter's sleety dribble,
　　An' cranreuch could! [3]

But Mousie, thou art no thy lane,
In proving foresight may be vain;
The best-laid schemes o' mice an' men
　　Gang aft agley,
An' lea'e us nought but grief an' pain,
　　For promis'd joy!

Still thou art blest, compar'd wi' me!
The present only toucheth thee:
But och! I backward cast my e'e,
　　On prospects drear!
An' forward, tho' I canna see,
　　I guess an' fear!

　　　　　　　　　　　　ROBERT BURNS

478 *A Prayer for Indifference*

Oft I've implor'd the Gods in vain,
　And pray'd till I've been weary;
For once I'll try my wish to gain
　Of Oberon, the fairy.

Sweet airy being, wanton sprite,
　That lurk'st in woods unseen,
And oft by Cynthia's silver light
　Tripst gaily o'er the green;

If e'er thy pitying heart was mov'd,
　As ancient stories tell,
And for th' Athenian maid, who lov'd,
　Thou sought'st a wondrous spell,

Oh! deign once more t' exert thy power;
　Haply some herb or tree,
Sov'reign as juice from western flower,
　Conceals a balm for me.

----

[1] without house or holding　　　　　　[2] suffer
　　　　　[3] crisp hoar-frost

I ask no kind return in love,
    No tempting charm to please;
Far from the heart such gifts remove,
    That sighs for peace and ease.

Nor ease nor peace that heart can know,
    Which, like the needle true,
Turns at the touch of joy or woe,
    But, turning, trembles too.

Far as distress the soul can wound,
    'Tis pain in each degree;
Bliss goes but to a certain bound,
    Beyond is agony.

Take then this treacherous sense of mine,
    Which dooms me still to smart;
Which pleasure can to pain refine,
    To pain new pangs impart.

Oh! haste to shed the sovereign balm,
    My shatter'd nerves new string;
And for my guest serenely calm,
    The nymph, Indifference, bring.

At her approach, see Hope, see Fear,
    See Expectation fly;
With Disappointment, in the rear,
    That blasts the promis'd joy.

The tears which pity taught to flow,
    My eyes shall then disown;
The heart which throbb'd at other's woe,
    Shall then scarce feel its own.

The wounds which now each moment bleed,
    Each moment then shall close,
And peaceful days shall still succeed
    To nights of sweet repose.

Oh, fairy self! but grant me this,
    This one kind comfort send;
And so may never-fading bliss
    Thy flowery paths attend!

So may the glow-worm's glimmering light
 Thy tiny footsteps lead
To some new region of delight,
 Unknown to mortal tread.

And be thy acorn goblets fill'd
 With heaven's ambrosial dew,
From sweetest, freshest flowers distill'd,
 That shed fresh sweets for you.

And what of life remains for me
 I'll pass in sober ease,
Half-pleas'd, contented will I be,
 Contented, half to please.

FRANCES MACARTNEY, MRS. GREVILLE

479 *A Man's a Man for a' that*

Is there, for honest Poverty
 That hings his head, an' a' that;
The coward slave–we pass him by,
 We dare be poor for a' that!
For a' that, an' a' that,
 Our toils obscure an' a' that,
The rank is but the guinea's stamp,
 The Man's the gowd for a' that.

What though on hamely fare we dine,
 Wear hoddin grey, an' a' that;
Gie fools their silks, and knaves their wine,
 A Man's a Man for a' that:
For a' that, an' a' that,
 Their tinsel show, an' a' that;
The honest man, tho' e'er sae poor,
 Is king o' men for a' that.

Ye see yon birkie ca'd 'a lord,'
 Wha struts, an' stares, an' a' that;
Tho' hundreds worship at his word,
 He's but a coof [1] for a' that:

<hr>

[1] brainless person

> For a' that, an' a' that,
>> His ribband, star, an' a' that;
> The man o' independent mind
>> He looks an' laughs at a' that.

> A prince can mak a belted knight,
>> A marquis, duke, an' a' that;
> But an honest man's aboon his might,
>> Gude faith, he mauna fa' [1] that!
> For a' that, an' a' that,
>> Their dignities an' a' that;
> The pith o' sense, an' pride o' worth,
>> Are higher rank than a' that.

> Then let us pray that come it may,
>> (As come it will for a' that,)
> That Sense and Worth, o'er a' the earth,
>> Shall bear the gree,[2] an' a' that.
> For a' that, an' a' that,
>> It's comin' yet for a' that.
> The Man to Man, the world o'er,
>> Shall brothers be for a' that.

ROBERT BURNS

480 *How No Age is Content*

Laid in my quiet bed, in study as I were,
I saw within my troubled head a heap of thoughts appear.
And every thought did shew so lively in mine eyes,
That now I sighed, and then I smiled, as cause of thought did
  rise.
I saw the little boy in thought how oft that he
Did wish of God to scape the rod, a tall young man to be.
The young man eke that feels his bones with pains opprest,
How he would be a rich old man, to live and lie at rest.
The rich old man that sees his end draw on so sore,
How he would be a boy again, to live so much the more.
Whereat full oft I smiled, to see how all these three,
From boy to man, from man to boy, would chop and change
  degree.

---

[1] attempt   [2] pre-eminence

And musing thus I think, the case is very strange,
That man from wealth, to live in woe, doth ever seek to
   change.
Thus thoughtful as I lay, I saw my withered skin,
How it doth show my dented chews, the flesh was worn so
   thin.
And eke my toothless chaps, the gates of my right way,
That opes and shuts as I do speak, do thus unto me say:
'Thy white and hoarish hairs, the messengers of age,
That shew, like lines of true belief, that this life doth assuage;
Bid thee lay hand, and feel them hanging on thy chin;
The which do write two ages past, the third now coming in.
Hang up therefore the bit of thy young wanton time:
And thou that therein beaten art, the happiest life define.'
Whereat I sighed, and said: 'Farewell! my wonted joy;
Truss up thy pack, and trudge from me to every little boy;
And tell them thus from me; their time most happy is,
If, to their time, they reason had, to know the truth of this.'

HENRY HOWARD, EARL OF SURREY

481 *Chorus*

Vain man, born to no happiness,
but by the title of distress,
Allied to a capacity
of Joy, only by misery;
whose pleasures are but remedies,
and best delights but the supplies
of what he wants, who hath no sense
but poverty and indigence:
Is it not pain still to desire
and carry in our breast this fire?
is it not deadness to have none,
and satisfied, are we not stone?
Doth not our Chiefest Bliss then lie
Betwixt thirst and satiety,
in the mid way? which is alone
in an half satisfaction:
and is not Love the middle way,
at which, with most delight we stay?

desire is total indigence,
But Love is ever a mixt sense
of what we have, and what we want,
and though it be a little scant
of satisfaction, yet we rest
in such an half possession best.
A half possession doth supply
the pleasure of variety,
and frees us from inconstancy
by want caus'd, or satiety;
He never lov'd, who doth confess
he wanted all he doth possess,
(Love to it self is recompense
besides the pleasure of the sense)
And he again, who doth pretend
that surfeited his Love took end,
Confesses in his Love's decay
his soul more mortal, than that clay
which carries it, for if his mind
be in it's purest part confin'd,
(for such Love is) and limited,
'tis in the rest, dying, or dead:
they pass their times in Dreams of Love
whom wavering passions gently move,
through a calm smooth-fac'd sea they pass,
but in the haven traffic glass:
they who love truly through the clime
of freezing North and scalding line,
Sail to their joys, and have deep sense
both of the loss, and recompense:
yet strength of passion doth not prove
Infallibly, the truth of love,
Ships, which to day a storm did find,
are since becalm'd, and feel no wind.

SIDNEY GODOLPHIN

482 *Work without Hope*

All Nature seems at work. Slugs leave their lair—
The bees are stirring–birds are on the wing–
And Winter slumbering in the open air,

Wears on his smiling face a dream of Spring!
And I the while, the sole unbusy thing,
Nor honey make, nor pair, nor build, nor sing.

Yet well I ken the banks where amaranths blow,
Have traced the fount whence streams of nectar flow.
Bloom, O ye amaranths! bloom for whom ye may,
For me ye bloom not! Glide, rich streams, away!
With lips unbrightened, wreathless brow, I stroll:
And would you learn the spells that drowse my soul?
Work without Hope draws nectar in a sieve,
And Hope without an object cannot live.

SAMUEL TAYLOR COLERIDGE

483   *Stanzas*

Often rebuked, yet always back returning
    To those first feelings that were born with me,
And leaving busy chase of wealth and learning
    For idle dreams of things which cannot be:

To-day, I will seek not the shadowy region:
    Its unsustaining vastness waxes drear;
And visions rising, legion after legion,
    Bring the unreal world too strangely near.

I'll walk, but not in old heroic traces,
    And not in paths of high morality,
And not among the half-distinguished faces,
    The clouded forms of long-past history.

I'll walk where my own nature would be leading:
    It vexes me to choose another guide:
Where the grey flocks in ferny glens are feeding;
    Where the wild wind blows on the mountain-side.

What have those lonely mountains worth revealing?
    More glory and more grief than I can tell:
The earth that wakes *one* human heart to feeling
    Can centre both the worlds of Heaven and Hell.

EMILY BRONTË

484 *Byzantium*

The unpurged images of day recede;
The Emperor's drunken soldiery are abed;
Night resonance recedes, night-walkers' song
After great cathedral gong;
A starlit or a moonlit dome disdains
All that man is,
All mere complexities,
The fury and the mire of human veins.

Before me floats an image, man or shade,
Shade more than man, more image than a shade;
For Hades' bobbin bound in mummy-cloth
May unwind the winding path;
A mouth that has no moisture and no breath
Breathless mouths may summon;
I hail the superhuman;
I call it death-in-life and life-in-death.

Miracle, bird or golden handiwork,
More miracle than bird or handiwork,
Planted on the star-lit golden bough,
Can like the cocks of Hades crow,
Or, by the moon embittered, scorn aloud
In glory of changeless metal
Common bird or petal
And all complexities of mire or blood.

At midnight on the Emperor's pavement flit
Flames that no faggot feeds, nor steel has lit,
Nor storm disturbs, flames begotten of flame,
Where blood-begotten spirits come
And all complexities of fury leave,
Dying into a dance,
An agony of trance,
An agony of flame that cannot singe a sleeve.

Astraddle on the dolphin's mire and blood,
Spirit after spirit! The smithies break the flood,
The golden smithies of the Emperor!
Marbles of the dancing floor

Break bitter furies of complexity,
Those images that yet
Fresh images beget,
That dolphin-torn, that gong-tormented sea.

WILLIAM BUTLER YEATS

485 *A Toccata of Galuppi's*

Oh Galuppi, Baldassaro, this is very sad to find!
I can hardly misconceive you; it would prove me deaf and
blind:
But although I take your meaning, 'tis with such a heavy mind!

Here you come with your old music, and here's all the good it
brings.
What, they lived once thus at Venice where the merchants
were the kings,
Where Saint Mark's is, where the Doges used to wed the sea
with rings?

Ay, because the sea's the street there; and 'tis arched by . . .
what you call
. . . Shylock's bridge with houses on it, where they keep the
carnival:
I was never out of England–it's as if I saw it all.

Did young people take their pleasure when the sea was warm
in May?
Balls and masks begun at midnight, burning ever to mid-day,
When they made up fresh adventures for the morrow, do you
say?

Was a lady such a lady, cheeks so round and lips so red,–
On her neck the small face buoyant, like a bell-flower on its
bed,
O'er the breast's superb abundance where a man might base
his head?

Well, and it was graceful of them–they'd break talk off and
afford
–She, to bite her mask's black velvet–he, to finger on his sword,
While you sat and played Toccatas, stately at the clavichord?

What? Those lesser thirds so plaintive, sixths diminished, sigh
on sigh,
Told them something? Those suspensions, those solutions—
'Must we die?'
Those commiserating sevenths—'Life might last! we can but
try!'

'Were you happy?'—'Yes.'—'And are you still as happy?'—
'Yes. And you?'
—'Then, more kisses!'—'Did *I* stop them, when a million
seemed so few?'
Hark, the dominant's persistence till it must be answered to!

So, an octave struck the answer. Oh, they praised you, I dare
say!
'Brave Galuppi! that was music! good alike at grave and gay!
'I can always leave off talking when I hear a master play!'

Then they left you for their pleasure: till in due time, one by
one,
Some with lives that came to nothing, some with deeds as well
undone,
Death stepped tacitly and took them where they never see the
sun.

But when I sit down to reason, think to take my stand nor
swerve,
While I triumph o'er a secret wrung from nature's close
reserve,
In you come with your cold music till I creep thro' every nerve.

Yes, you, like a ghostly cricket, creaking where a house was
burned:
'Dust and ashes, dead and done with, Venice spent what
Venice earned.
'The soul, doubtless, is immortal—where a soul can be dis-
cerned.

'Yours for instance: you know physics, something of geology,
'Mathematics are your pastime; souls shall rise in their degree;
'Butterflies may dread extinction,—you'll not die, it cannot
be!

'As for Venice and her people, merely born to bloom and drop,
'Here on earth they bore their fruitage, mirth and folly were the crop:
'What of soul was left, I wonder, when the kissing had to stop?

'Dust and ashes!' So you creak it, and I want the heart to scold.
Dear dead women, with such hair, too—what's become of all the gold
Used to hang and brush their bosoms? I feel chilly and grown old.

ROBERT BROWNING

486 *On the Tombs in Westminster Abbey*

Mortality, behold and fear!
What a change of flesh is here!
Think how many royal bones
Sleep within this heap of stones,
Hence remov'd from beds of ease,
Dainty fare, and what might please,
Fretted roofs, and costly shows,
To a roof that flats the nose:
Which proclaims all flesh is grass,
How the world's fair glories pass;
That there is no trust in health,
In youth, in age, in greatness, wealth:
For if such could have reprived,
Those had been immortal lived.
Know from this the world's a snare,
How that greatness is but care,
How all pleasures are but pain,
And how short they do remain:
For here they lie had realms and lands,
That now want strength to stir their hands;
Where from their pulpits seal'd with dust
They preach, 'In greatness is no trust.'

Here's an acre sown indeed
With the richest royal seed
That the earth did e'er suck in
Since the first man died for sin;
Here the bones of birth have cried
'Though Gods they were, as men have died.'
Here are sands, ignoble things,
Drop'd from the ruin'd sides of Kings;
With whom the poor man's earth being shown,
The difference is not easily known.
Here's a world of pomp and state
Forgotten, dead, disconsolate.
Think then this scythe that mows down kings,
Exempts no meaner mortal things.
Then bid the wanton lady tread
Amid these mazes of the dead;
And these, truly understood,
More shall cool and quench the blood
Than her many sports a day,
And her nightly wanton play:
Bid her paint till day of doom,
To this favour she must come.
Bid the merchant gather wealth;
The usurer exact by stealth;
The proud man beat it from his thought–
Yet to this shape all must be brought.

ANON. (?WILLIAM BASSE)

487 *Power*

Pass We the Ills, which each Man feels or dreads,
The Weight or fall'n, or hanging o'er our Heads;
The Bear, The Lion, Terrors of the Plain,
The Sheepfold scatter'd, and the Shepherd slain;
The frequent Errors of the pathless Wood,
The giddy Precipice, and the dang'rous Flood:
The noisome Pest'lence, that in open War
Terrible, marches thro' the Mid-day Air,
And scatters Death; the Arrow that by Night
Cuts the dank Mist, and fatal wings it's Flight;

The billowing Snow, and Violence of the Show'r,
That from the Hills disperse their dreadful Store,
And o'er the Vales collected Ruin pour;
The Worm that gnaws the ripening Fruit, sad Guest,
Canker or Locust hurtful to infest
The Blade; while Husks elude the Tiller's Care,
And Eminence of Want distinguishes the Year.

Pass we the slow Disease, and subtle Pain,
Which our weak Frame is destin'd to sustain;
The cruel Stone, with congregated War
Tearing his bloody Way; the cold Catarrh,
With frequent Impulse, and continu'd Strife,
Weak'ning the wasted Seats of irksome Life;
The Gout's fierce Rack, the burning Fever's Rage,
The sad Experience of Decay; and Age,
Her self the sorest Ill; while Death, and Ease,
Oft and in vain invok'd, or to appease,
Or end the Grief, with hasty Wings recede
From the vext Patient, and the sickly Bed.

Nought shall it profit, that the charming Fair,
Angelic, softest Work of Heav'n, draws near
To the cold shaking paralytic Hand,
Senseless of Beauty's Touch, or Love's Command,
Nor longer apt, or able to fulfill
The Dictates of it's feeble Master's Will.

Nought shall the Psalt'ry, and the Harp avail,
The pleasing Song, or well repeated Tale,
When the quick Spirits their warm March forbear;
And numbing Coldness has unbrac'd the Ear.

The verdant Rising of the flow'ry Hill,
The Vale enamell'd, and the Crystal Rill,
The Ocean rolling, and the shelly Shore,
Beautiful Objects, shall delight no more;
When the lax'd Sinews of the weaken'd Eye
In wat'ry Damps, or dim Suffusion lie.
Day follows Night; the Clouds return again
After the falling of the later Rain:

But to the Aged-blind shall ne'er return
Grateful Vicissitude: He still must mourn
The Sun, and Moon, and ev'ry Starry Light
Eclips'd to Him, and lost in everlasting Night.

Behold where Age's wretched Victim lies:
See his Head trembling, and his half-clos'd Eyes:
Frequent for Breath his panting Bosom heaves:
To broken Sleeps his remnant Sense He gives;
And only by his Pains, awaking finds He Lives.

Loos'd by devouring Time the Silver Cord
Dissever'd lies: unhonor'd from the Board
The Crystal Urn, when broken, is thrown by;
And apter Utensils their Place supply.
These Things and Thou must share One equal Lot;
Die and be lost, corrupt and be forgot;
While still another, and another Race
Shall now supply, and now give up the Place.
From Earth all came, to Earth must all return;
Frail as the Cord, and brittle as the Urn.

MATTHEW PRIOR

488 *The Vanity of Human Wishes*

Let observation with extensive view,
Survey mankind, from China to Peru;
Remark each anxious toil, each eager strife,
And watch the busy scenes of crowded life;
Then say how hope and fear, desire and hate,
O'erspread with snares the clouded maze of fate,
Where wav'ring man, betray'd by vent'rous pride,
To tread the dreary paths without a guide;
As treach'rous phantoms in the mist delude,
Shuns fancied ills, or chases airy good.
How rarely reason guides the stubborn choice,
Rules the bold hand, or prompts the suppliant voice,
How nations sink, by darling schemes oppress'd,
When vengeance listens to the fool's request.
Fate wings with ev'ry wish th' afflictive dart,
Each gift of nature, and each grace of art,

With fatal heat impetuous courage glows,
With fatal sweetness elocution flows,
Impeachment stops the speaker's pow'rful breath,
And restless fire precipitates on death.

But scarce observ'd the knowing and the bold,
Fall in the gen'ral massacre of gold;
Wide-wasting pest! that rages unconfin'd,
And crowds with crimes the records of mankind;
For gold his sword the hireling ruffian draws,
For gold the hireling judge distorts the laws;
Wealth heap'd on wealth, nor truth nor safety buys,
The dangers gather as the treasures rise . . .

Unnumber'd suppliants crowd Preferment's gate,
Athirst for wealth, and burning to be great;
Delusive Fortune hears th' incessant call,
They mount, they shine, evaporate, and fall.
On ev'ry stage the foes of peace attend,
Hate dogs their flight, and insult mocks their end.
Love ends with hope, the sinking statesman's door
Pours in the morning worshipper no more;
For growing names the weekly scribbler lies,
To growing wealth the dedicator flies,
From ev'ry room descends the painted face,
That hung the bright Palladium of the place,
And smok'd in kitchens, or in auctions sold,
To better features yields the frame of gold;
For now no more we trace in ev'ry line
Heroic worth, benevolence divine:
The form distorted justifies the fall,
And detestation rids th' indignant wall . . .

When first the college rolls receive his name,
The young enthusiast quits his ease for fame;
Through all his veins the fever of renown
Spreads from the strong contagion of the gown;
O'er Bodley's dome his future labours spread,
And Bacon's mansion trembles o'er his head.
Are these thy views? proceed, illustrious youth,
And Virtue guard thee to the throne of Truth!

Yet should thy soul indulge the gen'rous heat,
Till captive Science yields her last retreat;
Should Reason guide thee with her brightest ray,
And pour on misty Doubt resistless day;
Should no false Kindness lure to loose delight,
Nor Praise relax, nor Difficulty fright;
Should tempting Novelty thy cell refrain,
And Sloth effuse her opiate fumes in vain;
Should Beauty blunt on fops her fatal dart,
Nor claim the triumph of a letter'd heart;
Should no Disease thy torpid veins invade,
Nor Melancholy's phantoms haunt thy shade;
Yet hope not life from grief or danger free,
Nor think the doom of man revers'd for thee:
Deign on the passing world to turn thine eyes,
And pause awhile from letters, to be wise;
There mark what ills the scholar's life assail,
Toil, envy, want, the patron, and the jail.
See nations slowly wise, and meanly just,
To buried merit raise the tardy bust.
If dreams yet flatter, once again attend,
Hear Lydiat's life, and Galileo's end . . .

On what foundation stands the warrior's pride?
How just his hopes, let Swedish Charles decide;
A frame of adamant, a soul of fire,
No dangers fright him, and no labours tire;
O'er love, o'er fear, extends his wide domain,
Unconquer'd lord of pleasure and of pain;
No joys to him pacific sceptres yield,
War sounds the trump, he rushes to the field;
Behold surrounding kings their pow'rs combine;
And one capitulate, and one resign;
Peace courts his hand, but spreads her charms in vain;
'Think nothing gain'd,' he cries, 'till nought remain,
On Moscow's walls till Gothic standards fly,
And all be mine beneath the polar sky.'
The march begins in military state,
And nations on his eye suspended wait;
Stern Famine guards the solitary coast,
And Winter barricades the realms of Frost;

He comes, nor want nor cold his course delay;–
Hide, blushing Glory, hide Pultowa's day:
The vanquish'd hero leaves his broken bands,
And shews his miseries in distant lands;
Condemn'd a needy supplicant to wait,
While ladies interpose, and slaves debate.
But did not Chance at length her error mend?
Did no subverted empire mark his end?
Did rival monarchs give the fatal wound?
Or hostile millions press him to the ground?
His fall was destin'd to a barren strand,
A petty fortress, and a dubious hand;
He left the name, at which the world grew pale,
To point a moral, or adorn a tale.

All times their scenes of pompous woes afford,
From Persia's tyrant to Bavaria's lord.
In gay hostility, and barb'rous pride,
With half mankind embattled at his side,
Great Xerxes comes to seize the certain prey,
And starves exhausted regions in his way;
Attendant Flatt'ry counts his myriads o'er,
Till counted myriads soothe his pride no more;
Fresh praise is try'd till madness fires his mind,
The waves he lashes, and enchains the wind;
New pow'rs are claim'd, new pow'rs are still bestow'd,
Till rude resistance lops the spreading god;
The daring Greeks deride the martial show,
And heap their valleys with the gaudy foe;
Th' insulted sea with humbler thoughts he gains,
A single skiff to speed his flight remains;
Th' incumber'd oar scarce leaves the dreaded coast
Through purple billows and a floating host . . .

Where then shall Hope and Fear their objects find?
Must dull Suspense corrupt the stagnant mind?
Must helpless man, in ignorance sedate,
Roll darkling down the torrent of his fate?
Must no dislike alarm, no wishes rise,
No cries attempt the mercies of the skies?
Inquirer, cease, petitions yet remain,
Which heav'n may hear, nor deem religion vain.

Still raise for good the supplicating voice,
But leave to heav'n the measure and the choice.
Safe in his pow'r, whose eyes discern afar
The secret ambush of a specious pray'r.
Implore his aid, in his decisions rest,
Secure whate'er he gives, he gives the best.
Yet when the sense of sacred presence fires,
And strong devotion to the skies aspires,
Pour forth thy fervours for a healthful mind,
Obedient passions, and a will resign'd;
For love, which scarce collective man can fill;
For patience, sov'reign o'er transmuted ill;
For faith, that panting for a happier seat,
Counts death kind Nature's signal of retreat:
These goods for man the laws of heav'n ordain,
These goods he grants, who grants the pow'r to gain;
With these celestial Wisdom calms the mind,
And makes the happiness she does not find.

SAMUEL JOHNSON

489 *Now War is All the World about*

An Ode, upon occasion of His Majesties Proclamation in the
Year 1630. Commanding the Gentry to reside upon their
Estates in the Country.

Now War is all the World about,
And everywhere *Erynnis* reigns,
Or else the Torch so late put out,
        The stench remains.

Holland for many years hath been
Of Christian Tragedies the Stage,
Yet seldom hath she play'd a Scene
        Of Bloodier rage.

And *France* that was not long compos'd
With civil Drums again resounds,
And ere the old are fully clos'd,
        Receives new wounds.

The great *Gustavus* in the West,
Plucks the Imperial Eagles wing,
Than whom the earth did ne'er invest
    A fiercer King;

Revenging lost *Bohemia*,
And the proud wrongs which *Tilly* dud,
And tempereth the *German* clay
    With *Spanish* blood.

What should I tell of *Polish* Bands,
And the bloods boiling in the North?
'Gainst whom the furied *Russians*
    Their Troops bring forth

Both confident: This in his purse,
And needy Valor set on work;
He in his Axe; which oft did worse
    Th' invading *Turk*.

Who now sustains a *Persian* storm:
There Hell (that made it) suffers Schism:
This War (forsooth) was to reform
    Mahumetism.

Only the Island which we sow,
(A World without the World) so far
From present wounds, it cannot show
    An ancient scar.

White Peace (the beautifull'st of things)
Seems here her everlasting rest
To fix, and spreads her downy Wings
    Over the Nest:

As when great Jove, usurping Reign,
From the plagu'd World did her exile,
And tied her with a golden Chain
    To one blest Isle:

Which in a sea of plenty swam
And Turtles sang on ev'ry Bough,
A safe retreat to all that came
    As ours is now.

Yet we, as if some Foe were here,
Leave the despised Fields to Clowns,
And come to save ourselves as 'twere
                In walled Towns.

Hither we bring Wives, Babes, rich Clothes
And Gems; Till now my Soveraign
The growing evil doth oppose:
                Counting in vain

His care preserves us from annoy
Of Enemies his Realms t'invade,
Unless he force us to enjoy
                The peace he made.

To roll themselves in envied leisure,
He therefore sends the Landed Heirs,
Whilst he proclaims not his own pleasure
                So much as theirs.

The sap and blood o' th' Land, which fled
Into the Root, and chok'd the Heart,
Are bid their quick'ning pow'r to spread
                Through ev'ry part.

O! 'Twas an Act, not for my Muse
To celebrate, nor the dull Age,
Until the Country Air infuse
                A purer rage!

And if the Fields as thankful prove
For benefits receiv'd, as seed,
They will, to quite so great a love,
                A *Virgil* breed.

A *Tytirus*, that shall not cease
Th' *Augustus* of our World to praise
In equal Verse, Author of Peace
                And *Halcyon* days.

Nor let the Gentry grudge to go
Into those places whence they grew,
But think them blest they may do so.
                Who would pursue

The smoky glory of the Town,
That may go till his native Earth,
And by the shining Fire sit down
    Of his own hearth,

Free from the griping Scriveners Bands,
And the more biting Mercers Books;
Free from the bait of oiled hands
    And painted looks?

The Country too ev'n chops for rain:
You that exhale it by your power,
Let the fat drops fall down again
    In a full shower.

And you bright beauties of the time,
That waste your selves here in a blaze,
Fix to your Orb and proper Clime
    Your wand'ring rays.

Let no dark corner of the Land
Be unimbellisht with one Gem;
And those which here too thick do stand
    Sprinkle on them.

Believe me Ladies you will find
In that sweet life, more solid joys,
More true contentment to the mind
    Than all Town-toys.

Nor *Cupid* there less blood doth spill,
But heads his shafts with chaster love,
Not feathered with a Sparrows quill,
    But of a Dove.

There shall you hear the Nightingale
(The harmless Syren of the Wood)
How prettily she tells a tale
    Of Rape and Blood.

The Lyric Lark, with all beside
Of Natures feathered choir: and all
The Commonwealth of Flowers in 'ts pride
    Behold you shall.

The Lily (Queen) the (Royal) Rose,
The Gilly-flower (Prince of the blood)
The (Courtier) Tulip (gay in Clothes)
        The (Regal) Bud

The Violet (purple Senator),
How they do mock the pomp of State,
And all that at the surly door
        Of great ones wait.

Plant Trees you may, and see them shoot
Up with your Children, to be serv'd
To your clean Boards, and the fair'st Fruit
        To be preserv'd:

And learn to use their several Gums;
'Tis innocence in the sweet blood
Of Cherry, Apricocks and Plums
        To be imbru'd.
                SIR RICHARD FANSHAWE

490 *Kingdom*

My mind to me a kingdom is,
  Such present joys therein I find,
That it excels all other bliss
  That world affords or grows by kind.
Though much I want which most would have,
Yet still my mind forbids to crave.

No princely pomp, no wealthy store,
  No force to win the victory,
No wily wit to salve a sore,
  No shape to feed a loving eye;
To none of these I yield as thrall,
For why my mind doth serve for all.

I see how plenty suffers oft,
  And hasty climbers soon do fall;
I see that those which are aloft
  Mishap doth threaten most of all;
They get with toil, they keep with fear:
Such cares my mind could never bear.

Content I live, this is my stay,
  I seek no more than may suffice;
I press to bear no haughty sway;
  Look, what I lack my mind supplies.
Lo! thus I triumph like a king,
Content with that my mind doth bring.

Some have too much, yet still do crave;
  I little have, and seek no more.
They are but poor, though much they have,
  And I am rich with little store.
They poor, I rich; they beg, I give;
They lack, I leave; they pine, I live.

I laugh not at another's loss;
  I grudge not at another's gain;
No worldly waves my mind can toss;
  My state at one doth still remain.
I fear no foe, I fawn no friend;
I loathe not life, nor dread my end.

Some weigh their pleasure by their lust,
  Their wisdom by their rage of will;
Their treasure is their only trust,
  A cloaked craft their store of skill:
But all the pleasure that I find
Is to maintain a quiet mind.

My wealth is health and perfect ease,
  My conscience clear my choice defence;
I neither seek by bribes to please,
  Nor by deceit to breed offence.
Thus do I live; thus will I die;
Would all did so as well as I!

                              SIR EDWARD DYER

491 *Predestination*

By the hoof of the Wild Goat up-tossed
From the Cliff where She lay in the Sun,
      Fell the Stone
To the Tarn where the daylight is lost;
So She fell from the light of the Sun,
      And alone.

Now the fall was ordained from the first,
With the Goat and the Cliff and the Tarn,
    But the Stone
Knows only Her life is accursed,
As She sinks in the depths of the Tarn,
    And alone.

Oh, Thou who has builded the world!
Oh, Thou who has lighted the Sun!
Oh, Thou who hast darkened the Tarn!
    Judge Thou
The sin of the Stone that was hurled
By the Goat from the light of the Sun,
As She sinks in the mire of the Tarn,
    Even now–even now–even now!
RUDYARD KIPLING

492 *On Refusal of Aid between Nations*

Not that the earth is changing, O my God!
  Nor that the seasons totter in their walk,–
  Not that the virulent ill of act and talk
Seethes ever as a winepress ever trod,–
Not therefore are we certain that the rod
  Weighs in thine hand to smite thy world; though now
  Beneath thine hand so many nations bow,
So many kings:–not therefore, O my God!–

But because Man is parcelled out in men
  To-day; because, for any wrongful blow,
  No man not stricken asks, 'I would be told
Why thou dost thus;' but his heart whispers then,
  'He is he, I am I.' By this we know
  That our earth falls asunder, being old.
DANTE GABRIEL ROSSETTI

493 *The Second Coming*

Turning and turning in the widening gyre
The falcon cannot hear the falconer:
Things fall apart; the centre cannot hold;
Mere anarchy is loosed upon the world,

The blood-dimmed tide is loosed, and everywhere
The ceremony of innocence is drowned;
The best lack all conviction, while the worst
Are full of passionate intensity.

Surely some revelation is at hand;
Surely the Second Coming is at hand.
The Second Coming! Hardly are those words out
When a vast image out of *Spiritus Mundi*
Troubles my sight: somewhere in sands of the desert
A shape with lion body and the head of a man,
A gaze blank and pitiless as the sun,
Is moving its slow thighs, while all about it
Reel shadows of the indignant desert birds.
The darkness drops again; but now I know
That twenty centuries of stony sleep
Were vexed to nightmare by a rocking cradle,
And what rough beast, its hour come round at last,
Slouches towards Bethlehem to be born?

WILLIAM BUTLER YEATS

494 *Sight*

First the two Eyes, which have the Seeing Power,
Stand as one Watchman, Spy, or Sentinel,
Being placed aloft within the head's high Tower;
And though both see, yet both but one thing tell.

These Mirrors take into their little space
The Forms of moon and sun, and every star;
Of every body, and of every place
Which, with the world's wide arms, embraced are:

Yet their best object and their noblest use
Hereafter in another World will be;
When GOD in them shall heavenly light infuse,
That face to face they may their Maker see.

Here are they guides, which do the Body lead
Which else would stumble in eternal night;

Here in this world they do much knowledge *read*,
And are the Casements which admit most light:

They are her farthest-reaching instrument;
Yet they no beams unto their objects send:
But all the rays are from their objects sent;
And in the Eyes with pointed angles end.

If th' objects be far off, the rays do meet
In a sharp point, and so things seem but small;
If they be near, their rays do spread and fleet
And make broad points, that things seem great withal.

Lastly. Nine things to Sight requirèd are;
The Power to see! the Light! the Visible thing!
Being not too small! too thin! too nigh! too far!
Clear space! and Time, the Form distinct to bring.

Thus see we how the Soul doth use the Eyes,
As instruments of her quick power of sight;
Hence do th' Arts Optic, and fair Painting rise:
Painting, which doth all gentle minds delight!

SIR JOHN DAVIES

495 *As I ebb'd with the ocean of life*

I

As I ebb'd with the ocean of life,
As I wended the shores I know,
As I walk'd where the ripples continually wash you Paumanok,
Where they rustle up hoarse and sibilant,
Where the fierce old mother endlessly cries for her castaways,
I musing late in the autumn day, gazing off southward,
Held by this electric self out of the pride of which I utter
poems,
Was seiz'd by the spirit that trails in the lines underfoot,
The rim, the sediment that stands for all the water and all the
land of the globe.

Fascinated, my eyes reverting from the south, dropt, to follow
     those slender windrows,
Chaff, straw, splinters of wood, weeds, and the sea-gluten,
Scum, scales from shining rocks, leaves of salt-lettuce, left by
     the tide,
Miles walking, the sound of breaking waves the other side of
     me,
Paumanok there and then as I thought the old thought of
     likenesses,
These you presented to me, you fish-shaped island,
As I wended the shores I know,
As I walk'd with that electric self seeking types.

2

As I wend to the shores I know not,
As I list to the dirge, the voices of men and women wreck'd,
As I inhale the impalpable breezes that set in upon me,
As the ocean so mysterious rolls toward me closer and closer,
I too but signify at the utmost a little wash'd-up drift,
A few sands and dead leaves to gather,
Gather, and merge myself as part of the sands and drift.

O baffled, balk'd, bent to the very earth,
Oppress'd with myself that I have dared to open my mouth,
Aware now that amid all that blab whose echoes recoil upon me
     I have not once had the least idea who or what I am,
But that before all my arrogant poems the real Me stands yet
     untouch'd, untold, altogether unreach'd,
Withdrawn far, mocking me with mock-congratulatory signs
     and bows,
With peals of distant ironical laughter at every word I have
     written,
Pointing in silence to these songs, and then to the sand
     beneath.

I perceive I have not really understood anything, not a single
     object, and that no man ever can,
Nature here in sight of the sea taking advantage of me to dart
     upon me and sting me,
Because I have dared to open my mouth to sing at all.

3

You oceans both, I close with you,
We murmur alike reproachfully rolling sands and drift, knowing
    not why,
These little shreds indeed standing for you and me and all.

You friable shore with trails of débris,
You fish-shaped island, I take what is underfoot,
What is yours is mine, my father.

I too Paumanok,
I too have bubbled up, floated the measureless float, and been
    wash'd on your shores,
I too am but a trail of drift and débris,
I too leave little wrecks upon you, you fish-shaped island.

I throw myself upon your breast, my father,
I cling to you so that you cannot unloose me,
I hold you so firm till you answer me something.

Kiss me, my father,
Touch me with your lips as I touch those I love,
Breathe to me while I hold you close the secret of the murmur-
    ing I envy.

4

Ebb, ocean of life (the flow will return),
Cease not your moaning, you fierce old mother,
Endlessly cry for your castaways, but fear not, deny not me,
Rustle not up so hoarse and angry against my feet as I touch
    you or gather from you.

I mean tenderly by you and all,
I gather for myself and for this phantom looking down where
    we lead, and following me and mine.

Me and mine, loose windrows, little corpses,
Froth, snowy white, and bubbles,
(See, from my dead lips the ooze exuding at last,
See, the prismatic colours glistening and rolling),

Tufts of straw, sands, fragments,
Buoy'd hither from many moods, one contradicting another,
From the storm, the long calm, the darkness, the swell,
Musing, pondering, a breath, a briny tear, a dab of liquid or
    soil,
Up just as much out of fathomless workings fermented and
    thrown,
A limp blossom or two, torn, just as much over waves floating,
    drifted at random,
Just as much for us that sobbing dirge of Nature,
Just as much whence we come that blare of the cloud-
    trumpets,
We, capricious, brought hither we know not whence, spread
    out before you,
You up there walking or sitting,
Whoever you are, we too lie in drifts at your feet.

WALT WHITMAN

496 *Sonnet*

Cyriack, whose grandsire on the royal bench
    Of British Themis, with no mean applause,
    Pronounc't and in his volumes taught our laws,
    Which others at their bar so often wrench,
To-day deep thoughts resolve with me to drench
    In mirth, that after no repenting draws;
    Let Euclid rest, and Archimedes pause,
    And what the Swede intend, and what the French.
To measure life, learn thou betimes, and know
    Toward solid good what leads the nearest way;
    For other things mild Heav'n a time ordains,

And disapproves that care, though wise in show,
    That with superfluous burden loads the day,
    And when God sends a cheerful hour, refrains.

JOHN MILTON

497 Sonnet (on his having arrived at the age of twenty-three)

How soon hath time the subtle thief of youth,
    Stol'n on his wing my three-and-twentieth year!
    My hasting days fly on with full career,
    But my late spring no bud or blossom shew'th.
Perhaps my semblance might deceive the truth
    That I to manhood am arriv'd so near;
    And inward ripeness doth much less appear,
    That some more timely-happy spirits indu'th.
Yet be it less or more, or soon or slow,
    It shall be still in strictest measure eev'n
    To that same lot, however mean or high,
Toward which Time leads me, and the will of Heav'n
    All is, if I have grace to use it so,
    As ever in my great task master's eye.
                           JOHN MILTON

498 Sonnet (on his Blindness)

When I consider how my light is spent,
  Ere half my days, in this dark world and wide,
  And that one talent which is death to hide
  Lodg'd with me useless, though my soul more bent
To serve therewith my Maker, and present
  My true account, lest he returning chide,
  'Doth God exact day-labour, light deny'd?'
  I fondly ask. But Patience, to prevent
That murmur, soon replies, 'God doth not need
  Either man's work or his own gifts. Who best
  Bear his mild yoke, they serve him best. His state
Is kingly: thousands at his bidding speed
  And post o'er land and ocean without rest;
  They also serve who only stand and wait.'
                           JOHN MILTON

499 Sonnet

Milton! thou shouldst be living at this hour:
England hath need of thee: she is a fen
Of stagnant waters: altar, sword, and pen,

S

Fireside, the heroic wealth of hall and bower,
Have forfeited their ancient English dower
Of inward happiness. We are selfish men;
Oh! raise us up, return to us again;
And give us manners, virtue, freedom, power.
Thy soul was like a Star, and dwelt apart;
Thou hadst a voice whose sound was like the sea:
Pure as the naked heavens, majestic, free,
So didst thou travel on life's common way,
In cheerful godliness; and yet thy heart
The lowliest duties on herself did lay.

WILLIAM WORDSWORTH

500 *Sonnet*

It is not to be thought of that the Flood
Of British freedom, which, to the open sea
Of the world's praise, from dark antiquity
Hath flowed, 'with pomp of waters, unwithstood,'
Roused though it be full often to a mood
Which spurns the check of salutary bands,
That this most famous Stream in bogs and sands
Should perish; and to evil and to good
Be lost for ever. In our halls is hung
Armoury of the invincible Knights of old:
We must be free or die, who speak the tongue
That Shakespeare spake; the faith and morals hold
Which Milton held.–In every thing we are sprung
Of Earth's first blood, have titles manifold.

WILLIAM WORDSWORTH

501 *To Toussaint L'Ouverture*

Toussaint, the most unhappy man of men!
Whether the whistling Rustic tend his plough
Within thy hearing, or thy head be now
Pillowed in some deep dungeon's earless den;–

O miserable Chieftain! where and when
Wilt thou find patience! Yet die not; do thou
Wear rather in thy bonds a cheerful brow:
Though fallen thyself, never to rise again,
Live, and take comfort. Thou hast left behind
Powers that will work for thee; air, earth, and skies;
There's not a breathing of the common wind
That will forget thee; thou hast great allies;
Thy friends are exultations, agonies,
And love, and man's unconquerable mind.

WILLIAM WORDSWORTH

502 *On the Extinction of the Venetian Republic*

Once did She hold the gorgeous east in fee;
And was the safeguard of the west: the worth
Of Venice did not fall below her birth,
Venice, the oldest Child of Liberty.
She was a maiden City, bright and free!
No guile seduced, no force could violate;
And, when she took unto herself a Mate,
She must espouse the everlasting Sea.
And what if she had seen those glories fade,
Those titles vanish, and that strength decay;
Yet shall some tribute of regret be paid
When her long life hath reached its final day:
Men are we, and must grieve when even the Shade
Of that which once was great, is passed away.

WILLIAM WORDSWORTH

503 *The Tears of Peace*

Thus, by the way, to human loves interring,
These marginal, and secret tears referring
To my disposure (having all this hour
Of our unworldly conference, given power
To her late fainting issue to arise)
She raised herself and them, the progenies
Of that so civil desert, rising all;
Who fell with her; and to the funeral—

She bearing still the coffin—all went on.
And now gives Time her state's description.
Before her flew Affliction, girt in storms,
Gash'd all with gushing wounds, and all the forms
Of bane, and misery, frowning in her face;
Whom Tyranny, and Injustice, had in chase;
Grim Persecution, Poverty, and Shame;
Detraction, Envy, foul Mishap and lame;
Scruple of Conscience; Fear, Deceit, Despair;
Slander, and Clamour, that rent all the air;
Hate, War, and Massacre; uncrowned Toil;
And Sickness (t'all the rest the base and foil)
Crept after; and his deadly weight, trod down
Wealth, Beauty, and the glory of a Crown.
These usher'd her far off; as figures given
To show, these Crosses borne, make peace with heaven.
But now, made free from them, next her before;
Peaceful, and young, Herculean silence bore
His craggy club; which up aloft, he hild;
With which, and his fore-finger's charm he still'd
All sounds in air; and left so free mine ears,
That I might hear the music of the spheres,
And all the angels, singing, out of heaven;
Whose tunes were solemn, as to passion given;
For now, that Justice was the happiness there
For all the wrongs to Right, inflicted here.
Such was the passion that Peace now put on;
And on all went; when suddenly was gone
All light of heaven before us; from a wood,
Whose light foreseen, now lost, amaz'd we stood,
The sun still gracing us; when now, the air
Inflam'd with meteors, we discover'd, fair,
The skipping goat; the horse's flaming mane;
Bearded and trained comets; stars in wane;
The burning sword; the firebrand, flying snake;
The lance; the torch; the licking fire; the drake;
And all else meteors, that did ill abode;
The thunder child; the lightning leapt abroad;
And yet, when Peace came, in all heaven was clear;
And then did all the horrid wood appear;

Where mortal dangers more than leaves did grow;
In which we could not one free step bestow,
For treading on some murther'd passenger
Who thither was, by witchcraft, forced to err:
Whose face the bird hid that loves humans best;
That hath the bugle eyes and rosy breast,
And is the yellow Autumn's nightingale.
Peace made us enter here secure of all;
Where, in a cave, that through a rock did eat,
The monster Murther held his impious seat;
A heap of panting harts supported him,
On which he sate, gnawing a reeking limb
Of some man newly murther'd. As he ate,
His grave-digg'd brows, like stormy eaves did sweat;
Which, like incensed fens, with mists did smoke;
His hide was rugged as an aged oak
With heathy leprosies; that still he fed
With hot, raw limbs, of men late murthered.
His face was like a meteor, flashing blood;
His head all bristled, like a thorny wood;
His neck cast wrinkles, like a sea enrag'd;
And in his vast arms was the world engag'd
Bathing his hands in every cruel deed:
Whose palms were hell-deep lakes of boiling lead;
His thighs were mines of poison, torment, grief;
In which digg'd fraud, and treachery, for relief;
Religion's botcher, policy; and pride,
Oppression, slavery, flattery glorified,
Atheism, and tyranny, and gain unjust,
Frantic ambition, envy, shag-hair'd lust,
Both sorts of ignorance, and knowledge swell'd;
And over these, the old wolf avarice held
A golden scourge that dropt with blood and vapour,
With which he whipp'd them to their endless labour.
From under heaps cast from his fruitful thighs
(As ground, to all their damn'd impieties)
The mournful goddess drew dead Human Love;
Nor could they let her entry, though they strove;
And furnac'd on her all their venomous breath;
For though all outrage breaks the peace of death,

She coffin'd him; and forth to funeral
All help'd to bear him. But to sound it all,
My trumpet fails, and all my forces shrink.
Who can enact to life, what kills to think?
Nor can the soul's beams bear through blood and flesh,
Forms of such woe and height as now, afresh,
Flow'd from these objects; to see Poesy
Prepared to do the special obsequy
And sing the Funeral Oration;
How it did show, to see her tread upon
The breast of Death, and on a Fury lean;
How to her fist, as rites of service then,
A cast of ravens flew; on her shoulders, how
The fowls that to the Muses' queen we vow,
(The owl and heronshaw) sate; how, for her hair,
A hapless comet hurl'd about the air
Her curled beams, whence sparks, like falling stars,
Vanish'd about her; and with winds adverse
Were still blown back; to which the phoenix flew,
And, burning on her head, would not renew.
How her divine Oration did move
For th' unredeemed loss of Human Love;
Object man's future state to reason's eye;
The soul's infusion, immortality;
And prove her forms firm, that are here impress'd,
How her admired strains wrought on every breast;-
And made the woods cast their immanity [1]
Up to the air; that did to cities fly
In fuel for them; and, in clouds of smoke,
Ever hang over them; cannot be spoke;
Nor how to Human Love, to Earth now given,
A lightning stoop'd and ravish'd him to heaven,
And with him Peace, with all her heavenly seed:
Whose outward Rapture made me inward bleed;
Nor can I therefore my intention keep,
Since Tears want words, and words want tears to weep.

GEORGE CHAPMAN

[1] enormity

504 *To Detraction I present my Poesie*

Foul canker of fair virtuous action,
Vile blaster of the freshest blooms on earth,
Envy's abhorred child *Detraction*,
I here expose, to thy all-tainting breath
    The issue of my brain, snarl, rail, bark, bite,
    Know that my spirit scornes *Detraction*'s spite.

Know that the *Genius*, which attendeth on,
And guides my powers intellectual,
Holds in all vile repute *Detraction*,
My soul an essence metaphysical,
    That in the basest sort scorns *Critics*' rage,
    Because he knows his sacred parentage.

My spirit is not puft up with fatte fume
Of slimy Ale, nor *Bacchus*' heating grape.
My mind disdains the dungy, muddy scum
Of abject thoughts, and *Envy*'s raging hate.
    True judgement, slight regards Opinion,
    A sprightly wit, disdains Detraction.

A partial praise shall never elevate
My settled censure, of mine own esteem.
A cankered verdict of malignant Hate
Shall ne'er provoke me, worse my self to deem.
    Spite of despite, and rancor's villany,
    I am my self, so is my poesy.

JOHN MARSTON

505 *Prologue to Antonio's Revenge*

The rawish dank of clumsy winter ramps
The fluent summer's vein: and drizzling sleet
Chilleth the wan bleak cheek of the numb'd earth,
Whilst snarling gusts nibble the juiceless leaves,
From the nak'd shudd'ring branch; and peels the skin
From off the soft and delicate aspects.
O now, me thinks, a sullen tragic Scene
Would suit the time, with pleasing congruence.

May we be happy in our weak devoyer,
And all part pleas'd in most wish'd content:
But sweat of *Hercules* can ne'er beget
So blest an issue. Therefore, we proclaim,
If any spirit breathes within this round,
Uncapable of weighty passion
(As from his birth, being hugged in the arms,
And nuzzled twixt the breasts of happiness)
Who winks, and shuts his apprehension up
From common sense of what men were, and are,
Who would not know what men must be; let such
Hurry amain from our black visag'd shows:
We shall affright their eyes. But if a breast,
Nail'd to the earth with grief: if any heart
Pierc't through with anguish, pant within this ring:
If there be any blood, whose heat is choked
And stifled with true sense of misery:
If aught of these strains fill this consort up,
Th' arrive most welcome. O that our power
Could lackey, or keep wing with our desires;
That with unused paize [1] of style and sense,
We might weigh massy in judicious scale–
Yet here's the prop that doth support our hopes;
  When our Scenes falter, or invention halts,
  Your favour will give crutches to our faults.

JOHN MARSTON

506   *Rudel to the Lady of Tripoli*

I

I know a Mount, the gracious Sun perceives
First, when he visits, last, too, when he leaves
The world; and, vainly favoured, it repays
The day-long glory of his steadfast gaze
By no change of its large calm front of snow.
And underneath the Mount, a Flower I know,
He cannot have perceived, that changes ever
At his approach; and, in the lost endeavour

To live his life, has parted, one by one,
With all a flower's true graces, for the grace
Of being but a foolish mimic sun,
With ray-like flowers round a disk-like face.
Men nobly call by many a name the Mount
As over many a land of theirs its large
Calm front of snow like a triumphal targe
Is reared, and still with old names, fresh names vie,
Each to his proper praise and own account:
Men call the flower, the Sunflower, sportively.

II

Oh, Angel of the East, one, one gold look
Across the waters to this twilight nook,
–The far sad waters, Angel, to this nook!

III

Dear Pilgrim, art thou for the East indeed?
Go!–saying ever as thou dost proceed,
That I, French Rudel, choose for my device
A sunflower outspread like a sacrifice
Before its idol. See! These inexpert
And hurried fingers could not fail to hurt
The woven picture; 'tis a woman's skill
Indeed; but nothing baffled me, so, ill
Or well, the work is finished. Say, men feed
On songs I sing, and therefore bask the bees
On my flower's breast as on a platform broad:
But, as the flower's concern is not for these
But solely for the sun, so men applaud
In vain this Rudel, he not looking here
But to the East–the East! Go, say this, Pilgrim dear!

ROBERT BROWNING

507 *Ulysses*

It little profits that an idle king,
By this still hearth, among these barren crags,
Match'd with an aged wife, I mete and dole
Unequal laws unto a savage race,
That hoard, and sleep, and feed, and know not me.

I cannot rest from travel: I will drink
Life to the lees: all times I have enjoy'd
Greatly, have suffer'd greatly, both with those
That loved me, and alone; on shore, and when
Thro' scudding drifts the rainy Hyades
Vext the dim sea: I am become a name;
For always roaming with a hungry heart
Much have I seen and known; cities of men
And manners, climates, councils, governments,
Myself not least, but honour'd of them all;
And drunk delight of battle with my peers,
Far on the ringing plains of windy Troy.
I am a part of all that I have met;
Yet all experience is an arch wherethro'
Gleams that untravell'd world, whose margin fades
For ever and for ever when I move.
How dull it is to pause, to make an end,
To rust unburnish'd, not to shine in use!
As tho' to breathe were life. Life piled on life
Were all too little, and of one to me
Little remains: but every hour is saved
From that eternal silence, something more,
A bringer of new things; and vile it were
For some three suns to store and hoard myself,
And this gray spirit yearning in desire
To follow knowledge like a sinking star,
Beyond the utmost bound of human thought.

   This is my son, mine own Telemachus,
To whom I leave the sceptre and the isle—
Well-loved of me, discerning to fulfil
This labour, by slow prudence to make mild
A rugged people, and thro' soft degrees
Subdue them to the useful and the good.
Most blameless is he, centred in the sphere
Of common duties, decent not to fail
In offices of tenderness, and pay
Meet adoration to my household gods,
When I am gone. He works his work, I mine.

   There lies the port; the vessel puffs her sail:
There gloom the dark broad seas.   My mariners,

Souls that have toil'd, and wrought, and thought with me—
That ever with a frolic welcome took
The thunder and the sunshine, and opposed
Free hearts, free foreheads—you and I are old;
Old age hath yet his honour and his toil;
Death closes all: but something ere the end,
Some work of noble note, may yet be done,
Not unbecoming men that strove with Gods.
The lights begin to twinkle from the rocks:
The long day wanes: the slow moon climbs: the deep
Moans round with many voices. Come, my friends,
'Tis not too late to seek a newer world.
Push off, and sitting well in order smite
The sounding furrows; for my purpose holds
To sail beyond the sunset, and the baths
Of all the western stars, until I die.
It may be that the gulfs will wash us down:
It may be we shall touch the Happy Isles,
And see the great Achilles, whom we knew.
Tho' much is taken, much abides; and tho'
We are not now that strength which in old days
Moved earth and heaven; that which we are, we are;
One equal temper of heroic hearts,
Made weak by time and fate, but strong in will
To strive, to seek, to find, and not to yield.

ALFRED, LORD TENNYSON

508 *The Rubáiyát of Omar Khayyám*

Awake! for Morning in the Bowl of Night
Has flung the Stone that puts the Stars to Flight:
    And Lo! the Hunter of the East has caught
The Sultán's Turret in a noose of Light.

Dreaming when Dawn's left Hand was in the Sky
I heard a Voice within the Tavern cry,
    'Awake, my Little ones, and fill the Cup
Before Life's Liquor in its Cup be dry.'

And, as the Cock crew, those who stood before
The Tavern shouted–'Open then the Door!
　　You know how little while we have to stay,
And, once departed, may return no more.'

*　　*　　*

But come with old Khayyám, and leave the Lot
Of Kaikobád and Kaikhosrú forgot:
　　Let Rustum lay about him as he will,
Or Hátim Tai cry Supper–heed them not.

With me along some Strip of Herbage strown
That just divides the desert from the sown,
　　Where name of Slave and Sultán scarce is known,
And pity Sultán Máhmúd on his Throne.

Here with a Loaf of Bread beneath the Bough,
A Flask of Wine, a Book of Verse–and Thou
　　Beside me singing in the Wilderness–
And Wilderness is Paradise enow.

'How sweet is mortal Sovranty!'–think some:
Others–'How blest the Paradise to come!'
　　Ah, take the Cash in hand and wave the Rest;
Oh, the brave Music of a *distant* Drum!

Look to the Rose that blows about us–'Lo,
'Laughing,' she says, 'into the World I blow:
　　'At once the silken Tassel of my Purse
'Tear, and its Treasure on the Garden throw.'

The Worldly Hope men set their Hearts upon
Turns Ashes–or it prospers; and anon
　　Like Snow upon the Desert's dusty Face
Lighting a little Hour or two–is gone.

And those who husbanded the Golden Grain,
And those who flung it to the Winds like Rain,
　　Alike to no such aureate Earth are turn'd
As, buried once, Men want dug up again.

Think, in this batter'd Caravanserai
Whose Doorways are alternate Night and Day,
How Sultán after Sultán with his Pomp
Abode his Hour or two, and went his way.

*　　*　　*

Myself when young did eagerly frequent
Doctor and Saint, and heard great Argument
About it and about: but evermore
Came out by the same Door as in I went.

With them the Seed of Wisdom did I sow,
And with my own hand labour'd it to grow:
And this was all the Harvest that I reap'd–
'I came like Water, and like Wind I go.'

Into this Universe, and *why* not knowing,
Nor *whence*, like Water willy-nilly flowing:
And out of it, as Wind along the Waste,
I know not *whither*, willy-nilly blowing.

What, without asking, hither hurried *whence?*
And, without asking, *whither* hurried hence!
Another and another Cup to drown
The Memory of this Impertinence!

Up from Earth's Centre through the Seventh Gate
I rose, and on the Throne of Saturn sate,
And many Knots unravel'd by the Road;
But not the Knot of Human Death and Fate.

There was a Door to which I found no Key:
There was a Veil past which I could not see;
Some little Talk awhile of ME and THEE
There seemed–and then no more of THEE and ME.

Then to the rolling Heav'n itself I cried,
Asking, 'What Lamp had Destiny to guide
'Her little Children stumbling in the Dark?'
And–'A blind Understanding!' Heav'n replied.

Then to this earthen Bowl did I adjourn
My Lip the secret Well of Life to learn:
   And Lip to Lip it murmur'd–'While you live
'Drink!–for once dead you never shall return.'

I think the Vessel, that with fugitive
Articulation answer'd, once did live,
   And merry-make; and the cold Lip I kiss'd
How many Kisses might it take–and give!

        *   *   *

And lately, by the Tavern Door agape,
Came stealing through the Dusk an Angel Shape
   Bearing a Vessel on his Shoulder; and
He bid me taste of it; and 'twas–the Grape!

The Grape that can with Logic absolute
The Two-and-Seventy jarring Sects confute;
   The subtle Alchemist that in a Trice
Life's leaden Metal into Gold transmute.

The mighty Mahmúd, the victorious Lord,
That all the misbelieving and black Horde
   Of Fears and Sorrows that infest the Soul
Scatters and slays with his enchanted Sword.

But leave the Wise to wrangle, and with me
The Quarrel of the Universe let be:
   And, in some corner of the Hubbub coucht,
Make Game of that which makes as much of Thee.

For in and out, above, about, below,
'Tis nothing but a Magic Shadow-show,
   Play'd in a Box whose Candle is the Sun,
Round which we Phantom Figures come and go.

And if the Wine you drink, the Lip you press,
End in the Nothing all Things end in–Yes–
   Then fancy while Thou art, Thou art but what
Thou shalt be–Nothing–Thou shalt not be less.

While the Rose blows along the River Brink,
With old Khayyám the Ruby Vintage drink:
    And when the Angel with his darker Draught
Draws up to Thee–take that, and do not shrink.

*　　*　　*

And this I know: whether the one True Light,
Kindle to Love, or Wrath consume me quite,
    One Glimpse of It within the Tavern caught
Better than in the Temple lost outright.

Oh Thou, who didst with Pitfall and with Gin
Beset the Road I was to wander in,
    Thou wilt not with Predestination round
Enmesh me, and impute my Fall to Sin?

Oh, Thou, who Man of baser Earth didst make,
And who with Eden didst devise the Snake;
    For all the Sin wherewith the Face of Man
Is blacken'd, Man's Forgiveness give–and take!

EDWARD FITZGERALD

509 *Song*

All service ranks the same with God:
If now, as formerly he trod
Paradise, his presence fills
Our earth, each only as God wills
Can work–God's puppets, best and worst,
Are we; there is no last nor first.

Say not 'a small event!' Why 'small'?
Costs it more pain that this, ye call
A 'great event,' should come to pass,
Than that? Untwine me from the mass
Of deeds which make up life, one deed
Power shall fall short in or exceed!

ROBERT BROWNING

510 *Rebirth*

If any God should say
    'I will restore
The world her yesterday
    Whole as before
My Judgment blasted it'—who would not lift
Heart, eye, and hand in passion o'er the gift?

If any God should will
    To wipe from mind
The memory of this ill
    Which is mankind
In soul and substance now—who would not bless
Even to tears His loving-tenderness?

If any God should give
    Us leave to fly
These present deaths we live,
    And safely die
In those lost lives we lived ere we were born—
What man but would not laugh the excuse to scorn?

For we are what we are—
    So broke to blood
And the strict works of war—
    So long subdued
To sacrifice, that threadbare Death commands
Hardly observance at our busier hands.

Yet we were what we were,
    And, fashioned so,
It pleases us to stare
    At the far show
Of unbelievable years and shapes that flit;
In our own likeness, on the edge of it.

                    RUDYARD KIPLING

511 *Chaos*

In vain, in vain—the all-composing hour
Resistless falls: the Muse obeys the pow'r.

She comes! she comes! the sable throne behold
Of Night primeval, and of Chaos old!
Before her, Fancy's gilded clouds decay,
And all its varying rainbows die away.
Wit shoots in vain its momentary fires,
The meteor drops, and in a flash expires.
As one by one, at dread Medea's strain,
The sick'ning stars fade off th' ethereal plain;
As Argus' eyes, by Hermes' wand opprest,
Clos'd one by one to everlasting rest;
Thus at her felt approach, and secret might,
Art after Art goes out, and all is night.
See skulking Truth to her old cavern fled,
Mountains of casuistry heap'd o'er her head!
Philosophy, that lean'd on Heaven before,
Shrinks to her second cause, and is no more.
Physic of Metaphysic begs defence,
And Metaphysic calls for aid on sense!
See Mystery to Mathematics fly!
In vain! they gaze, turn giddy, rave, and die.
Religion, blushing, veils her sacred fires,
And unawares Morality expires.
Nor public flame, nor private, dares to shine;
Nor human spark is left, nor glimpse divine!
Lo! thy dread empire, Chaos! is restor'd;
Light dies before thy uncreating word:
Thy hand, great Anarch! lets the curtain fall;
And universal darkness buries all.

ALEXANDER POPE

512 *No Trust in Time*

Look how the flower which ling'ringly doth fade,
The morning's darling late, the summer's queen,
Spoil'd of that juice which kept it fresh and green,
As high as it did raise, bows low the head:
Right so my life, contentments being dead,
Or in their contraries but only seen,
With swifter speed declines than erst it spread,
And, blasted, scarce now shows what it hath been.

As doth the pilgrim therefore, whom the night
By darkness would imprison on his way,
Think on thy home, my soul, and think aright
Of what yet rests thee of life's wasting day:
   Thy sun posts westward, passed is thy morn,
   And twice it is not given thee to be born.
WILLIAM DRUMMOND

513 *On Time*

Fly, envious Time, till thou run out thy race:
Call on the lazy leaden-stepping Hours,
Whose speed is but the heavy plummet's pace;
And glut thyself with what thy womb devours,
Which is no more than what is false and vain,
And meerly mortal dross;
So little is our loss,
So little is thy gain!
For, when as each thing bad thou hast entomb'd,
And last of all thy greedy self consum'd,
Then long Eternity shall greet our bliss
With an individual kiss,
And Joy shall overtake us as a flood;
When every thing that is sincerely good,
And perfectly divine,
With Truth, and Peace, and Love shall ever shine
About the supreme Throne
Of him, t' whose happy-making sight alone,
When once our heav'nly-guided soul shall clime,
Then, all this earthy grossness quit,
Attir'd with Stars, we shall for ever sit,
   Triumphing over Death, and Chance, and thee O Time!
JOHN MILTON

514 *Elegy*

My prime of youth is but a frost of cares,
  My feast of joy is but a dish of pain,
My crop of corn is but a field of tares,
  And all my good is but vain hope of gain;
    The day is past, and yet I saw no sun,
    And now I live, and now my life is done.

My tale was heard and yet it was not told,
  My fruit is fallen and yet my leaves are green,
My youth is spent and yet I am not old,
  I saw the world and yet I was not seen;
    My thread is cut and yet it is not spun,
    And now I live, and now my life is done.

I sought my death and found it in my womb,
  I looked for life and saw it was a shade,
I trod the earth and knew it was my tomb,
  And now I die, and now I was but made;
    My glass is full, and now my glass is run,
    And now I live, and now my life is done.

CHIDIOCK TICHBORNE

515 *Sonet*

Fra bank to bank, fra wood to wood I rin,
  Ourhailit with my feeble fantasie;
Like til a leaf that fallis from a tree,
  Or til a reed ourblawin with the wind.
Twa gods guides me: the ane of tham is blind,
  Yea and a bairn brocht up in vanitie;
  The nixt a wife ingenrit of the sea,
And lichter nor a dauphin with 'hir fin.

Unhappy is the man for evirmair
  That tills the sand and sawis in the air;
  But twice unhappier is he, I lairn,
That feidis in his hairt a mad desire,
And follows on a woman throw the fire,
  Led be a blind and teachit be a bairn.

MARK ALEXANDER BOYD

516 *Arbor Vitae*

With honeysuckle, over-sweet, festoon'd;
With bitter ivy bound;
Terraced with funguses unsound;
Deform'd with many a boss
And closed scar, o'ercushion'd deep with moss;

Bunch'd all about with pagan mistletoe;
And thick with nests of the hoarse bird
That talks, but understands not his own word;
Stands, and so stood a thousand years ago,
A single tree.
Thunder has done its worst among its twigs,
Where the great crest yet blackens, never pruned,
But in its heart, alway
Ready to push new verdurous boughs, whene'er
The rotting saplings near it fall and leave it air,
Is all antiquity and no decay.
Rich, though rejected by the forest-pigs,
Its fruit, beneath whose rough, concealing rind
They that will break it find
Heart-succouring savour of each several meat,
And kernell'd drink of brain-renewing power,
With bitter condiment and sour,
And sweet economy of sweet,
And odours that remind
Of haunts of childhood and a different day.
Beside this tree,
Praising no Gods nor blaming, sans a wish,
Sits, Tartar-like, the Time's civility,
And eats its dead-dog off a golden dish.

COVENTRY PATMORE

517 *Finite Reason*

Dim, as the borrow'd beams of Moon and Stars
To lonely, weary, wand'ring Travellers
Is Reason to the Soul: And as on high
Those rolling Fires discover but the Sky
Not light us here; So Reason's glimmering Ray
Was lent, not to assure our doubtful way,
But guide us upward to a better Day.
And as those nightly Tapers disappear
When Day's bright Lord ascends our Hemisphere;
So pale grows Reason at Religion's sight;
So dies, and so dissolves in Supernatural Light.
Some few, whose Lamp shone brighter, have been led
From Cause to Cause to Nature's secret head;

And found that one first principle must be;
But what, or who, that UNIVERSAL HE;
Whether some Soul incompassing this Ball,
Unmade, unmov'd; yet making, moving All;
Or various Atoms' interfering Dance
Leapt into Form (the noble work of Chance,)
Or this great All was from Eternity;
Not ev'n the Stagirite himself could see;
And Epicurus guess'd as well as He.
As blindly grop'd they for a future State,
As rashly judg'd of Providence and Fate:
But least of all could their Endeavours find
What most concern'd the good of Human kind:
For Happiness was never to be found;
But vanish'd from 'em, like Enchanted ground.
One thought Content the Good to be enjoyed:
This, every little Accident destroyed:
The wiser Madmen did for Virtue toil,
A Thorny, or at best a barren Soil:
In Pleasure some their glutton Souls would steep,
But found their Line too short, the Well too deep,
And leaky Vessels which no Bliss cou'd keep.
Thus, anxious Thoughts in endless Circles roll,
Without a Centre where to fix the Soul:
In this wild Maze their vain Endeavours end:
How can the less the Greater comprehend?
Or finite Reason reach Infinity?
For what could fathom GOD were more than He.

JOHN DRYDEN

518 *Emblem*

A just man falleth seven times, and riseth up again; but the
wicked shall fall into mischief.–Prov. xxiv. 16.

'Tis but a foil at best, and that's the most
    Your skill can boast:
My slipp'ry footing fail'd me; and you tript,
    Just as I slipt:
My wanton weakness did herself betray
    With too much play:

I was too bold; he never yet stood sure,
    That stands secure:
Who ever trusted to his native strength,
    But fell at length?
The title's craz'd, the tenure is not good,
That claims by th' evidence of flesh and blood.

Boast not thy skill; the righteous man falls oft,
    Yet falls but soft:
There may be dirt to mire him, but no stones
    To crush his bones:
What if he staggers? nay, but case he be
    Foil'd on his knee?
That very knee will bend to Heav'n, and woo
    For mercy too.
The true-bred gamester ups afresh, and then
    Falls to 't again;
Whereas the leaden-hearted coward lies,
And yields his conquer'd life, or craven'd dies.

Boast not thy conquest; thou that ev'ry hour
    Fall'st ten times low'r;
Nay, hast not pow'r to rise, if not, in case,
    To fall more base:
Thou wallow'st where I slip; and thou dost tumble
    Where I but stumble:
Thou glory'st in thy slav'ries' dirty badges,
    And fall'st for wages:
Sour grief and sad repentance scours and clears
    My stains with tears:
Thy falling keeps thy falling still in ure;[1]
But when I slip, I stand the more secure.

Lord, what a nothing is this little span,
    We call a MAN!
What fenny trash maintains the smoth'ring fires
    Of his desires!
How slight and short are his resolves at longest:
    How weak at strongest!
Oh, if a sinner, held by that fast hand,
    Can hardly stand,

[1] use; practice

Good God! in what a desp'rate case are they,
    That have no stay!
Man's state implies a necessary curse;
When not himself, he's mad; when most himself,
    he's worse.

FRANCIS QUARLES

519 *Of His Divine Poems*

When we for Age could neither read nor write,
The subject made us able to indite;
The Soul, with nobler Resolutions deckt,
The Body stooping, does Herself erect:
No Mortal Parts, are requisite to raise
Her, that Unbodied can her Maker praise.
    The Seas are quiet, when the Winds give o'er;
So calm are we, when Passions are no more:
For then we know how vain it is to boast
Of fleeting Things, so certain to be lost.
Clouds of Affection from our younger Eyes
Conceal that emptiness, which Age descries.
    The Soul's dark Cottage, batter'd and decay'd,
Lets in new Light thro' chinks that time has made;
Stronger by weakness, wiser men become
As they draw near to their Eternal home.
Leaving the old, both Worlds at once they view,
That stand upon the threshold of the New.

EDMUND WALLER

520 *Behold, O Aspasia! I send you Verses*

Beauty! thou art a wanderer on the earth,
    And hast no temple in the fairest ile
Or city over-sea, where Wealth and Mirth
    And all the Graces, all the Muses, smile.

Yet these have always nurst thee with such fond,
    Such lasting love, that they have followed up
Thy steps thro' every land, and placed beyond
    The reach of thirsty Time thy nectar-cup.

Thou art a wanderer, Beauty! like the rays
    That now upon the platan, now upon
The sleepy lake, glance quick or idly gaze,
    And now are manifold and now are none.

I have call'd, panting, after thee, and thou
    Hast turn'd and lookt and said some pretty word,
Parting the hair, perhaps, upon my brow,
    And telling me none ever was prefer'd.

In more than one bright form hast thou appear'd,
    In more than one sweet dialect hast thou spoken:
Beauty! thy spells the heart within me heard,
    Griev'd that they bound it, grieves that they are broken.

                    WALTER SAVAGE LANDOR

521 *The Definition of Love*

My Love is of a birth as rare
As 'tis for object strange and high:
It was begotten by despair
Upon Impossibility.

Magnanimous Despair alone
Could show me so divine a thing,
Where feeble Hope could ne'er have flown
But vainly flapt its Tinsel Wing.

And yet I quickly might arrive
Where my extended Soul is fixt,
But Fate does Iron wedges drive,
And always crowds itself betwixt.

For Fate with jealous Eye does see
Two perfect Loves; nor lets them close:
Their union would her ruin be,
And her Tyrannic pow'r depose.

And therefore her Decrees of Steel
Us as the distant Poles have plac'd,
(Though Love's whole World on us doth wheel)
Not by themselves to be embrac'd.

Unless the giddy Heaven fall,
And Earth some new Convulsion tear;
And, us to join, the World should all
Be cramp'd into a *Planisphere*.

As Lines so Loves *oblique* may well
Themselves in every Angle greet:
But ours so truly *Parallel*,
Though infinite can never meet.

Therefore the Love which us doth bind,
But Fate so enviously debars,
Is the Conjunction of the Mind,
And Opposition of the Stars.

ANDREW MARVELL

522 *The Penitent Palmer's Ode*

Whilom in the Winter's rage
A Palmer old and full of age,
Sat and thought upon his youth,
With eyes, teares, and heart's ruth,
Being all with cares yblent,
When he thought on years misspent,
When his follies came to mind,
How fond love had made him blind,
And rapt him in a field of woes,
Shadowed with pleasure's shoes,
Then he sighed and said alas,
Man is sin, and flesh is grass.
I thought my mistress' hairs were gold,
And in her locks my heart I fold:
Her amber tresses were the sight
That wrapped me in vain delight:
Her Ivorie front, her pretty chin,
Were stales [1] that drew me on to sin:
Her starry looks, her Chrystal eyes,
Brighter then the Sun's arise:
Sparkling pleasing flames of fire,
Yok'd my thoughts and my desire,

[1] lures, decoys

That I gan crië ere I blin,[1]
Oh her eyes are paths to sin.
Her face was fair, her breath was sweet,
All her looks for love was meet:
But love is folly this I know,
And beauty fadeth like to snow.
Oh why should man delight in pride,
Whose blossom like a dew doth glide:
When these supposes toucht my thought,
That world was vain, and beauty nought,
I gan sigh and say alas,
Man is sin, and flesh is grass.

ROBERT GREENE

523 *The Thought*

If you do love as well as I,
Then every minute from your heart
   A thought doth part;
And winged with desire doth fly
Till it hath met in a straight line
   A thought of mine
So like to yours, we cannot know
Whether of both doth come or go,
   Till we define
Which of us two that thought doth owe.

I say then, that your thoughts which pass
Are not so much the thoughts you meant,
   As those I sent:
For as my image in a glass
Belongs not to the glass you see,
   But unto me,
So when your fancy is so clear,
That you would think you saw me there,
   It needs must be,
That it was I did first appear.

[1] ceased

Likewise, when I send forth a thought,
My reason tells me, 'tis the same
 Which from you came,
And which your beauteous image wrought;
Thus, while our thoughts by turns do lead,
 None can precede;
And thus while in each other's mind
Such interchanged forms we find,
 Our loves may plead
To be of more than vulgar kind.

May you then often think on me,
And by that thinking know 'tis true
 I thought on you:
I in the same belief will be,
While by this mutual address
 We will possess
A love must live, when we do die;
Which rare and secret property
 You will confess,
If you do love as well as I.

LORD HERBERT OF CHERBURY

524 *To Everlasting Oblivion*

Thou mighty gulf, insatiate cormorant,
Deride me not, though I seem petulant
To fall into thy chops. Let others pray
For ever their fair Poems flourish may.
But as for me, hungry *Oblivion*
Devour me quick, accept my orison:
 My earnest prayers, which do importune thee,
 With gloomy shade of thy still Empery,
 To vail both me and my rude poesy,
Far worthier lines in silence of thy state
Do sleep securely free from love or hate,
From which this living, ne'er can be exempt,
But whilst it breathes will hate and fury tempt.
Then close his eyes with thy all-dimming hand,
Which not right glorious actions can withstand.

Peace, hateful tongues, I now in silence pace,
Unless some hound do wake me from my place,
  I with this sharp, yet well meant poesy,
  Will sleep secure, right free from injury
  Of canker'd hate, or rankest villany.

JOHN MARSTON

525 *Tithonus*

The woods decay, the woods decay and fall,
The vapours weep their burthen to the ground,
Man comes and tills the field and lies beneath,
And after many a summer dies the swan.
Me only cruel immortality
Consumes: I wither slowly in thine arms,
Here at the quiet limit of the world,
A white-hair'd shadow roaming like a dream
The ever-silent spaces of the East,
Far-folded mists, and gleaming halls of morn.

Alas! for this gray shadow, once a man–
So glorious in his beauty and thy choice,
Who madest him thy chosen, that he seem'd
To his great heart none other than a God!
I ask'd thee, 'Give me immortality.'
Then didst thou grant mine asking with a smile,
Like wealthy men who care not how they give.
But thy strong Hours indignant work'd their wills,
And beat me down and marr'd and wasted me,
And tho' they could not end me, left me maim'd
To dwell in presence of immortal youth,
Immortal age beside immortal youth,
And all I was, in ashes. Can thy love,
Thy beauty, make amends, tho' even now,
Close over us, the silver star, thy guide,
Shines in those tremulous eyes that fill with tears
To hear me? Let me go: take back thy gift:
Why should a man desire in any way
To vary from the kindly race of men,
Or pass beyond the goal of ordinance
Where all should pause, as is most meet for all?

A soft air fans the cloud apart; there comes
A glimpse of that dark world where I was born.
Once more the old mysterious glimmer steals
From thy pure brows, and from thy shoulders pure,
And bosom beating with a heart renew'd.
Thy cheek begins to redden thro' the gloom,
Thy sweet eyes brighten slowly close to mine,
Ere yet they blind the stars, and the wild team
Which love thee, yearning for thy yoke, arise,
And shake the darkness from their loosen'd manes,
And beat the twilight into flakes of fire.

Lo! ever thus thou growest beautiful
In silence, then before thine answer given
Departest, and thy tears are on my cheek.

Why wilt thou ever scare me with thy tears,
And make me tremble lest a saying learnt,
In days far-off, on that dark earth, be true?
'The Gods themselves cannot recall their gifts.'

Ay me! ay me! with what another heart
In days far-off, and with what other eyes
I used to watch—if I be he that watch'd—
The lucid outline forming round thee; saw
The dim curls kindle into sunny rings;
Changed with thy mystic change, and felt my blood
Glow with the glow that slowly crimson'd all
Thy presence and thy portals, while I lay,
Mouth, forehead, eyelids, growing dewy-warm
With kisses balmier than half-opening buds
Of April, and could hear the lips that kiss'd
Whispering I knew not what of wild and sweet,
Like that strange song I heard Apollo sing,
While Ilion like a mist rose into towers.

Yet hold me not for ever in thine East:
How can my nature longer mix with thine?
Coldly thy rose shadows bathe me, cold
Are all thy lights, and cold my wrinkled feet
Upon thy glimmering thresholds, when the steam
Floats up from those dim fields about the homes
Of happy men that have the power to die,

And grassy barrows of the happier dead.
Release me, and restore me to the ground;
Thou seest all things, thou wilt see my grave:
Thou wilt renew thy beauty morn by morn;
I earth in earth forget these empty courts,
And thee returning on thy silver wheels.

ALFRED, LORD TENNYSON

526 *Evening in Paradise*

Now came still Eevning on, and Twilight gray
Had in her sober Liverie all things clad;
Silence accompanied, for Beast and Bird,
They to thir grassie Couch, these to thir Nests
Were slunk, all but the wakeful Nightingale;
She all night long her amorous descant sung;
Silence was pleas'd: now glow'd the Firmament
With living Saphirs: *Hesperus* that led
The starrie Host, rode brightest, till the Moon
Rising in clouded Majestie, at length
Apparent Queen unvaild her peerless light,
And o're the dark her Silver Mantle threw.

When *Adam* thus to *Eve*: Fair Consort, th' hour
Of night, and all things now retir'd to rest
Mind us of like repose, since God hath set
Labour and rest, as day and night to men
Successive, and the timely dew of sleep
Now falling with soft slumbrous weight inclines
Our eye-lids; other Creatures all day long
Rove idle unimploid, and less need rest;
Man hath his daily work of body or mind
Appointed, which declares his Dignitie,
And the regard of Heav'n on all his waies;
While other Animals unactive range,
And of thir doings God takes no account.
To morrow ere fresh Morning streak the East
With first approach of light, we must be ris'n,
And at our pleasant labour, to reform
Yon flourie Arbors, yonder Allies green,
Our walks at noon, with branches overgrown,
That mock our scant manuring, and require

More hands then ours to lop thir wanton growth:
Those Blossoms also, and those dropping Gumms,
That lie bestrowne unsightly and unsmooth,
Ask riddance, if we mean to tread with ease;
Mean while, as Nature wills, Night bids us rest.
   To whom thus *Eve* with perfet beauty adornd.
My Author and Disposer, what thou bidst
Unargu'd I obey; so God ordains,
God is thy Law, thou mine: to know no more
Is womans happiest knowledge and her praise.
With thee conversing I forget all time,
All seasons and thir change, all please alike.
Sweet is the breath of morn, her rising sweet,
With charm of earliest Birds; pleasant the Sun
When first on this delightful Land he spreads
His orient Beams, on herb, tree, fruit, and flour,
Glistring with dew; fragrant the fertil earth
After soft showers; and sweet the coming on
Of grateful Eevning milde, then silent Night
With this her solemn Bird and this fair Moon,
And these the Gemms of Heav'n, her starrie train:
But neither breath of Morn when she ascends
With charm of earliest Birds, nor rising Sun
On this delightful land, nor herb, fruit, floure,
Glistring with dew, nor fragrance after showers,
Nor grateful Eevning mild, nor silent Night
With this her solemn Bird, nor walk by Moon,
Or glittering Starr-light without thee is sweet.
But wherfore all night long shine these, for whom
This glorious sight, when sleep hath shut all eyes?
   To whom our general Ancestor repli'd.
Daughter of God and Man, accomplisht *Eve*,
Those have thir course to finish, round the Earth,
By morrow Eevning, and from Land to Land
In order, though to Nations yet unborn,
Ministring light prepar'd, they set and rise;
Least total darkness should by Night regaine
Her old possession, and extinguish life
In Nature and all things, which these soft fires
Not only enlighten, but with kindly heate
Of various influence foment and warme,

Temper or nourish, or in part shed down
Thir stellar vertue on all kinds that grow
On Earth, made hereby apter to receive
Perfection from the Suns more potent Ray.
These then, though unbeheld in deep of night,
Shine not in vain, nor think, though men were none,
That heav'n would want spectators, God want praise;
Millions of spiritual Creatures walk the Earth
Unseen, both when we wake, and when we sleep:
All these with ceaseless praise his works behold
Both day and night: how often from the steep
Of echoing Hill or Thicket have we heard
Celestial voices to the midnight air,
Sole, or responsive each to others note
Singing thir great Creator: oft in bands
While they keep watch, or nightly rounding walk
With Heav'nly touch of instrumental sounds
In full harmonic number joind, thir songs
Divide the night, and lift our thoughts to Heaven.

JOHN MILTON

527 *True Love*

She met me, Stranger, upon life's rough way,
And lured me towards sweet Death; as Night by Day,
Winter by Spring, or Sorrow by swift Hope,
Led into light, life, peace. An antelope,
In the suspended impulse of its lightness,
Were less aethereally light: the brightness
Of her divinest presence trembles through
Her limbs, as underneath a cloud of dew
Embodied in the windless heaven of June
Amid the splendour-wingèd stars, the Moon
Burns, inextinguishably beautiful:
And from her lips, as from a hyacinth full
Of honey-dew, a liquid murmur drops,
Killing the sense with passion; sweet as stops
Of planetary music heard in trance.
In her mild lights the starry spirits dance,
The sunbeams of those wells which ever leap
Under the lightnings of the soul—too deep

For the brief fathom-line of thought or sense.
The glory of her being, issuing thence,
Stains the dead, blank, cold air with a warm shade
Of unentangled intermixture, made
By Love, of light and motion: one intense
Diffusion, one serene Omnipresence,
Whose flowing outlines mingle in their flowing,
Around her cheeks and utmost fingers glowing
With the unintermitted blood, which there
Quivers, (as in a fleece of snow-like air
The crimson pulse of living morning quiver,)
Continuously prolonged, and ending never,
Till they are lost, and in that Beauty furled
Which penetrates and clasps and fills the world;
Scarce visible from extreme loveliness.
Warm fragrance seems to fall from her light dress
And her loose hair; and where some heavy tress
The air of her own speed has disentwined,
The sweetness seems to satiate the faint wind;
And in the soul a wild odour is felt,
Beyond the sense, like fiery dews that melt
Into the bosom of a frozen bud.–
See where she stands! a mortal shape indued
With love and life and light and deity,
And motion which may change but cannot die;
An image of some bright Eternity;
A shadow of some golden dream; a Splendour
Leaving the third sphere pilotless; a tender
Reflection of the eternal Moon of Love
Under whose motions life's dull billows move;
A Metaphor of Spring and Youth and Morning;
A Vision like incarnate April, warning,
With smiles and tears, Frost the Anatomy
Into his summer grave.
           Ah, woe is me!
What have I dared? where am I lifted? how
Shall I descend, and perish not? I know
That Love makes all things equal: I have heard
By mine own heart this joyous truth averred:
The spirit of the worm beneath the sod
In love and worship, blends itself with God.
T

Spouse! Sister! Angel! Pilot of the Fate
Whose course has been so starless! O too late
Belovéd! O too soon adored by me!
For in the fields of Immortality
My spirit should at first have worshipped thine,
A divine presence in a place divine;
Or should have moved beside it on this earth,
A shadow of that substance, from its birth;
But not as now:–I love thee; yes, I feel
That on the fountain of my heart a seal
Is set, to keep its waters pure and bright
For thee, since in those *tears* thou hast delight.
We–are we not formed, as notes of music are,
For one another, though dissimilar;
Such difference without discord, as can make
Those sweetest sounds, in which all spirits shake
As trembling leaves in a continuous air?

Thy wisdom speaks in me, and bids me dare
Beacon the rocks on which high hearts are wrecked.
I never was attached to that great sect,
Whose doctrine is, that each one should select
Out of the crowd a mistress or a friend,
And all the rest, though fair and wise, commend
To cold oblivion, though it is in the code
Of modern morals, and the beaten road
Which those poor slaves with weary footsteps tread,
Who travel to their home among the dead
By the broad highway of the world, and so
With one chained friend, perhaps a jealous foe,
The dreariest and the longest journey go.

True Love in this differs from gold and clay,
That to divide is not to take away.
Love is like understanding, that grows bright,
Gazing on many truths; 'tis like thy light,
Imagination! which from earth and sky,
And from the depths of human fantasy,
As from a thousand prisms and mirrors, fills
The Universe with glorious beams, and kills
Error, the worm, with many a sun-like arrow
Of its reverberated lightning. Narrow

The heart that loves, the brain that contemplates,
The life that wears, the spirit that creates
One subject, and one form, and builds thereby
A sepulchre for its eternity.

Mind from its object differs most in this:
Evil from good; misery from happiness;
The baser from the nobler; the impure
And frail, from what is clear and must endure.
If you divide suffering and dross, you may
Diminish till it is consumed away;
If you divide pleasure and love and thought,
Each part exceeds the whole; and we know not
How much, while any yet remains unshared,
Of pleasure may be gained, of sorrow spared:
This truth is that deep well, whence sages draw
The unenvied light of hope; the eternal law
By which those live, to whom this world of life
Is as a garden ravaged, and whose strife
Tills for the promise of a later birth
The wilderness of this Elysian earth.

PERCY BYSSHE SHELLEY

528 *The City of Dreadful Night*

Of all things human which are strange and wild
    This is perchance the wildest and most strange,
And showeth man most utterly beguiled,
    To those who haunt that sunless City's range;
That he bemoans himself for aye, repeating
How Time is deadly swift, how life is fleeting,
    How naught is constant on the earth but change.

The hours are heavy on him and the days;
    The burden of the months he scarce can bear;
And often in his secret soul he prays
    To sleep through barren periods unaware,
Arousing at some longed-for date of pleasure;
Which having passed and yielded him small treasure,
    He would outsleep another term of care.

Yet in his marvellous fancy he must make
 Quick wings for Time, and see it fly from us;
This Time which crawleth like a monstrous snake,
 Wounded and slow and very venomous;
Which creeps blindwormlike round the earth and ocean,
Distilling poison at each painful motion,
 And seems condemned to circle ever thus.

And since he cannot spend and use aright
 The little time here given him in trust,
But wasteth it in weary undelight
 Of foolish toil and trouble, strife and lust,
He naturally claimeth to inherit
The everlasting Future, that his merit
 May have full scope; as surely is most just.

O length of the intolerable hours,
 O nights that are as æons of slow pain,
O Time, too ample for our vital powers,
 O Life, whose woeful vanities remain
Immutable for all of all our legions
Through all the centuries and in all the regions,
 Not of your speed and variance *we* complain.

We do not ask a longer term of strife,
 Weakness and weariness and nameless woes;
We do not claim renewed and endless life
 When this which is our torment here shall close,
An everlasting conscious inanition!
We yearn for speedy death in full fruition,
 Dateless oblivion and divine repose.

*

Large glooms were gathered in the mighty fane,
 With tinted moongleams slanting here and there;
And all was hush: no swelling organ-strain,
 No chant, no voice or murmuring of prayer;
No priests came forth, no tinkling censers fumed,
And the high altar space was unillumed.

Around the pillars and against the walls
 Leaned men and shadows; others seemed to brood
Bent or recumbent in secluded stalls.

Perchance they were not a great multitude
Save in that city of so lonely streets
Where one may count up every face he meets.

All patiently awaited the event
    Without a stir or sound, as if no less
Self-occupied, doomstricken, while attent.
    And then we heard a voice of solemn stress
From the dark pulpit, and our gaze there met
Two eyes which burned as never eyes burned yet:

Two steadfast and intolerable eyes
    Burning beneath a broad and rugged brow;
The head behind it of enormous size.
    And as black fir-groves in a large wind bow,
Our rooted congregation, gloom-arrayed,
By that great sad voice deep and full were swayed:—

O melancholy Brothers, dark, dark, dark!
O battling in black floods without an ark!
    O spectral wanderers of unholy Night!
My soul hath bled for you these sunless years,
With bitter blood-drops running down like tears:
    Oh, dark, dark, dark, withdrawn from joy and light!

My heart is sick with anguish for your bale;
Your woe hath been my anguish; yea, I quail
    And perish in your perishing unblest.
And I have searched the heights and depths, the scope
Of all our universe, with desperate hope
    To find some solace for your wild unrest.

And now at last authentic word I bring,
Witnessed by every dead and living thing;
    Good tidings of great joy for you, for all:
There is no God; no Fiend with names divine
Made us and tortures us; if we must pine,
    It is to satiate no Being's gall.

It was the dark delusion of a dream,
That living Person conscious and supreme,
    Whom we must curse for cursing us with life;

Whom we must curse because the life He gave
Could not be buried in the quiet grave,
   Could not be killed by poison or by knife.

This little life is all we must endure,
The grave's most holy peace is ever sure,
   We fall asleep and never wake again;
Nothing is of us but the mouldering flesh,
Whose elements dissolve and merge afresh
   In earth, air, water, plants, and other men.

We finish thus; and all our wretched race
Shall finish with its cycle, and give place
   To other beings, with their own time-doom:
Infinite æons ere our kind began;
Infinite æons after the last man
   Has joined the mammoth in earth's tomb and womb.

We bow down to the universal laws,
Which never had for man a special clause
   Of cruelty or kindness, love or hate:
If toads and vultures are obscene to sight,
If tigers burn with beauty and with might,
   Is it by favour or by wrath of Fate?

All substance lives and struggles evermore
Through countless shapes continually at war,
   By countless interactions interknit:
If one is born a certain day on earth,
All times and forces tended to that birth,
   Not all the world could change or hinder it.

I find no hint throughout the Universe
Of good or ill, of blessing or of curse;
   I find alone Necessity Supreme;
With infinite Mystery, abysmal, dark,
Unlighted ever by the faintest spark,
   For us the flitting shadows of a dream.

O Brothers of sad lives! they are so brief;
A few short years must bring us all relief:
   Can we not bear these years of labouring breath?

But if you would not this poor life fulfil,
Lo, you are free to end it when you will,
   Without the fear of waking after death.–

The organ-like vibrations of his voice
   Thrilled through the vaulted aisles and died away;
The yearning of the tones which bade rejoice
   Was sad and tender as a requiem lay:
Our shadowy congregation rested still
As brooding on that 'End it when you will.'

JAMES THOMSON

529 *Echoes*

Out of the night that covers me,
   Black as the Pit from pole to pole,
I thank whatever gods may be
   For my unconquerable soul.

In the fell clutch of circumstance
   I have not winced nor cried aloud.
Under the bludgeonings of chance
   My head is bloody, but unbowed.

Beyond this place of wrath and tears
   Looms but the Horror of the shade,
And yet the menace of the years
   Finds, and shall find, me unafraid.

It matters not how strait the gate,
   How charged with punishments the scroll,
I am the master of my fate:
   I am the captain of my soul.

WILLIAM ERNEST HENLEY

530 *Sonnet on Chillon*

Eternal Spirit of the chainless Mind!
   Brightest in dungeons, Liberty! thou art,
   For there thy habitation is the heart–
The heart which love of thee alone can bind;

And when thy sons to fetters are consign'd–
  To fetters, and the damp vault's dayless gloom,
  Their country conquers with their martyrdom,
And Freedom's fame finds wings on every wind.
Chillon! thy prison is a holy place,
  And thy sad floor an altar–for 'twas trod,
Until his very steps have left a trace
  Worn, as if thy cold pavement were a sod,
By Bonnivard!–May none those marks efface!
  For they appeal from tyranny to God.

GEORGE GORDON, LORD BYRON

531 *To Mars*

Mars, most-strong, gold-helm'd, making chariots crack;
Never without a shield cast on thy back.
Mind-master, town-guard, with darts never driven;
Strong-handed; all arms, fort, and fence of heaven;
Father of victory, with fair strokes given;
Joint surrogate of justice, lest she fall
In unjust strifes a tyrant; general
Only of just men justly; that dost bear
Fortitude's sceptre; to heaven's fiery sphere
Giver of circular motion, between
That and the Pleiads that still wandering been;
Where thy still-vehemently-flaming horse
About the third heaven make their fiery course;
Helper of mortals; hear! As thy fires give
The fair and present boldnesses that strive
In youth for honour, being the sweet-beam'd light
That darts into their lives, from all thy height,
The fortitudes and fortunes found in fight.
So would I likewise wish to have the power
To keep off from my head thy bitter hour,
And that false fire, cast from my soul's low kind,
Stoop to the fit rule of my highest mind.
Controlling that so eager sting of wrath
That stirs me on still to that horrid scathe
Of war; that God still sends to wreak his spleen
(Even by whole tribes) of proud injurious men.

But O thou ever-blessed! give me still
Presence of mind to put in act, my will
Varied, as fits, to all occasion;
And to live free, unforced, unwrought upon;
Beneath those laws of peace that never are
Affected with pollutions popular
Of unjust hurt, or loss to any one;
And to bear safe the burthen undergone
Of foes inflexible, and inhumane hates;
Secure from violent and harmful fates.

GEORGE CHAPMAN

532 *Auguries of Innocence*

To see a World in a Grain of Sand
And a Heaven in a Wild Flower,
Hold Infinity in the palm of your hand
And Eternity in an hour.

A Robin Red breast in a Cage
Puts all Heaven in a Rage.
A dove house fill'd with doves & Pigeons
Shudders Hell thro' all its regions.
A dog starv'd at his Master's Gate
Predicts the ruin of the State.
A Horse misus'd upon the Road
Calls to Heaven for Human blood.
Each outcry of the hunted Hare
A fibre from the Brain does tear.
A Skylark wounded in the wing,
A Cherubim does cease to sing.
The Game Cock clip'd & arm'd for fight
Does the Rising Sun affright.
Every Wolf's & Lion's howl
Raises from Hell a Human Soul.
The wild deer, wand'ring here & there,
Keeps the Human Soul from Care.
The Lamb misus'd breeds Public strife
And yet forgives the Butcher's Knife.
The Bat that flits at close of Eve
Has left the Brain that won't Believe.

The Owl that calls upon the Night
Speaks the Unbeliever's fright.
He who shall hurt the little Wren
Shall never be belov'd by Men.
He who the Ox to wrath has mov'd
Shall never be by Woman lov'd.
The wanton Boy that kills the Fly
Shall feel the Spider's enmity.
He who torments the Chafer's sprite
Weaves a Bower in endless Night.
The Catterpiller on the Leaf
Repeats to thee thy Mother's grief.
Kill not the Moth or Butterfly,
For the last Judgment draweth nigh.
He who shall train the Horse to War
Shall never pass the Polar Bar.
The Beggar's Dog & Widow's Cat,
Feed them & thou wilt grow fat.
The Gnat that sings his Summer's song
Poison gets from Slander's tongue.
The poison of the Snake & Newt
Is the sweat of Envy's Foot.
The Poison of the Honey Bee
Is the Artist's Jealousy.
The Prince's Robes & Beggar's Rags
Are Toadstools on the Miser's Bags.
A truth that's told with bad intent
Beats all the Lies you can invent.
It is right it should be so;
Man was made for Joy & Woe;
And when this we rightly know
Thro' the World we safely go.
Joy & woe are woven fine,
A Clothing for the Soul divine;
Under every grief & pine
Runs a joy with silken twine.
The Babe is more than swadling Bands;
Throughout all these Human Lands
Tools were made, & Born were hands,
Every Farmer Understands.

Every Tear from Every Eye
Becomes a Babe in Eternity;
This is caught by Females bright
And return'd to its own delight.
The Bleat, the Bark, Bellow & Roar
Are Waves that Beat on Heaven's Shore.
The Babe that weeps the Rod beneath
Writes Revenge in realms of death.
The Beggar's Rags, fluttering in Air,
Does to Rags the Heavens tear.
The Soldier, arm'd with Sword & Gun,
Palsied strikes the Summer's Sun.
The poor Man's Farthing is worth more
Than all the Gold on Afric's shore.
One Mite wrung from the Labrer's Hands
Shall buy & sell the Miser's Lands;
Or, if protected from on high,
Does that whole Nation sell & buy.
He who mocks the Infant's Faith
Shall be mock'd in Age & Death.
He who shall teach the Child to Doubt
The rotting Grave shall ne'er get out.
He who respects the Infant's faith
Triumph's over Hell & Death.
The Child's Toys & the Old Man's Reasons
Are the Fruits of the Two seasons.
The Questioner, who sits so sly,
Shall never know how to Reply.
He who replies to words of Doubt
Doth put the Light of Knowledge out.
The Strongest Poison ever known
Came from Caesar's Laurel Crown.
Nought can deform the Human Race
Like to the Armour's iron brace.
When Gold & Gems adorn the Plow
To peaceful Arts shall Envy Bow.
A Riddle or the Cricket's Cry
Is to Doubt a fit Reply.
The Emmet's Inch & Eagle's Mile
Make Lame Philosophy to smile.

He who Doubts from what he sees
Will ne'er Believe, do what you Please.
If the Sun & Moon should doubt,
They'd immediately Go out.
To be in a Passion you Good may do,
But no Good if a Passion is in you.
The Whore & the Gambler, by the State
Licenc'd, build that Nation's Fate.
The Harlot's cry from Street to Street
Shall weave Old England's winding Sheet.
The Winner's Shout, the Loser's Curse,
Dance before dead England's Hearse.
Every Night & every Morn
Some to Misery are Born.
Every Morn & every Night
Some are Born to sweet delight.
Some are Born to sweet delight,
Some are Born to endless Night.
We are led to Believe a Lie
When we see not Thro' the Eye
Which was Born in a Night to perish in a Night
When the Soul Slept in Beams of Light.
God Appears & God is Light
To those poor Souls who dwell in Night,
But does a Human Form Display
To those who Dwell in Realms of day.

WILLIAM BLAKE

533 *Under Ben Bulben*

I

Swear by what the sages spoke
Round the Mareotic Lake
That the Witch of Atlas knew,
Spoke and set the cocks a-crow.

Swear by those horsemen, by those women,
Complexion and form prove superhuman,
That pale, long visaged company
That airs in immortality

Completeness of their passions won;
Now they ride the wintry dawn
Where Ben Bulben sets the scene.

Here's the gist of what they mean.

II

Many times man lives and dies
Between his two eternities,
That of race and that of soul,
And ancient Ireland knew it all.
Whether man die in his bed
Or the rifle knocks him dead,
A brief parting from those dear
Is the worst man has to fear.
Though grave-diggers' toil is long,
Sharp their spades, their muscles strong,
They but thrust their buried men
Back in the human mind again.

III

You that Mitchell's prayer have heard
'Send war in our time, O Lord!'
Know that when all words are said
And a man is fighting mad,
Something drops from eyes long blind,
He completes his partial mind,
For an instant stands at ease,
Laughs aloud, his heart at peace,
Even the wisest man grows tense
With some sort of violence
Before he can accomplish fate,
Know his work or choose his mate.

IV

Poet and sculptor, do the work,
Nor let the modish painter shirk
What his great forefathers did,
Bring the soul of man to God,
Make him fill the cradles right.

Measurement began our might:
Forms a stark Egyptian thought,
Forms that gentler Phidias wrought.
Michelangelo left a proof
On the Sistine Chapel roof,
Where but half-awakened Adam
Can disturb globe-trotting Madam
Till her bowels are in heat,
Proof that there's a purpose set
Before the secret working mind:
Profane perfection of mankind.

Quattro-cento put in paint,
On background for a God or Saint,
Gardens where a soul's at ease;
Where everything that meets the eye,
Flowers and grass and cloudless sky,
Resemble forms that are or seem
When sleepers wake and yet still dream,
And when it's vanished still declare,
With only bed and bedstead there,
That heavens had opened.
                    Gyres run on;
When that greater dream had gone
Calvert and Wilson, Blake and Claude,
Prepared a rest for the people of God,
Palmer's phrase, but after that
Confusion fell upon our thought.

V

Irish poets, learn your trade,
Sing whatever is well made,
Scorn the sort now growing up
All out of shape from toe to top,
Their unremembering hearts and heads
Base-born products of base beds.
Sing the peasantry, and then
Hard-riding country gentlemen,
The holiness of monks, and after
Porter-drinkers' randy laughter;

Sing the lords and ladies gay
That were beaten into the clay
Through seven heroic centuries;
Cast your mind on other days
That we in coming days may be
Still the indomitable Irishry.

VI

Under bare Ben Bulben's head
In Drumcliffe churchyard Yeats is laid.
An ancestor was rector there
Long years ago, a church stands near,
By the road an ancient cross.
No marble, no conventional phrase;
On limestone quarried near the spot
By his command these words are cut:

> *Cast a cold eye*
> *On life, on death.*
> *Horseman pass by!*

WILLIAM BUTLER YEATS

534 *To the Lady Margaret, Countess of Cumberland*

He that of such a height hath built his mind,
And rear'd the dwelling of his thoughts so strong,
As neither fear nor hope can shake the frame
Of his resolved pow'rs, nor all the wind
Of vanity or malice pierce to wrong
His settled peace, or to disturb the same;
What a fair seat hath he, from whence he may
The boundless wastes and wilds of man survey.

And with how free an eye doth he look down
Upon these lower regions of turmoil!
Where all the storms of passions mainly beat
On flesh and blood; where honour, pow'r, renown
Are only gay afflictions, golden toil;
Where greatness stands upon as feeble feet
As frailty doth, and only great doth seem
To little minds, who do it so esteem.

He looks upon the mightiest Monarchs' wars
But only as on stately robberies;
Where evermore the fortune that prevails
Must be the right; the ill-succeeding mars
The fairest and the best-fac't enterprize:
Great Pirate *Pompey* lesser Pirates quails;
Justice, he sees, as if seduced, still
Conspires with pow'r, whose cause must not be ill.

He sees the face of *Right* t'appear as manifold
As are the passions of uncertain man;
Who puts it in all colours, all attires,
To serve his ends and make his courses hold;
He sees, that let Deceit work what it can,
Plot and contrive base ways to high desires;
That the all-guiding Providence doth yet
All disappoint, and mocks his smoke of wit.

Nor is he mov'd with all the thunder-cracks
Of Tyrants' threats, or with the surly brow
Of power, that proudly sits on others' crimes,
Charg'd with more crying sins than those he checks;
The storms of sad confusion, that may grow
Up in the present, for the coming times,
Appall not him, that hath no side at all
But of himself, and knows the worst can fall.

Although his heart so near allied to earth;
Cannot but pity the perplexed State
Of troublous and distrest mortality,
That thus make way unto the ugly birth
Of their own sorrows, and do still beget
Affliction upon imbecility:
Yet seeing thus the course of things must run,
He looks thereon, not strange, but as foredone.

And whilst distraught Ambition compasses
And is incompast; whil'st as craft deceives
And is deceived; whil'st man doth ransack man,
And builds on blood, and rises by distress;
And th'inheritance of desolation leaves

To great expecting hopes; he looks thereon
As from the shore of peace with unwet eye,
And bears no venture in impiety.

Thus, Madam, fares that man that hath prepar'd
A rest for his desires, and sees all things
Beneath him, and hath learn'd this book of man,
Full of the notes of frailty, and compar'd
The best of glory with her sufferings:
By whom I see you labour all you can
To plant your heart, and set your thoughts as near
His glorious mansion as your pow'rs can bear.

Which, Madam, are so soundly fashioned
By that clear judgement that hath carried you
Beyond the feeble limits of your kind,
As they can stand against the strongest head
Passion can make; inured to any hue
The world can cast; that cannot cast that mind
Out of her form of goodness, that doth see
Both what the best and worst of earth can be.

Which makes, that, whatsoever here befals
You in the region of your self remain;
Where no vain breath of th'impudent molests,
That hath secur'd within the brazen walls
Of a clear conscience, that without all stain
Rises in peace, in innocency rests;
Whilst all what malice from without procures,
Shows her own ugly heart, but hurts not yours.

And whereas none rejoice more in revenge
Than women use to do; yet you well know,
That wrong is better checkt, by being contemn'd
Than being pursu'd; leaving him t'avenge
To whom it appertains; wherein you show
How worthily your clearness hath condemn'd
Base malediction, living in the dark,
That at the rays of goodness still doth bark.

Knowing the heart of man is set to be
The centre of this world, about the which

These revolutions of disturbances
Still roll; where all th'aspects of misery
Predominate; whose strong effects are such
As he must bear, being pow'rless to redress;
And that unless above himself he can
Erect himself, how poor a thing is man!

And how turmoil'd they are, that level lie
With earth, and cannot lift themselves from thence;
That never are at peace with their desires,
But work beyond their years, and even deny
Dotage her rest, and hardly will dispense
With death: that when ability expires,
Desire lives still: so much delight they have
To carry toil and travail to the grave.

Whose ends you see, and what can be the best
They reach unto, when they have cast the sum
And reckonings of their glory; and you know
This floating life hath but this Port of rest,
A heart prepar'd, that fears no ill to come:
And that mans greatness rests but in his show;
The best of all whose days consumed are
Either in war, or peace conceiving war.

This concord, Madam, of a well-tun'd mind
Hath been so set, by that all-working hand
Of heaven, that though the world hath done his worst
To put it out, by discords most unkind;
Yet doth it still in perfect union stand
With God and man, nor ever will be forc't
From that most sweet accord, but still agree
Equal in Fortunes inequality.

And this note (Madam) of your worthiness
Remains recorded in so many hearts,
As time nor malice cannot wrong your right
In th'inheritance of Fame you must possess;
You that have built you by your great deserts,
Out of small means, a far more exquisite
And glorious dwelling for your honoured name
Than all the gold that leaden minds can frame.

SAMUEL DANIEL

535 *Lines composed a few miles above Tintern
Abbey*

*Ou revisiting the bank of the Wye during a tour,
July 13, 1798*

Five years have past; five summers, with the length
Of five long winters! and again I hear
These waters, rolling from their mountain-springs
With a soft inland murmur.–Once again
Do I behold these steep and lofty cliffs,
That on a wild secluded scene impress
Thoughts of more deep seclusion; and connect
The landscape with the quiet of the sky.
The day is come when I again repose
Here, under this dark sycamore, and view
These plots of cottage-ground, these orchard-tufts,
Which at this season, with their unripe fruits,
Are clad in one green hue, and lose themselves
'Mid groves and copses. Once again I see
These hedge-rows, hardly hedge-rows, little lines
Of sportive wood run wild: these pastoral farms,
Green to the very door; and wreaths of smoke
Sent up, in silence, from among the trees!
With some uncertain notice, as might seem
Of vagrant dwellers in the houseless woods,
Or of some Hermit's cave, where by his fire
The Hermit sits alone.

                These beauteous forms,
Through a long absence, have not been to me
As is a landscape to a blind man's eye:
But oft, in lonely rooms, and 'mid the din
Of towns and cities, I have owed to them,
In hours of weariness, sensations sweet,
Felt in the blood, and felt along the heart;
And passing even into my purer mind,
With tranquil restoration:–feelings too
Of unremembered pleasure: such, perhaps,
As have no slight or trivial influence

On that best portion of a good man's life,
His little, nameless, unremembered, acts
Of kindness and of love, Nor less, I trust,
To them I may have owed another gift,
Of aspect more sublime; that blessed mood,
In which the burthen of the mystery,
In which the heavy and the weary weight
Of all this unintelligible world,
Is lightened:–that serene and blessed mood,
In which the affections gently lead us on,–
Until, the breath of this corporeal frame
And even the motion of our human blood
Almost suspended, we are laid asleep
In body, and become a living soul:
While with an eye made quiet by the power
Of harmony, and the deep power of joy,
We see into the life of things.
                                    If this
Be but a vain belief, yet, oh! how oft–
In darkness and amid the many shapes
Of joyless daylight; when the fretful stir
Unprofitable, and the fever of the world,
Have hung upon the beatings of my heart–
How oft, in spirit, have I turned to thee,
O sylvan Wye! thou wanderer thro' the woods,
How often has my spirit turned to thee!

And now, with gleams of half-extinguished thought,
With many recognitions dim and faint,
And somewhat of a sad perplexity,
The picture of the mind revives again:
While here I stand, not only with the sense
Of present pleasure, but with pleasing thoughts
That in this moment there is life and food
For future years. And so I dare to hope,
Though changed, no doubt, from what I was when first
I came among these hills; when like a roe
I bounded o'er the mountains, by the sides
Of the deep rivers, and the lonely streams,
Wherever nature led: more like a man
Flying from something that he dreads than one

Who sought the thing he loved. For nature then
(The coarser pleasures of my boyish days,
And their glad animal movements all gone by)
To me was all in all.–I cannot paint
What then I was. The sounding cataract
Haunted me like a passion: the tall rock,
The mountain, and the deep and gloomy wood,
Their colours and their forms, were then to me
An appetite; a feeling and a love,
That had no need of a remoter charm,
By thought supplied, nor any interest
Unborrowed from the eye.–That time is past,
And all its aching joys are now no more,
And all its dizzy raptures. Not for this
Faint I, nor mourn nor murmur; other gifts
Have followed; for such loss, I would believe,
Abundant recompense. For I have learned
To look on nature, not as in the hour
Of thoughtless youth; but hearing oftentimes
The still, sad music of humanity,
Nor harsh nor grating, though of ample power
To chasten and subdue. And I have felt
A presence that disturbs me with the joy
Of elevated thoughts; a sense sublime
Of something far more deeply interfused,
Whose dwelling is the light of setting suns,
And the round ocean and the living air,
And the blue sky, and in the mind of man:
A motion and a spirit, that impels
All thinking things, all objects of all thought,
And rolls through all things. Therefore am I still
A lover of the meadows and the woods,
And mountains; and of all that we behold
From this green earth; of all the mighty world
Of eye, and ear,–both what they half create,
And what perceive; well pleased to recognise
In nature and the language of the sense
The anchor of my purest thoughts, the nurse,
The guide, the guardian of my heart, and soul
Of all my moral being.
                    Nor perchance,

If I were not thus taught, should I the more
Suffer my genial spirits to decay:
For thou art with me here upon the banks
Of this fair river; thou my dearest Friend,
My dear, dear Friend; and in thy voice I catch
The language of my former heart, and read
My former pleasures in the shooting lights
Of thy wild eyes. Oh! yet a little while
May I behold in thee what I was once,
My dear, dear Sister! and this prayer I make,
Knowing that Nature never did betray
The heart that loved her! 'tis her privilege,
Through all the years of this our life, to lead
From joy to joy: for she can so inform
The mind that is within us, so impress
With quietness and beauty, and so feed
With lofty thoughts, that neither evil tongues,
Rash judgments, nor the sneers of selfish men,
Nor greetings where no kindness is, nor all
The dreary intercourse of daily life,
Shall e'er prevail against us, or disturb
Our cheerful faith, that all which we behold
Is full of blessings. Therefore let the moon
Shine on thee in thy solitary walk;
And let the misty mountain-winds be free
To blow against thee: and, in after years,
When these wild ecstasies shall be matured
Into a sober pleasure; when thy mind
Shall be a mansion for all lovely forms,
Thy memory be as a dwelling-place
For all sweet sounds and harmonies; oh! then,
If solitude, or fear, or pain, or grief,
Should be thy portion, with what healing thoughts
Of tender joy wilt thou remember me,
And these my exhortations! Nor, perchance–
If I should be where I no more can hear
Thy voice, nor catch from thy wild eyes these gleams
Of past existence–wilt thou then forget
That on the banks of this delightful stream
We stood together; and that I, so long
A worshipper of Nature, hither came

Unwearied in that service: rather say
With warmer love–oh! with far deeper zeal
Of holier love. Nor wilt thou then forget
That after many wanderings, many years
Of absence, these steep woods and lofty cliffs,
And this green pastoral landscape, were to me
More dear, both for themselves and for thy sake!

WILLIAM WORDSWORTH

536 *To Mr. Hobbes*

Vast Bodies of Philosophy
I oft have seen, and read,
But all are Bodies dead,
Or Bodies by Art fashioned;
I never yet the Living Soul could see,
But in thy Books and thee.
'Tis only God can know
Whether the fair Idea thou dost show
Agree intirely with his own or no.
This I dare boldly tell,
'Tis so like Truth, 'twill serve our Turn as well.
Just, as in Nature, thy Proportions be,
As full of Concord their Variety,
As firm the Parts upon their Centre rest,
And all so solid are, that they at least
As much as Nature, Emptiness detest.

Long did the mighty Stagirite retain
The universal Intellectual Reign,
Saw his own Country's short-liv'd Leopard slain;
The stronger Roman-Eagle did out-fly,
Oft'ner renew'd his Age, and saw that die.
Mecca it self, in spite of Mahomet, possess'd,
And chas'd by a wild Deluge from the East,
His Monarchy new planted in the West.
But as in time each great Imperial Race
Degenerates, and gives some new one place:
So did this noble Empire waste,
Sunk by degrees from Glories past,
And in the School-men's hands it perish'd quite at last.

Then nought but Words it grew,
And those all Barb'rous too.
It perish'd, and it vanish'd there,
The Life and Soul breath'd out became but empty Air.

The Fields which answer'd well the Ancient Plow,
Spent and out-worn return no Harvest now,
In barren Age wild and unglorious lie,
   And boast of past Fertility
The poor Relief of present Poverty.
   Food and Fruit we must now want:
   Unless new Lands we plant.
We break up Tombs with Sacrilegious Hands,
   Old Rubbish we remove;
To walk in Ruins, like vain Ghosts, we love,
   And with fond Divining Wands,
      We search among the dead
      For Treasures buried,
   Whilst still the Liberal Earth does hold
So many Virgin Mines of undiscover'd Gold.

The Baltique, Euxin, and the Caspian,
And slender-limb'd Mediterranean,
Seem narrow Creeks to thee, and only fit
For the poor wretched Fisher-boats of Wit.
Thy nobler Vessel the vast Ocean tries,
      And nothing sees but Seas and Skies,
      'Till unknown Regions it descries,
Thou great Columbus of the Golden Lands of new Philosophies.
      Thy Task was harder much than his,
      For thy learn'd America is
   Not only found out first by thee,
And rudely left to future Industry,
      But thy Eloquence and Wit
Has planted, peopled, built, and civiliz'd it.

      I little thought before,
      (Nor, being my own self so poor,
      Could comprehend so vast a Store)
   That all the Wardrobe of rich Eloquence

    Could have afforded half enough,
  Of bright, of new, of lasting Stuff,
To clothe the mighty Limbs of thy gigantic Sense.
Thy solid Reason like the Shield from Heaven
    To the Trojan Hero given,
Too strong to take a Mark from any mortal Dart,
Yet shines with Gold and Gems in every Part,
And Wonders on it grav'd by the learn'd Hand of Art,
    A Shield that gives Delight
    Even to the Enemies' Sight,
Then when they're sure to lose the Combat by't.

Nor can the Snow which now cold Age does shed
    Upon thy reverend Head,
Quench or allay the noble Fires within,
    But all which thou hast been,
    And all that Youth can be, thou'rt yet,
    So fully still dost thou
Enjoy the Manhood, and the Bloom of Wit,
And all the Natural Heat, but not the Fever too.
So Contraries on Ætna's Top conspire,
Here hoary Frosts, and by them breaks out Fire.
A secure Peace the faithful Neighbours keep
Th'embolden'd Snow next to the Flames does sleep.
    And if we weigh, like thee,
    Nature, and Causes, we shall see
    That thus it needs must be.
To Things Immortal Time can do no Wrong,
And that which never is to die, for ever must be young.
                     ABRAHAM COWLEY

537 *Character of the Happy Warrior*

Who is the happy Warrior? Who is he
That every man in arms should wish to be?
—It is the generous Spirit, who, when brought
Among the tasks of real life, hath wrought
Upon the plan that pleased his boyish thought:
Whose high endeavours are an inward light
That makes the path before him always bright:

Who, with a natural instinct to discern
What knowledge can perform, is diligent to learn;
Abides by this resolve, and stops not there,
But makes his moral being his prime care;
Who, doomed to go in company with Pain,
And Fear, and Bloodshed, miserable train!
Turns his necessity to glorious gain;
In face of these doth exercise a power
Which is our human nature's highest dower;
Controls them and subdues, transmutes, bereaves
Of their bad influence, and their good receives:
By objects, which might force the soul to abate
Her feeling, rendered more compassionate;
Is placable—because occasions rise
So often that demand such sacrifice;
More skilful in self-knowledge, even more pure,
As tempted more; more able to endure,
As more exposed to suffering and distress;
Thence, also, more alive to tenderness.
—'Tis he whose law is reason; who depends
Upon that law as on the best of friends;
Whence, in a state where men are tempted still
To evil for a guard against worse ill,
And what in quality or act is best
Doth seldom on a right foundation rest,
He labours good on good to fix, and owes
To virtue every triumph that he knows:
—Who, if he rise to station of command,
Rises by open means; and there will stand
On honourable terms, or else retire,
And in himself possess his own desire;
Who comprehends his trust, and to the same
Keeps faithful with a singleness of aim;
And therefore does not stoop, nor lie in wait
For wealth, or honours, or for worldly state;
Whom they must follow; on whose head must fall,
Like showers of manna, if they come at all:
Whose powers shed round him in the common strife,
Or mild concerns of ordinary life,
A constant influence, a peculiar grace;
But who, if he be called upon to face

Some awful moment to which Heaven has joined
Great issues, good or bad for human kind,
Is happy as a Lover; and attired
With sudden brightness, like a Man inspired;
And, through the heat of conflict, keeps the law
In calmness made, and sees what he foresaw;
Or if an unexpected call succeed,
Come when it will, is equal to the need:
–He who, though thus endued as with a sense
And faculty for storm and turbulence,
Is yet a Soul whose master-bias leans
To homefelt pleasures and to gentle scenes;
Sweet images! which, whereso'er he be,
Are at his heart; and such fidelity
It is his darling passion to approve;
More brave for this, that he hath much to love:–
'Tis finally, the Man, who, lifted high,
Conspicuous object in a Nation's eye,
Or left unthought-of in obscurity,–
Who, with a toward or untoward lot,
Prosperous or adverse, to his wish or not–
Plays, in the many games of life, that one
Where what he most doth value must be won:
Whom neither shape of danger can dismay,
Nor thought of tender happiness betray;
Who, not content that former worth stand fast,
Looks forward, persevering to the last,
From well to better, daily self-surpast;
Who, whether praise of him must walk the earth
For ever, and to noble deeds give birth,
Or he must fall, to sleep without his fame,
And leave a dead unprofitable name–
Finds comfort in himself and in his cause;
And, while the mortal mist is gathering, draws
His breath in confidence of Heaven's applause:
This is the happy Warrior: this is He
That every Man in arms should wish to be.

                                    WILLIAM WORDSWORTH

538 *Strange Meeting*

It seemed that out of battle I escaped
Down some profound dull tunnel, long since scooped
Through granites which titanic wars had groined.
Yet also there encumbered sleepers groaned,
Too fast in thought or death to be bestirred.
Then, as I probed them, one sprang up, and stared
With piteous recognition in fixed eyes,
Lifting distressful hands as if to bless.
And by his smile, I knew that sullen hall,
By his dead smile I knew we stood in Hell.
With a thousand pains that vision's face was grained;
Yet no blood reached there from the upper ground,
And no guns thumped, or down the flues made moan.
'Strange friend,' I said, 'here is no cause to mourn.'
'None,' said the other, 'save the undone years,
The hopelessness. Whatever hope is yours,
Was my life also; I went hunting wild
After the wildest beauty in the world,
Which lies not calm in eyes, or braided hair,
But mocks the steady running of the hour,
And if it grieves, grieves richlier than here.
For by my glee might many men have laughed,
And of my weeping something had been left,
Which must die now. I mean the truth untold,
The pity of war, the pity war distilled.
Now men will go content with what we spoiled.
Or, discontent, boil bloody, and be spilled.
They will be swift with swiftness of the tigress,
None will break ranks, though nations trek from progress.
Courage was mine, and I had mystery,
Wisdom was mine, and I had mastery;
To miss the march of the retreating world
Into vain citadels that are not walled.
Then, when much blood had clogged their chariot-wheels
I would go up and wash them from sweet wells,
Even with truths that lie too deep for taint.
I would have poured my spirit without stint
But not through wounds; not on the cess of war.
Foreheads of men have bled where no wounds were.

I am the enemy you killed, my friend.
I knew you in this dark; for so you frowned
Yesterday through me as you jabbed and killed.
I parried; but my hands were loath and cold.
Let us sleep now. . . .'

WILFRED OWEN

539 *Demogorgon's Speech*

This is the day, which down the void abysm
At the Earth-born's spell yawns for Heaven's despotism,
    And Conquest is dragged captive through the deep:
Love, from its awful throne of patient power
In the wise heart, from the last giddy hour
    Of dread endurance, from the slippery, steep,
And narrow verge of crag-like agony, springs
And folds over the world its healing wings.

Gentleness, Virtue, Wisdom and Endurance,
These are the seals of that most firm assurance
    Which bars the pit over Destruction's strength;
And if, with infirm hand, Eternity,
Mother of many acts and hours, should free
    The serpent that would clasp her with his length;
These are the spells by which to reassume
An empire o'er the disentangled doom.

To suffer woes which Hope thinks infinite;
To forgive wrongs darker than death or night;
    To defy Power, which seems omnipotent;
To love, and bear; to hope till Hope creates
From its own wreck the thing it contemplates;
    Neither to change, nor falter, nor repent;
This, like thy glory, Titan, is to be
Good, great and joyous, beautiful and free;
This is alone Life, Joy, Empire, and Victory.

PERCY BYSSHE SHELLEY

Book VIII
METAPHYSICAL VERSE

540 *Sonnet*

Muses that sing Love's sensual empery,
   And lovers kindling your enraged fires
At Cupid's bonfires burning in the eye,
   Blown with the empty breath of vain desires,
You that prefer the painted cabinet
   Before the wealthy jewels it doth store ye,
   That all your joys in dying figures set,
   And stain the living substance of your glory,
Abjure those joys, abhor their memory,
   And let my love the honour'd subject be
   Of love, and honour's complete history;
   Your eyes were never yet let in to see
The majesty and riches of the mind,
But dwell in darkness; for your God is blind.

GEORGE CHAPMAN

541 *Sonnet—To the Critic*

Methinks I see some crooked mimic jeer,
And tax my Muse with this fantastic grace,
Turning my papers asks, What have we here?
Making withal some filthy antic face.
I fear no censure, nor what thou canst say,
Nor shall my spirit one jot of vigour lose;
Think'st thou my wit shall keep the pack-horse way
That every dudgen low invention goes?
Since sonnets thus in bundles are imprest
And every drudge doth dull our satiate ear,
Think'st thou my love shall in those rags be drest,
That every dowdy, every trull, doth wear?
   Up to my pitch no common judgement flies;
   I scorn all earthly dung-bred scarabies.

MICHAEL DRAYTON

542 *The Good-morrow*

I wonder, by my troth, what thou, and I
Did, till we lov'd? were we not wean'd till then?
But suck'd on country pleasures, childishly?
Or snorted we in the Seven Sleepers' den?
'Twas so; but this, all pleasures fancies be.
If ever any beauty I did see,
Which I desired, and got, 'twas but a dream of thee.

And now good-morrow to our waking souls,
Which watch not one another out of fear;
For love all love of other sights controls,
And makes one little room, an every where.
Let sea-discoverers to new worlds have gone;
Let maps to other, worlds on worlds have shown,
Let us possess one world, each hath one, and is one.

My face in thine eye, thine in mine appears,
And true plain hearts do in the faces rest;
Where can we find two better hemispheres
Without sharp north, without declining west?
Whatever dies, was not mix'd equally;
If our two loves be one, or thou and I
Love so alike, that none do slacken, none can die.

JOHN DONNE

543 *The Ecstasy*

Where, like a pillow on a bed,
    A pregnant bank swell'd up, to rest
The violet's reclining head,
    Sat we two, one another's best.

Our hands were firmly cimented
    By a fast balm, which thence did spring;
Our eye-beams twisted, and did thread
    Our eyes upon one double string;

So t' entergraft our hands, as yet
    Was all the means to make us one;
And pictures in our eyes to get
    Was all our propagation.

As, 'twixt two equal armies, Fate
　　Suspends uncertain victory,
Our souls (which to advance their state
　　Were gone out) hung 'twixt her, and me.

And whilst our souls negotiate there,
　　We like sepulchral statues lay;
All day, the same our postures were,
　　And we said nothing, all the day.

If any, so by love refin'd,
　　That he soul's language understood,
And by good love were grown all mind,
　　Within convenient distance stood,

He (though he knew not which soul spake,
　　Because both meant, both spake the same)
Might thence a new concoction take,
　　And part far purer than he came.

This ecstasy doth unperplex
　　(We said) and tell us what we love;
We see by this, it was not sex;
　　We see, we saw not what did move:

But as all several souls contain
　　Mixture of things, they know not what,
Love, these mix'd souls, doth mix again,
　　And makes both one, each this and that.

A single violet transplant,
　　The strength, the colour, and the size
(All which before was poor and scant)
　　Redoubles still, and multiplies.

When love with one another so
　　Interanimates two souls,
That abler soul, which thence doth flow,
　　Defects of loneliness controls.

We then, who are this new soul, know,
　　Of what we are compos'd, and made,
For th'atomies of which we grow,
　　Are souls, whom no change can invade.

But, O alas! so long, so far
   Our bodies why do we forbear?
They are ours, though not we; we are
   Th'intelligences, they the sphere.

We owe them thanks, because they thus
   Did us, to us, at first convey,
Yielded their senses' force to us,
   Nor are dross to us, but allay.

On man heaven's influence works not so,
   But that it first imprints the air;
For soul into the soul may flow,
   Though it to body first repair.

As our blood labours to beget
   Spirits, as like souls as it can,
Because such fingers need to knit
   That subtle knot, which makes us man;

So must pure lovers' souls descend
   T' affections, and to faculties,
Which sense may reach and apprehend,
   Else a great prince in prison lies.

To' our bodies turn we then, that so
   Weak men on love reveal'd may look;
Love's mysteries in souls do grow,
   But yet the body is his book.

And if some lover, such as we,
   Have heard this dialogue of one,
Let him still mark us, he shall see
   Small change when we're to bodies gone.
                         JOHN DONNE

544 *The Canonisation*

For Godsake hold your tongue, and let me love,
   Or chide my palsy, or my gout,
   My five grey hairs, or ruin'd fortune flout,

U

With wealth your state, your mind with arts improve,
  Take you a course, get you a place,
   Observe his Honour, or his Grace,
Or the king's real, or his stamped face
  Contemplate; what you will, approve,
   So you will let me love.

Alas! alas! who's injur'd by my love?
  What merchant's ship have my sighs drown'd?
  Who says my tears have overflow'd his ground?
When did my colds a forward spring remove?
   When did the heats which my veins fill
   Add one more to the plaguy bill?
Soldiers find wars, and lawyers find out still
  Litigious men, which quarrels move,
  Though she and I do love.

Call us what you will, we are made such by love;
  Call her one, me another fly,
  We're tapers too, and at our own cost die,
And we in us find th'eagle and the dove.
   The phoenix riddle hath more wit
   By us; we two being one, are it;
So, to one neutral thing both sexes fit.
  We die and rise the same, and prove
  Mysterious by this love.

We can die by it, if not live by love,
  And if unfit for tomb or hearse
  Our legend be, it will be fit for verse;
And if no piece of chronicle we prove,
   We'll build in sonnets pretty rooms;
   As well a well-wrought urn becomes
The greatest ashes, as half-acre tombs,
  And by these hymns all shall approve
  Us canonised for love:

And thus invoke us, 'You whom reverend love
  Made one another's hermitage;
  You, to whom love was peace, that now is rage;

Who did the whole world's soul contract, and drove
      Into the glasses of your eyes
       (So made such mirrors, and such spies,
That they did all to you epitomise)
    Countries, towns, courts: Beg from above
    A pattern of your love!'

JOHN DONNE

545 *Madrigal*

My thoughts hold mortal strife;
I do detest my life,
And with lamenting cries,
Peace to my soul to bring,
Oft call that prince which here doth monarchise;
But he, grim-grinning king,
Who caitives scorns, and doth the blest surprise,
    Late having deckt with beauty's rose his tomb,
    Disdains to crop a weed, and will not come.

WILLIAM DRUMMOND

546 *Sonnet*

My lute, be as thou wast when thou didst grow
With thy green mother in some shady grove,
When immelodious winds but made thee move,
And birds on thee their ramage did bestow.
Sith that dear voice which did thy sounds approve,
Which us'd in such harmonious strains to flow,
Is reft from earth to tune those spheres above,
What art thou but a harbinger of woe?
Thy pleasing notes be pleasing notes no more,
But orphan wailings to the fainting ear,
Each stop a sigh, each sound draws forth a tear!
Be therefore silent as in woods before,
    Or if that any hand to touch thee deign,
    Like widow'd turtle, still her loss complain.

WILLIAM DRUMMOND

547 *Fair summer droops*

Fair summer droops, droop men and beasts therefore;
So fair a summer look for never more!
All good things vanish less than in a day,
Peace, plenty, pleasure, suddenly decay.
      Go not yet away, bright soul of the sad year,
      The earth is hell when thou leav'st to appear.

What, shall those flowers that decked thy garland erst,
Upon thy grave be wastefully dispersed?
O trees, consume your sap in sorrow's source;
Streams, turn to tears your tributary course.
      Go not yet hence, bright soul of the sad year,
      The earth is hell when thou leav'st to appear.
                      THOMAS NASHE

548 *The Grasshopper*
To my Noble Friend, Mr Charles Cotton

Oh thou that swing'st upon the waving hair
    Of some well-filled Oaten Beard,
Drunk ev'ry night with a Delicious tear
    Dropt thee from Heav'n, where now th'art rear'd.

The Joys of Earth and Air are thine intire,
    That with thy feet and wings dost hop and fly;
And when thy Poppy works thou dost retire
    To thy Carv'd Acorn-bed to lie.

Up with the Day, the Sun thou welcom'st then,
    Sport'st in the gilt-plats of his Beams,
And all these merry days mak'st merry men,
    Thy self, and Melancholy streams.

But ah the Sickle! Golden Ears are Cropt;
    Ceres and *Bacchus* bid good night;
Sharp frosty fingers all your Flowr's have topt,
    And what scythes spar'd, Winds shave off quite.

Poor verdant fool! and now green Ice! thy Joys
    Large and as lasting, as thy Perch of Grass,
Bid us lay in 'gainst Winter, Rain, and poise
    Their floods, with an o'erflowing glass.

Thou best of *Men* and *Friends*! we will create
    A genuine Summer in each other's breast;
And spite of this cold time and frozen Fate
    Thaw us a warm seat to our rest.

Our sacred hearths shall burn eternally
    As Vestal Flames, the North-wind, he
Shall strike his frost-stretch'd Wings, dissolve and fly
    This *Ætna* in Epitome.

Dropping *December* shall come weeping in,
    Bewail th'usurping of his Reign;
But when in show'rs of old Greeke we begin,
    Shall cry, he hath his Crown again!

Night as clear *Hesper* shall our Tapers whip
    From the light Casements where we play,
And the dark Hag from her black mantle strip,
    And stick there everlasting Day.

Thus richer than untempted Kings are we,
    That asking nothing, nothing need:
Though Lord of all what Seas embrace; yet he
    That wants himself, is poor indeed.

RICHARD LOVELACE

549 *On Shakespeare*

What needs my Shakespear for his honour'd Bones
The labour of an age in piled Stones,
Or that his hallow'd reliques should be hid
Under a Star-ypointing Pyramid?
Dear son of memory, great heir of Fame,
What need'st thou such weak witness of thy name!
Thou in our wonder and astonishment
Hast built thy self a live-long Monument.

For whilst, to th' shame of slow-endeavouring art,
Thy easie numbers flow, and that each heart
Hath from the leaves of thy unvalu'd Book
Those Delphick lines with deep impression took,
Then thou our fancy of it self bereaving,
Dost make us marble with too much conceiving;
And so Sepulcher'd in such pomp dost lie,
That Kings for such a Tomb would wish to die.

JOHN MILTON

550 *So tir'd are all my thoughts*

So tir'd are all my thoughts, that, sense and spirits fail:
Mourning I pine, and know not what I ail.
O what can yield ease to a mind
        Joy in nothing that can find?

How are my powers fore-spoke? What strange distaste is this?
Hence, cruel hate of that which sweetest is:
Come, come delight, make my dull brain
        Feel once heat of joy again.

The lover's tears are sweet, their mover makes them so;
Proud of a wound the bleeding soldiers grow.
Poor I alone, dreaming endure
        Grief that knows nor cause, nor cure.

And whence can all this grow? even from an idle mind,
That no delight in any good can find.
Action alone makes the soul blest:
        Virtue dies with too much rest.

THOMAS CAMPION

551 *Follow thy fair sun, unhappy shadow*

Follow thy fair sun, unhappy shadow,
Though thou be black as night,
And she made all of light,
Yet follow thy fair sun, unhappy shadow.

Follow her whose light thy light depriveth,
Though here thou liv'st disgrac't,
And she in heaven is plac't,
Yet follow her whose light the world reviveth.

Follow those pure beams whose beauty burneth,
That so have scorched thee,
As thou still black must be,
Till her kind beams thy black to brightness turneth.

Follow her while yet her glory shineth:
There comes a luckless night,
That will dim all her light;
And this the black unhappy shade divineth.

Follow still since so thy fates ordained;
The Sun must have his shade,
Till both at once do fade,
The Sun still proud, the shadow still disdained.

THOMAS CAMPION

552 *I lost the love of heaven*

I lost the love of heaven above,
  I spurned the lust of earth below,
I felt the sweets of fancied love,
  And hell itself my only foe.

I lost earth's joys, but felt the glow
  Of heaven's flame abound in me,
Till loveliness and I did grow
  The bard of immortality.

I loved, but woman fell away;
  I hid me from her faded flame.
I snatched the sun's eternal ray
  And wrote till earth was but a name.

In every language upon earth,
  On every shore, o'er every sea,
I gave my name immortal birth
  And kept my spirit with the free.

JOHN CLARE

553 *Dirge*

Chor.	Glories, pleasures, pomps, delights, and ease, Can but please The outward senses, when the mind Is or untroubl'd or by peace refin'd.
1st Voice	Crowns may flourish and decay, Beauties shine, but fade away.
2nd Voice	Youth may revel, yet it must Lie down in a bed of dust.
3rd Voice	Earthly honours flow and waste, Time alone doth change and last.
Chor.	Sorrows mingl'd with contents prepare Rest for care; Love only reigns in death; though art Can find no comfort for a broken heart.

JOHN FORD

554 *Koré*

Yea, she hath passed hereby and blessed the sheaves
And the great garths and stacks and quiet farms,
And all the tawny and the crimson leaves,
Yea, she hath passed with poppies in her arms
Under the star of dusk through stealing mist
And blest the earth and gone while no man wist.

With slow reluctant feet and weary eyes
And eyelids heavy with the coming sleep,
With small breasts lifted up in stress of sighs,
She passed as shadows pass amid the sheep
While the earth dreamed and only I was 'ware
Of that faint fragrance blown from her soft hair.

The land lay steeped in peace of silent dreams,
There was no sound amid the sacred boughs
Nor any mournful music in her streams,
Only I saw the shadow on her brows,
Only I knew her for the Yearly Slain
And wept, and weep until she come again.

EZRA POUND

555 *From 'In Memoriam'*

Lo, as a dove when up she springs
    To bear thro' Heaven a tale of woe,
    Some dolorous message knit below
The wild pulsation of her wings;

Like her I go; I cannot stay;
    I leave this mortal ark behind,
    A weight of nerves without a mind,
And leave the cliffs, and haste away

O'er ocean-mirrors rounded large,
    And reach the glow of southern skies,
    And see the sails at distance rise,
And linger weeping on the marge,

And saying; 'Comes he thus, my friend?
    Is this the end of all my care?'
    And circle moaning in the air:
' Is this the end? Is this the end?'

And forward dart again, and play
    About the prow, and back return
    To where the body sits, and learn
That I have been an hour away.

                  *

The Danube to the Severn gave
    The darken'd heart that beat no more;
    They laid him by the pleasant shore,
And in the hearing of the wave.

There twice a day the Severn fills;
    The salt sea-water passes by,
    And hushes half the babbling Wye,
And makes a silence in the hills.

The Wye is hush'd nor moved along,
    And hush'd my deepest grief of all,
    When fill'd with tears that cannot fall,
I brim with sorrow drowning song.

The tide flows down, the wave again
    Is vocal in its wooded walls;
    My deeper anguish also falls,
And I can speak a little then.

*

Oh yet we trust that somehow good
    Will be the final goal of ill,
    To pangs of nature, sins of will,
Defects of doubt, and taints of blood;

That nothing walks with aimless feet;
    That not one life shall be destroy'd,
    Or cast as rubbish to the void,
When God hath made the pile complete;

That not a worm is cloven in vain;
    That not a moth with vain desire
    Is shrivell'd in a fruitless fire,
Or but subserves another's gain.

Behold, we know not anything;
    I can but trust that good shall fall
    At last—far off—at last, to all,
And every winter change to spring.

So runs my dream: but what am I?
    An infant crying in the night:
    An infant crying for the light:
And with no language but a cry.

*

The wish, that of the living whole
    No life may fail beyond the grave,
    Derives it not from what we have
The likest God within the soul?

Are God and Nature then at strife,
    That Nature lends such evil dreams?
    So careful of the type she seems,
So careless of the single life;

That I, considering everywhere
>   Her secret meaning in her deeds,
>   And finding that of fifty seeds
She often brings but one to bear,

I falter where I firmly trod,
>   And falling with my weight of cares
>   Upon the great world's altar-stairs
That slope thro' darkness up to God,

I stretch lame hands of faith, and grope,
>   And gather dust and chaff, and call
>   To what I feel is Lord of all,
And faintly trust the larger hope.

*

'So careful of the type?' but no.
>   From scarped cliff and quarried stone
>   She cries, 'A thousand types are gone:
I care for nothing, all shall go.

'Thou makest thine appeal to me:
>   I bring to life, I bring to death:
>   The spirit does but mean the breath:
I know no more.' And he, shall he,

Man, her last work, who seem'd so fair,
>   Such splendid purpose in his eyes,
>   Who roll'd the psalm to wintry skies,
Who built him fanes of fruitless prayer,

Who trusted God was love indeed
>   And love Creation's final law—
>   Tho' Nature, red in tooth and claw
With ravine, shriek'd against his creed—

Who loved, who suffer'd countless ills,
>   Who battled for the True, the Just,
>   Be blown about the desert dust,
Or seal'd within the iron hills?

No more? A monster then, a dream,
　　A discord. Dragons of the prime,
　　That tare each other in their slime,
Were mellow music match'd with him.

O life as futile, then, as frail!
　　O for thy voice to soothe and bless!
　　What hope of answer, or redress?
Behind the veil, behind the veil.

•

When on my bed the moonlight falls,
　　I know that in thy place of rest
　　By that broad water of the west,
There comes a glory on the walls:

Thy marble bright in dark appears,
　　As slowly steals a silver flame
　　Along the letters of thy name,
And o'er the number of thy years.

The mystic glory swims away;
　　From off my bed the moonlight dies;
　　And closing eaves of wearied eyes
I sleep till dusk is dipt in gray:

And then I know the mist is drawn
　　A lucid veil from coast to coast,
　　And in the dark church like a ghost
Thy tablet glimmers to the dawn.

•

By night we linger'd on the lawn,
　　For underfoot the herb was dry;
　　And genial warmth; and o'er the sky
The silvery haze of summer drawn;

And calm that let the tapers burn
　　Unwavering: not a cricket chirr'd:
　　The brook alone far-off was heard,
And on the board the fluttering urn:

And bats went round in fragrant skies,
    And wheel'd or lit the filmy shapes
    That haunt the dusk, with ermine capes
And woolly breasts and beaded eyes;

While now we sang old songs that peal'd
    From knoll to knoll, where, couch'd at ease,
    The white kine glimmer'd, and the trees
Laid their dark arms about the field.

But when those others, one by one,
    Withdrew themselves from me and night,
    And in the house light after light
Went out, and I was all alone,

A hunger seized my heart; I read
    Of that glad year which once had been,
    In those fall'n leaves which kept their green,
The noble letters of the dead:

And strangely on the silence broke
    The silent-speaking words, and strange
    Was love's dumb cry defying change
To test his worth; and strangely spoke

The faith, the vigour, bold to dwell
    On doubts that drive the coward back,
    And keen thro' wordy snares to track
Suggestion to her inmost cell.

So word by word, and line by line,
    The dead man touch'd me from the past,
    And all at once it seem'd at last
The living soul was flash'd on mine,

And mine in his was wound, and whirl'd
    About empyreal heights of thought,
    And came on that which is, and caught
The deep pulsations of the world,

Æonian music measuring out
    The steps of Time–the shocks of Chance–
    The blows of Death. At length my trance
Was cancell'd, stricken thro' with doubt.

Vague words! but ah, how hard to frame
    In matter-moulded forms of speech,
    Or ev'n for intellect to reach
Thro' memory that which I became:

Till now the doubtful dusk reveal'd
    The knolls once more where, couch'd at ease,
    The white kine glimmer'd, and the trees
Laid their dark arms about the field:

And suck'd from out the distant gloom
    A breeze began to tremble o'er
    The large leaves of the sycamore,
And fluctuate all the still perfume,

And gathering freshlier overhead,
    Rock'd the full-foliaged elms, and swung
    The heavy-folded rose, and flung
The lilies to and fro, and said

'The dawn, the dawn,' and died away;
    And East and West, without a breath,
    Mixt their dim lights, like life and death,
To broaden into boundless day.

                    ALFRED, LORD TENNYSON

556 *Stanzas to* —

Well, some may hate, and some may scorn,
    And some may quite forget thy name;
But my sad heart must ever mourn
    Thy ruined hopes, thy blighted fame!
'Twas thus I thought, an hour ago,
    Even weeping o'er that wretch's woe;
One word turned back my gushing tears,
And lit my altered eye with sneers.

Then, 'Bless the friendly dust,' I said,
'That hides thy unlamented head!
Vain as thou wert, and weak as vain,
The slave of Falsehood, Pride, and Pain–
My heart has nought akin to thine;
Thy soul is powerless over mine.'
But these were thoughts that vanished too:
Unwise, unholy, and untrue:
Do I despise the timid deer,
Because his limbs are fleet with fear?
Or, would I mock the wolf's death-howl,
Because his form is gaunt and foul?
Or, hear with joy the leveret's cry,
Because it cannot bravely die?
No! Then above his memory
Let Pity's heart as tender be;
Say, 'Earth lie lightly on that breast,
And, kind Heaven, grant that spirit rest!'

EMILY BRONTË

557 *Stanzas*

I'll not weep that thou art going to leave me,
    There's nothing lovely here;
And doubly will the dark world grieve me,
    While thy heart suffers there.

I'll not weep, because the summer's glory
    Must always end in gloom;
And, follow out the happiest story–
    It closes with a tomb!

And I am weary of the anguish
    Increasing winters bear;
Weary to watch the spirit languish
    Through years of dead despair.

So, if a tear, when thou art dying,
    Should haply fall from me,
It is but that my soul is sighing,
    To go and rest with thee.

EMILY BRONTË

558 *The Death of Richard Wagner*

The world's great heart, whence all things strange and rare
Take form and sound, that each inseparate part
May bear its burden in all tuned thoughts that share
    The world's great heart—

The fountain forces, whence like steeds that start
Leap forth the powers of earth and fire and air,
Seas that revolve and rivers that depart—

Spake, and were turned to song: yea, all they were,
With all their works, found in his mastering art
Speech as of powers whose uttered word laid bare
    The world's great heart.

           ALGERNON CHARLES SWINBURNE

559 *The Bourne*

Underneath the growing grass,
   Underneath the living flowers,
   Deeper than the sound of showers:
   There we shall not count the hours
By the shadows as they pass.

Youth and health will be but vain,
   Beauty reckoned of no worth:
   There a very little girth
   Can hold round what once the earth
Seemed too narrow to contain.

           CHRISTINA ROSSETTI

560 *Ternissa! you are fled*

Ternissa! you are fled!
I say not to the dead,
But to the happy ones who rest below:
   For surely, surely, where
   Your voice and graces are,
Nothing of death can any feel or know.
   Girls who delight to dwell
   Where grows most asphodel,

Gather to their calm breasts each word you speak:
    The mild Persephone
    Places you on her knee,
And your cool palm smoothes down stern Pluto's cheek.
                    WALTER SAVAGE LANDOR

561 *The Appeal*

If grief for grief can touch thee,
    If answering woe for woe,
If any ruth can melt thee,
    Come to me now!

I cannot be more lonely,
    More drear I cannot be!
My worn heart throbs so wildly,
    'Twill break for thee.

And when the world despises,
    When Heaven repels my prayer,
Will not mine angel comfort?
    Mine idol hear?

Yes, by the tears I've poured thee,
    By all my hours of pain,
Oh, I shall surely win thee,
    Beloved, again!
                    EMILY BRONTË

562 *Brooding Grief*

A yellow leaf from the darkness
Hops like a frog before me—
—Why should I start and stand still?

I was watching the woman that bore me
Stretched in the brindled darkness
Of the sick-room, rigid with will
To die—
And the quick leaf tore me
Back to this rainy swill
Of leaves and lamps and traffic mingled before me.
                    DAVID HERBERT LAWRENCE

563 *Prayer for Forbearance*

Loërd, thou clepedest me
and I not ne answerëd thee
But wordës slow and sleepy:
'Thole [1] yet! Thole a little!'
But 'yiet' and 'yiet' was endëless,
and 'thole a little' a long way is.

ANON

564 *Sonnet*

Remember me when I am gone away,
　Gone far away into the silent land;
　　When you can no more hold me by the hand,
Nor I half turn to go yet turning stay.
Remember me when no more day by day
　You tell me of our future that you planned:
　Only remember me; you understand
It will be late to counsel then or pray.
Yet if you should forget me for a while
　And afterwards remember, do not grieve:
　For if the darkness and corruption leave
　A vestige of the thoughts that once I had,
Better by far you should forget and smile
　Than that you should remember and be sad.

CHRISTINA ROSSETTI

565 *Sleep not, dream not*

Sleep not, dream not; this bright day
Will not, cannot last for aye;
Bliss like thine is bought by years
Dark with torment and with tears.

Sweeter far than placid pleasure;
Purer, higher beyond measure;
Yet, alas! the sooner turning
Into hopeless, endless mourning ...

EMILY BRONTË

[1] bear with me

566 *Adieu! farewell earth's bliss*

Adieu! farewell earth's bliss!
This world uncertain is:
Fond are life's lustful joys,
Death proves them all but toys.
None from his darts can fly:
I am sick, I must die.
      Lord, have mercy on us!

Rich men, trust not in wealth!
Gold cannot buy your health;
Physic himself must fade;
All things to end are made;
The plague full swift goes by:
I am sick, I must die.
      Lord, have mercy on us!

Beauty is but a flower
Which wrinkles will devour:
Brightness falls from the air;
Queens have died young and fair;
Dust hath closed Helen's eye:
I am sick, I must die.
      Lord, have mercy on us!

Strength stoops unto the grave,
Worms feed on Hector brave,
Swords may not fight with fate,
Earth still holds ope her gate.
Come, come, the bells do cry,
I am sick, I must die.
      Lord, have mercy on us!

Wit with his wantonness
Tasteth death's bitterness:
Hell's executioner
Hath no ears for to hear
What vain art can reply:
I am sick, I must die.
      Lord, have mercy on us!

Haste, therefore, each degree
To welcome destiny:
Heaven is our heritage,
Earth but a player's stage:
Mount we unto the sky.
I am sick, I must die.
  Lord, have mercy on us!
     THOMAS NASHE

567 *Autumn*

Autumn hath all the summer's fruitful treasure;
Gone is our sport, fled is poor Croyden's pleasure.
Short days, sharp days, long nights come on apace:
Ah, who shall hide us from the winter's face?
Cold doth increase, the sickness will not cease,
And here we lie, God knows, with little ease.
 From winter, plague and pestilence, good Lord, deliver us!

London doth mourn, Lambeth is quite forlorn;
Trades cry, woe worth that ever they were born!
The want of term, is town and city's harm;
Close chambers we do want to keep us warm.
Long banished must we live from our friends:
This low-built house will bring us to our ends.
 From winter, plague and pestilence, good Lord, deliver us!
     THOMAS NASHE

568 *Discipline*

Throw away thy rod,
Throw away thy wrath:
 O my God,
Take the gentle path.

For my heart's desire
Unto thine is bent:
 I aspire
To a full consent.

Not a word or look
I affect to own,
        But by book,
And thy book alone.

Though I fail, I weep:
Though I halt in pace,
        Yet I creep
To the throne of grace.

Then let wrath remove;
Love will do the deed:
        For with love
Stony hearts will bleed.

Love is swift on foot;
Love's a man of war,
        And can shoot,
And can hit from far.

Who can scape his bow?
That which wrought on thee,
        Brought thee low,
Needs must work on me.

Throw away thy rod;
Though man frailties hath,
        Thou art God:
        Throw away thy wrath.

                                GEORGE HERBERT

569 *From 'The Marriage of Heaven and Hell'*

RINTRAH roars & shakes his fires in the burden'd air;
Hungry clouds swag on the deep.

Once meek, and in a perilous path,
The just man kept his course along
The vale of death.
Roses are planted where thorns grow,
And on the barren heath
Sing the honey bees.

Then the perilous path was planted,
And a river and a spring
On every cliff and tomb,
And on the bleached bones
Red clay brought forth;

Till the villain left the paths of ease,
To walk in perilous paths, and drive
The just man into barren climes.

Now the sneaking serpent walks
In mild humility,
And the just man rages in the wilds
Where lions roam.

Rintrah roars & shakes his fires in the burden'd air;
Hungry clouds swag on the deep.

WILLIAM BLAKE

570 *The Pontoon Bridge Miracle*

Prophets, preaching in new stars,
Have come in ships of sleep
And built a ghostly pontoon bridge that Michigan Avenue
Can keep.
Have built a causeway bright with sails
Where hares and tortoises may creep,
Where burbling bullfinches, laughing hyenas, whinnying
    Shetlands
Climb the steep.

Oh the harp-song of our sand-dunes
Up this arching avenue,
Oh the voices in the prophet-sails
Oh the lovers strolling slowly, two and two!

Though every Yankee patents some iron animals at last,
And does invent his own World's Fair,
And World's Fair tunes to cheer the air,
This is wild America, not orderly Timbuctoo.
So Barnum's old procession holds proud Michigan Avenue,

Again moves by up the pontoon bridge
To the Prophet Avenue.
The thought goes again through the night so dark,
Going up to the North-star ark,
Ostriches two and two,
Kangaroos, two and two, behemoths two and two,
Hippogriffs two and two, chimeras two and two.

Oh Radio, Oh Saxophone, Oh Slide Trombone, Oh Horns
   that moan:–
The lion, the lion, goes roaring from his cage,
Ten thousand years before your jazz he roared a deeper rage.
And Jumbo, great Jumbo, goes swaying left and right,
Ten thousand years before your jazz his trumpet shook the
   night.
But Jenny Lind outsings him still upon the heaven-born wind,
Stands up in Barnum's carriage on that bridge across the vast,
That pontoon span of comet-boats arching above the past,
That silvery bridge of dawn across the cold.
In the rigging of their ships the prophets old
Sing with her their songs across the cold.

So, come let us forget our ivory-towers, brothers,
Come let us be bold with our songs.

VACHEL LINDSAY

571 *The Passionate Man's Pilgrimage*
Supposed to be Written by One at the Point of Death

Give me my Scallop shell of quiet,
My staff of Faith to walk upon,
My Scrip of Joy, Immortal diet,
My bottle of salvation:
My Gown of Glory, hopes true gage,
And thus I'll take my pilgrimage.

Blood must be my body's balmer,
No other balm will there be given
Whilst my soul like a white Palmer
Travels to the land of heaven,
Over the silver mountains,
Where spring the Nectar fountains:

And there I'll kiss
The Bowl of bliss,
And drink my eternal fill
On every milken hill.
My soul will be a-dry before,
But after it, will ne'er thirst more.

And by the happy blissful way
More peaceful Pilgrims I shall see,
That have shook off their gowns of clay,
And go apparell'd fresh like me.
I'll bring them first
To slake their thirst,
And then to taste those Nectar suckets
At the clear wells
Where sweetness dwells,
Drawn up by Saints in Chrystal buckets.

And when our bottles and all we,
Are fill'd with immortality:
Then the holy paths we'll travel
Strew'd with Rubies thick as gravel,
Ceilings of Diamonds, Sapphire floors,
High walls of Coral and Pearl Bow'rs.

From thence to heaven's Bribeless hall
Where no corrupted voices brawl,
No Conscience molten into gold,
Nor forg'd accusers bought and sold,
No cause deferr'd, nor vain spent Journey,
For there Christ is the Kings Attorney:
Who pleads for all without degrees,
And he hath Angels, but no fees.

When the grand twelve million Jury,
Of our sins with sinful fury,
'Gainst our souls' black verdicts give,
Christ pleads his death, and then we live,
Be thou my speaker, taintless pleader,
Unblotted Lawyer, true proceeder,
Thou movest salvation even for alms:
Not with a bribed Lawyer's palms.

And this is my eternal plea,
To him that made Heaven, Earth and Sea,
Seeing my flesh must die so soon,
And want a head to dine next noon,
Just at the stroke when my veins start and spread
Set on my soul an everlasting head.
Then am I ready like a palmer fit,
To tread those blest paths which before I writ.

SIR WALTER RALEIGH

572 *The End Which Comes*

Then did Siddârtha raise his eyes, and see
Fast pacing towards the river-brink a band
Of wailing people; foremost one who swung
An earthen bowl with lighted coals; behind
The kinsmen, shorn, with mourning marks, ungirt,
Crying aloud, 'O Rama, Rama, Hear!
Call upon Rama, brothers;' next the bier,
Knit of four poles with bamboos interlaced,
Whereon lay–stark and stiff, feet foremost, lean,
Chapfallen, sightless, hollow-flanked, a-grin,
Sprinkled with red and yellow dust–the Dead,
Whom at the four-went ways they turned head first,
And crying 'Rama, Rama!' carried on
To where a pile was reared beside the stream:
Thereon they laid him, building fuel up–
Good sleep hath one that slumbers on that bed!
He shall not wake for cold, albeit he lies
Naked to all the airs–for soon they set
The red flame to the corners four, which crept,
And licked, and flickered, finding out his flesh
And feeding on it with swift hissing tongues,
And crackle of parched skin, and snap of joint;
Till the fat smoke thinned and the ashes sank
Scarlet and grey, with here and there a bone
White midst the grey–the total of the man.

Then spake the Prince: 'Is this the end which comes
To all who live?'

'This is the end that comes
To all,' quoth Channa; 'he upon that pyre–
Whose remnants are so petty that the crows
Caw hungrily, then quit the fruitless feast–
Ate, drank, laughed, loved, and lived, and liked life well.
Then came–who knows?–some gust of jungle wind,
A stumble on the path, a taint in the tank,
A snake's nip, half a span of angry steel,
A chill, a fishbone, or a falling tile,
And life was over and the man is dead.
No appetites, no pleasures, and no pains
Hath such; the kiss upon his lips is nought,
The fire-scorch nought; he smelleth not his flesh
A-roast, nor yet the sandal and the spice
They burn; the taste is emptied from his mouth,
The hearing of his ears is clogged, the sight
Is blinded in his eyes; those whom he loved
Wail desolate, for even that must go,
The body which was lamp unto the life,
Or worms will have a horrid feast of it.
Here is the common destiny of flesh:
The high and low, the good and bad, must die,
And then, 'tis taught, begin anew and live
Somewhere, somehow–who knows?–and so again
The pangs, the parting, and the lighted pile:–
Such is man's round.'
                    But lo! Siddârtha turned
Eyes gleaming with divine tears to the sky,
Eyes lit with heavenly pity to the earth;
From sky to earth he looked, from earth to sky,
As if his spirit sought in lonely flight
Some far-off vision, linking this and that,
Lost–past–but searchable, but seen, but known.
Then cried he, while his lifted countenance
Glowed with the burning passion of a love
Unquenchable, the ardour of a hope
Boundless, insatiate: 'Oh! suffering world;
Oh! known and unknown of my common flesh,
Caught in the common net of death and woe,
And life which binds to both! I see, I feel
The vastness of the agony of earth,

The vainness of its joys, the mockery
Of all its best, the anguish of its worst;
Since pleasures end in pain, and youth in age,
And love in loss, and life in hateful death,
And death in unknown lives, which will but yoke
Men to their wheel again to whirl the round
Of false delights and woes that are not false.
Me too this lure hath cheated, so it seemed
Lovely to live, and life a sunlit stream
For ever flowing in a changeless peace;
Whereas the foolish ripple of the flood
Dances so lightly down by bloom and lawn
Only to pour its crystal quicklier
Into the foul salt sea. The veil is rent
Which blinded me! I am as all these men
Who cry upon their gods and are not heard,
Or are not heeded—yet there must be aid!
For them and me and all there must be help!
Perchance the gods have need of help themselves,
Being so feeble that when sad lips cry
They cannot save! I would not let one cry
Whom I could save! How can it be that Brahm
Would make a world and keep it miserable,
Since, if, all-powerful, he leaves it so,
He is not good, and if not powerful,
He is not God?—Channa! lead home again!
It is enough! mine eyes have seen enough!'

Which when the King heard, at the gates he set
A triple guard; and bade no man should pass
By day or night, issuing or entering in,
Until the days were numbered of that dream.

SIR EDWIN ARNOLD

573 *Nox nocti indicat Scientiam*

When I survey the bright
        Cœlestial sphere:
So rich with jewels hung, that night
Doth like an Æthiop bride appear.

My soul her wings doth spread
And heaven-ward flies,
Th'Almighty's Mysteries to read
In the large volume of the skies.

For the bright firmament
Shoots forth no flame
So silent, but is eloquent
In speaking the Creator's name.

No unregarded star
Contracts its light
Into so small a Character,
Remov'd far from our human sight:

But if we stedfast look,
We shall discern
In it as in some holy book,
How man may heavenly knowledge learn.

It tells the Conqueror,
That far-stretcht pow'r
Which his proud dangers traffic for,
Is but the triumph of an hour.

That from the farthest North,
Some Nation may
Yet undiscovered issue forth,
And o'er his new got conquest sway.

Some Nation yet shut in
With hills of ice
May be let out to scourge his sin
'Till they shall equal him in vice.

And then they likewise shall
Their ruin have,
For as your selves your Empires fall,
And every Kingdom hath a grave.

Thus those Cœlestial fires,
            Though seeming mute,
The fallacy of our desires
With all the pride of life confute.

For they have watcht since first
            The World had birth:
And found sin in itself accurst,
And nothing permanent on earth.

WILLIAM HABINGTON

574 *The Aspiration*

How long, great God, how long must I
            Immur'd in this dark prison lie;
Where at the grates and avenues of sense,
My soul must watch to have intelligence;
Where but faint gleams of Thee salute my sight,
Like doubtful moonshine in a cloudy night:
            When shall I leave this magic sphere,
            And be all mind, all eye, all ear?

How cold this clime! And yet my sense
            Perceives e'en here Thy influence.
E'en here Thy strong magnetic charms I feel,
And pant and tremble like the amorous steel.
To lower good, and beauties less divine,
Sometimes my erroneous needle does decline,
            But yet, so strong the sympathy,
            It turns, and points again to Thee.

I long to see this excellence
            Which at such distance strikes my sense.
My impatient soul struggles to disengage
Her wings from the confinement of her cage.
Wouldst thou, great Love, this prisoner once set free,
How would she hasten to be link'd to Thee!
            She'd for no angels' conduct stay,
            But fly, and love-on, all the way.

JOHN NORRIS

575 *The Saving God*

Down in the depth of mine iniquity,
That ugly centre of infernal spirits,
Where each sin feels her own deformity,
In these peculiar torments she inherits,
　Depriv'd of human graces, and divine,
　Even there appears this *saving God* of mine.

And in this fatal mirrour of transgression,
Shews man as fruit of his degeneration,
The errour's ugly infinite impression,
Which bears the faithless down to desperation;
　Depriv'd of humane graces and divine,
　Even there appears this *saving God* of mine.

In power and truth, Almighty and eternal,
Which on the sin reflects strange desolation,
With glory scourging all the Spirits infernal,
And uncreated hell with unprivation;
　Depriv'd of humane graces, not divine,
　Even there appears this *saving God* of mine.

For on this spiritual Cross condemned lying,
To pains infernal by eternal doom,
I see my Saviour for the same sins dying,
And from that hell I fear'd, to free me come;
　Depriv'd of humane graces, not divine,
　Thus hath his death rais'd up this soul of mine.

FULKE GREVILLE, LORD BROOKE

576 *Death the Leveller*

The glories of our blood and state
　Are shadows, not substantial things;
There is no armour against fate;
　Death lays his icy hand on kings:
　　Sceptre and crown
　　Must tumble down,
And in the dust be equal made
With the poor crooked scythe and spade.

Some men with swords may reap the field,
    And plant fresh laurels where they kill:
But their strong nerves at last must yield;
    They tame but one another still:
        Early or late
        They stoop to fate,
And must give up their murmuring breath
When they, pale captives, creep to death.

The garlands wither on your brow;
    Then boast no more your mighty deeds;
Upon Death's purple altar now
    See, where the victor-victim bleeds.
        Your heads must come
        To the cold tomb:
Only the actions of the just
Smell sweet, and blossom in their dust.
JAMES SHIRLEY

577 *Christ's Triumph over Death*

So down the silver streams of Eridan,
On either side bank't with a lily wall,
Whiter than both, rides the triumphant Swan,
And sings his dirge, and prophesies his fall,
Diving into his wat'ry funeral:
    But Eridan to Cedron must submit
    His flow'ry shore, nor can he envy it,
If when Apollo sings, his swans do silent sit.

That heav'nly voice I more delight to hear,
Than gentle airs to breathe, or swelling waves
Against the sounding rocks their bosoms tear,
Or whistling reeds, that rutty Jordan laves,
And with their verdure his white head embraves,
    To chide the winds, or hiving bees, that fly
    About the laughing blooms of sallowie,
Rocking asleep the idle grooms that lazy lie.

And yet, how can I hear thee singing go,
When men incens'd with hate, thy death foreset?
Or else, why do I hear thee sighing so,

When thou, inflam'd with love, their life dost get?
That Love, and hate, and sighs, and songs are met;
   But thus, and only thus thy love did crave,
   To send thee singing for us to thy grave,
While we sought thee to kill, and thou sought'st us to save.

When I remember Christ our burden bears,
I look for glory, but find misery;
I look for joy, but find a sea of tears;
I look that we should live, and find him die;
I look for Angels' songs, and hear him cry:
   Thus what I look, I cannot find so well,
   Or rather, what I find, I cannot tell,
These banks so narrow are, those streams so highly swell.

Christ suffers, and in this, his tears begin,
Suffers for us, and our joy springs in this,
Suffers to death, here is his Manhood seen,
Suffers to rise, and here his Godhead is.
For Man, that could not by himself have ris,
   Out of the grave doth by the Godhead rise,
   And God, that could not die, in Manhood dies,
That we in both might live, by that sweet sacrifice.

Go giddy brains, whose wits are thought so fresh,
Pluck all the flo[w'r]s that Nature forth doth throw,
Go stick them on the cheeks of wanton flesh;
Poor idol, (forc't at once to fall and grow)
Of fading roses, and of melting snow:
   Your songs exceed your matter, this of mine,
   The matter, which it sings, shall make divine,
As stars dull puddles gild, in which their beauties shine.

Who doth not see drown'd in Deucalion's name,
(When earth his men, and sea had lost his shore)
Old Noah; and in Nisus' lock, the fame
Of Sampson yet alive; and long before
In Phaethon's, mine own fall I deplore:
   But he that conquer'd hell, to fetch again
   His virgin widow, by a serpent slain,
Another Orpheus was then dreaming poets feign.

That taught the stones to melt for passion,
And dormant sea, to hear him, silent lie,
And at his voice, the wat'ry nation
To flock, as if they deem'd it cheap, to buy
With their own deaths his sacred harmony:
   The while the waves stood still to hear his song,
   And steady shore wav'd with the reeling throng
Of thirsty souls, that hung upon his fluent tongue.
GILES FLETCHER

578 *Christ's Triumph After Death*

Had I a voice of steel to tune my song,
Were every verse as smoothly fil'd as glass,
And every member turned to a tongue,
And every tongue were made of sounding brass,
Yet all that skill, and all this strength, alas,
   Should it presume to gild, were misadvis'd,
   The place, where David hath new songs devis'd,
As in his burning throne he sits emparadis'd.

Most happy Prince, whose eyes those stars behold,
Treading ours under feet, now mayst thou powre
That overflowing skill, wherewith of old
Thou wont'st to comb rough speech, now mayst thou show'r
Fresh streams of praise upon that holy bower,
   Which well we heaven call, not that it rolls,
   But that it is the haven of our souls.
Most happy Prince, whose sight so heav'nly sight beholds.

Ah foolish Shepherds, that were wont esteem,
Your God all rough, and shaggy-hair'd to be;
And yet far wiser Shepherds than ye deem,
For who so poor (though who so rich) as he,
When, with us hermiting in low degree,
   He wash't his flocks in Jordan's spotless tide,
   And, that his dear remembrance aye might bide,
Did to us come, and with us liv'd, and for us died?

But now so lively colours did embeam
His sparkling forehead, and so shiny rays
Kindled his flaming locks; that down did stream
In curls, along his neck, where sweetly plays

X

(Singing his wounds of love in sacred lays)
  His dearest Spouse, Spouse of the dearest Lover,
  Knitting a thousand knots over, and over,
And dying still for love, but they her still recover.

Fair Egliset, that at his eyes doth dress
Her glorious face, those eyes, from whence are shed
Infinite belamóurs, where to express
His love, high God all heav'n as captive leads,
And all the banners of his grace dispreads,
  And in those windows, doth his arms englaze,
  And on those eyes, the Angels all do gaze,
And from those eyes, the lights of heav'n do glean their blaze.

But let the Kentish lad, that lately taught
His oaten reed the trumpet's silver sound,
Young Thyrsilis, and for his music brought
The willing spheres from heav'n, to lead a round
Of dancing Nymphs, and Herds, that sung, and crown'd
  Eclecta's hymen with ten thousand flow'rs
  Of choicest praise, and hung her heav'nly bow'rs
With saffron garlands, drest for Nuptial Paramours,

Let his shrill trumpet, with her silver blast,
Of faire Eclecta, and her Spousal bed,
Be the sweet pipe, and smooth Encomiast:
But my green Muse, hiding her younger head
Under old Chamus' flaggy banks, that spread
  Their willow locks abroad, and all the day
  With their own wat'ry shadows' wanton play,
Dares not those high amours, and love-sick songs assay.

Impotent words, weak side, that strive in vain,
In vain, alas, to tell so heav'nly sight,
So heav'nly sight, as none can greater feign,
Feign what he can, that seems of greatest might,
  Might any yet compare with Infinite?
  Infinite sure those joys, my words but light,
Light is the palace where she dwells. O blessed wight!
                     GILES FLETCHER

579 *The Ship of Death*

I

Now it is autumn and the falling fruit
and the long journey towards oblivion.
The apples falling like great drops of dew
to bruise themselves an exit from themselves.

And it is time to go, to bid farewell
to one's own self, and find an exit
from the fallen self.

II

Have you built your ship of death, O have you?
O build your ship of death, for you will need it.

The grim frost is at hand, when the apples will fall
thick, almost thundrous, on the hardened earth.

And death is on the air like a smell of ashes!
Ah! can't you smell it?
And in the bruised body, the frightened soul
finds itself shrinking, wincing from the cold
that blows upon it through the orifices.

III

And can a man his own quietus make
with a bare bodkin?

With daggers, bodkins, bullets, man can make
a bruise or break of exit for his life;
but is that a quietus, O tell me, is it quietus?

Surely not so! for how could murder, even self-murder,
ever a quietus make?

IV

O let us talk of quiet that we know,
that we can know, the deep and lovely quiet
of a strong heart at peace!

How can we this, our own quietus, make?

V

Build then the ship of death, for you must take
the longest journey, to oblivion.

And die the death, the long and painful death
that lies between the old self and the new.

Already our bodies are fallen, bruised, badly bruised,
already our souls are oozing through the exit
of the cruel bruise.

Already the dark and endless ocean of the end
is washing in through the breaches of our wounds,
already the flood is upon us.

O build your ship of death, your little ark
and furnish it with food, with little cakes, and wine
for the dark flight down oblivion.

VI

Piecemeal the body dies, and the timid soul
has her footing washed away, as the dark flood rises.

We are dying, we are dying, we are all of us dying
and nothing will stay the death-flood rising within us
and soon it will rise on the world, on the outside world.

We are dying, we are dying, piecemeal our bodies are dying
and our strength leaves us,
and our soul cowers naked in the dark rain over the flood,
cowering in the last branches of the tree of our life.

VII

We are dying, we are dying, so all we can do
is now to be willing to die, and to build the ship
of death to carry the soul on the longest journey.

A little ship, with oars and food
and little dishes, and all accoutrements
fitting and ready for the departing soul.

Now launch the small ship, now as the body dies
and life departs, launch out, the fragile soul
in the fragile ship of courage, the ark of faith
with its store of food and little cooking pans
and change of clothes,
upon the flood's black waste
upon the waters of the end
upon the sea of death, where still we sail
darkly, for we cannot steer, and have no port.

There is no port, there is nowhere to go
only the deepening blackness darkening still
blacker upon the soundless, ungurgling flood
darkness at one with darkness, up and down
and sideways utterly dark, so there is no direction any more
and the little ship is there; yet she is gone.
She is not seen, for there is nothing to see her by.
She is gone! gone! and yet
somewhere she is there.
Nowhere.

VIII

And everything is gone, the body is gone
completely under, gone, entirely gone.
The upper darkness is heavy as the lower,
between them the little ship
is gone

It is the end, it is oblivion

IX

And yet out of eternity a thread
separates itself on the blackness,
a horizontal thread
that fumes a little with pallor upon the dark.

Is it illusion? or does the pallor fume
A little higher?
Ah wait, wait, for there's the dawn,
the cruel dawn of coming back to life
out of oblivion

Wait, wait, the little ship
drifting, beneath the deathly ashy grey
of a flood-dawn.

Wait, wait! even so, a flush of yellow
and strangely, O chilled wan soul, a flush of rose.

A flush of rose, and the whole thing starts again.

X

The flood subsides, and the body, like a worn sea-shell
emerges strange and lovely.
And the little ship wings home, faltering and lapsing
on the pink flood,
and the frail soul steps out, into the house again
filling the heart with peace.

Swings the heart renewed with peace
even of oblivion.

Oh build your ship of death. Oh build it!
for you will need it.
For the voyage of oblivion awaits you.

D. H. Lawrence

580 *Vigil strange I kept on the field one night*

Vigil strange I kept on the field one night;
When you, my son and my comrade, dropt at my side that day,
One look I but gave which your dear eyes return'd with a look
    I shall never forget,
One touch of your hand to mine, O boy, reach'd up as you lay
    on the ground,
Then onward I sped in the battle, the even-contested battle,
Till late in the night reliev'd to the place at last again I made
    my way,
Found you in death so cold, dear comrade, found your body,
    son of responding kisses (never again on earth responding),
Bared your face in the starlight, curious the scene, cool blew
    the moderate night-wind,

Long there and then in vigil I stood, dimly around me the
   battle-field spreading,
Vigil wondrous and vigil sweet there in the fragrant silent night,
But not a tear fell, not even a long-drawn sigh, long, long I gazed,
Then on the earth partially reclining sat by your side leaning
   my chin in my hands,
Passing sweet hours, immortal and mystic hours with you,
   dearest comrade—not a tear, not a word,
Vigil of silence, love and death, vigil for you, my son and my
   soldier,
As onward silently stars aloft, eastward new ones upward stole,
Vigil final for you, brave boy (I could not save you, swift was
   your death,
I faithfully loved you and cared for you living, I think we
   shall surely meet again),
Till at latest lingering of the night, indeed just as the dawn
   appear'd,
My comrade I wrapt in his blanket, envelop'd well his form,
Folded the blanket well, tucking it carefully over head and
   carefully under feet,
And there and then and bathed by the rising sun, my son in
   his grave, in his rude-dug grave I deposited,
Ending my vigil strange with that, vigil of night and battle-
   field dim,
Vigil for boy of responding kisses (never again on earth
   responding),
Vigil for comrade swiftly slain, vigil I never forget, how as day
   brighten'd,
I rose from the chill ground and folded my soldier well in his
   blanket,
And buried him where he fell.

WALT WHITMAN

581 *If I could shut the gate*

If I could shut the gate against my thoughts
   And keep out sorrow from this room within,
Or memory could cancel all the notes
   Of my misdeeds, and I unthink my sin:

How free, how clear, how clean my soul should lie,
Discharg'd of such a loathsome company!

Or were there other rooms without my heart
That did not to my conscience join so near,
Where I might lodge the thoughts of sin apart
That I might not their clam'rous crying hear;
What peace, what joy, what ease should I possess,
Freed from their horrors that my soul oppress!

But, O my Saviour, who my refuge art,
Let thy dear mercies stand 'twixt them and me,
And be the wall to separate my heart
So that I may at length repose me free;
That peace, and joy, and rest may be within,
And I remain divided from my sin.

ANON

582 *Holy Sonnet*

This is my play's last scene; here heavens appoint
My pilgrimage's last mile; and my race
Idly, yet quickly run, hath this last pace;
My span's last inch, my minutes' latest point;
And gluttonous death will instantly unjoint
My body and soul, and I shall sleep a space;
But my'ever-waking part shall see that face,
Whose fear already shakes my every joint.
Then, as my soul, to'heaven her first seat, takes flight,
And earth-born body, in the earth shall dwell,
So fall my sins, that all may have their right,
To where they'are bred, and would press me, to hell.
Impute me righteous, thus purg'd of evil,
For thus I leave the world, the flesh, the devil.

JOHN DONNE

583 *A Hymn to God the Father*

Wilt Thou forgive that sin where I begun,
Which was my sin, though it were done before?

Wilt Thou forgive that sin, through which I run,
  And do run still, though still I do deplore?
    When Thou hast done, Thou hast not done,
      For I have more.

Wilt Thou forgive that sin which I have won
  Others to sin, and made my sin their door?
Wilt Thou forgive that sin which I did shun
  A year, or two: but wallowed in, a score?
    When Thou hast done, Thou hast not done,
      For I have more.

I have a sin of fear, that when I have spun
  My last thread, I shall perish on the shore;
But swear by Thy self, that at my death Thy Son
  Shall shine as he shines now, and heretofore;
    And, having done that, Thou hast done;
      I fear no more.

JOHN DONNE

584 *Holy Sonnet*

Death, be not proud, though some have called thee
Mighty and dreadful, for, thou art not so;
For those, whom thou think'st, thou dost overthrow,
Die not, poor Death, nor yet canst thou kill me.
From rest and sleep, which but thy picture, be,
Much pleasure, then from thee, much more must flow,
And soonest our best men with thee do go,
Rest of their bones, and soul's delivery.
Thou art slave to Fate, Chance, kings, and desperate men,
And dost with poison, war, and sickness dwell,
And poppy, or charms can make us sleep as well,
And better than thy stroke; why swell'st thou then?
One short sleep past, we wake eternally,
And Death shall be no more; Death, thou shalt die.

JOHN DONNE

585 *In the Glorious Assumption of Our Blessed Lady*

THE HYMN

Hark! she is call'd, the parting hour is come;
Take thy farewell, poor World, Heaven must go home.
A piece of heav'nly earth, purer and brighter
Than the chaste stars, whose choice lamps come to light
    her
Whilst through the crystal orbs, clearer than they
She climbs, and makes a far more Milky Way.
She's call'd! Hark, how the dear immortal dove
Sighs to his silver mate: Rise up, my love!
Rise up, my fair, my spotless one,
The winter's past, the rain is gone,
  The spring is come, the flow'rs appear,
No sweets (save thou) are wanting here.
         Come away, my love,
         Come away, my dove,
            Cast off delay;
          The court of heav'n is come
          To wait upon thee home;
            Come, come away.
  The flowers appear,
Or quickly would, wert thou once here.
The spring is come, or if it stay
'Tis to keep time with thy delay.
The rain is gone, except so much as we
Detain in needful tears to weep the want of thee.
          The winter's past,
          Or if he make less haste
His answer is, why she does so,
If summer come not, how can winter go?
          Come away, come away!
The shrill winds chide, the waters weep thy stay;
The fountains murmur; and each loftiest tree
Bows low'st his leafy top, to look for thee.
          Come away, my love,
          Come away, my dove, etc.

She's call'd again. And will she go?
When heav'n bids come, who can say no?
Heaven calls her, and she must away,
Heav'n will not, and she cannot, stay.
Go then, go glorious.
    On the golden wings
Of the bright youth of Heav'n, that sings
Under so sweet a burthen.   Go,
Since thy dread son will have it so:
And while thou goest, our song and we
Will, as we may, reach after thee.
Hail, Holy Queen of humble hearts!
We in thy praise will have our parts.
And though thy dearest looks must now give light
To none but the blest heavens, whose bright
Beholders, lost in sweet delight,
Feed for ever their fair sight
With those divinest eyes, which we
And our dark world no more shall see.
Though our poor eyes are parted so,
Yet shall our lips never let go
Thy gracious name, but to the last,
Our loving song shall hold it fast.
    Thy precious name shall be
    Thyself to us; and we
      With holy care will keep it by us,
        We to the last
        Will hold it fast,
And no Assumption shall deny us.
    All the sweetest showers
    Of our fairest flowers
    Will we strow upon it.
Though our sweets cannot make
It sweeter, they can take
Themselves new sweetness from it.

Mary, men and angels sing,
Maria Mother of our King.
Live rosy Princess, live, and may the bright
Crown of a most incomparable light

Embrace thy radiant brows. O may the best
Of everlasting joys bathe thy white breast.
Live our chaste love, the holy mirth
Of heaven, the humble pride of earth.
Live crown of women, queen of men,
Live mistress of our song; and when
Our weak desires have done their best,
Sweet angels come, and sing the rest.

RICHARD CRASHAW

586 *Regeneration*

A Ward, and still in bonds, one day
          I stole abroad,
It was high-spring, and all the way
          Primros'd and hung with shade;
          Yet, was it frost within,
                And surly winds
Blasted my infant buds, and sin
          Like Clouds eclips'd my mind.

Storm'd thus; I straight perceiv'd my spring
          Meer stage, and show,
My walk a monstrous, mountain'd thing
          Rough-cast with Rocks, and snow;
          And as a Pilgrim's Eye
                Far from relief,
Measures the melancholy sky
          Then drops, and rains for grief,

So sigh'd I upwards still, at last
          'Twixt steps, and falls
I reach'd the pinacle, where plac'd
          I found a pair of scales,
          I took them up and laid
                In th'one late pains,
The other smoke, and pleasures weigh'd
          But prov'd the heavier grains;

With that, some cried, *Away*; straight I
        Obey'd, and led
Full East, a fair, fresh field could spy
        Some call'd it, *Jacobs Bed*;
        A Virgin-soil, which no
        Rude feet ere trod,
Where (since he stept there,) only go
        Prophets, and friends of God.

Here, I repos'd; but scarce well set,
        A grove descried
Of stately height, whose branches met
        And mixt on every side;
        I entered, and once in
        (Amaz'd to see't,)
Found all was chang'd, and a new spring
        Did all my senses greet;

The unthrift Sun shot vital gold
        A thousand pieces,
And heaven its azure did unfold
        Checqur'd with snowy fleeces,
        The air was all in spice
        And every bush
A garland wore; Thus fed my eyes
        But all the Ear lay hush.

Only a little Fountain lent
        Some use for Ears,
And on the dumb shades language spent
        The Music of her tears;
        I drew her near, and found
        The Cistern full
Of divers stones, some bright, and round
        Others ill-shap'd, and dull.

The first (pray mark,) as quick as light
        Danc'd through the flood,
But, th'last more heavy than the night
        Nail'd to the Center stood;

I wonder'd much, but tir'd
    At last with thought,
My restless Eye that still desir'd
    As strange an object brought;

It was a bank of flowers, where I descried
    (Though 'twas mid-day,)
Some fast asleep, other broad-eyed
    And taking in the Ray,
    Here musing long, I heard
    A rushing wind
Which still increas'd, but whence it stirr'd
    No where I could not find;

I turn'd me round, and to each shade
    Dispatch'd an Eye,
To see, if any leaf had made
    Least motion, or Reply,
    But while I list'ning sought
    My mind to ease
By knowing, where 'twas, or where not,
    It whisper'd; *Where I please.*
Lord, then said I, *On me one breath,*
And let me die before my death!

Cant. Cap. 5. ver. 17.

Arise O north, and come thou South-wind, and blow upon my
garden, that the spices thereof may flow out.

                    HENRY VAUGHAN

587 *Holy Sonnet*

At the round earth's imagin'd corners blow
Your trumpets, angels, and arise, arise
From death, you numberless infinities
Of souls, and to your scatter'd bodies go,

All whom the flood did, and fire shall o'erthrow,
All whom war, dearth, age, agues, tyrannies,
Despair, law, chance, hath slain, and you whose eyes
Shall behold God, and never taste death's woe.
But let them sleep, Lord, and me mourn a space;
For, if above all these my sins abound,
'Tis late to ask abundance of Thy grace,
When we are there. Here on this lowly ground,
Teach me how to repent, for that's as good
As if Thou hadst seal'd my pardon with Thy blood.

JOHN DONNE

588 *Hymn to God, my God, in my Sickness*

Since I am coming to that Holy room,
    Where, with thy quire of saints for evermore,
I shall be made Thy Music; as I come
    I tune the instrument here at the door,
    And what I must do then, think here before;

Whilst my physicians by their love are grown
    Cosmographers, and I their map, who lie
Flat on this bed, that by them may be shown
    That this is my south-west discovery,
    Per fretum febris, by these straits to die;

I joy, that in these straits, I see my west;
    For, though their currents yield return to none,
What shall my west hurt me? As west and east
    In all flat maps (and I am one) are one,
    So death doth touch the Resurrection.

Is the Pacific sea my home? Or are
    The eastern riches? Is Jerusalem?
Anyan, and Magellan, and Gibraltar?
    All straits, and none but straits, are ways to them
    Whether where Japhet dwelt, or Cham, or Sem.

We think that Paradise and Calvary,
  Christ's cross and Adam's tree, stood in one place;
Look, Lord, and find both Adams met in me;
  As the first Adam's sweat surrounds my face,
  May the last Adam's blood my soul embrace.

So, in His purple wrapp'd, receive me Lord;
  By these His thorns, give me His other crown;
And as to others' souls I preach'd thy word,
  Be this my text, my sermon to mine own,
  Therefore that He may raise, the Lord throws down.

JOHN DONNE

589   *A Lyke-wake Dirge*

This ae night, this ae night,
  Every night and all,
Fire and fleet and candle light,
  And Christ receive thy soul.

When thou from hence away art past,
  Every night and all,
To Whinny-Muir thou com'st at last:
  And Christ receive thy soul.

If ever thou gavest hosen and shoon,
  Every night and all,
Sit thee down and put them on;
  And Christ receive thy soul.

If hosen and shoon thou ne'er gavst none
  Every night and all,
The whins shall prick thee to the bare bone;
  And Christ receive thy soul.

From Whinny-Muir when thou may'st pass,
  Every night and all,
To Brig o' Dread thou com'st at last;
  And Christ receive thy soul.

From Brig o' Dread when thou may'st pass,
Every night and all,
To Purgatory fire thou com'st at last;
And Christ receive thy soul.

If ever thou gavest meat or drink,
Every night and all,
The fire shall never make thee shrink;
And Christ receive thy soul.

If meat or drink thou ne'er gavst none,
Every night and all,
The fire will burn thee to the bare bone;
And Christ receive thy soul.

This ae night, this ae night,
Every night and all,
Fire and fleet and candle light,
And Christ receive thy soul.

ANON

590 *For the Baptist*

The last and greatest herald of heaven's King,
Girt with rough skins, hies to the deserts wild,
Among that savage brook the woods forth bring,
Which he than man more harmless found and mild:
His food was locusts, and what young doth spring,
With honey that from virgin hives distill'd;
Parch'd body, hollow eyes, some uncouth thing
Made him appear, long since from earth exil'd.
There burst he forth: 'All ye, whose hopes rely
On God, with me amidst these deserts mourn;
Repent, repent, and from old errors turn.'
Who listen'd to his voice, obey'd his cry?
    Only the echoes, which he made relent,
    Rung from their marble caves, 'Repent, repent!'
WILLIAM DRUMMOND

591　*Auras of Delight*

Beautiful habitations, auras of delight!
Who shall bewail the crags and bitter foam
And angry sword-blades flashing left and right
Which guard your glittering height,
That none thereby may come!
The vision which we have
Revere we so,
That yet we crave
To foot those fields of ne'er profaned snow?
　　　I, with heart-quake,
Dreaming or thinking of that realm of Love,
See, oft, a dove
Tangled in frightful nuptials with a snake;
The tortured knot,
Now, like a kite scant-weighted, flung bewitch'd
Sunwards, now pitch'd,
Tail over head, down, but with no taste got
Eternally
Of rest in either ruin or the sky,
But bird and vermin each incessant strives,
With vain dilaceration of both lives,
'Gainst its abhorred bond insoluble,
Coveting fiercer any separate hell
Than the most weary Soul in Purgatory
On God's sweet breast to lie.
And, in this sign, I con
The guerdon of that golden Cup, fulfill'd
With fornications foul of Babylon,
The heart where good is well-perceiv'd and known,
Yet is not will'd;
And Him I thank, who can make live again,
The dust, but not the joy we once profane,
That I, of ye,
Beautiful habitations, auras of delight,
In childish years and since had sometime sense and sight,
But that ye vanish'd quite,
Even from memory,
Ere I could get my breath, and whisper 'See!'
　　　But did for me

They altogether die,
Those trackless glories glimps'd in upper sky?
Were they of chance, or vain,
Nor good at all again
For curb of heart or fret?
Nay, though, by grace,
Lest, haply, I refuse God to His face,
Their likeness wholly I forget,
Ah, yet,
Often in straits which else for me were ill,
I mind me still
I *did* respire the lonely auras sweet,
I *did* the blest abodes behold, and, at the mountains' feet,
Bathed in the holy Stream by Hermon's thymy hill.

COVENTRY PATMORE

592 *For the Magdalene*

These eyes, dear Lord, once brandons of desire,
Frail scouts betraying what they had to keep,
Which their own heart, then others set on fire,
Their trait'rous black before thee here out-weep:
These locks, of blushing deeds the fair attire,
Smooth-frizzled waves, sad shelves which shadow deep,
Soul-stinging serpents in gilt curls which creep,
To touch thy sacred feet do now aspire.
In seas of care behold a sinking bark,
By winds of sharp remorse unto thee driven,
O! let me not expos'd be ruin's mark;
My faults confest, Lord, say they are forgiven.
    Thus sigh'd to Jesus the Bethanian fair,
    His tear-wet feet still drying with her hair.

WILLIAM DRUMMOND

593 *A Hymn, to the Name and Honour of the Admirable St. Teresa*

Foundress of the Reformation of the discalced Carmelites, both men and women; a woman for angelical height of specula- tion, for masculine courage of performance more than a woman; who yet a child outran maturity, and durst plot a martyrdom.

Misericordias Domini in Æternum Cantabo.

THE HYMN

Love, thou art absolute sole lord
Of life and death. To prove the word
We'll now appeal to none of all
Those thy old soldiers, great and tall,
Ripe men of martyrdom, that could reach down,
With strong arms, their triumphant crown;
Such as could with lusty breath,
Speak loud into the face of Death
Their great Lord's glorious Name, to none
Of those whose spacious bosoms spread a throne
For Love at large to fill: spare blood and sweat;
And see him take a private seat,
Making his mansion in the mild
And milky soul of a soft child.

  Scarce has she learnt to lisp the name
Of martyr; yet she thinks it shame
Life should so long play with that breath
Which spent can buy so brave a death.
She never undertook to know
What Death with Love should have to do;
Nor has she e'er yet understood
Why to show love, she should shed blood,
Yet though she cannot tell you why,
She can love, and she can die.

  Scarce has she blood enough to make
A guilty sword blush for her sake;
Yet has she a heart dares hope to prove
How much less strong is death than love.

    Be love but there; let poor six years
Be pos'd with the maturest fears
Man trembles at, you straight shall find
Love knows no nonage, nor the mind.
'Tis love, not years or limbs that can
Make the martyr, or the man.

    Love toucht her heart, and lo it beats
High, and burns with such brave heats;
Such thirsts to die, as dares drink up
A thousand cold deaths in one cup.
Good reason; for she breathes all fire;
Her white breast heaves with strong desire
Of what she may, with fruitless wishes
Seek for amongst her mother's kisses.

    Since 'tis not to be had at home
She'll travel to a martyrdom.
No home for hers confesses she
But where she may a martyr be.

    She'll to the Moors; and trade with them
For this unvalued diadem:
She'll offer them her dearest breath,
With Christ's name in't, in change for death.
She'll bargain with them; and will give
Them God, teach them how to live
In him: or, if they this deny,
For him she'll teach them how to die.
So shall she leave amongst them sown
Her Lord's blood, or at least her own.

    Farewell then, all the World! Adieu.
Teresa is no more for you.
Farewell, all pleasures, sports, and joys,
(Never till now esteemed toys)
Farewell, whatever dear may be,
Mother's arms or father's knee:
Farewell house, and farewell home!
She's for the Moors, and martyrdom.

    Sweet, not so fast! lo, thy fair Spouse
Whom thou seek'st with so swift vows,
Calls thee back, and bids thee come
T'embrace a milder martyrdom.

Blest powers forbid, thy tender life
Should bleed upon a barbarous knife;
Or some base hand have power to rase
Thy breast's chaste cabinet, and uncase
A soul kept there so sweet: O no,
Wise Heaven will never have it so.
Thou art Love's victim; and must die
A death more mystical and high.
Into Love's arms thou shalt let fall
A still-surviving funeral.
His is the dart must make the death
Whose stroke shall taste thy hallow'd breath;
A dart thrice dipp'd in that rich flame
Which writes thy Spouse's radiant Name
Upon the roof of Heaven; where aye
It shines, and with a sovereign ray
Beats bright upon the burning faces
Of souls which in that name's sweet graces
Find everlasting smiles: so rare,
So spiritual, pure, and fair
Must be th'immortal instrument
Upon whose choice point shall be sent
A life so lov'd: and that there be
Fit executioners for thee,
The fair'st and first-born sons of fire,
Blest seraphim, shall leave their quire,
And turn Love's soldiers, upon thee
To exercise their archery.

O how oft shalt thou complain
Of a sweet and subtle pain:
Of intolerable joys:
Of a death, in which who dies
Loves his death, and dies again,
And would for ever so be slain.
And lives, and dies; and knows not why
To live, but that he thus may never leave to die.

How kindly will thy gentle heart
Kiss the sweetly-killing dart!
And close in his embraces keep
Those delicious wounds, that weep

Balsam to heal themselves with. Thus
When these thy deaths, so numerous,
Shall all at last die into one,
And melt thy soul's sweet mansion;
Like a soft lump of incense, hasted
By too hot a fire, and wasted
Into perfuming clouds, so fast
Shalt thou exhale to Heaven at last
In a resolving sigh, and then
O what? Ask not the tongues of men.
Angels cannot tell; suffice
Thyself shalt feel thine own full joys,
And hold them fast for ever. There
So soon as thou shalt first appear,
The moon of maiden stars, thy white
Mistress, attended by such bright
Souls as thy shining self, shall come
And in her first ranks make thee room;
Where 'mongst her snowy family
Immortal welcomes wait for thee;
      O what delight, when reveal'd Life shall stand,
And teach thy lips heav'n with his hand;
On which thou now may'st to thy wishes
Heap up thy consecrated kisses.
What joys shall seize thy soul, when she,
Bending her blessed eyes on thee,
(Those second smiles of heav'n) shall dart
Her mild rays through thy melting heart!
      Angels, thy old friends, there shall greet thee,
Glad at their own home now to meet thee.
      All thy good works which went before
And waited for thee, at the door,
Shall own thee there; and all in one
Weave a constellation
Of crowns, with which the King thy spouse
Shall build up thy triumphant brows.
      All thy old woes shall now smile on thee
And thy pains sit bright upon thee
All thy sorrows here shall shine,
All thy sufferings be divine.

Tears shall take comfort, and turn gems,
And wrongs repent to diadems.
Ev'n thy deaths shall live; and new
Dress the soul that erst they slew.
Thy wounds shall blush to such bright scars
As keep account of the Lamb's wars.

    Those rare works where thou shalt leave writ
Love's noble history, with wit
Taught thee by none but him, while here
They feed our souls, shall clothe thine there.
Each heav'nly word, by whose hid flame
Our hard hearts shall strike fire, the same
Shall flourish on thy brows, and be
Both fire to us and flame to thee;
Whose light shall live bright in thy face
By glory, in our hearts by grace.

    Thou shalt look round about, and see
Thousands of crown'd souls throng to be
Themselves thy crown. Sons of thy vows
The virgin-births with which thy sovereign Spouse
Made fruitful thy fair soul, go now
And with them all about thee, bow
To him; put on, (he'll say,) put on
(My rosy love) that thy rich zone
Sparkling with the sacred flames
Of thousand souls, whose happy names
Heav'n keeps upon thy score. (Thy bright
Life brought them first to kiss the light,
That kindled them to stars). And so
Thou with the LAMB, thy lord, shalt go;
And wheresoe'er he sets his white
Steps, walk with HIM those ways of light
Which who in death would live to see,
Must learn in life to die like thee.

RICHARD CRASHAW

594 *The Flaming Heart*

*Upon the Book and Picture of the Seraphical Saint Teresa as
she is usually expressed with a Seraphim beside her*

Well-meaning readers! you that come as friends
And catch the precious name this piece pretends;
Make not too much haste to admire
That fair-cheek'd fallacy of fire.
That is a seraphim, they say,
And this the great Teresia.
Readers, be rul'd by me; and make
Here a well-plac'd and wise mistake;
You must transpose the picture quite,
And spell it wrong to read it right;
Read him for her, and her for him,
And call the saint the seraphim.
      Painter, what didst thou understand
To put her dart into his hand?
See, even the years and size of him
Shows this the mother seraphim.
This is the mistress flame; and duteous he
Her happy fire-works, here, comes down to see.
O most poor-spirited of men!
Had thy cold pencil kist her pen,
Thou couldst not so unkindly err
To show us this faint shade for her.
Why man, this speaks pure mortal frame;
And mocks with female frost Love's manly flame.
One would suspect thou meant'st to paint
Some weak, inferior, woman saint.
But had thy pale-fac'd purple took
Fire from the burning cheeks of that bright book,
Thou wouldst on her have heap'd up all
That could be found seraphical;
Whate'er this youth of fire wears fair,
Rosy fingers, radiant hair,
Glowing cheeks, and glistering wings,
All those fair and flagrant things,
But before all, that fiery dart
Had fill'd the hand of this great heart.

Do then, as equal right requires;
Since his the blushes be, and hers the fires,
Resume and rectify thy rude design;
Undress thy seraphim into mine;
Redeem this injury of thy art,
Give him the veil, give her the dart.
Give him the veil, that he may cover
The red cheeks of a rivall'd lover;
Ashamed that our world now can show
Nests of new seraphims here below.
Give her the dart, for it is she
(Fair youth) shoots both thy shaft and thee;
Say, all ye wise and well-pierc'd hearts
That live and die amidst her darts,
What is't your tasteful spirits do prove
In that rare life of her, and love?
Say, and bear witness. Sends she not
A seraphim at every shot?
What magazines of immortal arms there shine!
Heav'n's great artillery in each love-spun line.
Give then the dart to her who gives the flame;
Give him the veil, who kindly takes the shame.
But if it be the frequent fate
Of worse faults to be fortunate;
If all's prescription; and proud wrong
Hearkens not to an humble song;
For all the gallantry of him,
Give me the suff'ring seraphim.
His be the bravery of all those bright things,
The glowing cheeks, the glistering wings;
The rosy hand, the radiant dart;
Leave her alone the flaming heart.
Leave her that; and thou shalt leave her
Not one loose shaft, but Love's whole quiver;
For in Love's field was never found
A nobler weapon than a wound.
Love's passives are his activ'st part:
The wounded is the wounding heart.
O heart! the equal poise of Love's both parts,
Big alike with wound and darts,

Live in these conquering leaves; live all the same;
And walk through all tongues one triumphant flame.
Live here, great heart; and love and die and kill;
And bleed and wound; and yield and conquer still.
Let this immortal life where'er it comes
Walk in a crowd of loves and martyrdoms.
Let mystic deaths wait on't; and wise souls be
The love-slain witnesses of this life of thee.
O sweet incendiary! show here thy art,
Upon this carcass of a hard cold heart;
Let all thy scatter'd shafts of light that play
Among the leaves of thy large books of day,
Combin'd against this breast at once break in
And take away from me my self and sin;
This gracious robbery shall thy bounty be,
And my best fortunes such fair spoils of me.
O thou undaunted daughter of desires!
By all thy dower of lights and fires;
By all the eagle in thee, all the dove;
By all thy lives and deaths of love;
By thy large draughts of intellectual day,
And by thy thirsts of love more large than they;
By all thy brim-fill'd bowls of fierce desire,
By thy last morning's draught of liquid fire;
By the full kingdom of that final kiss
That seiz'd thy parting soul, and seal'd thee his;
By all the heav'ns thou hast in him
(Fair sister of the seraphim!)
By all of HIM we have in THEE;
Leave nothing of my SELF in me.
Let me so read thy life, that I
Unto all life of mine may die.

                                        RICHARD CRASHAW

595 *Hail holy light*

Hail holy light, ofspring of Heav'n first-born,
Or of th'Eternal Coeternal beam
May I express thee unblam'd? since God is light,
And never but in unapproached light
Dwelt from Eternitie, dwelt then in thee,

Bright effluence of bright essence increate.
Or hear'st thou rather pure Ethereal stream,
Whose Fountain who shall tell? before the Sun,
Before the Heavens thou wert, and at the voice
Of God, as with a Mantle didst invest
The rising world of waters dark and deep,
Won from the void and formless infinite.
Thee I re-visit now with bolder wing,
Escap't the *Stygian* Pool, though long detain'd
In that obscure sojourn, while in my flight
Through utter and through middle darkness borne
With other notes then to th'*Orphean* Lyre
I sung of *Chaos* and *Eternal Night*,
Taught by the heav'nly Muse to venture down
The dark descent, and up to reascend,
Though hard and rare: thee I revisit safe,
And feel thy sovran vital Lamp; but thou
Revisit'st not these eyes, that rowle in vain
To find thy piercing ray, and find no dawn;
So thick a drop serene hath quencht thir Orbs,
Or dim suffusion veild. Yet not the more
Cease I to wander where the Muses haunt
Cleer Spring, or shadie Grove, or Sunnie Hill,
Smit with the love of sacred song; but chief
Thee *Sion* and the flowrie Brooks beneath
That wash thy hallowd feet, and warbling flow,
Nightly I visit: nor somtimes forget
Those other two equal'd with me in Fate,
So were I equal'd with them in renown,
Blind *Thamyris* and blind *Mæonides*,
And *Tiresias* and *Phineus* Prophets old.
Then feed on thoughts, that voluntarie move
Harmonious numbers; as the wakeful Bird
Sings darkling, and in shadiest Covert hid
Tunes her nocturnal Note. Thus with the Year
Seasons return, but not to me returns
Day, or the sweet approach of Ev'n or Morn,
Or sight of vernal bloom, or Summers Rose,
Or flocks, or herds, or human face divine;
But cloud in stead, and ever-during dark
Surrounds me, from the chearful waies of men

Cut off, and for the Book of knowledg fair
Presented with a Universal blanc
Of Natures works to mee expung'd and ras'd,
And wisdome at one entrance quite shut out.
So much the rather thou Celestial light
Shine inward, and the mind through all her powers
Irradiate, there plant eyes, all mist from thence
Purge and disperse, that I may see and tell
Of things invisible to mortal sight.

JOHN MILTON

596 *At a Solemn Music*

Blest pair of Sirens, pledges of Heav'ns joy,
Sphear-born harmonious sisters, Voice, and Vers,
Wed your divine sounds, and mixt power employ,
Dead things with inbreath'd sense able to pierce;
And to our high-rais'd phantasie present
That undisturbed song of pure concent,
Ay sung before the saphire-coloured throne
To him that sits thereon
With saintly shout and solemn jubily;
Where the bright Seraphim in burning row
Their loud uplifted angel trumpets blow,
And the Cherubic host in thousand quires
Touch their immortal harps of golden wires,
With those just Spirits that wear victorious palms,
Hymns devout and holy psalms
Singing everlastingly:
That we on Earth, with undiscording voice,
May rightly answer that melodious noise;
As once we did, till disproportion'd sin
Jarr'd against nature's chime, and with harsh din
Broke the fair music that all creatures made
To their great Lord, whose love their motion sway'd
In perfect diapason, whilst they stood
In first obedience, and their state of good.
O may we soon again renew that song,
And keep in tune with Heaven, till God ere long
To his celestial consort us unite,
To live with him, and sing in endless morn of light.

JOHN MILTON

597 *The Windhover*

To Christ our Lord

I caught this morning morning's minion, king-
　　dom of daylight's dauphin, dapple-dawn-drawn Falcon, in
　　his riding
Of the rolling level underneath him steady air, and striding
High there, how he rung upon the rein of a wimpling wing
In his ecstasy! then off, off forth on swing,
　　As a skate's heel sweeps smooth on a bow-bend: the hurl
　　and gliding
Rebuffed the big wind. My heart in hiding
Stirred for a bird,–the achieve of, the mastery of the thing!

Brute beauty and valour and act, oh, air, pride, plume, here
　　Buckle! AND the fire that breaks from thee then, a billion
Times told lovelier, more dangerous, O my chevalier!

　　No wonder of it: shéer plód makes plough down sillion
Shine, and blue-bleak embers, ah my dear,
　　Fall, gall themselves, and gash gold-vermilion.
　　　　　　　　　　　　　　　　　GERARD MANLEY HOPKINS

598 *Epigram*

Paul's midnight voice prevail'd; his music's thunder
Unhing'd the prison-doors, split bolts in sunder:
And sitt'st thou here, and hang'st the feeble wing?
And whin'st to be enlarged? soul, learn to sing.
　　　　　　　　　　　　　　　　　FRANCIS QUARLES

599 *Hymn to the Night*

Ἀσπασίη, τρίλλιστος

I heard the trailing garments of the Night
　　Sweep through her marble halls!
I saw her sable skirts all fringed with light
　　From the celestial walls.

I felt her presence by its spell of might,
  Stoop o'er me from above;
The calm, majestic presence of the Night,
  As of the one I love.

I heard the sounds of sorrow and delight,
  The manifold, soft chimes,
That fill the haunted chambers of the Night,
  Like some old poet's rhymes.

From the cool cisterns of the midnight air
  My spirit drank repose;
The fountain of perpetual peace flows there,–
  From those deep cisterns flows.

O holy Night! from thee I learn to bear
  What man has borne before:
Thou layest thy finger on the lips of Care,
  And they complain no more.

Peace! Peace! Orestes-like I breathe this prayer!
  Descend with broad-winged flight,
The welcome, the thrice-prayed for, the most fair,
  The best beloved Night!
            HENRY WADSWORTH LONGFELLOW

600 *Sins' Round*

Sorry I am, my God, sorry I am,
That my offences course it in a ring.
My thoughts are working like a busy flame,
Until their cockatrice they hatch and bring:
And when they once have perfected their draughts,
My words take fire from my inflamed thoughts.

My words take fire from my inflamed thoughts,
Which spit it forth like the Sicilian Hill.
They vent the wares, and pass them with their faults,
And by their breathing ventilate the ill.
But words suffice not, where are lewd intentions:
My hands do join to finish the inventions.

My hands do join to finish the inventions:
And so my sins ascend three stories high,
As Babel grew, before there were dissensions.
Yet ill deeds loiter not: for they supply
New thoughts of sinning: wherefore, to my shame,
Sorry I am, my God, sorry I am.

GEORGE HERBERT

601 *Affliction*

Broken in pieces all asunder,
      Lord, hunt me not,
      A thing forgot,
Once a poor creature, now a wonder,
      A wonder tortur'd in the space
      Betwixt this world and that of grace.

My thoughts are all a case of knives,
      Wounding my heart
      With scatter'd smart,
As wat'ring pots give flowers their lives.
      Nothing their fury can control,
      While they do wound and pink my soul.

All my attendants are at strife,
      Quitting their place
      Unto my face:
Nothing performs the task of life:
      The elements are let loose to fight,
      And while I live, try out their right.

Oh help, my God! let not their plot
      Kill them and me,
      And also thee,
Who art my life: dissolve the knot
      As the sun scatters by his light
      All the rebellions of the night.

Then shall those powers, which work for grief,
      Enter thy pay,
      And day by day
Labour thy praise, and my relief;

With care and courage building me,
Till I reach heav'n, and much more, thee.
GEORGE HERBERT

602 *On Leaping Over the Moon*

I saw new Worlds beneath the Water lie,
New People; yea, another Sky
And Sun, which seen by Day
Might things more clear display.
Just such another
Of late my Brother
Did in his Travel see, and saw by Night,
A much more strange and wondrous Sight:
Nor could the World exhibit such another,
So Great a Sight, but in a Brother.

Adventure strange! No such in Story we
New or old, true or feigned, see.
On Earth he seem'd to move
Yet Heaven went above;
Up in the Skies
His body flies
In open, visible, yet Magic, sort:
As he along the Way did sport,
Over the Flood he takes his nimble Course
Without the help of feigned Horse.

As he went tripping o'r the King's high-way,
A little pearly river lay
O'r which, without a wing
Or Oar, he dar'd to swim,
Swim through the air
On body fair;
He would not use nor trust *Icarian* wings
Lest they should prove deceitful things;
For had he fall'n, it had been wondrous high,
Not from, but from above, the sky:

He might have dropt through that thin element
Into a fathomless descent;
Unto the nether sky
That did beneath him lie,

Y

And there might tell
What wonders dwell
On earth above. Yet doth he briskly run,
And bold the danger overcome;
Who, as he leapt, with joy related soon
How *happy he* o'r-leapt the Moon.

What wondrous things upon the Earth are done
Beneath, and yet above the sun?
Deeds all appear again
In higher spheres; remain
In clouds as yet:
But there they get
Another light, and in another way
Themselves to us *above* display.
The skies themselves this earthly globe surround;
W'are even here within them found.

On heav'nly ground within the skies we walk,
And in this middle centre talk:
Did we but wisely move,
On earth in heav'n above,
Then soon should we
Exalted be
Above the sky: from whence whoever falls,
Through a long dismal precipice,
Sinks to the deep abyss where *Satan* crawls
Where horrid Death and Despair lies.

As much as others thought themselves to lie
Beneath the moon, so much more high
Himself he thought to fly
Above the starry sky,
As *that* he spied
Below the tide.
Thus did he yield me in the shady night
A wondrous and instructive light,
Which taught me that under our feet there is,
As o'r our heads, a place of bliss.

To the same purpose; he, not long before
 Brought home from nurse, going to the door
  To do some little thing
  He must not do within,
   With wonder cries,
   As in the skies
He saw the moon, *O yonder is the moon*
 Newly come after me to town,
That shin'd at Lugwardin but yesternight,
 Where I enjoy'd the self-same light.

As if it had ev'n twenty thousand faces,
 It shines at once in many places;
  To all the earth so wide
  God doth the stars divide
   With so much art
   The moon impart,
They serve us all; serve wholly ev'ry one
 As if they served him alone.
While every single person hath such store,
 'Tis want of sense that makes us poor.
      THOMAS TRAHERNE

603 *To Saint Mary Magdalen*

Blessed Offendor: who thyself hast tried,
 how far a sinner differs from a Saint
 join thy wet eyes, with tears of my complaint,
 while I sigh for that grave, for which thou cried.
No longer let my sinful soul, abide
 in fever of thy first desires faint:
 but let that love which last thy heart did taint
 with pangs of thy repentance, pierce my side.
So shall my soul, no foolish virgin be
 with empty lamp: but like a Magdalen, bear
 for ointment box, a breast with oil of grace:
And so the zeal, which then shall burn in me,
 may make my heart like to a lamp appear
 and in my spouse's palace give me place.
      HENRY CONSTABLE

604 *The Gnat*

One night all tired with the weary day,
And with my tedious self, I went to lay
  My fruitless cares
  And needless fears
   Asleep.
The curtains of the bed, and of mine eyes
Being drawn, I hop'd no trouble would surprise
  That rest which now
  Gan on my brow
   To creep.

When lo a little fly, less than its name
(It was a Gnat) with angry murmur came.
  About she flew,
  And louder grew
   Whilst I
Fain would have scorn'd the silly thing, and slept
Out all its noise; I resolute silence kept,
  And laboured so
  To overthrow
   The fly.

But still with sharp alarms vexatious she
Or challenged, or rather mocked me.
  Angry at last
  About I cast
   My hand.
'Twas well night would not let me blush, nor see
With whom I fought; And yet though feeble she
  Nor her nor my
  Own wrath could I
   Command.

Away she flies, and her own triumph sings;
I being left to fight with idler things,
  A feebler pair
  My self and air.
   How true

A worm is Man, whom flies their sport can make!
Poor worm; true rest in no bed can he take,
      But one of earth,
      Whence he came forth
      And grew.

For there none but his silent sisters be,
Worms of as true and genuine earth as He,
      Which from the same
      Corruption came:
      And there
Though on his eyes they feed, though on his heart
They neither vex nor wake him; every part
      Rests in sound sleep,
      And out doth keep
      All fear.

                      JOSEPH BEAUMONT

605 *The Collar*

I struck the board, and cry'd, No more.
      I will abroad.
   What? shall I ever sigh and pine?
My lines and life are free; free as the road,
    Loose as the wind, as large as store.
      Shall I be still in suit?
   Have I no harvest but a thorn
   To let me blood, and not restore
   What I have lost with cordial fruit?
      Sure there was wine
Before my sighs did dry it: there was corn
     Before my tears did drown it.
   Is the year only lost to me?
     Have I no bays to crown it?
No flowers, no garlands gay? all blasted?
      All wasted?
   Not so, my heart: but there is fruit,
    And thou hast hands.
   Recover all thy sigh-blown age
On double pleasures: leave thy cold dispute
Of what is fit, and not. Forsake thy cage,

Thy rope of sands,
Which petty thoughts have made, and made to thee
Good cable, to enforce and draw,
And be thy law,
While thou didst wink and wouldst not see.
Away; take heed:
I will abroad.
Call in thy death's head there: tie up thy fears.
He that forbears
To suit and serve his need,
Deserves his load.
But as I rav'd and grew more fierce and wild
At every word,
Me thoughts I heard one calling, *Child*!
And I reply'd, *My Lord*.

GEORGE HERBERT

606 *The Retreat*

Happy those early days! when I
Shin'd in my Angel-infancy.
Before I understood this place
Appointed for my second race,
Or taught my soul to fancy ought
But a white, Celestial thought,
When yet I had not walkt above
A mile, or two, from my first love,
And looking back (at that short space,)
Could see a glimpse of his bright-face;
When on some *gilded Cloud*, or *flower*
My gazing soul would dwell an hour,
And in those weaker glories spy
Some shadows of eternity;
Before I taught my tongue to wound
My Conscience with a sinful sound,
Or had the black art to dispense
A sev'ral sin to ev'ry sense,
But felt through all this fleshly dress
Bright *shoots* of everlastingness.
    O how I long to travel back
And tread again that ancient track!

That I might once more reach that plain,
Where first I left my glorious train,
From whence th'inlightned spirit sees
That shady City of Palm trees;
But (ah!) my soul with too much stay
Is drunk, and staggers in the way.
Some men a forward motion love,
But I by backward steps would move,
And when this dust falls to the urn
In that state I came return.

HENRY VAUGHAN

607 *The Morning-Watch*

O Joys! Infinite sweetness! with what flowers,
And shoots of glory, my soul breaks, and buds!
            All the long hours
            Of night, and Rest
            Through the still shrouds
            Of sleep, and Clouds,
        This Dew fell on my Breast;
            O how it *Bloods*,
And *Spirits* all my Earth! hark! In what Rings,
And *Hymning Circulations* the quick world
            Awakes, and sings;
            The rising winds,
            And falling springs,
            Birds, beasts, all things
        Adore him in their kinds.
            Thus all is hurl'd
In sacred *Hymns*, and *Order*, The great *Chime*
And *Symphony* of nature. Prayer is
            The world in tune,
            A spirit voice,
            And vocal joys
        Whose *Echo is* heav'ns bliss
            O let me climb
When I lie down! The Pious soul by night
Is like a clouded star, whose beams though said
            To shed their light
            Under some Cloud

Yet are above,
And shine, and move
Beyond that misty shroud.
So in my Bed

That Curtain'd grave, though sleep, like ashes, hide
My lamp, and life, both shall in thee abide.

HENRY VAUGHAN

608 *The World*

I saw Eternity the other night
Like a great *Ring* of pure and endless light,
    All calm, as it was bright,
And round beneath it, Time in hours, days, years
        Driv'n by the spheres
Like a vast shadow mov'd, in which the world
    And all her train were hurl'd;
The doting Lover in his quaintest strain
        Did there Complain,
Near him, his Lute, his fancy, and his flights,
        Wit's sour delights,
With gloves, and knots the silly snares of pleasure
        Yet his dear Treasure
All scatter'd lay, while he his eye did pour
        Upon a flow'r.

The darksome States-man hung with weights and woe
Like a thick midnight-fog mov'd there so slow
    He did nor stay, nor go;
Condemning thoughts (like sad Eclipses) scowl
        Upon his soul,
And clouds of crying witnesses without
    Pursu'd him with one shout.
Yet dig'd the Mole, and lest his ways be found
        Workt under ground,
Where he did Clutch his prey, but one did see
        That policy,
Churches and altars fed him, Perjuries
        Were gnats and flies,
It rain'd about him blood and tears, but he
        Drank them as free.

The fearful miser on a heap of rust
Sate pining all his life there, did scarce trust
    His own hands with the dust,
Yet would not place one piece above, but lives
    In fear of thieves.
Thousands there were as frantic as himself
    And hugg'd each one his pelf,
The down-right Epicure plac'd heav'n in sense
    And scorn'd pretence
While others slipt into a wide Excess
    Said little less;
The weaker sort slight, trivial wares enslave
    Who think them brave,
And poor, despised truth sate Counting by
    Their victory.

Yet some, who all this while did weep and sing,
And sing, and weep, soar'd up into the *Ring*,
    But most would use no wing.
O fools (said I,) thus to prefer dark night
    Before true light,
To live in grots, and caves, and hate the day
    Because it shews the way,
The way which from this dead and dark abode
    Leads up to God,
A way where you might tread the Sun, and be
    More bright than he.
But as I did their madness so discuss
    One whisper'd thus,
This Ring the Bride-groom did for none provide
    But for his bride.

John, Cap. 2. ver. 16, 17.

All that is in the world, the lust of the flesh, the lust of the Eyes,
and the pride of life, is not of the father, but is of the world.
And the world passeth away, and the lusts thereof, but he that
doth the will of God abideth for ever.

                   HENRY VAUGHAN

609 *The Bird*

Hither thou com'st: the busy wind all night
Blew through thy lodging, where thy own warm wing
Thy pillow was. Many a sullen storm
(For which course man seems much the fitter born,)
   Rain'd on thy bed
   And harmless head.
And now as fresh and cheerful as the light
Thy little heart in early hymns doth sing
Unto that *Providence*, whose unseen arm
Curb'd them, and cloth'd thee well and warm.
  All things that be, praise him; and had
   Their lesson taught them, when first made.
So hills and valleys into singing break,
And though poor stones have neither speech nor tongue,
While active winds and stream both run and speak,
Yet stones are deep in admiration.
Thus Praise and Prayer here beneath the Sun
Make lesser mornings, when the great are done.

For each inclosed Spirit is a star
  Inlightning his own little sphere,
Whose light, though fetcht and borrowed from far,
  Both mornings makes, and evenings there.

But as these Birds of light make a land glad,
Chirping their solemn Matins on each tree:
So in the shades of night some dark fowls be,
Whose heavy notes make all that hear them, sad.

  The Turtle then in Palm-trees mourns,
   While Owls and Satyrs howl;
  The pleasant Land to brimstone turns
   And all her streams grow foul.

Brightness and mirth, and love and faith, all fly,
Till the Day-spring breaks forth again from high.
         HENRY VAUGHAN

610 *Wonder*

How like an Angel came I down!
   How bright are all things here!
When first among his Works I did appear
  O how their Glory did me crown!
The World resembled his ETERNITY,
   In which my Soul did walk;
  And evr'y thing that I did see
    Did with me talk.

The Skies in their Magnificence,
   The lovely lively Air,
Oh how divine, how soft, how sweet, how fair!
  The Stars did entertain my Sense;
And all the Works of God so bright and pure,
   So rich and great, did seem,
  As if they ever must endure
    In my Esteem.

A Native Health and Innocence
   Within my Bones did grow,
And while my God did all his Glories show
  I felt a vigor in my Sense
That was all Spirit: I within did flow
   With Seas of Life like Wine;
  I nothing in the World did know
    But 'twas Divine.

Harsh rugged Objects were conceal'd,
   Oppressions, Tears and Cries,
Sins, Griefs, Complaints, Dissentions, weeping Eyes,
  Were hid: And only things reveal'd
Which heavenly Spirits and the Angels prize:
   The State of Innocence
  And Bliss, not Trades and Poverties,
    Did fill my Sense.

The Streets seem'd paved with golden Stones,
   The boys and Girls all mine;
To me how did their lovely faces shine!
  The Sons of men all Holy ones,

In Joy and Beauty, then appear'd to me;
   And ev'ry Thing I found
(While like an Angel I did see)
   Adorn'd the Ground.

Rich Diamonds, and Pearl, and Gold
   Might ev'ry where be seen;
Rare Colors, yellow, blue, red, white, and green
   Mine Eyes on ev'ry side behold:
All that I saw, a Wonder did appear,
   Amazement was my Bliss:
  That and my Wealth met ev'ry where.
    No Joy to this!

Curs'd, ill-devis'd Proprieties
   With Envy, Avarice,
And Fraud, (those Fiends that spoil ev'n Paradise)
   Were not the Object of mine Eyes;
Nor Hedges, Ditches, Limits, narrow Bounds:
   I dreamt not ought of those,
  But in surveying all men's Grounds
    I found Repose.

For Property its self was mine,
   And Hedges, Ornaments:
Walls, Houses, Coffers, and their rich Contents,
   To make me Rich combine.
Clothes, costly Jewels, Laces, I esteem'd
   My Wealth by others worn,
For me they all to wear them seem'd,
    When I was born.

THOMAS TRAHERNE

611 *From 'St. Philip and St. James'*

Now the winds are all composure,
   But the breath upon the bloom,
Blowing sweet o'er each inclosure,
   Grateful off'rings of perfume.

Tansy, calaminth and daisies
    On the river's margin thrive;
And accompany the mazes
    On the stream that leaps alive.

Muse, accordant to the season,
    Give the numbers life and air;
When the sounds and objects reason
    In behalf of praise and pray'r.

All the scenes of nature quicken,
    By the genial spirit fann'd;
And the painted beauties thicken
    Colour'd by the master's hand.

Earth her vigour repossessing
    As the blasts are held in ward;
Blessing heap'd and press'd on blessing,
    Yield the measure of the Lord.

Beeches, without order seemly,
    Shade the flow'rs of annual birth,
And the lily smiles supremely
    Mention'd by the Lord on earth.

Cowslips seize upon the fallow,
    And the cardamine in white,
Where the corn-flow'rs join the mallow,
    Joy and health, and thrift unite.

Study sits beneath her arbour,
    By the bason's glossy side;
While the boat from out its harbour
    Exercise and pleasure guide.

Pray'r and praise be mine employment,
    Without grudging or regret,
Lasting life, and long enjoyment,
    Are not here, and are not yet.

Hark! aloud, the blackbird whistles,
    With surrounding fragrance blest,
And the goldfinch in the thistles
    Makes provision for her nest.

Ev'n the hornet hives his honey,
　　Bluecap builds his stately dome,
And the rocks supply the coney
　　With a fortress and a home.

But the servants of their Saviour,
　　Which with gospel-peace are shod,
Have no bed but what the paviour
　　Makes them in the porch of God.

CHRISTOPHER SMART

612　*The Nativity of Our Lord*

Where is this stupendous stranger,
　　Swains of Solyma, advise,
Lead me to my Master's manger,
　　Shew me where my Saviour lies?

O Most Mighty! O Most Holy!
　　Far beyond the seraph's thought,
Art thou then so mean and lowly
　　As unheeded prophets taught?

O the magnitude of meekness!
　　Worth from worth immortal sprung;
O the strength of infant weakness,
　　If eternal is so young!

If so young and thus eternal,
　　Michael tune the shepherd's reed,
Where the scenes are ever vernal,
　　And the loves be love indeed!

See the God blasphem'd and doubted
　　In the schools of Greece and Rome;
See the pow'rs of darkness routed,
　　Taken at their utmost gloom.

Nature's decorations glisten
　　Far above their usual trim;
Birds on box and laurel listen,
　　As so near the cherubs hymn.

Boreas now no longer winters
    On the desolated coast;
Oaks no more are riv'n in splinters
    By the whirlwind and his host.

Spinks and ouzels sing sublimely,
    'We too have a Saviour born';
Whiter blossoms burst untimely
    On the blest Mosaic thorn.

God all-bounteous, all-creative,
    Whom no ills from good dissuade,
Is incarnate, and a native
    Of the very world he made.
                      CHRISTOPHER SMART

613 *Quickness*

False life! a foil and no more, when
        Wilt thou be gone?
Thou foul deception of all men
That would not have the true come on.

Thou art a moon-like toil; a blind
        Self-posing state;
A dark contest of waves and wind;
A mere tempestuous debate.

Life is a fix'd, discerning light,
        A knowing Joy;
No chance, or fit; but ever bright,
And calm and full, yet doth not cloy.

'Tis such a blissful thing, that still
        Doth vivify,
And shine and smile, and hath the skill
To please without Eternity.

Thou art a toilsome mole, or less
        A moving mist
But life is, what none can express,
A quickness, which my God hath kist.
                      HENRY VAUGHAN

614 *Woefully Arrayed*

Woefully arrayed,
   My blood, man,
   For thee ran,
It may not be nay'd: [1]
   My body blue and wan,
Woefully arrayed.

Behold me, I pray thee, with thy whole reason,
And be not so hard-hearted, and for this encheason, [2]
Sith I for thy soul sake was slain in good season,
Beguiled and betrayed by Judas' false treason:
   Unkindly entreated,
   With sharp cord sore fretted,
   The Jews me threated:
They mowed, they grinned, they scorned me,
Condemned to death, as thou may'st see,
      Woefully arrayed.

Thus naked am I nailed, O man, for thy sake!
I love thee, then love me; why sleepest thou? awake!
Remember my tender heart-root for thee brake,
With pains my veins constrained to crake:
   Thus tugged to and fro,
   Thus wrapped all in woe,
   Whereas never man was so,
Entreated thus in most cruel wise,
Was like a lamb offered in sacrifice,
      Woefully arrayed.

Of sharp thorn I have worn a crown on my head,
So pained, so strained, so rueful, so red,
Thus bobbed, thus robbed, thus for thy love dead,
Unfeigned I deigned my blood for to shed:
   My feet and handes sore
   The sturdy nailes bore:
   What might I suffer more
Than I have done, O man, for thee?
Come when thou list, welcome to me,
      Woefully arrayed.

[1] denied   [2] cause

Of record thy good Lord I have been and shall be:
I am thine, thou art mine, my brother I call thee.
Thee love I entirely–see what is befall'n me!
Sore beating, sore threating, to make thee, man, all free:
    Why art thou unkind?
    Why hast not me in mind?
    Come yet and thou shalt find
  Mine endless mercy and grace–
  See how a spear my heart did race,[1]
      Woefully arrayed.

Dear brother, no other thing I of thee desire
But give me thine heart free to reward mine hire:
I wrought thee, I bought thee from eternal fire:
I pray thee array thee toward my high empire
    Above the orient,
    Whereof I am regent,
    Lord God ominpotent,
  With me to reign in endless wealth:
  Remember, man, thy soul's health.

        Woefully arrayed,
          My blood, man,
          For thee ran,
        It may not be nay'd:
          My body blue and wan,
        Woefully arrayed.

                JOHN SKELTON

615 *New Heaven, New War*

Come to your heaven, you heavenly quires!
Earth hath the heaven of your desires;
Remove your dwelling to your God,
A stall is now His best abode;
Sith men their homage do deny,
Come, angels, all their faults supply.

His chilling cold doth heat require,
Come, seraphins, in lieu of fire;

            [1] wound

This little ark no cover hath,
Let cherubs' wings His body swath;
Come, Raphael, this babe must eat,
Provide our little Tobie meat.

Let Gabriel be now His groom,
That first took up His earthly room;
Let Michael stand in His defence,
Whom love hath link'd to feeble sense;
Let Graces rock, when He doth cry,
And angels sing His lullaby.

The same you saw in heavenly seat,
Is He that now sucks Mary's teat;
Agnize [1] your King a mortal wight,
His borrowed weed lets not your sight;
Come, kiss the manger where He lies;
That is your bliss above the skies.

This little babe so few days old,
Is come to rifle Satan's fold;
All hell doth at His presence quake,
Though He Himself for cold do shake;
For in this weak unarmed wise
The gates of hell He will surprise.

With tears He fights and wins the field,
His naked breast stands for a shield,
His battering shot are babish cries,
His arrows, looks of weeping eyes,
His martial ensigns, cold and need,
And feeble flesh His warrior's steed.

His camp is pitched in a stall,
His bulwark but a broken wall,
The crib His trench, hay-stalks His stakes,
Of shepherds He His muster makes;
And thus, as sure His foe to wound,
The angels' trumps alarum sound.

My soul, with Christ join them in fight;
Stick to the tents that He hath pight [2];

[1] acknowledge, recognise   [2] pitched

Within His crib is surest ward,
This little babe will be thy guard;
If thou wilt foil thy foes with joy,
Then flit not from this heavenly boy.

ROBERT SOUTHWELL

616 *The Burning Babe*

As I in hoary Winter's night stood shivering in the snow,
Surpris'd I was with sudden heat, which made my heart to
glow;
And lifting up a fearful eye to view what fire was near,
A pretty Babe all burning bright, did in the air appear,
Who scorched with excessive heat, such floods of tears did
shed,
As though His floods should quench His flames which with
His tears were fed;
Alas! quoth He, but newly born, in fiery heats I fry,
Yet none approach to warm their hearts or feel my fire but I!
My faultless breast the furnace is, the fuel wounding thorns,
Love is the fire, and sighs the smoke, the ashes shame and
scorns;
The fuel Justice layeth on, and Mercy blows the coals,
The metal in this furnace wrought are men's defiled souls,
For which, as now on fire I am to work them to their good,
So will I melt into a bath to wash them in My blood:
With this He vanished out of sight, and swiftly shrank away,
And straight I called unto mind that it was Christmas-day.

ROBERT SOUTHWELL

617 *The Resurrection*

Can death be faithful or the grave be just
Or shall my tomb restore my scatter'd dust?
Shall ev'ry hair find out it's proper pore
And crumbled bones be joined as before
Shall long unpractis'd pulses learn to beat
Victorious rottenness a loud retreat
Or eyes eclipsed with a tedious night
May they once hope to resalute the light?

What if this flesh of mine be made the prey
Of scaly pirates cannibals at sea?
Shall living sepulchres give up their dead
Or is not flesh made fish then perished?
What if the working of a subtile flame
By an unkind embrace dissolve this frame
To ashes; and the whist'ling winds convey
Each atom to a quite contrary way–
Shall the small pilgrims that (perhaps) may pass
From grass to flesh and thence from flesh to grass
Travel until they meet and then embrace
So strictly as to grow the former face?
My God I know thy pow'rful word did frame
Out of pure nothing all that hath a name
From the bright Angels bathing in full streams
Of deathless joys to motes that dance in beams.
And shall I doubt but such a word can call
Flesh out of dust that out of less made all?
No no I am resolv'd, that when poor I
Shall slumb'ring in our mother's bosom lie
The circling worms shall loose their fast embrace
And kinder turfs that cover me give place:
The bands of death shall burst at the shrill sound
Of heaven's summons and I shall be found.
Then will I rise and dress me lord for thee
Who did'st by death undress thee lord for me.

NATHANIEL WANLEY

618 *The Coronet*

When for the Thorns with which I long, too long,
    With many a piercing wound,
    My Saviour's head have crown'd,
I seek with Garlands to redress that Wrong:
    Through every Garden, every Mead,
I gather flow'rs (my fruits are only flow'rs)
    Dismantling all the fragrant Towers
That once adorn'd my Shepherdess's head.
And now when I have summ'd up all my store,
    Thinking (so I my self deceive)
    So rich a Chaplet thence to weave

As never yet the king of Glory wore:
    Alas I find the Serpent old
    That, twining in his speckled breast,
    About the flow'rs disguis'd does fold,
    With wreaths of Fame and Interest.
Ah, foolish Man, that would'st debase with them,
And mortal Glory, Heaven's Diadem!
But thou who only could'st the Serpent tame,
Either his slipp'ry knots at once untie,
And disintangle all his winding Snare:
Or shatter too with him my curious frame:
And let these wither, so that he may die,
Though set with Skill and chosen out with Care.
That they, while Thou on both their Spoils dost tread,
May crown thy Feet, that could not crown thy Head.
ANDREW MARVELL

619 *To Heaven*

Good, and great God, can I not think of thee,
    But it must, straight, my melancholy be?
Is it interpreted in me disease,
    That, laden with my sins, I seek for ease?
O, be thou witness, that the reins dost know,
    And hearts of all, if I be sad for show,
And judge me after: if I dare pretend
    To aught but grace, or aim at other end.
As thou art all, so be thou all to me,
    First, midst, and last, converted one, and three;
My faith, my hope, my love: and in this state,
    My judge, my witness, and my advocate.
Where have I been this while exil'd from thee?
    And whither rap'd, now thou but stoop'st to me?
Dwell, dwell here still: O, being every-where,
    How can I doubt to find thee ever, here?
I know my state, both full of shame, and scorn,
    Conceiv'd in sin, and unto labour born,
Standing with fear, and must with horror fall,
    And destin'd unto judgement, after all.
I feel my griefs too, and there scarce is ground,
    Upon my flesh t'inflict another wound.

Yet dare I not complain, or wish for death
  With holy PAUL, lest it be thought the breath
Of discontent; or that these prayers be
  For weariness of life, not love of thee.

BEN JONSON

620 *Grief*

I tell you, hopeless grief is passionless;
  That only men incredulous of despair,
  Half-taught in anguish, through the midnight air
Beat upward to God's throne in loud access
Of shrieking and reproach. Full desertness
  In souls as countries lieth silent-bare
  Under the blanching, vertical eye-glare
Of the absolute Heavens. Deep-hearted man, express
Grief for thy Dead in silence like to death–
  Most like a monumental statue set
In everlasting watch and moveless woe
Till itself crumble to the dust beneath.
  Touch it; the marble eyelids are not wet:
If it could weep, it could arise and go.

ELIZABETH BARRETT BROWNING

621 *God's Grandeur*

The world is charged with the grandeur of God.
  It will flame out, like shining from shook foil;
  It gathers to a greatness, like the ooze of oil
Crushed. Why do men then now not reck his rod?
Generations have trod, have trod, have trod;
  And all is seared with trade; bleared, smeared with toil;
  And wears man's smudge and shares man's smell: the soil
Is bare now, nor can foot feel, being shod.

And for all this, nature is never spent;
  There lives the dearest freshness deep down things;
And though the last lights off the black West went
  Oh, morning, at the brown brink eastward, springs–
Because the Holy Ghost over the bent
  World broods with warm breast and with ah! bright wings.

GERARD MANLEY HOPKINS

622 *Thou art indeed just, Lord*

*Justus quidem tu es, Domine, si disputem tecum: verum-tamen
justa loquar ad te: Quare via impiorum prosperatur?* &c.

Thou art indeed just, Lord, if I contend
With thee; but, sir, so what I plead is just.
Why do sinners' ways prosper? and why must
Disappointment all I endeavour end?
⠀⠀⠀Wert thou my enemy, O thou my friend,
How wouldst thou worse, I wonder, than thou dost
Defeat, thwart me? Oh, the sots and thralls of lust
Do in spare hours more thrive than I that spend,
Sir, life upon thy cause. See, banks and brakes
Now, leavèd how thick! lacèd they are again
With fretty chervil, look, and fresh wind shakes
Them; birds build–but not I build; no, but strain,
Time's eunuch, and not breed one work that wakes.
Mine, O thou lord of life, send my roots rain.

GERARD MANLEY HOPKINS

623 *No worst, there is none*

No worst, there is none. Pitched past pitch of grief,
More pangs will, schooled at forepangs, wilder wring.
Comforter, where, where is your comforting?
Mary, mother of us, where is your relief?
My cries heave, herds-long; huggle in a main, a chief
Woe, world-sorrow; on an age-old anvil wince and sing–
Then lull, then leave off. Fury had shrieked 'No ling-
ering! Let me be fell: force I must be brief'.

O the mind, mind has mountains; cliffs of fall
Frightful, sheer, non-man-fathomed. Hold them cheap
May who ne'er hung there. Nor does long our small
Durance deal with that steep or deep. Here! creep,
Wretch, under a comfort serves in a whirlwind: all
Life death does end and each day dies with sleep.

GERARD MANLEY HOPKINS

624 *The Phoenix and the Turtle*

Let the bird of loudest lay,
On the sole Arabian tree,
Herald sad and trumpet be,
To whose sound chaste wings obey.

But thou shrieking harbinger,
Foul precurrer of the fiend,
Augur of the fever's end,
To this troop come thou not near.

From this session interdict
Every fowl of tyrant wing,
Save the eagle, feather'd king:
Keep the obsequy so strickt.

Let the priest in surplice white
That defunctive music can,
Be the death-divining swan,
Lest the requiem lack his right.

And thou treble-dated crow,
That thy sable gender mak'st
With the breath thou giv'st and tak'st,
'Mongst our mourners shalt thou go.

Here the anthem doth commence:
Love and constancy is dead;
Phoenix and the turtle fled
In a mutual flame from hence.

So they lov'd, as love in twain
Had the essence but in one;
Two distincts, division none:
Number there in love was slain.

Hearts remote, yet not asunder;
Distance, and no space was seen
'Twixt the turtle and his queen:
But in them it were a wonder.

So between them love did shine,
That the turtle saw his right
Flaming in the phoenix' sight;
Either was the other's mine.

Property was thus appal'd,
That the self was not the same;
Single nature's double name
Neither two nor one was call'd.

Reason, in itself confounded,
Saw division grow together;
To themselves yet either neither,
Simple were so well compounded,

That it cried, 'How true a twain
Seemeth this concordant one!
Love hath reason, reason none,
If what parts can so remain.'

Whereupon it made this threne
To the phoenix and the dove,
Co-supremes and stars of love,
As chorus to their tragic scene.

THRENOS

Beauty, truth, and rarity,
Grace in all simplicity,
Here enclos'd in cinders lie.

Death is now the phoenix' nest;
And the turtle's loyal breast
To eternity doth rest,

Leaving no posterity:
'Twas not their infirmity,
It was married chastity.

Truth may seem, but cannot be;
Beauty brag, but 'tis not she;
Truth and beauty buried be.

To this urn let those repair
That are either true or fair;
For these dead birds sigh a prayer.

WILLIAM SHAKESPEARE

Book IX

THE SYMPHONIC POEM

625 *Dream*

I

With camel's hair I clothed my skin,
  I fed my mouth with honey wild;
And set me scarlet wool to spin,
  And all my breast with hyssop filled;
Upon my brow and cheeks and chin
  A bird's blood spilled.

I took a broken reed to hold,
  I took a sponge of gall to press;
I took weak water-weeds to fold
  About my sacrificial dress.

I took the grasses of the field,
  The flax was bolled upon my crine;
And ivy thorn and wild grapes healed
  To make good wine.

I took my scrip of manna sweet,
  My cruse of water did I bless;
I took the white dove by the feet
  And flew into the wilderness.

II

The tiger came and played;
Uprose the lion in his mane;
The jackal's tawny nose
And sanguine dripping tongue
Out of the desert rose
And plunged its sands among;
The bear came striding o'er the desert plain.

Uprose the horn and eyes
And quivering flank of the great unicorn,
And galloped round and round;

662

Uprose the gleaming claw
Of the leviathan, and wound
In steadfast march did draw
Its course away beyond the desert's bourn.

I stood within a maze
Woven round about me by magic art,
And ordered circle-wise;
The bear more near did tread,
And with two fiery eyes,
And with a wolfish head
Did close the circle round in every part.

III

With scarlet corded horn,
With frail wrecked knees and stumbling pace
The scapegoat came:
His eyes took flesh and spirit dread in flame
At once, and he died looking towards my face.
RICHARD WATSON DIXON

626 *The Strayed Reveller*

The Portico of Circe's Palace. Evening.

A Youth. Circe.

The Youth:
　　Faster, faster,
　　O Circe, Goddess,
　　Let the wild, thronging train,
　　The bright procession
　　Of eddying forms,
　　Sweep through my soul!

　　Thou standest, smiling
　　Down on me; thy right arm,
　　Lean'd up against the column there,
　　Props thy soft cheek;
　　Thy left holds, hanging loosely,
　　The deep cup, ivy-cinctur'd,
　　I held but now.

Is it then evening
So soon? I see, the night-dews,
Cluster'd in thick beads, dim
The agate brooch-stones
On thy white shoulder.
The cool night-wind, too,
Blows through the portico,
Stirs thy hair, Goddess,
Waves thy white robe.

Circe:

Whence art thou, sleeper?

The Youth:

When the white dawn first
Through the rough fir-planks
Of my hut, by the chestnuts,
Up at the valley-head,
Came breaking, Goddess,
I sprang up, I threw round me
My dappled fawn-skin:
Passing out, from the wet turf,
Where they lay, by the hut door,
I snatch'd up my vine-crown, my fir-staff,
All drench'd in dew:
Came swift down to join
The rout early gather'd
In the town, round the temple,
Iacchus' white fane
On yonder hill.

Quick I pass'd, following
The wood-cutters' cart-track
Down the dark valley;–I saw
On my left, through the beeches,
Thy palace, Goddess,
Smokeless, empty:
Trembling, I enter'd; beheld
The court all silent,
The lions sleeping;
On the altar this bowl.

I drank, Goddess –
And sank down here, sleeping,
On the steps of thy portico.

Circe:

  Foolish boy! Why tremblest thou?
  Thou lovest it, then, my wine?
  Wouldst more of it? See, how glows,
  Through the delicate, flush'd marble,
  The red creaming liquor,
  Strown with dark seeds!
  Drink, then! I chide thee not,
  Deny thee not my bowl.
  Come, stretch forth thy hand, then–so–
  Drink, drink again!

The Youth:

  Thanks, gracious one!
  Ah, the sweet fumes again!
  More soft, ah me!
  More subtle-winding
  Than Pan's flute-music.
  Faint–faint! Ah me!
  Again the sweet sleep.

Circe:

  Hist! Thou–within there!
  Come forth, Ulysses!
  Art tired with hunting?
  While we range the woodland,
  See what the day brings.

Ulysses:

  Ever new magic!
  Hast thou then lur'd hither,
  Wonderful Goddess, by thy art,
  The young, languid-ey'd Ampelus,
  Iacchus' darling–
  Or some youth belov'd of Pan,
  Of Pan and the Nymphs?
  That he sits, bending downward

His white, delicate neck
To the ivy-wreathed marge
Of thy cup:–the bright, glancing vine-leaves
That crown his hair,
Falling forwards, mingling
With the dark ivy-plants,
His fawn-skin, half untied,
Smear'd with red wine-stains? Who is he,
That he sits, overweigh'd
By fumes of wine and sleep,
So late, in thy portico?
What youth, Goddess,–what guest
Of Gods or mortals?

Circe:

Hist! he wakes!
I lur'd him not hither, Ulysses.
Nay, ask him!

The Youth:

Who speaks? Ah! who comes forth
To thy side, Goddess, from within?
How shall I name him?
This spare, dark-featur'd,
Quick-ey'd stranger?
Ah! and I see too
His sailor's bonnet,
His short coat, travel-tarnish'd,
With one arm bare.–
Art thou not he, whom fame
This long time rumours
The favour'd guest of Circe, brought by the waves?
Art thou he, stranger?
The wise Ulysses,
Laertes' son?

Ulysses:

I am Ulysses.
And thou, too, sleeper?
Thy voice is sweet.
It may be thou hast follow'd

Through the islands some divine bard.
By age taught many things,
Age and the Muses;
And heard him delighting
The chiefs and people
In the banquet, and learn'd his songs,
Of Gods and Heroes,
Of war and arts,
And peopled cities
Inland, or built
By the grey sea.–If so, then hail!
I honour and welcome thee.

The Youth:
  The Gods are happy.
  They turn on all sides
  Their shining eyes:
  And see below them
  The Earth, and men.

  They see Tiresias
  Sitting, staff in hand,
  On the warm, grassy
  Asopus' bank:
  His robe drawn over
  His old, sightless head:
  Revolving inly
  The doom of Thebes.

  They see the Centaurs
  In the upper glens
  Of Pelion, in the streams,
  Where red-berried ashes fringe
  The clear-brown shallow pools,
  With streaming flanks, and heads
  Rear'd proudly, snuffing
  The mountain wind.

  They see the Indian
  Drifting, knife in hand,
  His frail boat moor'd to

A floating isle thick-matted
With large-leaved, low-creeping melon-plants,
And the dark cucumber.
He reaps, and stows them,
Drifting–drifting:–round him,
Round his green harvest-plot,
Flow the cool lake-waves:
The mountains ring them.

They see the Scythian
On the wide Stepp, unharnessing
His wheel'd house at noon.
He tethers his beast down, and makes his meal,
Mares' milk, and bread
Bak'd on the embers;–all around
The boundless waving grass-plains stretch, thick-starr'd
With saffron and the yellow hollyhock
And flag-leav'd iris flowers.
Sitting in his cart
He makes his meal: before him, for long miles,
Alive with bright green lizards,
And the springing bustard-fowl,
The track, a straight black line,
Furrows the rich soil: here and there
Clusters of lonely mounds
Topp'd with rough-hewn,
Grey, rain-blear'd statues, overpeer
The sunny Waste.

They see the Ferry
On the broad, clay-laden
Lone Chorasmian stream; thereon,
With snort and strain,
Two horses, strongly swimming, tow
The ferry-boat, with woven ropes
To either bow
Firm-harness'd by the mane:–a chief,
With shout and shaken spear,
Stands at the prow, and guides them; but astern,
The cowering Merchants, in long robes,
Sit pale beside their wealth

Of silk-bales and of balsam-drops,
Of gold and ivory,
Of turquoise-earth and amethyst,
Jasper and chalcedony,
And milk-barr'd onyx-stones.
The loaded boat swings groaning
In the yellow eddies.
The Gods behold them.

They see the Heroes
Sitting in the dark ship
On the foamless, long-heaving,
Violet sea:
At sunset nearing
The Happy Islands.

These things, Ulysses,
The wise bards also
Behold and sing.
But oh, what labour!
O Prince, what pain!

They too can see
Tiresias:–but the Gods,
Who give them vision,
Added this law:
That they should bear too
His groping blindness,
His dark foreboding,
His scorn'd white hairs;
Bear Hera's anger
Through a life lengthen'd
To seven ages.

They see the Centaurs
On Pelion;–then they feel,
They too, the maddening wine
Swell their large veins to bursting: in wild pain
They feel the biting spears
Of the grim Lapithae, and Theseus, drive,
Drive crashing through their bones: they feel
High on a jutting rock in the red stream

z

Alcmena's dreadful son
Ply his bow:—such a price
The Gods exact for song;
To become what we sing.

They see the Indian
On his mountain lake;—but squalls
Make their skiff reel, and worms
In the unkind spring have gnaw'd
Their melon-harvest to the heart: They see
The Scythian:—but long frosts
Parch them in winter-time on the bare Stepp,
Till they too fade like grass: they crawl
Like shadows forth in spring.

They see the merchants
On the Oxus' stream:—but care
Must visit first them too, and make them pale.
Whether, through whirling sand,
A cloud of desert robber-horse has burst
Upon their caravan: or greedy kings,
In the wall'd cities the way passes through,
Crush'd them with tolls; or fever-airs,
On some great river's marge,
Mown them down, far from home.

They see the Heroes
Near harbour:—but they share
Their lives, and former violent toil, in Thebes,
Seven-gated Thebes, or Troy;
Or where the echoing oars
Of Argo, first,
Startled the unknown Sea.

The old Silenus
Came, lolling in the sunshine,
From the dewy forest-coverts,
This way, at noon.
Sitting by me, while his Fauns
Down at the water-side
Sprinkled and smooth'd
His drooping garland,
He told me these things.

But I, Ulysses,
Sitting on the warm steps,
Looking over the valley,
All day long, have seen,
Without pain, without labour,
Sometimes a wild-hair'd Maenad;
Sometimes a Faun with torches;
And sometimes, for a moment,
Passing through the dark stems
Flowing-rob'd, the belov'd,
The desir'd, the divine,
Beloved Iacchus.

Ah cool night-wind, tremulous stars!
Ah glimmering water–
Fitful earth-murmur–
Dreaming woods!
Ah golden-hair'd, strangely-smiling Goddess,
And thou, prov'd, much enduring,
Wave-toss'd Wanderer!
Who can stand still?
Ye fade, ye swim, ye waver before me.
The cup again!

Faster, faster,
O Circe, Goddess,
Let the wild, thronging train,
The bright procession
Of eddying forms,
Sweep through my soul!

MATTHEW ARNOLD

627 *Gerontion*

*Thou hast nor youth nor age
But as it were, an after dinner sleep
Dreaming of both.*

Here I am, an old man in a dry month,
Being read to by a boy, waiting for rain.
I was neither at the hot gates
Nor fought in the warm rain
Nor knee deep in the salt marsh, heaving a cutlass,

Bitten by flies, fought.
My house is a decayed house,
And the jew squats on the window sill, the owner,
Spawned in some estaminet of Antwerp,
Blistered in Brussels, patched and peeled in London.
The goat coughs at night in the field overhead;
Rocks, moss, stonecrop, iron, merds.
The woman keeps the kitchen, makes tea,
Sneezes at evening, poking the peevish gutter.

                        I an old man,
A dull head among windy spaces.

Signs are taken for wonders. 'We would see a sign!'
The word within a word, unable to speak a word,
Swaddled with darkness. In the juvescence of the year
Came Christ the tiger

In depraved May, dogwood and chestnut, flowering judas,
To be eaten, to be divided, to be drunk
Among whispers; by Mr. Silvero
With caressing hands, at Limoges
Who walked all night in the next room;

By Hakagawa, bowing among the Titians;
By Madame de Tornquist, in the dark room
Shifting the candles; Fräulein von Kulp
Who turned in the hall, one hand on the door. Vacant shuttles
Weave the wind. I have no ghosts,
An old man in a draughty house
Under a windy knob.

After such knowledge, what forgiveness? Think now
History has many cunning passages, contrived corridors
And issues, deceives with whispering ambitions,
Guides us by vanities. Think now
She gives when our attention is distracted,
And what she gives, gives with such supple confusions
That the giving famishes the craving. Gives too late
What's not believed in, or if still believed,
In memory only, reconsidered passion. Gives too soon
Into weak hands, what's thought can be dispensed with
Till the refusal propagates a fear. Think

Neither fear nor courage saves us. Unnatural vices
Are fathered by our heroism. Virtues
Are forced upon us by our impudent crimes.
These tears are shaken from the wrath-bearing tree.

The tiger springs in the new year. Us he devours. Think at last
We have not reached conclusion, when I
Stiffen in a rented house. Think at last
I have not made this show purposelessly
And it is not by any concitation
Of the backward devils.
I would meet you upon this honestly.
I that was near your heart was removed therefrom
To lose beauty in terror, terror in inquisition.
I have lost my passion: why should I need to keep it
Since what is kept must be adulterated?
I have lost my sight, smell, hearing, taste and touch:
How should I use them for your closer contact?

These with a thousand small deliberations
Protract the profit of their chilled delirium,
Excite the membrane, when the sense has cooled,
With pungent sauces, multiply variety
In a wilderness of mirrors. What will the spider do,
Suspend its operations, will the weevil
Delay? De Bailhache, Fresca, Mrs. Cammell, whirled
Beyond the circuit of the shuddering Bear
In fractured atoms. Gull against the wind, in the windy straits
Of Belle Isle, or running on the Horn,
White feathers in the snow, the Gulf claims,
And an old man driven by the Trades
To a sleepy corner.
                              Tenants of the house,
Thoughts of a dry brain in a dry season.
                              THOMAS STEARNS ELIOT

628 L'Allegro

Hence, loathed Melancholy,
    Of Cerberus and blackest Midnight born
In Stygian cave forlorn.
    'Mongst horrid shapes, and shreiks, and sights unholy,

Find out some uncouth cell,
　Where brooding Darkness spreads his jealous wings,
And the night-raven sings;
　There under ebon shades, and low-brow'd rocks,
As ragged as thy locks,
　In dark Cimmerian desert ever dwell.
But com thou Goddess fair and free,
In Heav'n ycleap'd Euphrosyne,
And by men, heart-easing Mirth;
Whom lovely Venus at a birth,
With two sister Graces more
To ivy-crowned Bacchus bore:
Or whether (as som sager sing)
The frolick wind that breathes the spring,
Zephyr with Aurora playing,
As he met her once a-Maying,
There on beds of violets blew,
And fresh-blown roses washt in dew,
Filled her with thee a daughter fair,
So bucksom, blith, and debonair.
Haste thee Nymph, and bring with thee
Jest and youthful Jollity,
Quips and cranks, and wanton wiles,
Nods and becks, and wreathed smiles,
Such as hang on Hebe's cheek,
And love to live in dimple sleek;
Sport that wrincled Care derides,
And Laughter holding both his sides.
Com, and trip it as you go
On the light fantastick toe;
And in thy right hand lead with thee
The mountain-nymph, sweet Liberty;
And, if I give thee honour due,
Mirth, admit me of thy crue,
To live with her, and live with thee,
In unreproved pleasures free;
To hear the lark begin his flight,
And singing startle the dull night,
From his watch-towre in the skies,
Till the dappled dawn doth rise;
Then to com in spight of sorrow,

And at my window bid good-morrow,
Through the sweet-briar, or the vine,
Or the twisted eglantine,
While the cock with lively din,
Scatters the rear of darkness thin,
And to the stack, or the barn-dore,
Stoutly struts his dames before:
Oft list'ning how the hounds and horn
Chearly rouse the slumb'ring morn,
From the side of som hoar hill,
Through the high wood echoing shrill:
Som time walking not unseen
By hedge-row elms, on hillocks green,
Right against the eastern gate
Where the great Sun begins his state,
Roab'd in flames, and amber light,
The clouds in thousand liveries dight;
While the plowman, near at hand,
Whistles ore the furrow'd land,
And the milkmaid singeth blithe,
And the mower whets his sithe,
And every shepherd tells his tale
Under the hawthorn in the dale.
Streit mine eye hath caught new pleasures
Whilst the lantskip round it measures,
Russet lawns, and fallows gray,
Where the nibling flocks do stray,
Mountains on whose barren brest
The labouring clouds do often rest;
Meadows trim with daisies pide;
Shallow brooks, and rivers wide;
Towers and battlements it sees
Boosom'd high in tufted trees,
Where perhaps som beauty lies,
The cynosure of neighbouring eyes.
Hard by, a cottage chimney smokes
From betwixt two aged okes,
Where Corydon and Thyrsis met,
Are at their savoury dinner set
Of hearbs and other country messes,
Which the neat-handed Phillis dresses;

And then in haste her bowre she leaves,
With Thestylis to bind the sheaves;
Or if the earlier season lead,
To the tann'd haycock in the mead.
Some times with secure delight
The upland hamlets will invite,
When the merry bells ring round,
And the jocond rebecks sound
To many a youth, and many a maid
Dancing in the chequer'd shade;
And young and old com forth to play
On a sunshine holyday,
Till the live-long day-light fail,
Then to the spicy nut-brown ale,
With stories told of many a feat,
How Faery Mab the junkets eat.
She was pincht, and pull'd, she sed,
And by the Friar's lanthorn led,
Tells how the drudging goblin swet
To ern his cream-bowle duly set,
When in one night, ere glimpse of morn,
His shadowy flaile hath thresh'd the corn,
That ten day-labourers could not end,
Then lies him down the lubbar fend,
And, stretch'd out all the chimney's length,
Basks at the fire his hairy strength;
And crop-full out of dores he flings,
Ere the first cock his mattin rings.
Thus done the tales, to bed they creep,
By whispering winds soon lull'd asleep.
Towred cities please us then,
And the busy humm of men,
Where throngs of knights and barons bold,
In weeds of peace high triumphs hold,
With store of ladies, whose bright eies
Rain influence, and judge the prise
Of wit, or arms, while both contend
To win her grace, whom all commend.
There let Hymon oft appear
In saffron robe, with taper cleer,
And pomp, and feast, and revelry,

With mask, and antique pageantry,
Such sights as youthful poets dream
On summer eeves by haunted stream.
Then to the well-trod stage anon,
If Jonson's learned sock be on,
Or sweetest Shakespear fancies childe,
Warble his native wood-notes wilde.
And ever against eating cares,
Lap me in soft Lydian aires,
Married to immortal verse
Such as the meeting soul may pierce
In notes, with many a winding bout
Of lincked sweetness long drawn out,
With wanton heed, and giddy cunning,
The melting voice through mazes running;
Untwisting all the chains that ty
The hidden soul of harmony.
That Orpheus' self may heave his head
From golden slumber on a bed
Of heapt Elysian flowres, and hear
Such streins as would have won the ear
Of Pluto, to have quite set free
His half-regain'd Eurydice.
These delights, if thou canst give,
Mirth with thee, I mean to live.

JOHN MILTON

629 *To a Skylark*

Hail to thee, blithe Spirit!
   Bird thou never wert,
That from Heaven, or near it,
   Pourest thy full heart
In profuse strains of unpremeditated art.

Higher still and higher
From the earth thou springest
Like a cloud of fire;
The blue deep thou wingest,
And singing still dost soar, and soaring ever singest.

In the golden lightning
Of the sunken sun,
O'er which clouds are bright'ning,
Thou dost float and run;
Like an unbodied joy whose race is just begun.

The pale purple even
Melts around thy flight;
Like a star of Heaven,
In the broad daylight
Thou art unseen, but yet I hear thy shrill delight,

Keen as are the arrows
Of that silver sphere,
Whose intense lamp narrows
In the white dawn clear
Until we hardly see—we feel that it is there.

All the earth and air
With thy voice is loud,
As, when night is bare,
From one lonely cloud
The moon rains out her beams, and Heaven is overflowed.

What thou art we know not;
What is most like thee?
From rainbow clouds there flow not
Drops so bright to see
As from thy presence showers a rain of melody.

Like a poet hidden
In the light of thought,
Singing hymns unbidden,
Till the world is wrought
To sympathy with hopes and fears it heeded not:

Like a high-born maiden
     In a palace-tower,
Soothing her love-laden
     Soul in secret hour
With music sweet as love, which overflows her bower:

Like a glow-worm golden
     In a dell of dew,
Scattering unbeholden
     Its aëreal hue
Among the flowers and grass, which screen it from the view!

Like a rose embowered
     In its own green leaves,
By warm winds deflowered,
     Till the scent it gives
Makes faint with too much sweet those heavy-wingèd thieves:

Sound of vernal showers
     On the twinkling grass,
Rain-awakened flowers,
     All that ever was
Joyous, and clear, and fresh, thy music doth surpass:

Teach us, Sprite or Bird,
     What sweet thoughts are thine:
I have never heard
     Praise of love or wine
That panted forth a flood of rapture so divine.

Chorus Hymeneal,
     Or triumphal chant,
Matched with thine would be all
     But an empty vaunt,
A thing wherein we feel there is some hidden want.

What objects are the fountains
     Of thy happy strain?
What fields, or waves, or mountains?
     What shapes of sky or plain?
What love of thine own kind? what ignorance of pain?

With thy clear keen joyance
  Languor cannot be:
Shadow of annoyance
  Never came near thee:
Thou lovest–but ne'er knew love's sad satiety.

Waking or asleep,
  Thou of death must deem
Things more true and deep
  Than we mortals dream,
Or how could thy notes flow in such a crystal stream?

We look before and after,
  And pine for what is not:
Our sincerest laughter
  With some pain is fraught;
Our sweetest songs are those that tell of saddest thought.

Yet if we could scorn
  Hate, and pride, and fear;
If we were things born
  Not to shed a tear,
I know not how thy joy we ever should come near.

Better than all measures
  Of delightful sound,
Better than all treasures
  That in books are found,
Thy skill to poet were, thou scorner of the ground!

Teach me half the gladness
  That thy brain must know,
Such harmonious madness
  From my lips would flow
The world should listen then–as I am listening now.

PERCY BYSSHE SHELLEY

630 *The Passions, an Ode for Music*

When Music, Heav'nly Maid, was young,
While yet in early Greece she sung,
The Passions oft to hear her Shell,
Throng'd around her magic Cell,

Exulting, trembling, raging, fainting,
Possest beyond the Muse's Painting;
By turns they felt the glowing Mind,
Disturb'd, delighted, rais'd, refin'd.
Till once, 'tis said, when all were fir'd,
Fill'd with Fury, rapt, inspir'd,
From the supporting Myrtles round,
They snatch'd her Instruments of Sound,
And as they oft had heard a-part
Sweet Lessons of her forceful Art,
Each, for Madness rul'd the Hour,
Would prove his own expressive Pow'r.

First Fear his Hand, its Skill to try,
 Amid the Chords bewilder'd laid,
And back recoil'd he knew not why,
 Ev'n at the Sound himself had made.

Next Anger rush'd, his Eyes on fire,
 In Lightnings own'd his secret Stings,
In one rude Clash he struck the Lyre,
 And swept with hurried Hand the Strings.

With woful Measures wan Despair
 Low sullen Sounds his Grief beguil'd,
A solemn, strange, and mingled Air,
 'Twas sad by Fits, by Starts 'twas wild.

But thou, O Hope, with Eyes so fair,
 What was thy delightful Measure?
Still it whisper'd promis'd Pleasure,
 And bad the lovely Scenes at distance hail!

Still would Her Touch the Strain prolong,
 And from the Rocks, the Woods, the Vale,
She call'd on Echo still thro' all the Song;
 And, where Her sweetest Theme She chose,
 A soft responsive Voice was heard at ev'ry Close,
And Hope enchanted smil'd, and wav'd Her golden Hair.
And longer had She sung,–but with a Frown,
 Revenge impatient rose,

He threw his blood-stain'd Sword in Thunder down,
    And with a with'ring Look,
  The War-denouncing Trumpet took,
And blew a Blast so loud and dread,
Were ne'er Prophetic Sounds so full of Woe.
    And ever and anon he beat
    The doubling Drum with furious Heat;
And tho' sometimes each dreary Pause between,
    Dejected Pity at his Side,
    Her Soul-subduing Voice applied,
  Yet still He kept his wild unalter'd Mien,
While each strain'd Ball of Sight seem'd bursting from his Head.

Thy Numbers, Jealousy, to nought were fix'd,
    Sad Proof of thy distressful State,
Of diff'ring Themes the veering Song was mix'd,
    And now it courted Love, now raving call'd on Hate.

With Eyes up-rais'd, as one inspir'd,
Pale Melancholy sate retir'd,
And from her wild sequester'd Seat,
In Notes by Distance made more sweet,
Pour'd thro' the mellow Horn her pensive Soul:
    And dashing soft from Rocks around,
    Bubbling Runnels join'd the Sound:
Thro' Glades and Glooms the mingled Measure stole,
Or o'er some haunted Stream with fond Delay,
    Round an holy Calm diffusing,
    Love of Peace, and lonely Musing,
In hollow Murmurs died away.

But O how alter'd was its sprightlier Tone!
When Chearfulness, a Nymph of healthiest Hue,
    Her Bow a-cross her Shoulder flung,
    Her Buskins gem'd with Morning Dew,
Blew an inspiring Air, that Dale and Thicket rung,
    The Hunter's Call to Faun and Dryad known!
    The Oak-crown'd Sisters, and their chast-eye'd Queen,
    Satyrs and sylvan Boys were seen,
    Peeping from forth their Alleys green;
Brown Exercise rejoic'd to hear,
    And Sport leapt up, and seiz'd his Beechen Spear.

Last came Joy's Ecstatic Trial,
He with viny Crown advancing,
    First to the lively Pipe his Hand addrest,
But soon he saw the brisk awak'ning Viol,
    Whose sweet entrancing Voice he lov'd the best.
    They would have thought who heard the Strain,
    They saw in Tempe's Vale her native Maids,
    Amidst the festal sounding Shades,
To some unwearied Minstrel dancing,
    While as his flying Fingers kiss'd the Strings,
    Love fram'd with Mirth, a gay fantastic Round,
    Loose were Her Tresses seen, her Zone unbound,
    And He amidst his frolic Play,
    As if he would the charming Air repay,
    Shook thousand Odours from his dewy Wings.

O Music, Sphere-descended Maid,
Friend of Pleasure, Wisdom's Aid,
Why, Goddess, why to us deny'd?
Lay'st Thou thy antient Lyre aside?
As in that lov'd Athenian Bow'r,
You learn'd an all-commanding Pow'r,
Thy mimic Soul, O Nymph endear'd,
Can well recall what then it heard.
Where is thy native simple Heart,
Devote to Virtue, Fancy, Art?
Arise as in that elder Time,
Warm, Energic, Chaste, Sublime!
Thy Wonders in that God-like Age,
Fill thy recording Sister's Page—
'Tis said, and I believe the Tale,
Thy humblest Reed could more prevail,
Had more of Strength, diviner Rage,
Than all which charms this laggard Age,
Ev'n all at once together found,
Cæcilia's mingled World of Sound—
O bid our vain Endeavors cease,
Revive the just Designs of Greece,
Return in all thy simple State!
Confirm the Tales Her Sons relate!

WILLIAM COLLINS

631 *Ode to a Nightingale*

My heart aches, and a drowsy numbness pains
    My sense, as though of hemlock I had drunk,
Or emptied some dull opiate to the drains
    One minute past, and Lethe-wards had sunk:
'Tis not through envy of thy happy lot,
    But being too happy in thine happiness,—
        That thou, light-winged Dryad of the trees,
                In some melodious plot
    Of beechen green, and shadows numberless,
    Singest of summer in full-throated ease.

O, for a draught of vintage! that hath been
    Cool'd a long age in the deep-delved earth,
Tasting of Flora and the country green,
    Dance, and Provençal song, and sunburnt mirth!
O for a beaker full of the warm South,
    Full of the true, the blushful Hippocrene,
        With beaded bubbles winking at the brim,
                And purple-stained mouth;
    That I might drink, and leave the world unseen,
    And with thee fade away into the forest dim:

Fade far away, dissolve, and quite forget
    What thou among the leaves hast never known,
The weariness, the fever, and the fret
    Here, where men sit and hear each other groan;
Where palsy shakes a few, sad, last gray hairs,
    Where youth grows pale, and spectre-thin, and dies;
        Where but to think is to be full of sorrow
                And leaden-eyed despairs,
    Where Beauty cannot keep her lustrous eyes,
    Or new Love pine at them beyond to-morrow.

Away! away! for I will fly to thee,
    Not charioted by Bacchus and his pards,
But on the viewless wings of Poesy,
    Though the dull brain perplexes and retards:

Already with thee! tender is the night,
    And haply the Queen-Moon is on her throne,
        Cluster'd around by all her starry Fays;
                But here there is no light,
    Save what from heaven is with the breezes blown
        Through verdurous glooms and winding mossy ways.

I cannot see what flowers are at my feet,
    Nor what soft incense hangs upon the boughs,
But, in embalmed darkness, guess each sweet
    Wherewith the seasonable month endows
The grass, the thicket, and the fruit-tree wild:
    White hawthorn, and the pastoral eglantine;
        Fast fading violets cover'd up in leaves;
                And mid-May's eldest child,
    The coming musk-rose, full of dewy wine,
        The murmurous haunt of flies on summer eves.

Darkling I listen; and, for many a time
    I have been half in love with easeful Death,
Call'd him soft names in many a mused rhyme,
    To take into the air my quiet breath;
Now more than ever seems it rich to die,
    To cease upon the midnight with no pain,
        While thou art pouring forth thy soul abroad
                In such an ecstasy!
    Still wouldst thou sing, and I have ears in vain—
        To thy high requiem become a sod.

Thou wast not born for death, immortal Bird!
    No hungry generations tread thee down;
The voice I hear this passing night was heard
    In ancient days by emperor and clown:
Perhaps the self-same song that found a path
    Through the sad heart of Ruth, when, sick for home,
        She stood in tears amid the alien corn;
                The same that oft-times hath
    Charm'd magic casements, opening on the foam
        Of perilous seas, in faery lands forlorn.

Forlorn! the very word is like a bell
  To toll me back from thee to my sole self!
Adieu! the fancy cannot cheat so well
  As she is fam'd to do, deceiving elf.
Adieu! adieu! thy plaintive anthem fades
  Past the near meadows, over the still stream,
    Up the hill-side; and now 'tis buried deep
      In the next valley-glades:
  Was it a vision, or a waking dream?
    Fled is that music:–Do I wake or sleep?

JOHN KEATS

632 *Ode on a Grecian Urn*

Thou still unravish'd bride of quietness,
  Thou foster-child of silence and slow time,
Sylvan historian, who canst thus express
  A flowery tale more sweetly than our rhyme:
What leaf-fring'd legend haunts about thy shape
  Of deities or mortals, or of both,
    In Tempe or the dales of Arcady?
What men or gods are these? What maidens loth?
What mad pursuit? What struggle to escape?
  What pipes and timbrels? What wild ecstasy?

Heard melodies are sweet, but those unheard
  Are sweeter; therefore, ye soft pipes, play on;
Not to the sensual ear, but, more endear'd,
  Pipe to the spirit ditties of no tone:
Fair youth, beneath the trees, thou canst not leave
  Thy song, nor ever can those trees be bare;
    Bold lover, never, never canst thou kiss,
Though winning near the goal–yet, do not grieve;
  She cannot fade, though thou hast not thy bliss,
    For ever wilt thou love, and she be fair!

Ah, happy, happy boughs! that cannot shed
  Your leaves, nor ever bid the Spring adieu:
And, happy melodist, unwearied,
  For ever piping songs for ever new;

More happy love! more happy, happy love!
   For ever warm, and still to be enjoy'd,
     For ever panting, and for ever young;
All breathing human passion far above,
    That leaves a heart high-sorrowful and cloy'd,
     A burning forehead, and a parching tongue.

Who are these coming to the sacrifice?
   To what green altar, O mysterious priest,
Lead'st thou that heifer lowing at the skies,
   And all her silken flanks with garlands drest?
What little town by river or sea shore,
   Or mountain-built with peaceful citadel,
    Is emptied of this folk, this pious morn?
And, little town, thy streets for evermore
   Will silent be; and not a soul to tell
    Why thou art desolate, can e'er return.

O attic shape! Fair attitude! with brede
   Of marble men and maidens overwrought,
With forest branches and the trodden weed;
   Thou, silent form, dost tease us out of thought
As doth eternity: Cold Pastoral!
   When old age shall this generation waste,
    Thou shalt remain, in midst of other woe
Than ours, a friend to man, to whom thou say'st,
   Beauty is truth, truth beauty,—that is all
    Ye know on earth, and all ye need to know.

JOHN KEATS

633 From 'Prometheus Unbound'

Chorus of Spirits

From unremembered ages we
Gentle guides and guardians be
Of heaven-oppressed mortality;
And we breathe, and sicken not,
The atmosphere of human thought:
Be it dim, and dank, and gray,
Like a storm-extinguished day,

Travelled o'er by dying gleams;
  Be it bright as all between
Cloudless skies and windless streams,
  Silent, liquid, and serene;
As the birds within the wind,
  As the fish within the wave,
As the thoughts of man's own mind
  Float through all above the grave;
We make there our liquid lair,
Voyaging cloudlike, and unpent
Through the boundless element:
Thence we bear the prophecy
Which begins and ends in thee!

Ione

More yet come, one by one: the air around them
Looks radiant as the air around a star.

First Spirit

On a battle-trumpet's blast
I fled hither, fast, fast, fast,
'Mid the darkness upward cast.
From the dust of creeds outworn,
From the tyrant's banner torn,
Gathering 'round me, onward borne,
There was mingled many a cry—
Freedom! Hope! Death! Victory!
Till they faded through the sky;
And one sound, above, around,
One sound beneath, around, above,
Was moving; 'twas the soul of Love;
'Twas the hope, the prophecy,
Which begins and ends in thee.

Second Spirit

A rainbow's arch stood on the sea,
Which rocked beneath, immovably;
And the triumphant storm did flee,
Like a conqueror, swift and proud,
Between, with many a captive cloud,
A shapeless, dark and rapid crowd,

Each by lightning riven in half:
I heard the thunder hoarsely laugh:
Mighty fleets were strewn like chaff
And spread beneath a hell of death
O'er the white waters. I alit
On a great ship lightning-split,
And speeded hither on the sigh
Of one who gave an enemy
His plank, then plunged aside to die.

Third Spirit

I sate beside a sage's bed,
And the lamp was burning red
Near the book where he had fed,
When a Dream with plumes of flame
To his pillow hovering came,
And I knew it was the same
Which had kindled long ago
Pity, eloquence, and woe;
And the world awhile below
Wore the shade, its lustre made.
It has borne me here as fleet
As Desire's lightning feet:
I must ride it back ere morrow,
Or the sage will wake in sorrow.

Fourth Spirit

On a poet's lips I slept
Dreaming like a love-adept
In the sound his breathing kept;
Nor seeks nor finds he mortal blisses,
But feeds on the aereal kisses
Of shapes that haunt thought's wildernesses.
He will watch from dawn to gloom
The lake-reflected sun illume
The yellow bees in the ivy-bloom,
Nor heed nor see, what things they be;
But from these create he can
Forms more real than living man,
Nurslings of immortality!

One of these awakened me,
And I sped to succour thee.

PERCY BYSSHE SHELLEY

634   *The Leaden Echo and the Golden Echo*

(Maidens' song from St. Winefred's Well)

THE LEADEN ECHO

How to kéep—is there ány any, is there none such, nowhere
    known some, bow or brooch or braid or brace, láce, latch
    or catch or key to keep

Back beauty, keep it, beauty, beauty, beauty, . . . from
    vanishing away?

Ó is there no frowning of these wrinkles, rankèd wrinkles deep,

Dówn? no waving off of these most mournful messengers, still
    messengers, sad and stealing messengers of grey?

No there's none, there's none, O no there's none,

Nor can you long be, what you now are, called fair,

Do what you may do, what, do what you may,

And wisdom is early to despair:

Be beginning; since, no, nothing can be done

To keep at bay

Age and age's evils, hoar hair,

Ruck and wrinkle, drooping, dying, death's worst, winding
    sheets, tombs and worms and tumbling to decay;

So be beginning, be beginning to despair.

O there's none; no no no there's none:

Be beginning to despair, to despair,

Despair, despair, despair, despair.

THE GOLDEN ECHO

Spare!

There ís one, yes I have I have one (Hush there!);

Only not within seeing of the sun,

Not within the singeing of the strong sun,

Tall sun's tingeing, or treacherous the tainting of the earth's air,

Somewhere elsewhere there is ah well where! one,

One. Yes I can tell such a key, I do know such a place,

Where whatever's prized and passes of us, everything that's
    fresh and fast flying of us, seems to us sweet of us and
    swiftly away with, done away with, undone,

Undone, done with, soon done with, and yet dearly and
dangerously sweet

Of us, the wimpled–water-dimpled, not-by-morning-matchèd
face,

The flower of beauty, fleece of beauty, too too apt to, ah! to
fleet,

Never fleets móre, fastened with the tenderest truth

To its own best being and its loveliness of youth: it is an
everlastingness of, O it is an all youth!

Come then, your ways and airs and looks, locks, maiden gear,
gallantry and gaiety and grace,

Winning ways, air innocent, maiden manners, sweet looks,
loose locks, long locks, lovelocks, gaygear, going gallant,
girlgrace–

Resign them, sign them, seal them, send them, motion them
with breath,

And with síghs soaring, soaring síghs deliver

Them; beauty-in-the-ghost, deliver it, early now, long before
death

Give beauty back, beauty, beauty, beauty, back to God,
beauty's self and beauty's giver.

See; not a hair is, not an eyelash, not the least lash lost; every
hair

Is, hair of the head, numbered.

Nay, what we had lighthanded left in surly the mere mould

Will have waked and have waxed and have walked with the
wind what while we slept,

This side, that side hurling a heavyheaded hundredfold

What while we, while we slumbered.

O then, weary then whý should we tread? O why are we we so
haggard at the heart, so care-coiled, care-killed, so fagged,
so fashed, so cogged, so cumbered,

When the thing we freely fórfeit is kept with fonder a care,

Fonder a care kept than we could have kept it, kept

Far with fonder a care (and we, we should have lost it) finer,
fonder

A care kept.–Where kept? Do but tell us where kept, where.–

Yonder.–What high as that! We follow, now we follow.–

    Yonder, yes yonder, yonder,

Yonder.

GERARD MANLEY HOPKINS

635 *Kubla Khan*

In Xanadu did Kubla Khan
  A stately pleasure-dome decree:
Where Alph, the sacred river, ran
Through caverns measureless to man
  Down to a sunless sea.
So twice five miles of fertile ground
With walls and towers were girdled round:
And here were gardens bright with sinuous rills,
Where blossomed many an incense-bearing tree,
And here were forests ancient as the hills,
Enfolding sunny spots of greenery.

But oh! that deep romantic chasm which slanted
Down the green hill athwart a cedarn cover!
A savage place! as holy and enchanted
As e'er beneath a waning moon was haunted
By woman wailing for her demon-lover!
And from this chasm, with ceaseless turmoil seething,
As if this earth in fast thick pants were breathing,
A mighty fountain momently was forced,
Amid whose swift half-intermitted burst
Huge fragments vaulted like rebounding hail,
Or chaffy grain beneath the thresher's flail:
And 'mid these dancing rocks at once and ever
It flung up momently the sacred river.
Five miles meandering with a mazy motion
Through wood and dale the sacred river ran,
Then reached the caverns measureless to man,
And sank in tumult to a lifeless ocean:
And 'mid this tumult Kubla heard from far
Ancestral voices prophesying war!

    The shadow of the dome of pleasure
    Floated midway on the waves;
    Where was heard the mingled measure
    From the fountain and the caves.
It was a miracle of rare device,
A sunny pleasure-dome with caves of ice!

A damsel with a dulcimer
In a vision once I saw:
It was an Abyssinian maid,
And on her dulcimer she played,
Singing of Mount Abora.
Could I revive within me
Her symphony and song,
To such a deep delight 'twould win me,
That with music loud and long,
I would build that dome in air,
That sunny dome! those caves of ice!
And all who heard should see them there,
And all should cry, Beware! Beware!
His flashing eyes, his floating hair!
Weave a circle round him thrice,
And close your eyes with holy dread,
For he on honey-dew hath fed,
And drunk the milk of Paradise.

SAMUEL TAYLOR COLERIDGE

636 *Ode to the West Wind*

I

O wild West Wind, thou breath of Autumn's being,
Thou, from whose unseen presence the leaves dead
Are driven, like ghosts from an enchanter fleeing,

Yellow, and black, and pale, and hectic red,
Pestilence-stricken multitudes: O thou,
Who chariotest to their dark wintry bed

The wingèd seeds, where they lie cold and low,
Each like a corpse within its grave, until
Thine azure sister of the Spring shall blow

Her clarion o'er the dreaming earth, and fill
(Driving sweet buds like flocks to feed in air)
With living hues and odours plain and hill:

Wild Spirit, which art moving everywhere;
Destroyer and preserver; hear, oh, hear!

II

Thou on whose stream, mid the steep sky's commotion,
Loose clouds like earth's decaying leaves are shed,
Shook from the tangled boughs of Heaven and Ocean,

Angels of rain and lightning: there are spread
On the blue surface of thine aery surge,
Like the bright hair uplifted from the head

Of some fierce Maenad, even from the dim verge
Of the horizon to the zenith's height,
The locks of the approaching storm.   Thou dirge

Of the dying year, to which this closing night
Will be the dome of a vast sepulchre
Vaulted with all thy congregated might

Of vapours, from whose solid atmosphere
Black rain, and fire, and hail will burst: oh, hear!

III

Thou who didst waken from his summer dreams
The blue Mediterranean, where he lay,
Lulled by the coil of his crystalline streams,

Beside a pumice isle in Baiae's bay,
And saw in sleep old palaces and towers
Quivering within the wave's intenser day,

All overgrown with azure moss and flowers
So sweet, the sense faints picturing them! Thou
For whose path the Atlantic's level powers

Cleave themselves into chasms, while far below
The sea-blooms and the oozy woods which wear
The sapless foliage of the ocean, know

Thy voice, and suddenly grow gray with fear,
And tremble and despoil themselves: oh, hear!

IV

If I were a dead leaf thou mightest bear;
If I were a swift cloud to fly with thee;
A wave to pant beneath thy power, and share

The impulse of thy strength, only less free
Than thou, O uncontrollable! If even
I were as in my boyhood, and could be

The comrade of thy wanderings over Heaven,
As then, when to outstrip thy skiey speed
Scarce seemed a vision; I would ne'er have striven

As thus with thee in prayer in my sore need.
Oh, lift me as a wave, a leaf, a cloud!
I fall upon the thorns of life! I bleed!

A heavy weight of hours has chained and bowed
One too like thee: tameless, and swift, and proud.

V

Make me thy lyre, even as the forest is:
What if my leaves are falling like its own!
The tumult of thy mighty harmonies

Will take from both a deep, autumnal tone,
Sweet though in sadness. Be thou, Spirit fierce,
My spirit! Be thou me, impetuous one!

Drive my dead thoughts over the universe
Like withered leaves to quicken a new birth!
And, by the incantation of this verse,

Scatter, as from an unextinguished hearth
Ashes and sparks, my words among mankind!
Be through my lips to unawakened earth

The trumpet of a prophecy! O, Wind,
If Winter comes, can Spring be far behind?

PERCY BYSSHE SHELLEY

637 *Canto XVII*

So that the vines burst from my fingers
And the bees weighted with pollen
Move heavily in the vine-shoots:
　　　　　chirr–chirr–chirr-rikk–a purring sound,
And the birds sleepily in the branches.
　　　　　ZAGREUS! IO ZAGREUS!
With the first pale-clear of the heaven
And the cities set in their hills,
And the goddess of the fair knees
Moving there, with the oak-wood behind her,
The green slope, with white hounds
　　　　　leaping about her;
And thence down to the creek's mouth, until evening,
Flat water before me,
　　　　　and the trees growing in water,
Marble trunks out of stillness,
On past the palazzi,
　　　　　　　in the stillness,
The light now, not of the sun.
　　　　　　　Chrysophrase,
And the water green clear, and blue clear;
On, to the great cliffs of amber,
　　　　　　　Between them,
Cave of Nerea,
　　　she like a great shell curved,
And the boat drawn without sound,
Without odour of ship-work,
Nor bird-cry, nor any noise of wave moving,
Nor splash of porpoise, nor any noise of wave moving,
Within her cave, Nerea,
　　　　　she like a great shell curved
In the suavity of the rock,
　　　　　cliff green-gray in the far,
In the near, the gate-cliffs of amber,
And the wave
　　　　green clear, and blue clear,
And the cave salt-white, and glare-purple,
　　　　cool, porphyry smooth,
　　　　the rock sea-worn.

No gull-cry, no sound of porpoise,
Sand as of malachite, and no cold there,
    the light not of the sun.

Zagreus, feeding his panthers,
    the turf clear as on hills under light.
And under the almond-trees, gods,
    with them, *choros nympharum*. Gods,
Hermes and Athene,
        As shaft of compass,
Between them, trembled–
To the left is the place of fauns
    sylva nympharum;
The low wood, moor-scrub,
    the doe, the young spotted deer,
    leap up through the broom-plants,
        as dry leaf amid yellow.
And by one cut of the hills,
    the great alley of Memnons.
Beyond, sea, crests seen over dune,
Night sea churning shingle,
To the left, the alley of cypress.
        A boat came,
One man holding her sail,
Guiding her with oar caught over gunwale, saying:
'   There, in the forest of marble,
'   the stone trees–out of water–
'   the arbours of stone–
'   marble leaf, over leaf,
'   silver, steel over steel,
'   silver beaks rising and crossing,
'   prow set against prow,
'   stone, ply over ply,
'   the gilt beams flare of an evening.'
Borso, Carmagnola, the men of craft, *i vitrei*,
Thither, at one time, time after time,
And the waters richer than glass,
Bronze gold, the blaze over the silver,
Dye-pots in the torch-light,
The flash of wave under prows,
And the silver beaks rising and crossing.

Stone trees, white and rose-white in the darkness,
Cypress there by the towers,
Drift under hulls in the night.

'In the gloom the gold
Gathers the light about it.' . . .

Now supine in burrow, half over-arched bramble,
One eye for the sea, through that peek-hole,
Gray light, with Athene.
Zothar and her elephants, the gold loin-cloth,
The sistrum, shaken, shaken,
the cohort of her dancers.
And Aletha, by bend of the shore,
with her eyes seaward,
and in her hands sea-wrack
Salt-bright with the foam,
Koré through the bright meadow,
with green-gray dust in the grass:
'For this hour, brother of Circe.'
Arm laid over my shoulder,
Saw the sun for three days, the sun fulvid,
As a lion lift over sand-plain;
and that day,
And for three days, and none after,
Splendour, as the splendour of Hermes,
And shipped thence
to the stone place,
Pale white, over water,
known water,
And the white forest of marble, bent bough over bough,
The pleached arbour of stone,
Thither Borso, when they shot the barbed arrow at him,
And Carmagnola, between the two columns,
Sigismundo, after that wreck in Dalmatia.
Sunset like the grasshopper flying.

EZRA POUND

638 *Dejection: An Ode*

Late, late yestreen I saw the new Moon,
With the old Moon in her arms;

And I fear, I fear, my Master dear!
We shall have a deadly storm.
                          Ballad of Sir Patrick Spence

I

Well! If the Bard was weather-wise, who made
   The grand old ballad of Sir Patrick Spence,
   This night, so tranquil now, will not go hence
Unroused by winds, that ply a busier trade
Than those which mould yon cloud in lazy flakes,
Or the dull sobbing draft, that moans and rakes
      Upon the strings of this Æolian lute,
      Which better far were mute.
   For lo! the New-moon winter-bright!
   And overspread with phantom light,
   (With swimming phantom light o'erspread
   But rimmed and circled by a silver thread)
I see the old Moon in her lap, foretelling
   The coming-on of rain and squally blast.
And oh! that even now the gust were swelling,
   And the slant night-shower driving loud and fast!
Those sounds which oft have raised me, whilst they awed,
      And sent my soul abroad,
Might now perhaps their wonted impulse give,
Might startle this dull pain, and make it move and live!

II

A grief without a pang, void, dark, and drear,
   A stifled, drowsy, unimpassioned grief,
   Which finds no natural outlet, no relief,
      In word, or sigh, or tear—
O Lady! in this wan and heartless mood,
To other thoughts by yonder throstle woo'd,
   All this long eve, so balmy and serene,
Have I been gazing on the western sky,
   And its peculiar tint of yellow green:
And still I gaze—and with how blank an eye!
And those thin clouds above, in flakes and bars,
That give away their motion to the stars;
Those stars, that glide behind them or between,
Now sparkling, now bedimmed, but always seen:

Yon crescent Moon, as fixed as if it grew
In its own cloudless, starless lake of blue;
I see them all so excellently fair,
I see, not feel, how beautiful they are!

III

My genial spirits fail;
And what can these avail
To lift the smoth'ring weight from off my breast?
It were a vain endeavour,
Though I should gaze for ever
On that green light that lingers in the west:
I may not hope from outward forms to win
The passion and the life, whose fountains are within.

IV

O Lady! we receive but what we give,
And in our life alone does Nature live:
Ours is her wedding-garment, ours her shroud!
And would we aught behold, of higher worth,
Than that inanimate cold world allowed
To the poor loveless ever-anxious crowd,
Ah! from the soul itself must issue forth
A light, a glory, a fair luminous cloud
Enveloping the Earth–
And from the soul itself must there be sent
A sweet and potent voice, of its own birth,
Of all sweet sounds the life and element!

V

O pure of heart! thou need'st not ask of me
What this strong music in the soul may be!
What, and wherein it doth exist,
This light, this glory, this fair luminous mist,
This beautiful and beauty-making power.
Joy, virtuous Lady! Joy that ne'er was given,
Save to the pure, and in their purest hour,
Life, and Life's effluence, cloud at once and shower,
Joy, Lady! is the spirit and the power,
Which wedding Nature to us gives in dower,
A new Earth and new Heaven,

Undreamt of by the sensual and the proud–
Joy is the sweet voice, Joy the luminous cloud–
    We in ourselves rejoice!
And thence flows all that charms or ear or sight,
    All melodies the echoes of that voice,
All colours a suffusion from that light.

VI

There was a time when, though my path was rough,
  This joy within me dallied with distress,
And all misfortunes were but as the stuff
  Whence Fancy made me dreams of happiness:
For Hope grew round me, like the twining vine,
And fruits and foliage, not my own, seemed mine.
But now afflictions bow me down to earth.
Nor care I that they rob me of my mirth;
    But oh! each visitation
Suspends what nature gave me at my birth,
  My shaping spirit of Imagination.
For not to think of what I needs must feel,
  But to be still and patient, all I can;
And haply by abstruse research to steal
  From my own nature all the natural man–
This was my sole resource, my only plan:
Till that which suits a part infects the whole,
And now is almost grown the habit of my soul.

VII

Hence, viper thoughts, that coil around my mind,
    Reality's dark dream!
I turn from you, and listen to the wind,
  Which long has raved unnoticed.
    What a scream
Of agony by torture lengthened out
That lute sent forth! Thou Wind, that rav'st without,
  Bare crag, or mountain-tarn, or blasted tree,
Or pine-grove whither woodman never clomb,
Or lonely house, long held the witches' home,
  Me thinks were fitter instruments for thee,
Mad Lutanist! who in this month of showers,
Of dark-brown gardens, and of peeping flowers,

A A

Mak'st Devil's yule, with worse than wintry song,
The blossoms, buds, and timorous leaves among.
　　Thou actor, perfect in all tragic sounds!
Thou mighty Poet, even to frenzy bold!
　　　What tell'st thou now about?
　　　'Tis of the rushing of an host in rout,
　　With groans of trampled men, with smarting wounds–
At once they groan with pain, and shudder with the cold!
But hush! there is a pause of deepest silence!
　　And all that noise, as of a rushing crowd,
With groans, and tremulous shudderings–all is over–
　　It tells another tale, with sounds less deep and loud!
　　　A tale of less afright,
　　　And tempered with delight,
As Otway's self had framed the tender lay,
　　　'Tis of a little child
　　　Upon a lonesome wild,
Not far from home, but she hath lost her way:
And now moans low in bitter grief and fear,
And now screams loud, and hopes to make her mother hear.

VIII

'Tis midnight, but small thoughts have I of sleep:
Full seldom may my friend such vigils keep!
Visit her, gentle Sleep! with wings of healing,
　　And may this storm be but a mountain-birth,
May all the stars hang bright above her dwelling,
　　Silent as though they watched the sleeping Earth!
　　　With light heart may she rise,
　　　Gay fancy, cheerful eyes,
Joy lift her spirit, joy attune her voice;
To her may all things live, from pole to pole,
Their life the eddying of her living soul!
　　O simple spirit, guided from above,
Dear Lady! friend devoutest of my choice,
Thus mayest thou ever, evermore rejoice.
　　　　　　　　　　SAMUEL TAYLOR COLERIDGE

639 *The Scholar Gipsy*

Go, for they call you, Shepherd, from the hill;
  Go, Shepherd, and untie the wattled cotes:
    No longer leave thy wistful flock unfed,
  Nor let thy bawling fellows rack their throats,
    Nor the cropp'd grasses shoot another head.
      But when the fields are still,
    And the tired men and dogs all gone to rest,
      And only the white sheep are sometimes seen
      Cross and recross the strips of moon-blanch'd green
        Come, Shepherd, and again renew the quest.

Here, where the reaper was at work of late,
  In this high field's dark corner, where he leaves
    His coat, his basket, and his earthern cruse,
  And in the sun all morning binds the sheaves,
    Then here, at noon, comes back his stores to use;
      Here will I sit and wait,
    While to my ear from uplands far away
      The bleating of the folded flocks is borne,
      With distant cries of reapers in the corn–
        All the live murmur of a summer's day.

Screen'd is this nook o'er the high, half-reap'd field,
  And here till sun-down, Shepherd, will I be.
    Through the thick corn the scarlet poppies peep,
  And round green roots and yellowing stalks I see
    Pale pink convolvulus in tendrils creep:
      And air-swept lindens yield
    Their scent, and rustle down their perfum'd showers
      Of bloom on the bent grass where I am laid,
      And bower me from the August sun with shade;
        And the eye travels down to Oxford's towers:

And near me on the grass lies Glanvil's book–
  Come, let me read the oft-read tale again,
    The story of that Oxford scholar poor
  Of pregnant parts and quick inventive brain,
    Who, tir'd of knocking at Preferment's door,
      One summer morn forsook

His friends, and went to learn the Gipsy lore,
　And roam'd the world with that wild brotherhood,
　And came, as most men deem'd, to little good,
　　But came to Oxford and his friends no more.

But once, years after, in the country lanes,
　Two scholars whom at college erst he knew,
　Met him, and of his way of life inquir'd;
Whereat he answer'd, that the Gipsy-crew
　His mates, had arts to rule as they desir'd
　　The workings of men's brains,
And they can bind them to what thoughts they will:
　'And I,' he said, 'the secret of their art,
　When fully learn'd, will to the world impart:
　　But it needs heaven-sent moments for this skill.'

This said, he left them, and return'd no more,
　But rumours hung about the country side,
　That the lost Scholar long was seen to stray,
Seen by rare glimpses, pensive and tongue-tied,
　In hat of antique shape, and cloak of grey,
　　The same the Gipsies wore.
Shepherds had met him on the Hurst in spring,
　At some lone alehouse in the Berkshire moors,
　On the warm ingle-bench, the smock-frock'd boors
　　Had found him seated at their entering.

But, mid their drink and clatter, he would fly:
　And I myself seem half to know thy looks,
　And put the shepherds, Wanderer, on thy trace;
And boys who in lone wheatfields scare the rooks
　I ask if thou hast pass'd their quiet place;
　　Or in my boat I lie
Moor'd to the cool bank in the summer heats,
　Mid wide grass meadows which the sunshine fills,
　And watch the warm, green-muffled Cumner hills,
　　And wonder if thou haunt'st their shy retreats.

For most, I know, thou lov'st retired ground.
　Thee, at the ferry, Oxford riders blithe,
　　Returning home on summer nights, have met
　Crossing the stripling Thames at Bab-lock-hithe,
　　Trailing in the cool stream thy fingers wet,
　　　As the punt's rope chops round ; [1]
　And leaning backward in a pensive dream,
　　And fostering in thy lap a heap of flowers
　　Pluck'd in shy fields and distant Wychwood [2] bowers,
　　　And thine eyes resting on the moonlit stream.

And then they land, and thou art seen no more.
　Maidens, who from the distant hamlets come
　　To dance around the Fyfield elm in May,
　Oft through the darkening fields have seen thee roam,
　　Or cross a stile into the public way.
　　　Oft thou has given them store
　Of flowers–the frail-leaf'd, white anemone–
　　Dark bluebells drench'd with dews of summer eves–
　　And purple orchises with spotted leaves–
　　　But none hath words she can report of thee.

And, above Godstow Bridge, when hay-time's here
　In June, and many a scythe in sunshine flames,
　　Men who through those wide fields of breezy grass,
　Where black-wing'd swallows haunt the glittering Thames,
　　To bathe in the abandon'd lasher pass,
　　　Have often pass'd thee near
　Sitting upon the river bank o'ergrown ;
　　Mark'd thine outlandish garb, thy figure spare,
　　Thy dark vague eyes, and soft abstracted air ;
　　　But, when they came from bathing, thou wast gone !

At some lone homestead in the Cumner hills,
　Where at her open door the housewife darns,
　　Thou hast been seen, or hanging on a gate
　To watch the threshers in the mossy barns.
　　Children, who early range these slopes and late
　　　For cresses from the rills,

[1] variant: As the slow punt swings round
[2] woodland: 1853, 1854

Have known thee eyeing, all an April day,
  The springing pastures and the feeding kine;
  And mark'd thee, when the stars come out and shine,
    Through the long dewy grass move slow away.

In Autumn, on the skirts of Bagley Wood–
  Where most the Gipsies by the turf-edg'd way
  Pitch their smok'd tents, and every bush you see
With scarlet patches tagg'd and shreds of grey,
  Above the forest ground call'd Thessaly–
    The blackbird picking food
Sees thee, nor stops his meal, nor fears at all;
  So often has he known thee past him stray,
  Rapt, twirling in thy hand a wither'd spray,
    And waiting for the spark from heaven to fall.

And once, in winter, on the causeway chill
  Where home through flooded fields foot-travellers go,
  Have I not pass'd thee on the wooden bridge,
Wrapt in thy cloak and battling with the snow,
  Thy face towards Hinksey and its wintry ridge?
    And thou hast climb'd the hill,
And gain'd the white brow of the Cumner range;
  Turn'd once to watch, while thick the snow flakes fall,
  The line of festal light in Christ-Church hall–
    Then sought thy straw in some sequester'd grange.

But what–I dream!   Two hundred years are flown
  Since first thy story ran through Oxford halls,
  And the grave Glanvil did the tale inscribe
That thou wert wander'd from the studious walls
  To learn strange arts, and join a Gipsy tribe:
    And thou from earth art gone
Long since, and in some quiet churchyard laid;
  Some country nook, where o'er thy unknown grave
  Tall grasses and white flowering nettles wave–
    Under a dark-red-fruited yew-tree's shade.

No, no, thou hast not felt the lapse of hours,
    For what wears out the life of mortal men?
        'Tis that from change to change their being rolls;
    'Tis that repeated shocks, again, again,
        Exhaust the energy of strongest souls,
            And numb the elastic powers.
Till having us'd our nerves with bliss and teen,
    And tir'd upon a thousand schemes our wit,
        To the just-pausing Genius we remit
            Our well-worn life, and are—what we have been.

Thou hast not lived, why should'st thou perish, so?
    Thou hadst *one* aim, *one* business, *one* desire:
        Else wert thou long since number'd with the dead—
    Else hadst thou spent, like other men, thy fire.
        The generations of thy peers are fled,
            And we ourselves shall go;
But thou possessest an immortal lot,
    And we imagine thee exempt from age,
        And living as thou liv'st on Glanvil's page,
            Because thou hadst—what we, alas! have not!

For early didst thou leave the world, with powers
    Fresh, undiverted to the world without,
        Firm to their mark, not spent on other things;
    Free from the sick fatigue, the languid doubt,
        Which much to have tried, in much been baffled, brings.
            O life unlike to ours!
Who fluctuate idly without term or scope,
    Of whom each strives, nor knows for what he strives,
        And each half lives a hundred different lives;
            Who wait like thee, but not, like thee, in hope.

Thou waitest for the spark from Heaven: and we,
    Light half-believers of our casual creeds,
        Who never deeply felt, nor clearly will'd,
    Whose insight never has borne fruit in deeds,
        Whose vague resolves never have been fulfill'd;
            For whom each year we see

Breeds new beginnings, disappointments new;
　　Who hesitate and falter life away,
　　And lose to-morrow the ground won to-day—
　　　Ah! do not we, wanderer! await it too?

Yes, we await it, but it still delays,
　　And then we suffer; and amongst us one,
　　Who most has suffer'd, takes dejectedly
　His seat upon the intellectual throne;
　　　And all his store of sad experience he
　　　　Lays bare of wretched days;
　Tells us his misery's birth and growth and signs,
　　And how the dying spark of hope was fed,
　　And how the breast was sooth'd, and how the head,
　　　And all his hourly varied anodynes.

This for our wisest: and we others pine,
　　And wish the long unhappy dream would end,
　　And waive all claim to bliss, and try to bear,
　With close-lipp'd Patience for our only friend,
　　　Sad Patience, too near neighbour to Despair:
　　　　But none has hope like thine.
　Thou through the fields and through the woods dost stray,
　　Roaming the country-side, a truant boy,
　　Nursing thy project in unclouded joy,
　　　And every doubt long blown by time away.

O born in days when wits were fresh and clear,
　　And life ran gaily as the sparkling Thames;
　　Before this strange disease of modern life,
　With its sick hurry, its divided aims,
　　　Its heads o'ertaxed, its palsied hearts, was rife—
　　　　Fly hence, our contact fear!
　Still fly, plunge deeper in the bowering wood!
　　Averse, as Dido did with gesture stern
　　From her false friend's approach in Hades turn,
　　　Wave us away, and keep thy solitude!

Still nursing the unconquerable hope,
   Still clutching the inviolable shade,
     With a free onward impulse brushing through,
   By night, the silver'd branches of the glade–
     Far on the forest skirts, where none pursue,
       On some mild pastoral slope
   Emerge, and resting on the moonlit pales
     Freshen thy flowers as in former years
     With dew, or listen with enchanted ears,
       From the dark dingles, to the nightingales !

But fly our paths, our feverish contact fly !
   For strong the infection of our mental strife,
     Which, though it gives no bliss, yet spoils for rest;
   And we should win thee from thy own fair life,
     Like us distracted, and like us unblest.
       Soon, soon thy cheer would die,
   Thy hopes grow timorous, and unfix'd thy powers,
     And thy clear aims be cross and shifting made;
     And then thy glad perennial youth would fade,
       Fade, and grow old at last, and die like ours.

Then fly our greetings, fly our speech and smiles !
   –As some grave Tyrian trader, from the sea,
     Descried at sunrise an emerging prow
   Lifting the cool-hair'd creepers stealthily,
     The fringes of a southward-facing brow
       Among the Ægæan isles ;
   And saw the merry Grecian coaster come,
     Freighted with amber grapes, and Chian wine,
     Green bursting figs, and tunnies steep'd in brine;
       And knew the intruders on his ancient home,

The young light-hearted masters of the waves ;
   And snatch'd his rudder, and shook out more sail,
     And day and night held on indignantly
   O'er the blue Midland waters with the gale,
     Betwixt the Syrtes and soft Sicily,
       To where the Atlantic raves

Outside the Western Straits, and unbent sails
   There, where down cloudy cliffs, through sheets of foam,
   Shy traffickers, the dark Iberians come;
     And on the beach undid his corded bales.

MATTHEW ARNOLD

640 *To the Pious Memory of the Accomplisht Young Lady Mrs. Anne Killigrew*

Excellent in the Two Sister-Arts of Poesy and Painting

An Ode

Thou youngest Virgin-Daughter of the Skies,
   Made in the last Promotion of the *Blest*;
Whose Palms, new pluckt from Paradise,
In spreading *Branches* more sublimely rise,
   Rich with Immortal Green above the rest:
Whether, adopted to some Neighbouring Star,
Thou roll'st above us in thy wand'ring Race,
   Or, in Procession fixt and regular,
Mov'd with the Heavens' Majestic pace;
   Or, call'd to more Superior *Bliss*,
Thou tread'st, with Seraphims, the vast *Abyss*:
Whatever happy region is thy place,
Cease thy Celestial Song a little space;
(Thou wilt have time enough for Hymns Divine,
Since Heav'n's Eternal Year is thine.)
Hear then a Mortal Muse thy praise rehearse
     In no ignoble Verse;
But such as thy own voice did practise here,
When thy first Fruits of Poesy were given,
To make thyself a welcome Inmate there;
     While yet a young Probationer,
     And Candidate of Heav'n.

If by Traduction came thy Mind,
   Our Wonder is the less to find
A Soul so charming from a Stock so good;
Thy Father was transfus'd into thy *Blood*:
So wert thou born into the tuneful strain,
(An early, rich, and inexhausted Vein.)

But if thy Pre-existing Soul
Was form'd, at first, with Myriads more,
  It did through all the Mighty Poets roll
Who *Greek* or *Latin* Laurels wore,
And was that Sappho last, which once it was before.
  If so, then cease thy flight, O *Heav'n born Mind* !
Thou hast no *Dross* to purge from thy Rich Ore:
  Nor can thy Soul a fairer Mansion find
  Than was the *Beauteous* Frame she left behind:
Return, to fill or mend the Quire of thy Celestial kind.

  May we presume to say, that at thy *Birth*,
New joy was sprung in HEAV'N as well as here on *Earth* ?
For sure the Milder Planets did combine
  On thy *Auspicious* Horoscope to shine,
And ev'n the most Malicious were in Trine.
Thy *Brother-Angels* at thy *Birth*
  Strung each his Lyre, and tun'd it high,
    That all the People of the Sky
Might know a Poetess was born on Earth.
    And then if ever, Mortal Ears
    Had heard the Music of the Spheres!
    And if no clust'ring Swarm of *Bees*
On thy sweet Mouth distill'd their golden Dew,
    'Twas that, such vulgar Miracles
    Heav'n had not Leisure to renew:
  For all the *Blest* Fraternity of Love
Solemnis'd there thy *Birth*, and kept thy Holyday above.

    O Gracious God! How far have we
    Prophan'd thy Heav'nly Gift of Poesy!
    Made prostitute and profligate the Muse,
    Debas'd to each obscene and impious use,
    Whose Harmony was first ordain'd *Above*,
    For Tongues of *Angels* and for *Hymns* of *Love* !
Oh wretched We! why were we hurried down
    This lubric and adult'rate age,
(Nay, added fat Pollutions of our own)
    T'' increase the steaming Ordures of the Stage?
What can we say t' excuse our *Second Fall* ?
Let this thy *Vestal*, Heav'n, atone for all:

Her *Arethusian* Stream remains unsoil'd,
Unmixt with Foreign Filth and undefil'd,
Her Wit was more than Man, her Innocence a Child.

Art she had none, yet wanted none,
    For Nature did that Want supply:
So rich in Treasures of her Own,
    She might our boasted Stores defy:
Such Noble Vigour did her Verse adorn,
That it seem'd borrow'd, where 'twas only born.
Her Morals too were in her *Bosom* bred
    By great Examples daily fed,
What in the best of *Books*, her Father's Life, she read.
    And to be read her self she need not fear;
    Each Test, and ev'ry Light, her Muse will bear,
    Though *Epictetus* with his Lamp were there.
    Ev'n Love (for Love sometimes her Muse exprest),
Was but a Lambent-flame which play'd about her *Breast*:
    Light as the Vapours of a Morning Dream,
    So cold herself, whilst she such Warmth exprest,
    'Twas *Cupid* bathing in *Diana*'s Stream.

Born to the Spacious Empire of the Nine,
One wou'd have thought, she should have been content
To manage well that Mighty Government;
But what can young ambitious Souls confine?
    To the next Realm she stretcht her Sway,
    For *Painture* near adjoining lay,
A plenteous Province, and alluring Prey.
A *Chamber of Dependences* was fram'd,
(As Conquerors will never want Pretence,
    When arm'd, to justify th' Offence),
And the whole Fief, in right of Poetry she claim'd.
    The Country open lay without Defence;
For Poets frequent In-roads there had made,
    And perfectly could represent
    The Shape, the Face, with ev'ry Lineament;
And all the large Domains which the Dumb-sister sway'd;
    All bow'd beneath her Government,
    Receiv'd in Triumph wheresoe'er she went.
Her Pencil drew what'er her Soul design'd
And oft the *happy Draught* surpass'd the *Image* in her *Mind.*

The *Sylvan* Scenes of Herds and Flocks
And fruitful Plains and barren Rocks,
Of shallow *Brooks* that flow'd so clear,
The bottom did the top appear;
Of deeper too and ampler Floods
Which as in Mirrors, shew'd the Woods;
Of lofty Trees, with Sacred Shades
And Perspectives of pleasant Glades,
Where Nymphs of brightest Form appear,
And shaggy Satyrs standing near,
Which them at once admire and fear.
The Ruins too of some Majestic Piece,
Boasting the Pow'r of ancient *Rome* or *Greece*,
Whose Statues, Friezes, Columns, broken lie,
And, tho' defac'd, the Wonder of the Eye;
What *Nature*, *Art*, bold *Fiction*, e'er durst frame,
Her forming Hand gave Feature to the Name.
So strange a Concourse ne'er was seen before,
But when the peopl'd *Ark* the whole Creation bore.

The Scene then chang'd; with bold Erected Look
Our Martial King the sight with Reverence strook;
For, not content t' express his Outward Part,
Her hand call'd out the Image of his Heart,
His Warlike Mind, his Soul devoid of Fear,
His High-designing *Thoughts* were figur'd there,
As when, by Magic, Ghosts are made appear.
Our Phoenix queen was portray'd too so bright,
Beauty alone could *Beauty* take so right:
Her Dress, her Shape, her matchless Grace,
Were all observ'd, as well as heav'nly Face.
With such a Peerless Majesty she stands,
As in that Day she took the Crown from Sacred hands:
Before a Train of Heroines was seen,
In *Beauty* foremost, as in Rank, the Queen!
Thus nothing to her Genius was deny'd,
But like a *Ball* of Fire, the farther thrown,
Still with a greater *Blaze* she shone,
And her bright Soul broke out on ev'ry side.
What next she had design'd, Heaven only knows:
To such Immod'rate Growth her Conquest rose
That Fate alone its Progress could oppose.

Now all those Charms, that blooming Grace,
The well-proportion'd Shape and beauteous Face,
Shall never more be seen by Mortal Eyes;
In Earth the much-lamented Virgin lies!
   Not Wit nor Piety could Fate prevent;
   Nor was the cruel *Destiny* content
   To finish all the Murder at a blow,
   To sweep at once her *Life* and *Beauty* too;
But, like a hardn'd Felon, took a pride
   To work more mischievously slow,
And plunder'd first, and then destroy'd.
O double Sacrilege on things Divine,
To rob the Relic, and deface the Shrine!
   But thus *Orinda* died:
Heav'n, by the same Disease, did both translate,
As equal were their Souls, so equal was their fate.

Mean time, her *Warlike Brother* on the Seas
His waving Streamers to the Winds displays,
And vows for his Return, with vain Devotion, pays.
   Ah, Generous Youth! that Wish forbear,
   The Winds too soon will waft thee here!
   Slack all thy Sails, and fear to come,
Alas, thou know'st not, thou art wreck'd at home!
No more shalt thou behold thy Sister's Face,
Thou hast already had her last Embrace.
But look aloft, and if thou ken'st from far,
Among the *Pleïad*'s, a New-kindl'd star,
If any sparkles, than the rest, more bright,
'Tis she that shines in that propitious Light.

When in mid-Air the Golden Trump shall sound,
   To raise the Nations under ground;
   When in the Valley of *Jehosaphat*
The Judging God shall close the book of Fate;
   And there the last *Assizes* keep
   For those who Wake and those who Sleep;
   When rattling *Bones* together fly
   From the four Corners of the Sky,
When Sinews o'er the Skeletons are spread,
Those cloath'd with Flesh, and Life inspires the Dead;

The Sacred Poets first shall hear the Sound,
And foremost from the Tomb shall bound:
For they are cover'd with the lightest ground;
And straight, with in-born Vigour, on the Wing,
Like mounting Larks, to the New Morning sing.
There *Thou*, sweet Saint, before the Choir shalt go,
As Harbinger of Heav'n, the Way to show,
The Way which thou so well hast learn'd below.

JOHN DRYDEN

641 *An Horatian Ode upon Cromwell's Return from Ireland*

The forward youth that would appear
Must now forsake his muses dear,
   Nor in the shadows sing
   His numbers languishing.
'Tis time to leave the books in dust,
And oil th' unused armour's rust,
   Removing from the wall
   The corslet of the hall.
So restless Cromwell could not cease
In the inglorious arts of peace,
   But through advent'rous war
   Urged his active star.
And, like the three fork'd lightning, first
Breaking the clouds where it was nurst,
   Did through his own side
   His fiery way divide.
For 'tis all one to courage high
The emulous or enemy;
   And with such to inclose
   Is more then to oppose.
Then burning through the air he went,
And palaces and temples rent:
   And Caesar's head at last
   Did through his laurels blast.
'Tis madness to resist or blame
The force of angry heaven's flame:
   And, if we would speak true,
   Much to the man is due.

Who, from his private gardens, where
He liv'd reserved and austere,
    As if his highest plot
    To plant the bergamot,
Could by industrious valour climb
To ruin the great work of time,
    And cast the kingdom old
    Into another mould.
Though justice against fate complain,
And plead the ancient rights in vain:
    But those do hold or break
    As men are strong or weak.
Nature that hateth emptiness,
Allows of penetration less:
    And therefore must make room
    Where greater spirits come.
What field of all the civil wars,
Where his were not the deepest scars?
    And Hampton shows what part
    He had of wiser art.
Where, twining subtile fears with hope,
He wove a net of such a scope,
    That Charles himself might chase
    To Caresbrook's narrow case.
That thence the royal actor borne
The tragic scaffold might adorn:
    While round the armed bands
    Did clap their bloody hands.
He nothing common did or mean
Upon that memorable scene:
    But with his keener eye
    The axe's edge did try:
Nor call'd the gods with vulgar spite
To vindicate his helpless right,
    But bow'd his comely head,
    Down as upon a bed.
This was that memorable hour
Which first assur'd the forced pow'r.
    So when they did design
    The Capitol's first line,

A bleeding head where they begun,
Did fright the architects to run;
   And yet in that the State
   Foresaw its happy fate.
And now the Irish are asham'd
To see themselves in one year tam'd:
   So much one man can do,
   That does both act and know.
They can affirm his praises best,
And have, though overcome, confest
   How good he is, how just,
   And fit for highest trust:
Nor yet grown stiffer with command,
But still in the republic's hand:
   How fit he is to sway
   That can so well obey.
He to the commons feet presents
A kingdom, for his first years rents:
   And, what he may, forbears
   His fame to make it theirs:
And has his sword and spoils ungirt,
To lay them at the public's skirt.
   So when the falcon high
   Falls heavy from the sky,
She, having kill'd, no more does search,
But on the next green bough to perch;
   Where, when he first does lure,
   The Falconer has her sure.
What may not then our isle presume
While victory his crest does plume!
   What may not others fear
   If thus he crown each year!
A Caesar he ere long to Gaul,
To Italy an Hannibal,
   And to all states not free
   Shall clymacterick be.
The Pict no shelter now shall find
Within his party-colour'd mind;
   But from this valour sad
   Shrink underneath the plad:

Happy if in the tufted brake
The English hunter him mistake.
  Nor lay his hounds in near
  The Caledonian deer.
But thou the wars' and fortune's Son
March indefatigably on:
  And for the last effect
  Still keep thy sword erect;
Besides the force it has to fright
The spirits of the shady night,
  The same arts that did gain
  A pow'r must it maintain.

ANDREW MARVELL

642 *Alexander's Feast; or, the Power of Music*

An Ode in Honour of St. Cecilia's Day: 1697

i

'Twas at the Royal Feast, for *Persia* won,
    By *Philip*'s Warlike Son:
    Aloft in awful State
    The God-like Hero sate
    On his Imperial Throne;
  His valiant Peers were plac'd around;
Their Brows with Roses and with Myrtles bound.
  (So should Desert in Arms be Crown'd:)
The lovely *Thaïs* by his side,
Sat like a blooming *Eastern* Bride
In Flow'r of Youth and Beauty's Pride.
    Happy, happy, happy Pair!
      None but the Brave,
      None but the Brave,
  None but the Brave deserves the Fair.

Chorus

Happy, happy, happy Pair!
  None but the Brave,
  None but the Brave,
None but the Brave deserves the Fair.

ii

Timotheus plac'd on high
　　Amid the tuneful Quire
With flying Fingers touch'd the Lyre:
　　The trembling Notes ascend the Sky,
　　And Heav'nly Joys inspire.
The Song began from *Jove*;
Who left his blissful Seats above,
(Such is the Pow'r of mighty Love.)
A Dragon's fiery Form belied the God:
Sublime on Radiant Spires He rode,
When He to fair *Olympia* press'd:
And while He sought her snowy Breast:
Then, round her slender Waist he curl'd,
And stamp'd an Image of himself, a Sov'reign of the World.
　　The list'ning crowd admire the lofty Sound,
　　A present Deity, they shout around:
　　A present Deity, the vaulted Roofs rebound.
　　　　With ravish'd Ears
　　　　The Monarch hears,
　　　　Assumes the God,
　　　　Affects to nod,
　　　And seems to shake the Spheres.

Chorus

With ravish'd Ears
The Monarch hears,
Assumes the God,
Affects to nod,
And seems to shake the Spheres.

iii

The Praise of *Bacchus* then the sweet Musician sung,
　　Of *Bacchus* ever Fair, and ever Young:
　　　The jolly God in Triumph comes;
　　　Sound the Trumpets; beat the Drums;
　　　　Flush'd with a purple Grace
　　　　He shows his honest Face:
Now give the Hautboys breath; He comes, He comes.

Bacchus ever Fair and Young
　Drinking Joys did first ordain;
Bacchus' Blessings are a Treasure;
Drinking is the Soldier's Pleasure;
　　Rich the Treasure;
　　Sweet the Pleasure;
　Sweet is Pleasure after Pain.

Chorus

Bacchus' *Blessings are a Treasure,*
Drinking is the Soldier's Pleasure;
　　Rich the Treasure,
　　Sweet the Pleasure,
　Sweet is Pleasure after Pain.

iv

Sooth'd with the Sound the King grew vain;
　Fought all his Battles o'er again;
And thrice He routed all his Foes, and thrice he slew the slain.
The Master saw the Madness rise,
His glowing Cheeks, his ardent Eyes;
And while He Heav'n and Earth defied,
Chang'd his Hand, and check'd his Pride.
　　He chose a Mournful Muse,
　　Soft Pity to infuse;
　He sung *Darius* Great and Good,
　　By too severe a Fate,
　Fallen, fallen, fallen, fallen,
　　Fallen from his high estate,
　And welt'ring in his Blood:
　Deserted at his utmost Need
　By those his former Bounty fed;
　On the bare Earth expos'd He lies,
　With not a Friend to close his Eyes.
With down-cast Looks the joyless Victor sate,
　　Revolving in his alter'd Soul
　　　The various Turns of Chance below;
　　And, now and then, a Sigh he stole,
　　　And Tears began to flow.

Chorus

Revolving in his alter'd Soul
The various Turns of Chance below;
And, now and then, a Sigh he stole,
And Tears began to flow.

v

The Mighty Master smil'd to see
That Love was in the next Degree;
'Twas but a Kindred-Sound to move,
For Pity melts the Mind to Love.
    Softly sweet, in *Lydian* Measures,
    Soon he sooth'd his Soul to Pleasures.
War, he sung, is Toil and Trouble;
Honour but an empty Bubble.
    Never ending, still beginning,
Fighting still, and still destroying,
    If the World be worth thy Winning,
Think, O think, it worth Enjoying.
    Lovely *Thaïs* sits beside thee,
    Take the Good the Gods provide thee.
The Many rend the Skies, with loud applause;
So Love was Crown'd, but Music won the Cause.
    The Prince, unable to conceal his Pain,
        Gaz'd on the Fair,
        Who caus'd his Care,
    And sigh'd and look'd, sigh'd and look'd,
    Sigh'd and look'd, and sigh'd again:
At length, with Love and Wine at once oppress'd,
The vanquish'd Victor sunk upon her Breast.

Chorus

The Prince, unable to conceal his Pain,
    Gaz'd on the Fair
    Who caus'd his Care,
And sigh'd and look'd, sigh'd and look'd,
Sigh'd and look'd, and sigh'd again:
At length, with Love and Wine at once oppress'd,
The vanquish'd Victor sunk upon her Breast.

vi

Now strike the Golden Lyre again;
A louder yet, and yet a louder Strain.
Break his Bands of Sleep asunder,
And rouse him, like a rattling Peal of Thunder.
  Hark, hark, the horrid Sound
    Has rais'd up his Head;
    As awak'd from the Dead,
  And amaz'd, he stares around.
Revenge, revenge, *Timotheus* cries,
  See the Furies arise!
  See the Snakes that they rear,
  How they hiss in their Hair,
And the Sparkles that flash from their Eyes!
  Behold a ghastly Band,
  Each a Torch in his Hand!
Those are *Grecian* Ghosts, that in Battle were slain,
    And unburied remain
    Inglorious on the Plain:
    Give the Vengeance due
    To the Valiant Crew.
Behold how they toss their Torches on high,
  How they point to the *Persian* Abodes,
And glitt'ring Temples of their Hostile Gods.
The Princes applaud with a furious Joy;
And the King seized a Flambeau with Zeal to destroy;
    Thaïs led the Way,
    To light him to his Prey,
And, like another *Helen*, fir'd another *Troy*.

Chorus

And the King seiz'd a Flambeau with Zeal to destroy;
  Thaïs *led the Way,*
  To light him to his Prey,
And, like another Helen, *fir'd another* Troy.

vii

    Thus long ago,
  'Ere heaving Bellows learn'd to blow,
    While Organs yet were mute,
    Timotheus, to his breathing Flute

　　　　And sounding Lyre,
Could swell the Soul to rage, or kindle soft Desire.
　　　At last Divine *Cecilia* came,
　　　Inventress of the Vocal Frame;
The sweet Enthusiast, from her Sacred Store,
　　　Enlarg'd the former narrow Bounds,
　　　And added Length to solemn Sounds,
With Nature's Mother-Wit, and Arts unknown before.
　　　Let old *Timotheus* yield the Prize,
　　　　Or both divide the Crown:
　　　He rais'd a Mortal to the Skies:
　　　She drew an Angel down.

Grand Chorus

At last Divine Cecilia *came,*
Inventress of the Vocal Frame;
The sweet Enthusiast, from her Sacred Store,
Enlarg'd the former narrow Bounds,
And added Length to solemn Sounds,
With Nature's Mother-Wit, and Arts unknown before.
Let old Timotheus *yield the Prize,*
Or both divide the Crown:
He rais'd a Mortal to the Skies;
She drew an Angel down.

JOHN DRYDEN

643 *A Song to David*

O THOU, that sit'st upon a throne,
With harp of high majestic tone,
　　To praise the King of kings:
And voice of heav'n-ascending swell,
Which, while its deeper notes excel,
　　Clear, as a clarion, rings:

To bless each valley, grove and coast,
And charm the cherubs to the post
　　Of gratitude in throngs;
To keep the days on Zion's mount,
And send the year to his account,
　　With dances and with songs:

O Servant of God's holiest charge,
The minister of praise at large,
   Which thou may'st now receive;
From thy blest mansion hail and hear,
From topmost eminence appear
   To this the wreath I weave.

Great, valiant, pious, good, and clean,
Sublime, contemplative, serene,
   Strong, constant, pleasant, wise!
Bright effluence of exceeding grace;
Best man!–the swiftness and the race,
   The peril, and the prize!

Great–from the lustre of his crown,
From Samuel's horn, and God's renown,
   Which is the people's voice;
For all the host, from rear to van,
Applauded and embrac'd the man–
   The man of God's own choice.

Valiant–the word, and up he rose–
The fight–he triumph'd o'er the foes,
   Whom God's just laws abhor;
And arm'd in gallant faith he took
Against the boaster, from the brook,
   The weapons of the war.

Pious–magnificent and grand;
'Twas he the famous temple plann'd:
   (The seraph in his soul)
Foremost to give the Lord his dues,
Foremost to bless the welcome news,
   And foremost to condole.

Good–from Jehudah's genuine vein,
From God's best nature good in grain,
   His aspect and his heart;
To pity, to forgive, to save,
Witness En-gedi's conscious cave,
   And Shimei's blunted dart.

Clean–if perpetual prayer be pure,
And love, which could itself inure
    To fasting and to fear–
Clean in his gestures, hands, and feet,
To smite the lyre, the dance complete,
    To play the sword and spear.

Sublime–invention ever young,
Of vast conception, tow'ring tongue,
    To God th' eternal theme;
Notes from yon exaltations caught,
Unrivall'd royalty of thought,
    O'er meaner strains supreme.

Contemplative–on God to fix
His musings, and above the six
    The sabbath-day he blest;
'Twas then his thoughts self-conquest prun'd,
And heavenly melancholy tun'd,
    To bless and bear the rest.

Serene–to sow the seeds of peace,
Rememb'ring, when he watch'd the fleece,
    How sweetly Kidron purl'd–
To further knowledge, silence vice,
And plant perpetual paradise
    When God had calm'd the world.

Strong–in the Lord, who could defy
Satan, and all his powers that lie
    In sempiternal night;
And hell, and horror, and despair
Were as the lion and the bear
    To his undaunted might.

Constant–in love to God THE TRUTH,
Age, manhood, infancy, and youth–
    To Jonathan his friend
Constant, beyond the verge of death;
And Ziba, and Mephibosheth,
    His endless fame attend.

Pleasant–and various as the year;
Man, soul, and angel, without peer,
 Priest, champion, sage and boy;
In armour, or in ephod clad,
His pomp, his piety was glad;
 Majestic was his joy.

Wise–in recovery from his fall,
Whence rose his eminence o'er all,
 Of all the most revil'd;
The light of Israel in his ways,
Wise are his precepts, prayer and praise,
 And counsel to his child.

  * * * *

For ADORATION all the ranks
Of angels yield eternal thanks,
 And DAVID in the midst;
With God's good poor, which, last and least
In man's esteem, thou to thy feast,
 O blessed bridegroom, bidst.

For ADORATION seasons change,
And order, truth, and beauty range,
 Adjust, attract, and fill:
The grass the polyanthus cheques;
And polish'd porphyry reflects,
 By the descending rill.

Rich almonds colour to the prime
For ADORATION; tendrils climb,
 And fruit-trees pledge their gems;
And Ivis with her gorgeous vest
Builds for her eggs her cunning nest,
 And bell-flowers bow their stems.

With vinous syrup cedars spout;
From rocks pure honey gushing out,
 For ADORATION springs:
All scenes of painting crowd the map
Of nature; to the mermaid's pap
 The scaled infant clings.

The spotted ounce and playsome cubs
Run rustling 'mongst the flow'ring shrubs,
    And lizards feed the moss;
For ADORATION beasts embark,
While waves upholding halcyon's ark
    No longer roar and toss.

While Israel sits beneath his fig,
With coral root and amber sprig
    The wean'd advent'rer sports;
Where to the palm the jasmin cleaves,
For ADORATION 'among the leaves
    The gale his peace reports.

Increasing days their reign exalt,
Nor in the pink and mottled vault
    Th' opposing spirits tilt;
And, by the coasting reader spy'd,
The silverlings and crusions glide
    For ADORATION gilt.

For ADORATION rip'ning canes
And cocoa's purest milk detains
    The western pilgrim's staff;
Where rain in clasping boughs inclos'd,
And vines with oranges dispos'd,
    Embower the social laugh.

Now labour his reward receives,
For ADORATION counts his sheaves
    To peace, her bounteous prince;
The nectarine his strong tint imbibes,
And apples of ten thousand tribes,
    And quick peculiar quince.

The wealthy crops of whit'ning rice
'Mongst thyine woods and groves of spice,
    For ADORATION grow;
And, marshall'd in the fenced land,
The peaches and pomegranates stand,
    Where wild carnations blow.

The laurels with the winter strive;
The crocus burnishes alive
    Upon the snow-clad earth.
For ADORATION myrtles stay
To keep the garden from dismay,
    And bless the sight from dearth.

The pheasant shews his pompous neck;
And ermine, jealous of a speck,
    With fear eludes offence:
The sable, with his glossy pride,
For ADORATION is descried,
    Where frosts the wave condense.

The cheerful holly, pensive yew,
And holy thorn, their trim renew;
    The squirrel hoards his nuts:
All creatures batten o'er their stores,
And careful nature all her doors,
    For ADORATION shuts.

For ADORATION, DAVID's Psalms
Lift up the heart to deeds of alms;
    And he, who kneels and chants,
Prevails his passions to control,
Finds meat and med'cine to the soul,
    Which for translation pants.

For ADORATION, beyond match,
The scholar bulfinch aims to catch
    The soft flue's iv'ry touch;
And, careless on the hazel spray,
The daring redbreast keeps at bay
    The damsel's greedy touch.

For ADORATION, in the skies,
The Lord's philosopher espies
    The Dog, the Ram, and Rose;
The planet's ring, Orion's sword;
Nor is his greatness less ador'd
    In the vile worm that glows.

For ADORATION on the strings
The western breezes work their wings,
	The captive ear to soothe.–
Hark! 'tis a voice–how still, and small–
That makes the cataracts to fall,
	Or bids the sea be smooth.

For ADORATION, incense comes
From bezoar, and Arabian gums;
	And from the civet's furr:
But as for pray'r, or ere it faints,
Far better is the breath of saints
	Than galbanum and myrrh.

For ADORATION, from the down
Of dam'sins to th' anana's crown,
	God sends to tempt the taste;
And while the luscious zest invites,
The sense, that in the scene delights,
	Commands desire be chaste.

For ADORATION, all the paths
Of grace are open, all the baths
	Of purity refresh;
And all the rays of glory beam
To deck the man of God's esteem,
	Who triumphs o'er the flesh.

For ADORATION, in the dome
Of Christ the sparrows find an home;
	And on his olives perch:
The swallow also dwells with thee,
O man of God's humility,
	Within his Saviour's CHURCH.

Sweet is the dew that falls betimes,
And drops upon the leafy limes;
	Sweet Hermon's fragrant air:
Sweet is the lily's silver bell,
And sweet the wakeful tapers smell
	That watch for early pray'r.

Sweet the young nurse with love intense,
Which smiles o'er sleeping innocence;
    Sweet when the lost arrive:
Sweet the musician's ardour beats,
While his vague mind's in quest of sweets,
    The choicest flow'rs to hive.

Sweeter in all the strains of love,
The language of thy turtle dove,
    Pair'd to thy swelling chord;
Sweeter with ev'ry grace endu'd,
The glory of thy gratitude,
    Respir'd unto the Lord.

Strong is the horse upon his speed;
Strong in pursuit the rapid glede,
    Which makes at once his game;
Strong the tall ostrich on the ground;
Strong through the turbulent profound
    Shoots xiphias to his aim.

Strong is the lion–like a coal
His eyeball–like a bastion's mole
    His chest against the foes:
Strong the gier-eagle on his sail,
Strong against tide, th' enormous whale
    Emerges, as he goes.

But stronger still, in earth and air,
And in the sea, the man of pray'r:
    And far beneath the tide;
And in the seat to faith assign'd,
Where ask is have, where seek is find,
    Where knock is open wide.

Beauteous the fleet before the gale;
Beauteous the multitudes in mail,
    Rank'd arms and crested heads:
Beauteous the garden's umbrage mild,
Walk, water, meditated wild,
    And all the bloomy beds.

Beauteous the moon full on the lawn;
And beauteous, when the veil's withdrawn,
    The virgin to her spouse:
Beauteous the temple deck'd and fill'd,
When to the heav'n of heav'ns they build
    Their heart-directed vows.

Beauteous, yea beauteous more than these,
The shepherd king upon his knees,
    For his momentous trust;
With wish of infinite conceit,
For man, beast, mute, the small and great,
    And prostrate dust to dust.

Precious the bounteous widow's mite:
And precious, for extreme delight,
    The largess from the churl:
Precious the ruby's blushing blaze,
And alba's blest imperial rays,
    And pure cerulean pearl.

Precious the penitential tear;
And precious is the sigh sincere,
    Acceptable to God:
And precious are the winning flow'rs,
In gladsome Israel's feast of bow'rs,
    Bound on the hallow'd sod.

More precious that diviner part
Of David, ev'n the Lord's own heart,
    Great, beautiful, and new:
In all things where it was intent,
In all extremes, in each event,
    Proof—answ'ring true to true.

Glorious the sun in mid career;
Glorious th' assembled fires appear;
    Glorious the comet's train:
Glorious the trumpet and alarm;
Glorious th' almighty stretch'd-out arm;
    Glorious th' enraptur'd main:

Glorious the northern lights astream;
Glorious the song, when God's the theme:
　　Glorious the thunder's roar:
Glorious hosanna from the den;
Glorious the catholic amen;
　　Glorious the martyr's gore:

Glorious—more glorious is the crown
Of Him, that brought salvation down
　　By meekness, call'd thy Son;
Thou that stupendous truth believ'd,
And now the matchless deed's achiev'd,
　　DETERMIN'D, DAR'D, and DONE.

CHRISTOPHER SMART

644 *The Hound of Heaven*

I fled Him, down the nights and down the days;
I fled Him, down the arches of the years;
I fled Him, down the labyrinthine ways
　　Of my own mind; and in the mist of tears
I hid from Him, and under running laughter.
　　　　Up vistaed hopes I sped;
　　　　And shot, precipitated,
Adown Titanic glooms of chasmèd fears,
　　From those strong Feet that followed, followed after.
　　　　But with unhurrying chase,
　　　　And unperturbèd pace,
　　Deliberate speed, majestic instancy,
　　　　They beat—and a Voice beat
　　　　More instant than the Feet—
'All things betray thee, who betrayest Me.'

　　　　I pleaded, outlaw-wise,
By many a hearted casement, curtained red,
　　Trellised with intertwining charities;
(For, though I knew His love Who followèd,
　　　　Yet was I sore adread
Lest, having Him, I must have naught beside);
But, if one little casement parted wide,
　　The gust of His approach would clash it to.

Fear wist not to evade, as Love wist to pursue.
Across the margent of the world I fled,
  And troubled the gold gateways of the stars,
   Smiting for shelter on their clangèd bars;
          Fretted to dulcet jars
And silvern clatter the pale ports o' the moon.
I said to dawn, Be sudden; to eve, Be soon;
  With thy young skiey blossoms heap me over
        From this tremendous Lover!
Float thy vague veil about me, lest He see!
  I tempted all His servitors, but to find
My own betrayal in their constancy,
In faith to Him their fickleness to me,
  Their traitorous trueness, and their loyal deceit.
To all swift things for swiftness did I sue;
  Clung to the whistling mane of every wind.
     But whether they swept, smoothly fleet,
    The long savannahs of the blue;
        Or whether, Thunder-driven,
     They clanged his chariot 'thwart a heaven
Plashy with flying lightnings round the spurn o' their feet:-
  Fear wist not to evade as Love wist to pursue.
        Still with unhurrying chase,
        And unperturbèd pace,
     Deliberate speed, majestic instancy,
        Came on the following Feet,
        And a Voice above their beat-
  'Naught shelters thee, who wilt not shelter Me.'

I sought no more that after which I strayed
        In face of man or maid:
But still within the little children's eyes
     Seems something, something that replies;
They at least are for me, surely for me!
I turned me to them very wistfully;
But, just as their young eyes grew sudden fair
     With dawning answers there,
Their angel plucked them from me by the hair.
'Come then, ye other children, Nature's-share
With me' (said I) 'your delicate fellowship;
    Let me greet you lip to lip,

B B

Let me twine with you caresses,
　　　　Wantoning
With our Lady-Mother's vagrant tresses,
　　　　Banqueting
With her in her wind-walled palace,
Underneath her azured daïs,
Quaffing, as your taintless way is,
　　　　From a chalice
Lucent-weeping out of the dayspring.'
　　　　So it was done:
I in their delicate fellowship was one—
Drew the bolt of Nature's secrecies.
I knew all the swift importings
　　　On the wilful face of skies;
　　　I knew how the clouds arise
　　　Spumèd of the wild sea-snortings;
　　　　　All that's born or dies
　　　Rose and drooped with—made them shapers
Of mine own moods, or wailful or divine—
　　　With them joyed and was bereaven.
　　　I was heavy with the even,
　　　When she lit her glimmering tapers
　　　Round the day's dead sanctities.
　　　I laughed in the morning's eyes.
I triumphed and I saddened with all weather,
　　　Heaven and I wept together,
And its sweet tears were salt with mortal mine:
Against the red throb of its sunset-heart
　　　　I laid my own to beat,
　　　　And share commingling heat;
But not by that, by that, was eased my human smart.
In vain my tears were wet on Heaven's grey cheek.
For ah! we know not what each other says,
　　　These things and I; in sound *I* speak—
Their sound is but their stir, they speak by silences.
Nature, poor stepdame, cannot slake my drouth;
　　　Let her, if she would owe me,
Drop yon blue bosom-veil of sky, and show me
　　　The breasts o' her tenderness:
Never did any milk of hers once bless
　　　　My thirsting mouth.

Nigh and nigh draws the chase,
With unperturbèd pace,
Deliberate speed, majestic instancy;
And past those noisèd Feet
A voice comes yet more fleet–
'Lo! naught contents thee, who content'st not Me.'

Naked I wait Thy love's uplifted stroke!
My harness piece by piece Thou hast hewn from me,
And smitten me to my knee;
I am defenceless utterly,
I slept, methinks, and woke,
And, slowly gazing, find me stripped in sleep.
In the rash lustihead of my young powers,
I shook the pillaring hours
And pulled my life upon me; grimed with smears,
I stand amid the dust o' the mounded years–
My mangled youth lies dead beneath the heap.
My days have crackled and gone up in smoke,
Have puffed and burst as sun-starts on a stream.
Yea, faileth now even dream
The dreamer, and the lute the lutanist;
Even the linked fantasies, in whose blossomy twist
I swung the earth a trinket at my wrist,
Are yielding; cords of all too weak account
For earth with heavy griefs so overplussed.
Ah! is Thy love indeed
A weed, albeit an amaranthine weed,
Suffering no flowers except its own to mount?
Ah! must–
Designer infinite!–
Ah! must Thou char the wood ere Thou canst limn with it?
My freshness spent its wavering shower i' the dust;
And now my heart is as a broken fount,
Wherein tear-drippings stagnate, spilt down ever
From the dank thoughts that shiver
Upon the sighful branches of my mind.
Such is; what is to be?
The pulp so bitter, how shall taste the rind?
I dimly guess what Time in mists confounds;
Yet ever and anon a trumpet sounds

From the hid battlements of Eternity;
Those shaken mists a space unsettle, then
Round the half-glimpsèd turrets slowly wash again.
     But not ere him who summoneth
     I first have seen, enwound
With glooming robes purpureal, cypress-crowned;
His name I know, and what his trumpet saith.
     Whether man's heart or life it be which yields
     Thee harvest, must Thy harvest fields
     Be dunged with rotten death?

     Now of that long pursuit
     Comes on at hand the bruit;
    That Voice is round me like a bursting sea:
     'And is thy earth so marred,
     Shattered in shard on shard?
    Lo, all things fly thee, for thou fliest Me!
    Strange, piteous, futile thing,
Wherefore should any set thee love apart?
Seeing none but I makes much of naught' (He said),
'And human love needs human meriting:
     How hast thou merited—
Of all man's clotted clay the dingiest clot?
     Alack, thou knowest not
How little worthy of any love thou art!
Whom wilt thou find to love ignoble thee
     Save Me, save only Me?
All which I took from thee I did but take,
     Not for thy harms,
But just that thou might'st seek it in My arms.
     All which thy child's mistake
Fancies as lost, I have stored for thee at home:
     Rise, clasp My hand, and come!'

     Halts by me that footfall:
     Is my gloom, after all,
Shade of His hand, outstretched caressingly?
     'Ah, fondest, blindest, weakest,
     I am He Whom thou seekest!
Thou dravest love from thee, who dravest Me.'
                 FRANCIS THOMPSON

645 *Ode to Psyche*

O Goddess! hear these tuneless numbers, wrung
   By sweet enforcement and remembrance dear,
And pardon that thy secrets should be sung
   Even into thine own soft-conched ear:
Surely I dreamt to-day, or did I see
   The winged Psyche with awaken'd eyes?
I wander'd in a forest thoughtlessly,
   And, on the sudden, fainting with surprise,
Saw two fair creatures, couched side by side
   In deepest grass, beneath the whisp'ring roof
   Of leaves and trembled blossoms, where there ran
     A brooklet, scarce espied:
'Mid hush'd, cool-rooted flowers, fragrant-eyed,
   Blue, silver-white, and budded Tyrian,
They lay calm-breathing on the bedded grass;
   Their arms embraced, and their pinions too;
   Their lips touch'd not, but had not bade adieu,
As if disjoined by soft-handed slumber,
And ready still past kisses to outnumber
   At tender eye-dawn of aurorean love:
     The winged boy I knew;
But who wast thou, O happy, happy dove?
     His Psyche true!

O latest born and loveliest vision far
   Of all Olympus' faded hierarchy!
Fairer than Phoebe's sapphire-region'd star,
   Or Vesper, amorous glow-worm of the sky;
Fairer than these, though temple thou hast none,
    Nor altar heap'd with flowers;
Nor virgin-choir to make delicious moan
    Upon the midnight hours;
No voice, no lute, no pipe, no incense sweet
   From chain-swung censer teeming;
No shrine, no grove, no oracle, no heat
   Of pale-mouth'd prophet dreaming.

O brightest! though too late for antique vows,
   Too, too late for the fond believing lyre,

When holy were the haunted forest boughs,
   Holy the air, the water, and the fire;
Yet even in these days so far retir'd
   From happy pieties, thy lucent fans,
   Fluttering among the faint Olympians,
I see, and sing, by my own eyes inspired.
So let me be thy choir, and make a moan
    Upon the midnight hours;
Thy voice, thy lute, thy pipe, thy incense sweet
   From swinged censer teeming;
Thy shrine, thy grove, thy oracle, thy heat
   Of pale-mouth'd prophet dreaming.

Yes, I will be thy priest, and build a fane
   In some untrodden region of my mind,
Where branched thoughts, new grown with pleasant pain
   Instead of pines shall murmur in the wind:
Far, far around shall those dark-cluster'd trees
   Fledge the wild-ridged mountains steep by steep;
And there by zephyrs, streams, and birds, and bees,
   The moss-lain Dryads shall be lull'd to sleep;
And in the midst of this wide quietness
A rosy sanctuary will I dress
With the wreath'd trellis of a working brain,
   With buds, and bells, and stars without a name,
With all the gardener Fancy e'er could feign,
   Who breeding flowers, will never breed the same:
And there shall be for thee all soft delight
   That shadowy thought can win,
A bright torch, and a casement ope at night,
   To let the warm Love in!

JOHN KEATS

646 *Prothalamion*

Calme was the day, and through the trembling ayre,
Sweete breathing *Zephyrus* did softly play
A gentle spirit, that lightly did delay
Hot *Titans* beames, which then did glyster fayre:
When I whom sullein care,

Through discontent of my long fruitless stay
In princes Court, and expectation vayne
Of idle hopes, which still doe fly away,
Like empty shaddowes, did aflict my brayne,
Walkt forth to ease my payne
Along the shoare of silver streaming *Themmes*,
Whose rutty Bancke, the which his River hemmes,
Was paynted all with variable flowers,
And all the meades adorned with daintie gemmes,
Fit to decke maydens bowers,
And crowne their Paramours,
Against the Brydale day, which is not long:
    Sweet *Themmes* runne softly, till I end my Song.

There, in a Meadow, by the Rivers side,
A Flocke of *Nymphes* I chaunced to espy,
All lovely Daughters of the Flood thereby,
With goodly greenish locks all loose untyde,
As each had bene a Bryde,
And each one had a little wicker basket,
Made of fine twigs entrayled curiously,
In which they gathered flowers to fill their flasket:
And with fine Fingers, cropt full featously
The tender stalkes on hye.
Of every sort, which in that Meadow grew,
They gathered some; the Violet pallid blew,
The little Dazie, that at evening closes,
The virgin Lillie, and the Primrose trew,
With store of Vermeil Roses,
To decke their Bridegromes posies,
Against the Brydale day, which was not long:
    Sweet *Themmes* runne softly, till I end my Song.

With that, I saw two Swannes of goodly hewe,
Come softly swimming downe along the Lee;
Two fairer Birds I yet did never see:
The snow which doth the top of *Pindus* strew,
Did never whiter shew,
Nor *Jove* himself when he a Swan would be
For love of *Leda*, whiter did appeare:

Yet Leda was they say as white as he,
Yet not so white as these, nor nothing neare;
So purely white they were,
That even the gentle streame, the which them bare,
Seem'd foule to them, and bad his billowes spare
To wet their silken feathers, least they might
Soyle their fayre plumes with water not so fayre,
And marre their beauties bright,
That shone as heavens light,
Against their Brydale day, which was not long:
  Sweet *Themmes* runne softly, till I end my Song.

Eftsoones the *Nymphes*, which now had Flowers their fill,
Ran all in haste, to see that silver brood,
As they came floating on the Christal Flood.
Whom when they sawe, they stood amazed still,
Their wondring eyes to fill,
Them seem'd they never saw a sight so fayre,
Of Fowles so lovely, that they sure did deeme
Them heavenly borne, or to be that same payre
Which through the Skie draw *Venus* silver Teeme,
For sure they did not seeme
To be begot of any earthly Seede,
But rather Angels or of Angels breede:
Yet were they bred of *Somers-heat* they say,
In sweetest Season, which each Flower and weede
The earth did fresh aray,
So fresh they seem'd as day,
Even as their Brydale day, which was not long:
  Sweet *Themmes* runne softly, till I end my Song.

Then forth they all out of their baskets drew,
Great store of Flowers, the honour of the field,
That to the sense did fragrant odours yield,
All which upon those goodly Birds they threw,
And all the Waves did strew,
That like old *Peneus* Waters they did seeme,
When downe along by pleasant *Tempes* shore
Scattred with Flowres, through *Thessaly* they streeme,
That they appeare through Lillies plenteous store,
Like a Brydes Chamber flore:

Two of those *Nymphes*, meane while, two Garlands bound,
Of freshest Flowres which in that Mead they found,
The which presenting all in trim Array,
Their snowie Foreheads therewithall they crownd,
Whilst one did sing this Lay,
Prepar'd against that Day,
Against their Brydale day, which was not long:
   Sweete *Themmes* runne softly, till I end my Song.

Ye gentle Birdes, the worlds faire ornament,
And heavens glorie, whom this happie hower
Doth leade unto your lovers blisfull bower,
Joy may you have and gentle hearts content
Of your loves couplement:
And let faire *Venus*, that is Queene of love,
With her heart-quelling Sonne upon you smile,
Whose smile they say, hath vertue to remove
All Loves dislike, and friendships faultie guile
For ever to assoile.
Let endlesse Peace your steadfast hearts accord,
And blessed Plentie wait upon your bord,
And let your bed with pleasures chast abound,
That fruitfull issue may to you afford,
Which may your foes confound,
And make your joyes redound,
Upon your Brydale day, which is not long:
   Sweete *Themmes* run softly, till I end my Song.

So ended she; and all the rest around
To her redoubled that her undersong,
Which said, their bridale daye should not be long.
And gentle Eccho from the neighbour ground,
Their accents did resound.
So forth those joyous Birdes did passe along,
Adowne the Lee, that to them murmurde low,
As he would speake, but that he lackt a tong
Yet did by signes his glad affection show,
Making his streame run slow.
And all the foule which in his flood did dwell
Gan flock about these twaine, that did excell

The rest, so far, as *Cynthia* doth shend [1]
The lesser starres. So they enranged well,
Did on those two attend,
And their best service lend,
Against their wedding day, which was not long:
  Sweete *Themmes* run softly, till I end my song.

At length they all to mery *London* came,
To mery London, my most kyndly Nurse,
That to me gave this Lifes first native sourse:
Though from another place I take my name,
An house of auncient fame.
There when they came, whereas those bricky towres,
The which on *Themmes* brode aged backe doe ryde,
Where now the studious Lawyers have their bowers
There whylome wont the Templer Knights to byde,
Till they decayd through pride:
Next whereunto there stands a stately place,
Where oft I gayned gifts and goodly grace
Of that great Lord, which therein wont to dwell,
Whose want too well now feeles my freendles case:
But Ah here fits not well
Olde woes but joyes to tell
Against the bridale daye, which is not long:
  Sweete *Themmes* runne softly, till I end my Song.

Yet therein now doth lodge a noble Peer,
Great *Englands* glory and the Worlds wide wonder,
Whose dreadfull name, late through all *Spaine* did thunder,
And *Hercules* two pillors standing neere,
Did make to quake and feare:
Faire branch of Honor, flower of Chevalrie,
That fillest *England* with thy triumphs fame,
Joy have thou of thy noble victorie,
And endlesse happinesse of thine owne name
That promiseth the same:
That through thy prowesse and victorious armes,
Thy country may be freed from forraine harmes:

[1] surpass

And great *Elisaes* glorious name may ring
Through al the world, fil'd with thy wide Alarmes,
Which some brave muse may sing
To ages following,
Upon the Brydale day, which is not long:
   Sweete *Themmes* runne softly, till I end my Song.

From those high Towers, this noble Lord issuing
Like Radiant *Hesper* when his golden hayre
In th' *Ocean* billowes he hath Bathed fayre,
Descended to the Rivers open vewing,
With a great traine ensuing.
Above the rest were goodly to be seene
Two gentle Knights of lovely face and feature
Beseeming well the bower of anie Queene,
With gifts of wit and ornaments of nature,
Fit for so goodly stature:
That like the twins of *Jove* they seem'd in sight,
Which decke the Bauldricke [1] of the Heavens bright.
They two forth pacing to the Rivers side,
Received those two faire Brides, their Loves delight,
Which at th' appointed tyde,
Each one did make his Bryde.
Against their Brydale day, which is not long:
   Sweet Themmes runne softly, till I end my Song.
                        EDMUND SPENSER

647 Ode: Intimations of Immortality from Recollections of Early Childhood

The Child is father of the Man;
And I could wish my days to be
Bound each to each by natural piety.

I

There was a time when meadow, grove, and stream,
The earth, and every common sight,
    To me did seem
    Apparelled in celestial light,
The glory and the freshness of a dream.

[1] belt, girdle

It is not now as it hath been of yore;—
    Turn whereso'er I may,
      By night or day,
The things which I have seen I now can see no more.

II

    The Rainbow comes and goes,
    And lovely is the Rose,
    The Moon doth with delight
Look round her when the heavens are bare;
    Waters on a starry night
    Are beautiful and fair;
The sunshine is a glorious birth;
But yet I know, where'er I go,
That there hath past away a glory from the earth.

III

Now, while the birds thus sing a joyous song,
    And while the young lambs bound
      As to the tabor's sound,
To me alone there came a thought of grief:
A timely utterance gave that thought relief,
    And I again am strong:
The cataracts blow their trumpets from the steep;
No more shall grief of mind the season wrong;
I hear the Echoes through the mountains throng,
The Winds come to me from the fields of sleep,
    And all the earth is gay;
      Land and sea
    Give themselves up to jollity,
     And with the heart of May
    Doth every Beast keep holiday;—
      Thou Child of Joy,
Shout round me, let me hear thy shouts, thou happy
   Shepherd-boy!

IV

Ye blessèd Creatures, I have heard the call
    Ye to each other make; I see
The heavens laugh with you in your jubilee;

My heart is at your festival,
  My head hath its coronal,
The fulness of your bliss, I feel–I feel it all.
      Oh evil day! if I were sullen
      While Earth herself is adorning,
        This sweet May-morning,
      And the Children are culling
        On every side,
      In a thousand valleys far and wide,
      Fresh flowers; while the sun shines warm,
And the Babe leaps up on his Mother's arm:–
      I hear, I hear, with joy I hear!
      –But there's a Tree, of many, one,
A single Field which I have looked upon,
Both of them speak of something that is gone:
        The Pansy at my feet
        Doth the same tale repeat:
Whither is fled the visionary gleam?
Where is it now, the glory and the dream?

                    V

Our birth is but a sleep and a forgetting:
The Soul that rises with us, our life's Star,
      Hath had elsewhere its setting,
        And cometh from afar:
      Not in entire forgetfulness,
      And not in utter nakedness,
But trailing clouds of glory do we come
        From God, who is our home:
Heaven lies about us in our infancy!
Shades of the prison-house begin to close
        Upon the growing Boy,
            But He
Beholds the light, and whence it flows
        He sees it in his joy;
The Youth, who daily farther from the east
        Must travel, still is Nature's Priest,
        And by the vision splendid
        Is on his way attended;
At length the Man perceives it die away,
And fade into the light of common day.

VI

Earth fills her lap with pleasures of her own;
Yearnings she hath in her own natural kind,
And, even with something of a Mother's mind,
  And no unworthy aim,
  The homely Nurse doth all she can
To make her Foster-child, her Inmate Man,
  Forget the glories he hath known,
And that imperial palace whence he came.

VII

Behold the Child among his new-born blisses,
A six years' Darling of a pigmy size!
See, where 'mid work of his own hand he lies,
Fretted by sallies of his mother's kisses,
With light upon him from his father's eyes!
See, at his feet, some little plan or chart,
Some fragment from his dream of human life,
Shaped by himself with newly-learned art;
  A wedding or a festival,
  A mourning or a funeral;
   And this hath now his heart,
  And unto this he frames his song:
   Then will he fit his tongue
To dialogues of business, love, or strife;
   But it will not be long
  Ere this be thrown aside,
  And with new joy and pride
The little Actor cons another part;
Filling from time to time his 'humorous stage'
With all the Persons, down to palsied Age,
That Life brings with her in her equipage;
  As if his whole vocation
  Were endless imitation.

VIII

Thou, whose exterior semblance doth belie
  Thy Soul's immensity;

Thou best Philosopher, who yet dost keep
Thy heritage, thou Eye among the blind,
That, deaf and silent, read'st the eternal deep,
Haunted for ever by the eternal mind,–
     Mighty Prophet! Seer blest!
     On whom those truths do rest,
Which we are toiling all our lives to find,
In darkness lost, the darkness of the grave;
Thou, over whom thy Immortality
Broods like the Day, A Master o'er a Slave,
A Presence which is not to be put by;
     [To whom the grave
Is but a lonely bed without the sense or sight
     Of day or the warm light,
A place of thought where we in waiting lie; [1]]
Thou little Child, yet glorious in the might
Of heaven-born freedom on thy being's height,
Why with such earnest pains dost thou provoke
The years to bring the inevitable yoke,
Thus blindly with thy blessedness at strife?
Full soon thy Soul shall have her earthly freight,
And custom lie upon thee with a weight,
Heavy as frost, and deep almost as life!

IX

     O joy! that in our embers
     Is something that doth live,
     That nature yet remembers
     What was so fugitive!
The thought of our past years in me doth breed
Perpetual benediction: not indeed
For that which is most worthy to be blest;
Delight and liberty, the simple creed
Of Childhood, whether busy or at rest,
With new-fledged hope still fluttering in his breast:–
     Not for these I raise
     The song of thanks and praise;
    But for those obstinate questionings
    Of sense and outward things,
    Fallings from us, vanishings;

[1] See Notes.

Blank misgivings of a Creature
Moving about in worlds not realised,
High instincts before which our mortal Nature
Did tremble like a guilty Thing surprised:
  But for those first affections,
  Those shadowy recollections,
  Which, be they what they may,
Are yet the fountain-light of all our day,
Are yet a master-light of all our seeing;
  Uphold us, cherish, and have power to make
Our noisy years seem moments in the being
Of the eternal Silence: truths that wake,
  To perish never:
Which neither listlessness, nor mad endeavour,
  Nor Man nor Boy,
Nor all that is at enmity with joy,
Can utterly abolish or destroy!
  Hence in a season of calm weather
  Though inland far we be,
Our Souls have sight of that immortal sea
  Which brought us hither,
  Can in a moment travel thither,
And see the Children sport upon the shore,
And hear the mighty waters rolling evermore.

X

Then sing, ye Birds, sing, sing a joyous song!
  And let the young Lambs bound
  As to the tabor's sound!
We in thought will join your throng,
  Ye that pipe and ye that play,
  Ye that through your hearts today
  Feel the gladness of the May!
What though the radiance which was once so bright
Be now for ever taken from my sight,
  Though nothing can bring back the hour
Of splendour in the grass, of glory in the flower;
  We will grieve not, rather find
  Strength in what remains behind;
  In the primal sympathy

Which having been must ever be;
In the soothing thoughts that spring
Out of human suffering;
In the faith that looks through death,
In years that bring the philosophic mind.

XI

And O, ye Fountains, Meadows, Hills and Groves,
Forebode not any severing of our loves!
Yet in my heart of hearts I feel your might;
I only have relinquished one delight
To live beneath your more habitual sway.
I love the Brooks which down their channels fret,
Even more than when I tripped lightly as they;
The innocent brightness of a new-born Day
       Is lovely yet;
The Clouds that gather round the setting sun
Do take a sober colouring from an eye
That hath kept watch o'er man's mortality;
Another race hath been, and other palms are won.
Thanks to the human heart by which we live,
Thanks to its tenderness, its joys, and fears,
To me the meanest flower that blows can give
Thoughts that do often lie too deep for tears.

WILLIAM WORDSWORTH

648 *Samson hath Quit Himself*

Semichorus. While thir hearts were jocund and sublime,
Drunk with Idolatry, drunk with Wine,
And fat regorg'd of Bulls and Goats,
Chaunting thir Idol, and preferring
Before our living Dread who dwells
In *Silo* his bright Sanctuary:
Among them he a spirit of phrenzie sent,
Who hurt thir minds,
And urg'd them on with mad desire
To call in hast for thir destroyer;
They only set on sport and play
Unweetingly importun'd
Thir own destruction to come speedy upon them.

So fond are mortal men
Fall'n into wrath divine,
As thir own ruin on themselves to invite,
Insensate left, or to sense reprobate,
And with blindness internal struck.
   Semichorus. But he though blind of sight,
Despis'd and thought extinguish't quite,
With inward eyes illuminated
His fierie vertue rouz'd
From under ashes into sudden flame,
And as an ev'ning Dragon came
Assailant on the perched roosts,
And nests in order rang'd
Of tame villatic Fowl; but as an Eagle
His cloudless thunder bolted on thir heads.
So vertue giv'n for lost,
Deprest, and overthrown, as seem'd,
Like that self-begott'n bird
In the *Arabian* woods embost,
That no second knows nor third,
And lay e're while a Holocaust,
From out her ashie womb now teem'd
Revives, reflourishes, then vigorous most
When most unactive deem'd,
And though her body die, her fame survives,
A secular bird ages of lives.
   Manoa. Come, come, no time for lamentation now,
Nor much more cause, *Samson* hath quit himself
Like *Samson*, and heroicly hath finish'd
A life Heroic, on his Enemies
Fully reveng'd, hath left them years of mourning,
And lamentation to the Sons of *Caphtor*
Through all *Philistian* bounds. To *Israel*
Honour hath left, and freedom, let but them
Find courage to lay hold on this occasion,
To himself and Fathers house eternal fame;
And which is best and happiest yet, all this
With God not parted from him, as was feard,
But favouring and assisting to the end.
Nothing is here for tears, nothing to wail
Or knock the breast, no weakness, no contempt,

Dispraise, or blame, nothing but well and fair,
And what may quiet us in a death so noble.
Let us go find the body where it lies
Sok't in his enemies blood, and from the stream
With lavers pure and cleansing herbs wash off
The clotted gore. I with what speed the while
(*Gaza* is not in plight to say us nay)
Will send for all my kindred, all my friends
To fetch him hence and solemnly attend
With silent obsequie and funeral train
Home to his Fathers house: there will I build him
A Monument, and plant it round with shade
Of Laurel ever green, and branching Palm,
With all his Trophies hung, and Acts enroll'd
In copious Legend, or sweet Lyric Song.
Thither shall all the valiant youth resort,
And from his memory inflame thir breasts
To matchless valour, and adventures high:
The Virgins also shall on feastful days
Visit his Tomb with flowers, only bewailing
His lot unfortunate in nuptial choice,
From whence captivity and loss of eyes.
   Chorus. All is best, though we oft doubt,
What th' unsearchable dispose
Of highest wisdom brings about,
And ever best found in the close.
Oft he seems to hide his face,
But unexpectedly returns
And to his faithful Champion hath in place
Bore witness gloriously; whence *Gaza* mourns
And all that band them to resist
His uncontroulable intent,
His servants he with new acquist
Of true experience from this great event
With peace and consolation hath dismist,
And calm of mind all passion spent.

JOHN MILTON

649 *Lycidas*

In this Monody the Author bewails a learned Friend,
unfortunately drowned in his passage from Chester on the
Irish Seas, 1637; and, by occasion, foretells the ruin of our
corrupted Clergy, then in their height.

Yet once more, O ye laurels, and once more,
Ye myrtles brown, with ivy never-sear,
I come to pluck your berries harsh and crude,
And with forc'd fingers rude
Shatter your leaves before the mellowing year.
Bitter constraint and sad occasion dear
Compels me to disturb your season due;
For Lycidas is dead, dead ere his prime,
Young Lycidas, and hath not left his peer:
Who would not sing for Lycidas? he knew
Himself to sing, and build the lofty rhyme.
He must not flote upon his watery bear
Unwept, and welter to the parching wind,
Without the meed of som melodious tear.
  Begin then, Sisters of the sacred well,
That from beneath the seat of Jove doth spring,
Begin, and somewhat loudly sweep the string.
Hence with denial vain, and coy excuse:
So may some gentle Muse
With lucky words favour my destin'd urn,
And as he passes turn,
And bid fair peace be to my sable shrowd!
For we were nurst upon the self-same hill,
Fed the same flock, by fountain, shade, and rill.
  Together both, ere the high lawns appear'd
Under the opening eye-lids of the morn,
We drove a-field, and both together heard
What time the gray-fly winds her sultry horn,
Batt'ning our flocks with the fresh dews of night,
Oft till the star that rose, at ev'ning bright
Toward heav'ns descent had slop'd his westering wheel.
Meanwhile the rural ditties were not mute;
Temper'd to the oaten flute,
Rough Satyrs danc'd, and Fauns with clov'n heel

From the glad sound would not be absent long;
And old Damœtas lov'd to hear our song.
   But, O the heavy change, now thou art gon,
Now thou art gon and never must return!
Thee, Shepherd, thee the woods, and desert caves,
With wilde thyme and the gadding vine o'ergrown,
And all their echoes mourn.
The willows, and the hazel copses green,
Shall now no more be seen,
Fanning their joyous leaves to thy soft layes.
As killing as the canker to the rose,
Or taint-worm to the weanling herds that graze,
Or frost to flowers, that their gay wardrobe wear,
When first the white-thorn blows;
Such, Lycidas, thy loss to shepherd's ear.
   Where were ye, Nymphs, when the remorseless deep
Clos'd o're the head of your lov'd Lycidas?
For neither were ye playing on the steep
Where your old bards, the famous Druids, ly,
Nor on the shaggy top of Mona high,
Nor yet where Deva spreads her wisard stream.
Ay me! I fondly dream!
Had ye been there—for what could that have don?
What could the Muse herself that Orpheus bore,
The Muse herself for her inchanting son,
Whom universal nature did lament,
When by the rout that made the hideous roar,
His goary visage down the stream was sent,
Down the swift Hebrus to the Lesbian shore?
   Alass! what boots it with uncessant care
To tend the homely slighted shepherd's trade,
And strictly meditate the thankless Muse?
Were it not better don as others use,
To sport with Amaryllis in the shade,
Or with the tangles of Neæra's hair?
Fame is the spur that the clear spirit doth raise
(That last infirmity of noble mind)
To scorn delights, and live laborious dayes;
But the fair guerdon when we hope to find,
And think to burst out into sudden blaze,

Comes the blind Fury with th' abhorred shears,
And slits the thin-spun life. But not the praise,
Phœbus replied, and touched my trembling ears:
Fame is no plant that grows on mortal soil,
Nor in the glistering foil
Set off to th' world, nor in broad rumour lies,
But lives and spreads aloft by those pure eyes
And perfet witness of all-judging Jove;
As he pronounces lastly on each deed,
Of so much fame in Heav'n expect thy meed.

O fountain Arethuse, and thou honour'd floud,
Smooth-sliding Mincius, crown'd with vocal reeds,
That strain I heard was of a higher mood.
But now my oat proceeds,
And listens to the Herald of the Sea,
That came in Neptune's plea.
He ask'd the waves, and ask'd the fellon winds,
What hard mishap hath doom'd this gentle swain?
And question'd every gust of rugged wings
That blows from off each beaked promontory.
They knew not of his story;
And sage Hippotades their answer brings,
That not a blast was from his dungeon stray'd:
The air was calm, and on the level brine
Sleek Panope with all her sisters play'd.
It was that fatal and perfidious bark,
Built in th' eclipse, and rigg'd with curses dark,
That sunk so low that sacred head of thine.

Next Camus, reverend sire, went footing slow,
His mantle hairy, and his bonnet sedge,
Inwrought with figures dim, and on the edge
Like to that sanguine flower inscrib'd with woe.
Ah! who hath reft (quoth he) my dearest pledge?
Last came, and last did go,
The Pilot of the Galilean Lake;
Two massy keyes he bore of metals twain,
(The golden opes, the iron shuts amain)
He shook his miter'd locks, and stern bespake
How well could I have spar'd for thee, young swain,
Anow of such as for their bellies' sake,

Creep and intrude, and climb into the fold!
Of other care they little reck'ning make
Then how to scramble at the shearers' feast,
And shove away the worthy bidden guest.
Blind mouths! that scarce themselves know how to hold
A sheep-hook, or have learn'd ought els the least
That to the faithful herdman's art belongs!
What recks it them? What need they? They are sped;
And when they list, their lean and flashy songs
Grate on their scrannel pipes of wretched straw,
The hungry sheep look up, and are not fed,
But swoln with wind, and the rank mist they draw,
Rot inwardly, and foul contagion spread:
Besides what the grim woolf with privy paw
Daily devours apace, and nothing sed,
But that two-handed engine at the door,
Stands ready to smite once, and smite no more.
    Return, Alpheus, the dread voice is past,
That shrunk thy streams; return Sicilian Muse,
And call the vales, and bid them hither cast
Their bells, and flou'rets of a thousand hues.
Ye valleys low where the milde whispers use,
Of shades and wanton winds, and gushing brooks,
On whose fresh lap the swart star sparely looks,
Throw hither all your quaint enameld eyes,
That on the green terf suck the honied showres,
And purple all the ground with vernal flowres.
Bring the rathe primrose that forsaken dies,
The tufted crow-toe, and pale jessamine,
The white pink, and the pansie freakt with jeat,
The glowing violet,
The musk-rose, and the well-attir'd woodbine,
With cowslips wan that hang the pensive head,
And every flower that sad embroidery wears;
Bid amaranthus all his beauty shed,
And daffadillies fill their cups with tears,
To strew the laureat herse where Lycid lies.
For so, to interpose a little ease,
Let our frail thoughts dally with false surmise.
Ay me! while thee the shores, and sounding seas

Wash far away, whereere thy bones are hurl'd;
Whether beyond the stormy Hebrides,
Where thou perhaps under the whelming tide
Visit'st the bottom of the monstrous world;
Or whether thou, to our moist vows deny'd,
Sleep'st by the fable of Bellerus old,
Where the great Vision of the guarded mount
Looks toward Namancos and Bayona's hold.
Look homeward Angel now, and melt with ruth:
And, O ye dolphins, waft the haples youth.

Weep no more, woful shepherds weep no more,
For Lycidas, your sorrow, is not dead,
Sunk though he be beneath the watry floar,
So sinks the day-star in the ocean bed,
And yet anon repairs his drooping head,
And tricks his beams, and with new-spangled ore
Flames in the forehead of the morning sky:
So Lycidas sunk low, but mounted high,
Through the dear might of him that walk'd the waves,
Where other groves, and other streams along,
With nectar pure his oozy locks he laves,
And hears the unexpressive nuptial song,
In the blest kingdoms meek of joy and love.
There entertain him all the Saints above,
In solemn troops, and sweet societies
That sing, and singing in their glory move,
And wipe the tears for ever from his eyes.
Now Lycidas the shepherds weep no more;
Henceforth thou art the Genius of the shore,
In thy large recompense, and shalt be good
To all that wander in that perilous flood.

Thus sang the uncouth swain to th' oaks and rills,
While the still morn went out with sandals gray:
He touch'd the tender stops of various quills,
With eager thought warbling his Doric lay:
And now the sun had stretch'd out all the hills,
And now was dropt into the western bay;
At last he rose, and twitch'd his mantle blew:
To-morrow to fresh woods, and pastures new.

JOHN MILTON

650 *Adonais*

An Elegy on the death of John Keats, Author of
'Endymion', 'Hyperion', etc.

I weep for Adonais–he is dead!
O, weep for Adonais! though our tears
Thaw not the frost which binds so dear a head!
And thou, sad Hour, selected from all years
To mourn our loss, rouse thy obscure compeers,
And teach them thine own sorrow, say: 'With me
Died Adonais; till the Future dares
Forget the Past, his fate and fame shall be
An echo and a light unto eternity!'

Where wert thou, mighty Mother, when he lay,
When thy Son lay, pierced by the shaft which flies
In darkness? where was lorn Urania
When Adonais died? With veiléd eyes,
'Mid listening Echoes, in her Paradise
She sate, while one, with soft enamoured breath,
Rekindled all the fading melodies,
With which, like flowers that mock the corse beneath,
He had adorned and hid the coming bulk of Death.

Oh, weep for Adonais–he is dead!
Wake, melancholy Mother, wake and weep!
Yet wherefore? Quench within their burning bed
Thy fiery tears, and let thy loud heart keep
Like his, a mute and uncomplaining sleep;
For he is gone, where all things wise and fair
Descend;–oh, dream not that the amorous Deep
Will yet restore him to the vital air;
Death feeds on his mute voice, and laughs at our despair.

Most musical of mourners, weep again!
Lament anew, Urania!–he died,
Who was the Sire of an immortal strain,
Blind, old and lonely, when his country's pride,

The priest, the slave, and the liberticide,
Trampled and mocked with many a loathéd rite
Of lust and blood; he went, unterrified,
Into the gulf of death; but his clear Sprite
Yet reigns o'er earth; the third among the sons of light.

Most musical of mourners, weep anew!
Not all to that bright station dared to climb;
And happier they their happiness who knew,
Whose tapers yet burn through that night of time
In which suns perished; others more sublime,
Struck by the envious wrath of man or god,
Have sunk, extinct in their refulgent prime;
And some yet live, treading the thorny road,
Which leads, through toil and hate, to Fame's serene abode.

But now, thy youngest, dearest one, has perished—
The nursling of thy widowhood, who grew,
Like a pale flower by some sad maiden cherished,
And fed with true-love tears, instead of dew;
Most musical of mourners, weep anew!
Thy extreme hope, the loveliest and the last,
The bloom, whose petals nipped before they blew
Died on the promise of the fruit, is waste;
The broken lily lies—the storm is overpast.

To that high Capital, where kingly Death
Keeps his high court in beauty and decay,
He came; and bought with price of purest breath,
A grave among the eternal.—Come away!
Haste, while the vault of blue Italian day
Is yet his fitting charnel-roof! while still
He lies, as if in dewy sleep he lay;
Awake him not! surely he takes his fill
Of deep and liquid rest, forgetful of all ill.

He will awake no more, oh, never more!—
Within the twilight chamber spreads apace
The shadow of white Death, and at the door
Invisible Corruption waits to trace

His extreme way to her dim dwelling-place;
The eternal Hunger sits, but pity and awe
Soothe her pale rage, nor dares she to deface
So fair a prey, till darkness, and the law
Of change, shall o'er his sleep the mortal curtain draw.

Oh, weep for Adonais!–The quick Dreams,
The passion-wingéd Ministers of thought,
Who were his flocks, whom near the living streams
Of his young spirit he fed, and whom he taught
The love which was its music, wander not,–
Wander no more, from kindling brain to brain,
But droop there, whence they sprung; and mourn their lot
Round the cold heart, where, after their sweet pain,
They ne'er will gather strength, or find a home again.

And one with trembling hands clasps his cold head,
And fans him with her moonlight wings, and cries;
'Our love, our hope, our sorrow, is not dead;
See, on the silken fringe of his faint eyes,
Like dew upon a sleeping flower, there lies
A tear some Dream has loosened from his brain.'
Lost Angel of a ruined Paradise!
She knew not 'twas her own; as with no stain
She faded, like a cloud which had outwept its rain.

One from a lucid urn of starry dew
Washed his light limbs as if embalming them;
Another clipped her profuse locks, and threw
The wreath upon him, like an anadem,
Which frozen tears instead of pearls begem;
Another in her wilful grief would break
Her bow and wingéd reeds, as if to stem
A greater loss with one which was more weak;
And dull the barbéd fire against his frozen cheek.

Another Splendour on his mouth alit,
That mouth, whence it was wont to draw the breath
Which gave it strength to pierce the guarded wit,
And pass into the panting heart beneath

With lightning and with music: the damp death
Quenched its caress upon his icy lips;
And, as a dying meteor stains a wreath
Of moonlight vapour, which the cold night clips,
It flushed through his pale limbs, and passed to its eclipse.

And others came . . . Desires and Adorations,
Winged Persuasions and veiled Destinies,
Splendours, and Glooms, and glimmering Incarnations
Of hopes and fears, and twilight Phantasies;
And Sorrow, with her family of Sighs,
And Pleasure, blind with tears, led by the gleam
Of her own dying smile instead of eyes,
Came in slow pomp;–the moving pomp might seem
Like pageantry of mist on an autumnal stream.

All he had loved, and moulded into thought,
From shape, and hue, and odour, and sweet sound,
Lamented Adonais. Morning sought
Her eastern watch-tower, and her hair unbound,
Wet with the tears which should adorn the ground,
Dimmed the aereal eyes that kindle day;
Afar the melancholy thunder moaned,
Pale Ocean in unquiet slumber lay,
And the wild Winds flew round, sobbing in their dismay.

Lost Echo sits amid the voiceless mountains,
And feeds her grief with his remembered lay,
And will no more reply to winds or fountains,
Or amorous birds perched on the young green spray,
Or herdsman's horn, or bell at closing day;
Since she can mimic not his lips, more dear
Than those for whose disdain she pined away
Into a shadow of all sounds: a drear
Murmur, between their songs, is all the woodmen hear.

Grief made the young Spring wild, and she threw down
Her kindling buds, as if she Autumn were,
Or they dead leaves; since her delight is flown,
For whom should she have waked the sullen year?

To Phœbus was not Hyacinth so dear
Nor to himself Narcissus, as to both
Thou, Adonais: wan they stand and sere
Amid the faint companions of their youth,
With dew all turned to tears; odour, to sighing ruth.

Thy spirit's sister, the lorn nightingale
Mourns not her mate with such melodious pain;
Not so the eagle, who like thee could scale
Heaven, and could nourish in the sun's domain
Her mighty youth with morning, doth complain,
Soaring and screaming round her empty nest,
As Albion wails for thee: the curse of Cain
Light on his head who pierced thy innocent breast,
And scared the angel soul that was its earthly guest!

Ah, woe is me! Winter is come and gone,
But grief returns with the revolving year;
The airs and streams renew their joyous tone;
The ants, the bees, the swallows reappear;
Fresh leaves and flowers deck the dead Season's bier;
The amorous birds now pair in every brake,
And build their mossy homes in field and brere;
And the green lizard, and the golden snake,
Like unimprisoned flames, out of their trance awake.

Through wood and stream and field and hill and Ocean
A quickening life from the Earth's heart has burst
As it has ever done, with change and motion,
From the great morning of the world when first
God dawned on Chaos; in its stream immersed,
The lamps of Heaven flash with a softer light;
All baser things pant with life's sacred thirst;
Diffuse themselves; and spend in love's delight,
The beauty and the joy of their renewéd might.

The leprous corpse, touched by this spirit tender,
Exhales itself in flowers of gentle breath;
Like incarnations of the stars, when splendour
Is changed to fragrance, they illumine death

And mock the merry worm that wakes beneath;
Nought we know, dies. Shall that alone which knows
Be as a sword consumed before the sheath
By sightless lightning?—the intense atom glows
A moment, then is quenched in a most cold repose.

Alas! that all we loved of him should be,
But for our grief, as if it had not been,
And grief itself be mortal! Woe is me!
Whence are we, and why are we? of what scene
The actors or spectators? Great and mean
Meet massed in death, who lends what life must borrow.
As long as skies are blue, and fields are green,
Evening must usher night, night urge the morrow,
Month follow month with woe, and year wake year to sorrow.

He will awake no more, oh, never more!
'Wake thou,' cried Misery, 'childless Mother, rise
Out of thy sleep, and slake, in thy heart's core,
A wound more fierce than his, with tears and sighs.'
And all the Dreams that watched Urania's eyes,
And all the Echoes whom their sister's song
Had held in holy silence, cried ' Arise!'
Swift as a Thought by the snake Memory stung,
From her ambrosial rest the fading Splendour sprung.

She rose like an autumnal Night, that springs
Out of the East, and follows wild and drear
The golden Day, which, on eternal wings,
Even as a ghost abandoning a bier,
Had left the Earth a corpse. Sorrow and fear
So struck, so roused, so rapped Urania;
So saddened round her like an atmosphere
Of stormy mist; so swept her on her way
Even to the mournful place where Adonais lay.

Out of her secret Paradise she sped,
Through camps and cities rough with stone, and steel,
And human hearts, which to her aery tread
Yielding not, wounded the invisible

Palms of her tender feet where'er they fell:
And barbéd tongues, and thoughts more sharp than they,
Rent the soft Form they never could repel,
Whose sacred blood, like the young tears of May,
Paved with eternal flowers that undeserving way.

In the death-chamber for a moment Death,
Shamed by the presence of that living Might,
Blushed to annihilation, and the breath
Revisited those lips, and Life's pale light
Flashed through those limbs, so late her dear delight.
'Leave me not wild and drear and comfortless,
As silent lightning leaves the starless night!
Leave me not!' cried Urania: her distress
Roused Death: Death rose and smiled, and met her vain
    caress.

'Stay yet awhile! speak to me once again;
Kiss me, so long but as a kiss may live;
And in my heartless breast and burning brain
That word, that kiss, shall all thoughts else survive,
With food of saddest memory kept alive,
Now thou art dead, as if it were a part
Of thee, my Adonais! I would give
All that I am to be as thou now art!
But I am chained to Time, and cannot thence depart!

'O gentle child, beautiful as thou wert,
Why didst thou leave the trodden paths of men
Too soon, and with weak hands though mighty heart
Dare the unpastured dragon in his den?
Defenceless as thou wert, oh, where was then
Wisdom the mirrored shield, or scorn the spear?
Or hadst thou waited the full cycle, when
Thy spirit should have filled its crescent sphere,
The monsters of life's waste had fled from thee like deer.

'The herded wolves, bold only to pursue;
The obscene ravens, clamorous o'er the dead;
The vultures to the conqueror's banner true
Who feed where Desolation first has fed,

And whose wings rain contagion;–how they fled,
When, like Apollo, from his golden bow
The Pythian of the age one arrow sped
And smiled!–The spoilers tempt no second blow,
They fawn on the proud feet that spurn them lying low.

'The sun comes forth, and many reptiles spawn;
He sets, and each ephemeral insect then
Is gathered into death without a dawn,
And the immortal stars awake again;
So is it in the world of living men:
A godlike mind soars forth, in its delight
Making earth bare and veiling heaven, and when
It sinks, the swarms that dimmed or shared its light
Leave to its kindred lamps the spirit's awful night.'

Thus ceased she: and the mountain shepherds came,
Their garlands sere, their magic mantles rent;
The Pilgrim of Eternity, whose fame
Over his living head like Heaven is bent,
An early but enduring monument.
Came, veiling all the lightnings of his song
In sorrow; from her wilds Ierne [1] sent
The sweetest lyrist of her saddest wrong,
And Love taught Grief to fall like music from his tongue.

Midst others of less note, came one frail Form,
A phantom among men; companionless
As the last cloud of an expiring storm
Whose thunder is its knell; he, as I guess,
Has gazed on Nature's naked loveliness,
Actaeon-like, and now he fled astray
With feeble steps o'er the world's wilderness,
And his own thoughts, along that rugged way,
Pursued, like raging hounds, their father and their prey.

A pardlike Spirit beautiful and swift–
A Love in desolation masked;–a Power
Girt round with weakness;–it can scarce uplift
The weight of the superincumbent hour;

[1] Ireland (Gr.)

It is a dying lamp, a falling shower,
A breaking billow;–even whilst we speak
Is it not broken? On the withering flower
The killing sun smiles brightly: on a cheek
The life can burn in blood, even while the heart may break.

His head was bound with pansies overblown,
And faded violets, white, and pied, and blue;
And a light spear topped with a cypress cone,
Round whose rude shaft dank ivy-tresses grew
Yet dripping with the forest's noonday dew,
Vibrated, as the ever-beating heart
Shook the weak hand that grasped it; of that crew
He came the last, neglected and apart;
A herd-abandoned deer struck by the hunter's dart.

All stood aloof, and at his partial moan
Smiled through their tears; well knew that gentle band
Who in another's fate now wept his own,
As in the accents of an unknown land
He sung new sorrow; sad Urania scanned
The Stranger's mien, and murmured: 'Who art thou?'
He answered not, but with a sudden hand
Made bare his branded and ensanguined brow,
Which was like Cain's or Christ's–oh! that it should be so!

What softer voice is hushed over the dead?
Athwart what brow is that dark mantle thrown?
What form leans sadly o'er the white death-bed,
In mockery of monumental stone,
The heavy heart heaving without a moan?
If it be He, who, gentlest of the wise,
Taught, soothed, loved, honoured the departed one,
Let me not vex, with inharmonious sighs,
The silence of that heart's accepted sacrifice.

Our Adonais has drunk poison–oh!
What deaf and viperous murderer could crown
Life's early cup with such a draught of woe?
The nameless worm would now itself disown:
c c

It felt, yet could escape, the magic tone
Whose prelude held all envy, hate, and wrong,
But what was howling in one breast alone,
Silent with expectation of the song,
Whose master's hand is cold, whose silver lyre unstrung.

Live thou, whose infamy is not thy fame!
Live! fear no heavier chastisement from me,
Thou noteless blot on a remembered name!
But be thyself, and know thyself to be!
And ever at thy season be thou free
To spill the venom when thy fangs o'erflow:
Remorse and Self-contempt shall cling to thee;
Hot Shame shall burn upon thy secret brow,
And like a beaten hound tremble thou shalt–as now.

Nor let us weep that our delight is fled
Far from these carrion kites that scream below;
He wakes or sleeps with the enduring dead;
Thou canst not soar where he is sitting now–
Dust to the dust! but the pure spirit shall flow
Back to the burning fountain whence it came,
A portion of the Eternal, which must glow
Through time and change, unquenchably the same,
Whilst thy cold embers choke the sordid hearth of shame.

Peace, peace! he is not dead, he doth not sleep–
He hath awakened from the dream of life–
'Tis we, who lost in stormy visions, keep
With phantoms an unprofitable strife,
And in mad trance, strike with our spirit's knife
Invulnerable nothings.–*We* decay
Like corpses in a charnel; fear and grief
Convulse us and consume us day by day
And cold hopes swarm like worms within our living clay.

He has outsoared the shadow of our night;
Envy and calumny and hate and pain,
And that unrest which men miscall delight,
Can touch him not and torture not again;

From the contagion of the world's slow stain
He is secure, and now can never mourn
A heart grown cold, a head grown gray in vain;
Nor, when the spirit's self has ceased to burn,
With sparkless ashes load an unlamented urn.

He lives, he wakes–'tis Death is dead, not he;
Mourn not for Adonais,–Thou young Dawn,
Turn all thy dew to splendour, for from thee
The spirit thou lamentest is not gone;
Ye caverns and ye forests, cease to moan!
Cease, ye faint flowers and fountains, and thou Air,
Which like a mourning veil thy scarf hadst thrown
O'er the abandoned Earth, now leave it bare
Even to the joyous stars which smile on its despair!

He is made one with Nature: there is heard
His voice in all her music, from the moan
Of thunder to the song of night's sweet bird;
He is a presence to be felt and known
In darkness and in light, from herb and stone,
Spreading itself where'er that Power may move
Which has withdrawn his being to its own;
Which wields the world with never-wearied love,
Sustains it from beneath, and kindles it above.

He is a portion of the loveliness
Which once he made more lovely: he doth bear
His part, while the one Spirit's plastic stress
Sweeps through the dull dense world, compelling there,
All new successions to the forms they wear:
Torturing th' unwilling dross that checks its flight
To its own likeness, as each mass may bear;
And bursting in its beauty and its might
From trees and beasts and men into the Heaven's light.

The splendours of the firmament of time
May be eclipsed, but are extinguished not;
Like stars to their appointed height they climb,
And death is a low mist which cannot blot

The brightness it may veil. When lofty thought
Lifts a young heart above its mortal lair,
And love and life contend in it, for what
Shall be its earthly doom, the dead live there
And move like winds of light on dark and stormy air.

The inheritors of unfulfilled renown
Rose from their thrones, built beyond mortal thought,
Far in the Unapparent. Chatterton
Rose pale,—his solemn agony had not
Yet faded from him; Sidney, as he fought
And as he fell, and as he lived and loved
Sublimely mild, a Spirit without spot,
Arose; and Lucan, by his death approved:
Oblivion as they rose shrank like a thing reproved.

And many more, whose names on Earth are dark,
But whose transmitted effluence cannot die
So long as fire outlives the parent spark,
Rose, robed in dazzling immortality.
'Thou art become as one of us,' they cry.
'It was for thee yon kingless sphere has long
Swung blind in unascended majesty,
Silent alone amid an Heaven of Song.
Assume thy wingèd throne, thou Vesper of our throng!

Who mourns for Adonais? Oh, come forth,
Fond wretch! and know thyself and him aright.
Clasp with thy panting soul the pendulous Earth;
As from a centre, dart thy spirit's light
Beyond all worlds, until its spacious might
Satiate the void circumference: then shrink
Even to a point within our day and night;
And keep thy heart light lest it make thee sink
When hope has kindled hope, and lured thee to the brink.

Or go to Rome, which is the sepulchre,
Oh, not of him, but of our joy: 'tis nought
That ages, empires, and religions there
Lie buried in the ravage they have wrought;

For such as he can lend,–they borrow not
Glory from those who made the world their prey;
And he is gathered to the kings of thought
Who waged contention with their time's decay,
And of the past are all that cannot pass away.

Go thou to Rome,–at once the Paradise,
The grave, the city, and the wilderness;
And where its wrecks like shattered mountains rise,
And flowering weeds, and fragrant copses dress
The bones of Desolation's nakedness
Pass, till the spirit of the spot shall lead
Thy footsteps to a slope of green access
Where, like an infant's smile, over the dead
A light of laughing flowers along the grass is spread;

And gray walls moulder round, on which dull Time
Feeds, like slow fire upon a hoary brand;
And one keen pyramid with wedge sublime,
Pavilioning the dust of him who planned
This refuge for his memory, doth stand
Like flame transformed to marble; and beneath,
A field is spread, on which a newer band
Have pitched in Heaven's smile their camp of death,
Welcoming him we lose with scarce extinguished breath.

Here pause: these graves are all too young as yet
To have outgrown the sorrow which consigned
Its charge to each; and if the seal is set,
Here, on one fountain of a mourning mind,
Break it not thou! too surely shalt thou find
Thine own well full, if thou returnest home,
Of tears and gall. From the world's bitter wind
Seek shelter in the shadow of the tomb.
What Adonais is, why fear we to become?

The One remains, the many change and pass;
Heaven's light forever shines, Earth's shadows fly;
Life, like a dome of many-coloured glass,
Stains the white radiance of Eternity,

Until Death tramples it to fragments.–Die,
If thou wouldst be with that which thou dost seek!
Follow, where all is fled!–Rome's azure sky,
Flowers, ruins, statues, music, words, are weak
The glory they transfuse with fitting truth to speak.

Why linger, why turn back, why shrink, my Heart?
Thy hopes are gone before: from all things here
They have departed; thou shouldst now depart!
A light is passed from the revolving year,
And man, and woman; and what still is dear
Attracts to crush, repels to make thee wither.
The soft sky smiles,–the low wind whispers near:
'Tis Adonais calls! oh, hasten thither,
No more let Life divide what Death can join together.

That Light whose smile kindles the Universe,
That Beauty in which all things work and move,
That Benediction which the eclipsing Curse
Of birth can quench not, that sustaining Love
Which through the web of being blindly wove
By man and beast and earth and air and sea,
Burns bright or dim, as each are mirrors of
The fire for which all thirst; now beams on me,
Consuming the last clouds of cold mortality.

The breath whose might I have invoked in song
Descends on me; my spirit's bark is driven,
Far from the shore, far from the trembling throng
Whose sails were never to the tempest given;
The massy earth and spherèd skies are riven!
I am borne darkly, fearfully, afar;
Whilst, burning through the inmost veil of Heaven,
The soul of Adonais, like a star,
Beacons from the abode where the Eternal are.

PERCY BYSSHE SHELLEY

651 *When lilacs last in the dooryard bloom'd*

1

When lilacs last in the dooryard bloom'd,
And the great star early droop'd in the western sky in the night,
I mourn'd, and yet shall mourn with ever-returning spring.

Ever returning spring, trinity sure to me you bring,
Lilac blooming perennial and drooping star in the west,
And thought of him I love.

2

O powerful western fallen star!
O shades of night–O moody, tearful night!
O great star disappear'd–O the black murk that hides the star!
O cruel hands that hold me powerless–O helpless soul of me!
O harsh surrounding cloud that will not free my soul.

3

In the dooryard fronting an old farm-house near the white-
    wash'd palings,
Stands the lilac-bush tall-growing with heart-shaped leaves of
    rich green,
With many a pointed blossom rising delicate, with the perfume
    strong I love,
With every leaf a miracle–and from this bush in the dooryard,
With delicate-colour'd blossoms and heart-shaped leaves of
    rich green,
A sprig with its flower I break.

4

In the swamp in secluded recesses,
A shy and hidden bird is warbling a song.
Solitary the thrush,
The hermit withdrawn to himself, avoiding the settlements,
Sings by himself a song.

Song of the bleeding throat,
Death's outlet song of life (for well, dear brother, I know
If thou was not granted to sing thou would'st surely die).

5

Over the breast of the spring, the land, amid cities,
Amid lanes and through old woods, where lately the violets
  peep'd from the ground, spotting the grey débris,
Amid the grass in the fields each side of the lanes, passing the
  endless grass,
Passing the yellow-spear'd wheat, every grain from its shroud
  in the dark-brown fields uprisen,
Passing the apple-tree brows of white and pink in the orchards,
Carrying a corpse to where it shall rest in the grave,
Night and day journeys a coffin.

6

Coffin that passes through lanes and streets,
Through day and night with the great cloud darkening the
  land,
With the pomp of the inloop'd flags with the cities draped in
  black,
With the show of the States themselves as of crape-veil'd
  women standing,
With processions long and winding and the flambeaus of the
  night,
With the countless torches lit, with the silent sea of faces and
  the unbared heads,
With the waiting depôt, the arriving coffin, and the sombre
  faces,
With dirges through the night, with the shout and voices
  rising strong and solemn,
With all the mournful voices of the dirges pour'd around the
  coffin,
The dim-lit churches and the shuddering organs—where amid
  these you journey,
With the tolling, tolling bells' perpetual clang,
Here, coffin that slowly passes,
I give you my sprig of lilac.

7

(Nor for you, for one alone,
Blossoms and branches green to coffins all I bring,
For fresh as the morning, thus would I chant a song for you, O
  sane and sacred death.

All over bouquets of roses,
O death, I cover you over with roses and early lilies,
But mostly and now the lilac that blooms the first,
Copious I break, I break the sprigs from the bushes,
With loaded arms I come, pouring for you,
For you and the coffins all of you, O death.)

8

O western orb, sailing the heaven,
Now I know what you must have meant as a month since I
    walk'd,
As I walk'd in silence the transparent shadowy night,
As I saw you had something to tell as you bent to me night
    after night,
As you droop'd from the sky low down as if to my side (while
    the other stars all look'd on),
As we wander'd together the solemn night (for something I
    know not what kept me from sleep),
As the night advanced, and I saw on the rim of the west how
    full you were of woe,
As I stood on the rising ground in the breeze in the cool
    transparent night,
As I watch'd where you pass'd and was lost in the netherward
    black of the night,
As my soul in its trouble dissatisfied sank, as where you, sad
    orb,
Concluded, dropt in the night, and was gone.

9

Sing on there in the swamp,
O singer, bashful and tender, I hear your notes, I hear your call,
I hear, I come presently, I understand you,
But a moment I linger, for the lustrous star has detain'd me,
The star my departing comrade holds and detains me.

10

O how shall I warble myself for the dead one there I loved?
And how shall I deck my song for the large sweet soul that has
    gone?
And what shall my perfume be for the grave of him I love?

Sea-winds blown from east and west,
Blown from the Eastern sea and blown from the Western sea,
    till there on the prairies meeting,
These and with these and the breath of my chant,
I'll perfume the grave of him I love.

11

O what shall I hang on the chamber walls?
And what shall the pictures be that I hang on the walls,
To adorn the burial-house of him I love?

Pictures of growing spring and farms and homes,
With the Fourth-month eve at sundown, and the grey smoke
    lucid and bright,
With floods of the yellow gold of the gorgeous, indolent sinking
    sun, burning, expanding the air,
With the fresh sweet herbage under foot, and the pale green
    leaves of the trees prolific,
In the distance the flowing glaze, the breast of the river, with a
    wind-dapple here and there,
With ranging hills on the banks, with many a line against the
    sky, and shadows,
And the city at hand with dwellings so dense, and stacks of
    chimneys,
And all the scenes of life and the workshops, and the workmen
    homeward returning.

12

Lo, body and soul—this land,
My own Manhattan with spires, and the sparkling and hurrying
    tides, and the ships,
The varied and ample land, the South and the North in the
    light, Ohio's shores and flashing Missouri,
And ever the far-spreading prairies cover'd with grass and corn.
Lo, the most excellent sun so calm and haughty,
The violet and purple morn with just-felt breezes,
The gentle soft-born measureless light,
The miracle spreading bathing all, the fulfill'd noon,
The coming eve delicious, the welcome night and the stars,
Over my cities shining all, enveloping man and land.

13

Sing on, sing on, you grey-brown bird,
Sing from the swamps, the recesses, pour your chant from the
    bushes,
Limitless out of the dusk, out of the cedars and pines.

Sing on, dearest brother, warble your reedy song,
Loud human song, with voice of uttermost woe.

O liquid and free and tender!
O wild and loose to my soul–O wondrous singer!
You only I hear–yet the star holds me (but will soon depart),
Yet the lilac with mastering odour holds me.

14

Now while I sat in the day and look'd forth,
In the close of the day with its light and the fields of spring
    and the farmers preparing their crops,
In the large unconscious scenery of my land with its lakes and
    forests,
In the heavenly aerial beauty (after the perturb'd winds and
    the storms),
Under the arching heavens of the afternoon swift passing, and
    the voices of children and women,
The many-moving sea-tides, and I saw the ships how they
    sail'd,
And the summer approaching with richness, and the fields all
    busy with labour,
And the infinite separate houses, how they all went on, each
    with its meals and minutia of daily usages,
And the streets how their throbbings throbb'd, and the cities
    pent–lo, then and there,
Falling upon them all and among them all, enveloping me with
    the rest,
Appear'd the cloud, appear'd the long black trail,
And I knew death, its thought, and the sacred knowledge of
    death.

Then with the knowledge of death as walking one side of me,
And the thought of death close-walking the other side of me,
And I in the middle as with companions, and as holding the
    hands of companions,

I fled forth to the hiding receiving night that talks not,
Down to the shores of the water, the path by the swamp in the
   dimness,
To the solemn shadowy cedars and ghostly pines so still.

And the singer so shy to the rest receiv'd me,
The grey-brown bird I know receiv'd us comrades three,
And he sang the carol of death, and a verse for him I love.

From deep secluded recesses,
From the fragrant cedars and the ghostly pines so still,
Came the carol of the bird.

And the charm of the carol rapt me,
As I held as if by their hands my comrades in the night,
And the voice of my spirit tallied the song of the bird.

Come lovely and soothing death,
Undulate round the world, serenely arriving, arriving,
In the day, in the night, to all, to each,
Sooner or later delicate death.

Prais'd be the fathomless universe,
For life and joy, and for objects and knowledge curious,
And for love, sweet love—but praise! praise! praise!
For the sure-enwinding arms of cool-enfolding death.

Dark mother always gliding near with soft feet,
Have none chanted for thee a chant of fullest welcome?
Then I chant it for thee, I glorify thee above all,
I bring thee a song that when thou must indeed come, come
*   unfalteringly.*

Approach strong deliveress,
When it is so, when thou hast taken them I joyously sing the dead,
Lost in the loving floating ocean of thee,
Laved in the flood of thy bliss, O death.

From me to thee glad serenades,
Dances for thee I propose saluting thee, adornments and feastings
*   for thee,*

And the sights of the open landscape and the high-spread sky are
*   fitting,*
And life and the fields, and the huge and thoughtful night.

The night in silence under many a star,
The ocean shore and the husky whispering wave whose voice I
*   know,*
And the soul turning to thee, O vast and well-veil'd death,
And the body gratefully nestling close to thee.

Over the tree-tops I float thee a song,
Over the rising and sinking waves, over the myriad fields and the
*   prairies wide,*
Over the dense-pack'd cities all the teeming wharves and ways,
I float this carol with joy, with joy to thee, O death.

15

To the tally of my soul,
Loud and strong kept up the grey-brown bird,
With pure deliberate notes spreading filling the night.

Loud in the pines and cedars dim,
Clear in the freshness moist and the swamp-perfume,
And I with my comrades there in the night.

While my sight that was bound in my eyes unclosed,
As to long panoramas of visions.

And I saw askant the armies,
I saw as in noiseless dreams hundreds of battle-flags,
Borne through the smoke of the battles and pierc'd with
    missiles I saw them,
And carried hither and yon through the smoke, and torn and
    bloody,
And at last but a few shreds left on the staffs (and all in silence),
And the staffs all splinter'd and broken.

I saw battle-corpses, myriads of them,
And the white skeletons of young men, I saw them,
I saw the débris and débris of all the slain soldiers of the war,
But I saw they were not as was thought,

They themselves were fully at rest, they suffer'd not,
The living remain'd and suffer'd, the mother suffer'd,
And the wife and the child and the musing comrade suffer'd,
And the armies that remain'd suffer'd.

16

Passing the visions, passing the night,
Passing, unloosing the hold of my comrades' hands,
Passing the song of the hermit bird and the tallying song of my
soul,
Victorious song, death's outlet song, yet varying ever-altering
song,
As low and wailing, yet clear the notes, rising and falling,
flooding the night,
Sadly sinking and fainting, as warning and warning, and yet
again bursting with joy,
Covering the earth and filling the spread of the heaven,
As that powerful psalm in the night I heard from recesses,
Passing, I leave thee lilac with heart-shaped leaves,
I leave thee there in the door-yard, blooming, returning with
spring.

I cease from my song for thee,
From my gaze on thee in the west, fronting the west, com-
muning with thee,
O comrade lustrous with silver face in the night.

Yet each to keep and all, retrievements out of the night,
The song, the wondrous chant of the grey-brown bird,
And the tallying chant, the echo arous'd in my soul,
With the lustrous and drooping star with the countenance full
of woe,
With the holders holding my hand nearing the call of the bird,
Comrades mine and I in the midst, and their memory ever to
keep, for the dead I loved so well,
For the sweetest, wisest soul of all my days and lands—and
this for his dear sake,
Lilac and star and bird twined with the chant of my soul,
There in the fragrant pines and the cedars dusk and dim.

WALT WHITMAN

652 *From 'Ash Wednesday'*

Lady, three white leopards sat under a juniper-tree
In the cool of the day, having fed to satiety
On my legs my heart my liver and that which had been
    contained
In the hollow round of my skull. And God said
Shall these bones live? shall these
Bones live? And that which had been contained
In the bones (which were already dry) said chirping:
Because of the goodness of this Lady
And because of her loveliness, and because
She honours the Virgin in meditation,
We shine with brightness. And I who am here dissembled
Proffer my deeds to oblivion, and my love
To the posterity of the desert and the fruit of the gourd.
It is this which recovers
My guts the strings of my eyes and the indigestible portions
Which the leopards reject. The Lady is withdrawn
In a white gown, to contemplation, in a white gown.
Let the whiteness of bones atone to forgetfulness.
There is no life in them. As I am forgotten
And would be forgotten, so I would forget
Thus devoted, concentrated in purpose. And God said
Prophesy to the wind, to the wind only for only
The wind will listen. And the bones sang chirping
With the burden of grasshopper saying

Lady of silences
Calm and distressed
Torn and most whole
Rose of memory
Rose of forgetfulness
Exhausted and life-giving
Worried reposeful
The single Rose
Is now the Garden
Where all loves end
Terminate torment
Of love unsatisfied
The greater torment

Of love satisfied
End of the endless
Journey to no end
Conclusion of all that
Is inconclusible
Speech without word and
Word of no speech
Grace to the Mother
For the Garden
Where all love ends.

Under a juniper-tree the bones sang, scattered and shining
We are glad to be scattered, we did little good to each other,
Under a tree in the cool of the day, with the blessing of sand,
Forgetting themselves and each other, united
In the quiet of the desert. This is the land which ye
Shall divide by lot. And neither division nor unity
Matters. This is the land. We have our inheritance.

THOMAS STEARNS ELIOT

Book X
SATIRICAL VERSE

653 *Song*

Wake all the dead! What hoa! What hoa!
How soundly they sleep whose pillows lie low;
They mind not poor lovers who walk above
On the decks of the world in storms of love.
    No whisper now nor glance can pass
    Through wickets or through panes of glass;
For our windows and doors are shut and barr'd,
Lie close in the church, and in the churchyard.
    In every grave make room, make room!
The world's at an end, and we come, we come.

The State is now love's foe, love's foe;
'T has seiz'd on his arms, his quiver and bow;
Has pinion'd his wings, and fetter'd his feet,
Because he made way for lovers to meet,
    But O sad chance, his judge was old;
    Hearts cruel grow, when blood grows cold.
No man being young his process would draw.
Oh heavens that love should be subject to law!
    Lovers go woo the dead, the dead!
Lie two in a grave, and to bed, to bed!

                  SIR WILLIAM D'AVENANT

654 *Nano's Song*

Fools, they are the only nation
Worth men's envy, or admiration;
Free from care, or sorrow-taking,
Selves, and others merry-making:
All they speak, or do, is sterling.
Your Fool, he is your great man's dearling,
And your ladies' sport, and pleasure;
Tongue, and babble are his treasure.
E'en his face begetteth laughter,
And he speaks truth, free from slaughter;

781

He's the grace of every feast,
And, sometimes, the chiefest guest:
Hath his trencher, and his stool,
When wit waits upon the fool,
O, who would not be
Hee, hee, hee?

BEN JONSON

655 *Written in an Inn at Henley*

To thee, fair freedom! I retire
From flattery, cards, and dice, and din:
Nor art thou found in mansions higher
Than the low cot, or humble inn.

'Tis here with boundless pow'r, I reign;
And ev'ry health which I begin,
Converts dull port to bright champagne;
Such freedom crowns it, at an inn.

I fly from pomp, I fly from plate!
I fly from falsehood's specious grin!
Freedom I love, and form I hate,
And choose my lodgings at an inn.

Here, waiter! take my sordid ore,
Which lacqueys else might hope to win;
It buys, what courts have not in store;
It buys me freedom, at an inn.

And now once more I shape my way
Thro' rain or shine, thro' thick or thin,
Secure to meet, at close of day,
With kind reception, at an inn.

Whoe'er has travell'd life's dull round,
Where'er his stages may have been,
May sigh to think he still has found
The warmest welcome, at an inn.

WILLIAM SHENSTONE

656 *A Short Song of Congratulation*

Long-expected one and twenty
Ling'ring year at last is flown;
Pomp and Pleasure, Pride and Plenty
Great Sir John, are all your own.

Loosen'd from the Minor's tether,
Free to mortgage or to sell,
Wild as wind, and light as feather
Bid the Slaves of thrift farewell.

Call the Bettys, Kates, and Jennys
Ev'ry name that laughs at care,
Lavish of your Grandsire's guineas,
Show the Spirit of an heir.

All that prey on vice and folly
Joy to see their quarry fly,
Here the Gamester light and jolly,
There the Lender grave and sly.

Wealth, Sir John, was made to wander,
Let it wander as it will;
See the Jockey, see the Pander,
Bid them come, and take their fill.

When the bonny Blade carouses,
Pockets full, and Spirits high,
What are acres? What are houses?
Only dirt, or wet or dry.

If the Guardian or the Mother
Tell the woes of wilful waste,
Scorn their counsel and their pother,
You can hang or drown at last.

SAMUEL JOHNSON

657 *Horace Paraphrased*

There are a number of us creep
Into this world to eat and sleep,
And know no reason why they're born
But merely to consume the corn,
Devour the cattle, fowl and fish,
And leave behind an empty dish.
The crows and ravens do the same,
Unlucky birds of hateful name;
Ravens or crows might fill their place,
And swallow corn and carcases.
Then if their tombstone when they die
Ben't taught to flatter and to lie,
There's nothing better will be said
Than that 'They 've eat up all their bread,
'Drank up their drink and gone to bed.'

ISAAC WATTS

658 *To Helen*

(July 7th, 1836)

When some grim sorceress, whose skill
Had bound a sprite to work her will,
In mirth or malice chose to ask
Of the faint slave the hardest task,

She sent him forth to gather up
Great Ganges in an acorn cup;
Or Heaven's unnumbered stars to bring
In compass of a signet ring.

Thus Helen bids her poet write
The thanks he owes this morning's light;
And 'Give me,'–so he hears her say,–
'Four verses, only four, to-day.'

Dearest and best! she knows, if wit
Could ever half love's debt acquit,
Each of her tones and of her looks
Would have its four, not lines, but books.

WINTHROP MACKWORTH PRAED

659 *Is it possible?*

Is it possible
That so high debate,
So sharp, so sore, and of such rate,
Should end so soon and was begun so late?
Is it possible?

Is it possible
So cruel intent,
So hasty heat, and so soon spent,
From love to hate, and thence for to relent?
Is it possible?

Is it possible
That any may find,
Within one heart so diverse mind,
To change or turn as weather and wind?
Is it possible?

Is it possible
To spy it in an eye,
That turns as oft as chance on die,
The truth whereof can any try?
Is it possible?

Is it possible?
For to turn so oft;
To bring that low'st that was most aloft;
And to fall highest, yet to light soft;
It is possible.

All is possible;
Whoso list believe,
Trust therefore first, and after preve;
As men wed ladies by license and leave;
All is possible.

SIR THOMAS WYATT

660 *The Buddha at Kamákura*

'And there is a Japanese idol at Kamákura'

Oh ye who tread the Narrow Way
By Tophet-flare to Judgment Day,
Be gentle when the 'heathen' pray
    To Buddha at Kamakura!

To him the Way, the Law, Apart,
Whom Maya held beneath her heart,
Ananda's Lord the Bodhisat,
    The Buddha of Kamakura.

For though he neither burns nor sees,
Nor hears ye thank your Deities,
Ye have not sinned with such as these,
    His children at Kamakura;

Yet spare us still the Western joke
When joss-sticks turn to scented smoke
The little sins of little folk
    That worship at Kamakura—

The grey-robed, gay-sashed butterflies
That flit beneath the Master's eyes—
He is beyond the Mysteries
    But loves them at Kamakura.

And whoso will, from Pride released,
Contemning neither creed nor priest,
May feel the soul of all the East
    About him at Kamakura.

Yea, every tale Ananda heard,
Of birth as fish or beast or bird,
While yet in lives the Master stirred,
    The warm wind brings Kamakura.

Till drowsy eyelids seem to see
A-flower 'neath her golden *htee*
The Shwe-Dagon flare easterly
    From Burmah to Kamakura:

And down the loaded air there comes
The thunder of Thibetan drums,
And droned–'*Om mane padme oms*'–
    A world's width from Kamakura.

Yet Brahmans rule Benares still,
Buddh-Gaya's ruins pit the hill,
And beef-fed zealots threaten ill
    To Buddha and Kamakura.

A tourist-show, a legend told,
A rusting bulk of bronze and gold,
So much, and scarce so much, ye hold
    The meaning of Kamakura?

But when the morning prayer is prayed,
Think, ere ye pass to strife and trade,
Is God in human image made
    No nearer than Kamakura?

              RUDYARD KIPLING

661   *From 'The Masque of Anarchy'*

Stand ye calm and resolute,
Like a forest close and mute,
With folded arms and looks which are
Weapons of unvanquished war,

And let Panic, who outspeeds
The career of armèd steeds
Pass, a disregarded shade
Through your phalanx undismayed.

Let the laws of your own land,
Good or ill, between ye stand
Hand to hand, and foot to foot,
Arbiters of the dispute,

The old laws of England–they
Whose reverend heads with age are gray,
Children of a wiser day;
And whose solemn voice must be
Thine own echo–Liberty!

On those who first should violate
Such sacred heralds in their state
Rest the blood that must ensue,
And it will not rest on you.

And if then the tyrants dare
Let them ride among you there,
Slash, and stab, and maim, and hew,–
What they like, that let them do.

With folded arms and steady eyes,
And little fear, and less surprise,
Look upon them as they slay
Till their rage has died away.

Then they will return with shame
To the place from which they came,
And the blood thus shed will speak
In hot blushes on their cheek.

Every woman in the land
Will point at them as they stand–
They will hardly dare to greet
Their acquaintance in the street.

And the bold, true warriors
Who have hugged Danger in wars
Will turn to those who would be free,
Ashamed of such base company.

And that slaughter to the Nation
Shall steam up like inspiration,
Eloquent, oracular;
A volcano heard afar.

And these words shall then become
Like Oppression's thundered doom
Ringing through each heart and brain,
Heard again–again–again–

Rise like Lions after slumber
In unvanquishable number—
Shake your chains to earth like dew
Which in sleep had fallen on you—
Ye are many—they are few.

PERCY BYSSHE SHELLEY

662 *The Latest Decalogue*

Thou shalt have one God only; who
Would be at the expense of two?
No graven images may be
Worshipped, except the currency:
Swear not at all; for, for thy curse
Thine enemy is none the worse:
At church on Sunday to attend
Will serve to keep the world thy friend:
Honour thy parents; that is, all
From whom advancement may befall;
Thou shalt not kill; but need'st not strive
Officiously to keep alive:
Do not adultery commit;
Advantage rarely comes of it:
Thou shalt not steal; an empty feat,
When it's so lucrative to cheat:
Bear not false witness; let the lie
Have time on its own wings to fly:
Thou shalt not covet, but tradition
Approves all forms of competition.

ARTHUR HUGH CLOUGH

663 *If all the world were paper*

If all the world were paper,
    And all the sea were ink,
And all the trees were bread and cheese,
    How should we do for drink?

If all the world were sand-o,
    Oh, then what should we lack-o?
If, as they say, there were no clay,
    How should we take tobacco?

If all our vessels ran-a,
    If none but had a crack-a;
If Spanish apes ate all the grapes,
    How should we do for sack-a?

If friars had no bald pates,
    Nor nuns had no dark cloisters;
If all the seas were beans and peas,
    How should we do for oysters?

If there had been no projects,
    Nor none that did great wrongs;
If fiddlers shall turn players all,
    How should we do for songs?

If all things were eternal,
    And nothing their end bringing;
If this should be, then how should we
    Here make an end of singing?

ANON

664 *The Spirit's Song*

'There is no God,' the wicked saith,
    'And truly it's a blessing,
For what He might have done with us
    It's better only guessing.'

'There is no God,' a youngster thinks,
    'Or really, if there may be,
He surely didn't mean a man
    Always to be a baby.'

'There is no God, or if there is,'
    The tradesman thinks, 'twere funny
If He should take it ill in me
    To make a little money.'

'Whether there be,' the rich man says,
    'It matters very little,
For I and mine, thank somebody,
    Are not in want of victual.'

Some others, also, to themselves,
　　Who scarce so much as doubt it,
Think there is none, when they are well,
　　And do not think about it.

But country folks who live beneath
　　The shadow of the steeple;
The parson and the parson's wife,
　　And mostly married people;

Youths green and happy in first love,
　　So thankful for illusion;
And men caught out in what the world
　　Calls guilt, in first confusion;

And almost every one when age,
　　Disease, or sorrows strike him,
Inclines to think there is a God,
　　Or something very like Him.
　　　　　　　　　　　ARTHUR HUGH CLOUGH

665 *A Letter to the Hon. Lady Miss Margaret Cavendish-Holles-Harley*

My noble, lovely, little Peggy,
Let this, my First-Epistle, beg ye,
At dawn of morn, and close of even,
To lift your heart and hands to heaven:
In double beauty say your pray'r,
Our father first, then notre père;
And, dearest Child, along the day,
In ev'ry thing you do and say,
Obey and please my Lord and Lady,
So God shall love, and Angels aid, Ye.

If to these Precepts You attend,
No Second-Letter need I send,
And so I rest Your constant Friend,
　　　　　　　　　　　M.P.
　　　　　　　　　　　MATTHEW PRIOR

666 *Address to the Unco Guid, or The Rigidly Righteous*

My son, these maxims make a rule,
　An' lump them ay thegither;
The *Rigid Righteous* is a fool,
　The *Rigid Wise* anither:
The cleanest corn that e'er was dight
　May hae some pyles o' caff in;
So ne'er a fellow-creature slight
　For random fits o' daffin.

　　　　　Solomon, Eccles. ch. vii. verse 16.

O ye wha are sae guid yoursel,
　Sae pious and sae holy,
Ye've nought to do but mark and tell
　Your neibours' fauts and folly!
Whase life is like a weel-gaun mill,
　Supplied wi' store o' water;
The heapèt happer's ebbing still,
　An' still the clap plays clatter.

Hear me, ye venerable core,
　As counsel for poor mortals
That frequent pass douce Wisdom's door
　For glakit [1] Folly's portals:
I, for their thoughtless, careless sakes,
　Would here propone defences—
Their donsie [2] tricks, their black mistakes,
　Their failings and mischances.

Ye see your state wi' theirs compared,
　And shudder at the niffer; [3]
But cast a moment's fair regard,
　What maks the mighty differ?
Discount what scant occasion gave,
　That purity ye pride in;
And (what's aft mair than a' the lave)
　Your better art o' hidin.

---

[1] thoughtless　　　　[2] unlucky　　　　[3] exchange

Think, when your castigated pulse
    Gies now and then a wallop!
What ragings must his veins convulse,
    That still eternal gallop!
Wi' wind and tide fair i' your tail,
    Right on ye scud your sea-way;
But in the teeth o' baith to sail,
    It maks an unco lee-way.

See Social Life and Glee sit down,
    All joyous and unthinking,
Till, quite transmugrify'd, they're grown
    Debauchery and Drinking:
O would they stay to calculate
    Th' eternal consequences;
Or your more dreaded hell to state,
    Damnation of expenses!

Ye high, exalted, virtuous dames,
    Tied up in godly laces,
Before ye gie poor Frailty names,
    Suppose a change o' cases;
A dear-lov'd lad, convenience snug,
    A treach'rous inclination;
But, let me whisper i' your lug,
    Ye're aiblins [1] nae temptation.

Then gently scan your brother man,
    Still gentler sister woman;
Tho' they may gang a kennin [2] wrang,
    To step aside is human:
One point must still be greatly dark,
    The moving _Why_ they do it;
And just as lamely can ye mark,
    How far perhaps they rue it.

Who made the heart, 'tis He alone
    Decidedly can try us;
He knows each chord, its various tone,
    Each spring, its various bias:

[1] perhaps   [2] admittedly

Then at the balance let's be mute,
　　We never can adjust it;
What's done we partly may compute,
　　But know not what's resisted.

ROBERT BURNS

667 *The Elephant and the Bookseller*

The man who with undaunted toils,
Sails unknown seas to unknown soils,
With various wonders feasts his sight;
What stranger wonders does he write!
We read, and in description view
Creatures which Adam never knew;
For, when we risk no contradiction,
It prompts the tongue to deal in fiction.
Those things that startle me or you,
I grant are strange; yet may be true.
Who doubts that Elephants are found
For science and for sense renown'd?
Borri records their strength of parts,
Extent of thought, and skill in arts;
How they perform the law's decrees,
And save the state the hangman's fees;
And how by travel understand
The language of another land.
Let those, who question this report,
To Pliny's ancient page resort.
How learn'd was that sagacious breed!
Who now (like them) the Greek can read!
　　As one of these, in days of yore,
Rummaged a shop of learning o'er;
Not, like our modern dealers, minding
Only the margin's breadth and binding;
A book his curious eye detains,
Where, with exactest care and pains,
Were ev'ry beast and bird portray'd,
That e'er the search of man survey'd.
Their natures and their powers were writ,

With all the pride of human wit,
The page he with attention spread,
And thus remark'd on what he read:
    Man with strong reason is endow'd;
A beast scarce instinct is allow'd.
But let this author's worth be tried,
'Tis plain that neither was his guide.
Can he discern the diff'rent natures,
And weigh the power of other creatures,
Who by the partial work hath shown
He knows so little of his own?
How falsely is the spaniel drawn!
Did man from him first learn to fawn?
A dog proficient in the trade!
He the chief flatt'rer nature made!
Go, man, the ways of courts discern;
You'll find a spaniel still might learn.
How can the fox's theft and plunder,
Provoke his censure or his wonder?
From courtiers' tricks, and lawyers' arts,
The fox might well improve his parts.
The lion, wolf, and tiger's brood,
He curses, for their thirst of blood:
But is not man to man a prey?
Beasts kill for hunger, men for pay.
    The Bookseller, who heard him speak,
And saw him turn a page of Greek,
Thought, what a genius have I found!
Then thus address'd with bow profound:
    Learn'd Sir, if you'd employ your pen
Against the senseless sons of men,
Or write the history of Siam,
No man is better pay than I am;
Or, since you're learn'd in Greek, let's see
Something against the Trinity.
    When wrinkling with a sneer his trunk,
Friend, quoth the Elephant, you're drunk;
E'en keep your money, and be wise:
Leave man on man to criticise;
For that you ne'er can want a pen
Among the senseless sons of men.

They unprovoked will court the fray:
Envy's a sharper spur than pay.
No author ever spared a brother;
Wits are gamecocks to one another.

JOHN GAY

668 *To a Lady*
On her Passion for Old China

What ecstacies her bosom fire!
How her eyes languish with desire!
How blest, how happy should I be,
Were that fond glance bestow'd on me!
New doubts and fears within me war:
What rival's near? a china jar.

China's the passion of her soul;
A cup, a plate, a dish, a bowl,
Can kindle wishes in her breast,
Inflame with joy, or break her rest.

Some gems collect; some medals prize,
And view the rust with lover's eyes;
Some court the stars at midnight hours;
Some dote on Nature's charms in flowers!
But ev'ry beauty I can trace
In Laura's mind, in Laura's face;
My stars are in this brighter sphere,
My lily and my rose is here.

Philosophers more grave than wise
Hunt science down in butterflies;
Or fondly poring on a spider
Stretch human contemplation wider;
Fossils give joy to Galen's soul,
He digs for knowledge, like a mole;
In shells so learn'd, that all agree
No fish that swims knows more than he!
In such pursuits if wisdom lies,
Who, Laura, shall thy taste despise?

When I some antique jar behold,
Or white, or blue, or speck'd with gold,
Vessels so pure, and so refined,
Appear the types of woman-kind:
Are they not valued for their beauty,
Too fair, too fine, for household duty?
With flowers and gold and azure dyed,
Of ev'ry house the grace and pride?
How white, how polish'd is their skin,
And valued most when only seen!
She who before was highest prized,
Is for a crack or flaw despised;
I grant they're frail, yet they're so rare,
The treasure cannot cost too dear!
But man is made of coarser stuff,
And serves convenience well enough;
He's a strong earthen vessel made,
For drudging, labour, toil, and trade;
And when wives lose their other self,
With ease they bear the loss of delf.

Husbands more covetous than sage
Condemn this china-buying rage;
They count that woman's prudence little,
Who sets her heart on things so brittle.
But are those wise men's inclinations
Fixt on more strong, more sure foundations?
If all that's frail we must despise,
No human view or scheme is wise.
Are not ambition's hopes as weak?
They swell like bubbles, shine and break.
A courtier's promise is so slight,
'Tis made at noon, and broke at night.
What pleasure's sure? The miss you keep
Breaks both your fortune and your sleep,
The man who loves a country life,
Breaks all the comforts of his wife;
And if he quit his farm and plough,
His wife in town may break her vow.
Love, Laura, love, while youth is warm,
For each new winter breaks a charm,

D D

And woman's not like china sold,
But cheaper grows in growing old;
Then quickly choose the prudent part,
Or else you break a faithful heart.

JOHN GAY

669 *Lord Shaftesbury*

Some, by their monarch's fatal mercy grown,
From pardon'd rebels, kinsmen to the throne
Were raised in pow'r and public office high;
Strong bands, if bands ungrateful men could tie.
Of these the false *Achitophel*[1] was first,
A name to all succeeding ages curst.
For close designs and crooked counsels fit,
Sagacious, bold, and turbulent of wit,
Restless, unfixt in principles and place,
In pow'r unpleased, impatient of disgrace;
A fiery soul, which working out its way,
Fretted the pigmy body to decay:
And o'er informed the tenement of clay.
A daring pilot in extremity;
Pleas'd with the danger, when the waves went high
He sought the storms; but, for a calm unfit,
Would steer too nigh the sands to boast his wit.
Great wits are sure to madness near allied
And thin partitions do their bounds divide;
Else, why should he, with wealth and honour blest,
Refuse his age the needful hours of rest?
Punish a body which he could not please,
Bankrupt of life, yet prodigal of ease?
And all to leave what with his toil he won
To that unfeather'd two-legg'd thing, a son:
Got, while his soul did huddled notions try;
And born a shapeless lump, like anarchy.
In friendship false, implacable in hate,
Resolv'd to ruin or to rule the state;
To compass this the triple bond he broke;
The pillars of the public safety shook,
And fitted *Israel*[2] for a foreign yoke;

[1] Lord Shaftesbury   [2] England

Then, seiz'd with fear, yet still affecting fame,
Usurp'd a patriot's all-atoning name.
So easy still it proves in factious times
With public zeal to cancel private crimes:
How safe is treason and how sacred ill,
Where none can sin against the people's will,
Where crowds can wink; and no offence be known,
Since in another's guilt they find their own.
Yet, fame deserv'd, no enemy can grudge;
The statesman we abhor, but praise the judge.
In *Israel*'s courts ne'er sat an *Abbethdin* [1]
With more discerning eyes or hands more clean,
Unbrib'd, unsought, the wretched to redress;
Swift of dispatch and easy of access.
Oh, had he been content to serve the crown
With virtues only proper to the gown,
Or had the rankness of the soil been freed
From cockle that opprest the noble seed,
David [2] for him his tuneful harp had strung,
And Heav'n had wanted one immortal song.
But wild ambition loves to slide, not stand,
And fortune's ice prefers to virtue's land.
Achitophel, grown weary to possess
A lawful fame, and lazy happiness,
Disdain'd the golden fruit to gather free
And lent the crowd his arm to shake the tree.
Now, manifest of crimes, contriv'd long since,
He stood at bold defiance with his prince:
Held up the buckler of the people's cause
Against the crown; and skulk'd behind the laws.
The wish'd occasion of the plot he takes;
Some circumstances finds, but more he makes.
By buzzing emissaries, fills the ears
Of listening crowds, with jealousies and fears
Of arbitrary counsels brought to light,
And proves the King himself a *Jebusite*. [3]
Weak arguments! which yet he knew full well,
Were strong with people easy to rebel.

[1] Lord Chancellor   [2] King Charles II
[3] Papist

For, governed by the *moon*, the giddy *Jews* [1]
Tread the same track when she the prime renews:
And once in twenty years, their scribes record,
By natural instinct they change their lord.

JOHN DRYDEN

670 *An Epistle to Dr. Arbuthnot*

being the Prologue to the Satires

P. 'Shut, shut the door, good John!' fatigu'd, I said;
'Tie up the knocker, say I'm sick, I'm dead.'
The dogstar rages! nay, 'tis past a doubt,
All Bedlam, or Parnassus, is let out:
Fire in each eye, and papers in each hand,
They rave, recite, and madden round the land.

What walls can guard me, or what shades can hide?
They pierce my thickets, through my grot they glide,
By land, by water, they renew the charge,
They stop the chariot, and they board the barge.
No place is sacred, not the church is free,
Ev'n Sunday shines no sabbath-day to me:
Then from the Mint walks forth the man of rhyme,
Happy! to catch me, just at dinner time.

Is there a parson much bemus'd in beer,
A maudlin poetess, a rhyming peer,
A clerk, foredoom'd his father's soul to cross,
Who pens a stanza when he should engross?
Is there who, lock'd from ink and paper, scrawls
With desperate charcoal round his darken'd walls?
All fly to Twit'nam, and in humble strain
Apply to me, to keep them mad or vain.
Arthur, whose giddy son neglects the laws,
Imputes to me and my damn'd works the cause:
Poor Cornus sees his frantic wife elope,
And curses wit, and poetry, and Pope.

Friend to my life, (which did not you prolong,
The world had wanted many an idle song)
What drop or nostrum can this plague remove?
Or which must end me, a fool's wrath or love?

---

[1] English

A dire dilemma! either way I'm sped;
If foes, they write, if friends, they read me dead.
Seiz'd and tied down to judge, how wretched I!
Who can't be silent, and who will not lie.
To laugh, were want of goodness and of grace,
And to be grave, exceeds all power of face.
I sit with sad civility, I read
With honest anguish, and an aching head,
And drop at last, but in unwilling ears,
This saving counsel, 'Keep your piece nine years.'

 'Nine years!' cries he, who high in Drury Lane,
Lull'd by soft zephyrs thro' the broken pane,
Rhymes e're he wakes, and prints before term ends,
Oblig'd by hunger and request of friends:
'The piece, you think, is incorrect: why, take it,
I'm all submission: what you'd have it, make it.'

 Three things another's modest wishes bound,
'My friendship, and a prologue, and ten pound.'

* * * *

 There are, who to my person pay their court:
I cough like Horace; and, tho' lean, am short;
Ammon's great son one shoulder had too high,
Such Ovid's nose, and 'Sir! you have an eye-.'
Go on, obliging creatures, make me see
All that disgrac'd my betters, met in me.
Say for my comfort, languishing in bed,
'Just so immortal Maro held his head:'
And when I die, be sure you let me know
Great Homer died three thousand years ago.

 Why did I write? what sin to me unknown
Dipt me in ink, my parents', or my own?
As yet a child, nor yet a fool to fame,
I lisp'd in numbers, for the numbers came:
I left no calling for this idle trade,
No duty broke, no father disobey'd:
The Muse but serv'd to ease some friend, not wife,
To help me thro' this long disease, my life,
To second, Arbuthnot! thy art and care,
And teach, the being you preserv'd, to bear.

A. But why then publish? P. Granville the polite,
And knowing Walsh, would tell me I could write;
Well natur'd Garth inflam'd with early praise,
And Congreve lov'd, and Swift endur'd, my lays;
The courtly Talbot, Somers, Sheffield, read,
Ev'n mitred Rochester would nod the head,
And St. John's self (great Dryden's friends before)
With open arms receiv'd one poet more.
Happy my studies, when by these approv'd!
Happier their author, when by these belov'd!
From these the world will judge of men and books,
Not from the Burnets, Oldmixons, and Cooks.

Soft were my numbers; who could take offence
While pure description held the place of sense?
Like gentle Fanny's was my flow'ry theme,
A painted mistress, or a purling stream.
Yet then did Gildon draw his venal quill;
I wish'd the man a dinner, and sat still:
Yet then did Dennis rave in furious fret;
I never answer'd; I was not in debt.
If want provok'd, or madness made them print,
I wag'd no war with Bedlam or the Mint.

Did some more sober critic come abroad?
If wrong, I smil'd; if right, I kiss'd the rod.
Pains, reading, study, are their just pretence,
And all they want is spirit, taste, and sense.
Commas and points they set exactly right,
And 'twere a sin to rob them of their mite.
Yet ne'r one sprig of laurel grac'd these ribalds,
From slashing Bentley down to piddling Tibalds.
Each wight who reads not, and but scans and spells,
Each word-catcher that lives on syllables,
Ev'n such small critics some regard may claim,
Preserv'd in Milton's or in Shakespeare's name.
Pretty! in amber to observe the forms
Of hairs, or straws, or dirt, or grubs, or worms;
The things, we know, are neither rich nor rare,
But wonder how the devil they got there?

Were others angry? I excus'd them too;
Well might they rage, I gave them but their due.

A man's true merit 'tis not hard to find;
But each man's secret standard in his mind,
That casting weight pride adds to emptiness,
This who can gratify? for who can guess?
The bard whom pilfer'd pastorals renown,
Who turns a Persian tale for half a crown,
Just writes to make his barrenness appear,
And strains from hard bound brains eight lines a-year;
He, who still wanting, tho' he lives on theft,
Steals much, spends little, yet has nothing left;
And he, who now to sense, now nonsense, leaning,
Means not, but blunders round about a meaning;
And he whose fustian's so sublimely bad,
It is not poetry, but prose run mad:
All these my modest satire bad translate,
And own'd, that nine such poets made a Tate.
How did they fume, and stamp, and roar, and chafe?
And swear, not Addison himself was safe.

Peace to all such! but were there one whose fires
True genius kindles, and fair fame inspires,
Blest with each talent and each art to please,
And born to write, converse, and live with ease;
Shou'd such a man, too fond to rule alone,
Bear, like the Turk, no brother near the throne,
View him with scornful, yet with jealous eyes,
And hate for arts that caus'd himself to rise;
Damn with faint praise, assent with civil leer,
And without sneering, teach the rest to sneer;
Willing to wound, and yet afraid to strike,
Just hint a fault, and hesitate dislike;
Alike reserv'd to blame, or to commend,
A tim'rous foe, and a suspicious friend;
Dreading ev'n fools, by flatterers besieg'd,
And so obliging that he ne'er oblig'd;
Like Cato, give his little senate laws,
And sit attentive to his own applause;
While wits and Templers ev'ry sentence raise,
And wonder with a foolish face of praise.
Who but must laugh, if such a man there be?
Who would not weep, if Atticus were he!

What though my name stood rubric on the walls,
Or plaster'd posts, with claps in capitals?
Or smoking forth, a hundred hawkers' load,
On wings of winds came flying all abroad?
I sought no homage from the race that write;
I kept, like Asian monarchs, from their sight:
Poems I heeded (now be-rhym'd so long)
No more than thou, great George! a birthday song.
I ne'er with wits or witlings pass'd my days
To spread about the itch of verse and praise;
Nor like a puppy daggled through the town
To fetch and carry sing-song up and down;
Nor at rehearsals sweat, and mouth'd, and cried,
With handkerchief and orange at my side;
But sick of fops, and poetry, and prate,
To Bufo left the whole Castalian state.

Proud, as Apollo on his forked hill,
Sat full blown Bufo, puff'd by every quill:
Fed with soft dedication all day long,
Horace and he went hand in hand in song.
His library (where busts of poets dead
And a true Pindar stood without a head)
Receiv'd of wits an undistinguish'd race,
Who first his judgment ask'd, and then a place:
Much they extoll'd his pictures, much his seat,
And flatter'd ev'ry day, and some days eat:
Till grown more frugal in his riper days,
He paid some bards with port, and some with praise;
To some a dry rehearsal was assign'd,
And others (harder still) he paid in kind.
Dryden alone (what wonder?) came not nigh;
Dryden alone escap'd this judging eye:
But still the great have kindness in reserve;
He help'd to bury whom he help'd to starve.

May some choice patron bless each gray goose quill!
May every Bavius have his Bufo still!
So, when a statesman wants a day's defence,
Or envy holds a whole week's war with sense,
Or simple pride for flatt'ry makes demands;
May dunce by dunce be whistled off my hands!

Blest be the great! for those they take away,
And those they left me–for they left me Gay;
Left me to see neglected genius bloom,
Neglected die! and tell it on his tomb:
Of all thy blameless life the sole return
My verse, and Queensb'ry weeping o'er thy urn!
Oh let me live my own! and die so too!
'To live and die is all I have to do':
Maintain a poet's dignity and ease,
And see what friends, and read what books I please.
Above a patron, tho' I condescend
Sometimes to call a minister my friend:
I was not born for courts or great affairs,
I pay my debts, believe, and say my prayers;
Can sleep without a poem in my head,
Nor know, if Dennis be alive or dead.

Why am I ask'd, what next shall see the light?
Heav'ns! was I born for nothing but to write?
Has life no joys for me? or (to be grave)
Have I no friend to serve, no soul to save?
'I found him close with Swift'–'Indeed? no doubt
(Cries prating Balbus) something will come out.'
'Tis all in vain, deny it as I will;
'No, such a genius never can lie still:'
And then for mine obligingly mistakes
The first lampoon Sir Will or Bubo makes.
Poor guiltless I! and can I choose but smile,
When ev'ry coxcomb knows me by my style?

* * * *

Let Sporus tremble–A. What? that thing of silk,
Sporus, that mere white curd of asses' milk?
Satire or sense, alas! can Sporus feel?
Who breaks a butterfly upon a wheel?
P. Yet let me flap this bug with gilded wings,
This painted child of dirt, that stinks and stings;
Whose buzz the witty and the fair annoys,
Yet wit ne'er tastes, and beauty ne'er enjoys:
So well-bred spaniels civilly delight
In mumbling of the game they dare not bite.

Eternal smiles his emptiness betray,
As shallow streams run dimpling all the way.
Whether in florid impotence he speaks,
And, as the prompter breathes, the puppet squeaks;
Or at the ear of Eve, familiar toad,
Half froth, half venom, spits himself abroad,
In puns, or politics, or tales, or lies,
Or spite, or smut, or rhymes, or blasphemies;
His wit all seesaw between that and this,
Now high, now low, now master up, now miss,
And he himself one vile antithesis.
Amphibious thing! that acting either part,
The trifling head, or the corrupted heart!
Fop at the toilet, flatt'rer at the board,
Now trips a lady, and now struts a lord.
Eve's tempter thus the Rabbins have exprest,
A cherub's face, a reptile all the rest;
Beauty that shocks you, parts that none will trust,
Wit that can creep, and pride that licks the dust.

*   *   *   *

ALEXANDER POPE

671   *From 'Hudibras'*

For his *Religion* it was fit
To match his Learning and his Wit:
'Twas Presbyterian true Blue,
For he was of that stubborn Crew
Of Errant Saints, whom all men grant
To be the true Church *Militant*:
Such as do build their Faith upon
The holy Text of *Pike* and *Gun*;
Decide all Controversies by
Infallible *Artillery*;
And prove their Doctrine Orthodox
By Apostolick *Blows* and *Knocks*;
Call Fire, and Sword, and Desolation,
A *godly thorough Reformation*,
Which always must be carry'd on,
And still be doing, never done:

As if Religion were intended
For nothing else but to be mended.
A Sect whose chief Devotion lies
In odd perverse Antipathies:
In falling out with that or this,
And finding somewhat still amiss:
More peevish, cross, and splenetick,
Than Dog distract, or Monkey sick.
That with more care keep Holy-day
The wrong, than others the right way:
Compound for Sins they are inclin'd to,
By damning those they have no mind to.
Still so perverse and opposite,
As if they worship'd God for spight.
The self-same thing they will abhor
One way, and long another for.
Free-will they one way disavow,
Another, nothing else allow.
All Piety consists therein
In them, in other Men all Sin.
Rather than fail, they will defy
That which they love most tenderly:
Quarrel with *Minc'd-pies*, and *disparage*
Their best and dearest Friend *Plum-porridge*;
Fat *Pig* and *Goose* itself oppose,
And blaspheme *Custard* thro' the *Nose*.
Th'Apostles of this fierce Religion,
Like *Mahomet*'s, were Ass and Widgeon.
To whom our Knight, by fast Instinct
Of Wit and Temper, was so linkt.
As if Hypocrisy and Nonsense
Had got th'Advowson of his Conscience.

SAMUEL BUTLER

672 *A Letter from Rome*

Luther, they say, was unwise; like a half-taught German, he could not
See that old follies were passing most tranquilly out of remembrance;
Leo the Tenth was employing all efforts to clear out abuses;

Jupiter, Juno, and Venus, Fine Arts, and Fine Letters, the
   Poets,
Scholars, and Sculptors, and Painters, were quietly clearing
   away the
Martyrs, and Virgins, and Saints, or at any rate Thomas
   Aquinas:
He must forsooth make a fuss and distend his huge Witten-
   berg lungs, and
Bring back Theology once yet again in a flood upon Europe:
Lo you, for forty days from the windows of heaven it fell; the
Waters prevail on the earth yet more for a hundred and fifty;
Are they abating at last? the doves that are sent to explore are
Wearily fain to return, at the best with a leaflet of promise,–
Fain to return, as they went, to the wandering wave-tost
   vessel,–
Fain to re-enter the roof which covers the clean and the
   unclean,–
Luther, they say, was unwise; he didn't see how things were
   going;
Luther was foolish,–but, O great God! what call you Ignatius?
O my tolerant soul, be still! but you talk of barbarians,
Alaric, Attila, Genseric;–why, they came, they killed, they
Ravaged, and went on their way; but these vile, tyrannous
   Spaniards,
These are here still,–how long, O ye heavens, in the country
   of Dante?
These, that fanaticised Europe, which now can forget them,
   release not
This, their choicest of prey, this Italy; here you see them,–
Here, with emasculate pupils and gimcrack churches of Gesu,
Pseudo-learning and lies, confessional-boxes and postures,–
Here, with metallic beliefs and regimental devotions,–
Here, overcrusting with slime, perverting, defacing, debasing,
Michael Angelo's dome, that had hung the Pantheon in heaven,
Raphael's Joys and Graces, and thy clear stars, Galileo!

ARTHUR HUGH CLOUGH

673   *Invocation*

Bob Southey! You're a poet–Poet-laureate,
   And representative of all the race,

Although 'tis true that you turn'd out a Tory at
    Last,—yours has lately been a common case,—
And now, my Epic Renegade! what are ye at?
    With all the Lakers, in and out of place?
A nest of tuneful persons, to my eye
Like 'four and twenty Blackbirds in a pye;

'Which pye being open'd they began to sing'
    (This old song and new simile holds good),
'A dainty dish to set before the King,'
    Or Regent, who admires such kind of food;—
And Coleridge, too, has lately taken wing,
    But like a hawk encumber'd with his hood,—
Explaining metaphysics to the nation—
I wish he would explain his Explanation.

You, Bob! are rather insolent, you know,
    At being disappointed in your wish
To supersede all warblers here below,
    And be the only Blackbird in the dish;
And then you overstrain yourself, or so,
    And tumble downward like the flying fish
Gasping on deck, because you soar too high, Bob,
And fall, for lack of moisture quite a-dry, Bob!

And Wordsworth, in a rather long 'Excursion'
    (I think the quarto holds five hundred pages),
Has given a sample from the vasty version
    Of his new system to perplex the sages;
'Tis poetry—at least by his assertion,
    And may appear so when the dog-star rages—
And he who understands it would be able
To add a story to the Tower of Babel.

You—Gentlemen! by dint of long seclusion
    From better company, have kept your own
At Keswick, and, through still continued fusion
    Of one another's minds, at last have grown
To deem as a most logical conclusion,
    That Poesy has wreaths for you alone:
There is a narrowness in such a notion,
Which makes me wish you'd change your lakes for ocean.

I would not imitate the petty thought,
  Nor coin my self-love to so base a vice,
For all the glory your conversion brought,
  Since gold alone should not have been its price.
You have your salary; was't for that you wrought?
  And Wordsworth has his place in the Excise.
You're shabby fellows–true–but poets still,
And duly seated on the immortal hill.

Your bays may hide the boldness of your brows–
  Perhaps some virtuous blushes;–let them go–
To you I envy neither fruit nor boughs–
  And for the fame you would engross below,
The field is universal, and allows
  Scope to all such as feel the inherent glow:
Scott, Rogers, Campbell, Moore, and Crabbe, will try
'Gainst you the question with posterity.

For me, who, wandering with pedestrian Muses,
  Contend not with you on the winged steed,
I wish your fate may yield ye, when she chooses,
  The fame you envy, and the skill you need:
And recollect a poet nothing loses
  In giving to his brethren their full meed
Of merit, and complaint of present days
Is not the certain path to future praise.

He that reserves his laurels for posterity
  (Who does not often claim the bright reversion)
Has generally no great crop to spare it, he
  Being only injured by his own assertion;
And although here and there some glorious rarity
  Arise like Titan from the sea's immersion,
The major part of such appellants go
To–God knows where–for no one else can know.

If, fallen in evil days on evil tongues,
  Milton appeal'd to the Avenger, Time,
If Time, the Avenger, execrates his wrongs,
  And makes the word 'Miltonic' mean '*sublime*,'

He deign'd not to belie his soul in songs,
  Nor turn his very talent to a crime:
He did not loathe the sire to laud the Son,
But closed the tyrant-hater he begun.

Think'st thou, could he–the blind Old Man–arise
  Like Samuel from the grave, to freeze once more
The blood of monarchs with his prophecies,
  Or be alive again–again all hoar
With time and trials, and those helpless eyes,
  And heartless daughters–worn–and pale–and poor:
Would *he* adore a sultan? *he* obey
The intellectual eunuch Castlereagh?

Cold-blooded, smooth-fac'd, placid miscreant!
  Dabbling its sleek young hands in Erin's gore,
And thus for wider carnage taught to pant,
  Transferr'd to gorge upon a sister shore,
The vulgarest tool that Tyranny could want,
  With just enough of talent, and no more,
To lengthen fetters by another fix'd,
And offer poison long already mix'd.

An orator of such set trash of phrase
  Ineffably–legitimately vile,
That even its grossest flatterers dare not praise,
  Nor foes–all nations–condescend to smile,–
Not even a sprightly blunder's spark can blaze
  From that Ixion grindstone's ceaseless toil,
That turns and turns to give the world a notion
Of endless torments and perpetual motion.

A bungler even in its disgusting trade,
  And botching, patching, leaving still behind
Something of which its masters are afraid,
  States to be curb'd, and thoughts to be confin'd,
Conspiracy or Congress to be made–
  Cobbling at manacles for all mankind–
A tinkering slave-maker, who mends old chains,
With God and man's abhorrence for its gains.

If we may judge of matter by the mind,
    Emasculated to the marrow *It*
Hath but two objects, how to serve, and bind,
    Deeming the chain it wears even men may fit,
Eutropius of its many masters,–blind
    To worth as freedom, wisdom as to wit,
Fearless–because *no* feeling dwells in ice,
Its very courage stagnates to a vice.

                GEORGE GORDON, LORD BYRON

674 *Verses on the Death of Dr. Swift, D.S.P.D.*

Occasioned by reading a maxim in Rochefoucault

As Rochefoucault his maxims drew
From nature, I believe 'em true;
They argue no corrupted mind
In him; the fault is in mankind.

This maxim more than all the rest
Is thought too base for human breast;
'In all distresses of our friends
'We first consult our private ends,
'While nature kindly bent to ease us,
'Points out some circumstance to please us.'

If this perhaps your patience move
Let reason and experience prove.

We all behold with envious eyes,
Our equal raised above our size;
Who would not at a crowded show,
Stand high himself, keep others low?
I love my friend as well as you,
But would not have him stop my view;
Then let him have the higher post;
I ask but for an inch at most.

If in a battle you should find,
One, whom you love of all mankind,
Had some heroic action done,
A champion killed, or trophy won;
Rather than thus be over-topt,
Would you not wish his laurels cropt?

Dear honest Ned is in the gout,
Lies rackt with pain, and you without:
How patiently you hear him groan!
How glad the case is not your own!

What poet would not grieve to see,
His brethren write as well as he?
But rather than they should excel,
He'd wish his rivals all in Hell.

Her end when emulation misses,
She turns to envy, stings and hisses:
The strongest friendship yields to pride,
Unless the odds be on our side.

Vain human kind! Fantastic race!
Thy various follies, who can trace?
Self-love, ambition, envy, pride,
Their empire in our hearts divide:
Give others riches, power, and station,
'Tis all on me an usurpation.
I have no title to aspire;
Yet, when you sink, I seem the higher.
In Pope, I cannot read a line,
But with a sigh, I wish it mine:
When he can in one couplet fix
More sense than I can do in six:
It gives me such a jealous fit,
I cry, pox take him, and his wit.

Why must I be outdone by Gay,
In my own hum'rous biting way?

Arbuthnot is no more my friend,
Who dares to irony pretend;
Which I was born to introduce,
Refin'd it first, and shew'd its use.

St. John, as well as Pultney knows,
That I had some repute for prose;
And till they drove me out of date,
Could maul a Minister of State:

If they have mortified my pride,
And made me throw my pen aside;
If with such talents Heav'n hath blest 'em
Have I not reason to detest 'em?

To all my foes, dear Fortune, send
Thy gifts, but never to my friend:
I tamely can endure the first,
But, this with envy makes me burst.

Thus much may serve by way of proem,
Proceed we therefore to our poem.

The time is not remote, when I
Must by the course of nature die:
When I foresee my special friends,
Will try to find their private ends:
Tho' it is hardly understood,
Which way my death can do them good;
Yet, thus methinks, I hear 'em speak:
See, how the Dean begins to break:
Poor gentleman, he droops apace,
You plainly find it in his face:
That old vertigo in his head,
Will never leave him, till he's dead:
Besides, his memory decays,
He recollects not what he says;
He cannot call his friends to mind;
Forgets the place where last he din'd:
Plies you with stories o'er and o'er,
He told them fifty times before.
How does he fancy we can sit,
To hear his out-of-fashion'd wit?
But he takes up with younger folks,
Who for his wine will bear his jokes:
Faith, he must make his stories shorter,
Or change his comrades once a quarter:
In half the time, he talks them round;
There must another set be found.

For poetry, he's past his prime,
He takes an hour to find a rhyme:

His fire is out, his wit decay'd,
His fancy sunk, his muse a jade.
I'd have him throw away his pen;
But there's no talking to some men.

And, then their tenderness appears,
By adding largely to my years:
'He's older than he would be reckon'd,
'And well remembers Charles the Second.

'He hardly drinks a pint of wine;
'And that, I doubt, is no good sign.
'His stomach too begins to fail:
'Last year we thought him strong and hale;
'But now, he's quite another thing;
'I wish he may hold out till Spring.'

Then hug themselves, and reason thus;
'It is not yet so bad with us.'

In such a case they talk in tropes,
And, by their fears express their hopes:
Some great misfortune to portend,
No enemy can match a friend;
With all the kindness they profess,
The merit of a lucky guess,
(When daily howd'y's come of course,
And servants answer; *Worse and worse*)
Would please 'em better than to tell,
That, God be prais'd, the Dean is well.
Then he who prophecy'd the best,
Approves his foresight to the rest:
'You know, I always fear'd the worst,
'And often told you so at first:'
He'd rather choose that I should die,
Than his prediction prove a lie.
Not one foretells I shall recover;
But, all agree, to give me over.

Yet should some neighbour feel a pain,
Just in the parts, where I complain;
How many a message would he send?
What hearty prayers that I should mend?

Enquire what regimen I kept;
What gave me ease, and how I slept?
And more lament, when I was dead,
Than all the sniv'llers round my bed.

My good companions, never fear,
For though you may mistake a year;
Though your prognostics run too fast,
They must be verified at last.

Behold the fatal day arrive!
'How is the Dean? He's just alive.
'Now the departing prayer is read:
'He hardly breathes.   The Dean is dead.'
Before the passing-bell begun,
The news thro' half the town has run.
'O, may we all for death prepare!
'What has he left? And who's his heir?
'I know no more than what the news is,
' 'Tis all bequeath'd to public uses.
'To public use! A perfect whim!
'What had the public done for him!
'Mere envy, avarice, and pride!
'He gave it all:–But first he died.
'And had the Dean, in all the nation,
'No worthy friend, no poor relation?
'So ready to do strangers good,
'Forgetting his own flesh and blood?'

Now Grub-Street wits are all employ'd;
With elegies, the town is cloy'd:
Some paragraph in ev'ry paper,
To curse the Dean, or bless the Drapier.

The doctors tender of their fame,
Wisely on me lay all the blame:
'We must confess his case was nice;
'But he would never take advice:
'Had he been rul'd, for aught appears,
'He might have liv'd these twenty years:
'For when we open'd him we found,
'That all his vital parts were sound.'

From Dublin soon to London spread,
'Tis told at Court, the Dean is dead.

Kind Lady Suffolk in the spleen,
Runs laughing up to tell the Queen.
The Queen, so gracious, mild, and good,
Cries, 'Is he gone? 'Tis time he should.
'He's dead you say; why let him rot;
'I'm glad the medals were forgot.
'I promised them, I own; but when?
'I only was the Princess then;
'But now as Consort of the King,
'You know 'tis quite a different thing.'

Now, Chartres at Sir Robert's levee,
Tells, with a sneer, the tidings heavy:
'Why, is he dead without his shoes?'
(Cries Bob) 'I'm sorry for the news;
'Oh, were the wretch but living still,
'And in his place my good friend Will;
'Or, had a mitre on his head
'Provided Bolingbroke were dead.'

Now Curl his shop from rubbish drains;
Three genuine tomes of Swift's Remains.
And then to make them pass the glibber,
Revised by Tibbalds, Moore, and Cibber.
He'll treat me as he does my betters.
Publish my will, my life, my letters.
Revive the libels born to die;
Which Pope must bear, as well as I.

Here shift the scene, to represent
How those I love, my death lament.
Poor Pope will grieve a month; and Gay
A week; and Arbuthnot a day.

St. John himself will scarce forbear,
To bite his pen, and drop a tear.
The rest will give a shrug and cry,
I'm sorry; but we all must die.

Indifference clad in wisdom's guise,
All fortitude of mind supplies:
For how can stony bowels melt,
In those who never pity felt;
When *we* are lash'd, *they* kiss the rod;
Resigning to the will of God.

The fools, my juniors by a year,
Are tortur'd with suspense and fear.
Who wisely thought my age a screen,
When death approach'd, to stand between:
The screen remov'd, their hearts are trembling,
They mourn for me without dissembling.

My female friends, whose tender hearts
Have better learn'd to act their parts.
Receive the News in doleful dumps,
'The Dean is dead, (and what is trumps?)
'Then Lord have mercy on his soul.
'(Ladies I'll venture for the vole.)
'Six Deans they say must bear the pall.
'(I wish I knew what king to call.)
'Madam, your husband will attend
'The funeral of so good a friend.
'No Madam, 'tis a shocking sight,
'And he's engag'd to-morrow night!
'My Lady Club would take it ill,
'If he should fail her at Quadrille.
'He lov'd the Dean.   (I lead a heart.)
'But dearest friends, they say, must part.
'His time was come, he ran his race;
'We hope he's in a better place.'

Why do we grieve that friends should die?
No loss more easy to supply.
One year is past; a different scene;
No further mention of the Dean;
Who now, alas, no more is mist,
Than if he never did exist.
Where's now this fav'rite of Apollo?
Departed; and his works must follow:

Must undergo the common fate;
His kind of wit is out of date.
Some country squire to Lintot goes,
Enquires for Swift in verse and prose:
Says Lintot, 'I have heard the name:
'He died a year ago.' The same.
He searcheth all his shop in vain;
'Sir you may find them in Duck-lane:
'I sent them with a load of books,
'Last Monday to the pastry-cooks.
'To fancy they cou'd live a year!
'I find you're but a stranger here.
'The Dean was famous in his time;
'And had a kind of knack at rhyme:
'His way of writing now is past;
'The town hath got a better taste:
'I keep no antiquated stuff;
'But, spick and span I have enough.
'Pray, do but give me leave to shew 'em;
'Here's Colley Cibber's Birth-day Poem.
'This Ode you never yet have seen,
'By Stephen Duck, upon the Queen.
'Then, here's a Letter finely penn'd
'Against the Craftsman and his friend;
'It clearly shows that all reflection
'On ministers, is disaffection.
'Next, here's Sir Robert's Vindication,
'And Mr. Henly's last Oration:
'The hawkers have not got 'em yet,
'Your Honour please to buy a set?

  'Here's Wolston's Tracts, the twelfth edition;
' 'Tis read by ev'ry politician:
'The Country Members, when in town,
'To all their Boroughs send them down:
'You never met a thing so smart;
'The courtiers have them all by heart;
'Those Maids of Honour (who can read)
'Are taught to use them for their Creed.
'The Rev'rend author's good intention,
'Hath been rewarded with a pension:

'He doth an honour to his gown,
'By bravely running priest-craft down:
'He shews, as sure as God's in *Glo'ster*,
'That Jesus was a grand impostor:
'That all his miracles were cheats,
'Perform'd as jugglers do their feats:
'The Church had never such a writer:
'A shame, he hath not got a mitre!'

Suppose me dead; and then suppose
A club assembled at the Rose;
Where from discourse of this and that,
I grow the subject of their chat:
    And, while they toss my name about,
With favour some, and some without;
One quite indiff'rent in the cause,
My character impartial draws:

'The Dean, if we believe report,
'Was never ill received at Court:
'As for his works in verse and prose,
'I own my self no judge of those:
'Nor, can I tell what critics thought 'em:
'But, this I know, all people bought 'em;
'As with a moral view design'd
'To cure the vices of mankind:
'His vein, ironically grave,
'Expos'd the fool, and lash'd the knave:
'To steal a hint was never known,
'But what he writ was all his own.

'He never thought an honour done him,
'Because a Duke was proud to own him;
'Would rather slip aside, and choose
'To talk with wits in dirty shoes:
'Despis'd the fools with stars and garters,
'So often seen caressing Chartres:
'He never courted men in station,
'Nor persons had in admiration:
'Of no man's greatness was afraid,
'Because he sought for no man's aid.

'Though trusted long in great affairs,
'He gave himself no haughty airs:
'Without regarding private ends,
'Spent all his credit for his friends:
'And only chose the wise and good;
'No flatt'rers; no allies in blood;
'But succour'd virtue in distress,
'And seldom fail'd of good success;
'As numbers in their hearts must own,
'Who, but for him, had been unknown.

'With Princes kept a due decorum,
'But never stood in awe before 'em:
'He follow'd David's lesson just,
'In Princes never put thy trust.
'And, would you make him truly sour;
'Provoke him with a slave in power:
'The Irish Senate, if you named,
'With what impatience he declaimed!
'Fair LIBERTY was all his cry;
'For her he stood prepar'd to die;
'For her he boldly stood alone;
'For her he oft expos'd his own.
'Two Kingdoms, just as faction led,
'Had set a price upon his head;
'But, not a traitor could be found,
'To sell him for six hundred pound.

'Had he but spar'd his tongue and pen,
'He might have rose like other men:
'But, power was never in his thought;
'And, wealth he valu'd not a groat:
'Ingratitude he often found,
'And pitied those who meant the wound:
'But, kept the tenor of his mind,
'To merit well of human kind:
'Nor made a sacrifice of those
'Who still were true, to please his foes.
'He labour'd many a fruitless hour
'To reconcile his friends in power;

'Saw mischief by a faction brewing,
'While they pursu'd each others' ruin.
'But, finding vain was all his care,
'He left the Court in mere despair.

'And, oh! how short are human schemes!
'Here ended all our golden dreams.
'What St. John's skill in State affairs,
'What Ormond's valour, Oxford's cares,
'To save their sinking country lent,
'Was all destroy'd by one event.
'Too soon that precious life was ended,
'On which alone, our weal depended.
'When up a dangerous faction starts,
'With wrath and vengeance in their hearts:
'By solemn League and Cov'nant bound,
'To ruin, slaughter, and confound;
'To turn religion to a fable,
'And make the government a Babel:

'Pervert the law, disgrace the gown,
'Corrupt the senate, rob the crown;
'To sacrifice old England's glory,
'And make her infamous in story.
'When such a tempest shook the land,
'How could unguarded virtue stand?

'With horror, grief, despair the Dean
'Beheld the dire destructive scene:
'His friends in exile, or the Tower,
'Himself within the frown of Power;
'Pursued by base envenom'd pens,
'Far to the land of slaves and fens;
'A servile race in folly nurs'd,
'Who truckle most, when treated worst.

'By innocence and resolution,
'He bore continual persecution;
'While numbers to preferment rose;
'Whose merits were, to be his foes.

'When, ev'n his own familiar friends
'Intent upon their private ends;
'Like renegadoes now he feels,
'Against him lifting up their heels.

  'The Dean did by his pen defeat
'An infamous destructive cheat.
'Taught fools their int'rest how to know;
'And gave them arms to ward the blow.
'Envy hath own'd it was his doing,
'To save that helpless land from ruin,
'While they who at the steerage stood,
'And reapt the profit, sought his blood.

  'To save them from their evil fate,
'In him was held a crime of state.
'A wicked monster on the bench,
'Whose fury blood could never quench;
'As vile and profligate a villain,
'As modern Scroggs, or old Tressilian;
'Who long all justice had discarded,
'Nor fear'd he GOD, nor man regarded;
'Vow'd on the Dean his rage to vent,
'And make him of his zeal repent;
'But Heav'n his innocence defends,
'The grateful people stand his friends;
'Not strains of law, nor Judges' frown,
'Nor topics brought to please the Crown,
'Nor witness hir'd, nor jury pick'd,
'Prevail to bring him in convict.

  'In exile with a steady heart,
'He spent his Life's declining part;
'Where, folly, pride, and faction sway,
'Remote from St. John, Pope, and Gay.

  'His friendship there to few confin'd,
'Were always of the middling kind:
'No fools of rank, a mungril breed,
'Who fain would pass for lords indeed:
'Where titles give no right or power,
'And peerage is a wither'd flower,

'He would have held it a disgrace,
'If such a wretch had known his face.
'On rural squires, that kingdom's bane,
'He vented oft his wrath in vain:
'Biennial squires, to market brought;
'Who sell their souls and votes for naught;
'The nation stript go joyful back,
'To rob the Church, their tenants rack,
'Go snacks with thieves and rapparees,
'And, keep the peace, to pick up fees:
'In every job to have a share,
'A jail or barrack to repair;
'And turn the tax for public roads
'Commodious to their own abodes.

'Perhaps I may allow, the Dean
'Had too much satire in his vein:
'And seem'd determin'd not to starve it,
'Because no age could more deserve it.
'Yet, malice never was his aim;
'He lash'd the vice but spar'd the name.
'No individual could resent,
'Where thousands equally were meant.
'His satire points at no defect,
'But what all mortals may correct;
'For he abhorr'd that senseless tribe,
'Who call it humour when they jibe:
'He spar'd a hump or crooked nose,
'Whose owners set not up for beaux.
'True genuine dulness moved his pity,
'Unless it offer'd to be witty.
'Those, who their ignorance confess'd,
'He ne'er offended with a jest;
'But laugh'd to hear an idiot quote,
'A verse from Horace, learn'd by rote.

'He knew an hundred pleasant stories,
'With all the turns of Whigs and Tories:
'Was cheerful to his dying day,
'And friends would let him have his way.

'He gave the little wealth he had,
'To build a house for fools and mad:
'And shew'd by one satyric touch,
'No nation wanted it so much:
'That Kingdom he hath left his debtor,
'I wish it soon may have a better.'

JONATHAN SWIFT

675 *The Dean's Lady*

I

Next, to a Lady I must bid adieu–
Whom some in mirth or malice call a "*Blue*."
There needs no more–when that same word is said,
The men grow shy, respectful, and afraid;
Save the choice friends who in her colour dress,
And all her praise in words like hers express.

Why should proud man in man that knowledge prize,
Which he affects in woman to despise?
Is he not envious when a lady gains,
In hours of leisure, and with little pains,
What he in many a year with painful toil obtains?
For surely knowledge should not odious grow,
Nor ladies be despis'd for what they know;
Truth to no sex confin'd, her friends invites,
And woman, long restrain'd, demands her rights.
Nor should a light and odious name be thrown
On the fair dame who makes that knowledge known–
Who bravely dares the world's sarcastic sneer,
And what she is, is willing to appear.

'And what she is not!' peevish man replies,
His envy owning what his pride denies:
But let him, envious as he is, repair
To this sage Dame, and meet conviction there.

Miranda sees her morning levee fill'd
With men, in every art and science skill'd–
Men who have gain'd a name, whom she invites,
Because in men of genius she delights.

To these she puts her questions, that produce
Discussion vivid, and discourse abstruse:
She no opinion for its boldness spares,
But loves to show her audience what she dares;
The creeds of all men she takes leave to sift,
And, quite impartial, turns her own adrift.

Her noble mind, with independent force,
Her Rector questions on his late discourse;
Perplex'd and pain'd, he wishes to retire
From one whom critics, nay, whom crowds, admire—
From her whose faith on no man's dictate leans,
Who her large creed from many a teacher gleans;
Who for herself will judge, debate, decide,
And be her own 'philosopher and guide.'

Why call a lady *Blue*? It is because
She reads, converses, studies for applause;
And therefore all that she desires to know
Is just as much as she can fairly show.
The real knowledge we in secret hide,
It is the counterfeit that makes our pride.
'A little knowledge is a dangerous thing'—
So sings the Poet, and so let him sing:
But if from little learning danger rose,
I know not who in safety could repose.
The evil rises from our own mistake,
When we our ignorance for knowledge take;
Or when the little that we have, through pride,
And vain poor self-love view'd, is magnified.
Nor is your deepest Azure always free
From these same dangerous calls of vanity.

Yet of the sex are those who never show,
By way of exhibition, what they know.
Their books are read and prais'd, and so are they,
But all without design, without display.
Is there not One who reads the hearts of men,
And paints them strongly with unrivall'd pen?
All their fierce Passions in her scenes appear,
Terror she bids arise, bids fall the tear;

Looks in the close recesses of the mind,
And gives the finish'd portraits to mankind,
By skill conducted, and to Nature true,—
And yet no man on earth would call Joanna Blue!

Not so Miranda! She is ever prest
To give opinions, and she gives her best.
To these with gentle smile her guests incline,
Who come to hear, improve, applaud,—and dine.

Her hungry mind on every subject feeds;
She Adam Smith and Dugald Stewart reads;
Locke entertains her, and she wonders why
His famous Essay is consider'd dry.
For her amusement in her vacant hours
Are earths and rocks, and animals and flowers:
She could the farmer at his work assist,
A systematic agriculturist.
Some men, indeed, would curb the female mind,
Nor let us see that they themselves are blind;
But—thank our stars!—the liberal times allow,
That all may think, and men have rivals now.

Miranda deems all knowledge might be gain'd—
'But she is idle, nor has much attain'd;
'Men are in her deceiv'd: she knows at most
'A few light matters, for she scorns to boast.
'Her mathematic studies she resign'd—
'They did not suit the genius of her mind.
'She thought indeed the higher parts sublime,
'But then they took a monstrous deal of time!'

Frequent and full the letters she delights
To read in part; she names not him who writes—
But here and there a precious sentence shows,
Telling what literary debts she owes.
Works, yet unprinted, for her judgment come,
'Alas!' she cries, 'and I must seal their doom.
'Sworn to be just, the judgment gives me pain—
'Ah! why must truth be told, or man be vain?'

Much she has written, and still deigns to write,
But not an effort yet must see the light.
'Cruel!' her friends exclaim; 'unkind, unjust!'
But, no! the envious mass she will not trust;
Content to hear that fame is due to her,
Which on her works the world might not confer–
Content with loud applauses while she lives:
Unfelt the pain the cruel critic gives.

II

P.–Now where the Learned Lady? Doth she live,
Her dinners yet and sentiments to give–
The Dean's wise consort, with the many friends,
From whom she borrows, and to whom she lends
Her precious maxims?

　　　　　　F.–Yes, she lives to shed
Her light around her, but her Dean is dead.
Seen her I have, but seldom could I see:
Borrow she could not, could not lend to me.
Yet, I attended, and beheld the tribe
Attending too, whom I will not describe–
Miranda Thomson! Yes, I sometimes found
A seat among a circle so profound;
When all the science of the age combin'd
Was in that room, and hers the master-mind.
Well I remember the admiring crowd,
Who spoke their wonder and applause aloud;
They strove who highest should her glory raise,
And cramm'd the hungry mind with honied praise–
While she, with grateful hand, a table spread,
The Dean assenting–but the Dean is dead;
And though her sentiments are still divine,
She asks no more her auditors to dine.

Once from her lips came wisdom; when she spoke,
Her friends in transport or amazement broke.
Now to her dictates there attend but few,
And they expect to meet attention too;
Respect she finds is purchas'd at some cost,
And deference is withheld, when dinner's lost.

She, once the guide and glory of the place,
Exists between oblivion and disgrace;
Praise once afforded, now,–they say not why,
They dare not say it–fickle men deny;
That buzz of fame a new Minerva cheers,
Which our deserted queen no longer hears.
Old, but not wise, forsaken, not resign'd,
She gives to honours past her feeble mind,
Back to her former state her fancy moves,
And lives on past applause, that still she loves;
Yet holds in scorn the fame no more in view,
And flies the glory that would not pursue
To yon small cot, a poorly jointured *Blue*.

GEORGE CRABBE

676 *Mary the Cook-Maid's Letter to Dr. Sheridan*

Well; if ever I saw such another Man since my Mother bound my Head,

You a Gentleman! marry come up, I wonder where you were bred?

I am sure such Words does not become a Man of your Cloth,
I would not give such Language to a Dog, faith and troth.

Yes; you call'd my Master a Knave: Fie Mr. *Sheridan*, 'tis a Shame

For a Parson, who shou'd know better Things, to come out with such a Name.

Knave in your Teeth, Mr. *Sheridan*, 'tis both a Shame and a sin,

And the Dean my Master is an honester Man than you and all your kin:

He has more Goodness in his little Finger, than you have in your whole Body,

My Master is a parsonable Man, and not a spindle-shank'd hoddy doddy.

And now whereby I find you would fain make an Excuse,
Because my Master one Day in anger call'd you Goose.

Which, and I am sure I have been his Servant four Years since *October*,

And he never call'd me worse than Sweet-heart drunk or sober:

E E

Not that I know his Reverence was ever concern'd to my
knowledge,
Tho' you and your Come-rogues keep him out so late in your
Colledge.

   You say you will eat Grass on his Grave: a Christian eat
Grass!
Whereby you now confess your self to be a Goose or an
Ass:
But that's as much as to say, that my Master should die
before ye,
Well, well, that's as God pleases, and I don't believe that's a
true Story,
And so say I told you so, and you may go tell my Master;
what care I?
And I don't care who knows it, 'tis all one to *Mary*.
Every body knows, that I love to tell Truth and shame the
Devil,
I am but a poor Servant, but I think Gentle folks should be
civil.
Besides, you found fault with our Vittles one Day that you
was here,
I remember it was upon a *Tuesday*, of all Days in the
Year.
And *Saunders* the Man says, you are always jesting and
mocking,
Mary said he, (One Day, as I was mending my Master's
Stocking,)
My Master is so fond of that Minister that keeps the School;
I thought my Master a wise Man, but that Man makes him
a Fool.
Saunders said I, I would rather than a Quart of Ale,
He would come into our Kitchin, and I would pin a Dish-
clout to his Tail.
And now I must go, and get *Saunders* to direct this Letter,
For I write but a sad Scrawl, but my Sister *Marget* she
writes better.
Well, but I must run and make the Bed before my Master
comes from Pray'ers,
And see now, it strikes ten, and I hear him coming up
Stairs:

Whereof I could say more to your Verses, if I could write
    written hand,
And so I remain in a civil way, your Servant to command
Mary.
JONATHAN SWIFT

677 *The Merry Country Lad*

Who can live in heart so glad
As the merry country lad?
Who upon a fair green balk
May at pleasure sit and walk,
And amid the azure skies
See the morning sun arise,
While he hears in every spring
How the birds do chirp and sing:
Or before the hounds in cry
See the hare go stealing by:
Or along the shallow brook,
Angling with a baited hook,
See the fishes leap and play
In a blessed sunny day:
Or to hear the partridge call
Till she have her covey all:
Or to see the subtle fox,
How the villain plies the box;
After feeding on his prey,
How he closely sneaks away,
Through the hedge and down the furrow
Till he gets into his burrow:
Then the bee to gather honey;
And the little black-haired coney,
On a bank for sunny place,
With her forefeet wash her face,—
Are not these, with thousands moe
Than the courts of kings do know,
The true pleasing spirit's sights
That may breed true love's delights?
NICOLAS BRETON

678 *A Ballad upon a Wedding*

I tell thee, Dick, where I have been,
Where I the rarest things have seen;
　O, things without compare!
Such sights again cannot be found
In any place on English ground,
　Be it at wake or fair.

At Charing Cross, hard by the way,
Where we (thou know'st) do sell our hay,
　There is a house with stairs;
And there did I see coming down
Such folk as are not in our town,
　Forty at least, in pairs.

Amongst the rest, one pest'lent fine
(His beard no bigger though than thine)
　Walked on before the rest:
Our landlord looks like nothing to him:
The King (God bless him) 'twould undo him,
　Should he go still so drest.

At Course-a-Park, without all doubt,
He should have first been taken out
　By all the maids i' th' town:
Though lusty Roger there had been,
Or little George upon the Green,
　Or Vincent of the Crown.

But wot you what? the youth was going
To make an end of all his wooing;
　The parson for him stay'd:
Yet by his leave (for all his haste)
He did not so much wish all past
　(Perchance) as did the maid.

The maid (and thereby hangs a tale),
For such a maid no Whitsun-ale

Could ever yet produce:
No grape, that's kindly ripe, could be
So round, so plump, so soft as she,
   Nor half so full of juice.

Her finger was so small, the ring
Would not stay on, which they did bring,
   It was too wide a peck:
And to say truth (for out it must)
It looked like the great collar (just)
   About our young colt's neck.

Her feet beneath her petticoat,
Like little mice, stole in and out,
   As if they fear'd the light:
But O she dances such a way!
No sun upon an Easter-day
   Is half so fine a sight.

He would have kissed her once or twice,
But she would not, she was so nice,
   She would not do 't in sight,
And then she looked as who should say:
I will do what I list to-day,
   And you shall do 't at night.

Her cheeks so rare a white was on,
No daisy makes comparison
   (Who sees them is undone),
For streaks of red were mingled there,
Such as are on a Catherine pear
   (The side that's next the sun).

Her lips were red, and one was thin,
Compar'd to that was next her chin
   (Some bee had stung it newly);
But (Dick) her eyes so guard her face;
I durst no more upon them gaze
   Than on the sun in July.

Her mouth so small, when she does speak,
Thou'dst swear her teeth her words did break,
 That they might passage get;
But she so handled still the matter,
They came as good as ours, or better,
 And are not spent a whit.

If wishing should be any sin,
The parson himself had guilty been
 (She look'd that day so purely);
And did the youth so oft the feat
At night, as some did in conceit,
 It would have spoiled him surely.

Just in the nick the cook knocked thrice,
And all the waiters in a trice
 His summons did obey;
Each serving-man, with dish in hand,
Marched boldly up, like our trained band,
 Presented, and away.

When all the meat was on the table,
What man of knife or teeth was able
 To stay to be entreated?
And this the very reason was,
Before the parson could say grace,
 The company was seated.

The business of the kitchen's great,
For it is fit that men should eat;
 Nor was it there denied:
Passion o' me, how I run on!
There's that that would be thought upon
 (I trow) besides the bride.

Now hats fly off, and youths carouse;
Healths first go round, and then the house,
 The bride's came thick and thick:
And when 'twas nam'd another's health,
Perhaps he made it hers by stealth;
 And who could help it, Dick?

On the sudden up they rise and dance;
Then sit again and sigh, and glance:
　　Then dance again and kiss:
Thus several ways the time did pass,
Whilst ev'ry woman wished her place,
　　And every man wished his.

By this time all were stol'n aside
To counsel and undress the bride;
　　But that he must not know:
But yet 'twas thought he guess'd her mind,
And did not mean to stay behind
　　Above an hour or so.

When in he came (Dick), there she lay
Like new-fall'n snow melting away
　　('Twas time, I trow, to part);
Kisses were now the only stay,
Which soon she gave, as who would say,
　　God b' w' ye, with all my heart.

But, just as Heaven would have, to cross it,
In came the bridesmaids with the posset:
　　The bridegroon ate in spite;
For had he left the women to 't,
It would have cost two hours to do 't,
　　Which were too much that night.

At length the candle's out, and now
All that they had not done they do.
　　What that is, who can tell?
But I believe it was no more
Than thou and I have done before
　　With Bridget and with Nell.

　　　　　　　　　　SIR JOHN SUCKLING

679　*Tom Tatter's Birthday Ode*

Come all you jolly dogs, in the Grapes, and King's Head, and
　　Green Man, and Bell taps,
And shy up your hats–if you haven't hats, your paper and
　　woollen caps,

Shout with me and cry Eureka! by the sweet Parnassian River,
While echo, in Warner's Wood, replies, Huzza! the young
   Squire for ever!

And Vulcan, Mars, and Hector of Troy, and Jupiter and his
   wife,
And Phoebus, from his forked hill, coming down to take a
   knife,
And Mercury, and piping Pan, to the tune of 'Old King Cole,'
And Venus the Queen of Love, to eat an ox that was roasted
   whole.

Sir Mark, God bless him, loves good old times, when beards
   wag, and every thing goes merry,
There'll be drinking out of gracecups, and a Boar's head
   chewing rosemary,
Maid Marian, and a Morris dance, and the acting of quaint
   Moralities,
Doctor Bellamy and a Hobby horse, and many other Old
   Formalities.

But there won't be any Psalm-singing saints, to make us sad of
   a Monday,
But Bacchus will preach to us out of a barrel, instead of the
   methodist Bundy.
We'll drink to the King in good strong ale, like souls that are
   true and loyal,
And a fig for Mrs. Hanway, camomile, sage and penny-royal;
And a fig for Master Gregory, that takes tipsy folk into custody,
He was a wise man to-morrow, and will be a wiser man
   yesterday.

Come fill a bumper up, my boys, and toss off every drop of it!
Here's young Squire Ringwood's health, and may he live as
   long as Jason,
Before Atropos cuts his thread, and Dick Tablet, the bungling
   mason,
Chips him a marble tea-table, with a marble tea-urn a-top
   of it?
Quoth Tom in Tatters.

                                        THOMAS HOOD

680 *Captain Carpenter*

Captain Carpenter rose up in his prime
Put on his pistols and went riding out
But had got wellnigh nowhere at that time
Till he fell in with ladies in a rout.

It was a pretty lady and all her train
That played with him so sweetly but before
An hour she'd taken a sword with all her main
And twined him of his nose for evermore.

Captain Carpenter mounted up one day
And rode straightway into a stranger rogue
That looked unchristian but be that as may
The Captain did not wait upon prologue.

But drew upon him out of his great heart
The other swung against him with a club
And cracked his two legs at the shinny part
And let him roll and stick like any tub.

Captain Carpenter rode many a time
From male and female took he sundry harms
He met the wife of Satan crying 'I'm
The she-wolf bids you shall bear no arms.'

Their strokes and counters whistled in the wind
I wish he had delivered half his blows
But where she should have made off like a hind
The bitch bit off his arms at the elbows.

And Captain Carpenter parted with his ears
To a black devil that used him in this wise
O Jesus ere his threescore and ten years
Another had plucked out his sweet blue eyes.

Captain Carpenter got up on his roan
And sallied from the gate in hell's despite
I heard him asking in the grimmest tone
If any enemy yet there was to fight?

'To any adversary it is fame
If he risk to be wounded by my tongue
Or burnt in two beneath my red heart's flame
Such are the perils he is cast among.

'But if he can he has a pretty choice
From an anatomy with little to lose
Whether he cut my tongue and take my voice
Or whether it be my round red heart he choose.'

It was the neatest knave that ever was seen
Stepping in perfume from his lady's bower
Who at this word put in his merry mien
And fell on Captain Carpenter like a tower.

I would not knock old fellows in the dust
But there lay Captain Carpenter on his back
His weapons were the old heart in his bust
And a blade that shook between rotten teeth alack.

The rogue in scarlet and grey soon knew his mind
He wished to get his trophy and depart
With gentle apology and touch refined
He pierced him and produced the Captain's heart.

God's mercy rest on Captain Carpenter now
I thought him Sirs an honest gentleman
Citizen husband soldier and scholar enow
Let jangling kites eat of him if they can.

But God's deep curses follow after those
That shore him of his godly nose and ears
His legs and strong arms at the two elbows
And eyes that had not watered seventy years.

The curse of hell upon the sleek upstart
That got the Captain finally on his back
And took the red vitals of his heart
And made the kites to whet their beaks clack clack.

JOHN CROWE RANSOM

681 *A Farewell*

'And if I did, what then?
　Are you aggrieved therefore?
The sea hath fish for every man,
　And what would you have more?'

Thus did my mistress once
　Amaze my mind with doubt;
And popped a question for the nonce,
　To beat my brains about.

Whereto I thus replied:
　'Each fisherman can wish,
That all the seas at every tide
　Were his alone to fish.

'And so did I in vain,
　But since it may not be,
Let such fish there as find the gain,
　And leave the loss for me.

'And with such luck and loss
　I will content myself,
Till tides of turning time may toss
　Such fishers on the shelf.

'And when they stick on sands,
　That every man may see,
Then will I laugh and clap my hands,
　As they do now at me.'

GEORGE GASCOIGNE

NOTES

These notes are mainly to give the dates of publication of the poems and, where it is of interest, and where it is known, of their writing. Also, in those few cases where an extract only has been given, to state which portions are here printed. Only occasionally have allusions in the poems been explained.

Where a text different from that of the first appearance of the poem has been used, this has been noted. The figures refer to the numbers of the poems.

Book I

1. F. J. Child (*English and Scottish Popular Ballads*), no. 54a, who gives as his sources: (a) Sandys, *Christmas Carols*, p. 123, West of England; (b) Sandys, *Christmastide*, p. 241.
2. Balliol MS. 354. Printed in *Anglia*, xxvi, 175, and Chambers and Sidgwick, *Early English Lyrics*, 1926, p. 148.
3. Child, 36, with an emendation in the penultimate verse which, in Child's version, reads: 'An a' the fish came her tell but the proud machrell,/An she stood by the sea.'
4. *Minstrelsy of the Scottish Border*, 1802, II, iii, via Child (79).
5. *Percy's Reliques*, 1765.
6. Child, 12.
7. Scott's *Border Minstrelsy*, 1802-3.
8. *Chinese Poems*, 1946. After Ch'ên Tzŭ-lung (A.D. 1608-1647).
9. From 'the Eleventh Book of Homer's Odysseys', 1615.
10. The Induction to *The Mirour for Magistrates*, 1563, Stzs. 68-76.
11. *Troilus and Criseyde*, Book IV, Stzs. 32-49, c. 1380.
12. c. 1390.
13. First Sestiad, lines 1-182.
14. *Venus and Adonis*, lines 259-336.
15. *Tullie's Love*, 1589.
16. *Idea, The Shepheard's Garland*, 1593, Eclogue VIII.
17. 1819. First printed in *The Indicator*, May 10, 1820.
18. *The Heart of Midlothian*, 1818.
19. *Lyrical Poems*, 1887.
20. *Last Poems*, 1922.
21. *A Paradyse of Daynty Devises*, 1576. Compiled by Edwards.
22. *Poems*, 1881.
23. *Poems and Translations*, 1921.
24. From the end of the story 'Billy Budd, Foretopman', 1891. Publ. 1924.
25. *The Song of Hiawatha*, 1855, xix.

26. *The Defence of Guenevere and Other Poems*, 1858.
27. *Moments of Vision*, 1917.
28. From *Corythos*, 1859 version, lines 271–293.
29. From *Paradise Lost*, Book IV, lines 823 to end.
30. From *The Vision of Judgment*, Stzs. xxiv–xxxii.
    'Johanna Southcote, the aged lunatic, who fancied herself, and was believed by many followers, to be with child of a new Messiah, died in 1815. There is a full account of her in the *Quarterly Review*, vol. xxiv, p. 496.' Note in More's ed., Vol. XII.
31. Section xix, *Men and Women*, 1855.

BOOK II

32. From K. Sisam, *Fourteenth-Century Verse and Prose*.
33. From *Cymbeline*.
34. From *The Tempest*.
35. 1857.
36. *Historic Odes*, etc., 1864.
37. *Songs of Innocence*, 1789–1794.
38. From 'Golden Wings', *The Defence of Guenevere and Other Poems*. 1858.
39. 1847.
40. Child, 78. From the *Folk Lore Record*, I, 60, 1868.
41. *The Legend of Good Women*, F. Version, possibly about 1387.
42. *Love's Labour's Lost*.
43. *The Old Wives' Tale*, 1595.
44. From the Christ Church MS. ; before 1620.
45. T. Weelkes' *Airs or Fantastic Spirits*, 1608.
46. *Robin Goodfellow*, Part ii, 1628.
47. *The Masque of Augurs*, 1622.
48. *The Sad Shepherd*; pub. 1641.
49. *Sappho and Phao*, 1584.
50. *The Gypsies Metamorphosis*, 1621.
51. *Words for Music*, 1934.
52. *The Garlande of Laurell*, 1523.
53. *Twelfth Night*.
54. From *The Winter's Tale*.
55. Epilogue to *A Midsummer Night's Dream*.
56. *Patient Grissell*, 1603.
57. *Midas*, 1592.
58. From *The Ayres that were Sung and Played, at Brougham Castle* . . . 1618. Ed. George Mason and John Earsden.
59. *Pastorals, Containing Eglogues*, 1619. First printed with slight variants under 'Eglogs' in *Poems Lyrick and Pastorall*, 1606. The part of Eclogue ix here reprinted appeared as a song in *England's Helicon*, 1600.
60. From *David and Bethsabe*, 1599.
61. *Rosalynde*, 1590.
62. *The Second Booke of Songs or Ayres*, 1600.
63. *The First Booke of Songes or Ayres*, 1597.

64. *The Shepheardes Calendar*, 1579, Eclogue viii, August.
65. *Poems in Divers Humours*, 1598.
66. Eclog. vii. 1606 and 1619.
67. From *The Faithful Shepherdess*, V. i. 1610. Text 1679.
68. *Poems*, 1616.
69. From *Comus*. A Mask presented at Ludlow Castle, 1634.
70. Written c. 1620.
    Line 5 variant reading : Where are you when the sun shall rise ?
71. *Poems on several Occasions*, 1689.
72. From *The Impostors*, 1652.
73. *Death's Jest Book*, 1580.
74. From *Cymbeline*.
75. From *The Winter's Tale*.
76. The Definitive Complete Edition of the Poems of Emily Dickinson. London, 1933.
77. From *The Princess*, 1853.
78. *Selected Poems*, ed. Hazleton Spencer, Macmillan (N.Y.), 1931.
79. *Posthumous Poems*, 1824.
80. *Songs of Experience*, 1789–1794.
81. From *The Spanish Student*, 1843.
82. *The Forrest*, v, vi. This is two poems : each translates a part of Catullus's *Vivamus mea Lesbia*. Song v is in *Volpone*, 1607.
83. *Musicke of Sundrie Kindes* . . . 1607. A slightly different version in *Philis*, 1593.
84. *The Garlande of Laurell*, 1523.
85. From *Comus*. A Mask presented at Ludlow Castle, 1634.
86. From *Arcades*, 1633.
87. From *The Princess*, 1853.
88. From *As You Like It*.
89. 1642. The first part of the poem. For variants see edn. J. L. Weir, 1938. The last two lines of Stz. 2 run :

> That dares not put it to the touch,
> To gain or lose it all.

90. *Poems*, 1832. Version 1850.
91. From *Empedocles on Etna*, 1852.
92. *Unpublished Early Poems*, ed. Charles Tennyson, 1931.
93. From *Rosalynde*, 1590.
94. From *The Indian Emperour*, 1667.
95. *Hebrew Melodies*, 1815.
96. *Hesperides*, 1648.
97. *Ayres to Sing and Play to the Lute and Basse Viol*, 1618.
98. *Observations in the Art of English Poesie*, 1602.
99. *A Garlande of Laurell*, 1523.
100. *Miscellaneous Works*, 1702.
101. 1667. Another version, of 1671, may be found in the *Oxford Book of Seventeenth-Century Verse*.
102. *Menaphon*, 1589.
103. Ode vii. *Odes of Anacreon*, 1800.
104. From *King Arthur*, 1691.

105. From *The Rape of Lucrece*, IV, 6. About 1605.
106–110. From *Hesperides*.
111. From *The Silent Woman*.
112–114. *Hesperides*, 1648.
115. From *William Longbeard*, 1593.
116. From *Twelfth Night*.
117. *Forget-me-Not*, 1827.
118. *Poems*, 1807.
119. *The Winding Stair and Other Poems*, 1933.
120. *Posthumous Poems*, 1824.
121. *Hebrew Melodies*, 1815.
122. 1794.
123. 1808.
124. 1788.
125. 1791. Second version.
126. 1815.
127. 'Scotch Air' in *National Airs*, 1819–1828.
128. *Occasional Pieces*, 1814–1816.
129. *The Gentle Shepherd*, 1725.
130. 1783.
131. From *The Misfortunes of Elphin*, 1829.
132. From *Nightmare Abbey*, 1818.
133. *The Musical Miscellany*, v, 1731. Signora Cuzzoni was a famous
   Italian opera singer.

Book III

134. MS. Rawl. Poet 85, f. 123, 'Sr W.R.' Slightly dubious. First
   printed in Deloney's *The Garland of Good-will*, 1678.
135. *Divine Songs for Children*, 1715.
136. c. 1567.
137. First printed from MS. by Sir E. K. Chambers, *Poems and
   Masques*, 1912.
138–142. Some of Wyatt's poems first appeared in Tottel's Miscellany
   (1557). The first full edition was by Nott in the early nineteenth century. Our text is based on collation of the MSS.
   by Mr. Kenneth Muir.
138. The stanza beginning 'Love did assign . . .' is missing in
   some MSS.

   'And I alone
   Am left as . . . .'

   The MS. gives ' Armless as . . . '. Emendation (by Nott),
   generally accepted.

143. *The Third Booke of Ayres*, c. 1613.
144. *A Booke of Ayres*, 1601. Cf. No. 82.
145. *The Second Booke of Ayres*, 1613.
146. *Poems*, 1614.
147. *The Romaunt of the Rose*, c. 1369, Lines 21–131. This is
   a translation, this part almost certainly by Chaucer, of the
   French poem by Guillaume de Lorris (c. 1237).

148. From *Poems on Several Occasions*, 1727.
149. See note to 138. In the last stanza, some editors suggest:

'If that your heart doth not relent.'

150. *England's Helicon*, 1600, and *The Passionate Pilgrim*, 1599.
151. *The Passionate Pilgrim*, 1599.
152. From *The Mourning Garment*, 1590.
153. *Piscatorie Eclogues*, 1633, Eclog. IIII. The poem belongs to this Book only on the surface: it resembles a Drayton pastoral, but it is really a politico-moral poem, and might well go in Book IX next to *Lycidas*.
154. From *Caelica*, 1633.
155. From *The Muses Elizium*, 1630 ('The Fourth Nimphall').
156. *Songs and Sonets*, 1633.
157. *Tottel's Miscellany* (Songes and Sonnettes), 1557.
158. *Amoretti*, 1595. Sonnet I.
159. *Amoretti.* Sonnet LXXIII.
160. Sonnet LXI, from *Idea*, 1593.
161. See note to 138.
162. *Gebir*, etc., 1831. In the 'Ianthe' group.
163. Sonnet xviii.
164. Sonnet xxix.
165. Sonnet xxx.
166. Sonnet xxxiii.
167. Sonnet lv.
168. Sonnet lx.
169. Sonnet lxxiii.
170. Sonnet cxvi.
171. Sonnet cvi.
172. Sonnet cvii.
173. From *A Booke of Ayres*, 1601.
174. Sonnet vi, from *Idea*, 1593.
175. Sonnet xx, from *Idea*, 1593.
176. Sonnet cxxix.
177. Sonnet cxliv.
178–181. *Lucasta*, 1649.
182–183. *Poems* 1645.
184. From *Hero and Leander*, 1598. End of Fifth Sestiad.
185. John Dowland's *Songs and Airs*, 1597.
186. From Rowe's *The Fair Penitent*, 1702.
187. From *Cynthia's Revels*, 1601.
188. From *Under-Wood*, 1640 folio.
189. From *Castara*, Second Part, 1639.
190. *Lucasta.* Posthume Poems, 1655.
191–194. *Songs and Sonets*, 1633.
195. *Fragmenta Aurea*, 1646.
196. *The Last Remains of Sir John Suckling*, 1659.
197–198. From *Aglaura*, 1638.
199–200. *Poems etc. on Several Occasions*, 1691.
201. *Miscellany* (Hindmarsh), 1685.
202. From *The Broken Heart*, 1633.

203. *Fragmenta Aurea*, 1646.
204. *Miscellaneous Poems*, 1681.
205. From *Delia* 1592, Sonnet i.
206. From *Cleomenes*, 1692.
207-208. From *The Beggar's Opera*, 1728.
209. 'Sidera', xii.
210. From *The Countess of Pembroke's Arcadia*, 1598. The Thirde Booke or Acte.
    A shorter version from *The Arte of Poetry* may be found in *The Oxford Book of Sixteenth-Century Verse*.
211. From *Poems*, 1651.
212. From *Castara*, Pt. I, 1640.
213. *Posthumous Poems*, 1824.
214. From *Poetical Sketches* (1769-1778), pub. 1783.
215. c. 1793.
216. *Lyrical Ballads*, 1800. An earlier version appeared in *The Morning Post*, 21st Dec., 1799.
217. 1825. *Poems*. Blackwood, 1862.
218. From *Verses*, 1896.
219. 1893. To S. R. Crockett, from Vailima.
220. *Modern Love*, 1862, Stz. 1.
221. *Selected Poems*, ed. T. S. Eliot, London, 1935.

BOOK IV

222. *Poems*, 1870, 'Lyrics'.
223. *The Defence of Guenevere and Other Poems*, 1858.
224. *Poems*, 1817.
225. *The Temple*, 1633.
226. *Poems*, 1911. Ed. R. Bridges.
227. *Last Poems*, 1922.
228. *Hesperides*, 1648.
229. *The Devil's Law Case*, 1623.
230. 1802. *Poems*, 1807.
231. *New Poems*, 1867.
232. From trs. of *The Odyssey*, 1879.
233. 1819. *Literary Remains*, 1848.
234. *A Book of Ayres*, 1601.
235. 1854.
236. Tottel's *Miscellany*, 1557.
237. *Astrophel and Stella*, 1591.
238. *Delia*, 1592, Sonnet liiii.
239. Dated 1819. *Literary Remains*, 1848.
240. *Poems*, 1870, 'House of Life'. VI (b) subsequently omitted.
241. *Wuthering Heights and Agnes Grey . . . A Selection etc.*, 1850. Clement Shorter (and C. W. Hatfield), 1923.
242. *In the Seven Woods*, 1902.
243. 1802. *Poems*, 1807.
244. *At the Sign of the Lyre*. 1885. 'W. E. H.' is Henley.
245. 1802. *Poems*, 1807.
246. *Fortnightly Review*, May 1881.

247. *Poems*, 1870.
248. Harley MS. 9617. Doubtfully by King, ed. John Sparrow, 1925.
249. *New Poems*, 1897.
250. 'Eversley 1845', *Poems*, 1871.
251. *Poems*, 1807.
252. 1802. *Poems*, 1807.
253. 1804. *Poems*, 1807.
254. *Astrophel and Stella*, 1591.
255. *Posthumous Poems*, 1824.
256. Composed at Bracknell, April, 1814. *Alastor*, 1816.
257. *Idea*, 1593, Sonnet lxx.
258. *The Duchess of Malfi*, 1623.
259. *Christ's Company*, 1861.
260. *Cupid and Death : A Masque*, 1653.
261. 1658.
262. *Songs and Sonets*, 1633.
263. *The Plea of the Midsummer Fairies, etc.*, 1827.
264. *Ambarvalia*, 1849.
265. *Odes on Several Subjects*, 1746. Written in the beginning of the year 1746.
266. *Odes With other Lyrick Poesies*, 1619.
267. *Certaine Small Poems Lately Printed*, 1605.
268. 1915. *Moments of Vision*, 1917. Text from *Collected Poems*, 1919.
269. The beginning of *From Milton*, 1804–1808.
270. *Prometheus Unbound*, 1820.
271. *Atalanta in Calydon*, 1865.
272. *Hellas*, 1822.
273. *Cleopatra*, 1594.
274. *The King's Entertainment*, 1603.
275. *The Third Booke of Ayres*, n.d., c. 1613.
276. *Poems*, 1917.
277. *The Tribute*, 1837.
278. *Nepenthe*, 1835.
279. From *The Princess*, 1853.
280. First reprinted and assigned to Chatterton by Mr. E. H. W. Meyerstein in his *Life of Thomas Chatterton*, 1930. From *The Romantics*, ed. G. Grigson, 1942.
281–282. *Poetical Sketches* (1769–1778). Printed 1783.
283. *Posthumous Poems*, 1824.
284. *Devereux*, 1597.

    This since its appearance in Robert Allott's *English Parnassus*, 1600, where it was attributed to 'Ch. Marlowe' has, till recently, been accepted as a fragment of Marlowe's. It is, in fact, part of Markham's poem. (See T.L.S., Jan. 4, 1947, Article by John Crow.)
    We give the lines familiar as Marlowe's. The poem 'consists of 250 numbered *ottava rima* stanzas,' and two unnumbered. The 'Fragment' begins in the middle of Stanza 2 and breaks off in the middle of Stanza 5, which continues :

The Bower of Beauty; whence alone did flow
More heavenly streams than former age had seen,
Taking that current from that learned Hill
Where lodge the Mothers of admire and skill.

285. *The Second Booke of Ayres*, n.d., 1612–1613. Vivian in his edition prints another charming version, which omits the fourth stanza.

286. From *The Countess of Pembroke's Arcadia*, 1590.

287. *Arbasto*, 1584.

288. *Pericles and Aspasia*, 1836.

289. *The Lord's Maske*, 1613.

290. *Heroic Idylls*, 1863.

291. *Poems*, 1851.

292. *Hymen's Triumph*, 1615.

293. *Delia*, 1592. Later transferred to *Occasional Poems*.

294. *Tethy's Festival*, 1610.

295. *Castara*, Second Part, 1639.

296. Brit. Mus. Add. MSS. 33219.

297. *Poems and Translations*, 1647.

298. From Horace I. 11. *Verses and Translations*, 1862.

299. *The Lovers' Melancholy*, 1628.

300. *Miscellaneous Poems*, 1681.

> The original text has:
>
> Now, therefore, while the youthful hew
> Sits on thy face like morning glew. . . .
>
> The emendation 'dew' is usually accepted.

301. *Poems*, 1640.

302. *Psyche*, 1648.

303. *Endymion*, 1818, Book IV, 146–180.

304. Lansdowne MS. 777. *Oxford Book of Seventeenth-Century Verse*.

305. *The Phoenix Nest*, 1593.

306–308. 'Epigrammes', 1616 Folio. 'S.P.' Salamon Pavey: till recently supposed to be Salathiel Pavey. See *The Year's Work in English Studies*, xxiii, 120.

309. *Miscellaneous Poems*, 1681.

310. *Hesperides*, 1648.

311. *The Listeners*, 1912.

312. *The Tempest*.

313. *The White Divel*, 1612.

314. 1870.

315. *The Masque of Queens*, 1609. Folio, 1616.

316. *The Curse of Kehama*, 1810.

317. Whether it is legitimate to modernise Chatterton's false antique English may be doubted, but certainly to do so offers less impediment to the real poetry underlying the perverse original. The original version may be found in *The Rowley Poems of Chatterton*, ed. M. E. Hare, Oxford, 1911. This song comes from *Ælla: a Tragycal Enterlude*.

318. *The Old Wives' Tale*, 1595.

319. *The Third Booke of Ayres*, c. 1613.
320. *Hesperides*, 1648.
321. 1849.
322. 1865.
323. 1858. *Macmillan's Magazine*, Feb., 1861.
324. *Lyrical Ballads*, 1800.
325. Charles the First, Sc.v., *Posthumous Poems*, 1824.
326. *Death's Jest Book*, 1850.
327. *Poems by Currer, Ellis and Action Bell, 1846.* 'The following little piece has no title; but in it the genius of a solitary region seems to address his wandering and wayward votary, and to recall within his influence the proud mind which rebelled at times even against what it most loved.' (Note by Charlotte Brontë.)
328. *The Dynasts.* 1904–1908, Part III, Act VI, Sc.viii. The scene is Waterloo.
329. Published in *Hunt's Literary Pocket Book*, 1823.
330. From *Othello*.
331. *Complete Works*, ed. Shorter, 1910.
332. From *The Tragedy of Valentinian*, V. i. c. 1612. Text 1679.
333. The conclusion of the Second Part of *Christabel*, 1816.
334. *Menaphon*, 1589.
335. *Patient Grissill*, 1603.
336. From *A Midsummer Night's Dream*.
337. From *Cynthia's Revels*, 1600. Folio, 1616.
     'division': a musical term. 'Division in the musical nomenclature of the seventeenth and eighteenth centuries, were rapid passages-slow notes *divided* into quick ones . . . hence the word can be applied to quick consecutive passages'– Grove: *Dictionary of Music*.
338. *Poetical Miscellanies*, 1633.
339. *Tears for the Death of Moeliades*, 1613. Lines 97–142. Moeliades: Prince Henry.

O hyacinth, for aye your AI keep still.

AI, the exclamation of woe, the mark on the hyacinth to mourn for ever the death of Hyacinthus, who was turned into a blood-red flower when accidentally killed by Apollo. Cf. *Lycidas*, 'Like to that sanguine flow'r inscribed with woe'.
340. *The Third and Last Book of Songs or Aires*, 1603.
341. *Lyrical Ballads*, 1800.
     Usually classed with the 'Lucy' poems. Possibly, however, Wordsworth was writing about his spirit in a state of trance.
342. *Posthumous Poems*, 1824.
343. First published in *The Liberal*, 1822.
344. *Poems*, ed. Robert Bridges, 1918.
345. *Odes*, 1601.
346. *Noble Numbers*, 1647.
347–349. *Songs of Innocence*, 1789.
350–351. *Songs of Experience*, 1794.
352. c. 1800–1803.

353-354. *Songs of Experience*, 1794.
355. The opening lines of the Sixth Nimphall (*Muses Elizium*), 1630.
356. Written at the front during the early phase of the War of 1914–1918. Capt. the Hon. Julian H. F. Grenfell, D.S.O., died of wounds on May 26, 1915.
357. *Poems*, 1782.
358. *Poems*, 1640. 'dividing throat': trilling voice. See note to No. 337.
359. *Simonidea*, 1806. Revised version of 1846 given.
360. 1831. Included in *Pericles and Aspasia*, 1846.
361. *Hesperides*, 1640.
362. *Men and Women*, 1855.
363. 1818.
364. *Jerusalem*, 1804-1820, Chap. II, S. 52.
365. *Poems on Several Occasions*, 1709. A. R. Waller, 1907.
366. 'Anacreontics.' Works, 1710.
367-368. *Hesperides*.
369. *Miscellany Poems*, 1704.
    This is one of the earliest Jacobite Songs. Pan is James II, Syrinx, the Queen, and the Son, the baby who was later to to become 'the Old Pretender'.
370. *The Third Booke of Ayres*. c. 1613.
371. *Certain Elegant Poems*, 1647.
372. *Miscellaneous Works*, 1750.
373. *The Earthly Paradise*, 1868. 'An Apology' at the beginning.

BOOK V

374. *Sea Garden*, 1916.
375. *Poems*, 1833.
376. *Poems Dramatic and Lyrical*, 1893.
377-378. *The Poems of John Clare*. Ed. J. W. Tibble, 1935.
379-380. *Collected Poems*, 1936.
381. *Select Poems of William Barnes*, ed. Thomas Hardy. London (Humphrey Milford), 1922.
382-383. *Speculations*, 1924.
384. Sept, 28, 1881. *Poems*, 1918.
385. *Milton*, 1804, Book I, Section 34, line 28 to the end.
386. *Poems of Alexander Hume*, ed. A. Lawson. Scottish Text Society Publications, 1902.
387. 'Sea Drift' in *Leaves of Grass*.
388. *Sonnets and Miscellaneous Poems*, 1789.
389. 'The Flying Fish', Part II. *The Long Road*, 1926.
390-391. *Poems on Several Occasions*, 1689.
392. *The Tatler*, 17 Oct., 1710, No. 238.
393. 'In Hospital', *A Book of Verses*, 1888.
394. *The Long Road*, 1926.
395. *Chinese Poems*, 1946.
396. 'Mari Magno'. My Tale. *Collected Poems*, 1862.
397. *The Seasons*. Summer 1727, 1746 Version, lines 1103-1168
398. *The Seasons*. Autumn 1730, 1746 Version, lines 950-987.

399. *The Forrest.* Folio, 1616.
400. *Letters to Several Personages*, 1633.
401. *Miscellaneous Poems*, 1681.
402. *King Arthur*, 1691.
403–404. *Miscellaneous Poems*, 1681.
405. *The Shepherd's Week*, 1714. 'Tuesday or the Ditty: Marian.'
A mock pastoral which might with equal reason have been placed in Book X.
406. *The Faerie Queene*, 1590, Canto I, ix, Stzs. 21–36.
407. *The Faerie Queene*, 1590, Canto II, xii, Stzs. 70–80.
408. *Amoretti*, 1595. Sonnet lxiiii.
409. Published by Hunt in *The Examiner*, 1818.
410. *The Tatler*, May 7, 1709. No. 12.
411. *Gebir*, 1798, Book V, lines 1–120.
412. *Nereides; or Sea-Eclogues*, 1712. Eclogue x.
413. *Menaphon*, 1589.
414. Written 1919. *Michael Robartes and the Dancer*, 1921.
415. *Elegy* xvi, 1635.
416. *Sylvae*, 1685. Trs. from Lucretius. Latter part of Third Book. Line 200 to end.
417. *Divine Fancies*, 1632.
418. *New Verse*, 1925.
419. *Poems and Lyrics of the Joy of the Earth*, 1883.

BOOK VI

420. *Motley*, 1918.
421. *Poems*, Vol. II, 1939.
422. *Last Poems*, 1917.
423. *Cawdor*, 1929.
424. *Poems Dramatic and Lyrical*, 1893.
425. *Shorter Poems*, Book III. 1890.
426. *Shorter Poems*, Book I. 1890.
427. c. 1638.
428. *Miscellaneous Poems by Several Hands.* 1726. (Lewis's Miscellany.)
The first authentic edition. There is another pirated one, differing a good deal, of the same year, and a version in Pindaric form in Savage's Miscellany of 1725.
In this text the line in the last paragraph:

Search for Peace with all your skill

has been omitted. This is restored from the 1751 text.
429. *Odes on Several Subjects*, 1747.
430. Sent in a letter to Woodhouse, Sept. 22, 1819.
431. Fragments of *Death's Jest Book*, 1890.
432. *Poems*, 1821. Quatorzains, No. v.
433. *New Poems*, 1897.
434. *Miscellaneous Poems written by a Lady*, 1713.
435. *Childe Harold's Pilgrimage*, Canto III, 1816. Stanzas lxxxvi–xciii.

436. 1804. *Poems*, 1807.
437. *Lyrical Ballads*, 1800.
438. February, 1798.
439. 1770. Lines 1–96, 113–136, 193–264.
440. For Goldsmith's play. 1768.
441. *The Task*, 1785. 'The Time-Piece', lines 206–254.
442. *The Task*, 1785. 'The Garden,' lines 108–260.
443. *Pleasures of the Imagination*, 1744, Book III, lines 568–633 the end.
444. *Pleasures of the Imagination*, 1770. Book IV, lines 31–57.
445. 'Influence of Natural Objects in Calling Forth and Strengthening the Imagination in Boyhood and Early Youth', 1798. *The Friend*, Dec. 28, 1809.
446. *Men and Women*, 1855.
447. *Poems*, 1673.
448. *Horae Lyricae*, 1706, Book I.
449. *The Book of Los*, 1795, Chapter II.
450. *The London Magazine*, March 1822.
451. *The Germ*, 1850. Revised 1856 and 1870.
452. *Hyperion. A Fragment*, 1820, Book I, lines 1–71.
453. *Poems and Ballads*, Second Series, 1878.
454. Oct. 1816. First printed in *The Examiner*, Dec. 1, 1816.
455. *The Spleen. An Epistle* . . . 1737, lines 646–715, 814 to end.
456.   'In the June of 1797 some long-expected friends paid a visit to the author's cottage ; and on the morning of their arrival, he met with an accident, which disabled him from walking during the whole time of their stay. One evening, when they had left him for a few hours, he composed the following lines in the garden bower.'–Coleridge's note.
457. Works, 1717. Line 27. 'thy' for 'my' restores the earlier reading.
458. *Poems, Elegies, Paradoxes and Sonnets*, 1657. In line 30 we have adopted John Sparrow's emendation, 'life' for 'love'.
459. *Under-Wood*. Folio, 1640.
460. Feb. 9, 1646.
461. 1684. Oldham, the satirist, died in 1683.
462. *Collected Poems*, 1668. Thomas Wentworth, Earl of Strafford, was tried and executed in 1641.
463. 1751. Text 1768.
464. *Men and Women*, 1855.
465. March 13, 1726/1727. *Miscellanies*, 1727.
     Stella (Esther Johnson) died in 1729.
466. Epigrams, 101, Folio, 1616.
     Pooly : possibly 'foole' as in Harl. MS. 6917.
467. *The Angel in the House*, 'The Betrothal', 1854.
468. *Davison's Poetical Rhapsody*, 1602.
     'my two loves' : Sir Edward Dyer and Fulke Greville.
469. *Comedies and Tragedies*, 1679.
470. 1729. Separate publication.
     Stowe : Cobham's seat ; the centre of the 'Patriots'.
471. Prefixed to *Tiresias and Other Poems*, 1885.

BOOK VII

472. Rossetti MS.; accepting Keynes' reading of 'binds' for 'bends'.
473. From Michael Spark's *Crums of Comfort with Godly Prayers*, 7th Ed., 1728. Sparks (*fl.* 1640) apparently appropriated a version of the poem 'Hos ego versiculos' in Quarles's *Argalus and Parthenia*, 1629.
474. In a letter to his sister, 1818.
475. Written 1803. *Poems*, 1807. 'Memorials of a Tour in Scotland', 1803.
476. 1803.
477. 1785.
478. 'Annual Register', 1762. Oxford Book of Eighteenth-Century Verse.
479. 1794.
480. 'Tottel's Miscellany' (*Songes and Sonettes*), 1557. 'How no age is content with its own estate, and how the age of children is the happiest, if they had the skill to understand it.'
481. Goldolphin's poems were first printed by Saintsbury in 1906. Our text is from the edition from MS. by William Dighton, Clarendon Press, 1931.
482. 1825.
483. *Selections from Poems by Ellis Bell*, 1850.
484. *The Winding Stair and Other Poems*, 1933.
485. *Dramatic Lyrics*, 184- 185-.
        'toccata = an overture-a *touch* piece. Galuppi was a famous Italian composer of the eighteenth century. He was in London from 1741-1744.'-Note by R. B.
486. J. Weever's *Ancient Funeral Monuments*, 1631.
        A shorter version of this poem is usually ascribed to Francis Beaumont. Mr. Norman Ault (*Elizabethan Lyrics*) proposes Basse as the author of the version here printed.
487. 'Solomon', *Poems*, 1718, Book III, 'Power', lines 119-184.
488. 'In Imitation of the Tenth Satire of Juvenal', 1749. Lines 1-28, 73-90, 135-162, 189-240; 343 to end.
489. *Il Pastor Fido*, 1648 (Text of 1676), *Oxford Book of Seventeenth-Century Verse*.
490. Rawl. Poet. MS. No. 85. Often printed.
491. At the head of the story 'To be Filed for Reference' in *Plain Tales from the Hills*, 1888.
492. *Poems*, 1870.
493. *Michael Robartes and the Dancer*, 1921.
494. From *Nosce Teipsum*, 1599. Text, Bullen 1903.
495. First published in the *Atlantic Monthly*, April 1860, as 'Bardic Symbols', Sea-Drift, 1881.
496. 1655.
497. 1631. *Shorter Poems*, 1645.
498. *Sonnet xix*, 1655.
499. Sept., 1802. *Poems*, 1807.
500. *Morning Post*, April 16, 1803. *Poems*, 1807.
501. *Morning Post*, February 2, 1803. *Poems*, 1897.
        'François Dominique Toussaint, surnamed L'Ouverture,

was governor of St. Domingo, and chief of the African slaves enfranchised by the decree of the French Convention (1794). He resisted Napoleon's edict re-establishing slavery in St. Domingo, was arrested and sent to Paris in June 1802, and died there after ten months' imprisonment in April 1803.'– Hutchinson.

502. 1802 ? Poems, 1807.
503. Conclusion of *Euthymiœ Raptus* or *The Tears of Peace*, 1609. 'Referring back to the funeral of Love to which Peace was setting forth with a coffin. . . . Her "teares" in the language of the period, are her observations and lamentations made on the occasion and have formed the central part of the poem. They are "marginal" because they serve to gloss the main text of the "Death of Love".'–Note by Phyllis Brooks Bartlett, *The Poems of George Chapman*, Oxford, 1941.
504. *The Scourge of Villanie*, 1598.
505. *Antonio's Revenge*, 1609.
506. *Men and Women*, 1855.
507. *Poems*, 1842.
508. First version, 1859. Stzs. 1–3, 9–16, 27–35, 42–48, 56–58.
509. From *Pippa Passes*, 1841.
510. After the story 'At the Edge of the Evening', in *A Diversity of Creatures*, 1917.
511. Conclusion of *The Dunciad*. Final form 1743. The passage with variants originally concluded Book III of the 1728 version.
512. *Flowers of Sion*: or Spiritual Poems, 1630.
513. 1632–1633. *Shorter Poems*, 1645.
514. *Verses of Praise and Joy*, 1586. *Oxford Book of Sixteenth-Century Verse*.
515. The earliest extant text of this " Sonet " is given by James Fergusson in a transcription published in *The Times Literary Supplement*, May 12, 1950.
516. *The Unknown Eros*, Book 2, iii, 1877.
517. *Religio Laici*, 1682, lines 1–41.
518. *Emblems*, 1635, Book II, Emblem xiv.
519. *Poems*, 1686.
520. *Pericles and Aspasia*, 1835.
521. *Miscellaneous Poems*, 1681.
522. *Francesco's Fortune*, 1590.
523. *Poems*. Text G. C. Moore Smith, Oxford, 1923.
524. *The Scourge of Villanie*, 1598.
525. Published in 1860, but belongs to the 1833–1842 period.
526. *Paradise Lost*, 1667, Book IV, lines 598–688.
527. *Epipsychidion*, 1821, lines 72–189.
528. 1874. Sections xiii and xiv.
529. 'Echoes' IV ; in *A Book of Verses*, 1888.
530. In *The Prisoner of Chillon*, 1816.
531. Homer's Hymn to Mars from *The Crowne of all Homers Worckes*.
532. Pickering MS.
533. Sept. 4, 1938. *Last Poems and Two Plays*, 1939.

534. *Certaine Epistles*, 1601–1603.
535. *Lyrical Ballads*, 1798.
536. 'Pindaric Odes', *Works*, 1668.
537. Composed December 1805 or January 1806.
538. *Poems*, 1920.
539. *Prometheus Unbound*, 1820.

Book VIII

540. 'A Coronet for his Mistress Philosophie', *Ovid's Banquet of Sense*, 1595.
541. *Idea*, 1619, Sonnet xxxi.
542–544. *Songs and Sonnets*, 1633.
545–546. *Poems*, 1616, Second Part.
547. *Summer's Last Will and Testament*, 1600.
548. *Lucasta*, 1649.
549. Prefixed to the Second Edition of the Shakespeare *Folio*, 1632. Line 10, 'heart'. So 1645. Folio, 'part'.
550. *The Third Booke of Ayres*, 1613.
551. *A Booke of Ayres*, 1601.
552. *Poems of John Clare*, ed. Tibble, 1935.
553. *The Broken Heart*, 1633.
554. *Selected Poems.* Ed. T. S. Eliot, 1928. Originally in *Poems of Frederic Manning.*
555. *In Memoriam*, 1850, xii, xix, liv, lv, lvi, lxvii, xcv.
556–557. *Poems by Currer, Ellis and Acton Bell*, 1846.
558. *A Century of Roundels*, 1883. There are two on Wagner.
559. 17 Feb., 1854.
560. *Collected Works*, 1846. 'Hellenics.'
561. May 18, 1840. *Poems by Charlotte, Emily, and Anne Brontë.* New York, 1902.
562. *Some Imagist Poets*, 1916.
563. Fourteenth Century, New College, Oxford, MS. from *Religious Lyrics of the Fourteenth Century*, Carlton Brown, 1924.
564. July 25, 1849.
565. The first two verses of a fragmentary poem. *Complete Poems of Emily Brontë.* Ed. Clement Shorter, 1910.
566–567. *Summer's Last Will and Testament*, 1600.
568. *The Temple*, 1633.
569. 'The Argument' at the beginning, c. 1793.
570. 'Every Soul is a Circus', IV, *Selected Poems.*
571. *Daiphantus*, etc., to which this poem was added by An. Sc. Gentleman, 1604.
572. *The Light of Asia*, 1879, end of Book III. Siddartha: Buddha.
573. *Castara*, Third Part, 1640.
574. *A Collection of Miscellanies*, 1687.
575. *Cælicia*, 1633. Sonnet xcix.
576. From *The Contention of Ajax and Ulysses*, 1659.
577. 1610, Stzs. 1 to 8.
578. 1610, Stzs. 44 to the end. 'Kentish lad': Phineas Fletcher.
579. *Last Poems*, Florence, 1932; London, 1933.

580. *Drum-Taps*, 1865.
581. J. Danyel's *Songs for the Lute*, 1606.
582–584. *Divine Poems*, 1633.
585. *Sacred Poems*, 1652, with additional lines from the editions of 1636.
586. *Silex Scintillans: Sacred Poems and private Ejaculations*, 1655.
587. *Divine Poems*, 1633.
588. *Divine Poems*, 1635.
589. This dirge exists in several versions. The original seems to have belonged to the Cleveland district of Yorkshire. A later version, in Yorkshire dialect, is given in *Wit, Character, Folklore and Customs of the North Riding of Yorkshire*, by Richard Blakeborough, 1898, p. 123.
590. *Flowers of Zion*, 1630.
591. *The Unknown Eros*, Book 2, xi.
592. *Flowers of Zion*, 1630.
593–594. *Sacred Poems*, 1652.
595. *Paradise Lost*, 1667, Book III, lines 1–55.
596. 1632–1633. *Shorter Poems*, 1645.
597. 1877. *Poems*, 1918.
598. *Emblems*, 1635. Book V, Epigram x.
599. *Voices of the Night*, 1839.
600–601. *The Temple*, 1633.
602. *Poems of Felicity*. Ed. from the MS. by H. I. Bell, Oxford, 1910.
603. *Spirituall Sonnetes*, *c.* 1600.
604. *Psyche*, 1648.
605. *The Temple*, 1633.
606–609. *Silex Scintillans*, 1655.
610. See 602 above.
611–612. *Hymns and Spiritual Songs for the Feasts and Festivals of the Church of England*, appended to *The Psalms*, 1765.
613. *Silex Scintillans*, 1652.
614. 1475–1500.
615–616. *Saint Peters Complaint, newly augmented*, 1596.
617. Add. MS. 22472. Poems of N. W., Ed. L. C. Martin, Clarendon Press, 1928. Punctuation added.
618. *Miscellaneous Poems*, 1681.
619. *The Forrest*, 1641 Folio.
620. *Poems*, 1844.
621. 1877. Poems, 1918.
622. *Justus es*, etc., Jer. xii, 1. March 17, 1889. *Poems*, 1918.
623. 1885. *Poems*, 1918.
624. Robert Chester's *Love's Martyr*, 1601.

Book IX

625. *Christ's Company*, 1861.
626. *The Strayed Reveller, and Other Poems*. By A. 1849.
627. *Ara Vos Prec*, 1920. Text, *Poems 1919–1925*.
628. 1632–1634. *Shorter Poems*, 1645.
629. Composed at Leghorn, 1820.

630. *Odes on Several Subjects*, 1647.
631. Written May, 1819. *Annals of the Five Arts*, July 1819.
632. May, 1819. *Annals of the Five Arts*, No. XV (Jan. 1820 ?).
633. Act I, lines 672–751. Composed at Este, Sept., Oct. 1818.
634. 1882. *Poems*, 1918.
635. Composed May, 1798. First published 1816, with the sub-title 'or, a Vision in a Dream. A Fragment', and a long note on the circumstance of its composition.
636. Published with *Prometheus Unbound*, 1820.
637. *Draft of XXX Cantos*, 1933. Canto xvii.
638. Written 4 April, 1802. We give the version printed in *Sybilline Leaves*, 1817. For the much longer original version, and for the history and significance of the poem, see Ernest de Sélincourt, *Wordsworthian and Other Studies*, Oxford, 1947, pp. 57–76.
639. *Poems*, 1853.
640. 1686. Orinda : 'the matchless'. Mrs. Katherine Philips.
641. *Miscellaneous Poems*, 1681.
642. For St. Cecilia's Day, 1697.
643. 1763. Stzs. i–xvi: li–lxxxvi (the end).
644. *Poems*, 1893. Accepting the reading 'clatter' for 'chatter'.
645. 1819. *Lamia, Isabella*, etc., 1820.
646. 1596. To celebrate the double marriage of the Lady Elizabeth and the Lady Katherine Somerset, daughters of the Earl of Worcester.
647. *Poems*, 1807. The part in brackets (p. 747, ll. 12–15) is in the editions of 1807 and 1815, but is omitted in the 1820 and subsequent editions, in consequence of Coleridge's adverse criticism. See *Biographia Literaria*, chap. xxii.
648. *Samson Agonistes*, 1671. Conclusion. From line 1669 to end.
649. 'In this Monody the Author bewails a learned friend, unfortunately drown'd in his passage from Chester on the Irish Seas, 1637. And by occasion foretells the ruin of our corrupted clergy then in their height.'–Milton's Note. *Shorter Poems*, 1645.
650. 1821. Page 759. 'Pilgrim of Eternity': Byron. 'Ierne's sweetest lyrist': Moore. 'A phantom among men': Shelley.
651. First printed as a 'sequel' to *Walt Whitman's Drum-Taps*, New York, 1865, in memory of Abraham Lincoln, who was shot in Ford's theatre in Washington, Good Friday night, April 14, 1865, and died the next morning.
652. *Ash Wednesday*, 1930. Part II.

Book X

653. From *The Law Against Lovers*, 1662.
654. From *Volpone*, 1607. *Folio*, 1616.
655. *Dodsley's Collection*, 1758. *Works*, 1764.
656. *British Synonymy* (Mrs. Piozzi), 1794.
657. 'Miscellaneous Thoughts in Prose and Verse' in *Works*, 1753.
658. 7 July, 1836.

659. See note to Nos. 138–142.
660. *The Five Nations*, 1903.
661. *The Masque of Anarchy.* Pub. 1832. Stzs. lxxix–xci.
662. *Poems and Prose Remains*, 1869.
663. *Wit's Recreations*, 1691.
664. *Dipsychus.* Posthumously published.
665. *Miscellaneous Works*, 1746.
666. 1786.
667. *Fables*, 1726. No. x.
668. 1725. Separately published.
669. *Absalom and Achitophel*, Part I, 1681, lines 146–219.
670. Jan. 1735, lines 1–48, 115–282, 305–333. The Prologue to the Satires.
671. 1662. First part. Canto I, lines 189–236.
672. *Amours de Voyage*, 1858.
673. *Don Juan.* Canto I, 1819. Stzs. i–xv.
674. 1731. Printed 1739.
675. *Posthumous Tales. Works*, 1834.
676. *Miscellanies*, 1732.
677. *The Passionate Shepherd*, 1604.
678. *Fragmenta Aurea*, 1646. The wedding is that of Lord Broghill, later the Earl of Orrery, and Lady Margaret Howard, which took place in 1641.
679. Verses from *Tylney Hall*, 1834.
680. *Selected Poems*, New York, 1945.
681. 'The Adventures of Master F.I.', from *A Hundreth Sundrie Flowres*, 1578.

INDEX OF AUTHORS

The references are to the numbers of the poems

F F

INDEX OF FIRST LINES

The references are to pages

A

At length their long kiss severed, with sweet smart, 215.
A touch of cold in the Autumn night, 313.
At the round earth's imagin'd corners blow, 618.
Autumn hath all the summer's fruitful treasure, 592.
Avenge O Lord thy slaughter'd Saints, whose bones, 418.
Awake! for Morning in the Bowl of Night, 519.
A Ward, and still in bonds, one day, 616.
Away! the moor is dark beneath the moon, 227.
A widow bird sate mourning, 275.
A wind sways the pines, 268.
A yellow leaf from the darkness, 589.

B

Beautiful habitations, auras of delight, 622.
Beauty! thou art a wanderer on the earth, 531.
Before the beginning of years, 238.
Behold her, single in the field, 121.
Behold, slow-settling o'er the lurid grove, 331.
Behold what furies still, 240.
Being my selfe captyved here in care, 166.
Bid me to live, and I will live, 109.
Black pitchy night, companions of my woe, 228.
Blasted with sighs, and surrounded with tears, 186.
Blessed Offendor, who thyself hast tried, 639.
Blest pair of Sirens, pledges of Heav'n's joy, 633.
Blows the wind to-day, and the sun and the rain are flying, 203.
Bob Southey! You're a poet—Poet-laureate, 808.
Brave flowers, that I could gallant it like you, 222.
Bright star! would I were steadfast as thou art, 212.
Broken in pieces all asunder, 636.
Busy old fool, unruly Sun, 164.
But bringing up the rear of this bright host, 61.
But how can I describe the doleful sight, 16.
But, lo! from forth a copse that neighbours by, 30.
But see, the fading many-coloured woods, 333.
By our first strange and fatal interview, 365.
By the hoof of the Wild Goat up-tossed, 502.

C

Call for the robin-redbreast and the wren, 268.
Calme was the day, and through the trembling ayre, 738.
Can death be faithful or the grave be just, 655.
Captain Carpenter rose up in his prime, 837.
Care-charmer Sleep, son of the sable night, 214.
Care-charming sleep, thou easer of all woes, 279.
Careful Observers may foretell the Hour, 325.
Chaste Cloris doth disclose the shames, 160.
Chaste maids which haunt fair Aganippe's well, 283.
Chide, chide no more away, 258.
Children's voices in the orchard, 74.

N

O

70
71
72
74
75
76
77
79
83
85